THE
HARDEST
PLACE

THE HARDEST PLACE

THE AMERICAN MILITARY ADRIFT IN AFGHANISTAN'S PECH VALLEY

WESLEY MORGAN

RANDOM HOUSE • NEW YORK

Published in the United States by Random House, an imprint and division
of Penguin Random House LLC, New York.

RANDOM HOUSE and the HOUSE colophon are registered trademarks of Penguin
Random House LLC.

Library of Congress Cataloging-in-Publication Data
Names: Morgan, Wesley, author.
Title: The hardest place / Wesley Morgan.
Description: First edition. | New York : Random House, 2021
Identifiers: LCCN 2020011937 (print) | LCCN 2020011938 (ebook) |
ISBN 9780812995060 (hardcover; alk. paper) |
ISBN 9780812995077 (ebook)
Subjects: LCSH: Afghan War, 2001– —Campaigns—Afghanistan—
Pech Valley. | Afghan War, 2001– —Campaigns—Afghanistan—
Korangal Valley. | Afghan War, 2001– —Campaigns—
Afghanistan—Kunar (Province)
Classification: LCC DS371.4123.P43 M67 2020 (print) |
LCC DS371.4123.P43 (ebook) | DDC 958.104/742—dc23
LC record available at https://lccn.loc.gov/2020011937

Printed in the United States of America on acid-free paper

randomhousebooks.com

2   4   6   8   9   7   5   3   1

First Edition

*For the interpreters who risked and
sometimes lost their lives protecting
American soldiers and Marines
in the Pech valley and its tributaries.*

NOTE ON SPELLINGS

The towns and villages of Kunar and Nuristan have names that come from many languages: from Pashto, from Dari, and from Nuristani and Pashai languages that have no written form and in some cases are extinct. English transliterations vary. The name پیچ can be transliterated as "Pech" or "Pich," while وانت, pronounced "Want," has often been distorted into the two-syllable "Wanat" through a game of telephone involving Russian and American military map transliterations.

I HAVE TRIED to adopt spellings that are as close as possible to the way residents of the places pronounce the names without being unfamiliar to American veterans who served there, while preserving alternate spellings in quotations from Americans and from U.S. military documents. For places that have multiple names, I have used the name most familiar to the U.S. military (usually the Pashto one).

CONTENTS

RECURRING CHARACTERS

IN ORDER OF APPEARANCE

AMERICANS

JOE RYAN, Ranger battalion staff officer during Operation Winter Strike, 2003; Joint Special Operations Command (JSOC) task force staff officer at Bagram Airfield, 2007; commander of 1-327 Infantry (the "Bulldog" battalion) at FOB Blessing, 2010–2011; JSOC task force commander at Bagram, 2012; commanding general of Train-Advise-Assist Command East, 2018–2019

STAN McCHRYSTAL, JSOC commanding general, 2003–2008; commanding general of NATO's International Security Assistance Force (ISAF) and U.S. Forces—Afghanistan, 2009–2010

JIMMY HOWELL, 2-22 Infantry platoon leader during Operations Mountain Resolve and Winter Strike, 2003; Ranger platoon leader during Operation Red Wings recovery mission, 2005; commander of Viper Company, 1-26 Infantry in the Korengal, 2008–2009

KARL EIKENBERRY, commander of Combined Forces Command—Afghanistan in Kabul, 2005–2007; U.S. ambassador to Afghanistan, 2009–2011

CHRIS CAVOLI, commander of 1-32 Infantry (the "Chosin" battalion) at Jalalabad Airfield and FOB Blessing, 2006–2007

JOHN "MICK" NICHOLSON, commander of 3rd Brigade, 10th Mountain Division at FOB Salerno and Jalalabad Airfield, 2006–2007; ISAF operations director, 2010–2011; commanding general of NATO's Resolute Support mission and U.S. Forces—Afghanistan, 2016–2018

T.W., Asymmetric Warfare Group tactical advisor active in Kunar starting in 2004

DOUG SLOAN, commander of Bravo Company, 1-32 Infantry in the Korengal and Waygal, 2006; killed in action October 2006

BILL OSTLUND, battalion commander of 2-503 Infantry ("The Rock") at FOB Blessing, 2007–2008; JSOC task force commander and liaison to ISAF, Bagram and Kabul, 2009–2011

DAN KEARNEY, commander of Battle Company, 2-503 Infantry in the Korengal, 2007–2008; commander of Ranger Team Darby in eastern Afghanistan, 2011; JSOC task force staff officer at Bagram, 2014–2015 and 2016; 82nd Airborne Division battalion commander at Bagram, 2017–2018

BRETT JENKINSON, battalion commander of 1-26 Infantry (the "Blue Spaders") at FOB Blessing, 2008–2009; ISAF and U.S. Forces—Afghanistan staff officer, 2014

DREW POPPAS, commander of 1st Brigade, 101st Airborne Division at Jalalabad Airfield, 2010–2011; deputy commanding general of the 101st Airborne Division and Regional Command East, 2013

COLIN TULEY, commander of 2-35 Infantry (the "Cacti" battalion) at FOB Joyce, 2011–2012; JSOC task force commander at Bagram, 2013

LOREN CROWE, 1-26 Infantry platoon leader in northern Kunar and staff officer at FOB Blessing, 2008–2009; 2-35 Infantry staff officer at FOB Joyce and Gundog Company commander at FOB Blessing, 2011–2012

ARABS

OSAMA BIN LADEN, al-Qaida's Saudi founder and leader; killed 2011

AYMAN AL-ZAWAHIRI, bin Laden's Egyptian deputy and successor

ABU IKHLAS AL-MASRI, Egyptian al-Qaida operative involved in advising and assisting Afghan insurgents in Kunar and Nuristan; captured 2010

FAROUQ AL-QAHTANI, Qatari al-Qaida operative involved in advising and assisting Afghan insurgents in Kunar starting in 2009 and later al-Qaida's senior commander in eastern Afghanistan; killed 2016

AFGHANS

GULBUDDIN HEKMATYAR, former prime minister of Afghanistan; emir of Hizb-e Islami

KASHMIR KHAN, Hizb-e Islami commander who hosted Hekmatyar and Osama bin Laden in the Shigal valley after the 2001 battle of Tora Bora

HAJI RUHULLAH WAKIL, Jamaat al-Dawa leader detained by U.S. troops in 2002 and imprisoned at Guantánamo Bay

SABAR LAL MELMA, associate of Ruhullah imprisoned with him at Guantánamo Bay; killed 2011

HAMID KARZAI, president of Afghanistan, 2001–2014

MAWLAWI SHAHZADA SHAHID, Kunari cleric and member of Afghanistan's High Peace Council

HAJI GHAFOR, Hizb-e Islami commander in the Kantiwa valley

MAWLAWI ABDUL RAHIM, former chief of Korengal valley *shura;* Taliban shadow governor of Kunar, 2008–2012

HAJI MATIN, Korengal valley timber baron and Taliban commander; killed 2013

HAJI MOHAMMAD DAWRAN, commander from Sundray active in the Pech insurgency starting in 2003; killed 2013

AHMAD SHAH, insurgent commander targeted in Operation Red Wings; killed 2008

TAMIM NURISTANI, governor of Nuristan, 2006–2008 and 2011–2014

HAJI JUMA GUL, hotel owner and High Peace Council member from Want; killed 2011

HAJI ZALWAR KHAN, Korengal *shura* chief

HAJI ZALMAY YUSUFZAI, district governor in Pech valley's Watapur and Manogai districts

FARSHAD, interpreter to 1-32 Infantry, 2-503 Infantry, and 1-26 Infantry, 2006–2009

BURHAN, interpreter to 1-32 Infantry, 2-503 Infantry, 1-26 Infantry, 2-12 Infantry, 1-327 Infantry, and 2-35 Infantry, 2006–2012

ESMATULLAH, commander of 2/2 ANA battalion at FOB Blessing, 2010–2011

RAHMDEL HAIDARZAI, commander of 2/2 ANA battalion at FOB Blessing, 2011

DOST MOHAMMAD, Taliban shadow governor of Nuristan; killed 2013

TURAB KHAN, commander of 6/2 ANA battalion at FOB Blessing, 2011–2013

PROLOGUE

2010

The soldiers living in the concrete maze of Combat Outpost (COP) Michigan treated the Taliban fire that poured in from the mountains as though it were weather: bursts of machine-gun bullets were akin to drizzle, volleys of rocket-propelled grenades more like heavy rain.

I was sitting in the little base's recreational computer room, one of about twenty plywood buildings scattered around COP Michigan's gravel-covered grounds, when the thump of an explosion sounded from somewhere else on the fortified compound. The chatter of incoming and outgoing machine guns quickly joined the din, followed by the blasts of the outpost's mortars firing their own explosive shells up into the cloud-draped gray-and-green hills. "It might not be worth going out into that," a tall, blond soldier using one of the computers remarked to a friend sitting next to him. By the time a jet dropped a bomb on one of the insurgent firing positions, the attack had already subsided and infantrymen were sitting outside again in their one dedicated outdoor space, a little wooden deck outfitted with picnic tables, homemade Adirondack chairs, a pull-up bar, and a shroud of green plastic camouflage netting meant to shield the enclave from the view of Taliban spotters whose vantage points above otherwise offered a clear view of every inch of the valley-floor base. "That was a good one," one of the young soldiers on the deck said regretfully when the ground shook slightly and we watched the plume of smoke from the air strike rise from behind a tree-dotted ridge. He was sorry he'd forgotten to get his video camera out to record it for posterity and Facebook.[1]

The troops at COP Michigan during the summer of 2010 wore the black Screaming Eagle patch of the 101st Airborne Division on the shoulders of their camouflage fatigues. The seven hundred soldiers of their battalion, the division's 1-327 Infantry, nicknamed the Bulldogs, were two months into a deployment to four outposts in the valley formed by the fast-moving Pech River. Flying up the Pech in the passenger cabin of a Black Hawk helicopter in late July on my way to visit the Bulldog battalion, I'd gotten a bird's-eye look at the terrain surrounding it in Kunar Province, a hundred miles northeast of Kabul: wave after wave of peaks and ridges, rising another five or ten thousand feet from valley floors that were already three thousand feet above sea level. The valleys looked like the veins on a leaf: big ones like the Kunar River valley, which ran north to south through the province, were joined by tributaries like the Pech, which in turn were fed by the smaller tributaries that ran down side valleys so steep and narrow that some were more like canyons. Keep going up the Pech, and you would eventually leave Kunar and wind up in the next province to the north, Nuristan, a place famous in Afghanistan for having converted to Islam from an animist religion barely a century before.

Sharp spurs jutted out into the valley, forcing the river's course to curve around them and marking its junctions with small side valleys; viewed from a height, the spurs looked like the teeth in the open jaws of a crocodile. COP Michigan sat where one of these tributaries joined the Pech: on the opposite side of the flood-swollen river, two rocky teeth flanked the mouth of the Korengal valley, made famous by other journalists as the "valley of death" for the high toll that the fighting there had taken on a series of American units going back to a disastrous special operations mission in 2005. From 2006 until the spring of 2010, U.S. troops had maintained a cluster of bases inside the Korengal, outposts similar to Michigan but more compact; another unit had shuttered these bases just a few weeks before the Bulldog battalion deployed. The troops at Michigan knew just bits and pieces about what was going on inside the Korengal now. Local Taliban leaders had moved into the abandoned bases, intelligence reports said, although aerial footage from Predator drones and other surveillance aircraft didn't show any obvious signs of militant training camps or other alarming activity. Snippets of intercepted insurgent walkie-talkie chatter in Arabic—a foreign language in the country—suggested that back there somewhere, working with the local Taliban, were operatives of al-Qaida. It was the terrorist organization's presence as the guest of local militants that had drawn the American military into Afghanistan in the first place in 2001, into Kunar in 2002, into the Pech in 2003, and then into its tributaries.

What mattered to the troops at Michigan, though, was that the Korengal was where the fire was coming from during attacks on their base—especially the munitions that really made you think twice before stepping outside, such as shells from bazooka-like recoilless rifles and the finger-sized bullets of heavy machine guns. In his office inside the concrete-ringed plywood headquarters building, or operations center, the unexcitable company commander in charge of the outpost, Captain Dakota Steedsman, gave me a rundown of what his soldiers had experienced so far during their two months in the Pech. On his second day at Michigan, he recounted, a heavy machine gun, firing with surprising accuracy from a ridge two-thirds of a mile inside the Korengal, had pinned his men down and wounded a sergeant inside the base's little chow hall. Other soldiers had been wounded since, and one had died, a mechanic killed when a rocket-propelled grenade, or RPG, exploded in the tent where he was working. I should expect to see three or four attacks on the outpost each day during my stay, Steedsman told me, lasting anywhere between five and forty-five minutes, and I should be careful about going outside during them.

At 7:35 p.m., the third attack that day kicked off. Machine-gun rounds and RPGs snapped in from behind Ranger Rock, a big boulder overlooking the base just inside the Korengal, kicking up gravel and ricocheting off concrete blast barriers. Soldiers fired back with their own machine guns from the turrets of big, boxy armored trucks parked at intervals inside the perimeter walls. I tagged along with First Sergeant George Ehlschide—the senior man among the

enlisted troops the company commander, Steedsman, and his lieutenants oversaw—as he stepped out of the operations center and ran
through the labyrinth of concrete and dirt-filled barriers over to the
mortar pit.

"First Sergeant, you're not running around out here, are you?"
one mortarman asked. The first sergeant grunted. The mortarman
turned to me, the visiting reporter. "You came at a good time," he
joked. He and a few other soldiers were dropping rounds into three
mortar tubes, sending green-painted explosive shells arcing toward
grid coordinates they'd long since memorized, and then ducking
into a concrete shelter when the incoming fire got too close.

Some of the radio chatter had an urgent tone. Up above Michigan, fifteen or sixteen ill-trained soldiers from the U.S.-backed Afghan National Army (ANA) manned an observation post, or OP,
perched on the finger of rock that jutted directly across the Korengal's mouth. During the day, two Afghan flags were visible flying
over the post. Now its defenders were frantically contacting the
operations center on the radio, saying, through an interpreter, that
the incoming fire was too much for them. "Roger, I copy, possible
overrun of the OP," the senior mortarman said into his radio, suggesting insurgents might be about to capture the Afghan troops'
precarious position. I'd never heard anything like that before during
my "embeds" with American and British infantry units at outposts
around Afghanistan and Iraq. "Guys, stand your shit right by the
door, you understand? Full gear." Ehlschide, the first sergeant, cursed
and ran back to the operations center; I followed him.

The Afghan troops at the observation post were taking heavy
fire, but they weren't actually being overrun. Back inside the operations center, a fire-support specialist was on the radio with the crews
of two howitzers—huge guns that lobbed ninety-six-pound shells
in a high arc—at a bigger base four miles distant, feeding them coordinates of positions inside the Korengal that insurgents were
shooting from: "First grid, four two sierra x-ray delta seven seven
eight zero six six five zero. Second grid, x-ray delta seven . . ." As
the howitzer shells started exploding, scattering jagged steel fragments and chunks of the incendiary chemical white phosphorous a
mile and a half away up in the mountains, both the incoming and
the outgoing fire started to slacken. A soldier manning a radio asked

the room how many RPGs the enemy had fired since the attack began. "Fuck, your guess is as good as mine, but it's been ten or more," the captain answered. A fighter pilot arrived high overhead and checked in on the radio with his call sign, Viper 18. An Air Force targeting specialist sitting in the operations center with the soldiers sent him the coordinates of another Taliban position, and then there was a boom and a shudder of the earth as a thousand pounds of high explosive sprayed another thousand pounds of steel around its target somewhere on the wooded slopes above the Korengal.

The evening's attack was over—probably not because the air strike had killed any insurgents, but because they knew from long experience exactly how long it took American aircraft to arrive overhead and had packed up their weapons and scuttled off before the bomb dropped.

FOR THE SOLDIERS I was visiting, it had been just another night at COP Michigan; after two months in the valley, this kind of fighting was what they were accustomed to. For me, the war in the Pech was something different and surprising.

I was twenty-two years old, about the same age as many of the troops I was reporting on, and had been making trips to Iraq and Afghanistan as a freelance journalist for three years. The terrain here was so beautiful and rugged that it hardly seemed real, a sharp contrast to the dry hills, battered cities, and muggy farmlands I'd encountered elsewhere—a reaction many soldiers shared when arriving in Kunar or Nuristan after past deployments to Iraq or other parts of Afghanistan. And instead of a war of hidden bombs exploding from beneath the road, the field, the trail, or the floor, it was a war of firefights and firepower, where young infantrymen not only routinely fired their rifles and machine guns at the enemy but called in huge numbers of mortar shells (the Bulldog battalion had expended just over seven thousand so far on the deployment), howitzer shells (just over two thousand), rockets and missiles from attack helicopters, and satellite-guided bombs from jets (fifty-two so far when I arrived). I'd never seen anything like it, and no matter how inured to it they became, most soldiers who fought there would never see anything like it again in other valleys, provinces, or countries on later tours. "You get there, and the Pech delivered in every way. You really felt like you were doing what you signed up for," one veteran of the Pech would tell me later, echoing a sentiment I found to be common among sergeants and lieutenants who fought there.[2] "I call it 'Kunar syndrome.' For those of us who joined the infantry, that place is exactly what we envisioned," agreed another.[3]

The slightly larger base that housed the Bulldog battalion's headquarters was four miles beyond Michigan, farther up the Pech. Forward Operating Base (FOB) Blessing was the westernmost in the string of four outposts in the valley, and it was named after the first American soldier to die there, a sergeant named Jay Blessing who had been killed by a roadside bomb nearly seven years earlier while deployed with an elite Army special operations unit, the 75th Ranger Regiment. His name and those of dozens of other dead soldiers, along with a few Marines and Navy SEALs, were etched onto four marble plaques adorning a decorative blue parapet that overlooked the valley. Clouds drifted just above the villages on the slopes, and the flags of Afghanistan, the United States, and the U.S. Army waved above. Almost a hundred American troops had died in the Pech and its tributaries like the Korengal and Waygal by late July 2010, including four so far from the Bulldog battalion. At the memorial ceremonies, somber young soldiers would file into the plywood chapel downhill from the courtyard while a set of speakers played a mournful cello track from *Black Hawk Down,* the movie about the 1993 battle of Mogadishu that soldiers my age in Afghanistan and Iraq could often recite whole scenes from.

Farther downhill, on the flat part of the base closest to the Pech River, two howitzers boomed away day and night; if they weren't firing in support of COP Michigan, they were firing in support of the Bulldog battalion's other Pech outposts—COP Able Main and COP Honaker-Miracle, eight and eleven miles away—or sometimes at the hills just above FOB Blessing. The whole place had a strange, edge-of-the-map feeling to it, made stranger by the little frogs or toads that jumped around by my feet as I typed up notes from the day's patrols and interviews and the big monitor lizards that could be found sunning themselves on the rocks during breaks between rainstorms.

Even more surprising to me, though, was the way the senior American officer in the Pech, the Bulldog battalion's commander, Lieutenant Colonel Joseph Ryan, talked about the mission there when I sat down with him in his office in the battalion operations center, a single-story concrete building across a courtyard from the memorial plaques. Forty-one years old but with less gray in his high-and-tight haircut than some of his company commanders, Ryan was a West Point graduate from Pearl River, New York, and he had been in and out of Afghanistan and Iraq since the first months after September 11, 2001, as an officer in the night-raiding Rangers.

I had become accustomed to commanders in Afghanistan and Iraq promoting the counterinsurgency operations their units were conducting, even hyping them—rattling off numbers to indicate progress, making rosy predictions about the situations they would hand off to their successors. Joe Ryan didn't do that. It was the summer of President Barack Obama's Afghan surge, and with nearly a hundred thousand U.S. troops in the country, all the other battalions I'd visited over the past couple of months had been expanding, building new outposts in new districts. But Ryan talked about retracting. "Sometimes just your presence causes destabilization. We see that on our patrols here," he said. "Here, the time is done for coalition forces to keep spreading out into more places."

Since the Korengal pullout in April, he acknowledged—a move that likewise stood in contrast to the surge's aggressive approach elsewhere in the country—attacks on COP Michigan had increased, exactly as some opponents of the withdrawal in the military chain of command had warned they would. Michigan, in fact, was enduring more daily attacks than any other American outpost in eastern Afghanistan. That didn't mean that leaving had been the wrong call, though, Ryan argued. "We could've stayed there for five more years, banging our heads against the wall," he said of the abandoned outposts in the Pech's Korengal and Waygal side valleys, listing some of the defunct bases' names: Bella, Restrepo, the Ranch House.

Ryan wasn't convinced that he or his troops, or any other Americans, understood enough about what was going on within the complex coalition of insurgent factions in the Pech to definitively conclude that any particular change in the guerrillas' behavior was the result of U.S. actions. During the same period that attacks against

Michigan had risen, for example, the frequency of rocket and mortar strikes against FOB Blessing had decreased, and he didn't know why (although the soldiers in his staff's intelligence section had theories). "We often don't know, and won't know, why things happen," he said. "There's just a lot we will never know, no matter how good our intelligence collection is."

There was another thing Ryan didn't claim to know for sure: just what he and his men were doing in the Pech. "Why are we here?" he asked me. "Are we building a nation? Are we chasing terrorists? I read the same news as you do, and it doesn't always seem very clear."

WHAT WAS OBVIOUS in the Pech in the summer of 2010 was that U.S. forces and the Taliban had fought each other to a stalemate. For counterinsurgents as for insurgents, the cooperation of the people was everything, and in the Pech the people were sick and tired of both sides. Local children in the village outside Michigan, who tended to stare frostily at American patrols as they walked through town or flash them the middle finger, were so hardened to the violence that during gunfights they would often stroll through the cross fire, picking up expended brass shell casings so that they could sell them in the market.

Some of the patrols that I accompanied from FOB Blessing headed north, a short ways into a side valley called the Waygal. The officer in charge of these missions was one of the Bulldog battalion's fourteen platoon leaders, a lieutenant two years out of West Point named Alex Pruden, with whom I would stay in touch after leaving the Pech. Years later, Pruden would share a memory with me of the moment when the situation he and his thirty-odd soldiers were in crystallized for him. It had been the day of Afghanistan's parliamentary elections, a month after my visit, and the lieutenant was back at Blessing decompressing from a day of thrilling, nerve-racking firefights when his mind wandered to the science-fiction epic *Avatar,* which had hit theaters as the Bulldog battalion was getting ready to deploy. In the movie, human invaders with the mannerisms and high-and-tight haircuts of American military personnel are stationed at high-tech outposts on a stunningly gorgeous alien world called Pandora; they venture out into the lush jungle only in lumbering vehicles to exploit its natural resources. The analogy was imperfect but obvious. Pruden knew that unlike the marauding East India Company–like corporation in the movie, the U.S. military had come to the Pech with good intentions and that the valley had not been some idyllic Eden before Americans arrived. But it still felt as if he and the rest of the Bulldog battalion were the movie's space mercenaries and the Pech was Pandora.[4]

What was not obvious was how things had gotten this way and what really had brought U.S. forces into the area back in the early years of the war. In a conflict where units rotated every six or twelve months and passed down only small parts of their experience to their successors, the origins of American involvement in the Pech were murky, as were many events along the way. Why were the Pech bases even there? Ask a soldier at Michigan how long the outpost had been in existence, and you would get a shrug. It had been there when the Bulldog battalion deployed, and when the battalion before that deployed, and the battalion before that; as far as almost any of the troops living there were concerned, it had always been there. As for *why* the base had been established in the first place, who knew, and what did it matter? Life at the embattled outposts was what it was, and their garrisons were just trying to get through it, to the end of their year, not wondering about the decisions their predecessors had made or the ways in which American goals in the valley had morphed over the years.

After that first visit to the Pech, I would sift through thousands of pages of military documents and interview dozens and then hundreds of Americans and Afghans in an effort to piece together what had led up to the violent stalemate I saw there in the summer of 2010.

Parts of the story had already been told, vividly. Because the Pech was a hot spot of violence for American forces—"a place that is the hardest of the hard," as one of the four-star generals who oversaw the whole U.S. military enterprise in Afghanistan put it to me[5]—journalists had been gravitating toward it for several years, seeking stories about young Americans braving intense combat in mind-bogglingly severe terrain. It was the right place to find them. A pair of firefights on the same mountain above the Korengal in

2005 and 2007, a little over two years apart, would both yield Medals of Honor, and a paratroop company that spent fifteen months in the Waygal in 2007 and 2008 would earn two more of these rare valor awards, the highest the military could offer. The articles, news segments, and documentaries of one visiting reporter after another would make the Pech and the similarly austere regions abutting it in Kunar and Nuristan the public face of the war in Afghanistan just as the American public's attention was turning back to that war in 2008 and 2009 as the Bush administration's Iraq surge subsided.* These, along with the memoirs of veterans and the military's internal investigations into particularly deadly incidents, provided near-real-time records of some key events, helping to offset the fallibility of human memory that makes it difficult to reconstruct combat operations only from later interviews with participants.

The vast majority of American troops who fought in the Pech did their best, with the best of intentions, under the harshest of conditions. Afghans who worked alongside them played a vital role in illuminating how, nevertheless, one commander after another failed to accomplish what they set out to, and the subtle differences they saw play out as unit after unit rotated through, each talking the same talk of counterinsurgency but not always walking the same walk. "Each American unit had the same policy—to help people, build schools, train the ANA, fight the enemy," was how the long-serving interpreter who accompanied Joe Ryan everywhere he went in the Pech put it, "but really each commander had their own different policy."[6] District officials and village elders described what happened before, after, and in between periods of American activity, and talked about insurgent leaders they knew with a familiarity that U.S. intelligence personnel couldn't. They also shared their perspective on the accidental killings of civilians by artillery and air strikes that were a tragically persistent feature of U.S. involvement and a key factor in creating the hardened attitudes that Ryan and his men saw out on patrol in villages that had been much friendlier and

---

* For a time, the word "Korengal" became almost a stand-in for Afghanistan in popular media, referred to in video games and television shows like *House of Cards* when an Afghan place-name was required.

more willing to forgive mistakes a few years earlier. "Do not censor the pain and suffering of the people of Kunar and the Pech," one old man from a village a few miles west of Blessing urged me when I interviewed him and a group of his relatives in Kabul.[7]

Even at the height of news coverage of the war, when embedded reporters were regular visitors, much was happening in and around the Pech valley that neither they nor the infantry units they were covering could see, under cover of darkness and top secret classification. This was the part of the story—one separate from the everyday fighting yet inextricably linked with it—that proved both the most difficult to uncover and the most essential to understanding how events had played out: the role of American special operations troops and intelligence operatives.

In effect, throughout Afghanistan, while troops like those at Michigan and Blessing were fighting a daytime war, special operations forces like Army Rangers and Navy SEALs were fighting a nighttime one, hunting Taliban leaders and those rare al-Qaida terrorists who sometimes worked with them. It was these counter-terrorism troops, I would learn, who had led the way into the Pech and almost all of its tributaries, undertaking missions—and often leaving messes—that the regular infantry soldiers who arrived later were told little or nothing about. The one person in the Bulldog battalion who understood this part of the history of American involvement was its commander, Joe Ryan. That was because, during his time in the Rangers, he had been part of it, and would be part of it again as special operations units continued their mission from the air, with drones, when the price of combat operations on the ground had become too high.

Ryan had hinted at this backstory during my summer 2010 visit, acknowledging that he had been present during the long-ago operation that had cost a Ranger sergeant his life and left behind a base with his name. "We drove through this valley in Hilux pickup trucks," Ryan told me during one conversation at Blessing, sounding almost surprised at the memory and its contrast with the armored behemoths the Bulldog battalion drove everywhere. "When I came here in 2003, when Jay Blessing was still alive, this place was established to provide support to forward elements in Nuristan"—

Rangers who had ventured farther and higher into the wild province north of the Pech than almost any other American troops ever would.

Just what he and other special operations troops had been doing there, he didn't say, and at the time I didn't ask, not grasping how intertwined the stories of the daytime and nighttime wars of the infantry and the counterterrorism operatives were, that one half of the war couldn't be understood without the other. It was in this interplay between the visible and the hidden wars that the answers to my questions about what had led to the dramatic deadlock of 2010 lay.

Before it snowballed into the daily duel of bombs, rockets, and artillery that I saw at COP Michigan at the height of things, I would come to learn, America's war in the Pech had begun the same way it would end—with a manhunt.

PART I

INTO THE MOUNTAINS

2002–2005

Our response involves far more than instant retaliation and isolated strikes. Americans should not expect one battle, but a lengthy campaign unlike any other we have ever seen. It may include dramatic strikes, visible on TV, and covert operations, secret even in success.

—*George W. Bush, September 20, 2001*

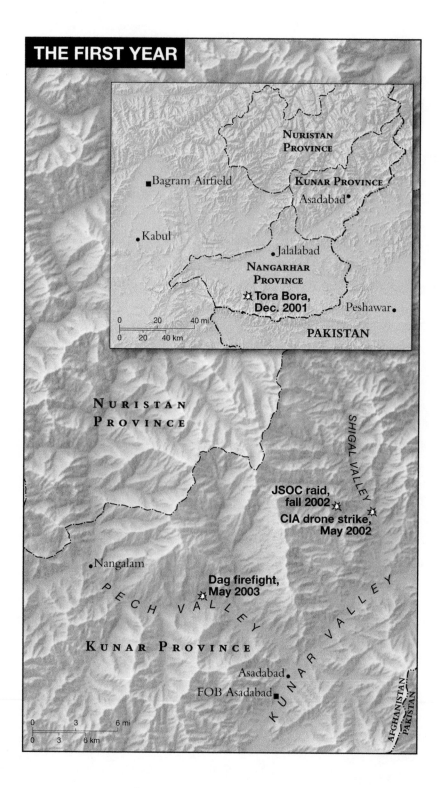

THE FIRST YEAR

NURISTAN
PROVINCE

■ Bagram Airfield   KUNAR PROVINCE
                     Asadabad●

● Kabul   ● Jalalabad
                 NANGARHAR
                 PROVINCE
             ☼ Tora Bora,
               Dec. 2001   Peshawar ●

0   20   40 mi
0   20   40 km   PAKISTAN

NURISTAN
PROVINCE
                                        SHIGAL VALLEY

                        JSOC raid,
                        fall 2002 ☼
                        CIA drone strike, ☼
                        May 2002

● Nangalam
              P E C H   V A L L E Y
                    Dag firefight,
                    May 2003 ☼

KUNAR   PROVINCE
                              KUNAR VALLEY
              Asadabad ●

         FOB Asadabad ■
                                        AFGHANISTAN
                                        PAKISTAN

0   3   6 mi
0   3   6 km

CHAPTER 1

AMERICA COMES TO KUNAR

2002–2003

IN SEARCH OF THE SHEIKH

American troops set up their first base in Kunar Province as the snow melted in the mountains in early 2002, the spring after the September 11 attacks and the ensuing autumn air war. They came trying to pick up a trail that had gone cold the previous December at the battle of Tora Bora, in another Afghan mountain range fifty miles to Kunar's south—the trail of Osama bin Laden.

I interviewed more than two hundred American veterans of Kunar before I found someone who knew firsthand how, why, and when U.S. troops entered the mountainous, nineteen-hundred-square-mile province and established the first of what would become a network of over a dozen remote outposts there. Tom Greer was a wiry former member of the Army's premier counterterrorist unit, Delta Force. In the spring of 2002, after leading the Delta team that came tantalizingly close to bin Laden at Tora Bora, he had been a major overseeing three small reconnaissance teams that paired some of the most highly trained commandos in the U.S. military with CIA officers and specialists in electronic eavesdropping. Wearing beards and local clothes and driving around in the Toyota Hilux pickup trucks that are ubiquitous in Afghanistan, the operators of these Advanced Force Operations teams were fanning out across the country's east, picking sites for little encampments. No one meant for these sites to become permanent, as most of them eventually did; they were just meant to be lily pads, places to set up radio relay points and get a good night's sleep in between reconnaissance forays into the mountains in Hiluxes or on all-terrain vehicles.[1]

The team that Tom Greer sent bouncing up Kunar's rocky, gravel-surfaced main road in a couple of pickup trucks sometime in the spring of 2002 was "SEAL heavy," he told me more than a decade later—made up mostly of operators from Delta Force's Navy equivalent, SEAL Team 6.[2] The SEALs and other personnel who accompanied them were entering a province of some 500,000 people "and an equal number of goats," as the author of a U.S. diplomatic cable a few years later would joke, where ribbons of green between the brown mountains housed fields of corn and wheat and groves of walnut trees, whose fruit the province is famous for.[3] Kunar was a conservative, rural place, where women were seldom seen outside except when working in the fields by their villages. The qualities that made it different from other eastern conservative, rural provinces—its historically complex relationship with the central government, the role of the timber trade in its economy, the Saudi-inspired brand of Islam that had become popular there during the war against the Soviets—were not obvious to special operators just starting to get the feel of the country many of them would come back to over and over again.

A couple of Delta Force operators had already visited Kunar during the fall air campaign, working in conjunction with the CIA, but they hadn't stayed.[4] This time the reconnaissance team stopped when it reached a dusty, rectangular compound a mile south of Asadabad, the provincial seat where the Pech River empties into the larger Kunar River, the province's spine. A site where there was already a fort of sorts was ideal, so that was where the SEALs made camp. Greer went up to visit the team once it was settled in. A Delta Force operator on a different recon team had recently named another new outpost Camelot. The SEALs had the honor of picking a nickname for the Asadabad camp, and they chose a less high-minded one: Puchi Ghar, because they were under the mistaken impression that *puchi ghar* meant "dog-shit mountain" in Pashto, and that was the vibe they got from the place.[5] (In fact, the phrase meant something like "crass mountain" and sounded nonsensical to Afghan ears.)

The compound didn't look like much, it was true—some broken-down mud-brick walls and buildings centered on a courtyard about five hundred feet long and five hundred feet wide, separated from the wide Kunar River by a road and some stands of trees. Locals called the compound Topchi Base because *topchi* was the Pashto word for "artillery," and the Soviets had based howitzers there.[6] More recently, Taliban fighters had used the site as a barracks, although their government had held little sway in Kunar outside Asadabad. No one imagined at the time that U.S. troops and CIA officers would occupy this base—eventually renamed Forward Operating Base Asadabad and then FOB Wright, after a Green Beret killed nearby in 2005, but often just called A-Bad—for twelve and a half years and continue to visit it even after that.

Of the seven thousand troops the United States had on the ground in Afghanistan that spring, when debris was still being cleared from the grounds of the World Trade Center, only a handful were directly involved in the hunt for Osama bin Laden. For the SEAL-led team that established FOB Asadabad, as for the other recon teams working in the east, picking up bin Laden's scent was priority number one. A top CIA official at Langley had recently stopped sending out a daily memo about progress on the bin Laden hunt, because there wasn't any, and CIA officers working out of an abandoned hotel in Kabul—their new station—were eager to use the military teams to get back on track.[7]

The Asadabad team was "looking for anything related to UBL, chasing his ghost up there," Greer recalled, using the government acronym for Usama bin Laden, then forty-five. "Any old fart that was rumored to be associated with UBL or an old acquaintance was on the target deck."[8] On May 6, within days of the special operations team's arrival, the CIA fired the first shot in America's war in Kunar, using one of its newly armed Predator drones to launch a Hellfire missile just outside a village in the Shigal valley northeast of Asadabad. The agency suspected that a pair of bin Laden's old Afghan allies from the 1980s, including the notorious warlord Gulbuddin Hekmatyar, were harboring him.[9]

To avoid tipping their hand, officials in Washington told reporters only that they had been targeting Hekmatyar, not bin Laden. Questioned about the strike during an exchange with reporters, President George W. Bush was cryptic about whom the intelligence agency had been trying to kill in Kunar: "I can assure you, when we go after individuals in the theater of war, it's because they intend to do some harm to America."[10]

WHEN ASKED AT a press conference less than a week after the September 11 attacks whether he wanted bin Laden killed, Bush had answered with the bellicosity of a gunfighter: "I want justice. And there's an old poster out west as I recall that says, 'Wanted: Dead or Alive.'"[11] The president did not mention bin Laden the next month when he announced the beginning of the U.S.-led aerial bombardment of Afghanistan, however. The military air campaign focused not on finding and striking individual al-Qaida leaders but on driving the Taliban regime from power and thereby removing the sanctuary from which al-Qaida had planned its attacks.[12]

For the first week or so after the attacks on New York and Washington, the CIA had had a good grasp on where bin Laden was, maybe better than his Taliban hosts did. According to the agency's station chief in Pakistan at the time, a CIA informant within al-Qaida made contact the Monday after the attacks to describe a town hall meeting the terrorist chief had just held with his followers near Jalalabad, the nearest big city to Kunar's south, straddling the highway from Kabul to Pakistan.[13]

Untouched by the air campaign, bin Laden next surfaced at Tora Bora in the White Mountains south of Jalalabad in early December 2001. There, the U.S. military's early unwillingness to commit ground troops beyond a handful of special operators to call in air strikes allowed bin Laden to slip away. As part of the meager American force sent to Tora Bora, Greer, the Delta Force major who later sent the SEALs to Kunar, had been there to hear the final, regretful radio broadcast bin Laden made to his followers in mid-December as the bombs fell in the mountains: "O youth of the nation. Crave death and life will be given to you."[14] Then bin Laden was gone, along with his Egyptian deputy, Dr. Ayman al-Zawahiri.

The way the U.S. government divvied up counterterrorism duties after the Taliban's ouster, the hunt for al-Qaida operatives in
Pakistan fell to the CIA, whose clandestine activities were more ac-
ceptable to Pakistan's leaders than a uniformed presence.[15] The hunt
inside Afghanistan would become one of the many responsibilities
of Operation Enduring Freedom, as the U.S. military mission in
Afghanistan had been named (and would remain named for thirteen
years). The hunters would come from Fort Bragg, North Carolina's
Joint Special Operations Command, or JSOC—the headquarters
responsible for overseeing Delta, Team 6, and other top-tier, top
secret military counterterrorism units.

JSOC mostly trained for quick, in-and-out missions like rescu-
ing hostages or securing loose nuclear weapons (although it had
some recent experience hunting war criminals in the Balkans). But
as the Fort Bragg command set up a headquarters compound for
itself in the rubble of Bagram, the huge Soviet-built airfield thirty
miles north of Kabul that would still serve as the hub for all U.S.
military activity in Afghanistan nearly two decades later, it was beginning a transformation into a long-term, global counterterrorist
decapitation machine, composed of many subordinate task forces
with inscrutable numbered code names, dedicated to hacking heads
off hydras.[16] Other military units that were claiming parts of Bagram's three-thousand-acre sprawl for their tent cities—helicopter
and paratroop units, units responsible for reconstruction or peacekeeping, and units from allied militaries—would come and go, as
would the JSOC task force's component units. But the Bagram
headquarters that JSOC was setting up to oversee its operations in
Kunar and every other corner of Afghanistan would be there for the
long haul—for much longer, it turned out, than it took to find bin
Laden.

WHERE THE TERRORIST chief had gone after Tora Bora was the
$25 million question. Some senior al-Qaida members had regrouped
at Bermel and Shah-e Kot in southeastern Afghanistan, and one
possibility was that bin Laden might be among them.[17] The CIA's
station chief in Islamabad suspected that bin Laden had fled east
from Tora Bora into Khyber, one of the "agencies" of Pakistan's

Federally Administered Tribal Areas, where Pashtun tribes ran things their own way and the Pakistani government had little control.[18] Another theory had him heading south from Tora Bora into a different tribal agency, Kurram, and from there to Waziristan, the region of the tribal areas where Arab militants had the longest history, dating to the early days of the jihad against the Soviets.

The chief of the CIA team at Tora Bora and the agency's deputy director for collection back at Langley both thought bin Laden had likely gone north, into Kunar.[19] None of al-Qaida's camps or regular safe houses had been located in the province.[20] But from Kunar he could have headed east into Pakistan or north into Nuristan, the even higher, hillier Afghan province to which Kunar was the gateway.

There was no hard intelligence proving that public enemy number one had headed one direction or another, just hints—including a tip that reached the agency suggesting that bin Laden and a small party had made their way into Kunar on horseback, spending their nights above the tree line.[21] Tantalizingly, studying aerial surveillance imagery, "We saw signs of people riding on horseback in the Pech valley," west of Asadabad, a former senior intelligence officer remembered. At CIA headquarters at Langley, intelligence officers compiled the information into a daily written update on the hunt for bin Laden that would make its way to President Bush's desk. The escape-on-horseback possibility made it in. "That excited the president as well as other readers" of the daily update, the intelligence officer recalled.[22]

Analysts at Langley "began to work every inch of the Pech" as well as other Kunari valleys, the officer said, poring over satellite images and signals intercepts for any clue about who the riders had been or where they had ended up. It was entirely possible, after all, that they had been locals and the agency was chasing the wrong lead.

At least some Arab militants had wound up in Kunar after Tora Bora, though. That was clear from the initial interrogation reports of other Arabs captured fleeing Tora Bora, people who had run in the Saudi bin Laden's and the Egyptian Zawahiri's circles and might know where they had gone, or at least where other Arabs had gone, who might in turn know.

The first Arab fighters had come to majority-Pashtun Afghanistan in the 1980s to join the insurgency that Afghan mujahidin were waging against the Soviets and the communist Afghan government. Of the more than ten thousand Arabs who came to the region during the jihad,[23] only a fraction ever actually fought inside Afghanistan, and most, including bin Laden, returned to their home countries in the early 1990s, hoping to practice there what they had learned in Afghanistan and Pakistan. After being expelled first from Saudi Arabia and then from Sudan, though, bin Laden returned to Afghanistan with the core leadership of al-Qaida in 1996. For the next five years, he and his followers circulated among the various camps and guesthouses in eastern and southern Afghanistan where Arabs belonging to different militant groups trained and mingled— all of them helping the Taliban with their war effort against the Northern Alliance, and some also preparing for jihad against America or repressive regimes in their home countries.[24] At the time of the September 11 attacks, by one estimate, there were as many as a thousand Arab militants in Afghanistan, perhaps one-fifth of whom were members of al-Qaida.[25] But now the United States and its allies were rounding up every Arab they could find from Kunduz to Kandahar. Wherever those detainees said there were more Arabs, Tom Greer sent one of the JSOC Advanced Force Operations recon teams, and a special operations outpost was born.[26]

One Libyan jihadi who wound up in American custody at Bagram and then at Guantánamo Bay Naval Base said that he had fled to Kunar when the bombing started.[27] Another early Guantánamo detainee, a Tunisian, told interrogators that when he went to fight at Tora Bora, he sent his family north to safety in Nuristan via Kunar.[28] And various other detainees claimed that among the Arabs who had fled to Kunar was a prominent jihadi named Hamza al-Qaiti, a Yemeni veteran of combat in the Balkans.[29] It was enough to warrant sending a JSOC team into the province to set up shop and start investigating.

IF BIN LADEN was still in Afghanistan at all, it was hard to think of a place better suited to his needs than Kunar or Nuristan, which mirrored the protective terrain of Tora Bora but on a much grander scale.[30] "I love the mountains," bin Laden had told a journalist in a 1996 interview at Tora Bora. "I really feel secure in the mountains. I really enjoy my life when I'm here."[31] The peaks around Asadabad were beautiful, tough, and deceptive; climb one, and the first thing you saw was higher peaks above, obscured from view from the valley floor, rising toward the snowcapped twelve- and fifteen-thousand-foot summits in the interior of the province, on either side of the Pech. It was a truism of the war in Kunar that no matter how high you went, there was always higher ground. And like Tora Bora, the craggy slopes of Kunar and Nuristan were thickly wooded.

These were key advantages, and U.S. intelligence knew that because bin Laden had traveled in Kunar and Nuristan in the years before September 11, he would be aware of them. Years later, bin Laden would write approvingly of Kunar's natural defenses from the Abbottabad compound where he eventually holed up. "Whoever can keep a low profile and take the necessary precautions should stay in the area, and those who cannot do so, their first option is to go to Nuristan, Kunar, Ghazni, or Zabul," he would write in a 2010 letter addressing where al-Qaida operatives could seek shelter from the CIA drone campaign pummeling them in Waziristan. "Kunar is more fortified due to its rougher terrain and the many mountains, rivers, and trees, and it can accommodate hundreds of the brothers without being spotted by the enemy. This will defend the brothers from [U.S.] aircraft."[32]

Bin Laden was right that Kunar's combination of steep slopes and unusually dense open-canopy forest would impede the American military's technological edge. Between the conifer forests and the mind-bogglingly steep mountainsides, there were almost no clearings big enough for helicopters to land anywhere near the remote villages that dotted the slopes of Kunar's canyon-like side valleys. The settlements themselves were frequently built right onto gradients so severe that the houses were stacked together, often on stilts, so that the front door of one building opened onto the roof of the next.

Above the tree line, in the alpine meadows that capped Kunar's tallest mountains above ten thousand feet, landing zones were more abundant, but the thin air made flying difficult for any but the most powerful helicopters in the Army inventory, twin-rotor Chinooks as big as school buses that were inviting targets for insurgent rocket-propelled grenades. And while you couldn't see helicopters until they were right on top of you in the deep blackness of a rural Afghan night, in the narrow valleys of Kunar you could hear them a long way out, the thump of rotors echoing off the valley walls. Flying down some of the narrower valleys felt like flying down a hallway.

It was one of the first things that the Delta reconnaissance commander Greer thought when he visited the SEALs at their new Asadabad firebase that first spring after September 11: *Terrible place for helicopters.*[33]

"WE BARELY HAD MAPS"

The problems Kunar's terrain posed came into focus in the early fall of 2002, when JSOC swung and missed in the most serious attempt the command had made to catch bin Laden since Tora Bora.

Over the summer, more Americans had arrived at FOB Asadabad. Fresh SEAL Team 6 and Delta Force operators replaced the Advanced Force Operations team, rotating in from Bagram for a few weeks at a time. "We did a lot of armed recons, checking out this valley or that valley in pickup trucks," remembered the Delta Force troop commander, a young officer with no idea he would tread the exact same ground sixteen years later, as a one-star general visiting a base still in use by Afghan troops and their American advisers.[34]

A handful of CIA officers and contractors took over one of the base's buildings, and a Green Beret team joined them to help the agency set up a unit of armed Afghans called a Counterterrorism Pursuit Team, or CTPT, nicknamed the Mohawks,* the first of many new Afghan security organizations the United States would create, train, and introduce to Kunar with varying degrees of success. The Mohawks acted as the agency's partners, accompanying

---

* Not knowing what "Mohawk" meant, many Kunaris called the CIA's Asadabad surrogate force the *Mahak,* and a member of the force a *Mahaki,* treating it as though it were a Pashto word.

CIA officers on missions, and surrogates—usually on the Afghan side of the border but sometimes crossing into Pakistan too.[35]

The biggest addition, crammed into green tents in the courtyard, was a company of more than a hundred young infantrymen from the 75th Ranger Regiment.[36] Rangers were a JSOC task force's brawn, backing up the much smaller teams of older Team 6 and Delta operators. Six months earlier, CIA officers on the ground at Tora Bora had urgently requested the deployment of Rangers to seal off potential escape routes. It was a common view in the intelligence and special operations communities that the military's failure to grant the request had allowed bin Laden to slip away.[37] No one wanted to make that mistake again. Belatedly on the ground in Afghanistan in force, the Rangers' job was to bail the small JSOC recon teams out of trouble and, when Delta or Team 6 launched a raid, to set up blocking positions to prevent anyone from getting away.

For the Rangers, life at FOB Asadabad was quiet and hot. One Ranger platoon leader, lacking an interpreter, talked to local people in Russian.[38] When the Rangers ventured north into Asadabad city on patrols, they, like the teenage Soviet draftees who had come before them, marveled at the frowning, red-faced rhesus monkeys sold as pets in the dusty bazaar.[39] Some adopted a monitor lizard as a mascot until their commander made them get rid of it.

The only luxuries were coffee and a makeshift gym area, which the young infantrymen collaborated with the older SEALs and Green Berets to improve.[40] There were downsides, like the dust, which necessitated the constant cleaning and re-cleaning of M4 rifles, and the lack of bathroom facilities, which required stirring barrels full of human waste while they burned. The upsides: being away from Bagram and the chiding superiors there, the thrill of driving Humvees up mountain roads far too narrow for them, and the possibility, however slim, of a firefight. "From a private's perspective, it was delightful," said one junior Ranger who was there that summer. "It felt like we were at the far end of the earth, which was everything we wanted—like we were in Indian country and any day some horde might descend on us. It was like, 'This is what I signed up for.'"[41]

. . .

THE ALERT FOR the big mission came as the heat and rain of the summer of 2002 were starting to subside and the nights were growing cold. According to one of the CIA's informants, a group of Arab escapees from Tora Bora was holed up in a mountainside village high in the Shigal valley, ten miles north of Asadabad. The Shigal had been the scene of the CIA's unsuccessful Predator strike in the spring, and the agency believed that the old mujahidin commander who controlled the valley, Haji Kashmir Khan, was harboring the Arabs there. Kashmir Khan's foreign guests kept to themselves and bought a lot of bread, the source said; the local people didn't know much about them and, because the foreigners spoke Arabic rather than Pashto, couldn't communicate with them.

It wasn't much, and a large Ranger force had already done an overnight hike up the Shigal in August and seen nothing unusual.[42] But the report was the closest thing in months to a lead on bin Laden or Zawahiri, and it came from a source the CIA deemed reliable. At Fort Bragg, JSOC's two-star commanding general, whose approval was required for risky operations, gave the "go" order.[43]

The gears of the JSOC raiding machine started turning. A constellation of aircraft arrived in the skies above the Shigal: a spy plane to listen for enemy communications; a Predator drone, which beamed grainy infrared video back to JSOC headquarters at Bagram and Fort Bragg; and then a wave of big twin-rotor MH-47 Chinook and smaller MH-60 Black Hawk helicopters, piloted by the elite Night Stalkers of the Army's 160th Special Operations Aviation Regiment.

The "bearded men with green eyes," as Afghan militants sometimes called American special operators for the glowing dots of their night-vision goggles, slid down thick nylon ropes into their landing zones, a procedure known as fast-roping that was particularly difficult in the mountains.[44] The Chinooks deposited more than a hundred Rangers into forest clearings above the target. Black Hawks swooped downhill to drop off several dozen SEAL Team 6 operators "on the X," or right in the village itself, but missed their mark and were unable to land; instead, another Chinook deposited a backup troop of SEALs on the target building, whose earth-covered roof was thick with the residents' crops. The heavily equipped frogmen's thin infrared aiming lasers swept every angle around them, bright green through their goggles but invisible to everyone else.

The Shigal mission was a "dry hole," in military terminology—a disappointing miss. The SEALs found some guns and medical supplies in a cave nearby, but nothing else. The only shooting that participants in the mission remembered was a few desultory rounds as the helicopters first arrived, as likely fired by frightened locals as by fleeing militants.[45]

The unforgiving terrain almost brought the mission to grief as surely as enemy resistance might have, however. As the Rangers hiked down the mountain in the blackness, weighed down with heavy body armor vests that were completely inappropriate for the terrain and altitude, first one of them tumbled off a cliff, then a second, then a third. One broke a femur and had to be medevaced. "It was the most rugged terrain I've ever seen," a Ranger on the mission said. "Absolutely inhospitable."[46]

The Black Hawks that inserted the SEALs could carry only a few operators apiece in the thin mountain air, and even then flying at that altitude was precarious for the single-rotor helicopters. During the first, abortive insertion attempt, one of the aircraft lost power. "You lose lift and there's no recovering from it at that altitude," said a Ranger who was watching via Predator drone feed from Bagram as the Black Hawk dropped suddenly and then slammed into the valley floor. For a moment it seemed as if it could be a complete disaster, but, amazingly, the pilot managed to make a "hard landing"—essentially a controlled crash. "It was like the hand of God was involved," the Ranger watching from Bagram remembered.[47] No one aboard was seriously hurt, but the helicopter's rotor blades were too badly damaged for it to fly. That meant that instead of leaving before daylight, the raid force was stuck there, guarding the wreck until another Chinook could fly up and haul the crippled Black Hawk out.[48]

The Night Stalkers who flew the SEALs to their targets were the best pilots in the Army, and their helicopters were outfitted with the latest infrared night-vision and terrain-mapping radar. Few places in Afghanistan or Iraq challenged the pilots and their aircraft the way

Kunar and Nuristan did. "When I came over that ridge, even under goggles, even with an [infrared] searchlight on, that terrain was unbelievable," recalled one of the Night Stalker pilots on the mission. "That area is the absolute worst. Down toward Khost, Gardez, Kandahar, the enemy is your problem, but up in Kunar it was always the terrain."[49]

As the Rangers piled into Humvees at the bottom of the mountain later that day for the ride back to FOB Asadabad, boys from a nearby school ran out to meet them, rightly expecting that the American troops would throw them candy, pens, and MREs, their packaged meals ready to eat. One child produced a drawing that he waved close enough for some of the Rangers to see. In crayon, crude but clear, the boy had sketched a big twin-rotor helicopter hauling out a smaller single-rotor bird under its belly.[50]

THE FALL 2002 Shigal raid was a wake-up call about another problem that would plague American military efforts in Kunar too: intelligence.

Kashmir Khan, the warlord of the Shigal, had indeed been in the valley at the time, he would acknowledge years later; he had heard the helicopters and run into the forest, he would tell an Afghan journalist.[51] Bin Laden was not there, but he had been until a few months earlier, staying as Kashmir Khan's guest just as the CIA suspected, and so had two of bin Laden's teenage sons and possibly Ayman al-Zawahiri as well.

The Shigal had been bin Laden's first hiding place after Tora Bora, a captured al-Qaida courier would later explain to American interrogators and other militants involved would later confirm to journalists. An Afghan militant commander had picked the al-Qaida Arabs up when they trudged down from the mountains during the December battle and driven them to Asadabad, where Kashmir Khan's fighters took charge of their security and escorted them up to a house overlooking the valley in a village called Khwarr. Gulbuddin Hekmatyar had joined them there in February, and they had all been in the Shigal until late spring, just as special operators were establishing themselves in the province. The May 6 CIA Predator strike, which very nearly killed Hekmatyar, convinced Kashmir

Khan that his guests needed to move on. If Kashmir Khan hadn't managed to avoid the Rangers' blocking positions as he fled the sound of the helicopters the night of the raid, he would almost certainly have been able to tell interrogators exactly where bin Laden had gone and when.[52]

Whatever the margin of error, the risky, complex JSOC raid had missed its mark, and the reason was that the intelligence behind it, while broadly accurate, hadn't been precise or timely enough. One special operations officer was surprised when he was "read in" on the information that prompted the raid and realized that instead of state-of-the-art signals intercepts or some signature visible to a satellite or high-flying spy plane—let alone a tip-off from inside al-Qaida—it amounted to little more than local rumors an informant had overheard. "I'm glad I got that kind of insight, because I really thought we had better information than that," he remembered.[53]

From an intelligence-collection standpoint, Afghanistan was a nightmare. The strong suit of America's intelligence community was signals intelligence. Using a globe-spanning network of spy planes, satellites, and listening stations, the National Security Agency (NSA) could suck up everything from walkie-talkie transmissions to cellular and satellite phone calls. But Afghanistan in 2002 had few phones for the NSA to exploit. The ability to track bin Laden through signals intelligence had dried up when he stopped using satellite phones in 1998, according to an NSA report; the more careful Zawahiri had never used the phones in the first place,[54] while their ally Hekmatyar's close call with a Predator strike in May had cured him of an incautious satellite phone habit.[55] The military did what it could to stir up signals intelligence in Kunar, but it wasn't much. Sometimes, for example, attack jets would thunder past a village in the middle of the night, dropping flares, in the hopes that militants hiding out there would wake up thinking a raid was under way and make calls that orbiting spy planes could pinpoint.[56]

Absent signals intelligence, the hunt for bin Laden and other senior al-Qaida figures came down to human intelligence—the cultivation and use of informants. There could hardly have been a more difficult place for U.S. intelligence collectors to break into than Kunar and Nuristan. Compounding the problems that intelligence collectors faced all over Afghanistan was the mountainous north-eastern region's diversity of languages. Kunaris were mostly members of Afghanistan's majority Pashtun ethnic group, but Kunaris spoke Pashto with a distinctive accent and vocabulary that was difficult enough to find interpreters versed in. The higher you went into Kunar-Nuristan's mountains and the thin valleys that wound between them—the places where high-value targets were most likely to hide—the more likely you were to find villages where Pashto was only a second language.

"Four or five of us would show up with a Pelican case full of cash, but it was really hard to develop local sources in the Pech and its tributary valleys because people spoke local dialects," remembered Ron Moeller, a CIA paramilitary officer who was working in eastern Afghanistan in 2002 and would deploy there again repeatedly.[57] In the 1960s, a Norwegian linguist visiting the Pech valley had counted nine languages in a ten-kilometer radius; some of those had died out by the end of the twentieth century, but a few remained, severely limiting the ability of outsiders to get a grip on what was going on.[58]

Even knowing where you were and whom you were talking to was difficult. "In 2002, we barely had maps," said a Ranger officer. "We basically had Russian maps."[59] He wasn't exaggerating. The maps of Kunar with the most accurate topography and up-to-date representations of settled areas were 1980s-vintage Soviet ones, the place-names in Russian. What was marked as a village on these maps might be a single dense settlement, or several smaller settlements spread out on a stretch of mountainside, or just a couple of residential compounds. Many settlements were not marked at all, or were marked with outdated or mangled names, or disappeared entirely when new U.S. military maps were transliterated from the Russian ones. The village of Kunyak in the Pech valley, for instance—the scene of a costly and controversial 1985 Soviet defeat—never made it onto American maps.[60] Other settlements had two or more names, a Pashto name and an older one in a valley-specific native language like Korengali or Gambiri.

When U.S. troops visited a village, a group of elders would typically appear to break bread with them, wearing the standard baggy two-piece *shalwar kameez* in white or brown that the Americans called man-jammies. A host would roll a mat on the ground for everyone to crouch around, and then someone would bring out an array of shallow metal dishes: big bowls of rice and chicken or mutton, along with little bowls of chopped tomatoes and onions or apples and oranges. Naan came out in stacks and was used to eat everything else. Tea with sugar or milk would be produced, or sometimes Pepsis or Mountain Dews. An interpreter would help exchange pleasantries and explain that the assembled elders were the village *shura,* or council.

Just as one had to hike up to false peaks to see the real ones above, there were sometimes layers of misinformation for visitors to work through. If Americans came back to the same village for a second visit, they might meet with an entirely different group of elders and realize that the old men who'd first presented themselves as the village *shura* had been surrogates, sent to the initial meeting with the strangers to feel them out, and sometimes to obfuscate. One special operations officer remembered hiking west into the mountains from Asadabad with his team and staying the night at a tiny settlement they hadn't been to before. Reading off his map, the officer asked the elders to confirm the name of their town, which they did. The next day the same villagers corrected themselves. The name on the map wasn't right at all, they said, providing the real one now that they felt more comfortable with the soldiers.[61]

ALL THIS MADE one of the core tasks of human intelligence collection, always difficult, much more so: figuring out when one was being deliberately misled by a source.

Tipsters would try to trick or use American intelligence officers desperate for good information in a land they understood poorly. "We really didn't understand the layers and layers of local dynamics and relationships at all," said Moeller, the CIA paramilitary officer.[62] In some cases, a source might point a CIA or Defense Intelligence Agency (DIA) case officer toward a rival in business or politics or some dispute over land or water, another U.S. government official who was working in Afghanistan in 2002 remembered; in other cases, "people were just making up stories because they knew we'd pay for it," he said. For $5,000 or even $500—and American intelligence and special operations teams had plenty of cash to hand out to sources—a tipster might go to some lengths to make up a convincing story about someone being associated with al-Qaida or having let an Arab militant sleep in his home.[63] He might also sell the same story, or a different version of it, to a CIA case officer at one base and a DIA case officer at another base in another province.[64] "We were played all the time, every day, on every issue," a case officer who did rotations at FOB Asadabad in the early part of the war said.[65]

Faulty intelligence had led to some of the worst defeats Soviet forces suffered in Kunar: both the May 1985 ambush at Kunyak, into which an infantry company was lured by false tips about a mujahidin cache of CIA-supplied anti-aircraft missiles, and an even bloodier episode a month earlier, when disinformation about a meeting of mujahidin leaders had led thirty *spetsnaz* commandos into an ambush in the Marawara valley near Asadabad, which only one man survived.[66]

In the quiet early days of the American war in Kunar, when a serious insurgency had yet to emerge, the consequences were less deadly, but in the long term no less serious: as elsewhere in Afghanistan, misunderstandings and faulty intelligence could, and did, result in American troops' squandering goodwill and creating distrust. The case of Haji Ruhullah Wakil, one of the wealthiest men in the Pech valley, which introduced Kunaris to the concept of indefinite detention at Guantánamo Bay, was an early stumbling block.

I interviewed Ruhullah in 2013 in the comfortable living room of an upscale house in Kabul, over tea and with caged birds chirping nearby. Charismatic and personable, with high cheekbones hidden under a long beard that forked into two points, Ruhullah was a political operator, not a fighter; he had opposed the Taliban in the years before their fall from Dubai and Peshawar, managing money and making plans. He was also a businessman who made much of his money off gem mines in western Kunar, far up his native Pech valley. Ruhullah's smuggling as well as his political connections made him a useful contact, and after September 11, by his account, both Pakistani and British intelligence operatives approached him for help getting into Afghanistan and raising militia forces for the battle of Tora Bora.[67] During the air war that fall, according to another rich Kunari who would become a close ally of the CIA's, agency case officers often visited Ruhullah's home in Peshawar, which Kunari opponents of the Taliban were using as a headquarters to orchestrate their actions in the province.[68]

Ruhullah was forty-two in August 2002. In the months since the fall of the Taliban, he had visited Kabul as a Kunari representative in the council that elected Hamid Karzai as Afghanistan's interim president, met with UN officials, and escorted a British government counternarcotics team around the province looking for poppy fields. He had been meeting with the American soldiers at FOB Asadabad too, he told a *New York Times* reporter who was visiting his Asadabad compound the evening of August 21 after a dinner in honor of Kunar's new governor, and the Americans seemed to think al-Qaida was regrouping in Kunar. "I told them, 'If there are al-Qaida, tell us and we'll take care of them,'" Ruhullah boasted to the visitors lounging on pillows on the floor of his home. "It's been three months, and they haven't caught any al-Qaida."[69]

Later that night, Ruhullah got a call from one of the interpreters at FOB Asadabad, speaking on behalf of an American officer. Could Ruhullah come to the base for a conversation? Ruhullah agreed, and drove to the American camp with a group of men from his compound.

The way Ruhullah remembered it, the meeting with the Americans was cordial, and it was only as he and his men were leaving FOB Asadabad that soldiers stopped the twelve of them, bound their wrists with plastic flex cuffs, and threw hoods over their heads. They were being "PUC'd," as the U.S. military lingo for detaining someone went. ("PUC" stood for "person under control" and rhymed with "duck.") Ruhullah spent the next couple of hours locked in a latrine, because the base didn't have enough holding cells for everybody. Then the Americans trundled him and one of his associates, another prominent Pech resident named Sabar Lal Melma, onto helicopters bound for Bagram.[70]

BOTH RUHULLAH AND Sabar Lal wound up in Guantánamo, as inmates numbers 798 and 801. Like many other Afghans detained by American special operations forces early in the war, both men would be held for years and then eventually released. The evidence against the detainees scooped up in the first year or so usually amounted to whatever tip-off had led U.S. troops to detain them and any statements interrogators had extracted from other detainees. That was how it was with Ruhullah and Sabar Lal, who were accused of helping al-Qaida fighters escape Tora Bora.[71]

The reports always specified that Ruhullah was a leader in an organization called Jamaat al-Dawa, which was true.[72] At his Guantánamo hearings over the next few years, Ruhullah would often struggle to explain to American officers what Jamaat was: not a secretive foreign terrorist group like al-Qaida, as they often assumed, but a Kunari political party that, like all political parties in rural Afghanistan, had armed men at its disposal and had been established as an anticommunist mujahidin group during the jihad. Sabar Lal was the head of a militia associated with Jamaat; he had fought against the Taliban and was now ostensibly acting as a government-sanctioned border guard commander.

It did not gain Ruhullah any points from the American viewpoint that, like most other Jamaat followers and a hefty proportion of Kunar's population, he was a Salafi, a Muslim who strove to practice Islam as it had been practiced in the time of the Prophet Muhammad in the seventh century. Instead of the South Asian form of Islam of most of Afghanistan (including the Taliban), Kunar's Salafis follow an Islamic doctrine inspired by Saudi Arabia's fundamentalist Wahhabi sect. Ruhullah's uncle, Jamaat's founder, had imported Wahhabi-style Salafism to Kunar in the late 1970s, along with Saudi money and the first handful of Saudi volunteer fighters after the anticommunist jihad began a few years later. Salafism had remained popular in Kunar after both the Soviets and most of the Saudis went home; Kunari Salafis could be found on all sides of the intra-mujahidin struggle for control of the province that followed the Soviet withdrawal, with some eventually siding for and some against the Taliban, whose presence in Kunar was not strong. To Americans who didn't understand the backstory, though, "Salafi" and "Wahhabi"—terms that, confusingly, Kunaris used interchangeably—smacked suspiciously of foreign influence and international terrorism, and drew their suspicion.

The allegations that Ruhullah had helped Arabs escape Tora

Bora might have been true, or they might not have been. Ruhullah denied he'd done anything wrong. "Since 1990, I fought these people, the Taliban and al-Qaida," he protested to a Guantánamo tribunal. "I don't know how they could call me an enemy combatant."[73]

The reports from informants about Ruhullah and Sabar Lal were specific: that on a particular day in November 2001, Sabar Lal had smuggled a group of nine Arab fighters out of Tora Bora and sequestered them at a compound Ruhullah owned far up the Pech, and that in February 2002, Ruhullah helped settle another group of Arabs in the remote Korengal valley west of Asadabad.[74] To many Kunaris, these reports were also plausible; Ruhullah was known as an opportunist who had ties to the same Pakistani intelligence apparatus that bankrolled the Taliban. But they were impossible to verify, especially after the fact. And whether the reports were true or not, the sources American intelligence personnel in Kunar were getting their information from just happened to be Ruhullah's rivals and enemies—in politics, business, or both. "He might have had some link to al-Qaida, I don't know," one former Afghan government official who knew Ruhullah recalled. "Everybody was affiliated with everybody. But in order to remove your rivals, you can make up links to al-Qaida."[75]

Ruhullah had many rivals. That was natural in Kunar, where rivalry among peers (*siali* in Pashto), rivalry among relatives (*turborwali*), and other species of rivalry were ubiquitous features of life. And because Ruhullah was one of the province's wealthiest and most prominent men, so were his rivals. After Asadabad became the first provincial seat the Soviets withdrew from in 1988, Jamaat and a rival mujahidin party, Hizb-e Islami, had fought bitterly for control of the city, and Kunari commanders vied for control of the rest of the province and its natural resources, chiefly timber and precious and semiprecious gems like emeralds, aquamarine, and tourmaline. When the Taliban lost Jalalabad in November 2001, the Jamaat and Hizb commanders, now more like robber barons, divvied Kunar up, trading government titles for territory or cash, control of this checkpoint for that lumberyard or mine. That was how Sabar Lal's militia wound up as the semiofficial border guard.

A trio of rival strongmen took the biggest shares: Matiullah Khan, a towering man from the Pech valley with a massive head and prominent nose whose men seized control of Asadabad; southern Kunar's Haji Jahan Dad, an old mujahid who liked to show off the communist bullet embedded in his finger and who moved into the governor's mansion in the city until a different governor arrived from Kabul; and the timber baron of northern Kunar, Malik Zarin, whose connections included Afghanistan's exiled royal family, its interim president, Hamid Karzai, and the CIA. Zarin and Jahan Dad both had long-standing reputations for predatory behavior and were widely disliked by many Kunaris, who viewed Zarin as a robber baron and Jahan Dad as a brigand. But both men had relationships with the Northern Alliance, the anti-Taliban movement based in northern Afghanistan that the United States threw its weight behind after September 11, so the CIA had effectively inherited them as allies during the fall 2001 air campaign. Zarin had escorted the first CIA officers into Kunar from Pakistan that autumn, and after FOB Asadabad was established, he had supplied the first batch of recruits for the Mohawk mercenary force that the agency paid and special operators at the base often worked with.[76]

"My father would tell the Americans, 'Listen to us, because we know the society and we can prevent bloodshed,'" Zarin's son remembered. "He was the leader of the area, so the Americans came to us for men and we gave them our men, and they came to us for information and we gave them information."[77]

Ruhullah didn't know which of the various groups of Americans at FOB Asadabad detained him and Sabar Lal—JSOC, CIA, Green Berets—and it still isn't clear more than a decade later. Nor was it clear exactly what tip led the Americans to bring the two men in. But the general outlines of what happened match with stories that were playing out with other U.S. units at other bases in other parts of Afghanistan.

As American military and intelligence personnel struggled to understand the confusing society and landscape they found themselves in the middle of, they had latched onto Kunar's big three warlords, caring less about who had fought for or against the Taliban than about who would give them information and militiamen.

Malik Zarin, the CIA's biggest ally in Kunar, was an ally of Ruhullah's as well. Working out of Ruhullah's home in Peshawar, the two had collaborated to help CIA officers understand what was going on in Kunar during the American bombing campaign in 2001.[78] But another of the province's big three was an avowed rival of Ruhullah's: Matiullah Khan, who got along well with American soldiers despite his previous support for the Taliban (he preferred to stress his anticommunist mujahidin credentials) and would soon be named provincial police chief.

Ruhullah and Matiullah had been at odds for years for two reasons: the two men were business competitors in the Pech's gem trade, and their families were engaged in a long-standing feud whose origins were murky but which had continued when the Taliban took power and Matiullah sided with them. "Matiullah joined the Taliban to take revenge against Ruhullah," one of Matiullah's relatives explained bluntly.[79] Matiullah's men had been in gunfights with Sabar Lal's in the western Pech in the recent past. Whether the tip that led to Ruhullah's detention came from him or from someone else (a warlord in neighboring Nangarhar Province who was also working closely with the Americans and despised Ruhullah is another plausible source[80]), Matiullah was happy to see Ruhullah go and insisted his new American friends had been right to arrest him.[81]

Both men would eventually be released, Sabar Lal in 2007 and Ruhullah the next year. The reasons the Guantánamo administrative review board put forward to explain their release were simple: in Sabar Lal's case, an acknowledgment of the obvious fact that the Kunari militia commander did not have prior knowledge of the September 11 attacks, and in Ruhullah's, a long list of ways in which he had opposed the Taliban. There was no explanation of exactly why they'd been detained in the first place.[82]

After his release, Ruhullah set up a new life for himself in Kabul, meeting with U.S. and Afghan officials and Western journalists (to whom he always proclaimed his innocence) and advocating on behalf of other repatriated Afghan Guantánamo inmates. For Sabar Lal, a darker fate awaited. Swept up in the first chapter of America's war in northeastern Afghanistan, he would be killed in a later one, shot during a 2011 JSOC raid on his Jalalabad home following accusations that he had been helping bankroll the Taliban, the movement he had been fighting against in the years before his detention.

.   .   .

CHIEF WARRANT OFFICER Brian Halstead arrived at FOB Asadabad shortly after Ruhullah's and Sabar Lal's August 2002 detention, as the second-in-command of a team of Green Berets. He had no inside information on how the detention went down, but thought what made their case unusual was mainly the two men's high profile and the fact that they made it all the way to Guantánamo. Many other people, he was confident, had wound up detained at Asadabad or Bagram, even if only briefly, because of tips motivated by grudges.

A profane wiseass with almost a decade in the Special Forces, Halstead tried to learn as much about the world he'd dropped into as he could, and the big three warlords seemed as good guides and points of entry into this complicated and alien place as any. They came with their own small armies and networks of informants, ready to go.

"A lot of us were left to make our own decisions," Halstead remembered. "Was a guy who'd been Taliban tainted forever? What did it mean that he'd been Taliban? Had he just accepted the Taliban as the government and that was it? What if he'd fought the Taliban before that?"[83]

But relying on the warlords came with trade-offs, to which Halstead, as a trained intelligence collector, was not blind. He worked most closely with Malik Zarin, and he knew that the timber baron was very calculating about what intelligence he fed his foreign friends. "These guys were the power back then," the Special Forces warrant officer explained. "Malik Zarin realized we were willing to give him all the guns and money he wanted, and he saw a great opportunity to use American forces as surrogates, risk fewer of his own people, and enrich himself, all by giving us information. It was always accurate, but I'm sure he was also using me to eliminate competition."[84]

Allying with strongmen known for preying on the weak also tainted American troops and intelligence officers with their predatory reputation. "The question a lot of Kunaris were asking was 'Who is whose proxy?' and the answer was getting harder to discern; it was hard to separate Malik Zarin's agenda from the American agenda," one Afghan American who worked with the troops at FOB Asadabad told me. "The one thing anyone in Kunar liked about the Taliban was that they had sidelined Malik Zarin. Now anyone standing up to him was on some list."[85]

But intelligence-wise, figures like Zarin, Matiullah, and Jahan Dad were the only game in town. The turbulent rivalries and feuds of Kunar just made it a dangerous game—for people like Ruhullah and Sabar Lal in the short term, and for Americans in the long term as detentions motivated by powerful men's grudges wore away at the goodwill Kunaris initially felt for the visitors in desert camouflage.

A WARRIOR FINDS HIS WAR

The vast majority of American soldiers who deployed to Kunar went there only once, spending six months or a year and then never seeing the place again. It was the system the military had used on peacekeeping missions in the 1990s; in long-haul missions like the Balkans and Afghanistan, soldiers couldn't be expected to stay until the job was done, whatever that meant.

Brian Halstead was that rare soldier who deployed to the same place twice: he went home to Fort Bragg in late 2002, spent six months stateside, and was then sent to Kunar again. This time around, Halstead was deploying with another exception, an eccentric, thirty-five-year-old Special Forces A-team commander who would never really leave Kunar, Captain Jim Gant.[86]

A small-framed man with a big forehead and graying hair, Gant was a warrior who'd been waiting his whole life to go to war. Like many American soldiers, he venerated the martial culture of ancient Sparta; he devoured books on the Spartans and had a tattoo of the Greek letter lambda, which adorned Spartan shields, on his left forearm. The book *The Green Berets,* on which John Wayne's iconic pro–Vietnam War movie was based, inspired Gant to join the Special Forces. By 2003, he'd worn the green beret and the accompanying blue-and-yellow Special Forces shoulder patch first as an enlisted soldier and then as an officer, but the closest he'd been to combat was advising Egyptian forces during Desert Storm.[87]

Kunar would be different, Gant knew the day he got off a Chinook at the dusty landing zone outside FOB Asadabad's perimeter wall in the spring of 2003. The place looked like a South Asian version of a setting for a Western; it was the frontier, the edge of American influence in Afghanistan, and the wild front line in America's retaliation for September 11. The base had grown over the winter but was still basically the same small rectangular compound, its walls supplemented by concertina wire and Hesco barriers, wire-framed baskets that soldiers filled with dirt and gravel. There were some plywood shacks now to help accommodate the base population, which had risen to a bit more than two hundred Americans (the Rangers had been replaced by paratroopers from the conventional Army's 82nd Airborne Division) plus their interpreters and the Mohawks, the CIA's local surrogates. One building was for the CIA team, one a command post for the Special Forces. Another, where the soldiers watched porn they'd brought over from the States, was nicknamed Heather's Heavenly Haven.[88]

Next to the front gate was a "wanted" poster in Pashto with Osama bin Laden's picture on it, advertising the $25 million reward for information leading to the terrorist leader and a Hotmail address where tips could be reported.[89] The bin Laden poster might as well have been a joke. No one in Kunar outside the American base, the little UN compound in Asadabad, and the governor's mansion was emailing anyone about anything; most Kunaris couldn't read, and cellular service, let alone internet service, was just starting to arrive. When Gant and Halstead showed video clips of the planes striking the Twin Towers to the Afghans they met with by way of explanation for their presence, some had heard of bin Laden and some hadn't; for most, "al-Qaida" was a new term. Yet fighters in the mountains harassed the base regularly with old Chinese and Soviet-bloc rockets and mortar shells, which usually flew far wide of their marks and even when they struck inside the base perimeter rarely hurt anyone.[90]

Who was doing the shooting and why, no one seemed to know, including the CIA personnel who rotated through the base but lacked the manpower to get out and investigate things on their own. Taliban, al-Qaida, Jamaat, Hizb—the military just called its opponents "ACM," for "anti-coalition militia." (Local people were little more specific, usually just calling the guerrillas *dushman*, "enemy," while the *dushman* themselves preferred *mujahidin*.) The only guidance that anyone gave Gant on his way to Kunar was a handwritten note the Special Forces battalion intelligence officer gave him at Bagram: "Kill or capture ACMs."[91] The intelligence staff at Bagram didn't know much about who the ACMs were; they were hoping that Gant's team and others like it would figure it out by catching some to interrogate.

KUNAR WAS EVERYTHING Gant hoped it would be. "I was born in Kunar," he would say when he returned to the province for a long-anticipated second tour years later. "I became a man there."[92] He and his Green Berets all grew beards, which had become de rigueur among American special operators since September 11. Besides helping build rapport with rural Pashtuns, who all had thick facial hair and saw it as a sign of maturity and seriousness, the beards helped lend the whole enterprise a rugged, adventurous feel. Gant and his men had $30,000 per month to spend on informants, food, or whatever else they saw fit, and not much oversight—the way Green Berets, the Army's "unconventional warriors," were trained to work. In their downtime, they swam naked in the river and drank Early Times whiskey they weren't supposed to have.[93]

When Gant came back to Kunar in 2010, the war in Afghanistan would be a different beast, centralized around sprawling headquarters full of senior officers, with written approvals required to go just about anywhere, and waged out of towering armored vehicles. None of that existed in 2003. If Gant wanted to go anywhere within ten kilometers of FOB Asadabad, all he had to do was send a short "who, what, when, where, why" summary up to his commander, then load up in Humvees or pickup trucks and go.[94] When Halstead just wanted a team to go somewhere on a hunch or on short notice, he grabbed Gant, who was restless and wanted to fight.[95]

Looking to tangle with the enemy, Gant started driving west with his seven-soldier team and whatever local forces they could scrounge up, along the rocky track that led from Asadabad up the Pech valley.

It worked. In late May, Halstead got a tip that a Taliban-affiliated bomb maker named Dr. Niamatullah was hiding out in a residential compound in a little town called Dag, eight miles up the Pech from Asadabad. That the Taliban were active at all in a valley where their pre-2001 presence had been minimal should have raised alarm bells. But with scant details about the enemy they were fighting or the local political context, the Green Berets didn't understand the full significance of that fact—that an anti-American insurgency was brewing and that it was uniting Kunaris of various parties, including ones who had previously opposed the Taliban regime, under a banner of opposition to foreign invaders.

The Pech was wide and prone to ferocious spring flooding, and the only two vehicle bridges had been broken for years. Dag was the site of a footbridge, one of the rickety-looking wooden ones that American troops liked to call Indiana Jones bridges. Leaving their Humvees on the far bank after dark, Gant's A-team walked across the bridge, trailing five pickups crammed with the CIA's Mohawk mercenaries in their olive-green fatigues.[96]

One of Halstead's local informants, whose pencil sketch of the target compound was the best "imagery" the Green Berets had to plan from, led the approach. Halstead and a militia commander knocked on the compound's front door and announced themselves, then broke it open and were greeted with gunfire. Shooting back, the American and Afghan troops hit some guerrillas—the Mohawks riddled Dr. Niamatullah with bullets as he escaped the compound and made for the river—but they also wounded two women. A CIA contractor who was helping lead the Mohawks somehow managed to fire on his own troops, but he didn't hit any of them.

Though it was hardly perfect, the Special Forces soldiers counted the Dag raid a success. Satisfying proof that they had killed not just an "ACM" but a bona fide Taliban operative came a few days later, when a Taliban media arm in Pakistan released an obituary, praising Niamatullah as the movement's loyal servant.[97] Gant and his A-team started driving up the Pech every week or two, because it seemed as if the enemy didn't want them to.[98] "You'd turn in to the Pech and right away you'd start seeing the smoke signals or flashlight signals" as insurgent spotters alerted one another that Americans were coming, a soldier remembered.[99]

A few days after the raid, Halstead attended a meeting in Asadabad to address what had happened with elders from Dag and other Pech towns. He brought along Kunar's new governor, Sayed Fazel Akbar, a friend of President Karzai's (they had even gone to Disneyland together[100]) who had recently returned to Afghanistan after five years living in the United States. Akbar was a mujahidin veteran from a prominent Kunari family, and Halstead hoped the new governor would be able to use the meeting to reconnect with people from the Pech and show that he was the new sheriff in town.

Instead, the Pech elders directed their complaints to the Americans, who, they well knew, had been the ones behind the Dag raid. Niamatullah was Taliban, they acknowledged; they understood why he'd been targeted. But they were outraged that the Americans had come for him at night and broken into his fortified home, where in Pashtun culture a man and especially his female relatives were supposed to be safe. It was hard for Halstead to take the critique seriously, although it was one that American commanders would have to address time and time again over the next decade, sometimes straight from President Karzai's mouth. Given their night-vision advantage, night was the only time the special operators at Asadabad were interested in launching dangerous raids, and they had hit the right house.

"They told us we couldn't be knocking down doors in the night, but I wasn't going to apologize," Halstead remembered. The response he gave the elders through an interpreter made perfect sense to the Special Forces warrant officer: *We're here to kill the people who attacked our cities. We'll be gone in the near future. So just cooperate. If we do knock on your door during the night, you should open it.*[101]

From the Kunari perspective, this was an unsatisfying response. Groups of elders had been pleading for the night raids to stop for a year, and the Dag mission was just the latest in a string of disrespectful and alarming episodes going back to the detention of Haji Ruhullah and Sabar Lal the previous summer. Although different groups of Americans came and went, their answers and excuses were always similar, and there was no sign that they would be leaving altogether anytime soon.

THE DOZEN OR SO CIA personnel at FOB Asadabad rotated every couple of months, and in these early days of the war, they ran the gamut from highly experienced paramilitary specialists to people who just weren't prepared for the job. First-tour officers and contractors with minimal combat-zone training abounded, and the agency selected its base chiefs "because they were up for management billets, not because they had specific knowledge of the area," explained Moeller, the paramilitary officer.[102] Halstead remembered his horror upon being told that one acting Asadabad base chief wasn't a case officer at all but an imagery analyst, with no training in handling sources.[103]

The worst was Dave Passaro, an angry, often-drunk thirty-seven-year-old Ranger veteran who had entered the CIA's armed contractor force at a time when it was relaxing its hiring standards to meet its expanding post–September 11 needs. What none of the soldiers at FOB Asadabad knew was that before joining the Army, Passaro had been fired from a Connecticut police force for assaulting a man who owed him money and, in court proceedings while in uniform, had been accused of beating his stepson with a flashlight while drunk. It would have been useful knowledge.

During the May Dag raid, Passaro had mistakenly fired on his own Mohawks, giving the Special Forces soldiers reason to wonder about his competence. Then, in June, Passaro started bugging Halstead and Gant to help him detain a man named Abdul Wali from a nearby valley who he'd heard was involved in the rocket attacks against FOB Asadabad. The Americans brought the middle-aged man's name to Governor Akbar, hoping to avoid a complicated raid into his home valley, and Akbar obliged, convincing Abdul Wali that the best way to clear his name would be to present himself for questioning at the U.S. base.

Halstead and Governor Akbar's teenage son Hyder were both there for Passaro's initial questioning of Abdul Wali, and both found the CIA contractor's behavior bizarrely aggressive—so aggressive that a worried soldier filming the session turned his camera off. Abdul Wali had reasonable answers for everything asked of him, but Passaro wasn't satisfied. Eventually he cuffed the Afghan and took him to a cell.

For the next three days, Passaro beat and abused Abdul Wali. Telling the paratroopers guarding the cell that he was subject to different rules from the military, he put the detainee in "stress positions," kept a sandbag over his head, beat him with a metal flashlight while apparently drunk, and kicked him in the crotch hard enough to lift him off the ground and cause internal injuries. Abdul Wali died his fourth day in the cell.[104]

CIA personnel had been using similar "enhanced interrogation techniques" on detainees at the agency's secret Salt Pit prison in Kabul for nearly a year, all with official sanction; one Afghan prisoner had already died there.[105] But Passaro, the CIA maintained, was a low-level rogue acting without permission. The agency pulled him out of Afghanistan the next week, and he was eventually sentenced to eight years in prison—the only CIA employee or contractor ever jailed for post–September 11 prisoner abuse. (After his eventual release, Passaro was unapologetic. "Man, I wasn't hired to be nice to those terrorists. I was there to get a job done," he would say in a 2015 interview. "Anything that I did to Abdul Wali, none of that constitutes torture. In hindsight, I wouldn't have done anything different.)[106] What other agency personnel at Asadabad did or didn't know about Passaro's actions at the time was kept under wraps during the court proceedings.

The damage was done, however. "The news of [Abdul Wali's] death spread quickly among the people and had a very negative impact on their perceptions of the Afghan government and the Americans," Governor Akbar explained in a letter to the judge who sentenced Passaro, noting that at least one old mujahidin commander from the Pech, called Najmuddin, had been planning to come down from the hills and join the government until Abdul Wali's killing deterred him. "The distrust of the Americans increased, [and] the security and reconstruction efforts of Afghanistan were dealt a blow."[107] Halstead agreed. "His actions were a terrible black eye," the Green Beret said. "I'm sure people still talk about it in Kunar. It was a lot harder for people to trust Americans and come talk to us when they thought they might get beaten to death with a flashlight."[108]

People in Kunar do still talk about the death of Abdul Wali, along with other incidents in 2002 and 2003 that they saw as abuses and missteps. In my interviews more than a decade after the events, in fact, Kunari notables like clerics and parliamentarians talked more often about these events than about the many civilian deaths that came later during years of intense fighting between local insurgents and American infantry units with their artillery and air support.[109]

A prominent Kunari cleric who, a decade later, would be appointed by the Karzai government to investigate civilian deaths in American drone strikes in Kunar, Mawlawi Shahzada Shahid, remembered his first interactions with Americans favorably. They had invited him to FOB Asadabad for a meal, talked to him about his life and his thoughts on the province's affairs, and asked him if he knew about September 11 (he did). "The Americans were afraid of the people and our food at first, but gradually they got closer and ate in our houses and saw that no one poisoned them," Shahzada joked of the relationship in those early days.

But the secretive detentions started to drain Kunaris' reservoir of goodwill. "People thought the Americans would practice human rights and follow the law, but they didn't," he said. "When they arrested us, there was no court to go to."[110] The widely known mistreatment of a few early detainees created an understandable fear that friends and family members who disappeared into the American detention system would be abused, and the number of Kunaris scooped up and sent off to the big U.S. prison facility at Bagram would only rise in the years to come.

A middle-aged man from the Pech named Shugrullah started by telling me about the Soviet entry into the province. He had been a small boy then, and he remembered what people said about how the Russian troops acted—how they looted and destroyed buildings, how they killed civilians indiscriminately. (In April 1979 at a village outside Asadabad, a team of Soviet military advisers helped direct a government commando unit's slaughter of more than a thousand men and boys.[111]) The Americans never did anything like that, Shugrullah stressed, as if to establish that he was not anti-American. "The American troops brought security," he said. "But then things got worse. They arrested innocent people, put sacks over people's heads, and dropped bombs based on wrong information and lies. The Americans didn't behave well, and that is why people fought against them."[112]

JIM GANT FLEW home in October 2003. It would be seven years before he returned to the province he'd come to love. When he left, no American had yet died in Kunar, but it was obvious that security was worsening and public opinion hardening. Amid rising attacks by militants, the UN had closed its Asadabad office a few weeks earlier.

"It was escalating," Gant remembered.[113] He was right. The guerrillas he had fought were the early members of an insurgency that would grow stronger in Kunar every year for many years to come. And as Gant made the long plane ride home to Fort Bragg, more than a thousand Army Rangers were flying in the opposite direction, from military bases in Georgia and the Pacific Northwest, on another JSOC man-hunting mission, a big one. They were bound for the Pech and its headwaters, deep in Nuristan.

CHAPTER 2

WINTER STRIKE

2003

"IT LOOKED LIKE DOOMSDAY"

Bagram Airfield buzzed with activity as the nights grew cold at the end of October 2003. For days, cargo jet after cargo jet had been churning through the main American military hub in Afghanistan. Descending steeply, unloading their cargo on the tarmac at the foot of the Salang mountains, and taking off again, the huge gray C–17s disgorged Humvees, helicopters, and hundreds of Rangers.

From the airfield's flight line, the newcomers headed to Bagram's JSOC compound, filling up rows of plywood huts that engineers were building near two huge, connected green tents that would soon house the counterterrorism command's operations center. For now, JSOC leaders were working out of a smaller, squat, Russian-built structure in the compound that SEAL Team 6 had been using as its forward headquarters.

The operations center in the little building was crammed with new arrivals from Fort Bragg, JSOC's stateside home, many of them staring up at a wall-mounted screen showing the slowly rotating video feed from a Predator drone. In the middle of the crowd was JSOC's new commander, Major General Stanley McChrystal. The forty-nine-year-old McChrystal, who had previously commanded

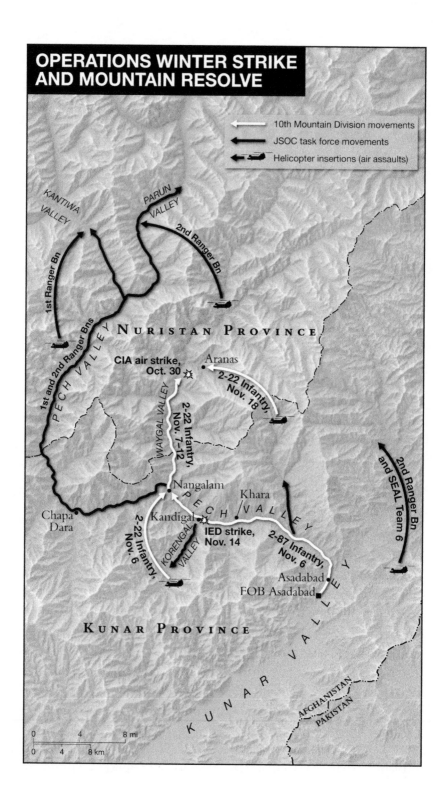

OPERATIONS WINTER STRIKE AND MOUNTAIN RESOLVE

→ 10th Mountain Division movements

→ JSOC task force movements

→ Helicopter insertions (air assaults)

KANTIWA VALLEY

PARUN VALLEY

1st Ranger Bn

2nd Ranger Bn

2nd Ranger Bn

1st and 2nd Ranger Bns

PECH VALLEY

NURISTAN PROVINCE

CIA air strike, Oct. 30 ☆

Aranas

2-22 Infantry, Nov. 18

WAYGAL VALLEY

2-22 Infantry, Nov. 7–12

Nangalam

Khara VALLEY

P E C H

Chapa Dara

2-22 Infantry, Nov. 6

Kandigal

IED strike, Nov. 14 ☆

KORENGAL VALLEY

2-87 Infantry, Nov. 6

2nd Ranger Bn and SEAL Team 6

Asadabad

FOB Asadabad

KUNAR PROVINCE

K U N A R   V A L L E Y

AFGHANISTAN

PAKISTAN

0   4   8 mi

0   4   8 km

the 75th Ranger Regiment, had been at JSOC's helm for less than a month, but he was already shaking up the counterterrorism command. Nearly half of his old regiment was getting ready to launch by helicopter, Humvee, and pickup truck into the valleys of Nuristan, north of the Pech, in search of a set of former mujahidin commanders suspected of having harbored or otherwise aided bin Laden after his escape from Tora Bora. The operation was called Winter Strike.

But on the night before Halloween, with Rangers and helicopters still flowing into Bagram, news arrived that threatened to upset the plans that had brought them to Afghanistan.[1] CIA officials were saying they had a target ready to go, based on a rare piece of specific intelligence: a cluster of houses on the side of a mountain in the Waygal valley twenty straight-line miles northwest of FOB Asadabad, outside a steeply sloping town called Aranas (pronounced "Uh-ronz") that was famous for its blacksmiths and silversmiths.[2]

In one of the houses on the mountain, an Afghan source working for the CIA claimed, was an Afghan warlord near the top of the agency's and JSOC's target lists: Gulbuddin Hekmatyar, who had briefly been the country's prime minister before the Taliban seized Kabul in 1997. A former American ally during the jihad against the Soviets, Hekmatyar had once accused the CIA's Islamabad station chief of plotting to assassinate him.[3] Now the agency was trying to do exactly that, using military resources. Hekmatyar was a longtime associate of bin Laden's, arguably closer to him than anyone in the Taliban.

The Predator circled, feeding video back to Bagram and the United States. At Langley, the CIA's director, George Tenet, wanted the cluster of buildings struck—ideally raided by SEALs or Rangers, but bombed if necessary. The memory of bin Laden's escape at Tora Bora was a powerful incentive against inaction.[4]

JSOC's commander, McChrystal, received the CIA's request from his own superiors at the Tampa, Florida, headquarters of U.S. Central Command, or CENTCOM, the military organization that oversaw the wars in both Iraq and Afghanistan. McChrystal was inclined to wait, according to a subordinate who was with him at the time. His forces would be ready to move in a few days, and the military wanted to confirm the agency's intelligence with one of its own sources, an Afghan informant handled by the DIA. "I'd be lying if I told you we were sure it was Hekmatyar, and because of the terrain we couldn't get our source up there to confirm," the JSOC officer who was with McChrystal at Bagram remembered.[5]

But the CIA informant's tip was tantalizingly specific, and top officials at Langley had much greater confidence in it.[6] Tenet asked CENTCOM to strike right away, Rangers or no Rangers. Armed aircraft headed toward the Waygal: a B-1 bomber high above with a weapons bay full of bombs, and, behind and below it, a slower-moving AC-130 Spectre gunship.[7]

AT THE SETTLEMENT on the mountainside, the hum of surveillance aircraft had been audible all day. The cluster of buildings consisted of several small houses, a guesthouse, a mosque, and a religious school. Late on October 30, most of the school's students left for their homes, because there wouldn't be any classes the next morning, Friday.[8] That left the members of a wealthy extended family, the Rabbanis, and their guests—among whom, according to the CIA's source, was Hekmatyar.[9]

After an evening Ramadan prayer at the mosque, the family members dispersed to their houses, according to one brother then in his thirties, Zabiullah Rabbani—except for another brother, Ahmad, their mother's favorite, who slept in the mosque.

"It was before midnight and everyone was getting ready for sleep when there was a big explosion," Zabiullah remembered. "All the windows and doors were knocked down." A satellite-guided bomb, dropped by the high-flying B-1, had struck the mosque, and when the dust settled, a raging fire illuminated the mountainside. A third brother, Mohammad—who had spent much of the day in the woods trying to lure back a herd of goats the circling surveillance planes had spooked—climbed to the roof of an intact building and shouted at the confused people spilling out of their houses to flee into the forest.[10]

The next set of bombs struck a few minutes after the first, according to Zabiullah. One hit the house belonging to an uncle, Niamatullah, and flattened it. As Zabiullah himself headed for the woods, he could see trees on fire, and he discerned a new, lower, growling sound overhead.[11] It was the propellers of the AC-130, a gray cargo plane retrofitted as a gunship. Manned by thirteen special operations airmen, with a howitzer and a variety of smaller guns bristling from its left side, an AC-130 would orbit a target, spitting shells at a central point. A secret 2002 report by al-Qaida fighters about their early encounters with Americans had warned of the AC-130 and the "evil sound" of its guns.[12] That was the next sound Zabiullah and his relatives heard.

Among the various headquarters monitoring the strike's progress was CENTCOM's air operations center in Qatar. "They struck the target as planned, but then a lot of people went running from the buildings, and that's where the AC-130 came in," recalled Major General Bob Elder, the Air Force officer overseeing the Qatar operations center—going after what the military called "squirters," people running from the target area.[13] At that point, the preplanned strike was over, and the gunship was on the hunt, using night-vision sensors that could pick out the heat of human forms.

The AC-130 circled the area, the flow of shells from its guns stretching down like a laser beam, visible because of the tracers. A young woman was cut down outside, running for the forest. Other people, including children, died in the woods as they tried to hide in caves and crevices. It went on long enough, according to a Rabbani family member from the nearest town, Aranas, for him and his neighbors to wake up and hike two miles, through a gorge and over a mountain ridge, to find that the cannon fire was still too heavy for them to get close.[14]

"When the planes went away at three or four in the morning, it was quiet again and we were all hiding on our own, not knowing who was dead or alive," said Zabiullah.[15] The mosque, school, guesthouse, and at least one house were in ruins, and dead livestock littered the ground. "It looked like doomsday," said the family member from Aranas who finally reached the scene at dawn.[16]

Within hours of the strike's end on the morning of October 31, phones were ringing in Kabul as people from Aranas contacted government officials. The reports said that six or more Rabbani family members and guests had died, including several young children.[17] "We did collateral damage calculations for every operation, and this one caused a lot of civilian casualties," said Elder, the Air Force general tracking the strike from Qatar. "I thought it was much worse than six people, frankly."[18]

There was no immediate suggestion—no radio traffic, phone call, or jihadist press release—that the strike had hit its mark and killed Hekmatyar. But neither was it possible for American intelligence to conclude, based on the reports, that he *hadn't* been there. There was no way to know one way or the other without putting boots on the ground at the scene.

GENERAL ABIZAID'S BIG-ASS OPERATION

Seven weeks earlier, the day before the second anniversary of September 11, al-Qaida's media arm had released a video of Osama bin Laden and Zawahiri picking their way across a rocky, wooded mountainside with the aid of walking sticks, accompanied by a voice-over from bin Laden. Both men wore standard rural Pashtun robes and *pakol* hats, and slung over bin Laden's back was his signature snub-nosed carbine. In the video's final scene, the two men sat together on a ledge, looking out over a vista of dense conifer forest, the signature vegetation of northeastern Afghanistan and the adjacent wilds of Pakistan.[19]

In Washington, the video served as a reminder that two years into the war in Afghanistan and six months after the invasion of Iraq, the terrorist masterminds who had stirred the colossus were still alive, apparently healthy, and somewhere they felt safe enough to stroll outdoors together. This reminder came just in time for presidential primary season in the United States and an accompanying spotlight on the results of the Bush administration's two wars. An audio recording from bin Laden followed a few weeks later, and soon Democratic presidential candidates were working the failure to find bin Laden into their campaign remarks.[20]

Bush's defense secretary, Donald Rumsfeld, was asking the same questions at the Pentagon. In a memo the week of the video release, Rumsfeld bemoaned the inability of the military and the intelligence community to find America's top targets. "I keep reading the . . . intel. It leaves one with the impression that we know a lot," he complained. "However, when one pushes on that information it is pretty clear we don't have actionable intelligence."[21]

In Tampa, CENTCOM's commander, General John Abizaid, ordered a new push in Afghanistan to pick up bin Laden's trail. The region the intelligence community brought to CENTCOM's attention for Winter Strike (or "General Abizaid's Big-Ass Operation," as some JSOC planners nicknamed it) was Nuristan, the even wilder and more rugged province to which Kunar was a gateway.[22]

Early modern Afghan chroniclers who referred to Kunar as a *yaghistan,* or lawless place, called its northern neighbor Kafiristan, or the land of infidels.[23] Until its conquest and conversion into Nuristan, the land of the enlightened, at the end of the nineteenth century, its inhabitants were wine-drinking animists, and the region was not recognized as part of Afghanistan at all.[24] One of the first Western visitors, an adventurer and mercenary who trekked up the Pech into Kafir territory in the 1820s, described it as "one huge fortress."[25]

The biggest clue pointing toward Nuristan was bin Laden's association with Gulbuddin Hekmatyar, the fundamentalist warlord the CIA had nearly killed in the U.S. government's debut combat operation in Kunar, the May 2002 Predator strike in the Shigal valley. Hekmatyar had spent much of the jihad in Pakistan, but Kunar and Nuristan had long been strongholds of his Hizb-e Islami mujahidin faction.[26]

Fifty-five years old, Hekmatyar often wore a black turban with glasses and a dress shirt, and with his long nose, severe brows, and drooping eyelids he bore a slight resemblance to the actor Christopher Lee. He was well known to the CIA, to say the least.[27] In the 1980s, via conduits in Pakistani intelligence, the agency had joined Saudi Arabia in funding and arming Hekmatyar's Hizb-e Islami—the mujahidin party that attracted the greatest share of visiting Arab militants[28]—against the Soviets. One of his men had been the first mujahidin commander to receive Stinger anti-aircraft missiles from the agency in 1986,[29] and a 1988 photo captured a meeting in Islamabad between Hekmatyar, the head of Pakistani intelligence, and U.S. officials, including the CIA director, William Webster.[30]

The relationship had not been a friendly one. The CIA always knew that Hekmatyar disliked the United States only a little less—or less urgently—than he did the Soviet Union, and Hekmatyar believed that the Americans were plotting to kill him at the same time that they were backing him.[31] While he was taking money and arms from the United States, Hekmatyar was also beginning his long relationship with bin Laden, then an upstart Saudi visitor to the war who had money but not much in the way of jihadist credentials. Hizb fighters escorted a twenty-eight-year-old bin Laden into Afghanistan on his first trip into the country and then on his first combat mission,[32] and during the 1987 battle of Jaji—the victory over Soviet troops that gave the thirty-year-old bin Laden combat credibility and allowed him to establish al-Qaida—Hekmatyar came to the young Saudi commander's aid when other Afghan mujahidin commanders abandoned him. That was not the kind of thing bin Laden forgot.[33] He grew closer to Hekmatyar and his party than to any other mujahidin faction; Hizb commanders rented land to al-Qaida for its first training camp and sold Stinger missiles to al-Qaida members as they battled the communists.[34]

After the Soviet withdrawal, Hekmatyar, like his Saudi friend, declared his enmity toward the United States, and the CIA cut ties. When bin Laden returned to Afghanistan in 1996 after a stint in Sudan, Hekmatyar helped make the arrangements, and when he flew into Jalalabad, Hekmatyar and other old friends welcomed him.[35] Bin Laden's association with the Taliban began only four months later, when the movement captured Jalalabad and inherited him as a guest.[36] Six months before September 11, a CIA analysis had singled out Hekmatyar as one of bin Laden's two most likely fallback hosts should the Taliban lose power[37]—an assessment that proved correct, with the Saudi terrorist even making arrangements about future sanctuary with his old Afghan friend in advance of the attacks.[38]

The Iranian government had expelled Hekmatyar in early 2002, retaliating for President Bush's "axis of evil" State of the Union address by unleashing him into Pakistan days after the speech. Since then, the CIA had been working to track down its old acquaintance.[39] Special operators had tried and failed to grab him when he left Iran in February.[40] The agency didn't know how close its drone strike in the Shigal had come to killing not only Hekmatyar but

Kashmir Khan, the legendary Hizb-e Islami military commander hosting him at the time; nor did it know that the strike had prompted Kashmir Khan to evacuate not only Hekmatyar but bin Laden and Zawahiri from the Shigal to a hiding spot close to the Pakistani border.[41] The agency's best guess as to Hekmatyar's location now was Nuristan or a neighboring part of Kunar. Old Hizb commanders there like Kashmir Khan, the CIA correctly guessed, might have helped bin Laden escape Tora Bora. If they or Hekmatyar could be found, they might provide the next critical piece of intelligence for the manhunt.[42] "It wasn't because we gave a shit about them," a CIA officer told me of his agency's interest in Hekmatyar and his associates. "It was because they might have information about 1 and 2," the intelligence community's number one and number two targets, bin Laden and Zawahiri.[43]

To reach these valleys north of the Pech, CENTCOM's commander, Abizaid, turned both to an infantry unit already in Afghanistan and to JSOC.

SEAL Team 6 operators had already raided Nuristani villages over the past year, flying in from Bagram and finding little of note.[44] But Abizaid knew that JSOC had the resources to do much more than launch a few raids. The command had the manpower and helicopters, in the form of Rangers and the 160th Special Operations Aviation Regiment, not only to launch into several Nuristani valleys in quick succession but to stay there for weeks afterward and comb through them. It also had the rare flexibility to move hundreds of men and their vehicles around the world with a few days' notice. Moreover, JSOC's new commander, Stan McChrystal, made no secret of his itch to escalate JSOC's role in the war on terror.

Within days of receiving the task, McChrystal had alerted the Ranger Regiment, and its biggest short-notice mobilization since the 1989 invasion of Panama got under way. "We didn't have a significant amount of intelligence at all," one of McChrystal's senior staff remembered. "We were going to use Rangers to make our intelligence, to develop up."[45] The Rangers would show up in remote places where old Hekmatyar associates felt safe and then see, through whatever kinds of interpreters they could scrounge up, what the locals would tell them about the people they were looking for.

But the unexpected order to get up to the site in the Waygal that the CIA had had bombed based on *its* intelligence came before most of the Rangers arrived at Bagram. So CENTCOM looked next to a unit of the ten-thousand-strong U.S. military force already in Afghanistan. The 1st Brigade, 10th Mountain Division (so named for its World War II service in the Italian Alps, not because it had any special mountain training) had deployed from Fort Drum in upstate New York over the summer. Spread across several bases from Bagram to Kandahar, the infantry brigade was already preparing for a supporting role in the movement into Nuristan when orders arrived to speed things up, get to FOB Asadabad and then the Waygal, and figure out whom the Air Force planes had killed.[46]

A WEEK AFTER the air strike, while the Rangers were still at Bagram rehearsing their missions into other valleys, a column of Humvees and cargo trucks left FOB Asadabad, where it had staged overnight, and headed up the Pech.

Driving under a cloudless sky with AH-64 Apache attack helicopters prowling overhead, the convoy carried a battalion of some five hundred 10th Mountain infantrymen, far more Americans than had been in the valley before. Their destination twenty road miles northwest was Nangalam, the settlement at the junction of the Pech and Waygal that, with a population of some ten thousand and a two-story hotel that towered over its other buildings, was the Pech valley's biggest town and a district administrative center.[47] There they were to establish a hasty staging and fire-support base for the next waves of troops: a sister 10th Mountain battalion slotted to land by helicopter and trek up the Waygal valley to the scene of the air strike, and then the Rangers heading farther afield.

The dirt-and-gravel road the convoy followed twisted westward along the north bank of the Pech River, threading the gaps between spurs that spread down from the mountains above either bank and interlocked like giant jack-o'-lantern teeth. The valley floor was a quarter of a mile wide in places, the road cushioned from the river by fields where people grew corn and rice in the summer and wheat in the winter. In other places it narrowed frighteningly, so the bulky Humvees could barely squeeze between the cliffs rising upward to their right and the ones plunging down toward the river on their left. The villages the convoy passed through were busy but not bustling; a substantial proportion of the valley's former residents remained in the Pakistani refugee camps to which they had fled more than twenty years earlier, during the war with the Soviets.[48]

No one had told the soldiers heading up the valley much about what they should expect, but some (including the battalion intelligence officer) had heard vague stories about how the Pech had swallowed up whole Soviet brigades and divisions, which lent the mission an ominous air.[49] These stories were wildly exaggerated, but they were rooted in kernels of truth that the 10th Mountain troops would not have found comforting. Fourteen miles up, the Humvees rumbled past Khara, a little village that had been the scene of one of the earliest defeats Soviet forces suffered at the hands of Afghan guerrillas after their December 1979 invasion.

Before dawn on May 11, 1980, soldiers of the Red Army's 66th Separate Motorized Rifle Brigade had headed up the Pech on a mission similar in concept to the one the 10th Mountain troops were now executing: one battalion driving up the valley by road, the other flying in by helicopter, with Nangalam as the objective. One Soviet company had been hiking across a barren field of rocks on the mountainside above Khara when it drifted out of visual contact with its sister units. A large force of mujahidin lurking higher on the mountain pounced, opening up with a combination of old bolt-action rifles and newer automatic weapons they had looted from government arsenals in Nangalam and Asadabad. Only with great difficulty was the company able to retreat down the mountain and take up defensive positions in a compound in Khara. There, the Soviet troops fought desperately into the night, pinned down by mortars and machine guns and with only brief spasms of artillery support from Asadabad.[50] Of ninety soldiers in the company, forty died, according to Soviet accounts. A lieutenant reaching the battlefield with reinforcements the next day found their bloated bodies "scattered like shards of broken glass."[51] After the battle of Khara, it had taken the Soviets three more days to fight their way up the Pech to Nangalam, which they found in ruins, already burned to the ground by Afghan communist forces in response to the first stirrings of the mujahidin uprising.[52]

Covering the same distance without anyone in the valley firing a shot, the 10th Mountain convoy pulled in to a rebuilt Nangalam on the afternoon of November 6, 2003, less than ten hours after they had left FOB Asadabad. One young soldier remembered being surprised, during a halt in the movement, to find that he had parked next to a field of cannabis; when some privates started grabbing what they could, a sergeant made everyone empty their pockets.[53] Arriving in Nangalam, a Humvee gunner was amazed by an everyday sight in the bazaar: a slaughtered cow bleeding into the same gutter where children were playing.[54]

The trucks halted in an open area just west of town, where some trees and a cluster of disused buildings sat between the mountains and the road. As the sun set, the 10th Mountain soldiers strung a concertina-wire perimeter and hung maps inside the two-story cinder-block structure that would be their command post. A pair of Chinooks flew up the valley, each dropping off a 105-millimeter howitzer, a big cannon capable of hurling a forty-pound shell eight miles.

AFTER DARK, MORE transport helicopters thumped up the valley. Five minutes out from the Nangalam landing zone, the soldiers inside, from 10th Mountain's 2-22 Infantry battalion,* nicknamed the Triple Deuce, stood up in the dim red light of the Chinooks' cabins.[55]

One of the Triple Deuce soldiers who piled out onto the steplike farming terraces above Nangalam when the birds touched down was an officer with no idea he would return to the Pech again and again: James Howell, a Texan eighteen months out of West Point, where he had played football and found the infantry an obvious branch choice. If you were going to be a soldier, he had reasoned as a cadet, why would you be anything but an infantryman? The Army was built around its infantrymen; the infantry branch was the heart of the whole animal.[56]

---

* 2nd Battalion, 22nd Infantry Regiment. An infantry battalion consists of several companies of one to two hundred soldiers. Each company is made up of several platoons, each led by a lieutenant and his older, more experienced platoon sergeant.

Now a lieutenant in the Triple Deuce battalion, Jimmy Howell was doing the job aspiring infantry officers dreamed of: leading a platoon of forty-odd young men, some of them older than he and some still in their teens, into the unknown. Along with half a dozen other rifle platoons, Howell and his men began marching up the Waygal valley a few hours later, before dawn on November 7.

Objective Winchester, as the site of the October 30 air strike was marked on the soldiers' maps, was ten miles up the gorge-like valley.[57] A German botanist had once called the Waygal the "green heart of the Hindu Kush," and it lived up to the name; uphill from the Americans' route of march, the lower edges of deep conifer forests were visible, something the Triple Deuce soldiers had not seen elsewhere in Afghanistan.[58] "We knew we were going into a pretty mountainous area and we knew it would be cold, but the mountains got more severe as we went north," Howell remembered.[59] The maps and satellite imagery he had studied before they got on the helicopters at Bagram didn't begin to convey the harshness, steepness, and spooky beauty of the terrain they hiked across. Signal mirrors flashed from the mountains, and the circling Apache attack helicopters occasionally let loose a few rounds at what looked like machine-gun nests hidden in the boulders or trees.[60] On the second night, the sky turned black as freezing rain kicked off a flash flood. But no one attacked.

Three days into the march, the Triple Deuce soldiers reached the base of the mountain below Objective Winchester. With local donkeys carrying their batteries and radios, three platoons started up the mountain. "Just imagine two and a half hours on the air stepper," a company first sergeant said of the climb. "It was straight up."[61] Howell and his soldiers ascended two thousand feet, part of the way via a stone staircase carved into the mountainside, to a *bandeh,* or shepherd's shack, from which they could provide covering fire while the other two platoons approached the compound that Air Force bombs had struck on October 30.[62] Nearing the objective, the soldiers were amazed to see A-10 attack jets flying *below* them through the valley.

Predictably, so many days after the strike, the site was deserted, with little evidence one way or another about who had died there. The bombs had clearly destroyed two buildings and damaged a third, but there were no bloodstains or remains; anyone killed had long since been buried elsewhere.[63] Nor, other than one old man with a bolt-action rifle, was there anyone nearby to talk to. When the weather cleared long enough for a Chinook to fly in, make a dangerous two-wheel "pinnacle landing," and deposit an interagency intelligence team to inspect the evidence, the experts could reach only one fairly firm conclusion: if Gulbuddin Hekmatyar had been at Objective Winchester at all, he had escaped.

Only as the Triple Deuce troops started to hike down again did a group of locals show themselves, twenty or so bearded men who appeared as suddenly and quietly as apparitions and approached the battalion commander. Eight civilians had died in the bombing, the men told the lieutenant colonel through an interpreter: Ahmad, the man killed by the first bomb that hit the mosque; an elderly aunt named Sayimid and three young children she was trying to take to shelter, Hamida, Bibi Shirini, and Zaki Ahmad Shah; Zahida, the young woman the AC-130 had killed as she ran for the woods; Hubaib, a baby who died when the gunship struck the cave where its mother was hiding; and a local holy man who lived there as the family's guest.[64] They wanted restitution, an apology—something.

With no obvious physical evidence that their claim was true, the men got nothing, and after a brief, tense exchange, the Triple Deuce troops continued toward the landing zone where they would be picked up and ferried back to the relative comfort of Bagram.[65]

CIVILIANS HAD INDEED died in the October 30 air strike—probably only civilians.

The central figure in the family that owned the settlement was a conservative cleric and prominent mujahidin veteran named Mawlawi Ghulam Rabbani, who had been away in Kabul at the time of the strike but who had lost two of his own adult children and several young grandchildren, nieces, and nephews in the mayhem.

Ghulam Rabbani and Hekmatyar had run in the same circles during the jihad of the 1980s; although Ghulam Rabbani had been with the rival Jamaat mujahidin party rather than Hekmatyar's Hizb-e Islami, he had overseen a distribution network in the passes and side valleys north of the Pech that supplied arms to guerrillas from both factions. After the Soviets left, Ghulam Rabbani had been the one person both Jamaat and Hizb could agree on as governor of Kunar when they took Asadabad, and he had gained a reputation as a bridge builder and peacemaker, mediating disputes among Nuristani communities and even working to arrange talks between the Northern Alliance and the Taliban.[66]

A senior intelligence official would later insist to me that Hekmatyar really had been at the mountainside settlement that night, staying with his old acquaintance from the jihad. "Hekmatyar and those with him escaped, but I'm quite certain he was there," the official said, although he wouldn't say how he could be so sure. He blamed the Air Force for striking the wrong houses.[67]

Survivors of the strike insisted that wasn't true—that Hekmatyar had never been there at all. "We are very deep Jamaatis," pointed out Ghulam Rabbani's son Zabiullah. "Even if we had invited Hekmatyar to our house, he wouldn't have come. He would never have trusted us."[68] Other accounts suggest Hekmatyar was in Pakistan at the time.[69]

In the weeks after the strike, Ghulam Rabbani visited Kabul, looking for answers. His trip ended in the fortified, eighty-acre presidential palace complex called the Arg, where he and a young relative acting as his translator met with President Karzai and David Sedney, the State Department's acting ambassador in Kabul at the time. Sedney had come to Kabul after a stint working Afghanistan issues on the National Security Council (NSC) staff, and Karzai invited him so that a senior American could see for himself the suffering that a U.S. error had caused.[70]

Describing the deaths of his relatives, Ghulam Rabbani showed Sedney and Karzai a photograph of one of the slain children and started to weep. Then he asked Sedney why America had bombed his home. He proffered a theory: Had American intelligence officers been talking to his neighbor, with whom he had a long-standing feud over water access rights (a common source of conflict in the Waygal)?[71] *Just tell me if my neighbor said I was sheltering someone who was against America,* Sedney remembered Ghulam Rabbani saying, with his relative and a government interpreter translating. *If he did, he was lying. Tell me it was him, and I will take revenge on him and his family.*

CIA officers had briefed Sedney on exactly what kind of intelligence had prompted the strike. The neighbor, he knew, had not been the agency's source. But because everything about the event was classified, he couldn't tell Ghulam Rabbani—or Karzai—even that much. The cleric left the meeting convinced that America had killed his family deliberately,[72] and the Afghan president left furious that the military, with all its high-tech surveillance systems, had been careless enough to launch a deadly strike based on what everything indicated was a false report. "Mawlawi Ghulam Rabbani was not the only one who wanted to know who had given the false intelligence," Karzai told me a decade and a half later. "The United States should have been more diligent, acted more carefully."[73]

In the years that followed, Ghulam Rabbani and members of his family would develop a theory about who had told the CIA that Hekmatyar was visiting them that night and why. "We knew the Americans wouldn't drop something from the sky on that exact house unless someone gave them information," said a family member who went on to work in the Afghan security apparatus.[74] So the Rabbanis appealed to a family friend, a longtime CIA ally known as Engineer Arif, who in 2003 had been the director of the National Directorate of Security (NDS), the Afghan intelligence service that was the CIA's main partner and proxy in Afghanistan.[75]

The CIA's sources, Engineer Arif told the family, had been two members of his own spy service, both of them Nuristanis: the first, a middle-aged NDS operative from the Wama area far up the Pech valley, and the other, a native of a town at the northern end of the Waygal. The Waygal was a small place, where members of prominent families knew and recognized each other, and once the Rabbani family had names to ask about, other reports emerged: one of the NDS men, it turned out, had been seen nearby, at another compound in the mountains outside Aranas, the day before the air strike.[76]

No American in a position to know would corroborate to me who the CIA's source on the ground was. But a former senior government official and a former JSOC officer both told me the source was an Afghan NDS operative, and there were only so many NDS officers who were of value in a place like the Waygal. Each of Nuristan's major valleys, including the Waygal, had its own language, a higher barrier from an intelligence standpoint than any geographic obstacle.* The two men were both native Waygali speakers, and it so happened that one was also the first cousin of a local notable who was well known as a close CIA ally.[77] "We're drawing conclusions. We're not sure. But there is evidence," a Rabbani family member told me of their circumstantial case.[78]

If Hekmatyar had not been there, why would these Nuristani NDS officers have led the CIA to believe that he *had* been? The family had a theory about that too: revenge.

In an ironic postscript to the agency's bloody proxy war against the Soviets in Afghanistan two decades earlier, its Afghan partner agency contained a cadre of former members of the communist-era Afghan secret police who had been trained by the ruthless professionals of the Soviet KGB.[79] The NDS operative from Wama was part of this KGB-trained contingent,[80] and during the jihad he and his Waygali colleague had both been part of the communist intelligence operation in Nuristan, working to penetrate mujahidin networks there. Among the mujahidin commanders they had faced off against were Hekmatyar and Ghulam Rabbani, both of whom had survived communist air strikes meant to kill them.[81] Now, years later, the Rabbani family contended, one or both of these men had used their influence with the CIA to get American bombs dropped on their old enemy's house, passing along a false report calculated to prompt a deadly air strike.

A former CIA officer who was in Afghanistan at the time but was not involved in the October 2003 strike didn't blink when I described the family's theory to him. "They were the best trained. They were actual intelligence officers," he said of the NDS's KGB-

---

* American soldiers often lumped all the province's languages together as "Nuristani," but they were actually five separate, mutually unintelligible languages (four of which U.S. troops encountered during Winter Strike). A 1948 expedition of Danish scholars had dubbed Nuristan an "ethnographic El Dorado."

trained core, but that cut both ways. "The crazy stuff was the stuff we would believe that NDS officers sold us. It always turned out to be business and family rivalries."[82] Adding plausibility to the Rabbanis' version of events, a later State Department assessment would single out one of the two operatives and describe the NDS apparatus he ran in Nuristan as "largely a criminal, bribe extraction organization," prone to falsifying intelligence.[83]

It was still only a theory, though. The former senior U.S. government official with direct knowledge of the events danced around an alternate, middle version, in between the CIA's line and the Rabbani family's. In this telling, the NDS operative or operatives really were tracking Hekmatyar in the Aranas area in the days leading up to the strike but, under pressure to deliver and perhaps motivated secondarily by their old grudge from the jihad, wrongly connected the final dots in placing him at the Rabbani settlement.

It would have been too big a risk for NDS officials to try to orchestrate an American air strike purely out of revenge, the former official said. "What if Hekmatyar was there, was being tracked, but these people lost him, and since this was a matter of very large significance to the U.S. government and the NDS people knew it, they believed he *could* have gone to that compound? They may have thought, 'He's likely there, so let's tell the Americans he *is* there, and if this guy we don't like is also killed, that's fine too.'"

The CIA, the former official suggested, should have pushed harder for the sources to explain how they had picked Hekmatyar back up. "But maybe," he said, "you're under such pressure from the White House to kill somebody that you don't ask that question."[84]

Twelve years later, the diplomat David Sedney, who knew the true answer but still couldn't reveal it because of classification, remained furious about the October 30 air strike outside Aranas. "I believe it was irresponsible militarily and morally to make that strike. It was a complete mistake, and it was decided outside the purview of the people on the ground," Sedney said. "Mawlawi Rabbani was known in every corner of every Nuristani valley for his role fighting the Soviets and as a religiously inspired and favored Muslim. He was a revered figure, and we killed his women and children and a holy man he had living with him. And we couldn't tell him why."[85]

RANGERS LEAD THE WAY

The intelligence that sent nearly half the 75th Ranger Regiment on a wild-goose chase in even snowier, higher valleys than the Waygal a week or so after the strike was not much better.

Until the end of October 2003, few Rangers were expecting to see Afghanistan again. JSOC's role in America's wars seemed to be wrapping up; home from the invasion of Iraq, the Ranger Regiment was getting back into the hum of training for the next big crisis. Then the news hit that McChrystal was taking command, and everything changed. Nicknamed the Pope in part for his well-known ascetic habits (he reportedly needed little sleep), McChrystal was a Ranger legend and former regimental commander, and he was famous for his single-minded drive. He was not going to let any unit under his command—least of all his treasured Rangers—sit on the sidelines training for a future war when a multitheater war on terror was already under way.[86]

The Rangers were the genie that, once let out of the bottle, would give JSOC the stamina and manpower to fight an endless war that the much smaller Delta Force and SEAL Team 6 squadrons could never have handled alone. The Ranger Regiment's three battalions, each seven hundred strong, were descendants of earlier Ranger units that had acted as amphibious shock troops and jungle commandos in World War II, light infantry and parachute raiders in Korea, and long-range scouts in Vietnam. The regiment's present specialty was seizing large, difficult targets like airfields, as Rangers had done during the 2001 and 2003 invasions of Afghanistan and Iraq. But flexibility was a Ranger virtue, one that McChrystal meant to put to use immediately by deploying the bulk of the regiment's 1st and 2nd Battalions from Savannah, Georgia, and Fort Lewis, Washington, to Afghanistan with barely two weeks' notice.[87]

One of the 1st Ranger Battalion officers in Savannah who got word to start planning for the sudden deployment was Major Joe Ryan, the black-haired officer from Pearl River, New York, who seven years later would command a 101st Airborne battalion in the Pech when I first visited the valley. His Army career was about to hit the first of four intersections with the story of American involvement in the Pech.

Ryan had grown up thirty miles from West Point and gone to baseball camp there, and he sought an appointment to the military academy as a teenager not because he wanted an Army career but because it seemed like a good college that was also free. After flirting during his cadet years with the idea of becoming a helicopter pilot, he opted for the infantry and found that it suited him. After stints at Fort Bragg and in Germany, he'd earned a slot in the Rangers, the pinnacle of infantry assignments.[88]

Ryan had been at 1st Ranger Battalion's Savannah base when al-Qaida struck the Twin Towers and the Pentagon, and by that first Christmas of the war he was downrange, commanding a Ranger company at the sprawling, notoriously smelly airfield complex outside Kandahar. The next time 1st Battalion deployed—the rotation during which it helped out on JSOC's dry-hole mission in the Shigal valley—he had been in Kansas, studying at the Army's staff college for mid-career officers and fretting about missing the action.

He needn't have worried. Back with 1st Battalion in the fall of 2003 as a major on the battalion staff, Ryan was told to report to regimental headquarters four hours away at Fort Benning. After a week of intensive planning there, he was back in Savannah the day before Halloween. He took his young children trick-or-treating and said goodbye to his wife for the second time since September 11, and then the battalion was off.[89]

ALTHOUGH THE RANGERS didn't make it in time for the botched air strike that kicked Winter Strike off, the turnaround from receiving McChrystal's orders to finding themselves at what seemed like the edge of civilization was still shockingly fast. It was the job of Rangers to be ready to go wherever, whenever, but to be at home in coastal Georgia and the Pacific Northwest one week and high in the crags of Nuristan the next was extreme.

The Savannah Rangers of 1st Battalion drew the primary target, ninety miles from Bagram: snowy Kantiwa, the valley surrounding one of the Pech's headwaters, a place where Hekmatyar's guerrillas had murdered a British journalist in 1987[90] and which bin Laden was rumored to have visited in 1996.[91]

Joe Ryan's role was to stay behind at Bagram and monitor the mission's progress by radio and Predator feed from JSOC's operations center. On everyone's mind, but particularly his, was the March 2002 battle of Shah-e Kot, the battalion's first, costly brush with Afghan mountain combat. Stuck in a Kandahar headquarters then as he was now at Bagram, Ryan had listened to the radio updates as a Chinook full of his Rangers had headed for a snowy mountaintop called Takur Ghar and then been brought down by an insurgent RPG. In the hours that followed, seven special operators had died, including four of Ryan's Rangers.

It didn't seem far-fetched that the enemy might put up a fight in the Kantiwa valley too. A small special operations team had gotten into a stiff firefight there during a brief visit back in March.[92] Everyone in the valley would know the Rangers were coming when the whop-whop-whop of the Chinooks' rotors echoed off the mountains, which rose to a staggering fifteen thousand feet above the eight-thousand-foot elevation of the valley floor where people lived, and the moon was gibbous, providing more illumination than the Night Stalker pilots were usually comfortable with.[93] Intelligence analysts had mapped out spots where anti-aircraft machine guns might be, and before the Chinooks took off, the battalion commander, Lieutenant Colonel Mike Kershaw, gathered his troops and gave a speech, stressing the risks associated with a large-scale night air-assault mission into a harsh environment.[94] "We were kind of thinking it was going to be a battle," one Ranger remembered.[95]

The higher into the mountains the Chinooks flew, the colder it got inside their metal cabins. In the operations center at Bagram, hearts were in throats when, barely a minute before the Chinooks touched down, Predator footage showed Kantiwa residents of all sizes and ages reacting to the sound of rotors by pouring out of their houses in dozens and hundreds. But the townspeople weren't coming out to fight; they were heading for the mountains, a procedure the older residents had practiced many times when faced with Soviet air raids.[96]

Once the helicopters were gone, the valley was silent—so quiet that when gunfire broke the calm, one Ranger platoon sergeant could hear the clack of the offending weapon's bolt being worked between shots. It was an old man firing a bolt-action rifle, which he dropped as the helmeted, heavily armed Rangers approached. "He was probably afraid we were there to rob him," the platoon sergeant speculated; he certainly wasn't a serious threat.[97] No further shots followed as the Rangers spread through town. Inside one house, the Rangers found an anti-aircraft machine gun disassembled and packed up in its box. There was no battle.

Some of the Rangers headed up a rocky spur that jutted into town—a hike that was torture for even the most physically fit soldiers, because they all had been at sea level just a few days earlier. At the top of the spur was a beige mud-brick fortress with loopholes for weapons instead of windows, a century-old structure that the Rangers camped out in and started calling the castle.

Joe Ryan was tracking the progress of the Rangers in the field by radio when he got the call from the battalion commander, Kershaw: He was to pack his things and get up to Kantiwa on the next helicopter. While the main body of the battalion flew in by Chinook, another group of Rangers had taken the ground route up the Pech, driving in pickups past 10th Mountain's Nangalam firebase and then thirty more miles to the mouth of the Kantiwa, where they continued by foot. During the march, the major in charge had fallen and hurt his ankle. Now Ryan, who had been expecting to spend the operation at Bagram, needed to fly up and replace him.[98]

ARRIVING, RYAN WAS agog: at the medieval-looking fortress; at the pristine beauty of the valley, accentuated by the shining snow and picturesque pines; and above all at the people, whose pale complexion and red hair he had known to expect but was shocked by all the same. Inside the fort, he found some Rangers manning radios and others lounging on a handful of animal-skin beds or curled up in sleeping bags in the dirt. Huge wooden beams formed the ceilings. Chickens and rats scurried around the castle's chilly chambers; much worse were the fleas.[99]

The Rangers' target in the Kantiwa was the don of the valley, a sixtyish associate of Hekmatyar's named Haji Ghafor. Tall, known for his ruthlessness and religious conservatism,[100] and said to possess a strikingly long white beard, Ghafor was the grandson of the fort's builder, and he had grown wealthy off Kantiwa's gem mines, which produced deep-red garnet. Like Mawlawi Ghulam Rabbani, he had fought against the Soviets (although in Ghafor's case as a direct subordinate of Hekmatyar in his party, Hizb) and then against the Taliban; he had supposedly been shot in the stomach a few years earlier during a skirmish with Taliban-aligned fighters in the Pech. Relatives of Ghafor's who were friendly with the CIA assured the agency that the old warlord wasn't involved with the insurgency or with Hekmatyar,[101] but American intelligence officers didn't believe them; they suspected Ghafor, as they did Ghulam Rabbani, of playing host to his old ally from the jihad.

Ghafor was nowhere to be found, of course. Some Kantiwa residents said that when he heard the sound of the helicopters, he had headed north on horseback. Just as likely, he had been among the exodus of people who left on foot as the Chinooks approached, disappearing right under the Rangers' noses. Either way, he was gone, and it seemed unlikely that he would come back while a hundred-plus Rangers were camped out in his family's fort, burning their firewood and, in Ryan's case, using one of their ornate silver bowls to shave each morning. The mission was a bust. Ryan remembered his time in the valley, which lasted until Christmas, as seventy-five days of boredom. "We wanted to find the enemy and kill them," he said. But "there just wasn't much going on up there, or much the people there could tell us."[102]

To reach the barer Parun valley, seven miles east of the Kantiwa across a thirteen-thousand-foot ridge, the West Coast Ranger element, 2nd Battalion, crawled all the way up the Pech in pickup trucks and then continued into the mountains on foot. Eaten to death by fleas and astonished by the snow and the trapped-in-time feel of the villages, the Fort Lewis Rangers stayed awhile but found nothing more than their 1st Battalion counterparts had in Kantiwa.[103] Some Rangers joked that a better name for the big mission would have been Operation Winter Strikeout.[104]

In both the Kantiwa and the Parun valleys, the Rangers were operating nearly blind, their main guides some of the CIA's Afghan CTPT surrogates (these ones nicknamed the Tigers rather than the

Mohawks). People in the first valley spoke one Nuristani language, people in the second another; although the troops in Kantiwa did have one Nuristani interpreter,[105] the balaclava-clad Tigers mostly just spoke Pashto, meaning that anything the locals wanted to say without the visitors' understanding, they could, even right in front of them. But for as long as JSOC's commander, McChrystal, wanted them there, they were stuck in the wilderness. Each day that November, Ranger patrols trekked up the mountains to investigate the campfires and caves—the mouths of gem mines—that they could spot through binoculars from below. Sometimes three or four feet of fresh snow stood in their way, ensuring that by the time they arrived at the site of a campfire, whoever had been there was long gone. The snowy woods contained everything from porcupines and weasel-like martens to jackals and wild pigs;[106] after spotting a white fox one day through his binoculars and being denied permission to shoot it, a platoon sergeant set up snares to try to catch the creature, but to no avail.[107]

After some initial caution, the local people helped entertain the Rangers too. When the main town in the Kantiwa celebrated the end of Ramadan, there was wrestling and a shot-put-like game, and 1st Battalion's commander, Kershaw, joined in a game of *buzkashi,* the famous polo-like Afghan sport that substituted a dead goat for a ball, which some Rangers recognized from *Rambo III.*

FOR A FLEETING moment one day in the Kantiwa, hopes soared. Ryan was in the radio room of the hilltop fort, as was the Ranger Regiment's commander, Colonel Craig Nixon, who was out visiting his far-flung troops. A Predator drone was overhead, and while both Ryan and Nixon listened, one of the satellite radios crackled with a message relayed from the drone's crew twelve time zones away in Nevada. An Air Force sensor operator there had spotted a group of men outside town, walking in a triangular formation, centered on a tall man in white robes. Osama bin Laden's height—six feet four inches—was well known, and the Predator crew was elated with their find.[108]

The Predator could seem like a silver bullet, a sci-fi tool that would penetrate the fog of war and allow the United States to stare into the world's lawless corners, in real time and undetected. But especially this early in the war, the Predator was a tool of narrow usefulness, and no place highlighted its limitations better than the mountains of Afghanistan's northeast.[109]

Predator crews often assumed that, flying at twenty thousand feet or more, their aircraft were inaudible on the ground,[110] but the higher you went in the mountains, the less true that was: during a 2002 mission, JSOC recon teams ten thousand feet up had heard a Predator as clearly as "a flying lawn mower" and watched militants, hearing it too, scurry for concealment.[111] And concealment, in Kunar and Nuristan, could be found in the nearest tree line, because an early Predator's cameras could not see through the needled branches of the pines, firs, and cedars that were common between six and ten thousand feet. Nor were the big remote-controlled aircraft invisible. It would come as a shock to some in the Predator community when a guerrilla commander captured in Kunar revealed in 2005 that every morning he could see the glint of the drone that was tracking him when the sun hit its wings at a certain angle, according to a longtime pilot's memoir.[112]

Even when a Predator had a clear view, its early-vintage cameras left much to be desired, producing black-and-white footage in which it was impossible to identify the objects blurry human figures were carrying, and color footage that was even worse.[113] The field of view was so narrow that the Ranger commander Nixon compared it to watching a football game through a soda straw from the fifty-yard line. "Back then, nobody knew what they were looking at or how to tell what was what," said CIA paramilitary officer Ron Moeller, who remembered the Kantiwa sighting briefly spurring excitement at the agency base where he was then deployed, elsewhere in Afghanistan.[114]

That day in November 2003, the sensor operators peering through the soda straw at a patch of ground outside the Kantiwa fort were deceiving themselves.

"There was a drone on-site," Nixon remembered. "The headquarters said, 'We see Osama bin Laden. Triangle formation with a tall man in a white robe. It's got to be his security detail and he's leading it.' In reality, I was there, I was looking from the fort down, and it was a group of kids with one adult playing soccer."[115]

. . .

AS THE WINTER weeks wore on, smaller groups of Rangers would head into other side valleys off the Pech whose names would become familiar later in the war but at the time were just strange foreign words. Marching or driving into the Korengal and Watapur valleys, 1st Battalion Rangers met more cagey locals and learned nothing useful. And when 2nd Battalion Rangers and some SEAL Team 6 operators flew into the Shigal valley for a rare daylight raid on the fort-like home of Kashmir Khan, he, like Haji Ghafor, had made himself scarce.[116]

Talking with Rangers from both battalions when he flew out for Thanksgiving, McChrystal got the message: they weren't finding anything, as Joe Ryan explained to the general in a detailed briefing at the Kantiwa fort.[117] Although Ryan and a platoon stayed on at the fort until just before Christmas, the JSOC commander gave the order for other Ranger units to start pulling back to Bagram. Nowhere near that many Americans would ever visit the Kantiwa or the Parun valley again. When Ryan finally left the Kantiwa at Christmas, he took with him the heavy metal bowl he'd been using to shave in. When he returned to the Pech six and a half years later as an infantry battalion commander, he would bring it with him, hoping to use it as a conversation starter with Haji Ghafor, by then no longer a wanted man. "He was a victim of circumstance more than anything else," Ryan said of the old man of the Kantiwa valley.[118]

Only years afterward did enough puzzle pieces come together to show that one key assumption of the decidedly spotty intelligence that prompted Winter Strike in Nuristan was actually correct, if a year out of date. Later accounts confirm that the hiding place in the Shigal to which a Hekmatyar loyalist delivered Osama bin Laden after Tora Bora was, in fact, a fort belonging to Kashmir Khan—one that had escaped JSOC's attention during its big 2002 mission in the same valley but that might have been the very one the SEALs and Rangers raided during Winter Strike.[119]

The troops in Kantiwa might have been chasing a red herring in Haji Ghafor, but the Rangers and SEALs looking for Kashmir Khan had come closer to bin Laden's trail than any of them knew, although not to bin Laden himself, who by then had moved on to deep isolation in Pakistan.[120]

CAMP BLESSING

During the weeks it was in the Parun, 2nd Ranger Battalion ran frequent convoys from FOB Asadabad up the Pech, driving as far as Nangalam in Humvees and the rest of the way in Hilux pickup trucks. After the first leg of the trip, the Rangers would rest at the firebase that the 10th Mountain troops had established outside town, sleeping in the open on the hillside while they waited for Hiluxes to take them up the valley into Nuristan.

One such convoy—a particularly large one of more than two dozen vehicles, a mix of Humvees and larger cargo trucks—left Asadabad and hung a left onto the hard-packed dirt of the Pech road before dawn on Friday, November 14. Humvees carrying a Ranger rifle platoon led the way and brought up the rear; in between were troops from a special operations logistics company, bringing fuel and other supplies for the Rangers in the field, and from 2nd Battalion's headquarters. In the driver's seat of one Humvee near the front of the column was the battalion's arms room sergeant, a gangly, pale-skinned native of Washington State named Jay Blessing.[121]

Blessing had followed the typical path that enlisted soldiers took into the Ranger Regiment: he'd joined right out of high school on a contract that promised him the chance to try out for the Rangers, because he'd heard they were the best and toughest outfit in the Army. He thrived in each phase of Army training and found humor in miseries that others griped about. During infantry basic training at Fort Benning, he'd enjoyed messing with his drill sergeants, a bold game to play. One night, a drill instructor ordered him to crawl around the barracks floor, meaning to wear the teenage recruit out in the oppressive Georgia heat, but Blessing was too physically fit; he crawled and crawled, leaving a slick trail of sweat and laughing the whole time, until the drill sergeant was laughing too.[122] From there Blessing had gone to airborne school and then

RIP, the Ranger Indoctrination Program. After passing both, he'd wound up in 2nd Battalion at Fort Lewis, half an hour south of his native Tacoma.

The Rangers, like other elite units, had a way of molding their members. "Once you get there, it's like finding everyone that's been missing from your life who's just like you," explained a friend of Blessing's who went through RIP with him. Blessing came in as a hip-hop fan but soon was listening to country music like everybody else. Rangers tended to be hard drinkers; Blessing liked few things more than to drive to some bar in his old Buick, so beat-up that you had to put new towels over the mold every day, and guzzle as much Busch Light or Mickey's Fine Malt Liquor as possible.[123]

Blessing was goofy and an oddball, friends remembered, but Ranger units had their own cultures and quirks, so he fit right in. Among 2nd Battalion's oddities was an affinity for cribbage, the card game with a wooden scoring board more often associated with the submarine service. The crotchety Marine veteran of Korea and Vietnam who was the battalion's civilian armorer, Ray Fuller, helped spread the game around. "What I remember most is the amount of beer that individual could drink, that and how him and Ray Fuller used to play cribbage all the time," a Ranger medic said of Blessing.[124]

After a year or two in their battalion, young Rangers went to Ranger School, the Army's grueling two-month leadership course in Georgia and Florida.* One of Blessing's lungs partially collapsed during Ranger School, and although he was able to finish the course without telling anyone (an ill-advised and practically superhuman feat), afterward he was pulled out of his platoon and sent to work with Fuller in the armorer's shop.

With a natural inclination for all things mechanical, Blessing took to the job. "Jay had that thing tore apart and put together again before any of the others had it tore apart," Ray Fuller remembered

---

* Ranger School and the 75th Ranger Regiment are separate institutions. Soldiers from all parts of the Army can attend Ranger School and earn the Ranger tab, becoming "Ranger qualified," while "Rangers"—members of the 75th Ranger Regiment—typically do not attend Ranger School until they have been with their Ranger battalion at least a year.

of Blessing's performance in an initial test he gave to potential assistants, quickly disassembling and reassembling a pistol. He became the old armorer's apprentice and sidekick, both in cards and in mastering the nuances of every firearm in the Ranger inventory. Whenever the arms room was open, the two men were there, either playing cribbage or replacing gas tubes on M4s or feeder pawls on machine guns and listening to a Fuller-approved country great: Johnny Cash, Waylon Jennings, or Kris Kristofferson, a favorite of the old Marine's. The duo deployed to Afghanistan together in the spring of 2002: Blessing, twenty-two, on his first war; Fuller, sixty-eight, on his third and last.

The next year Fuller retired; when 2nd Battalion deployed again for Winter Strike, Blessing, now a sergeant, was the old hand in the armorer's shop.[125]

BLESSING WAS HEADED up the Pech with the supply convoy on November 14 because there were machine guns to repair at a Ranger encampment in Nuristan, and with bad weather keeping helicopters out of the mountains, ground convoy was the quickest way to get there.

The day was dreary and drizzly, not too different from the fall Seattle weather 2nd Battalion had left behind. Despite the rain, there were fires burning at intervals on the peaks above the Pech; First Lieutenant Matt Work, the Ranger platoon leader in charge of the convoy, suspected they were signal fires, alerting people deeper in the valley of their arrival. By late morning, the convoy was four and a half miles short of Nangalam, at a spot where the mountain to the road's right rose so steeply that the stone houses hanging from it looked ready to slide off.[126] The trucks were just outside the village of Kandigal and the mouth of the Korengal side valley.

Matt Work had just noticed two men sitting on the hillside close to the road, watching the vehicles pass, when, at 11:05 a.m., an explosion boomed behind him and reverberated off the Pech valley's rocky walls.

Work called a halt and stepped out of his truck into the eerie silence that he would come to associate with the moments after attacks by improvised explosive devices, or IEDs. Two vehicles back,

Jay Blessing's Humvee was smoking. Someone had buried a small homemade bomb in the road, then waited until the first Humvees passed before using a trigger device to set it off when Blessing's vehicle was right on top of it.

The Humvee's other occupant was standing outside it, yelling, bleeding from his ears. Dust, smoke, and the putrid smell of the explosives hung in the cool air. Gatorade packets from inside the vehicle were scattered on the ground. Work barked for someone to chase after the two men he'd seen on the hillside and grab them.

There was a neat hole in the driver's-side floorboard, and neither driver nor driver's seat was still there. Work thought it looked almost as if Blessing had pulled the lever on an ejection seat, like in a fighter jet.

Through the rain Work saw other Rangers rushing down a steep embankment toward the north bank of the river. Blessing lay there by the water, where the blast had thrown him, bleeding from his nose and ears, one leg severed and the other badly damaged. A noncommissioned officer (NCO) performed CPR on Blessing's shirtless torso, his belly rising with each push on his chest, but to no avail. The Ranger sergeant from Tacoma did not survive.[127]

Twenty-three years old and on his second Afghanistan deployment, Jay Blessing was both the first man 2nd Battalion lost in the war on terror and the first American killed in Kunar or the Pech valley.

A medevac Black Hawk came to take Blessing and the wounded passenger away, and a patrol of Rangers ventured across a footbridge to the south side of the river to retrieve Blessing's missing leg. As Ranger and 10th Mountain reinforcements arrived, they swarmed Kandigal, scouring every cranny of every home in the little sawmill town for signs of the bomb's triggerman. Fifteen years and seven more deployments later, the patrol commander Work would remember November 14, 2003, as the longest, hardest day of his Army career. No one had much idea what to be looking for or where to look, and the search was fruitless. Whoever had initiated the blast might have been long gone—possibly in a black pickup truck that Work saw driving back up into the Korengal side valley before anyone could do anything about it—or he might have been right there, among the townspeople the soldiers angrily questioned (in the 10th Mountain troops' case, without the aid of anyone who spoke Pashto[128]). Some of the townspeople laughed at the troops as they searched futilely, Work remembered. No one was talking.[129]

AT BAGRAM, Sergeant Ray Fuller Jr.—the son of Blessing's old mentor and cribbage partner, Ray Fuller Sr.—heard the call come over the radio that an IED had struck a 2nd Battalion convoy. Next came the casualty report, including the identifying battle-roster number of the fallen Ranger. When Fuller checked the battalion roster, he knew it was Blessing.

Ignoring protocol, Ray Fuller Jr. called his own father in New Mexico, where he had retired after leaving the battalion, to tell him what had happened. Just a few months earlier, Blessing had paid the elder Fuller a surprise visit there, driving two thousand miles from Tacoma with his girlfriend. The younger Fuller had lost a close friend, but the elder one had lost something close to an adoptive son.[130]

"I just thought the world of Jay," Ray Fuller Sr. said simply when asked what he remembered about the young Ranger. A decade after Blessing's death, the eighty-year-old Marine kept a photo of Blessing on his mantel. "Jay was a splendid Ranger," he added. "I knew I could depend on him, no problem whatsoever." There was no higher praise in Fuller's vocabulary.[131]

The JSOC task force held a "ramp ceremony" for Blessing at Bagram. This was the ritual in which all available hands lined up while a flag-draped transfer case was carried into the hold of the cargo plane that would fly it to Dover Air Force Base in Delaware, the first stateside stop for the fallen of America's wars. The battalion chaplain, a former Ranger sergeant and combat veteran himself, read Psalm 23, and a major eulogized Blessing in a brief address, noting his affability and skill in the arms room as well as his widely known claim to fame: finishing Ranger School on one good lung.[132]

STAN MCCHRYSTAL HAD flexed JSOC's muscles in Winter Strike. But the operation was barely noticed outside the counterterrorism command, partly because it was classified and partly because it got no results. "Winter Strike's operational value was minimal," McChrystal judged.[133]

In the Waygal valley north of Nangalam, the October 30 air strike that preceded Winter Strike left behind a legacy of anger over the deaths of civilians and suspicion as to why America had struck at Mawlawi Ghulam Rabbani of all people, Nuristan's peacemaker. The CIA-directed air strike, the diplomat David Sedney believed, was the "original sin" of American involvement in the Waygal valley—an initial misstep so severe that Waygalis would never forget or forgive it.[134] That bitterness and mistrust would fester, waiting like a hidden booby trap for the next group of American soldiers to venture into the valley—who, because of the secrecy surrounding the strike, would only know about it what locals did, which wasn't much.

What Winter Strike left behind in the Pech proper was the firebase outside Nangalam. The hillside enclosure sat very close to where a company of Soviet troops had built and briefly manned a similar outpost in 1982. The Soviet outpost had been a temporary construction, abandoned after a few weeks,[135] and the Rangers who passed through Nangalam during Winter Strike had no reason to expect that their firebase would be any more permanent.

Several Rangers erected a small wooden cross at the foot of some rocks as a memorial to Jay Blessing, burning his initials into the wood in between the words "GOD BLESS" and the letters *RLTW:* "Rangers lead the way."[136]

But the Nangalam encampment itself would become a longer-lasting memorial. Within weeks of the conclusion of the fruitless lunge into Nuristan, soldiers at the base were calling it Camp Blessing.[137]

CHAPTER 3

THE A-CAMP

2004

THE BLESSING INK BLOT

As the old Soviet-bloc mortars and rocket launchers blasted a twenty-one-tube salute marking the Nangalam outpost's formal dedication as Camp Blessing in May 2004, Captain Ronald Fry felt a mixture of emotions: pride in what he and his Green Berets had achieved in the Pech with the help of its residents, sadness that he would soon leave the place forever, and worry about what would happen next in the valley.

A ginger-haired National Guardsman of thirty-two with a serious, thoughtful demeanor, Ron Fry was about to go home and trade the frontier life of a Green Beret officer in Afghanistan for that of a medical device salesman, his civilian job. His dozen-man Special Forces A-team 936 had rattled up the Pech road from Asadabad in Humvees and pickups the previous November as Winter Strike wound down. Their job—there wasn't a formal written order, just the say-so of a Green Beret major—was to take over the sloping, trapezoid-shaped stretch of ground the Rangers had been using as a jumping-off point and turn it into something more permanent.[1]

Hiring local labor instead of using the Navy engineers headquarters wanted to send out, Fry and his men set about creating an

"A-camp" like the ones Green Berets had served on in their Vietnam heyday: an outpost from which A-team 936 and the local allies it recruited could patrol and influence the surrounding area.[2] Where there weren't brick walls, workers had poured sand and gravel into Hesco baskets. Sandbag-and-plywood bunkers rose on the peaks above the base, elevated observation posts that gave early warning of attacks, disappearing into wispy white when clouds rolled down the valley. A squat, one-story, L-shaped cinder-block building at the foot of the mountain—an old tuberculosis clinic, a detail the team tried to forget—became the Green Berets' team house, their command post and barracks.[3] "It's like a scene out of a Vietnam movie," Fry wrote in his journal a week into the team's construction efforts, which included building a massive wooden front gate modeled on the one in John Wayne's *The Green Berets.*[4] In another nod to the 1968 film, the team named a stray dog they adopted after a character in the movie.

A cook the soldiers hired in town made enough rice, bread, and mutton or beef stew daily to feed the whole camp, buying his groceries in the shops of the Nangalam bazaar, where the Americans often strolled in baseball caps and T-shirts and won smiles by trying out Pashto phrases they'd picked up. Fry liked to visit Nangalam's hotel—at two stories, the town's biggest building—and eat yogurt with its owner as a treat. Many of the hotel trips resulted in hours of diarrhea in the camp latrine, but to Fry it was worth it—not just for the yogurt, but for the satisfaction people in the hotel seemed to take at a big, redheaded American sitting down with them on their own turf and trying their delicacies.[5]

The biggest building on Camp Blessing, a two-story schoolhouse, housed the hundred-plus local militiamen the team recruited, paid, armed, led, and outfitted in green camouflage. Fry had picked a Vietnam-era "tiger-stripe" pattern for the uniforms, paying for it with his own credit card. Every day for six months, American troops left the encampment's gates in fours and fives, accompanying groups of twenty or thirty militiamen as they walked into Nangalam or drove farther afield, visiting villages up and down the Pech, showing that a new force had come to the valley to keep it safe.

Fry was barely aware of it, because his austere postage stamp of land lacked email access or regular *Stars and Stripes* deliveries, but headlines at home that May centered on Iraq's implosion a year into the American-led occupation. Afghanistan was all but forgotten. In the six months since Winter Strike, however, he and his nine Green Berets—aided by two soldiers who specialized in civil-military affairs and propaganda, an Air Force special operator to call in air strikes, and forty young Marine Corps infantrymen—had turned their corner of the forgotten war into a little-noticed success story.

"When we left, I don't want to say it was a safe place," Fry said of Nangalam and the cluster of nearby villages, "but it was a very pro-American, pro-government place."[6]

A few soldiers from the A-team replacing Fry's had arrived in time for the ceremony too. Like many outgoing soldiers seeing their replacements for the first time, Fry looked at them with suspicion, wondering whether the newcomers had the right attitude, the one that had allowed A-team 936 to make headway in the Pech.

In military jargon, this turnover process, where a tired unit at the end of its deployment handed over the reins to a new one, was called a RIP/TOA—a "relief in place," culminating in a "transfer of authority" ceremony. Fry and the elders of Nangalam were both right to worry about the RIP/TOA. These turnovers—whether every six months, or every twelve, or every fifteen—would prove to be the bane of American efforts not only in the Pech but in dozens of other Afghan valleys and districts where the military struggled and often failed to maintain much consistency in its approach. Over the next few months, as the new A-team took the fight to a nearby side valley called the Korengal that Fry had deliberately avoided, the mood in the Pech changed, and war burst into Nangalam. By September 2004, when Fry was still readjusting to life selling pacemakers in Washington State, the hotel where he'd relished eating yogurt would be a burned-out ruin.

THE MISSION IN the Pech valley had passed from the hands of the man-hunting Joint Special Operations Command to Fry's small Green Beret team almost by default when JSOC's Rangers came out of the Pech empty-handed the previous Christmas.

No longer of interest to the generals in Tampa and Fort Bragg who had launched Operation Winter Strike because the mission had yielded no leads on bin Laden, the Pech became the site of an experiment by junior and mid-level officers of the Special Forces, the less secretive special operators who weren't part of JSOC and didn't share its counterterrorist mission.

In Kabul, Afghanistan's new national army was off to a painfully slow start. Because Green Berets specialized in training foreign troops, the top Special Forces colonels at Bagram wanted to start using their far-flung A-teams to set up supplementary local militias, which could assist the army as irregular forces later. The colonels chose the Pech as their first test case, because the steady stream of guerrilla attacks in the valley indicated a growing problem.[7]

Living at an A-camp in the valley, an A-team could work through its militia to slowly gather intelligence on al-Qaida and other militant figures, make the area difficult for them to live or move in, and start providing some services that Afghanistan's laughably weak government couldn't yet, like pop-up medical clinics. Accessible by road and equipped with two large buildings that no one else was using, the enclosure outside Nangalam that the Rangers and 10th Mountain troops had used as a staging point during the big operation seemed like a good site.

Ron Fry's A-team 936 had gotten to FOB Asadabad just a couple of weeks earlier, as Jim Gant's team was heading home. The A-team got the job.

In Nangalam, the Green Berets and Marines did what American troops did early on whenever they built a new outpost: bring in weight sets from FOB Asadabad and set up a makeshift gym. Then the team got to know the local officials who lived next door and started recruiting a militia, at a salary of $5 per day. To lead the new force, Fry and his soldiers found older men who had fought the Soviets as mujahidin; each new recruit reached out to his family and found brothers and cousins in need of work. Flouting rules that required them to send all captured weapons to the rear, the special operators used any weapons they found in buried caches on their patrols—there were many—to supplement the assault rifles and old bolt-action weapons the recruits brought from home. Within a week, A-team 936 had more than a hundred men on the payroll of its Afghan Security Force, as the militia was blandly called, and the

Americans were introducing the young Afghan "indig"* to jumping jacks and push-ups.

Green Berets were supposed to be soldier-statesmen, able to work in far-flung places with little support from other American units. Recruiting throughout the Army, the Special Forces put experienced NCOs and captains through a year of training at Fort Bragg before they earned their beret and blue Special Forces "long tab." Fry, who'd joined the Army as a lieutenant after ROTC at Brigham Young University, had gone through Special Forces selection and qualification after a stint in Kosovo with the 82nd Airborne; Jim Gant, in the same Special Forces officer group, sat behind Fry during classroom lessons. While Gant went to an active-duty A-team, Fry chose to join the smaller pool of A-teams in the part-time National Guard.

When A-team 936 first arrived, a rumor ran through Nangalam that "Commander Ron" and his men were Muslim because of their beards. Fry set the record straight, but he jumped on the distinction the townspeople had spotted between his Green Berets and the infantry troops who had been around during Winter Strike. Besides being clean shaven, the Rangers and 10th Mountain infantrymen who had set the outpost up habitually wore helmets, and locals talked about how some of the "helmeted soldiers" had broken down doors and frightened people. Fry talked up what made his men, who usually just wore baseball caps or round *pakols,* different. Where the helmeted soldiers had only come for a short while, his team was here to stay until spring, he said; where the helmeted soldiers had been interested only in finding the enemy, his team wanted to get to know Nangalam and its people.[8]

"All SF guys are trained in this stuff," Fry pointed out.[9] Counterinsurgency was a core Special Forces mission, one John F. Kennedy had charged the Green Berets with in 1961 when he officially blessed their eponymous headgear and tasked them with helping fight the world's brushfire wars against communism. What A-team 936 was doing at Camp Blessing, recruiting a local irregular force

---

* Pronounced "in-didge," Green Beret shorthand for "indigenous troops" since Vietnam.

and acting as its mentors and leaders, looked almost exactly like the final exercise that all Special Forces candidates went through in the North Carolina woods before earning their tabs and berets. But not all A-teams took to the subtler parts of the job the way 936 did, the statesman part of the soldier-statesman balance. Many—like Jim Gant's team—were more interested in getting into gunfights.

No Special Forces team was really prepared for counterinsurgency in Afghanistan in 2003, at least not by the standards to which Green Berets trained in peacetime. (The Army was not even prepared to use the word "counterinsurgency," because it didn't yet acknowledge publicly that it faced insurgencies in Afghanistan and Iraq.) In theory, A-teams were supposed to speak the language of the country they expected to work in, but none specialized in Pashto. A-team 936 had a Pacific focus: Ron Fry spoke Mandarin, and other team members spoke Thai and Korean, languages as useless in Afghanistan as the team's scuba expertise.[10] To talk to anyone, Fry and his soldiers relied on civilian interpreters and on their militiamen.

Further, as National Guardsmen, the team's soldiers didn't train together as often as their active-duty counterparts, and they were at war for the first time. But being a team of "weekend warriors" brought advantages too. The team's members ranged in age from thirty to fifty, older than on an active-duty team, a fact some Pech elders pointed out with appreciation. (The team's oldest member, whom the militiamen called *kaka,* or uncle, had been a Green Beret long enough to tell stories about training to carry a backpack-sized nuclear bomb into Russia to blow up on the Trans-Siberian Railroad.[11]) Some had civilian professions that helped them relate to people in the Pech: one NCO was a platinum miner, and another had spent time working as a gem trader in Southeast Asia, jobs that townspeople who supplemented their income pulling colorful crystals of kunzite and tourmaline out of mountain caves nodded their heads at knowingly.

It didn't hurt that half the Utah-based A-team's members were Mormons, a fact Fry realized with some surprise gave his men some common ground with the deeply religious people of the Pech. American soldiers of all stripes swore like sailors, and after only limited exposure Afghans were liable to recognize, and take offense at, common obscenities, but the Mormon Green Berets didn't curse at all. Nor did they drink, unlike the many A-teams that took advantage of the loose oversight afforded Special Forces and kept contraband liquor on base—a vice local people inevitably became aware of through the rumor mill of base workers and interpreters.[12]

FRY USED DIFFERENT analogies to describe what his team was doing in the Pech. In one, he contrasted it with the JSOC man-hunting foray that had left Camp Blessing behind for him to inherit. "They're constantly trying to squash cockroaches," he said of the Rangers. "We're trying to make the building uninhabitable for cockroaches," and doing it on the cheap, through local irregulars.

"The key terrain is the people," Fry added, putting it another way. "We have a cause and the enemy has a cause and we're trying to show the people in the middle that ours is to their benefit. It's the ink-blot theory." The idea was simple: by working closely with local forces to secure a small area, like Nangalam and a circle of villages around it, "you deny the enemy a sanctuary and make that a secure spot, and then you make that spot wider and bigger," as Fry put it. On a map, the circle of security would grow like a drop of ink soaking into paper.[13]

Fry was using a metaphor—counterinsurgency by "ink blot" or "oil spot"—that would have been familiar to his father in Vietnam and to British and French troops who employed it to describe their tactics in Algeria, Malaya, and elsewhere. Those midcentury counterinsurgents were, in turn, borrowing the term from French officers who had coined it to describe their approach to colonial pacification in Indochina, Madagascar, and Morocco.[14]

After its Vietnam heyday, the ink-blot method and the word "counterinsurgency" itself had dropped out of the official doctrine and mainstream lingo of the U.S. Army, which preferred to forget the whole thing and focus on preparing for tank battles with the Soviets.[15] Some in Special Forces kept up on it, however, including Fry's boss back at Bagram, a colonel who saw Green Berets apply the lessons of Vietnam counterinsurgency in Latin America. Fry had read about ink-blot counterinsurgency in reference to the British in Malaya, but his description of the ink-blot theory in the Pech closely matched what the term's French originator had described a century before: pacification "not by mighty blows, but as a patch of oil spreads, through a step by step progression, playing alternately on all the local elements, utilising the divisions between tribes and between their chiefs."[16]

The physical size of the ink blot was dictated in part by the limitations of old-fashioned firepower: its circumference was the range of Camp Blessing's mortars, waist-high metal tubes that leaned on bipods in a sandbag-lined pit. Within the mortars' three-and-a-half-mile range, the militia could patrol on foot with just a couple of Green Berets accompanying them. If someone shot at them, one of the Americans could call back to Blessing, and within a minute or so ten-pound shells would start exploding on the offending ridge and quiet things down. Only once, in March, did the camp itself come under attack, other than the occasional harassing rocket fired from the reverse sides of the surrounding ridges.

Beyond the mortars' protective envelope—past the villages of Sundray east of base and Wodi Geram to the west—patrols had to rely on the machine guns on their Humvees and pickup trucks, and the insurgents knew it. Firing from deep rock maws high on the mountainside, often protected by slabs of stone ten or twenty feet thick, local militants knew they were safe until American airpower showed up, and they learned quickly how long it took to get there. When a B-52 bomber or A-10 Warthog attack plane finally arrived overhead forty-five minutes or an hour in and got on the radio with A-team 936's Air Force air controller, the firefight would stop abruptly.

Every version of the ink-blot theory called for counterinsurgents to get to know the people they lived among as well as possible and to help provide them with basic services in order to win their loyalty (the idea often simplified, and mocked, as "winning hearts and minds").[17] One basic need in rural Afghanistan was medical care, especially for women, and running simple clinics was bread-and-butter work for an A-team's medics. Fry's medics, one of whom was a cardiac nurse in civilian life and another a pharmacist, ran regular clinics, treating everything from scrapes to serious illnesses. The clinics also gave locals an excuse to speak to Americans behind closed doors, rather than walking up to them when they were on patrol and risking being spotted by an insurgent spy or sympathizer, so the team's intelligence sergeants regularly attended the clinics too.

AS THE SPRING of 2004 arrived, A-team 936's members saw more evidence every day of the depth of the bond they and their militiamen had formed with the residents of Nangalam and the outlying villages. Fry himself had doubts until one tragic day a week before the end-of-tour base dedication ceremony. The captain was out in town on patrol when a pack of scraggly, half-wild dogs appeared. Dogs had bitten two Marines in Nangalam already, so when the biggest hound in the pack got too close and loud for comfort, Fry raised his rifle and shot it. To the Special Forces captain's horror, after it passed through the dog, the bullet ricocheted off a rock and hit a middle-aged man named Ahmad, who was standing in a nearby doorway, square in the forehead.

Fry had killed an innocent man, and he expected the consequences to be dire. Within a few hours, angry townspeople were demonstrating outside Camp Blessing's gate. But to his surprise, local elders and two mullahs who'd worked with a Special Forces chaplain calmed the crowd down by explaining that the shooting had been an honest mistake by a man they all knew, Commander Ron. At a *shura* two days later where Fry asked what he could do to make amends, instead of demanding the A-team pull up stakes and leave the valley as he feared they would, the elders suggested Fry negotiate compensation with the grieving family: an offering of goats, cash, and rice, and a heartfelt apology.[18]

The forbearance and forgiveness of the Nangalam *shura* and the bereaved family brought Fry to tears. "It was only then that we knew how close we were to the people," he said.[19] When he told a visiting CBS crew a few days later that he hoped to come back to the Pech someday and walk the hills with his sons, he meant it.[20] Nangalam and its environs had proven a friendly place with friendly people who wanted to both help and be helped: absorbent paper for the counterinsurgent ink blot to soak into.

Looking at the Blessing ink blot in the spring of 2004, that was an honest, reasonable assessment. But that rosy picture would not last long. When the Ranger officer Joe Ryan returned to the Pech six years later, leading a seven-hundred-man infantry battalion instead of a small A-team, he and his own boss would use the ink-blot analogy too—to justify pulling out. Years of insurgent brutality and American missteps, they would argue to their superiors in 2010, had turned the Pech from paper to plastic, a nonabsorbent substance the ink would never soak into.[21]

In May 2004, a new Green Beret team was about to make some of those missteps as it ventured into a Pech side valley Ron Fry had spent six months avoiding: the Korengal.

THE TIMBER WAR

When Jim Gant had crossed the wood-and-rope footbridge across the Pech a year earlier, in June 2003, and climbed into a pickup truck for the spine-compressing ride up the Korengal, he had been one of the first Americans to venture any distance up the valley since an anthropology doctoral student had trekked up and been turned away nearly forty years earlier.[22] In the years since, outside visitors had been rare. Soviet troops had ventured into the Korengal only during large offensives like those they mounted in the Pech in 1980 and 1985, typically winding up in serious firefights when they did so.[23] American intelligence collectors had first heard of the Korengal in the summer of 2002, when the name popped up as one of the valleys to which a group of Arabs had supposedly fled after Tora Bora.[24] Since then, SEAL Team 6 operators from Bagram had poked around the valley mouth on reconnaissance missions and at least one nighttime raid.[25]

Gant and his team were visiting not for a raid but for a meet and greet and to discuss a recent dispute between the Korengalis and one of the police officials they worked with, who was along for the trip and had recently had some trouble in the valley. A delegation of Korengalis met them on the south side of the bridge and ushered them into waiting pickups—the only type of vehicle suited to the dirt road that curled precariously along the valley's western slope—and up they went, into the gorge-like cut in the mountains.[26]

There was no valley floor to speak of; the villages, like the road, were carved into the mountainside, the stone and mud dwellings supported on stilts and adorned with wooden window frames and balconies whose bright turquoises and oranges jumped out from the brown-and-green landscape. Corn grew on lush, thin terraces. Some roofs were topped with grass for goats to graze on, others with satellite dishes. Above and below the towns stretched the forest, its dark green marred here and there by geometric shapes—evidence of the commercial logging that was the Korengal's livelihood.

The trucks stopped in Dokalbat, one of several villages clustered five miles back: "the only flat spot in that whole damn valley," as a Green Beret on the trip put it.[27] The Korengali elders who had gathered in a small room there, sitting on mattresses, wore red-dyed beards and kohl-like black powder around their eyes, and the team's interpreter, aided by Hyder Akbar, the governor's teenage Afghan American son, talked with them in Pashto. The Korengalis were a mountain tribe of the dwindling Pashai ethnic group (their ancestors had converted to Islam a century or so before the Kafirs of Nuristan[28]), and for them Pashto was a second language. Many of the attendees talked quietly in their own Korengali tongue throughout the *shura,* producing background chatter that no one among the visitors could understand.

There was rice, naan, mutton, and cold soda for everyone, but the gathering was short and tense. Gant's boss, the Green Beret company commander from Asadabad, explained what they were doing there, in a scene Hyder Akbar recorded for the radio show *This American Life.* The police official they'd brought along had recently had some trouble during a visit to the valley, the Green Beret major said; there had been a fight. The Korengalis weren't paying their taxes and were cutting down trees in violation of a recent ban by the Karzai government in Kabul. Everybody had to obey the police official, the major scolded, offering an off-key analogy about how he followed "the official system" when he had to pay a speeding ticket back in the United States, and they had better stop cutting down trees. "President Karzai has imposed a, I want to call it, it's a moratorium—anyway he's preventing people from cutting down all the trees," the major said, sounding confused by his own message. "His reason is, unless you have a program to regrow the trees, it's going to have a bad effect."[29]

Before the Green Berets left, a younger man who had been quiet during the *shura* approached Gant with a warning: *Don't come close to our valley again. If you do, we will fight.*[30]

After that, nearly every patrol that pushed more than a few hundred yards up the Korengal took warning volleys of gunfire—the exception being a Ranger company that stayed overnight during Winter Strike and found the valley tense but quiet.[31]

During their six months in the Pech the following year, Ron Fry and his intelligence sergeants listened as Pech valley informants intimated that the people behind the rocket attacks on Camp Blessing and bombs and ambushes aimed at convoys on the Pech road were Korengalis. Special Forces officers and intel sergeants, like all intelligence collectors, are trained to regard informants' claims with an eye toward ulterior motives. When it came to sources from the Pech valley proper pointing fingers at the neighboring Korengal, there was a big one: the timber business.

"The Americans were a tool, used by the Safis in the Pech to rid them of their competition in the timber trade," a Korengali elder would complain years later, referring to the Safi Pashtun tribe to which most residents of the Pech proper belonged.[32] Gant hadn't grasped it at the time, but when he visited the Korengal, he and his team were the first Americans of many to be used as muscle by one side in an economic war over wood. Safi timber barons controlled access to the Korengal, and a few days earlier the police commander—really a figure in the U.S.-backed warlord Haji Jahan Dad's militia—had visited with what the Korengalis saw as an unfair price hike for the role he played in getting Korengali timber to market, resulting in a brawl. Gant's Green Berets brought that commander along on their trip, took his side in the dispute without understanding it, and left only after their major insisted that one of the Korengali elders pose for a photo op with his opponent, shaking hands.[33]

WOOD WAS A way of life in Kunar and Nuristan, which were home to the largest and richest remaining forest ecosystem in Afghanistan, a country that is mostly dry and brown.[34] Growing up, children heard stories from their fathers and grandfathers about how dark and deep the forest was, and how much deeper and darker it once had been. Yarns about encounters with white-chested bears and huge troops of monkeys were standard fare. In some places, hunters' tales had been passed down from the pre-Islamic past about giant forest spirits whose houses, hidden inside the rock, were guarded by the leopards that really did still roam the dim green light of the forest's densest parts.[35]

Wood was also a multimillion-dollar business, and the Korengal was at the heart of it.

Kunar's forests had two layers. A band of leafy hardwood forest stood on the lower slopes, near most of the villages; Kunaris relied on this tier's small evergreen oaks and birches for everything from firewood to animal feed to toothbrush twigs. Up between six and ten thousand feet, hidden from the valley floor by ridges and false peaks, stood the second layer: forests of conifers with bright green needles and drooping branches. Wide spaces separated the trunks of the pines, cedars, firs, spruces, and junipers that grew in this layer, but around the forest's edge and in the places where the trees were oldest and largest, the upper branches meshed together into a canopy, under which lived everything from small mammals, musk deer, and chattering parakeets to jackals, lynx, monkeys, and the occasional bear and leopard.

Kunaris called the conifers *nakhtar.* An East India Company botanist who visited the Pech in 1840 wrote admiringly that a *nakhtar* was "a large tree, seventy to eighty feet high: one of average size measured fourteen feet in girth, four feet from the base," its lower branches often used by locals for torches.[36] A century and a half later, Kunar's forests had shrunk, but high in the Korengal and a few other side valleys like the Watapur there were still conifer forests so thick that people called them jungles. American soldiers who made it up to these areas tended to be shocked at first that such places could exist in Afghanistan. The scenery reminded some of them of the wooded mountains of the Pacific Northwest, others of Endor, the forest moon in *Return of the Jedi.*

In 2010, the U.S. Agency for International Development (USAID) would belatedly lend a Yale-trained forester named Harry Bader to the military to study Kunar's timber trade. Bader had spent time working in the Balkans, where he helped develop techniques to identify mass grave sites through thick canopies and had been kidnapped by Serb forces, and in Iraq. He was fascinated by the wild woods he found in Kunar and by villagers' relationship with them. "The forest is as important to some of these communities now as it was two thousand years ago, and that's not hyperbole," he told me. In recent decades, in fact, wood had become more important than ever—specifically the Himalayan or deodar cedars that made up some 15 to 20 percent of the conifer forest.[37]

Light, strong, aromatic, and resistant to rot and insects, deodar cedar had always been used for construction in Kunar, but as Bader learned, the jihad of the 1980s was what turned the cedar trade into an international business. Carried across the border to Pakistan by donkeys, bought by Pakistani timber barons in Peshawar, and then shipped across the Indian Ocean from Karachi, cedar from Kunar came to be prized by pious, ultra-wealthy Arabs of the Persian Gulf who were backing the jihad financially. "In the Gulf states, it was called jihad wood," Bader found. "You'd want the cabinetry in your mansion in Dubai done in this cedar, because you would be supporting the mujahidin."[38]

Bader, who had grown up on a farm in Iowa, explained the rapid evolution of the cedar business with an analogy. "Corn was important to my grandfather and my great-grandfather and they grew a lot of it, but now, if you're a farmer in Iowa, you *only* grow corn," he said. "That's what happened to deodar cedar in Kunar."[39] The introduction of chain saws sped things along.[40]

With some of Kunar's best cedar and less flat ground to grow crops than some other Pech side valleys, the Korengal went all in on logging starting in the late 1980s, as foreign demand for the wood rose. A decade later, the business had made the leading Korengali families rich. (The Rangers who trekked in during Winter Strike were amazed by the size and quantity of the felled cedars they saw being stockpiled in the valley and by the mansion-like scale of some of the houses they saw.[41]) In answer to concerns about deforestation raised by foreign environmental organizations like the UN Environment Programme (UNEP) and by his own finance minister, a U.S.-educated technocrat and future president named Ashraf Ghani, Hamid Karzai had issued a decree in 2002 banning logging in Afghanistan altogether.[42]

Years later, it would become clear that reports of deforestation in

Kunar—including an influential UN study[43]—were alarmist and seriously flawed.* In 2010, Bader and his team would often take a Black Hawk up to sites where there wasn't supposed to be so much as a twig left and find dense stands of trees that clearly had not been cut since the time of the East India Company botanist's visit 170 years earlier.[44] But by then, the damage of Karzai's timber ban was done. "The ban criminalized an activity that everyone had to participate in to live," Bader explained. "Everyone was always going to defy it. So it made everyone vulnerable to arrest; corrupt government officials could send anyone to prison who crossed them."[45]

In the Korengal (which Bader never studied specifically), that dynamic permanently altered the commercial balance between the Korengalis and the Safi Pashtun timber barons who profited off them, and it drew the American military into a conflict over timber that it did not understand. Far from stopping logging in the Korengal, the ban gave the very Safi strongmen who acted as middlemen in the trade—American allies like Matiullah Khan, the Pech gem baron who was Kunar's police chief, and Jahan Dad, the thuggish timber baron in charge of provincial border guards—a pretext to intervene in it and extort ever-higher levies for wood's safe passage. The Korengalis kept cutting trees, now illegally, which gave their business partners the power to arrest them at will, and the strongmen-cum-officials kept buying, transporting, and selling the timber because the ban's vague language only explicitly forbade the cutting of trees, not the resulting commerce.[46] Matiullah Khan kept armed police in Kandigal, controlling the Korengal's front door, while Jahan Dad's border guards controlled the back door over the mountains into a pair of perpendicular valleys that led down to the Kunar River.

---

* Unable to visit Kunar to see firsthand how cedar was logged, the UN Environment Programme team relied on low-resolution satellite imagery, and when a Wildlife Conservation Society team tried in 2006 to replicate the UNEP results with the same imagery, it couldn't. Later studies, including Bader's, would find that the timber barons actually avoided the environmentally dangerous practice of clear-cutting and that the high-altitude conifer forests the timber ban targeted were consequently doing fine, ecologically speaking. True deforestation was occurring only in the lower oak forests and wouldn't spread to the conifer forest until 2011 as the Americans began their long pullout from Kunar and the Taliban moved to take over the province's whole timber industry.

As both strongmen squeezed the Korengal, the *shura* that governed the valley's logging operations turned to the Taliban for help. The Korengal's most prominent and respected elder, a Salafi cleric named Mawlawi Abdul Rahim (who had fought under Haji Ghafor during the jihad and whom U.S. intelligence suspected of having harbored Arabs after the battle of Tora Bora), had had ties with the Taliban government before September 11. Abdul Rahim became the valley's liaison to Taliban officials in Pakistan, and before long Taliban fighters were arriving, bringing weapons and helping local men stage attacks to keep away competitors like the police and border guards and any Americans who accompanied them. In return, the Korengalis paid the Taliban a fee, and Taliban fighters were able to use the Korengal as a training ground and base area—their main foothold in a province where the movement had been weak before September 11.

Ron Fry didn't know all the details of which U.S.-backed officials were exploiting the timber ban to get the better of the Korengalis, or of the Korengalis' evolving dance with the Taliban. Though he knew Jim Gant, the two hadn't so much as seen each other during their A-teams' fleeting overlap at FOB Asadabad in the fall, let alone discussed what Gant had learned on his brief visit to the valley.

But Fry grasped that what was going on in the Korengal was an economic affair, motivated by the Korengalis' desire to preserve their now-illegal wealth, and he didn't think it sounded like his A-team's business. Further, he doubted the reports informants gave to his intel sergeants about Korengali participation in attacks on Pech-road convoys or the rocketing of Camp Blessing. The informants relaying these reports were almost exclusively Pech Safis, and Fry well knew that Pech Safis were responsible for many of those attacks. Nobody liked admitting that his brother, son, cousin, or friend had taken part in an attack; doing so risked the economic relationship between one's village and the Special Forces A-camp. Even setting aside the timber issue, which Fry understood only in the vaguest terms, blaming the Korengal was an easy out.

"The Korengal wasn't exporting fighters. The Korengalis weren't coming out and fucking with us," Fry explained. "It didn't make sense for us to go in there just to get shot at. So we made the decision not to go kick a hornet's nest."[47]

DIFFERENT A-TEAM, DIFFERENT WAR

At Fort Bragg, another A-team was reading the same intelligence reports as Fry and reaching a different conclusion. "We knew well ahead of time where the turds were hiding," recalled Sergeant First Class Luke,* a senior NCO on A-team 361, referring to the guerrillas the team hoped to capture or kill during their six months at Camp Blessing. "They were in the Korengal."[48]

Luke flew into Nangalam on May 16, the day of the ceremony formally naming the base Blessing. The rest of A-team 361 followed over the next few days. The incoming Green Berets were more experienced than Fry's men; most were on their third Afghan tour since September 11, a fact that seemed to leave them uninterested in what the outgoing Utah National Guardsmen had to say about the lessons they'd learned in the Pech. "They weren't sponges, so to speak," Fry said. "It was, 'When can we have your room? Are you gone yet?'"[49]

Fry was right to be nervous. What was happening was a kind of "mission creep" inevitable in a war run on a system of unit rotation: the kind that happened when two units, identical on paper, passed the baton and turned out to have seriously divergent mindsets and plans. Both dozen-man A-teams were built the same, and the Green Berets on them had gone through the same selection and training at Fort Bragg. There the similarities ended. In the words of its French originators, the oil-spot method of counterinsurgency required "a collection of rare qualities"—very much the ones Green Berets, as "unconventional warriors," were supposed to have.[50] "Initiative, intelligence, and energy" both teams had in abundance. But compared with A-team 936, Fort Bragg team 361 fell short in the "prudence, calm, and perspicacity" department. The two teams were a case study in a Special Forces identity crisis that would play out throughout the war on terror.

As sometimes happened on A-teams where young captains were nominally in charge of a close-knit group of far more experienced NCOs, A-team 361's sergeants marginalized their captain and ran

---

* Luke asked that his full name not be used.

things their own way, with Luke and the team's intel sergeant playing outsized roles. Luke, an Idaho native, had joined the Special
Forces at age thirty-six to get away from the spit and polish of the
infantry, where he'd already had a long career. Now past forty, he
had plenty of gray in his deployment beard. A-team 361 had been
on a peacetime deployment in the Persian Gulf the day New York
and Washington were attacked, and the jubilant reactions Luke had
seen there colored his perceptions of Muslims. But he was a competent light infantryman with a knack for inspiring battlefield courage
even in ragtag irregular troops whose religion he disliked and with
whom he had nothing in common. And as a soldier in the war on
terror, he saw his job as punishing the enemy.[51]

Luke and the other Green Beret sergeants on A-team 361 were
happy to inherit the Nangalam militia force that A-team 936 had
recruited and trained, but they didn't intend to use the force the way
the Utah soldiers had, on local patrols that built up trust between
the militiamen and the people inside their protective ink blot. To
Luke, the dichotomy Fry drew between going out and crushing
cockroaches and staying closer afield to keep the cockroaches away
made no sense. He had a force of more than a hundred armed militiamen, trained by fellow Green Berets. What he wanted to do with
them was go find the cockroaches and kill them. "There's a reason
to train the [militia], and that reason is to do offensive operations,"
he said.[52]

A-team 361 also inherited an attached platoon of Marines at
Camp Blessing. Based out of Camp Lejeune, North Carolina, three
hours from 361's Fort Bragg home, the forty-odd infantrymen of
First Platoon, Kilo Company, 3/6 Marines were young—many had
been high-school seniors less than a year earlier—and like all good
Marines they were champing at the bit to find and fight the enemy.
To many of them, A-team 936's slow-and-steady approach had been
frustrating, and the arrival of a new team with an aggressive attitude
was a breath of fresh air.[53]

The new Green Berets swore the way the Marines did, kept
contraband liquor on hand for special occasions, and treated the
Marines like younger brothers. To the Marines' delight, Luke supplemented the camp dog with a pair of rhesus monkeys he bought
in the bazaar, one of whom, Mr. Peepers, liked to come along on

patrols. (When he felt as if his American friends were threatened—usually by an Afghan child—the red-faced Mr. Peepers would work his eyebrows up and down dramatically and make menacing noises.) Instead of eating the same food as the militiamen, Luke and his team brought their own Army cook and finagled little luxuries through the shoestring supply system: steak, lobster, and ice cream bars flown or trucked out to Blessing. The Marines loved it.[54]

The oldest Marine at the outpost, sent to help the platoon's lieutenant keep things in order, was Gunnery Sergeant Bill Bodette, and he couldn't have been happier with the A-team switch out. Tall, with deep-set eyes, one permanently arched eyebrow, and the high-and-tight haircut of a drill instructor, Bodette was an imposing figure. In any line of work besides the infantry, the drinking, brawling gunnery sergeant wouldn't have been the person you looked to for adult supervision. Bodette and Luke got along like long-lost brothers from the day they met. "These were real Special Forces soldiers and they didn't take no shit," the Marine gunny said of A-team 361. "They wanted to fight."[55]

Nangalam residents had the same impression, and at least some of them approved. "Commander Ron and Commander Luke were both good people, much better than the other officers who came later," one native of the town, Anayat Rahman, told me long afterward, referring to Fry and Luke. Anayat Rahman was close to the militia leaders at Blessing and often shared tips with them and their Green Beret handlers about where insurgents were. What he perceived as A-team 936's hesitance to act on that information and go after the enemy—especially militants in the Korengal—had frustrated him.

"Commander Ron was a *jirga* guy," he said, using the Pashto word for the big meetings of elders and local notables that Fry had made regular appearances at. "Commander Luke was not a *jirga* guy. He was our district governor and our police. He liked to fight, and he was the first to fight the Korengalis."[56]

BY DAY, A-TEAM 361 and the Marines and militiamen (for whose uniforms Luke had special patches tailored, depicting a skull and sword superimposed on the Afghan flag) kept patrolling the ink blot just as Ron Fry's men had, talking to people and developing sources. Bodette, known in Nangalam as Commander Gunny, looked on these missions—the bread and butter of the previous A-team's version of counterinsurgency—skeptically. "We got along good with most of the townspeople, but the Taliban were mixed in with them. I probably shook a Taliban guy's hand and didn't know it," he recalled, stating an obvious truth of counterinsurgency work with frustration.[57]

By night, Luke and Bodette drove east along the Pech road to contested areas just outside the reach of Camp Blessing's mortars, near the riverbank village of Sundray, and picked fights. Where Ron Fry's team had mainly gotten around in pickup trucks and on foot, A-team 361 relied on its Humvees—armed with .50-caliber heavy machine guns and Mk 19 grenade launchers that burped out explosive shells the size of Red Bull cans at a rate of sixty per minute—and on a pair of British Land Rovers that they'd gotten their hands on and tricked out with machine guns and bazooka-like recoilless rifles like something out of *Mad Max*. After dark, the Green Berets and Marines would head east on the Pech road, using one group of gun trucks as bait for an insurgent attack while another patrol set up heavy weapons in a hidden ambush position. The resulting fights typically ended inconclusively after half an hour when Air Force jets roared onto station.[58]

"If we thought there were bad people there, that's where we went," Luke said.[59] But the fighters A-team 361 was tangling with around Sundray—local Salafis led by a wealthy Sundray resident named Haji Mohammad Dawran—weren't the ones the team was really interested in. The real draw lay over the next ridge, in the Korengal.

The A-team's intel sergeant had been studying reports about the Korengal for weeks back at Fort Bragg. He spent most of his first month at Blessing helping Luke build "target packets"—files that pulled together all the known information about particular guerrillas or their hideouts—to support proposals for operations into the valley, which Special Forces headquarters back at Bagram had to approve.[60]

One of the Korengali insurgents on whom the Green Berets were able to assemble a target packet was the owner of an expensive band saw, which sliced felled cedar trunks into more easily portable cants—a key figure in the valley's timber business who informants said was instrumental in the Korengal's alliance with the Taliban.[61] "There was huge money in that lumber industry, and that was how they were funding their operations," Luke said. By leaving the Korengal alone, he reasoned, A-team 936 had been allowing an infection to grow.[62]

BESIDES WANTING TO go after the enemy where he felt safe, Luke and his intel sergeant were drawn to the Korengal by the purported presence there of one of the only actual al-Qaida operatives U.S. intelligence was aware of in all of Afghanistan: an Arab jihadi called Abu Ikhlas al-Masri.

No one knew Abu Ikhlas's real name. The one he went by was a *kunya,* a common form of Arabic pseudonym, and *al-Masri* just meant "the Egyptian." Before leaving Egypt as a young man in the 1980s, he had spent time in prison for militant activity there. One rumor had it that he had been a cellmate of Omar Abdel-Rahman, the "blind sheikh" imprisoned for his links to the 1993 World Trade Center bombing,[63] and according to another he traveled from Egypt to Afghanistan alongside Ayman al-Zawahiri, the future leader of al-Qaida.[64] During the jihad, he'd been known for his skill repairing weapons, especially the big DShK heavy machine guns that Afghans called "Dushkas."[65] When most of his fellow Arab volunteers returned to their home countries in the early 1990s, Abu Ikhlas stayed and built a life for himself in Kunar, learning Pashto, marrying at least one woman from the Pech,[66] and running small businesses in Asadabad like an auto-repair shop and a construction company that built concrete columns for mosques.

In the eyes of many Kunaris who knew him in the 1990s, Abu Ikhlas had essentially become Afghan. "I don't know what he became later, but at that point he was pretty much a local," one Kunari told me of him.[67] When he wasn't working downtown, he helped train Islamist militants of various stripes at Topchi Base, the future site of FOB Asadabad, reportedly specializing in explosive devices, including the improvised mines that would later be called IEDs.[68]

It is not clear how or when Abu Ikhlas became a member of

al-Qaida. It might have been when Zawahiri and a faction of the Egyptian militants in Afghanistan merged with al-Qaida in the late 1990s, or it might not have been until early 2002, when he left his family and public life in Asadabad and took to the hills. "When the Americans and NDS were looking for Arabs, Abu Ikhlas fled to the Korengal with Mawlawi Abdul Rahim and Dawran, who were the first to fight the Americans in the Pech valley," a Kunari who worked closely with the CIA at the time told me.[69] There, Abu Ikhlas became one of the earliest members of Kunar's anti-American, antigovernment insurgency, teaching Taliban and Hizb-e Islami fighters alike how to build roadside bombs and opening up a link to the money and resources of al-Qaida in Pakistan. A mullah from Nangalam who had taught Abu Ikhlas at Asadabad's main mosque remembered the day he received a letter, unsigned but in handwriting he recognized as his Egyptian pupil's, explaining what he was doing: he was taking up arms against the American occupiers, Abu Ikhlas wrote, and the elderly cleric should not cooperate with the infidels or the puppet government they supported if he knew what was good for him.[70] The role of the trainer, financier, and all-around adviser was a familiar one for al-Qaida, which had been training and assisting local militants on battlefields from Somalia to Afghanistan well before it ventured into international terrorism.[71]

Abu Ikhlas was on the radar of the CIA officers at FOB Asadabad by the end of their first summer there, but there was little to go on.[72] Like any smart guerrilla, he was careful to avoid speaking on the phone, the best way U.S. intelligence had of keeping tabs on someone. By the time an informant reported he had visited a village somewhere, he was always long gone—if he had been there at all. Sometimes it turned out that a subordinate had simply played a recorded message from him at the village mosque. Some informants who had met him said he was tall, others that he was stocky, and one that he had scars on one side of his body from a mine explosion (though whether it was a mine he stepped on, a mine he was defusing, or an IED he was building was not specified).[73] Ron Fry imagined that the Egyptian jihadi was in his early forties. In fact he was a decade older. Years later, after a lucky break finally led to Abu Ikhlas's capture in 2010, interrogators met a thin, balding man with a long face and widely separated eyes—hardly the intimidating commander many Americans had pictured as their opponent.

Fry knew little about Abu Ikhlas except that he played an active role in the Pech insurgency; the one time militants launched a concerted attack on Camp Blessing during Fry's deployment, in March, informants quickly identified Abu Ikhlas as the assault's planner.[74] "He was basically my counterpart," Fry guessed. The Special Forces captain was overseeing the training and employment of a group of local fighters in the Pech on one side of the war, and Abu Ikhlas was doing the same on the other side, like a jihadi version of a Green Beret adviser.[75] (A later report from an informant would describe how, when Abu Ikhlas visited a town in the mountains above the Pech, he asked a local cell leader to provide his six bravest and most dedicated young fighters to go back to Bajaur in Pakistan with him for training.[76]) There was a $20,000 bounty on Abu Ikhlas's head; Abu Ikhlas, in turn, made it known that he would give $10,000 to whoever killed the commander of Camp Blessing.[77]

"The al-Qaida guys were few and far between, so with Abu Ikhlas, it became like a Where's Waldo thing," recalled Ron Moeller, the CIA paramilitary officer.[78] "He was al-Qaida, and al-Qaida was kind of a phantom back then," a case officer who spent time at Asadabad agreed. "He was the only true al-Qaida guy that we knew of. . . . So he was a big target."[79]

There were, in fact, other members of al-Qaida who still spent time on the right side of the Afghan border in 2003 and 2004; the Americans in Kunar at the time just didn't know about them. One who made trips in the province without attracting American attention was another Egyptian veteran of the jihad, Abu Ubaydah al-Masri, who visited to oversee battlefield advisers like Abu Ikhlas. Abu Ubaydah would later become al-Qaida's emir or commander for eastern Afghanistan and be linked to terrorist plots in Europe.[80] Abu Ikhlas, by comparison, was more locally focused guerrilla than international terrorist. Al-Qaida documents captured in later years would name Abu Ubaydah, not Abu Ikhlas, as the head of the group's Kunar operations during the 2003–2005 period.[81]

But because Abu Ikhlas was a better-known figure in Kunar, American intelligence became aware of him earlier and received more frequent and detailed reports about him, and he became a target of tantalizing interest to the CIA team at FOB Asadabad and their attached "Omega team" of JSOC operators.* Anytime a tip or a cell phone intercept hinted at his presence, off the Omega team went with the CIA's Mohawk local troops, chasing the ghost, and in Asadabad the Mohawks took to harassing Abu Ikhlas's wife and children at their home.[82]

The focus on Abu Ikhlas, a midlevel operative who had had nothing to do with September 11 or other international terrorist attacks, exemplified a kind of tunnel vision in the American military and intelligence community that bin Laden himself understood and said openly that he hoped to exploit. The United States was "easy for us to bait and provoke," bin Laden said in a fall 2004 videotape filmed somewhere in Pakistan as American special operators and intelligence officers were busy running down every hint of an Arab in eastern Afghanistan. "All we have to do is send two mujahidin to the furthest point east to raise a piece of cloth on which 'al-Qaida' is written in order to make the generals race there" and commit military resources.[83]

America's eight-year search for Abu Ikhlas would bear bin Laden's assessment out. The CIA's focus on Abu Ikhlas solidified A-team 361's assessment of the middle-aged Egyptian jihadi: he was the biggest cockroach in need of squashing in the greater Pech, and the valley where informants most often placed him was the Korengal, where intercepted Arabic walkie-talkie transmissions confirmed at least the occasional presence of Arabs. "The local thugs up there were influenced by Abu Ikhlas and his boys," Luke guessed. "He had gone up there to hide and he was teaching them 'This is how you do it,'" sharing expertise on ambushes and bomb making.[84]

With approval from Bagram, the team started driving its gun trucks up the precarious Korengal road in early June. The point was to get in fights, and get in fights they did. During their first Korengal mission, Luke and the other Green Berets and Marines found

---

* Each SEAL Team 6 contingent to rotate through Bagram farmed out some of its operators to Omega teams at various CIA border outposts, where they helped lead surrogate units like the Mohawks on missions and provided the agency's link to military air support.

themselves in an on-again, off-again long-range firefight as Korengali fighters tried without success to scare the visitors off.[85]

Each mission after that was bigger than the last. The Green Berets returned on July 3 with more men and more firepower—not just the Marines and militiamen from Blessing but a sister Special Forces team and some signals intelligence specialists from FOB Asadabad. Coming under heavy fire on their way back out of the valley, the Americans suffered one Marine lightly wounded, called in bombs and strafing runs from jets overhead, and had to abandon two pickup trucks because they were too badly riddled with bullets.[86]

Three weeks after that, A-team 361 launched an even bigger mission, dubbed Operation Chainsaw, this time in concert with a whole company of nearly two hundred Marines who flew onto the Korengal's eastern ridgeline in Chinooks and "cleared" downhill from their landing zones. Predictably, the Marines and Green Berets found little; insurgent commanders in the Korengal had to know, after two incursions, that more were coming. "Once the enemy realized there was a company of Marines in the valley, they went to ground," the captain who led the Marine air-assault mission speculated reasonably. The most frightening moment in the operation was when an Army medevac bird—an unarmed Black Hawk with a big red cross painted on its side—had to evacuate a Marine who'd been hit by a tumbling rock. As the medevac helicopter hovered, an RPG soared out of nowhere and exploded disquietingly close to its tail.[87] Neither Abu Ikhlas nor any other insurgent leader was anywhere to be found, and the close call with the helicopter foreshadowed tragedies to come.

IT SHOULD HAVE come as no surprise that the summer's Korengal missions had little immediate result. As Winter Strike had already shown, insurgents in Kunar and Nuristan were too smart to contest most big offensive "clearance" operations.

Each time the Americans entered the side valley, however, they were putting the squeeze on the Korengal's illegal lumber operation. On every visit, the Green Berets and Marines set up a temporary patrol base on the grounds of a sawmill four miles into the valley, perched on its western side. The Korengal Lumberyard, as they called the place, offered a commanding view of the valley floor, and the lumber stacked there provided cover during firefights.

The sawmill was the property of the Korengal's wealthiest businessman, a red-bearded Salafi named Haji Matin. Later, when a whole U.S. infantry company occupied the Korengal valley floor, using the lumberyard as its permanent base, and Haji Matin stood at the head of the valley's relentless insurgency, a story gained currency that Matin had turned against the United States after an American air strike destroyed one of his homes and killed part of his family.[88] Whether this story is fact or fiction is almost impossible to say so long after the fact and without talking to Matin himself, who died in a JSOC drone strike in 2013, a decade after he took up arms. It is probably somewhere in between; air strike or no, by the end of the summer of 2004, Matin had every economic reason to fight the United States. According to reports that reached U.S. troops at FOB Asadabad that fall, the price of timber in Kunar had risen 30 percent in a year.[89]

So it also should not have come as a surprise that when the Korengali insurgents struck back, they would target Camp Blessing, the home of Americans who were interfering with their business.

A month after Operation Chainsaw, at the end of August 2004, the Green Berets at Blessing started to hear an alarming amount of chatter on the walkie-talkies with which they kept tabs on insurgent radio communications. The guerrillas spoke to each other in code so transparent that if they hadn't been talking about their preparations for a major attack, it would have seemed laughable, referring to RPGs and machine guns as "bananas" and "logs."

"That night, we knew they were coming, but we didn't know when," Luke recalled. He and the other soldiers feared that a frontal assault on the base was imminent, like the ones their Green Beret forerunners had often faced at remote A-camps in Vietnam.[90] They were right. Blessing's defenders—fewer than usual because the Marine platoon had been temporarily pulled out for another job—were waiting at their battle positions when rockets and mortars started raining down with far greater volume and accuracy than A-team 361 had ever seen before. The incoming fire quickly knocked one of the camp's mortars out of operation, wounding the senior militiaman manning it.

The battle nearly became a disaster when the militiamen manning Observation Post Comanche, one of the fortified satellite positions on the peaks surrounding Blessing, abandoned their post and attacking guerrilla fighters took over the OP and turned its DShK heavy machine gun around to fire down into the main base. The gun's huge .51-caliber tracers looked to Luke like glowing baseballs as they streaked down at Camp Blessing, and the team rushed to position a Humvee where its own heavy machine gun could duel with the DShK. When the fire from OP Comanche abruptly stopped, though, it wasn't due to good shooting by the Green Berets in the Humvee; when the base defenders reoccupied the OP after the battle, they found the heavy machine gun there intact, with no evidence that any insurgents had been hurt. Probably, the Americans figured, the DShK had simply jammed. Had it kept firing much longer, it almost certainly would have wounded or killed someone down below.[91]

When A-10 attack jets and then an AC-130 gunship arrived and started looping overhead, blasting their cannon at every group of guerrillas they spotted in the hills and on the outskirts of Nangalam, the fight petered out. No Americans had been hurt or killed. But in town, the hotel where Ron Fry had enjoyed stopping for yogurt during his deployment was on fire and would burn to the ground by morning. It was a common rumor among later units at Blessing that A-team 361 had called in a bomb strike directly on the hotel, but Luke denied that. His guess was that rockets or cannon fire from the A-10s had set fire to a small, adjacent sawmill and the resulting blaze had consumed the hotel.[92]

The August 30 battle never made it into the annals of the war, and most of the thousands of American troops who fought in the Pech later would never hear of it. But it made an impression in town. "I remember that battle very well," Anayat Rahman, the wealthy Nangalam resident who was close to Luke, said of the fight. "Commander Luke came out into the market and fought very bravely until the planes came."[93] The war had come to Nangalam.

Less than a month later, on September 23, the insurgents reprised their attack, again starting out with a barrage of rockets and then targeting the base with increasingly accurate mortar and RPG fire that blew up an empty pickup truck inside the perimeter. The commander of the Marine battalion in eastern Afghanistan, Lieutenant Colonel Dale Alford, was visiting Blessing, and his guard detail joined in the defense while he walked the perimeter, encouraging the defending troops in his thick, profanity-laced northern Georgia drawl. This time the battle culminated when a group of the attacking militants—a couple dozen—rallied in the field south of the camp's main gate, by the river, seemingly in preparation for launching a frontal attack, and a low-flying A-10 delivered a five-hundred-pound bomb right into their midst.[94]

Alford was impressed by the discipline and skill of the attacking locals. Despite taking what had to have been heavy casualties, they were able to speedily drag away all of their dead and wounded, leaving behind only a few blood trails by the time any of the heavily equipped Americans ventured out to look for them. (This was why Soviet troops had called the guerrillas they fought in Kunar *dukhov,* Russian for "ghosts" or "spooks.") "They could drag sons of bitches away faster than anybody I've ever seen," Alford said with admiration, judging Blessing's attackers against the Arab jihadis his battalion would face a year later in Iraq. "There in the Pech valley, you didn't find a fucking dead enemy soldier. They hauled 'em away."[95]

THE TWIN ATTACKS on Camp Blessing at the end of the summer of 2004 were premonitions of what was to come in the Pech and its tributary valleys as the war there escalated and the U.S. military established outposts in ever-more-remote locations. The same disciplined infantry tactics—focusing first on crucial defensive positions like mortar pits and observation posts in the hopes of crippling the base's ability to fend off a penetration of the perimeter, enduring heavy casualties but leaving practically no trace afterward that they'd ever been there—would recur in one outpost assault after another, always the most alarming day of any unit's deployment. As Luke said, "They were trying to overrun us"—a bold tactic that only a handful of U.S. bases in Afghanistan ever faced, most of them in Kunar and Nuristan.[96]

No one could say for sure who the attackers had been. That many if not most of them were disaffected locals of the Pech and its side valleys was clear. In some nearby villages from which fallen insurgents hailed, Luke was told, families carried the dead through town the next day to their burial sites.[97] But informants named a who's who of Pech guerrilla leaders: Abu Ikhlas of al-Qaida; Mullah Dawran, the commander from Sundray who had joined the insurgency after initially opposing the Taliban; Mawlawi Monibullah, a Waygali cleric and son of an old Hizb commander who had recently thrown in his lot with the Taliban; and a young Salafi commander called Ahmad Shah, who, like Abu Ikhlas, was purported to use the Korengal as a base. Some fighters had come from the district west of Nangalam, Chapa Dara, where one of the Blessing indig militiamen had been making enemies for the Americans in his spare time, extorting money from local gem dealers by threatening to tell his Green Beret friends that they were with al-Qaida or the Taliban.[98]

The reports that A-team 361 latched onto were the ones implicating the Korengal. After a summer of escalating American intrusions into their valley, it seemed highly plausible to Luke and the team's intel sergeant that the Korengalis were hitting back, even if they were doing so in collaboration with Pashtun and Waygali guerrilla cells for added manpower.

The team's response was further escalation: more trips into the Korengal. "We kept going back up the road into the Korengal," Luke explained—sometimes just the A-team, sometimes with the Marines, and, on two occasions, just the Marines by themselves on big helicopter assaults that turned up nothing. "It became kind of a free-fire zone."[99] A year and a half after Jim Gant first visited it, the Korengal valley was fast becoming a self-fulfilling prophecy (or, in militarese, a "self-licking ice cream cone"): a place where American military activity was driving insurgent attacks, and insurgent attacks were driving American military activity.

A GAME OF TELEPHONE

When Justin Bellman stepped off the helicopter at Camp Blessing in late October 2004, Luke met him at the landing zone, baseball cap on his head and chattering monkey on his shoulder. A Marine lieutenant on his first combat deployment, Bellman was to be Blessing's third commander.[100] With A-team 361's tour coming to an end, the

Green Beret colonels back at Bagram were rotating out too, and the incoming Special Forces headquarters was not interested in continuing the Pech valley counterinsurgency experiment. So Bellman and eighty other Marines, fresh from their home station in Hawaii, were inheriting it.

Versions of this story were playing out in many places in Iraq and Afghanistan: with Special Forces A-teams in short supply and high demand, and little continuity between the Special Forces groups that rotated every six months with their own strategies and priorities, conventional infantry units were taking over missions started by special operators, often with little preparation or understanding of the work of the units that had preceded them.

During a brief overlap period, the homeward-bound Green Berets handed Bellman a wad of cash to pay the indig and the keys to a storage unit full of so many captured weapons that it reminded the lieutenant of the movie *The Boondock Saints.* Then they were gone, and Forward Operating Base Blessing, the local militiamen the Green Berets had recruited, and the security of the Pech valley were the responsibility of a group of Marines of whom the twenty-six-year-old Bellman was one of the oldest.

Like Jim Gant, Ron Fry, and Luke before him, Bellman couldn't escape another film comparison: Blessing, with its sandbagged fighting positions and tiger-stripe-clad indig defenders, looked like something out of a Vietnam war movie.[101] He didn't know this was partly by design, a deliberate tribute on the part of Fry's Green Beret team. Nor did he know much else about what A-team 936 had accomplished in the Pech earlier that same year; all the information he got came from the mouths of Luke and the other A-team 361 soldiers.

This was a common and debilitating problem, yet one that was all but impossible to avoid. No one knew how long American involvement in Afghanistan or Iraq would last, and soldiers couldn't be deployed forever. People had to rotate out. The periods of deployment the different services came up with varied—six or seven months for Green Berets and Marines, twelve or fifteen months for the regular Army, three or four months for JSOC troops—but only a handful of servicemen ever stayed for more than sixteen months at a stretch. The result was a counterinsurgency fought like a game of telephone. It was a rare unit in Afghanistan that had an accurate understanding of how the base it occupied had come into being, or of what had been transpiring outside that base's gates more than one rotation into the recent past.

The problem was hardly new. It had bedeviled the Soviets, who fought their war in Afghanistan in two-year increments, and it was famously said that in Vietnam (where soldiers rotated as individuals, not as units) the U.S. Army had fought not one ten-year-long war but ten one-year-long ones. Nearly a decade later, at a reunion of his team, Ron Fry performed an experiment: he read aloud an excerpt from a 1970 RAND Corporation report on Army failures in Southeast Asia. "The Army in Vietnam is like a recording tape that is erased every twelve months," the paper's author, also a Special Forces officer, had observed. "I am convinced that the twelve-month tour condemns us to learning the same lessons over and over again."[102] Fry replaced "Vietnam" with "Afghanistan" and "twelve" with "six" and asked his former teammates what they thought of the analysis of the war they'd fought in. *Spot-on,* was the consensus.[103]

The switch-off from Ron Fry's A-team 936 to Luke's A-team 361 and then to Justin Bellman's Hawaii Marines, and the resulting escalation in the Korengal valley—all in the space of a year—exemplified the discontinuity of purpose that this shortcoming created.

Bellman had been at Camp Blessing for barely a day when one of the grizzled Green Berets he was replacing asked him a question: "Do you want to get into a firefight?" He did.

"They took me out to the Korengal Lumberyard, where they knew we were going to get into a firefight, and damned if we didn't," Bellman remembered. As he excitedly reported on his adventure to his superiors that evening via secure internet chat, Bellman didn't give much thought to how, when, or why the A-team he was replacing had gotten entangled in the wooded side valley, nor was he aware that the A-team before *them* had deliberately avoided the place. The battle-hardened special operators he was taking over from said that to protect Camp Blessing, you had to push off toward the sound of guns in the Korengal. That was enough for him.[104]

CHAPTER 4

RED WINGS

2005

A MEETING IN PESHAWAR

The two dozen militant leaders who convened at the Yasir Hotel in the Pakistani city of Peshawar in April 2005 came from disparate corners of the Pech and its tributaries, answering a call from a Taliban commander named Mawlawi Monibullah. A few came from Aranas in the Waygal valley, north of Nangalam, where Monibullah was from, according to the informant who described the Yasir Hotel meeting the month after it occurred. From the Korengal came the timber baron Haji Matin, whose sawmill the Marines at FOB Blessing had been visiting regularly in the months since they inherited the Pech mission.[1]

Almost none of the men had been affiliated with the Taliban a year or two earlier. Even those who had taken up arms against the Americans early had done so under the banners of their old mujahidin parties, Jamaat and Hizb-e Islami; Monibullah's father was one of the elderly Hizb commanders JSOC and the CIA had been looking for during Operation Winter Strike. Now, though, these younger commanders had pledged allegiance to the Peshawar *shura,* a new Taliban leadership council and font of money and weapons. From their own hideouts deeper in Pakistan, the Taliban's fugitive top leaders had established the Peshawar *shura* to aid the growing local insurgency in Kunar and Nuristan and bring it under Taliban control.[2]

Among the younger commanders in attendance was one who went by the nom de guerre Ahmad Shah—or, as the informant who saw him at the hotel meeting in Peshawar called him, Commander Ismail. A young Salafi with ties to Hizb, Ahmad Shah had established himself as a small-time commander in the Korengal, using it as a base for machine-gun and RPG attacks against Marine convoys on the Pech road, but he hailed from another isolated valley, called the Dara-e Nur, twenty miles south across the mountains. Ahmad Shah helped supply other up-and-coming militants with arms and money, taking advantage of connections he'd forged with the Pakistani intelligence service, the ISI, whose funding and provision of safe haven for the resurgent Taliban were a frustrating open secret by 2005.[*]

According to some accounts, Ahmad Shah had been fighting against the Taliban when American troops arrived in Afghanistan, like many Salafis from Kunar and Nangarhar.[3] As far as U.S. intelligence could make out, he had made his debut as a guerrilla commander in Kunar in late 2003, just around the time of Operation Winter Strike. That October 30 (coincidentally the same night as the botched CIA-directed air strike in the Waygal that killed the young children of the veteran mujahidin cleric Mawlawi Rabbani), Ahmad Shah and a band of fighters had come down from the mountains and torched one of the Pech's only police stations. An insurgent cameraman had filmed the young commander lecturing the station's policemen and then letting them go, disarmed.[4] Now he was taking money and arms from the Taliban as well as the ISI.

In contrast to more experienced militants like the Egyptian al-Qaida operative Abu Ikhlas, Ahmad Shah was sloppy about his communications security, speaking regularly with subordinates and

---

[*] Sixty miles from Kunar, Peshawar had been the epicenter of the ISI's efforts to fund and arm Afghan mujahidin groups in the 1980s, when the Pakistani spy service was the main distributor of American and Saudi funds for the anticommunist insurgency. By 2005, the ISI was harboring and supporting the Peshawar *shura* in much the same way, under the noses of intelligence personnel at the U.S. consulate.

colleagues by satellite phone. The NSA—upon which the military was coming to rely ever more heavily as cell and satellite phone use rose in Afghanistan—was listening.[5] Each time Ahmad Shah made or received a call, a new set of grid coordinates went next to his photo and code name, Objective Fairbanks, on military target lists. By the time the informant reported on the Yasir Hotel meeting, Ahmad Shah was back in Afghanistan, and his satellite phone calls were coming from two villages high on the ridge that formed the Korengal valley's eastern wall, running from the Abbas Ghar sub-peak up to the higher Sawtalo Sar. Three thousand feet above the Pech valley floor and four miles back, accessible only by foot trail, and inhabited by people whose livelihoods were tied up with the hard-pressed cedar trade and with the Taliban, the two villages, Chichal and Kandlay, made perfect hideouts.[6]

"He was a known guy who would pop up on our radar," an intelligence officer who spent time at the CIA's Asadabad base recalled of Ahmad Shah, who by the spring of 2005 had been linked to several IED attacks against Marine convoys on the Pech road. "He was like a lumber-smuggling murderer."[7] What Ahmad Shah was *not* was an al-Qaida operative, the category of targets within the purview of the CIA and the JSOC task force at Bagram. He was a local combatant in the bigger war that neither al-Qaida nor JSOC's Rangers and SEAL Team 6 operators had much to do with yet in 2005: the day-to-day struggle between American and NATO troops and the Taliban-led insurgency that was engulfing more of Afghanistan's east and south each fighting season.

There was another group of SEALs at Bagram too, however, housed down the street in a separate compound and with a different mission and chain of command. To the officer who headed up this second group of frogmen at the giant airbase, Lieutenant Commander Erik Kristensen of Little Creek, Virginia's, SEAL Team 10, Ahmad Shah seemed like a promising target.

IN THE SMALL world of Navy special operators, Kristensen was an unassuming giant—beloved, respected, and more than a little unusual. Six feet four with bright red hair, a lover of karaoke and reading, he accumulated nicknames wherever he went: Spider on his prep-school football team; Special K and Big E in the Navy. The son of an admiral, he had made it through SEAL training in Coronado, California (called BUD/S), at twenty-seven, pushing the age cutoff, after seeing friends become frogmen and catching the bug.[8] Before that, he had served on a destroyer and in a small-boat unit and taught English at the U.S. Naval Academy, his alma mater, while earning a master's degree at nearby St. John's College. He'd been a standout at the little liberal arts college just as he was in the Navy: "the kind of student who makes your whole teaching career feel worth it," as one faculty member who led Kristensen through discussions of Herodotus and Thucydides put it.[9] A word people often used to describe him was "mellow," which was not typical of SEALs. In a culture of pickup drivers, he drove a Volvo station wagon. His favorite books were Herman Melville's *Omoo* and *Moby-Dick*.[10]

Kristensen was on his first combat deployment, heading up a group of about forty frogmen drawn from the Navy's "vanilla" SEAL teams, the bigger community from which SEAL Team 6 recruited. The Team 6 operators at Bagram spent their days sequestered in the JSOC compound with the Rangers and Night Stalkers—working out, playing video games, occasionally venturing out on missions against suspected al-Qaida targets, and rehearsing for the "big op" to get bin Laden in Pakistan. Kristensen and his frogmen were part of the parallel "white" special operations task force, made up mostly of Green Beret teams, that was deeply involved in the larger war against the Taliban-led insurgency. In this Green Beret–dominated task force, Kristensen's SEALs were the odd men out, their main task in Afghanistan not quite clear. At a time when "things were very slow," as one of the frogmen recalled, it was the SEAL lieutenant commander's job to keep his unit busy.[11]

Kristensen figured cooperation with other branches of the American military was his unit's way into the war. Soon after arriving at Bagram in the early spring of 2005 and growing a bushy red deployment beard, he began to make the rounds, visiting different groups of American personnel at Bagram and beyond: Green Berets, Rangers, the CIA. Whatever they were doing, his message went, his SEALs could help.[12]

The first unit to take Kristensen up on his offer was the Green Beret A-team at FOB Asadabad, which enlisted some of his SEALs to come along on a raid into the heights near the Pakistani border. Targeting a militant who had killed a Green Beret with an IED on the Kunar valley road over the winter, the April 5 mission was a success.[13] It wasn't long before Kristensen was looking at hitting another Kunar target, this time alongside Marines he had met during a visit to Asadabad.[14]

The Hawaii-based 2/3 Marines had just relieved a sister battalion of responsibility for Kunar when some of its officers met Kristensen late in the spring, but they were already looking at the same target he was, one of the few in the province whose location could often be pinpointed with signals intelligence: Ahmad Shah.

The Pech was the Marine battalion's most active sector, and FOB Blessing, where nearly a hundred Marines now lived with their local militia partners, was the battalion's most remote outpost. Blessing was connected to Asadabad only by the narrow Pech road, along which Ahmad Shah's men had already laid several ambushes and IEDs. Among the PowerPoint files 2/3 Marines had inherited from their outgoing sister unit was a rough plan for how to go after Ahmad Shah in the Korengal using whatever aircraft could be rustled up. SEALs from the team before Kristensen's had gone along with the previous Marines on an uneventful winter mission into the Korengal, and when the Marine planners approached the Night Stalker pilots of the 160th Special Operations Aviation Regiment about getting their help, the special operations task force insisted that some of the troops on the ground would have to be special operators for them to get involved. This was Kristensen's entry point. During an early-June meeting in Asadabad, Kristensen and the operations officer* of the Marine battalion, Major Tom Wood, agreed to reprise the ad hoc partnership.[15]

Flying back to Bagram together for a couple of days of planning, Kristensen and Wood hashed out the details of the mission. The Marines gave it a name: Operation Red Wings, in keeping with a string of recent air assaults named after hockey teams.[16]

---

* The operations officer is the third-ranking officer in a battalion (after the commander and executive officer), responsible for the portion of the headquarters staff charged with planning and tracking operations. Other staff sections include intelligence, communications, and personnel.

Red Wings involved two of the three U.S. military "tribes" in Afghanistan from the get-go: Kristensen and his frogmen hailed from the Green Beret–led "white" special operations task force, and the Marines were from the conventional force. To get the Marines and SEALs onto a treacherously wooded nine-thousand-foot ridge a hundred miles from Bagram in the middle of the night, the JSOC task force would get involved. A period of low moonlight was coming up, and the regular Army Chinook crews at Bagram weren't allowed to fly in a place as tough as the Korengal under those conditions. But the Night Stalkers specialized in dangerous nocturnal flying, and with terrain-mapping radar and infrared sensors their helicopters were uniquely outfitted for it; while working with conventional troops like the Marines was unusual for the Night Stalker crews, inserting special operations teams into dangerous places in the dead of night was their bread and butter.[17]

AT THE HEART of the Red Wings plan was a simple, if risky, helicopter assault not unlike others Kristensen's SEALs had conducted since arriving in Afghanistan, albeit in tougher terrain.

Flying from Jalalabad, the nearest airfield, in the dead of night, the Night Stalkers would get their big MH-47 Chinooks as close as possible to the target village of Chichal, where Ahmad Shah's satellite phone had most recently been picked up. They would hover while Kristensen and thirty other frogmen fast-roped off the helicopters' rear ramps into a clearing on the ridge that planners had picked out from aerial photos. While the frogmen broke into the four compounds from which most of the satellite phone intercepts originated, more Chinooks would deposit a hundred or so Marines, who would cordon the area off to prevent Ahmad Shah from escaping. When the Chinooks landed to pick up the SEALs and their detainees, the Marines would stay behind, taking the opportunity to hike downhill into the Korengal for a week or more of turning over rocks and talking to locals to elicit intelligence—less exciting work than a night raid but often far more useful in the long run.[18]

That much of the plan was straightforward. With intercepts of Ahmad Shah's phone coming in only every few days, though, how would Kristensen's assault force know which of the target compounds in Chichal to search first, or whether the militant commander was still in the area at all? If the SEALs didn't hit the right compound first, there was a strong chance their quarry would disappear into the forest, Marine cordon force or no Marine cordon force, because he knew the ground and they didn't.

With most of the Air Force's small Predator drone fleet busy in Iraq, there wasn't going to be persistent aerial surveillance of the target ahead of time. To confirm Ahmad Shah's presence and trigger the raid, an early version of the plan had called for the same Asadabad-based Green Berets with whom Kristensen had collaborated on the April border raid to infiltrate the area on foot.[19] When the mission was delayed and the Green Beret team rotated home, Kristensen tapped some of his own men to take their place and adjusted the plan. Twenty-four hours ahead of the planned raid, four SEALs would fast-rope out of a Chinook a mile from Chichal and fifteen hundred feet above it, on the south side of a ninety-three-hundred-foot summit called the Sawtalo Sar, then creep overnight to a position close enough to get a good look at the place through their sniper scopes. If they spotted someone who looked enough like the blurry black-and-white shot they had of Ahmad Shah, the raid the next night would be a go.[20]

Scouting in small teams in unfriendly territory—"special reconnaissance"—was a core SEAL mission, one the frogmen prided themselves on. But Kunar was an inhospitable place for that kind of job, with its excruciatingly difficult terrain and built-in network of insurgent spotters in the form of the walkie-talkie-equipped goatherds who spent the warm months roaming the highest slopes, living out of mountainside *bandehs*.

Other military units had already learned tough lessons about the feasibility of working undetected in Kunar's mountains, especially after noisy helicopter insertions. Two autumns earlier, for instance, during Operation Winter Strike, helicopters had dropped off a long-range surveillance team from the 10th Mountain Division on the Abbas Ghar, from which the Sawtalo Sar rises. Inserted two days after an IED killed Jay Blessing near the Korengal's mouth, the team's job had been to watch out for guerrillas coming down from the side valley to plant bombs on the Pech road. They had been spotted, or compromised, almost immediately, and soon afterward endured a barrage of RPG and machine-gun fire that wounded one team member before air support got there. "Trying to hide from everyone who lived up there was like me trying to hide from my own dog in my backyard," the wounded scout remembered.[21]

With little sharing of lessons between conventional troops and special operators, Kristensen and the other SEALs planning Red Wings were probably not aware of that episode, but they received warnings from various quarters about the risks of flying a small scout team in ahead of time. The Green Berets who were originally going to be part of the mission, for instance, planned to hike all the way from FOB Asadabad over two nights, an arduous ten-mile movement over seven- and eight-thousand-foot ridges that they nonetheless preferred over the idea of a Chinook's thumping rotors tipping their hand. At Bagram, a Ranger officer who had worked in similar terrain during Winter Strike cautioned that the vegetation on the mountaintop would likely prevent the SEAL recon team from seeing as far or as clearly as they thought they would be able to, even with their sniper scopes and other optics.[22]

FOB Asadabad was one of the few places with any institutional knowledge of Kunar: working on short deployments just three or four months long, the CIA and DIA personnel who lived in the mud-walled buildings along the base's northern wall, and the JSOC operators who supported them, frequently came back for repeat stints. When the SEAL Team 10 and Marine officers putting Red Wings together visited Asadabad during the mission planning, according to two sources who were there at the time, CIA officers questioned whether the plan entailed too much risk for too small-time of a target, cautioning that the Korengal was too dangerous and remote a place for a four-man recon team, especially one inserted by helicopter.[23] "What I saw was a very experienced [CIA] chief of base telling the SEALs not to put the four guys in," one Army officer who was present for that meeting said. "It was too high risk."[24]

"We were overconfident," said one SEAL involved. Rather than blanch at the objections being raised by various sister units at Bagram and Asadabad, he remembered, "We were all thinking, 'Finally! We're going somewhere where there's something going on!'"

Approval for the mission lay not with the CIA or the JSOC task force but with the two-star conventional Army general at Bagram to whom the "white" special operations task force answered, Major General Jason Kamiya. When Kristensen briefed the general and his staff, no one raised any questions.[25] "General Kamiya slapped the table and said we were good to go," remembered Wood, the Marine operations officer, who was happy to let Kristensen do the talking.[26]

"They briefed it really competently," said a staff officer who heard the presentation and who didn't remember hearing about the objections other organizations had raised. "It didn't seem crazy at the time."[27]

COMPROMISED

The leaders taking part in Operation Red Wings met for a final rehearsal on the afternoon of Monday, June 27, in the Marines' big green operations center tent at Jalalabad Airfield. The assembled troops walked through the two-stage plan and went over the latest intelligence on Ahmad Shah: the last hit on his phone in Chichal had been three days earlier.[28]

Among the SEALs sitting in on the rehearsal in Jalalabad's jungle-humid heat were the four who'd been tapped to insert later that night for the initial reconnaissance phase of the mission. The recon team's leader was a fine-featured twenty-nine-year-old from Long Island on his first combat deployment, Lieutenant Michael Murphy, who wore the patch of a friend's New York City Fire Department ladder company on his combat uniform. With him were three SEAL petty officers (the Navy equivalent of sergeants): Danny Dietz, the radioman, and Marcus Luttrell and Matt Axelson, both snipers. All came from a SEAL unit that trained for a very different kind of low-visibility operation—piloting underwater submersibles—but during the war on terror had been tapped for reconnaissance operations on land because they trained more extensively for them than other SEALs did.[29] Murphy, a quiet, humble officer who was well aware of his inexperience, was an ancient Sparta enthusiast like Jim Gant, which the recon team's call sign reflected: Spartan.[30]

The Chinook carrying the four SEALs took off between sunset and moonrise Monday night. While a sister aircraft hung back at FOB Asadabad with Kristensen aboard in case something went wrong, the insertion helicopter headed toward the blackness of the Sawtalo Sar mountain that loomed above the Korengal and Shuryak side valleys. Inside, the team leader, Mike Murphy, and the three other frogmen were loaded for reconnaissance, not sustained combat—green forest camouflage fatigues, lightweight helmets, no body armor or machine guns, their heaviest weapons a couple of rifle-mounted grenade launchers. Their most important tools were the sniper scopes through which they would try to spot Ahmad Shah, the grainy photo they'd been given of him, and satellite communications gear with which to report back to the Marine and SEAL operations centers at Jalalabad and Bagram.[31]

The Chinook dipped down toward the summit three times without dropping off the SEALs, finding the trees around the clearings too tall for the insertion rope, before descending to a spot just below the ridge, on the opposite side of the Sawtalo Sar from the target village.[32] It took six minutes of hovering, an excruciating eternity for a boxcar-sized target like a Chinook, for the flight crew to negotiate the treetops and settle the helicopter low enough for the four SEALs to fast-rope into the clearing. One Night Stalker remembered it as the most difficult nighttime insertion he was ever involved in. Then, after cutting loose the rope when the crew member who tried to pull it back aboard found it tangled with vegetation, the Chinook was off.[33]

Under clouds that obscured a half-moon, Murphy, Axelson, Dietz, and Luttrell began their movement across the upper Sawtalo Sar's patchwork of small meadows, denuded logging sites, rock formations, and stands of conifers. In the operations tent at Jalalabad, Kristensen and other SEALs and Marines monitored Spartan's foot movement (just a mile point to point, but much farther on the ground) by radio, listening as the twenty-five-year-old radioman, Dietz, checked in at one planned waypoint after another. Finally, Dietz reported that he and his teammates had made it around the Sawtalo Sar and reached their hide site overlooking Chichal. Kristensen and the other SEALs at Jalalabad filed back into the Chinooks and headed for Bagram to get some daytime sleep ahead of the next night's raid.

Kristensen and most of the other frogmen and Night Stalkers involved in the insertion were just beginning their day on June 28 when radios at Jalalabad, Bagram, and Asadabad crackled to life with a disheartening message from the team in the field. Whether through dumb luck or by discovering the severed insertion rope that the frogmen had hastily buried when they landed, someone had found recon team Spartan's hide site.[34] "'Compromised' was the word he used," remembered one person who heard the midday transmission from one of the SEALs in the CIA's Asadabad radio room.[35] The sounds of a gunfight were briefly audible, and then the call cut off abruptly.[36] "No location or specifics were given before the transmission stopped," one military postmortem noted.[37] Either the mountains were too much for Dietz's small satellite radio, or the firefight had forced him to cut the transmission short, or he'd been shot.

At least one more call would come through around 1:45 p.m., nearly two hours after the first. By then the military machine required to rescue or reinforce the embattled recon team had come to life, but it was not running smoothly or quickly.

OPERATION RED WINGS included a contingency plan: a Marine platoon was standing by at Jalalabad as a designated quick-reaction force, and when the call about the compromise came, the Marines were ready to go, geared up and practicing fast-rope insertions for the raid that night. But the Marines, and the regular Army Black Hawk helicopters at Jalalabad set aside to fly them, could not launch without an order from the Army division headquarters at Bagram, and as noon came and went, then one o'clock, then two o'clock, that order did not come.[38]

The explanation for the delay has never been made public and remains frustratingly unclear to many troops involved. One possibility is that the Black Hawks were waiting on an escort of Apache attack helicopters, which was not immediately available.[39] Whatever the reason, at Bagram, Erik Kristensen ran out of patience. Instead of waiting around, he grabbed his frogmen and the Night Stalker crews who were supposed to fly them on the raid that night and organized a second quick-reaction force, taking advantage of what was effectively a loophole in the complex organizational structure of U.S. forces in Afghanistan: while the Marines and regular Army helicopters answered to the Army division headquarters and needed to wait for its say-so, the Night Stalkers did not.

Awakened from their pre-mission sleep, the SEALs and Night Stalkers drove out in pickups to the tarmac where the Chinooks allocated for the coming night's mission were waiting. One truck carried Kristensen and his subordinate Lieutenant Michael McGreevy. McGreevy had been the top man in his class at both BUD/S and Ranger School.[40] Ten weeks earlier, at the start of the deployment, he had led some of the same SEALs into another on-the-fly rescue effort. Aboard a pair of Black Hawks en route to a fast-rope training session in southeastern Afghanistan, word had come over the radio that a Green Beret team nearby was in a firefight, its team sergeant shot through both legs and bleeding out. The Navy lieutenant had unhesitatingly volunteered his platoon's services and landed in the middle of the battle with his men. The frogmen's to-the-sound-of-the-guns approach had been welcome; maneuvering around a hilltop, McGreevy had helped the Green Berets outflank the retreating enemy, with a SEAL sniper killing one of them.[41]

Now the Night Stalker pilot joined McGreevy and Kristensen by the Chinooks as they talked through a similarly bold impromptu plan. All any of them knew was that the recon team was in a tight spot somewhere on the Sawtalo Sar; it wasn't clear where exactly they were, let alone where the enemy was. With their teammates in danger, that didn't bother the two SEAL officers. "Just get us to the highest place possible, and we'll fight down and find our guys," the Army aviator remembered McGreevy telling him.[42]

Finally, some four hours after the compromise call, two Chinooks laden with SEALs lifted off from Bagram bound for the Sawtalo Sar via Jalalabad, flying under the call signs Turbine 33 and Turbine 34.[43] Aboard the lead Chinook, Turbine 33, were Kristensen and the Night Stalker officer acting as the rescue force's air mission commander, Major Stephen Reich.

Like his Navy contemporary Kristensen, the thirty-four-year-old Reich was a rising star and the object of admiration in his world: after West Point, where he had studied Arabic and set the baseball team's all-time win record with his ninety-mile-per-hour fastball, he had played briefly for an Orioles farm team but chose to return to the Army as an aviator instead of pursuing an athletic career.[44] Like Kristensen too, Steve Reich was reserved but supremely confident and unafraid to challenge the status quo. The previous fall, when he and a subordinate officer had been learning how to fly their Night Stalker company's older D-model MH-47s at Fort Campbell, Reich had stopped at a particular item on the preflight checklist, which in the culture of Army aviation is akin to scripture in its inviolability. "In a crisis, the most conservative course of action will be the right one," the checklist read, or words to that effect. Reich didn't want his crew to take that step literally, he had told them over the intercom. In a crisis he was going to make the best decision possible, and it might not be the most conservative.[45]

On the afternoon of June 28, when crisis hit, Reich and his own boss, a Night Stalker lieutenant colonel, did not make the conservative decision. The conservative decision would have been to allow the established plan to play out: to wait for nightfall to launch, when the Night Stalkers and SEALs were already slated to fly; to sit back while division headquarters debated whether to launch the Marine quick-reaction force from Jalalabad. But the four frogmen on the ground might not live that long, and there was an unwritten rule in the Night Stalkers: "If we put them in, we take them out." Reich volunteered to head an ad hoc rescue mission himself from the jump seat of Turbine 33, between and behind the pilots, Chris Scherkenbach and Corey Goodnature.[46]

It was the fastest solution at a moment when time was of the essence—so fast that key staff officers in both the black and the white special operations task forces didn't know it was happening until the Chinooks were already in the air.[47] But with JSOC and conventional forces operating on different radio frequencies, and neither obliged to talk to the other nor used to doing so, it also introduced a new wrinkle into an already complex situation. Landing briefly around 3:30 p.m., Kristensen and Reich learned that division headquarters had, at last, given the go-ahead to the Marine quick-reaction force. It had just taken off, aboard Black Hawks escorted by a pair of Apaches.

That meant that once the Night Stalker Chinooks were in the air again, two separate quick-reaction forces were headed for the Sawtalo Sar, neither one communicating directly with the other.

Back at the JSOC compound at Bagram, the Night Stalker staff officers monitoring the progress of Steve Reich's two Chinooks didn't know the conventional quick-reaction force was in the air.[48] At division headquarters just down the street, the reverse was true: division staff officers had no idea that Night Stalker aircraft were en route.[49]

TURBINE 33 AND Turbine 34 sped over Kunar's mountains through gathering rain clouds at 150-plus knots, eight SEALs in each bird's roomy cabin. In the interest of speed, the Night Stalkers had declined an offer from the Apache pilots to fly in first and scan the mountaintop; the attack helicopters were still lagging to the south, and letting them catch up would have taken precious minutes.[50] Turbulence rocked Steve Reich's aircraft, Turbine 33, as it sped over a saddle into the Shuryak and the Sawtalo Sar came into view.[51] The Chinook slowed into a hover over a treeless part of the ridge close to Spartan's original insertion site. Kristensen and the seven other SEALs aboard were preparing to slide down ropes from the rear ramp to the ground.[52]

The Apaches and the Black Hawks full of Marines were lagging to the south, but the lead Black Hawk crew was close enough to see what came next, at 4:15 p.m.—a bright red flash.

At first the Black Hawk crew thought it was a flare, fired by one of the four SEALs trapped on the mountain, but next came a larger explosion. One of Ahmad Shah's men on the Sawtalo Sar had fired a shoulder-launched rocket at the lead MH-47 from close range, and it had hit its mark, flying in Turbine 33's open rear ramp and exploding under the engines.[53] The doomed helicopter's "tail first sank down in the air, and then . . . it fell into the mountain side and there was another explosion," the Black Hawk crew reported afterward.[54]

Turbine 34 was banking right to follow its sister Chinook in when it happened. "By the time I completed the turn we could find nothing of the aircraft," its pilot said later. "There was just a large column of smoke."[55]

Turbine 33 was down, with all sixteen sailors and soldiers aboard killed, including the SEAL and Night Stalker commanders Kristensen and Reich, whose loss would shake the worlds of Naval Special Warfare, Army aviation, and the service academies where both men had been beloved.[56]

IT'S A MAD, MAD, MAD, MAD WORLD

In JSOC's Bagram operations center, "there was disbelief when the first report came in," an officer on duty at the time remembered.[57] A routine if risky kill/capture mission had suddenly transformed into a disaster of the highest military priority, but with a nasty storm front building over central Kunar, the crash site, on the Shuryak side of the Sawtalo Sar, was all but inaccessible.

There were only a handful of Predator drones in Afghanistan, but Air Force crews launched one after another into Kunar, risking the delicate remote-controlled planes to black clouds that swallowed two of them (one lost to lightning and one to ice). When a third Predator, diverted from a CIA mission, finally made it through and started delivering black-and-white aerial footage of the crash site, Turbine 33's burning wreck stood out as a high-contrast bloom on screens from Bagram to Tampa.[58] It was clear that nobody aboard the helicopter could have survived, but that evening, despite the weather, manned aircraft that shared the skies with the Predator spotted a tantalizing hint that one or more of the four Spartan SEALs might be alive: the crews of an AC-130, an A-10, and a P-3 surveillance plane all briefly saw what they thought was an infrared strobe light moving around on the mountain.[59]

The mission to recover the bodies of those killed in the crash and find the missing frogmen quickly became one of the largest and most dangerous combat search-and-rescue missions since Vietnam.[60] As it did so, the whole effort fell victim to the complicated command-and-control lines that governed and separated the three military tribes in Afghanistan. Murphy's team had never filed a formal escape-and-evasion plan with the Air Force at Bagram, just with Kristensen. Now, with Kristensen and the other SEAL and Night Stalker leaders who best understood the recon team's plan all dead, confusion reigned.[61] As one soldier involved put it, "Everything reverted to the most logjammed it could be in terms of command and control."[62]

At Jalalabad, the Marine operations tent filled up with representatives of each uniformed tribe. "A Special Forces lieutenant colonel, SEALs, Marines, JSOC, everybody is trying to be in charge," a Night Stalker officer said of the chaotic scene he found at the airfield.[63] JSOC won out: given the news while touring Gettysburg battlefield in Pennsylvania, JSOC's commander, Major General Stan McChrystal, put the SEAL Team 6 commander at Bagram in charge of the recovery effort. A huge, invisible circle was drawn on everyone's map with the crash site at its center, which only special operations forces were to enter.[64]

With the weather keeping helicopters at bay, the first efforts to reach the crash site fell to commandos moving by ground from Jalalabad and FOB Asadabad, the closest special operations base to the Shuryak and Korengal. Two different columns of Green Berets, CIA paramilitary officers with their local Mohawk surrogates, Rangers, and SEALs headed west into the mountains in succession in Humvees and pickup trucks. When the trail became too narrow for the vehicles, they continued by foot, a movement so grueling in the heat, humidity, and rain that even the Mohawks were soon falling out of line and a donkey died. One Team 6 operator administered IVs to ward off dehydration, hanging them from bushes during brief stops. Others jettisoned ammunition along the way to lessen the weight they were carrying.[65]

The frustrated overland efforts reminded one Asadabad-based intelligence officer of the 1963 movie *It's a Mad, Mad, Mad, Mad World,* where different parties bumbled and stumbled over one another in a race to reach a trove of stolen cash. "People kept looking at the map and saying, 'Oh it's not that far!'" the intelligence officer remembered. "Much of the ground rescue mission was based on that flawed premise." Although the crash site on the eastern face of the Sawtalo Sar was separated from Asadabad by just nine map miles, the combination of severe weather and severer terrain meant it might as well have been on another planet, and the relief troops' progress slowed to a crawl as they paused to await an emergency parachute drop of bottled water.[66]

The first troops to actually reach Turbine 33's crash site flew in— fifty-odd Rangers and a small group of SEALs. Leading them was a friend of Steve Reich's from West Point, a 2nd Ranger Battalion company commander, Major Pat Work (the brother of the Ranger officer who had been on the scene when an IED killed Jay Blessing). Work had been in the Pech for Winter Strike, as had many of his Rangers, including one of the platoon leaders, Jimmy Howell, the West Point football player from Texas who had led the way into the town of Aranas in the Waygal valley during 10th Mountain's part of the 2003 operation.[67]

Forced to turn back by the weather when they launched in MH-47s a few hours after the crash, the Night Stalkers flying the Rangers and SEALs in tried again on the night of June 29, more than twenty-four hours after Turbine 33 had gone down. This time the weather cooperated, but it was a high-risk insertion. With no good landing zones available and the specter of a second shoot-down looming, the Chinooks hovered one at a time above a tiny clearing two and a half miles south of the crash site long enough for the Rangers to slide down ninety-foot ropes.

Understanding what kind of terrain they were heading into from their Winter Strike experience, the Rangers had stripped the back plates out of their body armor to minimize weight and were carrying little but water, batteries, and ammunition. But the height involved was at the outer edge of the envelope for a feasible fast-rope insertion, especially on treacherous sloping ground. Through their night-vision goggles, the Night Stalker crew chiefs could see some of the Rangers plummeting the last few feet after the ropes ended and then tumbling down the mountain. One Ranger, a platoon radioman, broke his ankle when his platoon sergeant landed on top of him, but kept the injury to himself as the force began its punishing hike toward the Sawtalo Sar.

The Rangers and the frogmen accompanying them—who included both Team 6 operators and surviving members of Kristensen's unit—reached the wreck of Turbine 33 around dawn on Thursday, June 30, guided in by the smoke they could see as the sun came up. Half headed uphill to secure a perimeter and scour the bunker-like fighting positions Ahmad Shah's men had left behind, while Jimmy Howell and his two dozen Rangers made for the crash site itself.[68]

The scene on the muddy mountainside was predictably grim.

"We came up on it and it was still smoking, just smoking on the side of the mountain," remembered one of the Team 6 operators who hiked in with the Rangers, Chief Petty Officer James Hatch.[69] The Chinook had trailed wreckage across a football-field-sized area as it rolled down the mountain. There was no fuselage left at all; the largest recognizable parts—the engines—had come to rest just downhill from a large rock formation and were still burning. White ash coated the ground where jet fuel had been burning, and twisted metal detritus lay here and there: casings from bullets that had cooked off in the inferno, battered helmets, scorched sights, and flashlights from rifles.[70]

As the day wore on, more troops arrived, including a team of cadaver-sniffing dogs and SEAL and Ranger officers who set up a command post atop the Sawtalo Sar's summit. The smell of the fire and the human remains in the hot sun made the Team 6 operator Hatch think of a mass grave he had encountered during a deployment to Bosnia. When it started to overwhelm him, Hatch would look up at the beauty of the mountain; aside from the occasional hooting of monkeys, it reminded him of his native Utah.[71]

By sunset, the Rangers and SEALs had recovered fifteen of the sixteen sets of remains at the crash site and lined them up in heavy rubber body bags they had lugged in. The corpses that had not been incinerated in the fire appeared to have been mostly left alone; the only uniform items insurgents had obviously stripped from them were their boots.[72]

THE FOUR SPARTAN frogmen were still out there, alive or dead, and the next morning the search for them began in earnest. Fanning out down the Sawtalo Sar's slopes and down the adjoining Abbas Ghar, Rangers, SEALs, Mohawks, and 82nd Airborne paratroopers—the latest arrivals—found mostly empty caves and *bandehs* and villagers who would say nothing useful. Now and again, militants would probe the American base camp atop the mountain, and a Team 6 fire-support specialist would talk A-10s in on gun runs to drive the attackers off.[73] One paratroop patrol got into a fight with a group of guerrillas who, when cornered in a cave, turned out to be carrying

American night-vision goggles and radios, clearly looted either from the Turbine 33 crash site or from the missing SEALs.[*][74]

That evening, working off signals intercepts and Predator footage, JSOC called in an Air Force bomb strike on a house in Chichal, the village Kristensen's assault mission was supposed to have targeted.[75] Jimmy Howell's Ranger platoon got the job of hiking down to Chichal to see whom the six satellite-guided bombs had killed, if anyone. Predictably, the terrain slowed the Rangers' movement to a snail's pace, and by the time Howell got to Chichal, the debris from the strike had been cleaned up and no weapons were in evidence; the dead, the villagers claimed, had been civilians.[76]

THE MARINE LIEUTENANTS in charge at FOB Blessing, whose troops actually lived in the Pech, had been told only the bare bones about Operation Red Wings or its aftermath. Now, with JSOC running a massive recovery effort right in the Marines' backyard, they were out of the loop.[77] So when an old man walked up to the gate guards at Blessing two nights into the disaster saying he had information about a lost American, the Marine base commander who sat down with him, First Lieutenant Matt Bartels, wasn't sure what to think. Bartels knew that Red Wings had gone badly and that a helicopter had crashed on the Sawtalo Sar, but that an American might be alive and missing was news to him.

When the old man said he came from the Shuryak valley and was a relative of a man named Mohammad Gulab, though, Bartels's ears perked up. Mohammad Gulab was a contact he had inherited from his fellow Marine lieutenant Justin Bellman, the previous base commander. A former mujahidin fighter in his early thirties, Gulab came to Nangalam regularly to help represent the Shuryak at district-wide *shuras* and made a point of breaking bread with the Marines at Blessing when he did so and sharing information with them.[78]

---

[*] Other debris from the June 28 battle would show up in militant hiding spots around the Shuryak and Korengal in years to come, including Marcus Luttrell's helmet with a Velcro patch of the Texas flag attached to it, which paratroopers found in another cave in 2007.

Then the old man produced a sheet of green lined paper from a waterproof military field notebook. There was a brief note scrawled on it—from the lost American, the old man said. "No code name on it, no nothing, signed his name in cursive. He was like, 'I am down, send help,'" Bartels remembered. He couldn't make out the signature, but it started with an *L,* and after the Marine lieutenant typed out a message explaining the situation on the military's secure internet chat system, phones in the Blessing operations room started ringing furiously.[79]

Intelligence personnel and SEALs at Asadabad and Bagram correctly suspected that the signature belonged to Marcus Luttrell, the twenty-nine-year-old petty officer from Texas who was the missing recon team's sniper and medic.[80] Almost as soon as Bartels had scanned the note and emailed it out, a helicopter showed up at Blessing and disgorged a group of bearded special operators, who, over the Marine lieutenant's objections, grabbed the old man, cuffed and hooded him, threw him into the back of the helicopter, and took off.[81]

At the Asadabad intelligence compound, a combination of special operators and CIA and DIA officers questioned the old man, trying to figure out where exactly Luttrell was hiding or being held and whether he was the only one still alive. "He looked about a thousand years old, but he was probably about sixty," one intelligence officer remembered of the man, who said there was only one American and that he was wounded but safe in a village in the Shuryak whose name his questioners did not recognize. Finally, a DIA officer thought to ask the man for the names of some of the insurgents from his village—the only names U.S. intelligence kept much track of—in case the place was marked with a different name on American military maps. That worked: cross-referencing the names with intelligence reports on file yielded a village marked on U.S. maps as Salar Ban, a mile and a half from Chichal on the opposite side of the Abbas Ghar.[82] A Team 6 operator remembered that after some initial confusion when he was shown a satellite image of the village, the old man even pointed out a house.[83]

At Bagram, JSOC officers began planning the rescue mission, and early on July 2 a Ranger platoon, a Green Beret team, and a group of SEALs all headed toward Salar Ban, while a separate

Ranger element headed up from the Pech valley floor with the old man from the village as a guide. There had been sightings of Taliban all around the village, but under the cover of a monsoon-like rainstorm the Rangers and Green Berets, who made it there ahead of the frogmen, passed them without contact.[84] Apparent confirmation that the search was not in vain came later in the day. Nine time zones away at Fort Meade, Maryland, an NSA analyst scanning search-and-rescue frequencies caught the tail end of what an NSA document described as "a deep male voice speaking American English."[85] Luttrell was alive.

Unsure exactly where they might find him, the Rangers lucked out when a plane overhead picked up a faint signal from an emergency beacon just outside Salar Ban, giving them a set of grid coordinates.[86] The next morning they lucked out again: Luttrell's rescuer, Gulab, was moving the wounded SEAL along a trail outside the village just as the rescue patrol approached, and the two groups stumbled upon each other. The first friendly face the hurt and ailing sailor saw belonged to an Afghan Mohawk sporting a George W. Bush reelection campaign cap.[87]

An Air Force rescue crew flying a gray HH-60 Pave Hawk came for Luttrell after dark, swooping into a Ranger-held landing zone while A-10s and an AC-130 pummeled the surrounding ridges to prevent another helicopter from being shot down. After the Pave Hawk's pararescue medic shouted a preplanned identity confirmation question and heard the wounded SEAL's answer, he was hustled inside and the helicopter was off.[88] That same day, Rangers found two of Luttrell's teammates, both dead, lying in the draw between Salar Ban and the ridge above, their bodies stripped of weapons and equipment. At Bagram on the Fourth of July, fellow SEALs identified the bodies as those of the radioman Danny Dietz and the recon team leader Mike Murphy, the latter recognizable by the red FDNY "Engine 53/Ladder 43" patch on his dirty uniform and the Celtic cross tattooed on his left arm.

IN BETWEEN SURGERIES at Bagram's military hospital, Luttrell told debriefers what had happened. Murphy and Dietz had both died in a ferocious insurgent attack on the team on June 28, well before the launch of any quick-reaction force, he explained, and his own survival had been a very close call.

After a team of goatherds discovered them, the Spartan team frogmen had retreated from their hide site as fast as they could, climbing for the better part of an hour across a plunging draw before stopping to take stock on the Sawtalo Sar's northeastern spur.[89] That was where a group of Ahmad Shah's fighters had found them. Luttrell assumed that the goatherds had tipped the enemy off to the team's location, but Gulab later told *Newsweek* that Ahmad Shah's men, who had been scouring the mountain for the SEALs all morning after hearing the Chinook overnight, actually stumbled on the team separately and then tracked them quietly to a place with terrain favorable for an attack.[90]

There was no way to know how many attackers there were, but a dozen men with a machine gun and an RPG or two would have been enough to pin the SEALs down, given their lack of heavy weapons and their location, trapped between cliff-like slopes below them and antagonists who knew the terrain well above them. "It was a drop-off on three sides and there was only one way in and one way out," Luttrell said later.[91] With rifle, machine-gun, and RPG fire coming in from two directions, the radioman struggled to maintain a satellite radio connection with higher headquarters long enough to relay the team's coordinates, and the four sailors retreated down the spur into the gully-like draw below them in long, bone-crushing jumps and tumbles.

One after another, each SEAL was shot. According to Luttrell, Dietz was hit first, in the hand as he moved into the open to try to get a better angle with his satellite antenna and then fatally in the face. The next to go was Murphy, who, Luttrell said, climbed onto a boulder after already having been shot once and managed to briefly contact headquarters on the team's backup Iridium satellite phone before being killed.[92] The last Luttrell saw of his final teammate, Matt Axelson, was when an RPG exploded between them. The blast knocked Luttrell, who was already shot in one leg, farther down the gully and left him unconscious.

"It got so intense that I actually put my weapon down and covered my ears because I couldn't stand to hear him die," Luttrell would elaborate years later, remembering Murphy's final moments. "All I wanted him to do was stop screaming my name."[93]

The only other eyewitnesses to the clash were Ahmad Shah's fighters, including two cameramen, whose video footage captured small teams of fighters pushing forward amid the rocks and trees, firing downhill at the trapped sailors. On the insurgent video, the last audible shots from the SEALs' M4s and sniper rifles rang out at 1:59 p.m., while Erik Kristensen and Steve Reich were still struggling to get permission to launch a rescue force.[94]

That first night, after he came to, it had probably been Luttrell's infrared strobe that Air Force and Navy pilots overhead had spotted; the wounded frogman had been able to hear the aircrews calling out to him on an emergency frequency, but had been afraid insurgents would hear him if he responded.[95] Only because Gulab stumbled on him soon afterward—and because Gulab was able to convince others in Salar Ban that it was worth sheltering him—did Luttrell survive. Resisting both threats of violence and offers of pickup trucks and property in Peshawar from Ahmad Shah's men, the villagers in Salar Ban harbored him for four days, first in a building in town and then in a cave, until the Ranger rescue patrol arrived.

Discovering Matt Axelson's fate took nearly another week. A twenty-seven-year-old from Cupertino, California, with curly blond hair, Axelson had gone through SEAL sniper school with Luttrell and was among the Texas frogman's closest friends. Nicknamed Cool Hand Luke for his passing resemblance to Paul Newman and for his unflappable refusal to rise to the bait when ribbed, Axelson had died with his teammates on June 28,[96] but villagers found his body and buried it. Perhaps nervous that they would be held responsible for the SEAL's death, the villagers did not reveal this to the troops still searching the Sawtalo Sar and the Abbas Ghar until July 10.

That night at Bagram, after Axelson's body had been returned to the airbase, American servicemen and contractors lined the base's main road by the hundreds as the casket was driven from mortuary affairs to the tarmac for the flight home.[97]

.   .   .

BEFORE OPERATION RED WINGS, only sixty-nine Americans had died in combat in Afghanistan.[98] The loss of nineteen special operators on the Sawtalo Sar raised that toll by more than a quarter in the space of an afternoon—a shock to a country and military that had mostly written Afghanistan off as a war already won.

The mission also went down as the first in the Afghan war to earn an American serviceman the military's highest award for valor, the Medal of Honor. President Bush would present the medal and its distinctive sky-blue ribbon to Lieutenant Michael Murphy's parents more than two years later, after an extensive Navy review of the events that had transpired that Tuesday in 2005.

By the time Luttrell's account of Murphy's actions began to spread in the tight-knit world of Navy special operations, the Army had awarded its first post–September 11 Medal of Honor to a fallen soldier for his actions in Iraq, and the Marine Corps was in the process of doing the same. Senior officers at Naval Special Warfare Command in Coronado, California, felt that Murphy's bravery in climbing onto the boulder to place a final satellite phone call, as Luttrell recounted it, was of the same caliber and warranted the same recognition. It was not a rubber-stamp case, however. By Navy regulation, high-level valor awards like the Medal of Honor required "a minimum of two notarized witness statements."[99] There weren't two surviving witnesses to what happened on the Sawtalo Sar on the afternoon of June 28—just one battered, grief-stricken hospital corpsman second class.

In the bestselling book *Lone Survivor,* Luttrell and a co-author (a British writer of naval-themed thrillers) would later present a version of Red Wings that blended facts with novelistic embellishment—writing, for instance, that Ahmad Shah was "one of Osama bin Laden's closest associates"[100] and inflating the number of attackers to an implausible "140 men minimum."[101] But that all lay in the future as Naval Special Warfare Command assembled a two-hundred-page Medal of Honor nomination packet for admirals at the Pentagon to consider. Some Rangers involved in Luttrell's recovery doubted that the firefight had been as long or as intense as Luttrell indicated even then, based on how few shell casings of the caliber the SEALs had been using they had found around the scene of the fight.[102] But officers who read the rough, emotional testimony that Luttrell gave during his summer 2005 debriefing—which formed the cornerstone of the nomination packet—got the sense that it was the most detailed and accurate account he was able to provide given the medical condition he was in and the gaps in his memory. Back then, he put the number of attackers in the low dozens.[103]

To fill the gaps and get around the two-eyewitness rule, Navy officers and intelligence analysts wove Luttrell's sworn statement, notes on the calls that made it through to headquarters on June 28, photographs of the battlefield, and summaries of intercepted enemy communications together into a detailed, still-classified "all-source reconstruction." "It was very different from the packet you'd get if three people saw a guy throw himself on a grenade or something like that, and the board was uncomfortable with that," a Navy officer close to the process recalled. "It was contentious."[104] Nevertheless, after long deliberations, the board of admirals approved the nomination packet, paving the way for Murphy to receive the first Medal of Honor awarded to a SEAL since Vietnam and for his three teammates, including Luttrell, to receive the service's next-highest valor award, the Navy Cross. Not since 1975 had such a raft of top-tier valor medals been awarded for a single engagement.[105]

Unstated in the nomination packets were any conclusions Navy investigators had reached about the failures of Red Wings—the ways in which the tragedy might have been avoided.

It is a military axiom that "the enemy has a vote"—meaning that no matter how good a plan is, in war, a skillful or lucky adversary can derail it and inflict losses or defeat. That axiom held true in Red Wings: Ahmad Shah had gotten lucky, but he had also correctly identified the American military's fervor for recovering its own as a potential weakness and exploited it, effectively bringing the whole U.S. military campaign in Afghanistan to a standstill for a week as a result. "We certainly know that when the American army comes under pressure and they get hit, they will try to help their friends," Ahmad Shah said of his group's actions on June 28 later that year, speaking from behind a ski mask in a mountain hideout. "It is the law of the battlefield."[106]

But poor planning and the muddled lines of organization of conventional and special operations troops in Afghanistan also contributed to the disaster. In later years, special operations raid teams would routinely bring liaison officers from nearby infantry units along on their missions and launch them from the conventional outposts like FOB Blessing that were closest to the target sites. In 2005, no such arrangement was in place, nor did the SEALs likely know that a conventional scout team from the 10th Mountain Division had been discovered on the Abbas Ghar just nineteen months earlier, although other special operators had warned them about similar compromised missions. No effective system existed for conventional and special operations units to share hard-learned lessons, let alone pass them down from rotation to rotation. All cooperation was ad hoc, and that created risk, despite the best intentions of the SEAL and Marine officers whose hasty collaboration created and launched the operation.

"We weren't integrated. The interface points were doomed" was how the 2/3 Marine battalion's second-in-command at the time of Red Wings put it, noting with frustration that protocol had prevented Kristensen's SEALs from sharing their radio frequencies with the Marines ahead of the mission. "We violated the basics of being prepared, rehearsing, walking through it, and at the end of the day it cost guys' lives."[107]

That the mission's planners expected a four-man reconnaissance team, after being inserted by noisy Chinooks, to remain undetected and not be overrun if compromised was the most glaring problem. "I remember thinking to myself on the mountain, 'How the fuck would anybody sneak into this place, especially with a helicopter as loud as a Who concert?'" said James Hatch, the Team 6 chief who roped in with the Rangers and tried to focus on the scenery when the smells reminded him of a Balkan mass grave. "You're not sneaking around up there, especially in an MH-47. These were great Americans, but to think they were going to sneak in undetected was insanity."[108]

Almost everyone I interviewed about Red Wings repeated another charge: that the complex parallel chains of command governing conventional and special operations units not only militated against effective planning for the joint mission but also created a cascade of confusion in the hours after Murphy's four-man team was compromised.[109] "I remember crying because everything was so screwed up, literally crying," an intelligence officer involved said.

"At every level it was fucked up. It was like in Oz when they pull back the curtain and there's not a lot there."[110]

More fundamentally, some questioned the decision to risk troops going after a mid-level local enemy commander like Ahmad Shah whose operations were confined to one or two provinces. One officer who wondered about that risk-reward calculus was the top American commander in Afghanistan, Lieutenant General Karl Eikenberry, who had arrived in Kabul six weeks before Red Wings. As a commander with political and strategic responsibilities, not tactical ones, Eikenberry hadn't been briefed on the mission before it happened. The first he heard of four SEALs being inserted into the wilds of Kunar was on the afternoon of June 28 when a staff officer interrupted a meeting with Pakistani diplomats to pass him a note laying out the bare outlines of the unfolding tragedy.[111]

When the commanders of all three military tribes involved delivered a postmortem to Eikenberry at his request, he was taken aback by what he learned. "The risks inherent in inserting a small element in such a remote location did not seem to match the payoff of potentially netting a small-time commander of local insurgents," he said a decade later.[112]

But there was no public reckoning with what had gone wrong during Red Wings, and not much of one in the Night Stalker or SEAL communities back in the United States, either. A Night Stalker pilot involved in every phase of the affair was surprised never to be interviewed for any joint investigation of the operation and recovery.[113] An internal SEAL review was conducted, according to friends of Kristensen's, but if so, its distribution was so limited that even Hatch and other Team 6 operators involved in the recovery were never aware of it.[114] "There was never a full, 100 percent, down-to-the-details examination of what led to it, and that has always disturbed me," Hatch told me.[115]

It seemed to Hatch that the Navy held up the heroism of those involved without acknowledging the mistakes in planning and execution that helped cause their deaths. "There's a deep pain" among survivors, he wrote later, "when you take a version of their story and just tell the parts that allow it to be a legendary epic about flawless heroism. When you uphold only the hero image, you deny those same heroes the ability to commit mistakes," creating a "distorted reality."[116]

"WERE WE THE BEES, OR WERE WE THE HONEY?"

If those were the factors that led to the disaster, what the disaster in turn led to was American military escalation in Kunar—focused on the Korengal.

From the vantage point of FOB Blessing, things seemed to Matt Bartels, the Marine lieutenant in charge of the base, as if they were going well in the Pech proper, much as they had to Ron Fry's Green Beret team a little over a year before. Bartels and his Marines were patrolling daily, getting along with the residents of Nangalam and surrounding villages, bringing in tips, and maintaining the Blessing ink blot, inside which combat was a rarity.[117] Viewed from the Marine battalion headquarters at Jalalabad, however, the Pech looked like an increasingly violent and problematic place. Less than a month after Red Wings, on July 24, a bomb went off under a Humvee in the Marine battalion commander's column as he went up the Pech to visit Blessing. The vehicle flipped end over end, and only a combination of armor and luck saved the Marines inside from being killed. That IED and others like it, Marine intelligence officers suspected, had been planted by Ahmad Shah's men, working from inside their Korengal sanctuary.[118]

The issue of sanctuary—of places where the Taliban and other insurgents could rest and plan attacks unmolested—was at the heart of America's problems in Afghanistan. Just to the east of the Afghan provinces where Marines and soldiers were fighting commanders like Ahmad Shah, Pakistan provided the Taliban-led insurgency with a huge and permanent safe haven. It was in Peshawar, if the informant's spring report from the city was to be believed, that Ahmad Shah and other militants had gotten their marching orders for the 2005 fighting season in Kunar. But, frustratingly, that problem was beyond the U.S. military's power to affect, especially the conventional military. Pakistan was the business of the State Department, the CIA, and the Pakistanis. Even the border passes through which militants traveled back and forth between Kunar and Pakistan were out of the Marines' reach; that politically sensitive "battle space" was the purview of special operators and the CIA.

The Korengal, on the other hand, was a sanctuary right under American commanders' noses: a nest of guerrilla leaders as diverse as Ahmad Shah, Abu Ikhlas al-Masri, and Haji Matin that was on the right side of the border and therefore within their reach. "We'd hear all the time about Arabs and Chechens* being deep in the Korengal," the 2/3 Marine battalion's intelligence officer, Captain Scott Westerfield, remembered.[119] In the aftermath of Red Wings, the valley increasingly looked to U.S. officers at Asadabad, Jalalabad, Khost, and Bagram like a cancer that needed to be excised. "After a while you started to realize that if you were looking to get into a fight, pretty much any of these valleys would do, but at the time the Korengal seemed like it had a different vibe, with the outside fighters they were hosting in there," explained the Marine battalion commander, Lieutenant Colonel Jim Donnellan.[120]

Ahmad Shah's activities after his triumph on the Sawtalo Sar reinforced that impression. In early August, a two-hour-long propaganda video of combat in Kunar started circulating by DVD in Afghanistan and Pakistan and hitting the web in the Arab world. Ahmad Shah's men were its stars. Titled *The War of the Oppressed,* it spliced together video of the July 24 IED strike on the Pech road with vivid combat footage from the June 28 battle and shots of Mike Murphy's and Danny Dietz's dead bodies and their captured weapons, helmets, military identification cards, and other equipment.[121]

Videotaped proof of successful attacks was the currency with which small-time militant leaders negotiated for men, money, and resources with the Taliban's Peshawar *shura.* Ahmad Shah's videographers had captured some of the most compelling such footage of the war so far, raising his stock tremendously. That the video was

---

* Afghans often use the term "Chechen" to describe Caucasian-looking or Russian-speaking militants not just from Chechnya but from other parts of Russia, the Caucasus, and Central Asia. If Arab fighters were like big game for the U.S. military in Afghanistan, real Chechens were more like unicorns—reported but never definitively, with none ever taken alive, a legend born at the intersection of misinformation from Afghan sources and misunderstanding by American troops.

released by a propaganda group linked to al-Qaida, not just the Taliban, was especially worrying. "The events of Red Wings were an incredible boon to the enemy," said Westerfield, the Marine intelligence officer, who tracked such videos closely. Partly because he had ambushed and killed a group of elite special operators, but especially because he had gotten it on film, "at that point Ahmad Shah became the preeminent enemy commander in Kunar."[122]

Both military and intelligence assets started being diverted from other tasks to go after a commander who a few weeks earlier had been seen as small fry. "You get caught up in the chase," one CIA Afghanistan hand said of the elevation of Ahmad Shah on target lists. "I was guilty of it too. I don't think anybody had the foresight to stand up and say, 'This is a bad idea.'"[123]

THE CAUSES OF the violence emanating from the Korengal—the details of the Taliban-timber nexus that Jim Gant had stumbled into two years earlier and that Green Beret A-team 361 had exacerbated—were not obvious to commanders or staffs back at Jalalabad and Bagram, which were responsible for monitoring numerous provinces, each with its own set of problems. But a reaction was ready in the Marine battalion's playbook: more and bigger offensive operations.

It was in the collective DNA of Marine leaders that the purpose of any infantry unit was to pursue the enemy and, upon finding him, not let go. "There's very few things that are going to change a Marine infantry battalion's collective mindset when it comes to finding and fixing the enemy," recalled Major Tom Wood, who, as the 2/3 battalion's operations officer, had helped Erik Kristensen plan Red Wings and now took the lead on planning additional offensive missions into the Korengal and other Pech side valleys. "We wanted to be able to go up the Pech without being attacked, and all of our kinetic activity was taking place up there, so we moved more troops up there."[124] At Blessing, plywood huts multiplied to house the new arrivals, which included a company headquarters and the crews of a pair of 105-millimeter howitzers. Some of the operations involved the bulk of the battalion, with different companies marching up different side valleys, typically with some Afghan soldiers in tow.

Donnellan, the battalion commander, hoped that bringing those government troops along would help set the stage for a future in which Afghan forces, not Americans, patrolled Afghan valleys. "When it comes to the utility versus the futility of big battalion ops, bringing those Afghan troops in was at least connecting them to a remote place they couldn't and wouldn't have gone otherwise," he said. "That was the main benefit of those battalion operations." In practice, though, the small Afghan units' performance was unimpressive. Donnellan had drilled into his Marines that there was no place on the battlefield they couldn't go, that they shouldn't "be afraid of the bogeyman." So it was with horror that he watched his Afghan counterpart's first interaction with a group of Korengali elders. "The elder asks him why Afghan troops haven't been up here before, and the guy says, 'We were afraid to come because you shoot at anybody who comes in your valley.' I could've killed him," Donnellan remembered.[125]

Years later, both Donnellan and Wood would question whether they and their fellow Marines might not have been giving insurgent commanders what they wanted by reacting to the Red Wings tragedy and the IED strikes on the Pech road with such large-scale missions. "I was all too ready to go in there with these big battalion-sized ops," Donnellan reflected. "In hindsight, what we should have done was go in with a lot more Afghans and a lot fewer Americans." In the immediate aftermath of Operation Red Wings, it seemed better to be safe than sorry.[126]

"Were we the bees, or were we the honey?" wondered Wood.[127]

But in the summer of 2005, as hundreds more Marines arrived in the Pech for offensive operations that scoured the Korengal, Shuryak, Chowkay, and Watapur valleys and more Americans were wounded and killed in ones and twos,[128] few in the military chain of command were asking that question.

PART II

THE PECH BUBBLE

2006–2010

How is it that despite the presence of artillery and the regular army in Kunar, they couldn't prevent a few wretched people from causing such trouble?

—*Emir Abd al-Rahman Khan (1890)*

Our rucksacks are packed and our boots are on tight.
Our magazines are loaded and we're ready for a fight.
From Restrepo to Phoenix where the Pech River runs,
And straight to Vimoto, hear the wrath of her guns.

—*lyrics by 173rd Airborne Brigade medics (2008)*

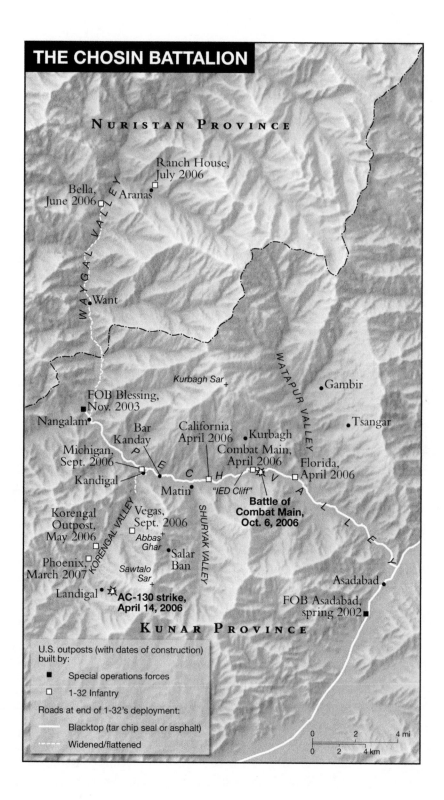

THE CHOSIN BATTALION

NURISTAN PROVINCE

Ranch House,
July 2006

Bella,
June 2006 Aranas

WAYGAL VALLEY

•Want

Kurbagh Sar +

WATAPUR VALLEY

•Gambir

FOB Blessing,
Nov. 2003

Nangalam•

Bar
Kanday

California,
April 2006

•Kurbagh

•Tsangar

Michigan,
Sept. 2006

P E

C H

Combat Main,
April 2006

Florida,
April 2006

Kandigal

Matin•

"IED Cliff"

V A

Battle of
Combat Main,
Oct. 6, 2006

Korengal
Outpost,
May 2006

Vegas,
Sept. 2006

SHURYAK VALLEY

L L E Y

KORENGAL VALLEY

Abbas +
Ghar

•Salar
Ban

Phoenix,
March 2007

Sawtalo
Sar +

Asadabad •

Landigal •

AC-130 strike,
April 14, 2006

FOB Asadabad,
spring 2002 ■

KUNAR PROVINCE

U.S. outposts (with dates of construction)
built by:

■ Special operations forces

☐ 1-32 Infantry

Roads at end of 1-32's deployment:

——— Blacktop (tar chip seal or asphalt)

----- Widened/flattened

0   2   4 mi

0   2   4 km

CHAPTER 5

THE PLUNGE

2006

COUNTERTERRORISM THROUGH COUNTERINSURGENCY

As Lieutenant Colonel Christopher Cavoli stood among the pines and cedars on the eastern slope of the Abbas Ghar, with the Korengal valley over the ridge and the Shuryak behind and below him, he could hear the dying sobs over the radio of the first of many men his soldiers would kill.

It was April 10, 2006, day one of Operation Mountain Lion—the largest offensive in northeastern Afghanistan since Winter Strike in 2003, the first big mission for Cavoli's infantry battalion, and the start of an ambitious new phase in America's war in the Pech. From here on out, the Pech and its side valleys would be the day-in, day-out focus and home not just of a Special Forces A-team or a few dozen Marines but of the bulk of a seven-hundred-man battalion. Cavoli commanded the first of five Army infantry battalions that would spend their tours in the Pech: the 10th Mountain Division's 1-32 Infantry.

A cerebral forty-one-year-old with two Ivy League degrees and a compact stature, Chris Cavoli had been waiting for his turn to fight in Afghanistan since September 11, 2001, when, as a major working a staff job at the Pentagon, he had spent the day helping man the main triage point outside the smoking building. He had taught at Ranger School and spent his summers as a boy climbing and skiing around the village in the Italian Alps where his father's family lived, and he relished each day he spent in the mountains; Kunar was no exception. But the hike up the Abbas Ghar—toward the scene of the tragedy that had unfolded nine months earlier during Operation Red Wings—was a grueling shock for soldiers who, despite the "Mountain" tabs on their shoulders, had trained in the cold flatness of upstate New York near the Canadian border.

Cavoli and ninety of his men had driven up the Shuryak in pickup trucks as far as the road went. Now they had a day and a half to ascend the Abbas Ghar before the main phase of Mountain Lion began and helicopters started delivering hundreds more troops onto the heights around the Korengal. The soldiers were wearing gray camouflage fatigues—the Army's ill-conceived new replacement for desert beige—which, far from helping them blend in, stood out brightly against the greens and browns of the mountain. On the slopes of neighboring ridges, insurgent spotters were tracking their slow ascent and comparing notes over the walkie-talkies that were essential gear for guerrillas and goatherds alike in Kunar.

The Americans' Afghan interpreters were listening in, and when one spotter revealed his location, Cavoli encouraged the fire-support officer who followed him everywhere to call for fire from the battalion mortarmen waiting down on the Pech road. The interpreters gave a blow-by-blow as the spotter reported in to his comrades.

"I'm behind a rock," the invisible man reported after the first salvo missed him. "I'm safe."

The next group of shells were white phosphorous rounds, packed with a waxy pale chemical that, upon detonation and contact with the air, burned at five thousand degrees Fahrenheit and produced billowing white smoke. The Marines in the Pech had been pairing high-explosive rounds with white phosphorous ones for months, using the harsh clouds from the WP shells to smoke enemy fighters out of their caves and crevices and into the open where the standard high-explosive shells could kill them. Troops called the mixed fire missions "shake and bake," and Cavoli, recognizing their potential in mountains where the enemy was never more than a few feet from the cover of boulders and caves, had instructed his soldiers to embrace the tactic.

On the radio, the spotter's tone changed from fearful to despairing as the shake-and-bake barrage peppered his patch of mountainside. "I can't breathe," he gasped. "I must move." Wounded either by the high-explosive shells' shrapnel or by the glowing white phosphorous fragments, he died as Cavoli's soldiers, amped up by their first contact with the enemy, listened in.[1]

Cavoli and his men spent that night outside Salar Ban—where the old man who had taken Marcus Luttrell's note to FOB Blessing approached them and introduced himself—before continuing their ascent up the draw where the other recon team SEALs had fought to the death. Struggling up the steep slope as much with hands as feet, sometimes tumbling down, often hoisting themselves up by hanging on to exposed tree roots, the soldiers of the 1-32 Infantry battalion were getting their first taste of the unforgiving, usually low-tech war that would be theirs for the rest of a deployment that would run sixteen months, almost three times as long as any other American troops had spent in the Pech. Facing an enemy who didn't wear body armor or other heavy gear and was expert at vanishing into the trees and the folds of the mountains, Cavoli's soldiers often felt as if they spent their days locked in firefights not with people but with rocks and cliffs. For all the U.S. military's technological prowess, the grinding day-to-day combat would be more like something out of Korea (where 1-32 Infantry had earned the nickname Chosin during the vicious December 1950 battle at the frozen Chosin Reservoir) than the higher-tech war that the American public, and many American troops, expected. The key weapons available to Cavoli's soldiers were not drones or smart bombs but machine guns and old-fashioned mortars and artillery, often firing shake-and-bake missions.

The waves of Chinooks and Black Hawks came the next night, April 11, ferrying hundreds of 10th Mountain soldiers and Marines—along with troops from the infant Afghan National Army—into clearings along the Abbas Ghar and in the higher mountains to the Korengal's south. Over the next few weeks, the plan went, the Chosin battalion and the other troops involved in Mountain Lion would scour the Korengal and leave behind a small outpost there, manned jointly by American and Afghan soldiers, the first new long-term base in the Pech or its side valleys since the establishment of FOB Blessing in 2003. That outpost would become the center of a new ink blot and deny insurgents like Ahmad Shah and Abu Ikhlas al-Masri the use of the Korengal as a safe haven from which to attack the Pech road.

The first gunshots to ring out on night two were some harassing rounds aimed in the direction of the snow-coated Sawtalo Sar summit, where Colonel John "Mick" Nicholson, Cavoli's superior, had set up a hasty command post in the same clearing that had served as a Ranger command post during the recovery of the bodies of the men killed on Turbine 33. The rest of the night was quiet as the troops deposited in the mountain landing zones prepared to descend into the Korengal.[2]

"I think they're hiding," Nicholson told an embedded journalist who had flown in with his soldiers. "They think this is like other operations where we come in for three or four days. This will be different."[3]

CHRIS CAVOLI AND Mick Nicholson made an odd-looking pair—Lieutenant Colonel Cavoli five feet six, his round, expressive face topped by a rapidly balding crown; Colonel Nicholson gaunter, much taller, with a brush of silver hair that looked dignified even in crew-cut form. Nicholson had an almost aristocratic bearing befitting a former first captain, or top cadet, of his West Point class, and his manner of speech was polished and succinct. Cavoli talked in sentences so long and complex and often studded with profanity that they sometimes struggled to hold the multilayered ideas he was trying to express.

There were similarities too. Both men were Army brats. Both had attended elite universities: Nicholson, oddly, had left West Point for Georgetown, intending to take premed classes there, only to change his mind and go back to the military academy after earning his civilian bachelor's degree; Cavoli had done ROTC at Princeton and later earned a master's degree at Yale. And Afghanistan was each man's second war—Nicholson's first had been Grenada in 1983, Cavoli's Iraq in 1991—but a war to which they were already connected by virtue of where they had been on September 11, 2001. Like Cavoli, Nicholson had been working at the Pentagon at the time; when American Airlines Flight 77 crashed into the building's northwest side, it destroyed Nicholson's office on a day when he happened to be out moving into a new house. Both men's style of leadership was to trust and empower subordinates to an extreme degree and then help them when necessary. Both were ambitious and confident: in the plans they laid for the long deployment to Kunar and Nuristan, in their lives, and in their careers. (Both would become four-star generals, and Nicholson would lead the whole U.S. and NATO mission in Afghanistan a decade later.)

The two colonels were bound for Afghanistan at a time when not only the U.S. public but the government and the military itself seemed almost to have forgotten about their four-and-a-half-year-old war there. In weekly videoconferences hosted by CENTCOM, the relative time devoted to Iraq and Afghanistan was a telling indicator of how the headquarters prioritized its missions in the two countries, Operation Iraqi Freedom and Operation Enduring Freedom, OIF and OEF. Iraq's descent into civil war often took up the first fifty or fifty-five minutes of an hour-long session before it was the turn of the Afghan war commander, Lieutenant General Karl Eikenberry (also a survivor of the attack on the Pentagon), to give a rushed OEF update. That disparity was echoed in the allocation of troops (130,000 in Iraq versus 23,000 in Afghanistan), helicopters, and drones.[4] Nicholson liked to compare Afghanistan to the Pacific in World War II, a secondary theater of war that never got the manpower or matériel it needed, because Europe came first. To a peer on Eikenberry's staff, that seemed too generous. Really, he said, Afghanistan was more like the little-remembered and even more meagerly resourced China-Burma-India theater.[5]

Nor did the Pentagon seem eager to face facts about how bad the situation in Afghanistan was becoming. Bizarrely, given that units on the ground had been using the term since 2003, there was a reluctance in the building even to officially acknowledge that what the United States and its allies faced there was an insurgency at all. "There was almost this Orwellian non-speak about what we were facing," Nicholson remembered. He knew his 3rd Brigade, 10th Mountain Division would be facing an insurgency, whatever the

Pentagon wanted to call it, so he assigned his officers books on Algeria, Malaya, and Indochina and brought in a family friend, the Vietnam historian and former Army and CIA officer Lewis Sorley, to talk about the counterinsurgency lessons the Army had learned in Southeast Asia and then mostly thrown away: separating the insurgents from the population, partnering with local troops, the same midcentury lingo of ink blots and oil spots that Ron Fry had learned about in the Special Forces schoolhouse and brushed up on before coming to the Pech.[6]

HEADED FOR A forgotten and foundering war, Nicholson attempted to impose direction onto his brigade's impending deployment. With more than a dozen Afghan provinces to cover, the brigade would have to concentrate somewhere, and he chose to plunge into Kunar and Nuristan, starting with the Korengal during April 2006's Operation Mountain Lion and then leapfrogging north into Nuristan, building new outposts as they went.

Kunar and Nuristan were where Nicholson felt his soldiers could make a difference. In the other hot spot he considered, farther south in Paktika and Khost, the Taliban-led insurgency's base areas were inside Pakistan and therefore untouchable. (A huge militia force answering to the CIA also guarded the border there.) In Kunar, the Korengal presented a promising target for action on the right side of the border, where his troops could build a new outpost and a new ink blot.

There was another dimension to the decision too. Some rank-and-file troops who flew into the Korengal for Mountain Lion were under the impression that al-Qaida operatives had planned the September 11 attacks there, or somewhere nearby.[7] That wasn't true, but it was a distortion of a real consideration that played heavily into Nicholson's and Cavoli's planning. Of all the provinces in eastern Afghanistan, Kunar and Nuristan were the two where the U.S. intelligence community believed al-Qaida maintained the most regular presence, and they bordered a region of Pakistan that the CIA suspected was the hideout of the top al-Qaida leaders whose trail had gone cold four years earlier.

That was of self-evident importance to officers who had witnessed the destruction of September 11. Both men knew the rough outlines of the intelligence about bin Laden's suspected escape route from Tora Bora that had pulled special operations forces to Kunar and Nuristan in 2002 and 2003, and had been briefed about Abu Ikhlas, the main al-Qaida figure the military and intelligence community were aware of in Afghanistan.

As an aide to the chairman of the Joint Chiefs two years earlier, Cavoli had co-authored a study on how local guerrillas and global terrorists interacted to form a "global insurgency." "Local insurgents welcome the global insurgents because they bring weapons, skills, volunteers, and a commitment to the local fight," he had written, while the global terrorists gained sanctuary and followers. Cavoli judged that Kunar and Nuristan—where a small number of foreign jihadis like Abu Ikhlas embedded themselves among local mujahidin like Ahmad Shah's and Haji Matin's fighters—fit the model to a T, better than anywhere else in Afghanistan.[8]

Years later, evidence would emerge that al-Qaida advisers were working quietly with Afghan guerrillas in other parts of eastern Afghanistan at the time too, not just in the two provinces the 10th Mountain leaders zeroed in on. According to a tribute video the terrorist group released in 2010 honoring several al-Qaida operatives killed on Afghan soil that year, Arabs who had been fighting with the Taliban in 2006 included three Saudis in the provinces of Zabul, Paktika, and Khost.[9] But the intelligence available to military commanders like Nicholson and Cavoli at the time didn't reflect that; it just highlighted Abu Ikhlas, with his higher profile and long history in Kunar.

"Our purpose as a nation for being in Afghanistan in the first place was al-Qaida and terrorist organizations, and the only place in all of Regional Command East that had a known al-Qaida operative was Kunar, where Abu Ikhlas was," remembered Nicholson.[10]

Nicholson and Cavoli still cannot speak about the role that intelligence agencies like the CIA, DIA, and NSA played in aiming them toward Kunar-Nuristan and the Pech, but they and other 10th Mountain Division leaders made the rounds in Washington before deploying. Kunar was a good place to go to fight enemies connected to al-Qaida, intelligence officials affirmed. More than that, it was the gateway to Nuristan, and a heavier U.S. military presence on the ground in both Kunar and Nuristan might create opportunities for the CIA and DIA to recruit new sources in the parts of Pakistan that Kunar and Nuristan bordered, Bajaur Agency and Chitral District.

The mountainous, wooded, often snowbound terrain of this Pakistani region northwest of Peshawar mirrored Kunar's and Nuristan's, and there were indications that it might be a hub of upper-level al-Qaida activity. Some in the intelligence community also believed that after his 2002 stint in Kunar, Osama bin Laden had moved to Chitral; at Langley, a team of analysts was poring over imagery from potential compounds in the district "square yard by square yard," according to a former senior intelligence officer, looking for clues.[11] A senior al-Qaida figure linked to the deadly July 2005 subway bombings in London was based in Bajaur—Abu Ubaydah al-Masri, who also oversaw the activity of Abu Ikhlas and other Arab advisers in Kunar and sometimes visited them there.[12] And there were strong indications that Zawahiri and other senior bin Laden subordinates had relocated to Bajaur in 2004 after a Pakistani military operation displaced them from Waziristan.[13] A lead on Zawahiri's location in the opening weeks of 2006 had prompted a rare air strike under CIA authority inside Bajaur, killing dozens of religious-school students but not Zawahiri.[14]

The intelligence community was eager for the military to take any action that might facilitate the development of new sources with knowledge of al-Qaida activities in Bajaur and Chitral, where the CIA's information was "spotty and irregular."[15] New military offensives in Kunar and Nuristan could push militants around and force them to talk to their leaders back in Pakistan, where the NSA was intercepting more communications than ever. And new outposts in remote Nuristani districts could create new opportunities for CIA and DIA case officers to recruit local agents, like cross-border smugglers or merchants, who moved back and forth among places the intelligence community was interested in.

"Our interest in Kunar was as a means to an end," said the CIA paramilitary officer Ron Moeller, who deployed to Afghanistan again over the winter as the main liaison between the agency and the 10th Mountain Division headquarters at Bagram. "We gave lip service to Kunar because the conventional forces wouldn't expand into Nuristan until after Kunar and the Pech. Mountain Lion became this convenient foundation."[16]

"We weren't that interested in people in Afghanistan, but you had to develop source networks aimed to the east," in Pakistan, added another CIA officer who was in Afghanistan at the time. "Everyone believed that bin Laden would be in Chitral or Bajaur, but we couldn't set up bases there. The closest place the military could set up bases was in Kunar and Nuristan."[17] The idea was that "we could dislocate the enemy, get them to stir things up and communicate, and that might allow the counterterrorism guys to go after the people they were there to get," echoed a military officer involved in the pre-deployment consultations with the intelligence community that informed the brigade's opening moves.[18]

The theory was misguided, at least partly. Bin Laden wasn't in Bajaur or Chitral; he was already living in Abbottabad, in Pakistan's developed interior. Once again—as when the CIA's interest in Nuristan launched the Rangers on Winter Strike and left behind FOB Blessing—top-level pressure to pick up bin Laden's trail was causing U.S. intelligence to look in the right direction too late and helping draw American troops there as a result. This time it wouldn't be a few small special operations teams or a couple of Marine platoons that stayed behind after the offensive but the bulk of an infantry battalion: hundreds of soldiers, enough to dot the Pech with many new ink blots.

COUNTERTERRORISM THROUGH COUNTERINSURGENCY in the Pech's daunting mountains was a much different kind of campaign from the Humvee-mounted war of highway convoys and urban raids the Army was fighting in Iraq. Not every infantry battalion in the Army would have been up to the task Chris Cavoli and his seven hundred soldiers were looking at, a year of bare-bones light infantry combat on hellish terrain. But as he boarded a passenger jet at Fort Drum in March 2006 for the first leg of his long trip, leaving behind his wife, Christina, and five- and seven-year-old sons for the longest deployment of his career, Cavoli was sure that the Chosin battalion could do it.

Every unit in the Army had its own character, history, and

culture—passed along, as on a Navy warship or a professional sports team, even as individual members came and went, and influenced especially by its leaders. Some battalions, particularly airborne ones, were cocky, while some had inferiority complexes; some worked on methodical planning, some on initiative and collective muscle memory.

The Chosin battalion was not cocky—people sometimes called its attitude humble—but it was tough. "Some Army units are your pit bulls, and that's what these guys were, they were pit bulls," one Army counterinsurgency adviser said of Chosin and the rest of Nicholson's 3rd Brigade, 10th Mountain Division.[19] By virtue of its location at freezing Fort Drum, 10th Mountain tended to draw soldiers from the Northeast—New England, New York, rural Pennsylvania—who wanted to be closer to home than the Army's other big bases allowed, giving its battalions "a blue-collar Yankee feel."[20]

"It was a battalion of meat eaters," said Cavoli's senior NCO, Command Sergeant Major Jimmy Carabello, a career Ranger and paratrooper from Massachusetts who'd wanted to join the infantry since watching *The Longest Day* as a boy. "If a battalion had to go to Kunar and Nuristan, it was the right battalion to send."[21]

During visits to both of the Army's pre-deployment exercise hubs—the Joint Readiness Training Center at Fort Polk, Louisiana, and the National Training Center at Fort Irwin, California—Cavoli had his companies rehearse long dismounted missions until they practically forgot what the Humvees they'd driven around Iraq in 2004 looked like. He drilled his lieutenants on machine-gun tactics; as far as he was concerned, making the best possible use of his machine guns was a platoon leader's most important job. Documents that Cavoli distributed to his subordinates didn't mention the bigger counterterrorism purpose they were supposed to be fulfilling in the Pech, which was above the pay grade (and the security clearance) of a lieutenant or sergeant. They stressed infantry basics—*remember to shave, change your socks daily, be able to report immediately on the disposition of all your men and the next likely enemy threat*—and what Cavoli saw as the two sides of the counterinsurgency tactics they would be employing: protecting the population and pursuing the enemy.

"The population is not the enemy—they are stuck between us

and the bad guys," one of Cavoli's PowerPoint briefings to his lieutenants noted. "Respect the population—don't call them 'haji' or anything else demeaning."

The flip side of counterinsurgency came two slides later: "Hunt the enemy ruthlessly and kill him where he lives. . . . Trick him, bait him, fool him, kill him."[22]

MOUNTAIN LION

In Kunar, an old friend of Cavoli's was pleased to hear the Army was sending more troops to the Pech, and more pleased still when he learned that Cavoli was leading them.

T.W. (who asked that his full name not be published) was a forty-six-year-old member of the Asymmetric Warfare Group, or AWG, a new unit the Army had set up to study and react to the IED threat. A lifelong, prolific hunter, physical endurance fanatic, and veteran of low-profile combat deployments in Central America, T.W. was also one of the Army's few genuine mountain warfare experts—a "Rembrandt of mountain combat," as Cavoli put it—except that he wasn't in the Army anymore. T.W. had retired after twenty years as a Ranger and Delta Force operator shortly before September 11, then come right back to work for what would become AWG, this time as one of its first armed civilian contractors. After a bomb blast wounded him in Iraq, he had shifted over to Afghanistan in 2004, where he set to work studying the worsening IED problem. To the amazement of the young infantrymen and engineers whose patrols he often accompanied (in whose eyes he was both an ancient and a kind of superman), his preferred method of clearing a road for a convoy of Humvees was to hike up into the hills above the route and scout for wires—often alone, often at a run.

Kunar was T.W.'s kind of place. Just about anytime he was deployed (he would make sixteen trips to Afghanistan), he found his way there. In that time, he would see one lieutenant colonel after another command infantry battalions in the Pech, most of them rising stars in the Army. None impressed him as much as Cavoli, whom he'd first met more than a decade earlier when both men were serving as Ranger School instructors. Cavoli had qualities T.W.

valued highly: aggressiveness, a deep trust in his subordinates, and an enthusiasm for the minutiae of infantry work. "Chris Cavoli is a guy who preached the importance of understanding the basics, like understanding the terrain," he said appreciatively. "He could analyze terrain as good as anybody I ever saw." T.W. saw a need in the Pech for more American troops to tackle a worsening problem, and that was the kind of commander he hoped would lead them.[23]

T.W.'s trips to the Pech started because that was where the bombs took him. Part of his job was to analyze as many IED blast sites as possible as soon as he could after the bombs detonated. As the Pech road emerged as one of Afghanistan's IED hot spots in 2005—sometimes called IED Alley, with one perilous drop-off nicknamed IED Cliff—T.W. kept coming back.[24] By early 2006, the Pech was the most heavily IED'd road in Afghanistan,[25] the problem solved neither by repeated Marine missions into the Korengal in the months that followed Red Wings nor by a ban on further Korengal missions that division headquarters then imposed due to fears about losing another helicopter full of troops there.[26]

When a new set of Hawaii-based Marines took over at FOB Blessing in January 2006, they drove through four ambushes on the Pech road in their first week. Three weeks in, they lost a twenty-one-year-old lance corporal, Billy Brixey, to a bomb that flipped a Humvee over. Two weeks after that, insurgents killed eight soldiers from the new Afghan National Army in an IED-initiated ambush on the road.[27]

The nerve-racking task of trying to find the bombs on the Pech road before they blew up fell to a group of Army Reserve engineers called a route-clearance patrol, whose missions T.W. often accompanied. On March 12, 2006, the route-clearance patrol had been surveying the river crossing at the Korengal mouth and were heading back down the Pech past Dag, the village where Jim Gant had gotten into his first firefight in 2003, when a bomb exploded underneath the lead Humvee.

Manning a gun in the turret of the next Humvee back, T.W. saw the blast hurl one soldier out of the targeted truck. By the time the former special operator was able to dismount and approach the blast site, three of the four engineers who'd been inside were dead and the fourth, with both legs severed, was dying. Among those killed was a skinny, charismatic, twenty-nine-year-old engineer with whom T.W. had worked elsewhere in Afghanistan, Staff Sergeant Joseph Ray.[28] T.W. had seen bad days already in his career and would see many more, but years later, when some of the memories had become foggy, the events of March 12, 2006, still stood out clearly in his mind's eye.[29]

Not all of the IEDs showing up on the Pech road were coming out of the Korengal, but T.W. felt sure that many of them were. Hard evidence was frustratingly hard to come by, but tips from informants consistently pointed to the Korengal as the most prolific IED production area off the Pech,[30] and Ahmad Shah's men, thought to be based in the heights within easy marching distance of many of the blast sites, were filming and openly taking credit for some of the attacks in Taliban propaganda videos.

The Marine officers at Jalalabad Airfield responsible for the Pech agreed, and with an idea of where their tormentors were, they chafed at the ban on Korengal missions over the winter. All they needed was permission, and it was clear to everyone that when the 10th Mountain Division headquarters rotated in from Fort Drum shortly ahead of Mick Nicholson's and Chris Cavoli's troops, the Korengal would be back on the table.[31]

BY THE TIME of the engineers' deaths on March 12, the green tent city that edged up against the Jalalabad Airfield tarmac was struggling to hold both the Marines and the thousand-plus 10th Mountain troops who were arriving to stage and plan for Operation Mountain Lion.

Under the plan that Nicholson's staff sent up to Bagram for approval, the better part of three battalions would converge on the Korengal by air and ground, more troops than had been in the Pech since Winter Strike. Cavoli's Chosin battalion, 1–32 Infantry, would secure the Pech road and hold the ridges above the Korengal, using their commanding positions to call in mortars, artillery, and air strikes on any insurgents who dared to come out and fight. Marine battalion 1/3, meanwhile, would enter the Korengal from two directions, some platoons landing by helicopter in clearings deep inside the target valley while others pushed up by ground from the ford site where the Korengal joined the Pech. And another 10th Mountain unit—3-71 Cavalry, commanded by Lieutenant Colonel Joseph Fenty, a lanky, red-faced super-marathoner who had been among Cavoli's closest friends since the two shared a trailer during a Balkan peacekeeping deployment—would block the passes high around the soaring Chalas Ghar mountain where the Korengal joined the perpendicular valleys that descended toward the Kunar River.

Together, Cavoli's men and the Marines would scour the villages beyond the Sawtalo Sar where Ahmad Shah, Haji Matin, and Abu Ikhlas were thought to be hiding, trying to capture or kill them. They would also establish an outpost on the grounds of Haji Matin's sawmill four and a half miles into the valley. After a few weeks, the Marines would go home to Hawaii, and the cavalry would move to a new sector to the northeast. One of Cavoli's platoons would stay behind at the new Korengal Outpost while the rest of his battalion prepared for follow-on missions north of the Pech, into Nuristan.[32] Some ANA soldiers would stay in the Korengal too; the base there was supposed to become an Afghan government outpost, although with the ANA still effectively in its infancy four years into the war, this proved to be a fantasy.

The big column of Chosin battalion Humvees and ANA pickup trucks passed FOB Asadabad and headed up the Pech on April 9. After bumping up and down on the dirt road for six hours, some platoons peeled off to set up temporary firebases along the route. Cavoli's main convoy spent the night at one of them and in the morning set out for the mouth of the Shuryak. In Bar Kanday, children swarmed the trucks, and an eager shop owner listed to Cavoli all the things the market town wanted from America: schools, a medical clinic, a "micro-hydro" power unit to generate electricity from the Pech River.[33] The movement up the Shuryak was excruciatingly slow; to make it up the Abbas Ghar in time for the big air assault, Cavoli hired some local pickup trucks on the spot to lug gear up the winding Shuryak road after it became too treacherous for Humvees.

Soldiers who'd seen contour maps of their objective and satellite imagery on FalconView, the military's version of Google Earth, were shocked to actually look up from the valley at the steepness of the ridge above. Many of the ninety men who accompanied Cavoli up the Abbas Ghar were soon gasping from exhaustion. When the party finally crested the ridge after their first, exhilarating contact with the enemy (when the shake-and-bake mortar mission killed the enemy spotter), a look back down into the Shuryak showed a serene scene of women and children working on the thin emerald agricultural terraces below, and then, as if on cue, all the little figures started running for their villages at once. This, an ANA captain helpfully explained through an interpreter, was a bad sign.[34]

Once the overwhelming size of the force ringing and entering the Korengal became clear, though, the guerrillas did what they had been doing in the area for three years when faced with superior American numbers: they faded away. Chinooks and Black Hawks deposited no fewer than eleven Marine platoons around the valley overnight; Mick Nicholson and his command team landed atop the still-snowy Sawtalo Sar and hiked down; and another two hundred Marines walked up the Korengal to Haji Matin's lumberyard with a Predator and an AC-130 gunship guarding them from above. As the Marine, Army, and ANA platoons searched one village after another in the days that followed (always with the Americans planning the missions and the ANA just tagging along), they found little of note—even in villages that were known insurgent bases—and sometimes no people at all.[35]

There were occasional reminders of the tragedy that had occurred over the summer. On the fifth day in the valley, a Marine patrol detained five unarmed men it suspected of being insurgents, one of whom was wearing hiking boots of the same kind U.S. special operators often wore and carrying a piece of a U.S. radio; another patrol found scorched shards of Turbine 33's fuselage inside a mountain *bandeh*. Unsatisfying, long-distance firefights crackled across the valley once a day or so as someone shot at the intruding American patrols from across a draw or stream and then sought to avoid the succession of machine-gun and mortar fire, then shake-and-bake artillery salvos from the howitzers at Blessing and Asadabad, and then air strikes.[36]

How many insurgents all that ordnance was actually killing was impossible to say. One sniper team, exploring a camouflaged hole they stumbled on near their mountaintop hide site, found it was one of several entrances to a deep cave that some guerrillas seemed to have been using for shelter, taking advantage of both its scenic view of the valley and the complete protection its thick rock ceiling offered from air strikes and artillery. How many more invisible, impenetrable caves and tunnels dotted the mountain slopes, never to be found by Americans, was anyone's guess.[37]

For Cavoli's bored troops on the Abbas Ghar, strung out among little ridgetop observation posts built from sandbags, tree branches, and camouflage poncho liners called woobies, the only entertainment available was watching the howitzer shells burst among the conifers and rock formations. For Cavoli himself, the days alternated between tedium and excitement. Once, he had a helicopter drop off a case of Bitburger nonalcoholic beer for his command group to sip while they watched ninety-six-pound howitzer shells arc in from FOB Asadabad toward one face of a ridge and then the other, chasing a slippery group of enemy fighters back and forth. At other times, he had little enough to do that he called his friend Joe Fenty on a Thuraya satellite phone just to chat.[38] Photos Cavoli's operations officer took showed him in moments of annoyance (with his hand against his furrowed brow while he talked to headquarters) and humor, as in one where the small-framed lieutenant colonel posed, grinning ear to ear, surrounded by indifferent goats.

THE SCARCITY OF targets and unwillingness of the Korengali insurgents to engage a large American force were frustrating to Nicholson, who hoped Operation Mountain Lion would net Abu Ikhlas, Ahmad Shah, or at least Haji Matin and repeatedly stressed to his subordinates the importance of striking quickly when an informant's tip or a signals intercept came in. With routine support from one of the few Predator drones in Afghanistan, a high-altitude U-2 spy plane, a signals intelligence plane, and an AC-130 gunship with its night optics, the brigade had more access to surveillance gadgetry during Mountain Lion than it ever would again during the deployment, and Nicholson wanted to make the most of it. But acting on a piece of intelligence about a high-value target quickly enough to have any hope of success came with risks, as Nicholson and his officers learned the hard way during Mountain Lion's first week.

On April 14, a satellite phone intercept placed an insurgent tied to Abu Ikhlas and Haji Matin, code-named Objective Boring I, in the village of Landigal, situated in a draw running down into the Korengal from the Sawtalo Sar. When a Marine patrol entered Landigal, it took fire and a group of men fled up the draw to an outlying cluster of houses. An orbiting Predator beamed footage of the scene onto laptop-like video terminals at the Marine command post down below, at the Korengal Lumberyard, and Nicholson's voice came over the radio with clear directions. "Colonel Nicholson was like, 'You need to kill or capture those guys,'" a Marine major present remembered. "We didn't want these guys to get away."[39]

In Landigal, the Marine lieutenant whose men had been fired on, Jesse Wolfe, got a request from the lumberyard command post to approve a bomb strike by an A-10 attack jet. Wolfe could barely see the cluster of buildings his commanders wanted to bomb, so he declined to call for a strike. But Nicholson and the Marine battalion commander ordered the strike anyway, and the A-10 dropped two bombs. One hit the house the Predator had seen the fleeing fighters enter.[40]

After dark, as Wolfe and his Marines were hiking up the draw with some ANA soldiers to inspect the damage, two things happened in quick succession. First, late at night, the CIA base at Asadabad called the lumberyard with a tip. According to one of the agency's sources, Haji Matin was hiding in a cave next to a house in the vicinity of Landigal. Second, fifteen minutes later, an AC-130 arrived on station and spotted a group of figures moving around a streambed very close to the house the A-10 had bombed—little black forms that seemed to dart into the mouth of a cave when the gunship circled overhead.

With the AC-130 short on fuel and a narrowing window of opportunity to kill Boring I or perhaps Haji Matin, the Marine battalion commander at the lumberyard authorized the circling gunship to open fire with its 105-millimeter howitzer, the biggest gun it carried. "We thought we had them dead to rights," the battalion operations officer recalled.[41]

Down below, the Marine platoon commander Wolfe got word of the impending strike moments before it happened, as he was approaching the site of the original A-10 strike. He emphatically radioed back that the AC-130 should hold its fire; the danger to him and his men was too great. But it was too late. By the time Wolfe's urgent message made it through a series of radio relays to the lumberyard—a game of telephone necessitated by the dips, rises, and cliffs that disrupted a clear radio signal from inside the Landigal draw—the gunship had already started belching howitzer shells down into a spot in the streambed just six hundred feet from the alarmed Marines and ANA.[42]

What Wolfe and his men discovered when they reached the site of the AC-130 strike at dawn horrified the Marine lieutenant. There was no cave complex, although Wolfe could see how an arrangement of boulders in the streambed might have looked like one in the grainy footage produced by a Predator's or AC-130's sensors. The first person Wolfe saw in the early-morning gloom was an old man in blood-soaked robes. At the old man's feet was a pile of children's bodies and body parts. From the heads and torsos, Wolfe counted seven dead children. Nearby, an old woman was badly hurt. From the wounds and the gore-spattered boulders in the streambed, it was obvious that it was the AC-130's handiwork. There was no evidence of any insurgents, alive or dead; Boring I popped back up on the radio a few days later. Haji Matin, wherever he was, had escaped.[43]

Talking to the men of the village and later watching the "gun tape" the AC-130 had recorded, Wolfe thought he understood what had happened. After the A-10 strike, the families in the little settlement in the draw had sent all their children to the streambed for protection under the supervision of the old woman, in case there were more bombs. That was where the AC-130 had found them and mistaken them, moving among the rocks, for insurgents entering and exiting a cave.[44]

For the Marine lieutenant, the Landigal strike was an appalling tutorial on the ability of American power to harm innocents for no good reason. For the brigade commander Nicholson, three echelons up in the military hierarchy and still running a major offensive operation, it was a sad lesson in the limits of surveillance technology.[45] But it did not dampen his determination to hunt down the guerrilla commanders who were Operation Mountain Lion's targets.

Two nights later there was an even more promising lead when two intelligence sources tipped off their handlers that Abu Ikhlas was holed up in a house in Salar Ban, the village that had sheltered the wounded SEAL Marcus Luttrell and through which Chris Cavoli had passed on his way up the Abbas Ghar a week earlier. The two sources offered matching physical descriptions, and a Prophet radio-intercept device pinpointed what seemed as though it might be the house. This time there was no question of using airpower; the house was right in the village. But when one of Cavoli's platoons got there, it found nothing, perhaps misled by the Prophet system, which the brigade's operators were learning to use on the fly.[46]

If Abu Ikhlas really was in Salar Ban that night, it was probably the closest American troops would get to him for nearly five more years. "Anybody of consequence probably got the hell out of there as soon as they realized the size of the operation," Nicholson guessed.[47]

FOUR WEEKS INTO the operation, at the beginning of May, Mountain Lion was winding down. No major insurgent leaders had been captured or killed, but Nicholson and Cavoli were optimistic that they had been displaced from the Korengal, and Cavoli meant to keep them out with the outpost that his men were establishing at the lumberyard, a small postage stamp of brown straddling the Korengal road four hundred feet above the valley floor.

On the night of May 4, three days before the scheduled flag raising at the lumberyard outpost, Cavoli shared a helicopter back to Jalalabad with Joe Fenty, the friend and peer whose 3-71 Cavalry squadron had been plugging up the high southern exits of the Korengal. After a month separated in the mountains, the infantry battalion commander was thrilled to have the chance to catch up with his cavalry colleague and to congratulate Fenty in person on the birth of his first child, a daughter, back at Fort Drum. But free time for two commanders in a war zone, collectively coordinating the complex movements of more than a thousand soldiers, was scant. When Fenty boarded another Chinook the next night to oversee the extraction of his troopers from tiny landing zones scattered around the 10,800-foot Chalas Ghar mountain south of the Korengal, the two men had been able to catch up only cursorily.

Less than three hours after Fenty's Chinook took off from Jalalabad, a lieutenant walked into Cavoli's office with a stricken look on his face and bad news. After a month of good luck flying in the mountains, a bird had gone down, not to enemy fire, but to a rotor strike on a tree in a tiny high-altitude landing zone—Joe Fenty's bird, call sign Colossal 31.[48]

A drone arrived over the Chalas Ghar soon afterward and broadcast back a grim picture: the Chinook had tumbled to the bottom of a ravine far below the landing zone and was burning furiously. Only in the light of the next day, when the fire had finally exhausted itself, would Marines and Air Force pararescuemen be able to reach the incongruously peaceful-looking little poppy field where Colossal 31 had come to rest and confirm what was already obvious within minutes of the crash: none of the ten soldiers aboard could have survived.

AT THE FLAG-RAISING ceremony at the new Korengal Outpost, or KOP, two days later, the mood was somber. In the May days ahead, while Cavoli flew home with his friend's remains and attended his funeral at Arlington National Cemetery, one of his platoons settled in, fortifying the KOP's sawmill site with sandbags and Hesco barriers and sleeping in structures made from stacked lumber and blue tarps. When they weren't digging in or resting, they trekked from one end of the valley to another, getting to know its strange sights and sounds (the big porcupines sometimes visible through night-vision goggles, the hollering of monkeys in the trees, very rarely a leopard or other big cat), its terrain features (hidden natural springs, seemingly endless staircases carved into the rock), and its people, with their henna-dyed beards and black eyeliner. The lieutenant leading them joked that the patrols were not movements to contact but "movements to village elder."[49]

It was the calm before the storm. At the end of May, the KOP absorbed the first of what would soon become routine withering attacks from multiple directions as the Korengal valley attempted to reject its new outpost like a body rejecting an organ. Two weeks after that, the Chosin battalion lost its first soldier when a sniper, Sergeant Russell Durgin, was fatally shot in the head during a night ambush patrol near Landigal.

The 10th Mountain officers overseeing operations in Kunar figured the attacks would soon pass. Korengali elders routinely assured the troops patrolling from the KOP that any insurgents in the valley were outsiders like Ahmad Shah and Abu Ikhlas, the same assurances they had given Nicholson himself during a *shura* at the lumberyard when Operation Mountain Lion kicked off.

With American troops now effectively enforcing a permanent blockade on the Korengal's livelihood by occupying its main sawmill, and with one of the valley's communities reeling from the mistaken killing of seven of its children by American airpower, taking those assurances at face value was optimistic, to say the least. It would take many more months—and several more deaths—for the soldiers of the Chosin battalion in the Korengal to learn what Ron Fry's Special Forces A-team had suspected in 2004: that the insurgency there was not a group of outside militants but the product of a strong alliance between outsiders and the people of the Korengal itself.

"At that first *shura* we held the day after we flew in, we were sitting down with essentially the elders of the insurgency in the valley," Nicholson observed later. "But we didn't know that at the time. We thought the Korengali population was being coerced by outsiders like Ahmad Shah and Abu Ikhlas."[50]

"ENDSTATE: CAVOLISTAN"

Asked how he coped with the death of his best friend in the Army, Joe Fenty, and with the deaths of his own soldiers that began a few weeks later with Russ Durgin, Chris Cavoli answered that he took comfort in his Catholic faith and that it helped that Nicholson ordered him to escort Fenty's body home, giving him a rest and time to grieve away from his men. Beyond that he wasn't sure; he had just pushed through the way soldiers have to. "I don't know," he said. "I've been told I have a lot of energy. I guess I'm a pretty focused person when there's something to do."[51]

There was plenty to do; the bulk of the Chosin battalion's deployment still lay ahead. To T.W., the Asymmetric Warfare Group operator five years Cavoli's senior who was his adviser and friend, Fenty's death seemed to leave the Chosin commander with greater energy and determination than ever. When Cavoli returned to his Jalalabad Airfield command post from his somber trip stateside, it was on to the next objective: Aranas, the town high in Nuristan's Waygal valley north of FOB Blessing that another 10th Mountain battalion had fruitlessly searched in November 2003 after the CIA-directed air strike nearby that shattered the unlucky family of Mawlawi Ghulam Rabbani and kicked off Operation Winter Strike.

Nicholson and Cavoli wanted to get to Aranas for the same reasons the CIA had homed in on the town two and a half years before: signals intelligence and reports from informants, many of them passed along to 10th Mountain by the agency, showed that it was a regular stopping point for wanted militants.[52] "Of the enemy leaders we were focusing on, all of them—100 percent—had been to . . . Aranas in the past year," Cavoli wrote later: Abu Ikhlas, Ahmad Shah, the Nuristani Taliban commander Mawlawi Monibullah (who was from Aranas), and even Haji Ghafor, the Hizb-e Islami commander the Rangers had been looking for during Winter Strike.[53] One report from an informant placed Ahmad Shah in Want, on the Waygal valley floor halfway between Blessing and Aranas, as recently as April 9, suggesting he had already moved on from the Korengal to the even less accessible Waygal by the time Mountain Lion kicked off.[54]

Aranas fit Cavoli's model of "global insurgency" even better than the Korengal did. The town and other villages far up the Waygal valley were not only stopping points for the occasional al-Qaida operative but longtime sanctuaries and recruiting grounds for another transnational terrorist group, Lashkar-e-Taiba, the jihadist organization that in 2008 would kill more than 160 people in a shocking seaborne attack on the Indian city of Mumbai.

The Pakistani militants who started Lashkar-e-Taiba, the Army of the Pure, were adherents of a conservative brand of Islam called Ahl-e Hadith, a South Asian analogue to the Saudi-style Salafism that later became popular in nearby Kunar. They enjoyed extensive support from Pakistan's ISI spy agency and had spent the 1990s fighting against Indian troops in Kashmir on Pakistan's behalf. By

2006, though, the U.S. intelligence community was learning about broader terrorist plots by the group and about connections between some of its members and al-Qaida.[55] Top al-Qaida leaders assumed that some of the Lashkar-e-Taiba operatives they dealt with were reporting back on them to Pakistani intelligence,[56] but in Bajaur the al-Qaida field commander Abu Ubaydah was using Lashkar-e-Taiba members to transport weapons into Kunar.[57]

Each autumn since the early 1990s, Lashkar-e-Taiba recruiters had visited Aranas and left for Kashmir—just 175 miles away—with local recruits. Many young Aransi men spent a few months in Kashmir and then came home for good, but others joined the jihadi group on a permanent basis. Some acted as cadre to train new recruits. According to the Kunari journalist Bilal Sarwary, others served as radiomen, foiling Indian signals intelligence by speaking in their native Waygali language, like a Nuristani version of Navajo code talkers.[58]

As Mountain Lion wound down, Nicholson ordered Cavoli to get to Aranas and clear it of insurgents by August 1. That was an ambitious goal for a battalion that had just established one new outpost in notoriously contested terrain and still had several platoons guarding the Pech road against IEDs. When Cavoli's operations officer and sergeant major began to sketch out a plan for the northward plunge in mid-May, superimposing arrows, unit icons, and question marks over a crude map on a whiteboard under the only half-joking heading "Endstate: Cavolistan," they had their doubts. How much could one Army infantry battalion with some ragtag Afghan government partners really accomplish in a year? When Cavoli got his hands on the whiteboard and started adding his own thoughts, though, the colonel's confident energy—and his answers for every question they posed—quieted them.[59]

THE JOB OF getting to Aranas fell to 1–32 Infantry's Bravo Company,* based at FOB Blessing and commanded by a six-foot-three former

---

* Nicknamed Battle Company, but referred to here as Bravo Company to avoid confusion with the Battle Company, 2–503 Infantry, that is the focus of chapter 7.

enlisted mortarman named Douglas Sloan. At forty, Sloan was almost as old as Cavoli—much older than the battalion's other captains—and he sported a rebellious mustache that hinted at a crude and mischievous irreverence that his soldiers loved. (Sloan had spent much of Operation Mountain Lion with his privates hanging in the wind, exposed through holes in his tattered gray camouflage pants, which hadn't stood up well to field conditions in the Korengal. When anyone asked, he'd say he wasn't putting on a new uniform until his soldiers got new uniforms too.)

Examining satellite maps with red stars marking the locations of cell phone intercepts, Doug Sloan struggled to plan an air assault on Aranas. When he and Cavoli flew over the town in a Black Hawk, they saw no potential landing zones close enough to maintain the element of surprise. Instead, the Bravo Company commander proposed moving up the Waygal bit by bit, first driving ten miles up the valley from Blessing to a tiny market village, called Bella (pronounced "Bay-luh") in Pashto or Jameshgal-nisha in Waygali, and establishing a mortar firebase and helicopter landing zone there. That would enable the next stage of the advance, and it would give Sloan a chance to see how the people of Aranas reacted before actually approaching the town.[60]

The road up the Waygal valley wound along a cliff, and beyond the district seat, Want, it was much too narrow for Humvees. That forced Sloan's men to continue to Bella in the beige Ford pickup trucks their ANA colleagues drove—a violation of theater-wide restrictions, meant to cut down on IED deaths, that since 2005 had barred U.S. troops from traveling in "nonstandard" vehicles like pickup trucks.[61]

In later years, commanders in Afghanistan would follow those restrictions to the letter, but it never occurred to Cavoli to allow a narrow road and some rules on the books at a rear-area headquarters to stand in his troops' way. "The reality of the terrain dictated it," Cavoli explained: on a road like the one up the Waygal, the choice wasn't between dangerous pickup trucks and safe Humvees but between pickup trucks "and fucking walking."[62] In the balance between protection and mobility, the latter seemed the obvious choice to Cavoli; it was the choice the infantry doctrine he'd been raised on dictated, and he knew his own boss, Nicholson, would agree and back him up.

To T.W., who was in and out of the Pech as the Waygal advance got under way, the two colonels' willingness to underwrite this risky move in spite of the rules was a breath of fresh air; more and more in his travels, he saw troops buttoned up in Humvees, somewhat safer from IEDs but less mobile. Within two years, as IED casualties in Afghanistan mounted and higher headquarters tightened the restrictions meant to prevent them, the bold movement Sloan's company made up the Waygal in late June 2006 would be not only impossible but difficult for troops and their commanders even to imagine.

The trip up the narrow road to Bella was hair-raising. "Mirrors would break off on the left side, and you'd have tires hanging halfway off the cliff on the right side," one NCO said of the ride, which he made in the back of an ANA pickup. "Halfway up I smelled weed, and the ANA driver of my truck was stoned out of his mind."[63] But no trucks fell off the side, and there were no IEDs. Two days after setting out from FOB Blessing, Sloan's troops and the ANA were filling sandbags, stringing concertina wire, and setting up lean-tos under blue tarps in a bend in the Waygal River that would become Firebase Bella.

The outpost site itself was "a fishbowl that ten guys with two machine guns could wreak havoc on," as one Marine captain embedded with the ANA troops as a combat adviser observed.[64] But it was the only flat spot for miles around, and without the landing zone and mortar firebase that it afforded, it wouldn't be possible to push on to Aranas, two and a half miles northeast and two thousand feet higher up.[*]

On June 27, with 120-millimeter mortars in place at Bella, a platoon and some accompanying ANA set out for their main objec-

---

[*] To support Sloan's advance up the Waygal, an artillery unit had moved two 155-millimeter howitzers to FOB Blessing. That put Aranas within range of howitzer support, but the mountains surrounding the town were so steep that the howitzers, which fired their shells in a relatively shallow arc, still wouldn't be able to hit some of the northern slopes. Putting 120-millimeter mortars at Bella solved that problem.

tive, crossing the narrow but fast-moving Waygal River on a pulley-gondola system that locals used (the only way there was). The patrol passed through the outlying settlement that the CIA had disastrously ordered bombed in 2003—where a shepherd fed the soldiers goat, rice, and okra and filled them in about the tragedy there—and then approached the rickety wooden bridge at Aranas's eastern edge.[65]

Instead of an ambush or IED, the platoon was greeted by a delegation of curious elders. Sloan came up from Bella the next day and accepted the men's invitation, relayed through an interpreter, to come into town. After meeting with an assembled *shura* that seemed neither hostile nor overly friendly, Sloan called Cavoli by satellite radio. An aggressive assault operation wouldn't be necessary to get into Aranas, he said. He was there already and intended to stay.[66]

CAVOLI AGREED, and he made the trip up himself two days later, on June 30, crossing the river in the pulley-drawn gondola and hiking up to Aranas with his sergeant major and some intelligence personnel from the Asadabad CIA base.

In a *shura* in front of Aranas's main mosque, an ANA officer introduced Cavoli, and then, through an interpreter translating into Pashto (the second language of most people in town), the colonel explained his intentions with his usual energy and earnestness. After promising financial restitution for the 2003 air strike outside town, he explained that his men had come looking for enemies of the United States and the Afghan government like Ahmad Shah and that they wanted to stay and build a base. If the town agreed to this, he promised, his men would enter homes only if invited, and they would reward Aranas with the material benefits of American nation building: a school, a generator, a paved road.[67]

The *shura* attendees were seated on the ground in two groups, Cavoli observed, and the groups reacted to his brief speech differently: one (including a charismatic elder who claimed to have fired U.S.-supplied Stinger anti-aircraft missiles during the jihad against the Soviets) with muted enthusiasm, and the other with stony faces. The latter, Cavoli guessed, were the town's conservatives, men who had fought in Kashmir or otherwise approved of Aranas's long-standing relationship with militants or were followers of Mawlawi

Monibullah, the Aransi cleric who was a rising figure in the Taliban. What the compact American commander was confidently proposing was a whole new order, and the elders doing the talking responded that the *shura* would need time to think it over.

The next morning a much smaller *shura* assembled, and Ghulam Saffar, the man who claimed to have been a Stinger operator, spoke for them: the Americans and their ANA friends could stay and build a base. Pleased—the Chosin battalion was a month ahead of the schedule Nicholson had set for it—Cavoli headed back down the mountain, leaving it to Doug Sloan to sort out the details.

Offering a year's rent up front to prove he meant to stay, Sloan garrisoned thirty-odd American and ANA soldiers in an abandoned one-story schoolhouse located at the upper edge of the steeply sloping town. Concertina wire and fighting positions went up around the perimeter, and with the help of local hires the soldiers began the weeks-long work of digging, picking, and blasting at the rock surface above the building's flat roof to make room for a Black Hawk to land. On the radio with Cavoli, Sloan reported that the schoolhouse looked like a ranch-style American home, and so the Ranch House, the most northerly, inaccessible, and precarious outpost any U.S. unit would establish in the Pech or its side valleys, was born.

THE FIRST MONTH at the Ranch House was quiet—much quieter than the first at the Korengal Outpost. An ANA officer who had religious training and knew some of the town's mullahs was particularly well received and would even give guest sermons at the main mosque. True to Cavoli's promise, the soldiers at the Ranch House entered no homes uninvited. For the most part, no one invited them, but there were encouraging exceptions, like a town doctor who struck up a friendship with Doug Sloan; the doctor had a taste for whiskey, which the CIA officers at Asadabad (to whom the military's ban on alcohol did not apply) were happy to supply.

The militant leaders the Chosin battalion had hoped to find were gone, of course, but Nicholson, Cavoli, and Sloan all figured that if there were ever a good place to collect information about their comings and goings, that place was Aranas. Early conversations with locals who acknowledged Ahmad Shah's visits and provided information on other local militants seemed to bear that out. The Bella outpost proved an unexpected source of intelligence too. Although almost no one actually lived in Bella, the little market and medical clinic there both drew travelers, like itinerant salesmen, with knowledge of goings-on not just elsewhere in Nuristan but across the Pakistani border in Bajaur and Chitral, the areas that interested the CIA.

Then the other shoe dropped.

Because helicopters couldn't land at the Ranch House yet, the troops there hired local donkey trains to haul supplies up from Firebase Bella, and during the second week of August someone intercepted one of these low-tech, unmanned logistics patrols, killing the donkeys and burning the supplies. Then, on August 11, as a twenty-two-soldier patrol was hiking the same route up to the Ranch House from Bella, insurgents struck, waiting until the patrol's point man had passed below their concealed positions high on the mountain before unleashing a barrage of machine-gun fire and RPGs on a particularly narrow and barren stretch of the trail.

As the fire intensified, the lead team was torn apart, its sergeant hit and two of its junior soldiers, Specialist Rogelio Garza and Private First Class James White, blown down the mountainside by an RPG volley that killed them both. Pinned against a cliff face, the rest of the patrol could not move or return effective fire—except for the sixth soldier in line, a private first class named Andrew Small who had graduated from high school in southern Maine barely a year earlier.

Carrying a light machine gun called a squad automatic weapon, or SAW, Small dropped to the bare ground and started spitting out long bursts of 5.56-millimeter rounds, drawing enemy fire toward himself and away from the men behind him. The teenage soldier's solitary defense bought the staff sergeant leading the patrol, who was also wounded, enough time to gather his men and then organize a counterattack when Air Force jets arrived overhead. Reaching Small's position, the other soldiers in the patrol found two empty ammunition drums next to his dead body and a third empty drum attached to his SAW—evidence that he had fought until he had no more rounds to fire and then succumbed to his wounds.[68]

After the ambush, a delegation of elders visited the Ranch House to share their condolences. The *shura*'s sympathy was cold comfort to the soldiers whose friends had died,[69] especially after the identities of some of the attackers emerged: rather than outside militants, according to informants in town, they had been local men from the pro-Lashkar-e-Taiba and pro-Taliban faction that had opposed allowing the Americans into Aranas, at least one of them a native of a nearby village whose brother had died fighting for the group in Kashmir.[70]

The lieutenant whose soldiers had been killed in the ambush, a bookish-looking University of Pennsylvania graduate named Erik Malmstrom, worried that the attack was an inevitable consequence of Americans' stepping into a closed society whose complex local politics they didn't, and perhaps couldn't, understand.

"I think that things were going on beneath the surface that we weren't fully aware of at the time," Malmstrom speculated reasonably. "The insurgents had probably scattered and then were planning to hit us. Momentum was probably building to something like August 11."[71]

Cavoli was more optimistic. His takeaway from the engagement was that his men had shown the Aransis that they weren't going anywhere, even in the face of casualties, and that the enemy, by staging the attack so close to Aranas, had shown the townspeople that they weren't above putting civilian lives at risk.[72]

TWO WEEKS AFTER the ambush, Cavoli wrote a lengthy newsletter to his soldiers' families in upstate New York, attempting to explain what their loved ones were doing in the Pech, Korengal, and Waygal. By then the Chosin battalion had been deployed nearly six months, and twelve of its seven hundred soldiers had died. Unknown to the families or most of the battalion's soldiers, some recent intelligence had suggested their counterinsurgency gamble might be paying counterterrorism dividends—like an intelligence report that the same week as the Aranas ambush a Taliban commander in Kunar had "refused an offer from senior Taliban officials for additional Arab fighters," noting how hard it was to protect the one al-Qaida adviser he already had with so many more American troops around.[73]

"If we are to create hope for these people, the first step is to keep the enemy away from them," Cavoli wrote in his newsletter—what he believed he had taken a step toward doing by establishing the KOP and the Ranch House. "The enemy will not just go away; he will need to be faced down and chased away—by your valiant loved ones, who will continue to show the people of Afghanistan and of America what it means to fight for right. This doesn't come free. . . . We have lost many soldiers here, fine young men and women."

Continuing, the colonel drew a connection—a much-simplified one—between the counterinsurgency and the counterterrorism missions that had prompted the battalion's plunge into the mountains and that he hoped might be starting to pay off:

> Their efforts and their sacrifice have been in the service of a just cause, and an important one. The enemy we fight is not some strange group of unknowns in a far-off land; this enemy is the direct enemy of the United States, the very groups and their associates who launched the attacks of 9/11, 2001. . . . We are winning. But we aren't there yet.[74]

Cavoli believed what he wrote. But the finish line was further off than he, his soldiers, or their families knew.

CHAPTER 6

WHERE THE ROAD ENDS . . .

2006–2007

INK BLOTS, INK LINES

By the fall of 2006, seven months into their deployment, the Chosin battalion soldiers in the Pech valley knew to expect attacks on nights when the moon was full. But when machine-gun bullets and RPGs started raking the skin-and-bones outpost called Combat Main around 11:30 p.m. on Friday, October 6, coming from the mountains both north and south of the Pech, the sheer volume of the fire came as a shock.[1]

Sitting by the radio in the green tent that served as his command post, Captain Rob Stanton, the senior officer at Combat Main, dropped to the ground when he saw glowing green tracer rounds start piercing the tent's canvas sides. After a few moments crouching for cover behind a hardened storage box called a Pelican, making radio calls for help, Stanton, a blond thirty-one-year-old who had been at the top of his West Point class, crawled out of the tent and made a run for his Humvee, parked next to a huge boulder on the base perimeter.[2]

Once he was outside in the moonlight, Stanton could see clusters of muzzle flashes blinking in the mountains all around like fireflies. From the number of flickering clusters, he figured there had to be a hundred or so attackers, split into many small teams and all of them far above Combat Main, where only the base's heaviest weapons—its mortars and .50-caliber heavy machine guns—could possibly reach them.[3] Showing impressive planning and fire discipline, the guerrillas hit exactly those weapons' positions first: the Humvees with their mounted machine guns, sandbagged posts where other machine guns were located, the mortar pit, the medics' aid station, and Stanton's own green command post tent, recognizable by its clutch of antennas.[4]

"They pinpointed all our key locations in the first volley," Stanton recalled. "They had us pinned down," and with the command post tent ripped to shreds and the radios inside mostly destroyed, communications with FOB Asadabad, the site of the two big howitzers that could save the day, were lost.[5] It was an infantry leader's nightmare.

Squeezed between the river and the road just short of IED Cliff (almost on the spot where a bomb had mortally wounded Lance Corporal Billy Brixey at the beginning of the year), Combat Main was named for the unit that occupied it, the Chosin battalion's Combat Company, which Stanton commanded. In the months since Operation Mountain Lion, while its sister companies fought high in the Korengal and Waygal side valleys, Combat Company had drawn the job of securing the Pech valley proper. The two-hundred-strong company and a smattering of ANA troops had occupied three small outposts along the Pech road: Firebase Florida, Firebase California, and Combat Main, the company headquarters, in between them.

Even compared with the austere conditions at the Korengal Outpost and the Ranch House, Combat Main and its two satellite firebases were haphazard affairs, just collections of tents and Humvees ringed by concertina wire and sandbagged heavy weapons positions. Their purpose was to guard a U.S.-funded road construction project that was getting under way in the Pech with the object of making it harder to plant IEDs along the route (dirt was much more fertile ground for bombs than asphalt). No one knew how long paving the Pech road would take. "Just pack your rucksack," the Chosin battalion commander, Chris Cavoli, had told Stanton when he sent him up from Jalalabad to oversee security for the road project. "I'll tell you when it's time to come back."[6] Because the job was a temporary (if open-ended) one, Cavoli had instructed Stanton to keep construction at his firebases light—no digging in or bringing out concrete barricades like those that formed the walls of larger bases.[7]

With the withering attack preventing Combat Main's defenders from effectively returning fire on the night of October 6, Stanton rued that order. The company's senior medic was shot in the throat, and a platoon sergeant in the back. Six RPGs blew up around one machine gunner. At the sandbag-ringed mortar pit, the mortar crews did what they could, but, badly exposed, one mortarman was shot through the femur. A Javelin antitank missile (the outpost's only long-range precision weapon, used like a sniper rifle firing $80,000 bullets) silenced one mountain machine-gun position,[8] but there were so many more that the mortar pit and most of the machine-gun crews were pinned down.

One soldier who wasn't pinned down was the company's forty-four-year-old senior NCO, First Sergeant John Mangels, who had been in the Humvee where he always slept when the attack kicked off. Flat-footed and color-blind, Mangels had originally been an Army personnel clerk before tricking his way into the infantry. Now on his third war, he was admiringly described by one lieutenant as "an excellent NCO, borderline batshit crazy."[9]

Climbing into his Humvee's turret, Mangels started pouring tracers into the hills to mark enemy positions for other machine gunners, disregarding the hail of incoming gunfire and flying shrapnel until he was shot in the face and knocked unconscious.

"Roger, I just woke up," Mangels replied when he came to in his turret and realized that Stanton was urgently asking for him over the radio. "I got hit in the fucking side of the head. Right now I'm bleeding all over the place. I got a hole in the top of my head right now." (After punching through his cheekbone, the bullet had traveled a short distance through the first sergeant's brain, leaving fragments as it went, and then mangled the top of his ear as it exited his head.)

Did Mangels need help? Stanton asked.

"No, you're fine, I don't think it's bleeding that much anymore.

There's just fucking blood all over my truck, that's all," the first sergeant's gravelly voice called back. After figuring out where the entry and exit wounds were and getting his bearings, he kept fighting.[10]

A little later, a lieutenant spotted Mangels taking a breather, standing in the moonlight amid the chaos smoking a cigarette. "Hey, First Sergeant, do you know you're bleeding everywhere?" the surprised lieutenant yelled when he saw the dark stains on Mangels's face and gray body armor vest.

"No shit, Lieutenant," Mangels answered. "How many casualties you got?" Then he walked off and got back to work, his nonchalance boosting the spirits of every soldier who saw him.[11]

The battle abated only when reinforcements arrived from the neighboring Florida and California firebases and started blotting out one mountainside fighting position after another with guided anti-tank missiles from their Humvees. That quieted the firing down enough for Combat Main to get its radios working better, arrange artillery fire from Asadabad, and summon a team of Apache attack helicopters from Jalalabad, the nearest airfield, which did their best to chase the insurgent attackers as they retreated higher into the mountains.[12]

The troops at Combat Main didn't know it (two years was an eternity in a war of rotations), but they'd endured and repulsed the largest attack on an American outpost in the Pech since Green Beret A-team 361's defense of FOB Blessing against two onslaughts in the fall of 2004. The attack on Combat Main followed a similar pattern to the 2004 attacks on Blessing. It involved different insurgent groups, from both the north and the south sides of the Pech. The tactics the guerrillas used were those of disciplined mountain infantrymen, with an early focus on knocking out heavy weapons, command posts, and radios. And it appeared to be a reaction to American military activity (although it was always hard to ascribe motivations to militants who rarely left behind even one wounded man for intelligence personnel to question).

In 2004, Pech-area insurgents had waited and planned for months after FOB Blessing was established and became involved in blockading the Korengal timber trade, then slammed the base. The battle of Combat Main, it was hard not to guess, was the insurgents' way of showing their displeasure not just with the establishment of new firebases in the Pech valley but with what those firebases were guarding: the beginnings of a paved road.

FOR THE TOP American general in Afghanistan, Karl Eikenberry, road building had become a mantra and a key part of his counterinsurgency strategy: where the road ended, he liked to say, the insurgency began.[13] (By the time of the little-noticed October 2006 battle of Combat Main, everyone from President Bush to Senators Joe Biden and John Kerry was repeating that line after visiting Eikenberry in Kabul.) The Pech exemplified Eikenberry's catchphrase: unless you counted the precarious tracks up the Korengal and Waygal as roads, the road literally ended where those valleys joined the Pech, and it was out of those same valleys and the heights between them that insurgents were coming to attack low-ground bases like Blessing and Combat Main.

Pacification through road building and other infrastructure projects was hardly a new strategy in post–September 11 Afghanistan. When British troops marched into Kunar in 1840, the lack of roads had made their progress painstakingly slow, and the track up the Pech had been too narrow for their artillery pieces to fit.[14] During the conquest of Kafiristan half a century later, the army of the Afghan crown had built new roads to facilitate its advance, including up the Pech;[15] some Kafir leaders professed that they would rather convert to Islam than accept the building of roads that they rightly saw as the physical manifestations of their forced incorporation into the Afghan state.[16] Starting in the late nineteenth century, Europe's great powers and eventually the United States all invested in road, rail, and bridge projects in Afghanistan. And under the pre-2001 Taliban regime, Osama bin Laden had used road-building projects to make himself useful to his Afghan hosts.[17]

Not many of the projects stood up to the country's unforgiving landscape and weather. In James Michener's 1963 novel, *Caravans,* a young American diplomat comes across a string of exquisitely constructed bridges, all standing uselessly detached from a nearby road because their German engineer failed to anticipate that Afghanistan's torrential spring floods would quickly wash out their approaches.[18] The elements were little kinder to road projects initiated by the Soviets in the 1980s or by Western development organizations during a flurry of well-intentioned spending that followed the Soviet withdrawal. By 2004, the U.S. Agency for International Development (after some short-lived resistance from the Bush administration, thinking of its 2000 election campaign promises to avoid "nation building") was spending hundreds of millions of dollars paving the same Kabul-Kandahar highway that the Soviets had paved.[19] In Kunar and Nuristan, rain and snowmelt had undone much of the widening and flattening that aid groups like CARE International had performed on the Pech road the previous decade.[20]

For American counterinsurgents like Eikenberry and Cavoli, paved roads were appealing on several levels, from the political and the strategic to the purely tactical.

In 2005, Eikenberry had used the promise of a road project to induce the former Northern Alliance commanders of the Panjshir valley north of Kabul to integrate their men and arms into the ANA. The road opened up the Panjshir's commercial opportunities and also extended the government's physical reach into the valley, a win-win situation that Eikenberry was eager to replicate in rural provinces where the government's influence was geographically limited and the Taliban-led insurgency was gaining strength. Soon, USAID and military units called provincial reconstruction teams were funding road projects in numerous eastern and southern provinces, and Eikenberry, in a twist on the ink-blot theory of counterinsurgency, was touting paved roads as "ink lines."[21]

"You look at the roads in one way, as military supply lines, and they allow you to project power," Eikenberry explained, by allowing troops to get by Humvee to places otherwise accessible only by helicopter or pickup truck. "You look at them another way, as winning over villagers and Afghan locals who say, 'A road coming my way will help us economically, so we'll help defend the road,' and you start to open up and connect things. So the theory went."[22]

CHRIS CAVOLI KNEW Eikenberry about as well as a lieutenant colonel could know a lieutenant general; he had served under "the Eik" as a lieutenant in a prestigious paratroop unit in Italy, and on September 11, when both men were at the Pentagon, the younger man called the older at home and was relieved to find out he had survived the attack. He was well aware of Eikenberry's road strategy, and he bought into it wholesale. But three echelons lower in the chain of command and much closer to the vicious fight that was developing in the Pech, Cavoli had reasons for embracing road paving that were different from the general's, more narrowly tactical. Roads of dirt and rock, he was convinced, were killing his soldiers due to their vulnerability to IEDs, and paved roads could save them.[23]

When Winston Churchill briefly commanded an infantry battalion during World War I, he compared the job to command of a warship; like a captain in a destroyer's passageways, he'd been able to walk the trenches and see most of his soldiers as many as three times a day.[24] A battalion commander in Vietnam, often with a dedicated personal helicopter, could hop from one part of his sector to another at a moment's notice. But in the resource-strapped Afghan theater in 2006, helicopter support was a rare luxury, typically available in Kunar only in dire combat emergencies, and the Chosin battalion was spread out across sixty miles (the straight-line distance between the Ranch House in Aranas and the battalion operations center at Jalalabad Airfield). So for Cavoli, the routine task that the modern Army called battlefield circulation—visiting his troops—was a logistical ordeal, one that kept him bumping along dirt roads in Humvees many hours per day most days of the week: from Jalalabad, where his headquarters staff were, to the FOBs that housed his company commanders, to the ragged firebases where a dozen lieutenants and their platoon sergeants oversaw the young NCOs in charge of the battalion's forty-odd squads and sections, and back again, over and over.

These hundreds of men (and a few female medics) were connected to Cavoli and to one another by three things: radios, helicopters, and roads, only the latter two of which could deliver essential supplies like food, batteries, and ammunition. "We had to use the roads because there was almost no aviation available to lift anybody," said the Asymmetric Warfare Group adviser T.W. Paving the roads where he and his troops drove became Cavoli's obsession. He wanted asphalt laid on the Pech road, and fast.

That task fell to the provincial reconstruction team, or PRT, at

FOB Asadabad, a mix of National Guardsmen, Army Reservists, and Navy engineers who happened to be led by a Princeton classmate of Cavoli's, Commander Ryan Scholl. Nicknamed Doc, Scholl was a standout fighter pilot who'd been inspired to join the Navy in part by *Top Gun,* and he was as surprised as anyone when he learned that his next assignment would be in Kunar rather than on an aircraft carrier.*[25]

The previous PRT, which Scholl's team replaced soon after Cavoli and the Chosin battalion deployed, had made efforts to build roads in Kunar, but without much success. An Indian-owned construction company's USAID-funded effort to widen and flatten the Kunar valley road from Jalalabad to Asadabad for eventual paving was the only active road improvement project in the province. The outgoing PRT had negotiated a contract to begin preparatory work on the Pech road in 2005, but the Kunari contractor had quickly backed out on the grounds that the Pech was too dangerous. Worse, the December 2005 death of the old PRT's first sergeant in an IED strike had devastated the small, ill-prepared team so badly that it ceased to do much but visit Kunar's governor in his compound in Asadabad. "All the knowledge about the road projects had really been in that first sergeant's brain," a Foreign Service officer who arrived at FOB Asadabad in early 2006 as the State Department's representative to the PRT was dismayed to discover.[26]

With dozens more soldiers and sailors than the outgoing team, the new Asadabad PRT was in a far better position to undertake the difficult task Cavoli was asking of it, and Doc Scholl and the engineers on his team threw themselves into the work. "Chris needed a hardball road because his guys were getting blown up," Scholl remembered, and that was rationale enough for him.[27]

What Scholl proposed after a couple of weeks' familiarization

---

* There was a method to the military's seeming madness in sending fighter pilots and nuclear submariners to run reconstruction projects in a landlocked, rural country starting in 2006. Run for two years by an Army stretched thin by two wars, the PRT program had been undermanned and sometimes staffed by Army officers passed over for battalion command or otherwise at career dead ends. The Pentagon hoped to revitalize the PRTs by putting them under the leadership of some of the Navy's and Air Force's stars and tapping into those two services' less depleted manpower resources.

with the Pech, however, was less quick-and-dirty counter-IED project and more "micro-development plan for the Pech valley," as Cavoli put it[28]—a more intensive and longer-term undertaking than the infantry battalion commander had been imagining, but one he supported wholeheartedly after it was pitched to him. The existing, dead-in-the-water Pech road improvement contract for $1.3 million would be scrapped. In its place, the PRT would pay another Afghan construction company $7.4 million not only to widen the Pech road from one lane to two and pave it with two layers of asphalt-topped gravel but to build an array of add-ons to increase the road's usefulness to residents and therefore its longevity: micro-hydroelectric generators to bring villages electricity, ten fortified checkpoints for a (largely theoretical) police force, a traffic circle in Nangalam, and bridges at key sites like the mouth of the Shuryak to connect isolated communities to their neighbors across the river. The Kabul-based construction outfit to which the PRT awarded the contract, Unique Builders, was required to hire a high percentage of the labor for all this from within a certain distance of the construction site, which, it was hoped, would cut down on theft and destruction of equipment and also suck young men away from the insurgency by giving them another way to earn cash.[29]

THE JOB OF guarding the road as it was built—its workers, their construction equipment, and their camps—fell to Rob Stanton's Combat Company, working out of Firebases California, Florida, and Combat Main.

With a low-key, relaxed leadership style, Stanton had a charisma that not only made him popular with his men but served him better with the residents of the Pech villages than what little counter-insurgency and reconstruction training the Army had given him. He certainly hadn't been trained to coach a machine-pistol-toting old mujahidin commander (now serving as a district governor) on how to write a tax code or to inspect the quality of roadwork, but those were among the things he found himself doing in between grueling patrols into the hills to seek out and fight insurgents.[30]

Some of Stanton's sergeants and lieutenants struggled with the work, frustrated by long *shuras* that didn't seem like what they'd joined the infantry to do. Others thrived. The best warrior-diplomat–aid worker in the company was Michael Harrison, a lieutenant who exuded the earnest enthusiasm of a Peace Corps volunteer. Embracing the aspects of counterinsurgency that annoyed some other soldiers—learning the names of hundreds of local people, sitting for hours with elders—Harrison earned the respect and affection of practically everyone he dealt with. Children constantly came by the flea-ridden patch of rocky ground that was Firebase California to see him and sell sodas, kebabs, and bread to his men, and before long it was common for people to point out IEDs to his patrols before they could go off—exactly the payoff that living in close quarters with a local population was supposed to yield.[31]

But the soldiers of Combat Company had to stay adept at the harsher side of counterinsurgency too, frequently defending their firebases from attacks and hiking thousands of feet up to scout and lay ambushes on the same boulder-strewn mountainsides north of the Pech where *spetsnaz* and other nimble Soviet light infantry had roamed twenty years earlier on similar missions.[32] After a Chinook insertion so high up that Apaches couldn't follow, the battalion scout platoon once spent more than a week above twelve thousand feet, climbing around the two highest peaks a dozen miles north of the river, where insurgents were reported to be using a series of high-altitude trails to cross between the Waygal and the Watapur side valleys.

Unlike in later years, when tens of thousands more American troops were on the ground in Afghanistan and concern over civilian casualties led to Byzantine approval procedures, junior leaders—often sergeants—were trusted to employ every type of munition they had or could reach by radio: mortars and guided antitank missiles, cascades of howitzer shells, and, on occasions when jets or helicopters were available, air strikes.[33] "White phosphorous is your friend," Mike Harrison wrote in a best-practices memo; TOW and Javelin antitank missiles, which could reliably hit moving human targets at long ranges, were even better. "On the rare occasion that you can observe [insurgent] forces, it is imperative that the enemy is destroyed and not allowed to escape unscathed."[34]

Those were sentences that it was hard to imagine the smiling alliance builder and *shura* holder so beloved by the Pech's children uttering, but there wasn't a contradiction. These were the two sides of counterinsurgency, the one impossible without the other.

THE SUMMER MONTHS dragged into fall like this, with the soldiers of Combat Company patrolling the Pech's towns and fighting off attacks on their outposts while they watched the road project progress by inches and feet. Before any gravel or pavement could be laid, the existing road had to be widened and flattened, and various landownership disputes worked out. At a July 30 meeting in Asadabad, Unique Builders promised that the gravel for the first layer would be laid within a week, but a week later the gravel laying still hadn't started. "It was always going to be next week, or the week after," one officer remembered.[35]

By the time cold weather put construction on hold, the company had put only preliminary layers of rock-studded tar on the three short stretches of road most vulnerable to IEDs—fulfilling the narrowest purpose of the road project but falling well short of the lofty development goals for which the PRT had earmarked millions of dollars.[36] In the meantime, the men of Combat Company remained vulnerable in their outposts, which Cavoli insisted not be built up into forts that would present a psychological barrier between them and the people of the Pech.

Only the savage October 6 battle of Combat Main—in which First Sergeant Mangels heroically kept fighting with bullet fragments in his brain—persuaded the battalion commander to soften his line and allow Stanton to build more fortifications at his outposts. It was the same quick, practical evolution that the only Soviet outpost to last more than a few weeks in the Pech, in nearby Bar Kanday, had undergone in the summer of 1982: the Soviet company commander and his soldiers had started out living in tents, but as the daily mortar and machine-gun attacks from the mountains intensified, they dug in until they were living almost completely underground.[37]

Even after the command post tent at Combat Main gave way to a sandbagged bunker and Hesco barriers replaced concertina wire on the perimeter, the Pech outposts remained Spartan affairs, nothing like the mazes of concrete that typified equivalent bases in Iraq.

A few weeks after the Combat Main battle, Mick Nicholson visited Firebase Florida with the brigade's senior NCO, Command Sergeant Major James Redmore. The tallest Hescos at the outpost were just four feet high, meaning that the soldiers there slept in quarters that were far dirtier and more cramped than berths on a submarine, without room to stand up, almost like animal dens.

Redmore was a no-nonsense former Delta Force operator. When he crawled out of one of these "hobbit hole" bunkers, he was in tears. "Sir, I can't believe you guys are living like this," Stanton remembered him saying.

"Well, they stop bullets, Sergeant Major," Stanton replied.[38]

"APPROPRIATE, ATTAINABLE, AND CONGRUENT WITH OUR INTERESTS"

While one of the Chosin battalion's companies fought for the Pech road under Rob Stanton, two others manned the more remote and even more vulnerable new bases in two of the Pech's side valleys, the Korengal and Waygal.

Overseeing the latter effort was Doug Sloan, Bravo Company's tall, gregarious, mustached commander. Newly promoted to major in a quick ceremony in Aranas, Sloan split his time between FOB Blessing and his two tiny bases high in the Waygal, the fishbowl mortar firebase at Bella and the Ranch House outpost in Aranas, perched so high on the mountain that helicopters flew *up* to get to it.[39]

In the operation Sloan was running in the Waygal, the two threads of American operations in eastern Afghanistan—counterinsurgency and counterterrorism—intersected. The hope of collecting better intelligence on terrorist leaders and other militants was what had motivated Cavoli to send Sloan up to Aranas to build the Ranch House. There were early indications that that move was paying off: of the Chosin battalion's three main enemy targets, the two of greatest interest to the counterterrorism operatives at JSOC and the CIA, Abu Ikhlas al-Masri and Ahmad Shah, both seemed to have moved north after Operation Mountain Lion pushed them out of the Korengal. Persistent tips and satellite phone intercepts placed Ahmad

Shah in the mountains north of Aranas, and Cavoli had high hopes that the troops at the Ranch House would be able to pinpoint him for an air or artillery strike or else kill him in combat.

The Waygal valley's other draw was as the gateway to a province that Cavoli and Nicholson believed had the essential ingredient for successful counterinsurgency and development: an energetic, aggressive representative of the central government in the person of its governor, an Afghan American in his late forties named Tamim Nuristani.

Tamim was a controversial figure, adept at charming those whose help he wanted; won over by his alluringly lofty goals for his ancestral province and the confidence with which he pitched them, Cavoli described the governor as "regal" and "urbane."[40] Although he had participated in the jihad in Kunar and Nuristan, Tamim had grown up in Kabul and lived most of his adult life as an expatriate in India, Germany, and the United States, where at one point he owned several pizza franchises in Sacramento. He was from a prominent Nuristani family, however, a fact he made the most of. Haji Ghafor, the old mujahidin commander the Rangers had hunted during Winter Strike, was a cousin, and Tamim had spent many days escorting CIA officers to remote parts of the province and trying to explain various local feuds to them. After the fall of the Taliban, he had moved back to Kabul and ingratiated himself with President Hamid Karzai by campaigning for him in Nuristan. In 2005, Karzai had rewarded him with Nuristan's governorship.[41]

Governors, in the centralized post-2001 Afghan system, were really just representatives of the central government. Lacking the ability to collect taxes, provincial governments were financially reliant on Kabul and on outside aid. No Afghan governor confronted more acute difficulties in governing than Tamim. Responsible for a mountainous expanse with practically no roads, it was nearly impossible for him even to get around his province, and his provincial center, the hamlet of Pashki in the Parun valley by one of the headwaters of the Pech, was so remote that one U.S. diplomat wrote in 2005 that "obvious geographic realities" would probably prevent it from ever functioning as a "normal provincial capital."[42]

Not only did Tamim reject that assessment, he painted a picture for anyone who would listen of a not-too-distant future Parun that was an economically prosperous tourist magnet—a kind of out-doorsman's paradise whose picturesque forests and waterfalls would draw wealthy adventurers, mountaineers, skiers, hunters, and the like from the Persian Gulf, South Asia, and even the West. To many people, this sounded fantastical, and it turned out to be. But the idea was inspired by Nuristan's history. Afghanistan's kings had long maintained lodges in Nuristan to hunt the area's markhor wild goats, and after the province was opened up to foreign hunters in the 1960s, proposals on how to turn Nuristan into a tourist destination persisted until Afghanistan descended into civil war.[43]

From the day he took office in 2005, Tamim promised he could revive these plans and deliver prosperity to the country's least hospitable province—just as soon as foreign donors connected the Parun and other Nuristani valleys to the outside world with modern roads.

Five American officers who had the resources to help were the road-building general Eikenberry and his subordinates Nicholson, Cavoli, Scholl, and Sloan. Eikenberry had already earmarked funds for an eventual multiyear, multimillion-dollar Nuristan road expansion program when Cavoli escorted the general up to the Parun valley for a visit in the spring of 2006, just after Mountain Lion. Peering up at the same pristine forests and jagged peaks that Rangers had seen covered in snow earlier in the war and enjoying the salty goat cheese and other food his hosts offered, Cavoli couldn't help but think of the little mountain towns in northern Italy where his family was from and where he'd summered as a child. He was fascinated.[44]

Over the summer, contracts started to be awarded to Afghan construction companies. Cavoli huddled with Tamim for two days at Blessing in the fall, talking future plans and bonding in the base's dining hall over steak, lobster, and discussions of American football and basketball that left the American colonel charmed. There were foreign jihadis hiding out in Nuristan's valleys, the governor claimed: Arabs, even Chechens, all on the payroll of the ISI, Pakistan's intelligence service. (Tamim probably understood that Chechens—real, imagined, or misidentified—were the white whales of the military targeting world and that the prospect of hunting them would be hard for American commanders and intelligence officers to resist.) He quoted Eikenberry's axiom to Cavoli, telling the colonel,

"Where roads go, the enemy leaves," and he promised to name the completed road connecting the Parun valley to the Pech "Eikenberry Road."

"It is hard to overstate Tamim's enthusiasm for roads," Cavoli wrote after the visit in a report to his superiors. "Gov Nuristani is our best bet for Nuristan," he concluded optimistically. "His vision for Nuristan is appropriate, attainable, and congruent with our interests."[45]

TAMIM WANTED THE Americans to focus their efforts on the Parun.[46] But the counterterrorism angle that had drawn the Chosin battalion to Aranas, along with the Bella and Ranch House outposts' need for a reliable ground resupply route, dictated that the Waygal be the first step in the Nuristan road-building program. With winter would come weather that kept helicopters away from Doug Sloan's little bases for weeks at a time, which made improving the Waygal road to the point where Humvees could traverse it a priority. As insurgents began to harass the Ranch House with occasional attacks in the fall, Doc Scholl's PRT signed a $300,000 contract with a Waygali construction business to widen and level the road, the first steps toward the eventual paving that would hinder IED emplacement. At the same time, Cavoli dispatched an engineer platoon to install a pair of Humvee-capable bridges in Want, the district seat halfway up the valley.

As the engineers got to work on the bridges, Want (marked on American maps as "Wanat") was warm and receptive. No one was friendlier than the town's most prominent resident, a hook-nosed former mujahidin commander named Haji Juma Gul, who owned Want's biggest building, its two-story hotel. American involvement in Want would eventually bring Juma Gul's life to an untimely and mysterious end, but in 2006 he couldn't have been happier to see Americans in town—let alone American development aid—and he fed the Army engineers a hot breakfast several times a week. As a gesture of thanks, the engineer platoon leader gave Juma Gul a bottle of maple syrup, which the old man took to carrying around town, sampling the syrup with his finger as he went about his business. Over tea, he explained his affection for America: he had a son

living in the United States, and he had first met an American decades earlier, when he helped facilitate the travels in the Waygal of
an anthropologist and archaeologist named Louis Dupree. When
the engineers finished their work, Juma Gul told the departing platoon leader he looked forward to working with more Americans
and offered a gift of his own: a wooden oil pot carved with the images of snakes, goats, and other animals, either a relic of the Waygal's
pre-Islamic past or a more recent piece meant to evoke it.[47]

Sloan, meanwhile, ranged the length of the valley, leading patrols
to secure the emerging road project and to visit and get to know as
many Waygali villages as possible. Beloved by his men for his irrepressible latrine humor and devil-may-care attitude (a former enlisted soldier, he was nearing the twenty-year retirement mark and
didn't expect to stay in the Army much longer), Sloan's outgoing
confidence made an impression on the Waygalis he dealt with too.
"He was the man. He was a great leader, and he did everything he
wanted," recalled Sloan's interpreter, a tall, Kabul-raised Nuristani
with a gentle manner who would go on to interpret for three more
American company commanders in the area and would later act as
my interpreter on a Pech visit. "The people didn't complain about
him. He knew how to talk to an Afghan, how to satisfy him. When
he detained someone, he knew how to explain it well. People would
whisper afterward, 'Major Sloan was right.'"[48]

But for all the enthusiasm for the road and the American presence that Bravo Company and the engineers heard in *shuras,* there
were other, conservative factions in the Waygal who were biding
their time—the militants and militant sympathizers, like the Aransi
cleric turned regional Taliban commander Mawlawi Monibullah,
who had publicly opposed the establishment of the Ranch House
outpost and had staged the deadly ambush on an American patrol in
August.

THE OPPONENTS OF the road and the American presence killed
Doug Sloan on Halloween.

On the night of October 30 (three years to the day after the first
American bombs had fallen in the Waygal, destroying a family and
kicking off U.S. involvement there), Bravo Company camped out-

side Want at the end of a tough mountain patrol. The engineers working on the bridges grilled burgers and steaks for the weary infantrymen. Scheduled to hand over command of his company to a younger officer in just a couple of days, Sloan was in fine form, joking and farting theatrically for his soldiers' entertainment.[49] The next morning he and his men climbed into Humvees and headed north for Bella, driving along a road that was just wide enough now to accommodate the boxy armored trucks but still a long way from being paved.

Sloan and two other soldiers were in the lead truck. A mile south of Bella, a bomb went off beneath it, killing all three of them. When the counter-IED adviser T.W. reached the scene a few hours later to do the blast analysis, the vehicle was still burning and cooking off ammunition. Putting out the fire, sanitizing the site, and dragging the twisted shards of metal up to Bella by pickup truck and by hand took days.[50]

At Bella in the week that followed, T.W. was surprised and touched by the stream of visitors, mostly village elders, who came to the outpost to offer their condolences, sometimes traveling miles to do so.

"Some of the sergeants were saying they were just coming down to recon the base, but I didn't think so," T.W. said. "People were bringing gifts that they wanted given to his family. He had quite a following up there."[51] But the attack was a sharp reminder of many Waygalis' behind-the-scenes opposition to the coming of the Americans and their road.[52]

IT WASN'T LONG after Sloan's death that heavy snow began to blanket the Waygal, halting work on the road project well short of where Cavoli and Sloan had hoped. Firebase Bella and the Ranch House remained "air-centric," or mainly reliant for resupply on scarce military helicopters (and some rickety old Russian-made birds from a Kabul company called Supreme Air) that were at the mercy of the weather and commitments elsewhere in the east.

The coming of winter weather also hampered the counterterrorism and intelligence-collection missions that had brought Sloan to the Waygal, both by limiting the reach of the Bravo Company patrols on the ground and by interfering with finicky surveillance platforms like Predator drones.

True to Cavoli's and Nicholson's theory that increased presence would lead to increased human intelligence, the Bella and Ranch House outposts had produced some new sources for intelligence personnel on the ground, and partnership with Tamim Nuristani yielded access to the governor's own network of informants. Cross-referencing of sources' tips with signals intelligence intercepts brought the Chosin battalion tantalizingly close to killing Ahmad Shah, their biggest target besides the elusive Abu Ikhlas, more than once. In September, hits on Ahmad Shah's phone had just begun to pop up in the Parun valley over the mountains from the Waygal when a panicky Tamim called Cavoli up and confirmed it: Ahmad Shah and dozens of his fighters, Tamim said, were driving around the valley in stolen police pickups, setting up roadblocks and menacing the precarious government enclave there. Similar scenarios played out every few weeks that fall as Ahmad Shah appeared in one spot or another in the mountains north of the two Waygal outposts.

The devil was in finding a way to act on the intelligence. When Ahmad Shah's cell phone was tracked to Amshuz—a standoffish village barely two miles from Bella that was marked as "Amesozeh" on American maps and alternately known to locals by the Waygali name Ameshdesh—it looked on a map as if the man responsible for the worst loss of American life in the Afghan war were right under Bravo Company's nose. But Amshuz was high on a mountainside, protected by cliffs, and impossible to sneak up on. "In that kind of terrain," said Doug Sloan's replacement, "if they just go to the next valley over, they might as well be on a different planet."[53] The arrival of foot upon foot of snow before Christmas made the troops at Bella and the Ranch House all but static; they had access to "over-whites" that allowed them to blend into the snow (rarely, if ever, used in a combat zone since Korea), but no snowshoes or skis or the training to patrol in them.

Nor was the JSOC task force at Bagram likely to risk a helicopter raid force of SEALs or Rangers for anything but the hardest of intelligence, even when the target was Ahmad Shah. Joe Ryan, the Ranger major who had stayed at Tamim Nuristani's and Haji Ghafor's family fortress in the Kantiwa valley during Winter Strike, was back in Afghanistan as the task force operations officer that winter. "We weren't against going up there, but somebody had to show us the money," he remembered.[54]

So the weapons of choice became artillery (which could reach only so far up the valley), a long-range missile launcher called a HIMARS (a JSOC asset, for whose tall firing arc the sky had to be cleared of commercial airliners), and, when available, drones (which were at the mercy of the weather).

Once, when Ahmad Shah was crossing a mountain pass into artillery range, Cavoli and Nicholson thought they had the militant dead to rights. Then division headquarters denied the artillery fire mission in favor of a more precise Predator strike, only for winter clouds to momentarily obscure the Predator's view, interrupting the continuous visual lock on a target that the rules of engagement required to launch a Hellfire missile.

"We had a shot at him and we blew it," said Nicholson. "Up there, with the mountains and the weather, the clouds would roll in and the Predator couldn't see through the clouds and you'd lose him and then you'd have to start all over."[55] Nevertheless, the two colonels believed that just by being at Bella and the Ranch House, their men were denying an important chunk of ground—albeit a small one—to enemy leaders.

THE SECURITY BUBBLE

Chris Cavoli was at Jalalabad Airfield when the bad news came. It was late January 2007; the Chosin battalion had been in Afghanistan for nearly eleven months, and the end was in sight. Fresh commanders from the 82nd Airborne had already arrived at the airfield and were planning out the first moves they would make once they took over from the tired 10th Mountain troops.

Then the division commander called Nicholson, who called Cavoli, who in turn called his company commanders and then assembled his headquarters troops, climbed up on a John Deere tractor, and told them that the end wasn't in sight anymore. The whole brigade's deployment had been extended from twelve months to sixteen. They would be in Afghanistan for the start of another fighting season.[56]

Ten days earlier, Secretary of Defense Robert Gates had made his first visit to Afghanistan since President Bush had named him to succeed Donald Rumsfeld. From the day he was sworn in, Gates's focus, like the Army's and the president's, was Iraq, but he was immediately confronted with grim reports from the "forgotten theater" too. Karl Eikenberry, nearing the end of his tour as the top commander in Kabul, and 10th Mountain Division leaders at Bagram were all but begging for more troops to beat back the growing Taliban-led insurgency. What Eikenberry and 10th Mountain wanted—a second U.S. Army infantry brigade to supplement Nicholson's 3rd Brigade[57]—was pocket change compared with the thirty-thousand-troop surge the White House and Pentagon were about to order to Iraq. As the Army juggled units to meet the demands of two wars, however, no fresh brigade was immediately available for Afghanistan. To achieve what Bush called the "silent surge" there, 3rd Brigade would have to stay in the field four extra months.[58]

Tours had occasionally been extended before in the war on terror, but that was cold comfort. "The extension hit the brigade like a kick in the balls," said T.W. (who, as a contractor, had been in and out of the country on short stints since the 10th Mountain troops deployed). "Morale pretty much went in the drink at that point."[59]

Nowhere was the extension a harder pill to swallow than in the Korengal, where Cavoli's unhappy Attack Company had already spent eight months in combat more punishing and persistent than almost anything their comrades in Bravo and Combat Companies saw. One platoon leader remembered keeping the news to himself for as many minutes as he could bear. His soldiers were already skinny and dirty, their uniforms tattered, a sunken look on many of their faces, and the knowledge that they would soon be home was a big part of what was keeping them going. The company had lost eight soldiers already, and if they were going to be in the Korengal when the weather started warming up again, it seemed inevitable that more would join them.[60]

. . .

WHEN HE HAD taken over at the Korengal Outpost in late May 2006, Attack Company's commander, Captain Jim McKnight, had had little idea of the ordeal that lay ahead of him and his men. Compact at five feet five and younger than his fellow company commanders at twenty-eight, the dark-haired McKnight was a devout Christian who almost never swore and had entered the Army after graduating from the conservative Virginia college Washington and Lee. Impressed by his record in the Ranger Regiment—where he had parachuted into western Iraq during the 2003 invasion—Cavoli put McKnight in charge of Attack Company shortly before the deployment. He did not know, at the time, how miserable a task that company in particular would draw.

Nowhere in the Korengal was safe. Where the Pech valley floor outposts and the Ranch House came under occasional sustained attack, the KOP was machine-gunned, rocketed, mortared, and harassed with rifle fire almost every day, sometimes for several hours. The firefights McKnight and his men faced as they patrolled the Korengal were as relentless as the summer heat, some weeks numbering as many as thirty. Soldiers were sprayed with RPG shrapnel and shot, starting with Russ Durgin, the sniper sergeant killed on a night mission in June.

Others tumbled down mountains, including McKnight, who plummeted from a trail to the valley floor early in the summer, suffering two broken ribs, a chipped spine, and a concussion. McKnight was already subject to his troops' suspicion and dislike because of the emotional distance he maintained from them and his strict enforcement of rules that other commanders tended to ignore, like bans on pets and pornography. His several-week absence for medical treatment did not help. Never popular the way Stanton and Sloan were, he became the object of his men's contempt, blamed for everything that went wrong in the Korengal.[61]

When Attack Company listened in on insurgent walkie-talkie chatter, it mostly wasn't Pashto (let alone Arabic), but rather Korengali, a language for which the KOP didn't have an interpreter until late in the summer. That was suggestive, but what convinced McKnight of the deeply native character of the Korengal insurgency beyond any doubt was an incident in early August. After a firefight south of the KOP, a group of Attack Company soldiers followed a blood trail to find a rare wounded insurgent. On the wounded guerrilla's person was a handwritten record of Taliban payments, which showed that practically every village and every family in the southern Korengal had members on the Taliban payroll.

By the time McKnight and his officers fully understood that Korengalis were driving the insurgency in the valley, not outsiders as they had assumed going in and as the elders always claimed, Attack Company's situation was becoming untenable. McKnight had come in expecting the KOP to get its supplies of ammunition, fuel, and water by helicopter, but with the even more remote Ranch House outpost relying on the same method, helicopter resupply flights slowed to a trickle. To stay supplied, Attack Company had to start patrolling the narrow dirt road up from the Pech, the only ground route to the KOP.[62]

Described by one soldier as "stacked rocks on the wall of a canyon, covered in moon dust,"[63] the Korengal road was a perfect venue for snipers and IED emplacers. On August 17, one of McKnight's three platoons was inching along the road in Humvees when an insurgent firing from the rocks above managed to hit two soldiers *inside* their truck, one of them fatally. Two days later, after a brief rest outside the valley, the same platoon was headed back into the Korengal with some new medics for the company when a bomb went off under another of its Humvees. Three soldiers died, including a twenty-one-year-old female medic who had sometimes sung at other soldiers' memorial ceremonies. The platoon leader, whose first wedding anniversary it was, survived with burns over nearly half of his body.

Cavoli's response to the four deaths on the road was to lock the Korengal down. When the district governor in Nangalam, a polished bureaucrat named Mohammad Rahman Danish, declared a blockade on the valley, barring the entry of basic goods like sugar, flour, and cooking oil, Cavoli gave his edict teeth, complementing the contingent of police in Kandigal with a major battalion operation.

The mission was formally dubbed Big North Wind, but one Chosin officer half jokingly started all his planning session notes with the heading "FUCK THE KORENGAL (FTK)."[64] The operation's aim was to isolate and punish the villages of the southern

Korengal where most of the enemy fighters seemed to be coming from and simultaneously reward the smaller Pashtun community near the valley's mouth, showing both groups the material benefits of cooperating with the U.S. military. At the same time, the plan went, Army engineers would widen and flatten the road so that it could support five-ton cargo trucks and continue their work installing a prefabricated Bailey bridge across the Pech at the ford site at the Korengal's mouth, opening a reliable ground supply route to the KOP.[65]

AS OPERATION Big North Wind began, McKnight's troops scoured the Korengal, marching deep into the valley's south on exhausting long-distance foot patrols. Some platoons headed to villages that Americans hadn't visited since Mountain Lion in the spring. On one such mission up on the Sawtalo Sar, a squad made two rare sightings: a pair of desert-camouflage-clad insurgents who seemed not to have expected Americans to venture up that far; and, to the surprise of the patrol's point man, a trio of huge black wildcats sniffing around the insurgents' hastily abandoned campfire.[66] Atop the Abbas Ghar and the Sawtalo Sar, meanwhile, other troops kept watch through new thermal sights that allowed them to pick out the heat signatures of human bodies. Whenever the soldiers manning the air-conditioner-sized thermal sensor units spotted the glowing blobs of guerrillas trying to sneak up on Attack Company in the valley below, they would call for shake-and-bake fire missions from the howitzers at Asadabad and Blessing. As the operation intensified, the big guns fired so often into the Korengal that stocks of high-explosive and white phosphorous shells back at Bagram ran low.[67]

Coming at the end of a dry summer, the artillery barrage had an unintended effect: the bright-burning white phosphorous fragments sparked blazing fires in the bands of conifer forest that surrounded the Korengal.[68] Viewed from inside the valley, the effect produced by the fires and blankets of smoky haze was spooky, especially through night vision, like a trippy scene from *Apocalypse Now,* as one lieutenant put it.[69] From above, the pillar of smoke on the horizon helped guide fighter pilots in from as far away as Jalalabad.[70]

The destruction the artillery wrought in the forests was un-planned, but Cavoli welcomed it: the point of Big North Wind and the accompanying Afghan government blockade was to apply eco-nomic pressure to the Korengal. While his men were patrolling the hills and calling in cascades of ordnance, the battalion commander had made the harrowing drive up the Korengal road himself and temporarily set up shop at the KOP, intending to deliver a pointed message to the valley's elders in a series of *shuras* there. The cedars that were burning were the source of the wealth not only of Haji Matin, the timber baron running the Korengal insurgency, but of many of the elders with whom Cavoli would be trying to negoti-ate.[71]

Two elders who acted as the Korengal's liaisons to the American intruders, Haji Shamshir Khan and his relative Haji Zalwar Khan, kicked the first *shura* off, delivering a well-worn speech whose thrust was that Pakistanis and Arabs, not Korengalis, were responsible for the fighting. Cavoli didn't want to hear it. "I hear you telling a lot of stories about how the bad guys are coming in and oppressing you," the colonel responded when it was his turn to speak. "Well, I'm going to tell you a story. It's a story about a long, cold, hungry winter," without sugar or cooking oil.[72] The road project his bat-talion was undertaking, he continued, would go only as far as the KOP. The villages in the north of the valley would benefit from it, but the ones in the south would be shut out because of their refusal to cooperate.

A month into Big North Wind, Cavoli and his officers were starting to think it was working. The Bailey bridge was complete and the ground supply route to the KOP open, and one of McKnight's platoons had taken over a *bandeh* overlooking the road—dubbing it Firebase Reno*—to guard against IEDs and ambushes. In the command post at the KOP, the lone Korengali-speaking inter-preter who listened in on the valley's walkie-talkie traffic reported what Cavoli hoped were signs of a building fissure between the wealthy elders who called the shots in the Korengal and the fighters and their families who bore the brunt of the fighting and the block-

---

* Over the winter, this outpost would be relocated farther up the western slope of the Abbas Ghar and renamed Firebase Vegas.

ade. Insurgent radiomen discussed the forest fires in agitated tones, clearly worried to see the precious resource they were fighting to protect burning away.[73] Sometimes, angry wives could be heard berating their insurgent husbands in the hills over the lack of cooking oil in the villages.[74]

But then came Ramadan, the Islamic fast month, and over American objections the Pech district governor, Rahman, lifted the blockade out of religious respect.

The reprieve was supposed to be temporary, but it gave Haji Matin and his associates an opening for a tactic that Kunaris had been using for decades when they were unhappy with government appointees: a smear campaign. Using business contacts to bring the allegations to the attention of politicians in Kabul, the Korengal *shura* accused Rahman of taking bribes (which, like most officials of his station, he was, according to interpreters who knew him[75]), benefiting from the illegal lumber trade (an ironic accusation), even selling weapons to insurgents. The point wasn't for the accusations to stick, just to circulate enough complaints to get Rahman suspended or removed from office.[76]

It worked. Under the black cloud of an official investigation, Rahman lacked the authority to restart the blockade when Ramadan ended; the legs were pulled out from under Big North Wind, and the possible social fissure in the valley that Cavoli was hoping the operation would cause was averted.[77] The fighting remained lethal—a beloved platoon medic and two other soldiers, one American and one Afghan, were killed in early October—but Attack Company and the Korengali insurgents had reached a kind of stalemate.

OUTFOXED BY THE Korengali elders, Cavoli adjusted how the valley fit into his concept of what the Chosin battalion was doing in the Pech.

Instead of ink blots or ink lines, the phrase Cavoli had come up with to describe his battalion's war was the "security bubble." The inside of the bubble included the Pech proper, where road building and development were taking place under the protection of Combat Company, and the first couple of miles inside the Korengal, where cooperative villages were being rewarded. The bubble's edge was where the inevitable fighting happened as the enemy pushed back, the violent terrain beyond the KOP where Attack Company was fighting for its life. There, Cavoli told McKnight, his job was just to fight—to keep the Korengali insurgents busy far from the interior of the bubble.[78]

Attack Company, under this framework, was a combat sponge, soaking up the Korengali insurgents' time, energy, and supplies. This was not an easy mission for soldiers to wrap their minds around, let alone embrace, given the severe conditions they were enduring. One seasoned platoon sergeant acquired a steady twitching in his arms, a symptom of combat stress. Overall, the company developed a tense, angry culture where the general dislike for McKnight among enlisted soldiers congealed into something more like hatred.[79]

McKnight took solace in his religion. "Your personal faith will be tried over and over," he wrote that winter in a report on lessons learned from the deployment. He addressed the subject of morale in prolonged combat directly: "When an uncomfortable soldier tells you that his morale is low, it shows you what an unseasoned baby he is. You'll really know what morale is when your men are too afraid to go back outside the wire. At that point, morale is impacting mission." It was important, he added, to give one's soldiers "ample opportunity before they deploy to figure out where they're going if they die."[80]

When the extension hit in January 2007, the troops about whom Cavoli worried most were McKnight's (and McKnight himself). Attack Company was worn down, and it seemed very possible that the right thing to do was swap it out with another company that hadn't lost so many men. By radio, Cavoli asked McKnight what he thought.

The captain said he needed a day to think about it and talk it over with some of his soldiers. The next day McKnight recommended to Cavoli that the company stay so that veterans, not a new unit with a steep learning curve, would be in the valley when the weather and the fighting heated up. That, he and his men knew—even if they didn't like it—would save lives. It was one tough call that McKnight didn't recall hearing many complaints about.[81]

Attack Company was on its thirteenth deployed month when, at the end of March 2007, McKnight sent his troops out to build yet another firebase (the battalion's ninth, and the third in the Korengal) as part of a battalion-wide spring push. Occupying a house at the top of a village a kilometer south of the KOP, two dozen soldiers used logs and sandbags to fortify the structure into a compact bunker, which they called Firebase Phoenix. On the fourth evening the platoon spent in the house, insurgents slammed them, firing from a flat hilltop right above the new base and from the next village up, Aliabad (where Shamshir Khan and Zalwar Khan were from). A shell from a recoilless rifle punched through a Hesco barrier and exploded by a machine-gun position, wounding three soldiers and killing a machine gunner named Chris Wilson.[82]

After the fight, the platoon rotated back to the KOP for a brief rest and some hot food. Cavoli visited them there; one soldier was so upset he couldn't eat, just shake silently. When he saw the colonel, McKnight started weeping, and then so did Cavoli. Why, the colonel wondered aloud to his subordinate, did this loss hurt so much, when the battalion had already lost so many others?

Cavoli knew why, really; it was because Wilson was the first soldier killed after the extension and after he had made the call to keep Attack Company in the Korengal four more long months. Cavoli teared up recalling it. "I will always live with the question, 'Should I have left that company, and Jim, there that long?'" he told me at his home in Virginia years afterward, when he was a brigadier general working at the Pentagon. "I did it because those guys were fucking experts in that place. If I'd rotated another company in there, I probably would have saved some psychological scars, but there'd be more dead guys on our side because of it."[83]

AS THE CHOSIN battalion's long deployment drew to an end and Doc Scholl's PRT handed its road projects off to a new Navy-led team, much had changed in the Pech.

The Pech valley road was two lanes wide all the way out to FOB Blessing (which itself had expanded to accommodate Cavoli's battalion headquarters), and the whole distance was paved either with tar-and-rock chip seal or, closer to Asadabad, with actual asphalt, which the construction company had started laying down in the spring.[84] Local businessmen had built a pair of gas stations along the route, and travel time from one end to the other was down from five hours to two and a half. Three newly constructed bridges spanned the Pech. In Nangalam, a four-story hotel—practically a skyscraper by Kunar standards—was rising by the freshly paved and lit traffic circle. "The bottom line is that, in Kunar, [U.S. forces and the Afghan government] have sharply reduced insurgent activity over the past year," a cable from the PRT's State Department representative noted sunnily. "The Kunari people generally support the [government], and except for the Korengal valley there are no areas under enemy control. Our presence and engagement have paid off, so far."[85]

The two side-valley road projects were still in their infancy, meanwhile. Local workers had widened the Waygal road as far as Want to a width of five meters—a comfortable size for Humvees—and had started work as far as Bella, but no paving had occurred either there or on the loose-dirt Korengal road, parts of which were still just two and a half meters wide, narrower than a Humvee itself.[86]

How much the Chosin battalion's counterinsurgency project in Kunar and Nuristan had contributed to the secret counterterrorism role that had helped drive it was hard to say. With only a small number of case officers in Afghanistan, the CIA had ultimately never given much support to the expansion it had encouraged Nicholson and 10th Mountain Division headquarters to undertake. No CIA personnel had relocated to the new outposts in the Pech and its side valleys.

"Whenever we'd visit, it was a one-and-done sort of thing. We never stayed long enough to develop assets. We weren't resourced that way," said Ron Moeller, the agency's liaison to 10th Mountain. "If there wasn't any al-Qaida around, we were gone. So our guys never actually established collection teams up there. The efforts didn't wind up being mutually supporting." Instead, besides a handful of the Army's own tactical-level intelligence collectors, "it was basically a bunch of infantry guys trying to play intel collector" at the new bases.[87] The CIA itself had built one new base in Kunar, called Falcon Base, and was in the process of constructing a smaller listening post, but both were along the border, where they could have been built without the military's expansion into the Pech and Nuristan. And the agency was no closer to locating bin Laden or Zawahiri—the former of whom had actually moved on from the border region Kunar abutted to deep isolation in Abbottabad, 120 miles inside Pakistan.

The new Pech outposts' presence did seem to have pushed some militants away. Ahmad Shah had moved on from the Waygal by mid-2007, relocating across the border, where he was out of the military's reach, for example.* That deterrent effect would last only as long as the outposts themselves did, however—if that long—and ANA and Afghan police forces were a long way from being able to take any of them over.

The price had been high.

For some Chosin battalion veterans, the sixteen-month deployment that finally ended in June 2007 was a high point in life—an unrepeatable experience that pushed them to find and beat other challenges, a leadership school like few others. Several of Cavoli's lieutenants went on to the Ranger Regiment, Green Berets, and other elite units, while others left the Army for high-prestige jobs and graduate schools. Combat Company's commander, Rob Stanton, chose to stay in the Army and the infantry; so did his star soldier-peacemaker, Mike Harrison. Cavoli took pride in that.

But there was "another version" too, Cavoli acknowledged: "It crushes people. There's a lot of human debris left behind from a deployment like that."[88]

Post-combat stress afflicted the toughest of the tough. "I was forty-four years old, and Kunar made me a man," said John Mangels, the first sergeant who was the hero of the October 6 battle of Combat Main and finished the deployment after medical treatment despite the bullet fragment still lodged in his brain. "But I'm not ashamed to say it took me until 2010 to deal with the stupid shit that gets in your head. When you come back, your switch doesn't turn

---

* Ahmad Shah vanished from the annals of America's war in the Pech in 2007 as suddenly as he had appeared in 2003, popping back up in Bajaur. His death there in April 2008 was publicly reported as the result of a shoot-out with Pakistani security forces, but some U.S. military personnel suspected it had something to do with a spurt of cross-border activity by the CIA's Kunari surrogates around that time.

off."[89] Attack Company was "in tatters" when Jim McKnight passed the flag to Mike Harrison, its ranks plagued by discipline problems like drunk driving and drug abuse that the other Chosin companies also saw but at less alarming levels.[90] One lieutenant would dream of the Korengal almost every night for four years, even when he was deployed with the Rangers to other tough areas of Afghanistan and Iraq.[91] Cavoli would flash back to the Pech at unexpected times. Once, when he was in the chair of a prosthodontist who was trying to mitigate the damage done by months of grinding his teeth in Kunar, the smell of the drill burning through enamel reminded Cavoli so vividly of the odor of shake-and-bake artillery missions that he began to weep and had to leave.[92]

While he was in command in Afghanistan, the human cost was hard for the laser-focused Cavoli to see—not least the toll the deployment and especially the extension took on spouses, parents, and children at home, including his own.

The realization that the Pech hadn't left him, his family, or seven hundred other families kicked the colonel the same June night that he got back to Fort Drum. After Cavoli and his wife had put their two young sons to bed, the phone rang. It was Cavoli's brother, and the colonel jumped out of bed to talk to him.

Cavoli's son, age eight, had gotten up when he heard the phone ring too and bumped into his father in the hall.

The younger Cavoli had been around for a lot of late-night phone calls over the past sixteen months as his mother was alerted to fresh casualties downrange. He knew what they usually meant.

"Is anybody dead?" he asked.[93]

CHAPTER 7

ROCK AVALANCHE

2007

"IF IT IS IMPOSSIBLE, WE WILL DO IT"

The ceremony ending the Chosin battalion's sixteen long months in the Pech took place on a sunny morning in June 2007, on the grounds of a newly enlarged FOB Blessing, sprawling nearly to the Pech River, where brick-and-mortar buildings now outnumbered tents and plywood shacks.

In a tree-lined courtyard on Blessing's east side, a sand-colored podium faced three rows of black folding chairs. American commanders and sergeants major sat in the front row, Afghan officials and interpreters in the rear two rows. Behind them stood a smattering of headquarters soldiers: the outgoing Chosin troops in fatigues that had faded to brown, and their replacements, fresh from the U.S. Army base in Vicenza, Italy, in crisp gray-green ones. The assembled soldiers and civilians listened to brief speeches, and Chris Cavoli posed for pictures with the Afghan officials he had befriended during his time in Kunar and would never see again. The ceremony's centerpiece was an old-fashioned ritual, a throwback to the age of knights: the casing of the nylon guidon that bore 1-32 Infantry's heraldic crest—its "colors"—and the uncasing of the incoming 2-503 Infantry's.

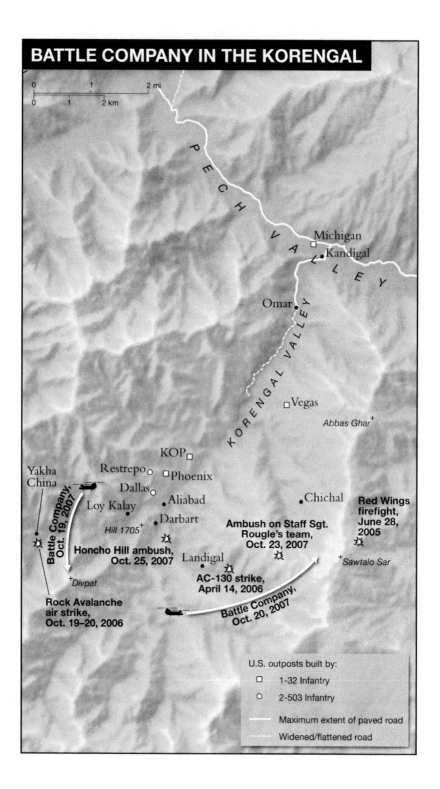

BATTLE COMPANY IN THE KORENGAL

0 1 2 mi
0 1 2 km

P E C H   V A L L E Y

Michigan
Kandigal

Omar

K O R E N G A L   V A L L E Y

Vegas

Abbas Ghar⁺

KOP

Restrepo   Phoenix
Dallas
Loy Kalay   Aliabad   Chichal   Red Wings
Yakha   firefight,
China   June 28,
Battle Company, Oct. 19, 2007   2005
          Hill 1705⁺   Darbart
                              Ambush on Staff Sgt.
          Honcho Hill ambush,   Rougle's team,
          Oct. 25, 2007   Oct. 23, 2007
                     Landigal
                                              ⁺Sawtalo Sar
          ⁺Divpat   AC-130 strike,
                               April 14, 2006
          Rock Avalanche   Battle Company,
          air strike,   Oct. 20, 2007
          Oct. 19–20, 2006

U.S. outposts built by:

☐   1-32 Infantry

○   2-503 Infantry

———   Maximum extent of paved road

– – –   Widened/flattened road

While the assembled soldiers stood at attention, Cavoli and a senior NCO furled their battalion's dark blue guidon with its clutch of multicolored campaign streamers and stowed it in a green canvas tube for the trip home to Fort Drum. Then came the uncasing of the colors of the new battalion by its commander, the man inheriting the complex counterinsurgency mission that Cavoli had shaped: Lieutenant Colonel William Ostlund.

BILL OSTLUND WAS forty-one years old, tall enough to look over the top of Cavoli's head, with arresting blue eyes, a jawline out of Hollywood, and a gravelly voice that some of his men could imitate to a T. He was a rising star in a service where he had spent more than half his life. Enlisting in the Army as a teenager because the Marine Corps couldn't guarantee him an infantry slot, he had joined the Rangers as a private just in time to miss the parachute assault on Grenada, to his immense frustration. After four years lugging around a heavy recoilless rifle in Savannah's 1st Ranger Battalion, Ostlund had returned to his native Nebraska for college, then come back into the Army as a lieutenant in time to earn his Combat Infantryman Badge with the 101st Airborne Division in Desert Storm. Twelve years later, with a master's degree from Tufts University's Fletcher School under his belt, he was among the thousand soldiers from the Italy-based 173rd Airborne Brigade who parachuted into northern Iraq during the 2003 invasion.[1]

"Billy" to his friends and "Wild Bill" to the paratroopers he commanded, Ostlund had made an impression everywhere he went in the Army, earning fierce loyalty from his peers and subordinates and acquiring influential patrons. A soldier who was a fellow private in the Rangers and served with Ostlund twice more as an officer called him "one of the most natural soldiers and leaders ever to put on a pair of fatigues."[2] Many who encountered him were as struck by his outlook on the Army and the world as by his tactical proficiency and charismatic leadership. "He is somebody who really, truly believes in America, in America's mission, in American exceptionalism, and that American soldiers' job on earth is to protect the weak and do good," said Lady Emma Sky, a British diplomat who served with Ostlund in Iraq. "For him, there's a human hierarchy, and on top of that hierarchy is the American soldier."[3] Ostlund had been raised Roman Catholic, but an officer who taught with him at West Point quipped that it seemed as if America and its army were his religion.[4]

Now the Army had rewarded Ostlund for his standout service with command of a storied paratroop battalion widely regarded as one of the Army's best: the 173rd Airborne's 2-503 Infantry, nicknamed The Rock for its role in an audacious 1945 parachute assault on the cliff-top fortress of Corregidor in the Philippines.

The Rock was not a humble outfit; not many airborne units were. The unit's reputation and its choice location, two hours' drive from Milan and Bologna, attracted NCOs from the Ranger Regiment and lieutenants who had been West Point first captains or ROTC graduates of top universities, and Italy's drinking age, eighteen, made Vicenza a highly appealing post for junior paratroopers. Where the Chosin battalion had had to clean house before deployment, getting rid of undesirables and deploying undermanned, The Rock was actually *over*manned. Their commander tried to reinforce his men's impression of themselves as an elite force. When brigade headquarters wanted to suspend training for parachute operations in the run-up to deployment, because they clearly wouldn't be doing any parachute jumps downrange, Ostlund pushed back. Being up to speed on jump operations, he argued, was as important for his men's confidence, their sense of being not just infantrymen but *paratroopers,* as it was for any potential practical application.[5]

At Ostlund's direction, the title slides of the PowerPoint briefings his staff produced were adorned with this line: "If it is possible, it's been done. If it is impossible, we will do it." What the Army was asking of The Rock—to take over and complete an ambitious program mixing counterinsurgency, counterterrorism, and economic development that another battalion had initiated in one of Afghanistan's most violent and socially complex environments—might or might not have been impossible, but it was made all the more difficult by the circumstances of the battalion's deployment. Ever since returning from their last tour, to Afghanistan's flatter, more arid south, in early 2006, The Rock had been preparing for an Iraq deployment, with exercises that stressed close-quarters urban combat drills and convoy operations, not high-altitude foot patrolling and long-range firefights. Only in February 2007, when the same "silent surge" that extended the Chosin battalion's deployment upended the Army's unit rotation schedule for Afghanistan, did new orders come down redirecting The Rock from Iraq to Kunar.

With barely three months until deployment, there was little time for mountain warfare training or familiarization with the languages of northeastern Afghanistan. The best the Army could do was to fly a handful of hardened 10th Mountain soldiers to Europe, where they showed the paratroopers photos of the daunting terrain they would face and stressed the importance of artillery and mortars, and to send Ostlund and a few other leaders to the Pech for a whirlwind familiarization trip. The colonel was confident that his paratroopers' grounding in basic combat tasks and their enviable esprit de corps would see them through, but after getting a glimpse of the kind of fighting they were heading into, he also understood that their preparation for the Pech was a far cry from the long train-up that the Chosin battalion had enjoyed.

At a pre-deployment event in Vicenza to which he brought his three young sons, Ostlund gave an impromptu speech in which he tried to impress upon his men both how dangerous and different this tour was going to be and the seriousness with which he took his responsibility to back them up and give them the tools and support they needed to beat the enemy. More than one paratrooper— including a sergeant who would earn the Medal of Honor on the blackest day of the deployment, July 13, 2008—remembered the gist of the brief speech's heartfelt kicker, made the more forceful by the presence of Ostlund's three young boys in the audience: "During this deployment I will care about you men more than I care about my sons."[6]

AS THE PARATROOPERS of The Rock arrived at FOB Blessing and the Pech outposts in late May 2007, Ostlund, like Chris Cavoli before him, turned to the tactical advisers of the Asymmetric Warfare Group to help his men get their bearings and survive the first, especially dangerous weeks on the ground. When T.W., the advisory group's resident Kunar expert, walked into the expanded, modernized operations center at Blessing and got his first look at the Pech's new battalion commander, he recognized his face but took a moment to place it: the two men had first crossed paths more than twenty years earlier, when T.W. was a Ranger sergeant in Savannah and Ostlund was a private first class there. The advisory group's senior officer in the area, Lieutenant Colonel George Sterling, was an old friend of Ostlund's too, from their lieutenant days. Along with a small number of other Asymmetric Warfare Group contractors and soldiers, T.W. and Sterling had an unusual front-row seat as one American commander and his battalion replaced another in one of Afghanistan's most difficult areas of operation.

On paper, Chosin and The Rock, like any two Army light infantry battalions, looked very much the same. They were organized almost identically; with the exception of parachute training, their junior soldiers had come from the same training pipeline; their commanders came from the Army's top tier of infantry officers; and the PowerPoint briefings that outlined the units' missions identified the same priorities and "lines of effort."

There were subtle yet important differences, however, beyond the two units' varying levels of Afghanistan-specific training and the obvious fact that one battalion was exhausted and worn down at the end of a long tour while the other was fresh. Some were internal to the battalions, the product of distinct unit cultures and Chris Cavoli's and Bill Ostlund's dissimilar personalities, while others were externally imposed. Sometimes, the differences were invisible to the new unit itself—it knew only one way of doing things—but glaring to old hands like T.W. and the Afghan interpreters The Rock inherited when it arrived in the Pech.

By mid-2007, the language and tactics of population-based counterinsurgency that Ron Fry, Chris Cavoli, and other unit commanders had stumbled onto on their own had become the Army's new orthodoxy, adopted into doctrine and popularized by the four-star commander overseeing President Bush's surge in Iraq, General David Petraeus. Ostlund embraced the new counterinsurgency canon enthusiastically; he counted Petraeus among his mentors and kept in touch with him by email. (He was also a friend and former West Point office mate of one of the main drafters of the new counterinsurgency field manual Petraeus had commissioned.) He quickly drilled its catchphrases into his captains and lieutenants: ink blots, white space, separation of the people from the enemy, and "money is ammunition," Petraeus's oft-quoted encouragement to spend cash freely on development projects.

But the commander of The Rock was a population-centric counterinsurgent because his beloved Army had adopted population-centric counterinsurgency as the way forward, not because the methods it entailed came naturally to him. As one of T.W. and George Sterling's Asymmetric Warfare Group colleagues observed, Ostlund was "a warrior, the Patton of the Pech,"[7] always more comfortable and more expert in the traditional tasks of an infantry commander that the Army had raised him to perform. Unlike Cavoli, who had developed a deep affection for many of the officials, elders, and interpreters he worked with in Kunar, Ostlund found Afghans hard to relate to. The only two Afghan civilians he ever grew to trust were the provincial governor Fazlullah Wahidi and the towering Pech district governor, Haji Zalmay Yusufzai.[8]

When I interviewed Zalmay years later and asked him which American commanders he'd gotten along with best, his answer was unhesitating: Cavoli and Ostlund were the two best, he said, and Ostlund was "the very best," because he "took the suggestions of the Afghan government and could make the local villages forget civilian casualties."[9] But after the interview, my translator—a former interpreter to both battalions named Farshad—laughed and offered another explanation: "Haji Zalmay could get things from Colonel Ostlund—money, food, those kind of things."[10] Money was ammunition after all.

During meetings with Afghans, Ostlund could keep his interpreter on the edge of his seat with his direct, sometimes domineering demeanor. "Sometimes I put flowers on Colonel Ostlund's sentences so that the people he was talking to wouldn't hold grudges in their hearts," admitted another interpreter, a skinny, sensitive young man Ostlund inherited from Cavoli.[11] The colonel's blunt approach bled over to how his soldiers interacted with Afghans, some outsiders who worked alongside The Rock in the Pech contended. As a third interpreter put it, Ostlund's men "were the bravest of all the American soldiers, but they were also more rude, and the people complained about them more."[12]

In T.W.'s view, The Rock's attitude affected the way the battalion operated in the field, not just in the *shura* room. "This is hard for me to say, because I'm an offensive-minded guy, but in my experience those guys were heavy with the hammer, and that leaves a scar with the locals," he said of the paratroopers.[13]

Unit transitions were dangerous times for Afghan civilians as well as for American troops just getting used to their new environment, and as The Rock's platoons began patrolling their sectors, the scarring started early. Late in the afternoon on June 11, two days after Ostlund uncased The Rock's colors at Blessing, a patrol was out in Kandigal bazaar when a red pickup truck came around a corner too quickly for the soldiers' comfort. Like all deploying American troops, the paratroopers had been briefed on the threat of car bombs—a very real danger in Iraq, though never in Kunar—and they fired warning shots above the truck to signal it to slow down. When it kept coming, they opened fire into the windshield, and it veered into a tree. Three teenage boys, who were unarmed and whom locals insisted were not insurgents, were killed.[14]

Officers at nearby Firebase Michigan apologized profusely and were quick to pay compensation in cash and sheep and to offer to build a school and riverbank retaining wall in Kandigal as a goodwill gesture.[15] The platoon leader at Michigan was in the mold of Mike Harrison; in the months to come, he would befriend many locals. But there was a cumulative effect. Seven months earlier, an errant round launched by one of the Chosin battalion's mortar crews had killed a little girl in Matin, two miles down the Pech road from Kandigal, during the Eid holiday. Four months before that, near Dag, a nervous American machine gunner had killed three local policemen in their car in an incident very similar to the one in Kandigal. With each civilian death, no matter the American response, the scar tissue built up, and residents of the Pech grew less willing to forgive.

THE BIGGEST DIFFERENCE was where the two battalions started. Rather than initiating a program of outpost and road building, Ostlund was inheriting one that was well under way and had already undergone several incremental expansions.

Hidden beneath these layers of expansion was the narrow, practical purpose for which Cavoli and Doc Scholl had actually begun 1-32 Infantry's and the PRT's road improvement projects: IED prevention. With their pragmatic origins obscured by the passage of a year's time and by the undeniable economic boom that they had brought to the Pech proper, Ostlund and his officers viewed paved roads and associated development projects through a fundamentally different lens— a lens where both ambitions and expectations were much higher. Nowhere was the contrast sharper than in the Korengal.

A few weeks before The Rock deployed, a new provincial reconstruction team had arrived in Asadabad. In its briefings, it labeled Kunar "the province of opportunities."[16] Impressed with the results of the road in the Pech proper, the new PRT's commander—a nuclear engineer, picked from among the Navy's rising stars like Doc Scholl before him—proposed allocating funds for a radical expansion of the bare-bones Korengal road project that the Chosin battalion had initiated at the end of the previous summer. The Korengal road still didn't have any asphalt on it, and with every rainstorm boulders tumbled down the mountain and blocked its path, but workers were widening and flattening its dirt surface enough that five-ton trucks would soon be able to drive all the way to the KOP with supplies.

The next step, the newly arrived Navy officer suggested, could be to extend the road all the way up the Korengal, over a pass nine miles up the valley near the Chalas Ghar mountain, and back down to the Kunar River via the adjoining Chowkay valley, where a new American outpost was under construction.[17]

Cavoli had been at the end of his rope with the Korengal at the time, exhausted by the casualties he had taken there but certain that if American troops pulled out—as his own operations officer was advocating at the time[18]—the same Korengali guerrillas who had been fighting Attack Company would come down from the hills and start attacking the Pech road, slowing or preventing its completion. Part of him wondered whether pushing a road of any kind much deeper into the Korengal (let alone over an eighty-two-hundred-foot pass that would inevitably be snowed in for much of every winter) wasn't a pie-in-the-sky dream. But the new PRT commander's can-do attitude impressed him, so he offered his tentative support, reasoning that it was worth trying anything that might eventually improve the lot of the next company in the Koren-gal.[19] "Well," the PRT commander remembered Cavoli quipping darkly, "either we do that, or we build a big fucking dam and fill the place up."[20]

When The Rock arrived, $11 million in PRT funds were already lined up, and Ostlund backed the Korengal road expansion with fervor. He was "an optimist who believed in believing," in his own words, and what he believed in 2007—and for many years afterward—was that his paratroopers and the PRT held the keys to a revolutionary improvement in the lives of the Korengal's residents in the form of a road up their valley and down the Chowkay.[21] Much work remained to be done on the Pech road, but it appeared to have transformed the main valley, bringing cell towers and medical clinics and fish and chicken farms, creating connections between villages and the government, and allowing the Pech's young men to earn a better wage from (U.S.-funded) construction contractors than from the Taliban.[22] A road, the colonel was sure, could transform the Korengal in the same way. Instead of being at the violent edge of the security bubble, the side valley's villages could be inside it. If it sounded far-fetched, fine; doing the impossible was The Rock's business.

THE BOYS OF BATTLE COMPANY

To push economic progress and the writ of the government into the Korengal, Ostlund tapped his youngest but most combat-tested company commander, Captain Daniel Kearney of Battle Company.[23]

When Ostlund had gone looking for captains to bring to Vicenza, a friend told him that despite his youth, Dan Kearney was a must-have.[24] The twenty-seven-year-old father of a new baby boy, Kearney had grown up around the infantry, the son of a highly regarded officer who had commanded the Italy-based brigade and was now a three-star special operations general. During a year of combat in the volatile Iraqi city of Mosul, he had been a standout lieutenant, leading a platoon in brutal urban combat and temporarily taking over a company when his commander was wounded in a suicide bombing. Six feet four, with blunt features and a gap between his front teeth, Kearney was big, burly, loud, profane, and brimming with confidence in himself and "the boys," as he always called his troops. If he didn't know a soldier's name, he just addressed him as "paratrooper" or "dude." "The caricature of Dan Kearney would just be him yelling at the top of his lungs and everyone running around and doing what he said," said a friend and fellow company commander.[25] Many of Kearney's NCOs found him arrogant and inflexible, and his boys either loved or detested him. It wasn't unknown for a group of paratroopers at the KOP to jump up and hum Darth Vader's "Imperial March" at his approach.[26]

Before leaving Italy, The Rock's company commanders had received lessons-learned memos from the 10th Mountain company commanders they were replacing. Jim McKnight's three-page note from the KOP read like a warning: "In closing, you're not going to Iraq. You are going to Mountain Phase of Ranger School with real bullets."[27] Kearney had shrugged it off; whatever the Korengal threw at him, he figured, it couldn't be worse than Mosul. He and his boys, he remembered thinking, would "go into the valley, quell it in a few months, and then move someplace else." If McKnight and Attack Company had gotten stuck there for their whole deployment, they must have been doing something wrong.[28]

At the KOP and its two satellite outposts, Firebases Vegas and Phoenix, at the end of May, Kearney found a company of outgoing troops who looked more ragged and worn down than he could imagine his paratroopers ever being. Some of his men were shaken by it. One young machine gunner—who, the first night at the KOP, thought the monkeys shrieking outside the outpost were Taliban[29]— remembered being frightened: the men of Attack Company looked angry and on edge, but they were so physically fit and tactically proficient that he knew they couldn't be lazy, crazy, or incompetent.[30] Kearney saw it differently. It seemed to him that McKnight had failed to keep a lid on unsoldierly behavior that the daily stress of living and fighting in the Korengal for a year had brought on: wearing tattered uniforms, openly talking shit about their commander, even, in a few cases, drinking alcohol and using drugs. He and his boys could do better.[31]

. . .

THE LAST OF McKnight's soldiers were still at the KOP on June 5, waiting for their lifts out, when Kearney's Second Platoon left the wire for its second no-training-wheels patrol, climbing up the big hill called 1705, where the Korengal split into two branches, to investigate what someone thought looked like a cave. Hill 1705 (so named for its height in meters) had been the scene of one of the toughest fights of Attack Company's deployment, when McKnight and one of his platoons fought off a four-sided ambush during Operation Big North Wind.

As the Battle Company patrol climbed uphill, it was attacked from three sides. One of the paratroopers on the patrol was Private First Class Timothy Vimoto, a nineteen-year-old whose father, the brigade sergeant major, had been at the KOP just hours earlier for the transfer ceremony between Attack and Battle Companies.

Within a few seconds of the start of the firefight, "Vimoto had fired his weapon, turned back around to another soldier to say, 'Let's get these motherfuckers,' and his head snapped back," remembered the NCO who led the patrol. Vimoto had been shot twice, fatally. A sergeant carried his body back down the mountain.[32]

Kearney was undeterred. "I want to extend the security bubble, because wherever I can place troops and provide security is where I'm going to be able to have an influence on the populace," he explained to the journalists Sebastian Junger and Tim Hetherington on the first of several visits they would make to Battle Company. "Right now the road ends at the Korengal Outpost, and where the road ends is where the Taliban begins."

The captain was hitting all of the counterinsurgency talking points. But he was already starting to figure out for himself what Attack Company had learned: that in the Korengal, the population and the insurgency could not be separated, no matter what, because they were the same. "Getting these people to push out the insurgency, basically push out their family members, is going to be the hard part," he acknowledged to the embedded journalists in the same briefing.[33]

Each day and each night, Kearney's paratroopers would listen to music on their iPods as they shouldered sixty to eighty pounds of body armor, water, ammunition, radios, batteries, and shoulder-launched rockets. Then they would file out the gate and face the next long-distance gunfight. Aliabad, the village two thousand feet south of Firebase Phoenix where the Korengal *shura* leaders Haji Shamshir Khan and Haji Zalwar Khan were from, became the line in the sand; pass the six-two grid line there, and a patrol could count on getting hit with some combination of machine-gun, RPG, and recoilless-rifle fire. Phoenix itself reliably took fire right before and right after the evening call to prayer. These were the rules of life in the southern Korengal.

At the end of August, Battle Company inched deeper south, building another outpost, the Korengal's fourth. For this one, Kearney had selected a flat hilltop five hundred feet above and fifteen hundred feet west of Phoenix, looking down into the nettlesome village of Loy Kalay. Building a new base on that hilltop would both take away a position the enemy often used to attack Phoenix and offer views past Loy Kalay down the western fork of the valley toward Yakha China, a guerrilla base area that Battle Company couldn't easily reach.

Under a bright moon, a platoon hiked up to the hilltop and started digging and breaking rocks. All day every day the paratroopers filled sandbags and Hescos in the sweltering heat, stopping only to fight off enemy attacks. They named the new outpost after a popular medic killed in July, the second Battle Company paratrooper to die: Observation Post Restrepo.[*][34]

To end—if not win—their firefights, the paratroopers adopted tactics they'd inherited from Attack Company, refining them to make better use of air support. With several thousand more U.S. and other NATO troops deployed in the country than a year earlier, more jets, drones, attack helicopters, and huge B-1 bombers were patrolling the Afghan skies, waiting to help when a troops-in-contact alert went out. Many pilots soon became familiar with the Korengal and the radio call signs of the paratroopers fighting there. Battle Company was just one of sixty U.S. and allied infantry companies spread out around Afghanistan, but on some days its gunfights with insurgents in the valley accounted for a staggering 70 percent of all the bombs NATO jets were dropping in the entire country.[35]

---

[*] Firebase Phoenix was renamed OP Vimoto at the same time, but most of the paratroopers there kept calling the base by its original name.

Approval for air strikes rested with Ostlund and the two majors on his staff, one of whom was always in Blessing's operations center, monitoring the progress of any ongoing fights by radio and sometimes drone feed and awaiting requests for support. Ostlund's tendency was to give Kearney, whom he trusted implicitly, whatever firepower he asked for. If anything, he wanted more aerial weapons at his men's disposal, at one point telling his old commander Petraeus in an email that he wished the jets supporting his battalion could carry Mark 77 incendiary bombs, the little-used modern successor to napalm, which he thought would be more effective than standard munitions at killing insurgents inside caves or under boulders.[36]

At brigade headquarters at Jalalabad, however, the amount of ordnance being dumped on the Korengal raised eyebrows. Civilian casualties from air strikes were on the rise in Afghanistan, and in June the four-star U.S. commander in Kabul had urged his subordinate commanders to curb their use of heavy munitions in the first of several "tactical directives" that top American generals would write over the years as civilian casualties from air strikes persisted.[37]

But suggestions from the brigade commander or his staff that Battle Company was overdoing it angered Ostlund, who felt that the officers back in Jalalabad either didn't understand how easily the terrain allowed the enemy to survive heavy ordnance or were just plain risk averse. Once, after a Predator spent all morning tracking a group of men as they walked through the wilds of the southern Korengal with a train of donkeys, unloaded the donkeys' cargo in Aliabad practically under the noses of the paratroopers at OP Restrepo (who were also watching), and then headed back into the forest, Kearney requested an air strike and brigade denied it.

Ostlund flew to Jalalabad the next day for a scheduled commanders' conference indignant and armed with a PowerPoint presentation laying out what had happened. "There were at least three majors in here [at brigade headquarters] watching the same Predator feed, holding back permission to engage," his notes complained. "If we [were] right and failed to engage 7 donkeys worth of chow and ammo will I go to jail or just have to write condolence letters?"[38]

Ostlund's men were living a contradiction of counterinsurgency combat. A conflicted T.W. could see both sides of the issue. Battle

Company, he observed, was "heavy on the stick versus the carrot," and that risked killing civilians. But "in the Korengal, you needed the stick to stay alive."[39] That was the dilemma.

PROTESTATIONS FROM ELDERS like Zalwar Khan and Shamshir Khan to the contrary, it was obvious to everyone in Battle Company that most of the people they were fighting and calling in air strikes on were natives of the Korengal—the elders' nephews, sons, and grandsons, all answering to the timber baron turned commander Haji Matin, who was Zalwar Khan's cousin. (A lieutenant tasked with keeping track of family relationships in the valley thought that Shamshir Khan had a nephew fighting in the hills, and Zalwar Khan one if not two sons.[40]) When Kearney's men patrolled through Korengali villages, the stares they got made it seem as if even the youngest children wanted them dead or gone, and many of the paratroopers quickly came to hate the Korengalis in return. "I thought they were all bad," one sergeant remembered. "They creeped me out. Their beards, the way they dyed their palms—they were very creepy. It was almost like they were aliens."[41]

Dealing with the elders got to Kearney too. It wasn't in the captain's nature to engage with Afghans in the indirect way they were used to, and it got harder as more of his soldiers were maimed and killed, but because he was the most senior American in the Korengal, the task of "smoking the peace pipe" with them, as he sometimes put it, fell to him by default. At least once a week, a group of Korengali elders visited the KOP for a *shura* that Kearney presided over through an interpreter. The scene as the old men walked through the outpost to the base's *shura* room was invariably bizarre, a vivid illustration of the clash of cultures that was occurring in the valley: hunched, weathered Korengalis with red or purple beards, yellow teeth, long robes, and neat vests filing past young, cleanshaven, often shirtless young paratroopers whose heavily muscled limbs and chests were inked with martial imagery and angry English phrases like "INFIDEL" and "DAMN THE VALLEY."

At first, Kearney took a conciliatory tone in the *shuras,* hoping to avoid the types of angry deadlocks that he had seen Jim McKnight get into. *Just forget about everything that happened with McKnight and*

Attack Company, he would urge Shamshir Khan and Zalwar Khan and the other elders squatting in front of him, *and we can all start over with a clean slate.*[42] That was wishful thinking, and it didn't last long. Soon, "Kearney would get emotional fast," making accusations and letting his anger get the best of him, said T.W., who attended many of the *shuras.* "It would wind up getting confrontational, and both sides would shut down."[43]

Only rarely did anyone in the company get real insight into the lives of the guerrillas they were fighting, beyond what could be gleaned from listening to the terse conversations of enemy spotters on their walkie-talkies. "We called them all Taliban, but take that with a grain of salt because I don't know what the heck they really were," Kearney said.[44]

Once, though, a fighter from the southern Korengali town of Ashat, between OP Restrepo and Yakha China, unexpectedly presented himself at the gate of FOB Blessing, explaining that he was "tired of fighting and tired of living in the mountains" and wanted to surrender to Afghan government officials.

Through an interpreter, an American officer asked the man when and why he had first joined the insurgency. He answered that two years earlier, American troops in Kandigal had detained him for a week for no good reason. Angry, he'd gone into the mountains and joined Haji Matin's men. "It is difficult for people to talk to the Coalition forces in the Korengal because they are often upset," the Korengali continued, according to a military summary of the conversation. The officer talking with him was Kearney's friend and fellow company commander Captain Matt Myer. Myer shot back that it was hard for Kearney and the other Battle Company leaders not to be upset when so many of their soldiers had died. His comrades in the mountains felt the same way, the man replied, and Americans had killed far more Korengalis—more than three hundred, he said—than vice versa.[45]

It was undeniable, however, that there were foreign jihadis in the Korengal too, fighting alongside the native Korengalis in small numbers. Like Green Beret A-team 361 back in 2004, the signals intercept team at the KOP occasionally overheard walkie-talkie chatter in languages other than Pashto and Korengali. Urdu, spoken in Pakistan, was one language that the KOP interpreters could readily identify when they heard it, and now and again there were snippets of Arabic; a Battle Company lieutenant who had studied Arabic at West Point once overheard a conversation that he thought was in the distinctive Egyptian dialect.[46]

The puzzle was what the foreign jihadis were doing there—fighting, obviously, but how did they fit into what seemed mostly to be an indigenous insurgency?

The Arabs, the battalion intelligence shop guessed, as well as the "Chechens" who were occasionally reported based on Russian-sounding intercepts, were probably playing a role not unlike American Green Berets: al-Qaida trainers and advisers, answering to Abu Ikhlas, who visited to teach tactical lessons to Korengali fighters and recruit some for further instruction at camps in Pakistan.[47] That matched how the intelligence community saw al-Qaida's role. A DIA report that fall estimated the group had more trainers and advisers in Afghanistan in 2007 than at any time since at least early 2002, suggesting that the deterrent effect 10th Mountain observed a year earlier had been short-lived.[48] The Korengali elders always denied that they had any dealings with the Arab visitors, but years later Zalwar Khan would admit to an American researcher that he had routinely corresponded with them through an intermediary, arranging for them to stay out of the villages.[49]

Much more numerous than the Arabs were Taliban recruits from the Pashtun heartland in southeastern Afghanistan and the tribal areas of Pakistan—not foreign jihadis like the Arabs, but still people who would never have set foot in the Korengal if there hadn't been American troops there to fight. In the four years since the Korengal *shura* first invited the Taliban in to help protect the valley's timber interests, the alliance had deepened. As the insurgency grew, it was formalizing its structure; the Peshawar *shura* was appointing provincial "shadow governors" inside Afghanistan to oversee both local guerrilla cells and Taliban troops coming in from Pakistan, and would soon name one of the most prominent members of the Korengali tribe, an elderly cleric named Mawlawi Abdul Rahim, as the Taliban shadow governor for Kunar. And the intensity of the fighting in the valley in Attack Company's time, U.S. intelligence learned, had in early 2007 spurred Taliban commanders in Peshawar to order more men and weapons to the Korengal.[50]

Kearney and the battalion intelligence shop speculated that the Taliban were using the Korengal as a testing ground for trainees, sending recruits there as a kind of capstone exercise after they received basic training at camps in Pakistan and before they were sent (if they survived) to fight in other Afghan provinces.[51] Hiking across the border from Pakistan at the Nawa Pass south of Asadabad, small groups of fighters would follow the same "ratline," as the U.S. military called the series of trails, that mujahidin fighters had used in the 1980s: across the Kunar River near Pashat, then up the Chowkay valley or Narang valley to where they converged with the Korengal below the Chalas Ghar mountain. "They would come to the Korengal to kind of get their version of a CIB," Kearney said, referring to the U.S. Army's Combat Infantryman Badge. "Go to the Korengal and get your fight on, and then get pushed out to other areas."[52] Arriving in the spring with the warm weather, the outside fighters would go back to Pakistan in the late fall when it got cold (a pattern familiar throughout Afghanistan), leaving just the native Korengalis to fight over the winter.

This rough understanding of the interplay between native and outside insurgents in the Korengal contributed to the defining experience of Battle Company's deployment: Operation Rock Avalanche.

SEARCH AND ATTACK

"We knew where the bad guys were down in Yakha China," Kearney recalled of the impetus for Rock Avalanche. "I knew and the boys knew, but without helicopters we just couldn't get to them."[53] Where Mick Nicholson had turned a blind eye to the Chosin battalion's use of pickup trucks, ATVs, and other unarmored vehicles that theater regulations technically prohibited U.S. troops from traveling in, Ostlund's brigade commander enforced the rules strictly.[54] That placed many towns high in the mountains that the 10th Mountain troops had been able to visit on their own outside The Rock's reach—except by helicopter.

The only reliable way to secure use of the carefully husbanded pool of Chinooks at Bagram, commanders and staffs throughout

Afghanistan knew, was with a big air-assault mission. Once approved by headquarters at Bagram and in Kabul, a "named operation" would lock in helicopters (and other scarce assets like a Predator) for several days. Such an operation had to be scheduled weeks in advance—sequenced with other battalions' operations and timed for a part of the month when there was enough moonlight for Chinooks to fly in the mountains but not enough to dangerously silhouette them—which made it impossible to act on time-sensitive intelligence like a tip-off or signals intercept indicating where an insurgent bigwig was going to be on a specific day. Instead, The Rock's planning section timed the operation to hit insurgent base areas far back in the Korengal just before the onset of cold weather and departure of outsiders for Pakistan. Then over the winter, the plan went, Battle Company would have an easier time garnering local support for the Korengal road project without constantly fighting for their lives.[55]

As the nights in the mountains grew cold in late October 2007, the battalion's scattered outposts were the scene of methodical preparation for Rock Avalanche. At the KOP, Kearney's troops, who would kick the operation off, built a giant sand table inside the command post building, denoting contour lines with string and the Chinooks and Black Hawks that would fly them south to Yakha China with little models hanging from the rafters.[56]

The plan was for a "sequenced search and attack" with helicopters ferrying one company of paratroopers after another to half a dozen objectives over the course of four nights. First, Kearney and his men would fly to Yakha China, where they would search for weapons caches and host a visit by Ostlund and the Navy PRT commander to try to sell the villagers on the Korengal road project. Then the helicopters would return and ferry Battle Company up to the Sawtalo Sar while the sister companies Able and Chosen searched a pair of villages below in the Shuryak—uncharted territory where, as one paratrooper joked, the Taliban "could've been training Yetis" for all Battle Company knew.[57] Meanwhile, a company of the 82nd Airborne, on loan to The Rock for the operation, would land farther south and higher up, on the slopes of the towering Chalas Ghar where the valleys converged. In what had become the typical way of using the understrength ANA unit that shared The Rock's outposts with the paratroopers, a small number of Afghan soldiers would tag along with their Marine advisers. (For American officers, the unreliability of many ANA troops under fire was a strong disincentive to working closely with them or giving them independent roles to play on missions.)

"The purpose of this operation is to separate the enemy from the population, stabilize Central Kunar, and set the conditions for a transformed environment," the plan that The Rock sent up to Kabul for approval explained optimistically. The whole thing would last six days.[58]

FOR EVERYONE EXCEPT Battle Company, Rock Avalanche went quietly, like so many large operations in the Pech before. Able Company lugged heavy machine guns and automatic grenade launchers into the Shuryak and set them up on tripods, anticipating heavy fighting; there was hardly any.[59] And up on the Chalas Ghar, the visiting 82nd Airborne company found nothing but deep, fresh snow.[60]

Every tough sector in Afghanistan and Iraq had its "heart of darkness," and Yakha China was Battle Company's. Out of the reach of American patrols, insurgents could rest indoors there, zero their weapons, stash large weapons like DShK heavy machine guns, and meet with commanders like Haji Matin or visiting Arab trainers. Although the little town was just three miles from the KOP as the crow flies, to Kearney and his men it might as well have been on the moon. Many of the paratroopers believed, incorrectly, that American troops had never set foot there at all.*

Just a couple of minutes after they boarded Chinooks and Black Hawks at the KOP on the night of October 19, Kearney and his soldiers were piling back out onto cold mountain clearings above Yakha China. Scattered gunfights began within fifteen minutes as the paratroopers stumbled upon small groups of insurgents or vice versa. One fighter, apparently carrying a backpack full of RPGs, exploded in flames when a paratrooper shot him.[61]

---

* Attack Company had gone to Yakha China fourteen months earlier during Operation Big North Wind; before that, Marines had visited during April 2006's Operation Mountain Lion and August 2005's Operation Whalers.

From their hilltop position, Kearney and the Air Force targeting specialist at his side called in fire from a bevy of aircraft: an AC-130, a pair of Apache attack helicopters, and a B-1 bomber with a belly full of satellite-guided munitions. After the AC-130 crew watched a group of more than a dozen armed men run inside a house, Kearney got permission from Ostlund—who was watching the same scene via drone feed in the Blessing operations center—and then ordered a strike. The gunship and then the Apaches swept in, perforating the building with cannon and rocket fire.[62]

Kearney called up an estimate of twenty enemy killed, but he was worried. "I'm not going to lie," he acknowledged to a reporter accompanying him for the operation. "Some are probably civilians."[63]

When a platoon walked into Yakha China in the morning and started searching the place, the enemy fighters who'd been there the night before had disappeared, leaving behind just an old shotgun, some RPGs, and some jihadist literature in Pashto and Arabic. But outside the town's mosque were the corpses of five women and children, shrouded with blankets, and a group of elders who angrily explained that the planes and helicopters had killed them. Seven more women and children with shrapnel wounds appeared as American medics got to work.[64]

Ostlund flew out to Yakha China the next day, stepping out of a Black Hawk onto the roof of a house. Facing off with Zalwar Khan and the village's elders, the colonel stood and gave a stern, slow *shura* speech that he had given many times before: The Rock and the Afghan government were there to help; they weren't enemies of Islam. His men could be doing real good for the valley if they weren't busy fighting. Foreign jihadis were duping Korengalis into fighting against their own country for a meager wage.[65]

The message did not resonate—not surprisingly, given that this was at least the third major instance of civilian deaths in a U.S. air strike on a Korengali village in a little over two years. The Yakha China elders unenthusiastically agreed to start coming to Kearney's weekly *shuras* at the KOP. But after the helicopters picked the paratroopers up that night and flew them over to the Sawtalo Sar, signals intelligence picked up predictable, disappointing walkie-talkie chatter: after talking it over among themselves, the elders had given the insurgents hidden outside town permission to keep fighting the Americans.

BATTLE COMPANY SPENT the next two nights on the upper slopes of the Sawtalo Sar, resting for a few hours after searching mountainside *bandehs* and chasing some heat signatures that turned out to be burning fragments from white phosphorous artillery rounds. From their position in a grove of spruces near the summit, some of the paratroopers thought they could see the scorched remains of Turbine 33. The enemy was close by, hidden by the rocks and trees and stumps; the sandal-packed trails they used were all around, and the second day on the mountain the paratroopers could hear the guerrillas on the radio and once or twice even hear their voices in the chilly fall air.[66] The mountaintop "was probably the eeriest place I've ever been," remembered one junior paratrooper.[67]

Battalion planners had hoped that Battle Company's sequential helicopter landings would push insurgents out of the Korengal and into other companies' blocking positions in the Shuryak and on the Chalas Ghar. Instead, while Kearney and his men were in Yakha China, a group of insurgents moved unnoticed onto the Korengal side of the Sawtalo Sar *from* the Shuryak side, and they were lurking there when Battle Company landed on the mountain. A group of them struck hard a little before noon on Tuesday, October 23, day four of Rock Avalanche.

After painstakingly scaling a steep cliff uphill from Landigal, a group of enemy fighters darted from the tree line and attacked a fighting position manned by three paratroopers on the top of a small rise. In the opening seconds of the fight, the guerrillas killed Staff Sergeant Larry Rougle and wounded both of the men with him, got close enough to strip the weapons and night-vision goggles off them, and then disappeared.[68]

The leader of a scout-sniper team and a Ranger veteran, Rougle was only twenty-five years old but already on his sixth combat deployment since September 11. He was what Ostlund liked to call a "Rock star," revered throughout the battalion, and his loss was a hard pill for the soldiers on the mountain to swallow. "Rougle was kind of a god to these kids," said the brigade psychologist, a former enlisted soldier who spent much of his time with Battle Company. "They all expected they might die by that point, but they didn't think Rougle could die."[69]

Of most immediate concern was the equipment the attackers had made off with. Losing a pair of night-vision goggles meant Battle Company would have to stop using infrared identification lights in the valley, because whoever had the goggles would now be able to see them too, and Ostlund didn't want the machine gun and rifles showing up in a Taliban propaganda video like the rifles and helmets Ahmad Shah's fighters had taken off the SEALs killed on the same mountaintop during Operation Red Wings. So even though the operation's planned phases were winding down and battalion intelligence estimated that the insurgents had lost forty men and been "severely disrupted,"[70] Ostlund gave Battle Company one more job. The missing American weapons were still out there, probably hidden somewhere near Landigal, and he and Kearney wanted them back.

After a brief rest at the KOP, two platoons headed back up the Sawtalo Sar before light on October 25. While Battle Company stood guard outside town, Ostlund flew into Landigal and, after delivering much the same speech he'd given in Yakha China over the weekend, demanded the return of the missing weapons and equipment. As in Yakha China, the message didn't seem to make an impression. The Landigal elders told Ostlund that the insurgents around were foreigners, that they knew nothing about them and could do nothing about them. The missing items were nowhere to be found.

AS THEY FILED back down the spur they called Honcho Hill that evening at the close of Rock Avalanche, the twenty-odd paratroopers of Battle Company's lead platoon walked into an ambush. A Shadow drone and two Apaches were overhead, but hidden in the trees, the ten or fifteen attackers who opened fire at close range with RPGs, rifles, and machine guns were invisible to their infrared cameras. The Apache pilots, and soldiers watching the Shadow feed back at Blessing and the KOP, could see muzzle flashes, but they couldn't make out any details of the fracas below.

What was happening was a textbook L-shaped ambush laid at a bend in the trail, pinning down the rear of the platoon (where a medic, Specialist Hugo Mendoza, was fatally hit) and reducing the fight to a melee at a range of a few feet between the attackers and the six paratroopers of the lead American squad. "They hit us in an ambush from about thirty meters away from about fifteen different fighting positions," remembered one of those six, Specialist Salvatore Giunta, who was amazed at the volume of incoming machine-gun fire and at the enemy's willingness to attack when they could hear the Apaches overhead. "They had cover, they had concealment, and they had the benefit of elevation on us."[71]

The team leader, Sergeant Joshua Brennan, was used to walking point—he'd been shot in the calf doing it back in August—and he was on point on the night of October 25. He went down badly hurt in the first volley of RPGs, as did the soldier behind him. Throwing hand grenades, three soldiers managed to reach the second wounded man despite the storm of machine-gun fire. While a staff sergeant started first aid, Sal Giunta kept going, looking for Brennan, his closest friend in the battalion.

A few meters down the trail, during a strange, sudden lull in the shooting, Giunta saw him: two enemy fighters were dragging Brennan away by his hands and feet as fast as they could. That was probably what the insurgents who attacked Rougle had been hoping to do too: grab a wounded American, or at least a body. Opening fire with his M4, Giunta killed one of the fighters and hit the other one, forcing him to let go of Brennan and run.

Hit six times and torn up by the RPG shrapnel, Brennan survived long enough for a medevac Black Hawk to get him to FOB Asadabad but died at the small combat surgical hospital there. That night, as the operation ended, an AC-130 was back overhead, hammering targets.[72]

JUST EIGHT DAYS before Rock Avalanche, President Bush had presented a posthumous Medal of Honor to the family of Michael Murphy, the SEAL lieutenant killed fighting on the Sawtalo Sar on June 28, 2005. Embroiled in their own war in the Korengal, the paratroopers of Battle Company had hardly noticed, if at all. But back at the KOP after the operation ended, it seemed clear to Kearney that Sal Giunta's actions on a spur of the same mountain met the bar for the nation's top valor award too.

Giunta was not a role model like Larry Rougle, but he was a good paratrooper—a twenty-two-year-old Iowan who had joined the Army because he wanted to fight in a war and had completed one Afghanistan tour already before deploying to the Korengal, a place he'd come to despise.[73] His actions had kept the body of an American serviceman from falling into enemy hands—the nightmare scenario that had prompted the massive, weeks-long search for the SEAL bodies on the Sawtalo Sar after Red Wings. It also seemed probable to Kearney that during the minutes when Giunta was the front-most unwounded soldier on the trail on Honcho Hill, his actions had saved more lives by preventing other militants from pushing farther up the trail past the incapacitated wounded.

The battalion put together a nomination packet in the cold days after Rock Avalanche. In a ceremony at the White House in 2010, Giunta—by then a sergeant and a veteran of a third Afghanistan deployment—would become the first serviceman of the post-Vietnam era to survive the actions for which he was nominated and live to wear the Medal of Honor around his neck.

WHITE SPACE

During their first five months on the ground, up through the night Joshua Brennan and Hugo Mendoza died on Honcho Hill, Kearney's paratroopers had gotten into more than 200 firefights (sometimes 10 or more in a single day), and besides their seven dead they had taken twenty-seven wounded. In the ten months that followed, they would lose just a single paratrooper killed and thirteen wounded in 144 firefights. That was still far in excess of what most American and allied infantry companies in Afghanistan experienced, but it was a significant reduction.[74]

Along with the downturn in violence came a slight but perceptible thaw in relations between Battle Company's officers and the village elders they dealt with. Shamshir Khan started inviting Kearney to join him for lunch on his porch in Aliabad; Zalwar Khan remained standoffish in public but behind closed doors began to joke and make small talk with the paratroop officers, even to ask them about their lives at home and whom they planned to vote for in the 2008 presidential election. (Zalwar Khan's understanding was that the candidates would be "Bush again or the wife of Clinton."[75])

This was the "white space" that Rock Avalanche had been intended to create, and Battle Company used it to revamp the stalled Korengal road construction project. A few weeks after the operation, thirty Korengalis were at work widening and flattening the road below Firebase Phoenix. Some elders began to admit the road sounded like a good idea, even in public, which they hadn't done before. It was enough to get anyone's hopes up, especially the irrepressibly optimistic Ostlund. In February 2008, citing the valley elders' shift in tone at *shuras* and in closed-door meetings, the colonel predicted to Kunar's governor that Battle Company was close to "turning the Korengal to the government."[76]

Whether the opening to work on the road was actually attributable to Rock Avalanche was a matter of debate, however.

Ostlund was sure it was. The operation had worked as planned, he maintained, killing enough key enemy personnel to put the Korengal insurgency on its back foot. In *shuras* with the Korengali elders over the winter, he would use the mission as a talking point. Ostlund "advised [the elders] that another Rock Avalanche is just an order away," notes on one such meeting read, adding a summary of what the colonel said next: "We have the power to fly into your safe havens and cause destruction and kill your sons who have been paid a slave's wage to fight a fool's war. Progress will enter the Korengal, with or without your cooperation."[77] The battalion would continue to launch more air-assault missions along the same lines whenever it could muster the helicopters: Rock Thrust in March 2008, Rock Nitro in April, Rock Penetrator in May, but never again with much combat, because the enemy melted away ahead of the missions.

Not everyone who participated in Rock Avalanche agreed with Ostlund's assessment. His own operations officer acknowledged that because the operation had been timed to coincide with the departure of insurgents for their winter hibernation in Pakistan, its actual effects were impossible to tease out from the drop in enemy activity that would have come with the cold weather anyway.[78] A more severe skeptic was T.W., who had flown with the 82nd Airborne company up onto the snowy Chalas Ghar, the least eventful part of the operation. T.W. had seen the Marines and the Chosin battalion launch big multicompany air assaults in the Pech before The Rock. "It don't work," he said of the tactic. "It might work other places in Afghanistan, but not there. In the environment we're talking about, with constant observation by the enemy, big operations that brief well on paper—pushing the enemy this way or that way, movements to contact—they just don't work in the Pech and those capillary valleys. You can't drive wild game like that, because wild game is just going to use the terrain to their advantage and split up."[79]

The problem was this. Any offensive operation big enough to secure helicopters and other resources from division was also too big to conceal ahead of time from the enemy's network of observers and informants and impossible to launch on short enough notice to be tied to timely intelligence. It was also unlikely to do much damage unless the enemy cooperated and threw themselves at American forces, accepting heavy losses in order to inflict smaller ones. And even if an operation really did inflict enough casualties to cause a lull in daily fighting in a particular area, the lull could last for only so long.

George Sterling, Ostlund's old friend from their lieutenant days who worked with T.W. in the Pech, was conflicted. "Bill and I talked at length about the need for balancing the carrot and the stick, but in that area the enemy will fuck you up if you don't take the fight to them," Sterling said. "Here's where Bill and I split. Those big operations didn't do much. I mean, Rock Avalanche did buy some time and space, but for what? You can't maintain the pressure after going in there hard like that."[80]

AS WARM WEATHER crept back into the valley in April and The Rock got ready for its second fighting season, the threatening Taliban "night letters" that the Korengali road workers had been receiving over the winter gave way to a reprise of the savage violence that had brought Attack Company's work on the same road to a halt: murders, beheadings. Battle Company was powerless to stop it; the Korengal security bubble didn't even extend as far as the soldiers could see from their outposts. Work ground to a halt. The first couple of kilometers of the road were paved with asphalt, but the progress was nothing like what the PRT-funded plan for a route up the Korengal and back down the Chowkay had envisioned at the start of the deployment.

Ostlund never wavered in his insistence that building the road was possible (if The Rock didn't finish it, the next unit could) and would transform life in the Korengal.[81] And while Kearney was in the valley, he echoed to his own paratroopers the confident encouragement that the colonel was giving him, hyping every foot of road progress and touting the importance of the two new outposts they had built, OP Restrepo and OP Dallas (a little fortress constructed in March 2008 yet another fraction of a mile up the valley).

But later, Kearney wondered to what extent he'd been overselling what progress he did see just to make the daily ordeal of life and combat in the Korengal worthwhile.

"Counterinsurgency works at a glacial pace, and we were making glacial-pace progress. I was also drinking my own Kool-Aid," Kearney said years later, when he'd been back to Afghanistan several more times with the Ranger Regiment and the Kool-Aid was out of his system. "I was a one-man IO machine keeping my boys' morale up."[*82] By then American involvement in the Korengal had ended—the road had never grown much beyond where Battle Company left it—and Kearney was dubious that the outposts he and his soldiers had built or the patrols they had gone on every day had really accomplished much besides killing an unknown number of young men who were fighting Americans. The promises of security that he and his officers had made to gain the cooperation of elders and road workers seemed particularly overoptimistic.

" 'Security bubble' was an improper term, because honestly we never secured anybody," he reflected. "We told them we were going to provide security, when that was an unattainable goal."[83]

★ IO stands for "information operations," a category that includes propaganda operations.

CHAPTER 8

A VALLEY TOO FAR

2007–2008

"THEY'RE INSIDE THE WIRE"

At FOB Blessing and the Ranch House and Bella outposts to its north, The Rock's Chosen Company inherited a very different war from Battle Company's in June 2007. For the deployment's first three months, while the Korengal boiled with firefights, it hardly seemed as if there were a war going on in the Waygal valley at all.

Where Dan Kearney was big, brash, and loud, Chosen Company's commander, Captain Matthew Myer, was lankier, more easygoing, and more patient, a third-generation West Pointer with a sardonic sense of humor who had led a platoon of Bradley armored vehicles for a year in Iraq before coming to The Rock. Now in charge of two infantry platoons—one with him at Blessing, patrolling Nangalam and its environs, and the other up in the Waygal—Matt Myer faced less immediate challenges than his friend Kearney did at the KOP, but ones that worried him all the same.

The way the outgoing 10th Mountain captain had explained it to Myer before heading home, a winter snowed in at Bella and the Ranch House had yielded dividends with the residents of the adjacent towns; the Waygal was a place where American troops had a good thing going.[1] Myer wasn't so sure. The whole setup in the

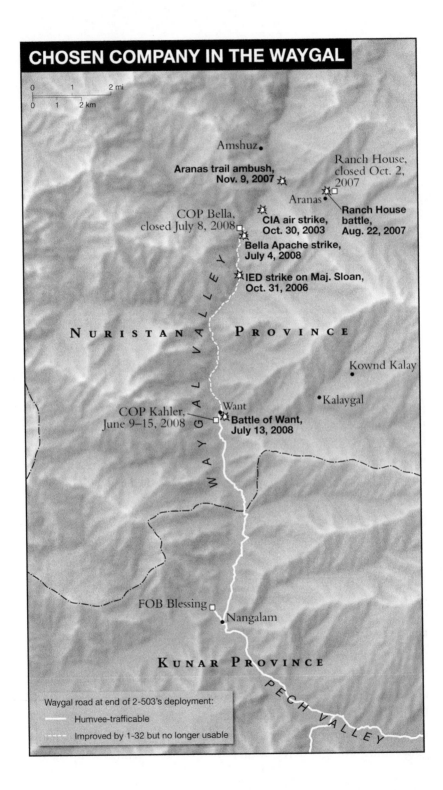

CHOSEN COMPANY IN THE WAYGAL

0   1   2 mi

0   1   2 km

Amshuz

**Aranas trail ambush,
Nov. 9, 2007**

Ranch House,
closed Oct. 2,
2007

Aranas

**CIA air strike,
Oct. 30, 2003**

**Ranch House
battle,
Aug. 22, 2007**

COP Bella,
closed July 8, 2008

**Bella Apache strike,
July 4, 2008**

**IED strike on Maj. Sloan,
Oct. 31, 2006**

N U R I S T A N   P R O V I N C E

WAYGAL VALLEY

Kownd Kalay

Kalaygal

Want

COP Kahler,
June 9–15, 2008

**Battle of Want,
July 13, 2008**

FOB Blessing

Nangalam

K U N A R   P R O V I N C E

PECH VALLEY

Waygal road at end of 2-503's deployment:

——— Humvee-trafficable

- - - - Improved by 1-32 but no longer usable

valley troubled him, starting with the fact that it physically separated him from his most isolated platoon by ten miles. That the platoon itself was split in two, half at Bella and half at the Ranch House, bothered the captain even more. The distance and rough terrain between the two outposts would prevent one from quickly reinforcing the other when the lurking enemy that had killed Doug Sloan the previous fall eventually broke silence and attacked.

Then there was the matter of resupply. Local workers had made progress widening and flattening the Waygal road during 10th Mountain's tour, but mostly in the lower half of the valley, well short of Bella. Resupply convoys of Humvees tried to make it all the way to Bella two or three times over the summer of 2007 but found the road too narrow, and when a local contractor was hired to drive bottled water up from Blessing in pickup trucks, insurgents killed the first driver to make the trip.[2] Because U.S. troops could no longer drive in pickup trucks in the Waygal themselves, per theater rules, the Ranch House and Bella bases were, in military lingo, "air-centric"—completely reliant on helicopters for resupply. (Army Chinooks and Black Hawks brought in military items like ammunition and radio codebooks, while a company called Supreme Air flew food and water in on old unarmed Russian aircraft.)

The outpost that worried Myer most was the Ranch House, the aerie in the clouds that Sloan had established and named a year earlier on the edge of the mountainside town of Aranas. The steeply sloped, flea-infested base included a main building on top of which helicopters could land, some plywood huts, and a concertina-wire perimeter punctuated by six wood-and-sandbag bunkers, four of them manned by paratroopers, one by some ANA soldiers, and one by locally hired Aransi security guards. The half platoon there couldn't get out and do much. Even a short foot patrol into Aranas for a *shura* was a hike, and anything farther out was a major expedition, requiring days of planning and leaving just a skeleton crew at the base. Myer thought that with the Ranch House, 10th Mountain had extended themselves too far.[3]

Myer's recommendation that the Ranch House be shut down was welcome at battalion and brigade headquarters. The biggest disconnect between the 173rd Airborne Brigade and 10th Mountain was over how to deal with Nuristan. Lieutenant General Karl

Eikenberry, the highest-ranking proponent of U.S. military–assisted development in Nuristan, had rotated home over the winter, leaving less interest in the remote province at International Security Assistance Force (ISAF) headquarters in Kabul. Nevertheless, in his final weeks in the Pech, Chris Cavoli had remained bullish on Nuristan, even collaborating with the Navy commander in charge of the Nuristan provincial reconstruction team on plans to build a "green" self-sustaining PRT base in Governor Tamim Nuristani's government enclave in the Parun valley, over the mountains from the Waygal.[4]

Upon taking charge in Jalalabad, the 173rd's commander, Colonel Charles "Chip" Preysler, pulled the plug on that plan. Where his predecessors had seen in Tamim a credible partner with a vision for a prosperous future, Preysler saw a snake-oil salesman peddling unrealistic dreams. Leaving Aranas made plenty of sense to him, and to Bill Ostlund too.[5] "I did not understand, and Chris could not adequately explain, the need for the Ranch House," said Ostlund, who had first raised questions about the Pech's northernmost base when Cavoli gave him a tour during his brief pre-deployment visit.[6] That Cavoli had sent troops to Aranas in the first place partly at the urging of the intelligence community did not impress Ostlund. Haji Ghafor, the old mujahidin commander whom the CIA had traced to Aranas in 2005, had since moved much deeper into Nuristan, far out of reach,[7] and having troops at the Ranch House had never helped Cavoli catch Ahmad Shah, who had now relocated to Bajaur in Pakistan.[8] "An infantry platoon on a mountainside is not a national intelligence collection mechanism," Ostlund judged. "They didn't even have LLVI," the next echelon of signals intelligence above an interpreter with a walkie-talkie tuned to the Taliban's frequency.[9] When Ostlund visited the Ranch House, he would reassure the worried NCOs there that the outpost's days were numbered.[10]

But closing the Ranch House was a difficult proposition for the same reasons that resupplying or reinforcing it was. Disassembling an air-centric base took helicopters, which were in short supply and had to come out of the same pool of aircraft that supported resupply runs and air-assault missions like Rock Avalanche. With no fighting in the Waygal, no immediate threat, the closure of the Ranch House was a priority, but it wasn't a *top* priority, so it would have to wait.

. . .

THE SUMMER OF calm at the Ranch House ended at 4:55 a.m. on August 22 when a rocket-propelled grenade lanced out of the early-morning fog—the signal for guerrillas who had crept close to the base overnight to unleash a ferocious assault. The first explosion was followed by rifle fire and then heavy, sweeping machine-gun fire and more RPGs that blanketed the interior of the outpost. The ruckus snapped alert the twenty-two Americans there, many of whom, along with the ANA and local Aransi security guards at two of the perimeter strongpoints, were still asleep when the shooting started.[11]

The fire was coming from every direction—some from across the Aranas gorge, meant to pin the Americans at the outpost down and knock out their communications, and some from very, very close. One paratrooper, still in flip-flops and a T-shirt, started to shoot back with his grenade launcher and was amazed to see the first round he fired bounce harmlessly off the boulder he'd been aiming at; the rock and the insurgent behind it were evidently less than forty-six feet away, the arming distance for a 40-millimeter grenade.[12] The aim of the attacking force was clear: to storm over the Ranch House's perimeter wire and kill, wound, or drag off as many Americans as they could before reinforcements could arrive by foot or helicopter.

The First Platoon leader, Matthew Ferrara, a thin-featured runner, was the only officer at the outpost. An earnest lieutenant who had an older brother in the Army and two younger ones on the path to join, Ferrara had spent the past three months immersing himself in the counterinsurgency tasks that some other soldiers eschewed, taking detailed notes on every conversation he had with Aransis and learning every elder's name so that an interpreter wouldn't have to remind him.[13] Now he was facing a trial by fire of the traditional infantry tasks that West Point and Ranger School had taught him.

The first thing the lieutenant saw in the early-morning light was ANA soldiers and Aransi security guards running downhill, the wrong direction, fleeing the two strongpoints they manned. With the aid of long wooden boards, the insurgent assault force climbed over the concertina-wire perimeter into the base.[14] Helping themselves to a stash of RPGs inside the bunker the ANA had abandoned, the attackers fired so many grenades at the next strongpoint in their way that the Chosen Company paratroopers inside had to retreat from it too, leaving one of their own wounded inside, pinned in the rubble. All the American defenders of a fourth strongpoint were wounded.

As the camouflage-clad enemy fighters moved deeper into the base, shouting to each other in Waygali and Pashto and dashing from strongpoint to boulder to plywood shed, Matt Ferrara went back into his command post to call for mortar support from Bella. With incredible calm, he transmitted a message no American commander thought he would ever say or hear: "They're inside the wire." Shortly afterward Ferrara's voice cut out. RPGs had destroyed the satellite antenna on the command post's roof, forcing the lieutenant to abandon the building.[15]

Firing their M4s, throwing hand grenades at enemy fighters thirty feet away, and using 60-millimeter mortars as handheld weapons, Staff Sergeants Erich Phillips and David Dzwik and five junior paratroopers managed to hang on to the central area around the Ranch House's mortar pit. Their last-ditch defense blunted the enemy's downhill penetration and gave Ferrara the time he needed to talk in a pair of A-10 Warthog attack planes.

Responding to the lieutenant's distress call, the Air Force jets' pilots had homed in on the smoke twisting above the horizon from the outpost's fifth strongpoint, which RPG blasts had set aflame. As the A-10s approached, Ferrara guided them in, explaining that his own position was marked with bright orange rubber visibility panels and that a wounded American was stranded alone in one of the guard towers.[16]

When the slow-moving gray "Hawgs"—their cruciform shapes more reminiscent of World War II dive-bombers than of other modern jets—swooped in for the first time just over an hour into the fight, dropping flares, relief swept through the troops around Ferrara. But to do any good, the A-10 pilots would have to do what the howitzers and mortars couldn't—fire right into the base, "danger close." Accepting the risk of friendly fire, the lieutenant channeled the thunderous burp of the planes' car-sized Gatling guns (designed to punch through the armor of Soviet tanks) onto the perimeter strongpoints that the enemy had seized. That stopped the attackers cold, and they fell back the way they'd come, dragging their wounded and dead with them.[17]

MORE THAN TWO and a half hours after the shooting started, the first medevac Black Hawk arrived. Eleven of the twenty-two Americans at the Ranch House had been wounded, but, miraculously, all were alive. One Aransi security guard had been killed and one ANA soldier fatally wounded. Chosen Company estimated ten enemy dead, but there was only one body left behind, on a trail about a hundred feet from the perimeter. It was Mawlawi Hazrat Omar, an Aransi militant commander linked to Ahmad Shah and the Taliban's Peshawar *shura*. Hazrat Omar had already been wounded earlier in the summer leading an attack on the nearest police station, down on the Waygal valley floor. In the dead militant's pockets and pouches was a trove of intelligence: payroll documents, photos, plans. There was also a video that showed him briefing his men before the assault just the way a Ranger School graduate would, off a sand table and detailed diagram of the Ranch House, using a rifle's cleaning rod as a pointer and requiring back briefs of key points from his subordinates.[18]

Matt Ferrara would be awarded the Silver Star for his actions on August 22, 2007, and the Army recognized mortarman Erich Phillips—a twenty-five-year-old who had joined the Army after the Marine Corps rejected him over a teenage arrest record[19]—with an even higher award, the Distinguished Service Cross, second only to the Medal of Honor. The battle of the Ranch House, in the eyes of commanders from Myer and Ostlund up to division, was an alarming example of a piece of Army folk wisdom: when soldiers on the ground are put into positions where they commit acts of desperate heroism, something has gone wrong.

The battle had vividly demonstrated the outpost's physical vulnerability and the dangerous length of time it took to reinforce. Besides those obvious tactical issues, officers at Blessing, Jalalabad, and Bagram saw it as a betrayal of Chosen Company by the community of Aranas. Counterinsurgents were supposed to protect the people, separating them from the insurgents. The grateful protected community was supposed to do its part by letting the counterinsurgents know when the insurgents were around. But the attacking force had staged beforehand at a schoolhouse right in Aranas and retreated there afterward to regroup and treat their wounded. How many townspeople had seen or heard Hazrat Omar and his men moving into position in town overnight and passively allowed the attack to happen? How many had actively helped the attackers drag away their casualties? Worse, the Americans remaining at the Ranch House soon learned that the Aransi security guards hadn't just fled their post during the battle. A few days before the fight, Ferrara had fired the local foreman in charge of the guards. In apparent retaliation, an Army report concluded, the foreman had then "used his detailed knowledge of the camp's defenses to lead . . . fighters inside the perimeter and attack the barracks at close range."[20] Three days after the battle, at a *shura* for delegations from all over the Waygal, Matt Myer demanded a list of names of Waygali men who'd participated in the attack. He didn't get them.[21]

Getting out of the Ranch House was now a high priority both for The Rock and for division headquarters, but marshaling the required helicopters still took five more weeks—a tense time for Ferrara and the other paratroopers still manning the outpost. Finally, at the end of September, the lieutenant told a *shura* of Aranas elders that he and his platoon were leaving but hoped the *shura* would keep in touch. He gave the Aranas schoolteacher a box of pencils, crayons, and glue as a parting gift.[22] For the next three days, Chinooks came and went, lifting out supplies and equipment. Then, on October 2, the paratroopers set the Ranch House base on fire and flew away.

Chosen Company was not done with Aranas, however, nor Aranas with Chosen Company.

FIRST PLATOON GOT a month to decompress at Blessing: they ran Humvee patrols along the smooth pavement of the Pech road, worked out and played video games at the FOB gym in their downtime, and spent an uneventful few days in the Shuryak during Operation Rock Avalanche. Then, in early November, Ferrara and his men headed up to Bella to start a winter rotation at what was now the northernmost outpost in The Rock's corner of Afghanistan.

The paratroopers had been at Bella only a few days when a message arrived from Aranas: the elders wondered if Ferrara would come visit them, now that he was back in their neck of the woods. Ever the good soldier-diplomat, Ferrara jumped at the chance. His soldiers were not so happy; they'd just *left* Aranas, after killing an unknown number of Aransis in a pitched battle. Specialist Kyle White, Ferrara's radioman, didn't trust the townspeople's intentions. When Ferrara announced they would be taking the elders up on the invitation, the twenty-year-old paratrooper from Seattle was so anxious he was nauseated. He wasn't alone. "There were guys who were sick, throwing up from nerves, because you had this feeling in your stomach like something bad was going to happen," White remembered of the hours before the return-to-Aranas patrol headed out after dark on November 8.[23]

The patrol comprised Ferrara, a squad and a half of his paratroopers, a squad of ANA and their Marine combat adviser, and two interpreters. Their overnight march through the mountains went quietly, and the *shura* in Aranas the next day, November 9, was heavily attended. Instead of the handful of elders who had usually shown up when the paratroopers were living next door, it seemed as if every man in town were there, staring, listening intently, and carrying on side conversations that Ferrara's interpreter (who spoke only Pashto, not Waygali) couldn't understand.[24] As the patrol left town again late in the afternoon, taking a different trail back toward Bella this time, the paratroopers watched nervously as a group of men started to follow them, then split off onto a parallel trail above them on the same mountain.[25]

Just short of the junction of the Aranas gorge with the Waygal valley, the patrol walked onto a narrow stretch of trail unshielded by foliage. "On the right was a cliff going straight up," the platoon forward observer later wrote. "To the left was a cliff going straight down. The terrain was rocky shale, rough as shit, nowhere to go."[26] Above were boulders; below was a tree-lined gorge with a thin stream at the bottom of it. The setting sun was in the paratroopers' and ANA soldiers' eyes. "Hey, let's get through this area quick," someone said over the radio.[27]

The soldiers heard a couple of cracks first, then a cacophony of machine-gun fire and RPGs from across the gorge and across the

Waygal. At the rear of the single-file column, the Afghan troops mostly ran back uphill or disappeared into the trees. In the kill zone at the front, accurate fire felled one paratrooper after another. Shot in the arm, the squad leader judged that the best chance for survival was jumping down the cliff into the two-hundred-foot-deep gorge. By the time he and his men had tumbled down the near-vertical slope, four of them had been killed. At the bottom of the ravine, the squad leader helped the five other survivors consolidate, dragging one wounded soldier into a cave and treating another who'd been shot through both legs.

Behind the lead squad on the trail was Ferrara's headquarters group: the lieutenant, his forward observer, the Marine combat adviser, two interpreters, and White, the radioman.

Feeling numb, White started emptying M4 magazines toward the muzzle flashes he could see across the gorge, his only cover from the RPGs exploding around him the trunk of a scrawny tree.[28] Around him, in between blasts, White could see the damage the enemy fire was doing. Matt Ferrara lay dead in a pile of rocks, shot in the head. The forward observer and the Marine adviser were nearby, both wounded badly. Exposed and with bullets hitting the cliff behind him and even snapping through his shirt, White ran to one wounded man and then the other, applying tourniquets and packing wounds. Despite his efforts, the Marine sergeant bled to death on the trail. Grabbing the dead Marine's radio (his own had been shot), White managed to get a call for fire through to Bella, and mortar and howitzer shells started falling, then bombs from a B-1.[29]

Recovering first the wounded and then the eight dead—six Americans and two ANA—took a pair of medevac Black Hawks all night, working one above the other to hoist casualties up from the mountain and the ravine below. While the medevacs were refueling, another Black Hawk filled in, locating some of the bodies and an eerie group of moving, flashing infrared strobe lights that turned out to represent not soldiers but just their helmets, tumbling slowly down the stream toward the Waygal junction.[30]

IN THE MONTHS before November 9, said Chosen Company's first sergeant, "We went everywhere and did everything."[31] After the six deaths on the Aranas trail, that changed. It was a while before enough walking wounded and replacements trickled in for First Platoon even to start patrolling again, and then it was with what the new lieutenant who took Matt Ferrara's place remembered as "kind of a sad resignation."[32] Instead of hiking up to villages in the mountains to hold *shuras,* he would ask the elders to come visit him at Bella.[33] The American bubble of influence in the Waygal had shrunk to a small pocket, and Aranas, the town that had drawn U.S. attention to the valley in the first place, wasn't in it.

Matt Myer did not think that the Waygal had completely turned against his company. The insurgents were just one segment of a complex society; many, he thought, were just teenagers who became "enchanted by the fighter lifestyle" after encountering bands of militants while tending their villages' goats in the mountains, joining the fight without their elders ever knowing.[34] But the captain already knew from his time in Iraq how hard it could be for soldiers to understand, or even tolerate, local people who seemed ungrateful and unwilling to pick a side.[35]

In the wake of what seemed like repeated betrayals by whole Waygali communities, an angry bitterness descended on much of Chosen Company.[36] The company first sergeant made clear to a visiting Army historian how he felt about patrols where his men handed out trinkets like Beanie Babies to local children, and by implication about the people of the Waygal who did not provide information about their insurgent neighbors and relatives. "I hate that shit," he fumed. "Someone shoots at you from a house and then your commanders want you to go back to that same house and say, 'Would you like some stuffed animals, some toys or cookies?' Fuck you. How about I put a bullet in your head? . . . Not that I would, but that's what I'm thinking."[37]

Some of the Afghan interpreters Myer and his men had inherited from 10th Mountain thought Chosen Company had it backward. In their view, Waygalis had turned on the company in part because the paratroopers treated them with less respect and understanding than their predecessors had, lashing out at whole communities after tragedies that most people had no hand in.[38] Farshad, the tall, quiet Nuristani from Kabul who had been Doug Sloan's interpreter before he was Matt Myer's (and who would be my interpreter in the

Pech years later), thought that to many Aransis—including some who hadn't supported the American presence initially but had seen the economic benefits as their friends got road construction and base security jobs—it was actually the pullout from the Ranch House that seemed like a betrayal and turned them against Chosen Company. "They would complain about the people, that they were lying or not cooperating. That's okay, I accept that, but it does not make things easier," Farshad said of Myer's paratroopers. "Eventually, the relationship between the people and Chosen Company was completely broken."[39]

When I interviewed a group of Waygali men a decade later about their experience with Americans, several of them described the falling-out in similar terms. "We dealt with Colonel Cavoli and his men as brothers and friends and cooked for them and believed their promises, but they lied to us when they promised us a road," one middle-aged man said. Mullah Mohammad Afzal, a senior member of the Aranas *shura* who spent a year in detention at Bagram because 10th Mountain officers suspected him of collaborating with the enemy, agreed. "The Americans acted like Afghan politicians," he said. "They promised they would build roads and clinics, and then they didn't."[40]

There was one American who had spent more time in the Waygal valley than any other and who was in a position to comment thoughtfully on this chicken-and-egg question of who had betrayed whom: David Katz, a tall, irascibly opinionated State Department diplomat who happened to have spent sixteen months in the Waygal in the 1970s doing fieldwork for an anthropology dissertation, visited the valley occasionally in the years since, and stayed in touch with Waygali friends during subsequent postings in Pakistan. He had just finished a tour with the Nuristan PRT when the Ranch House was attacked, and could only follow with horror the news of the tragedy unfolding.

Like many diplomats and academic area specialists, Katz had had a difficult time working with the military while deployed to western Nuristan with the PRT. The Army taught infantry officers to abhor inaction and indecision, which could cost lives on the battlefield. It also told them, in the age of counterinsurgency, that they should try to learn something about the culture they were operating in.* The problem, as Katz saw it, was that in a society as multilayered and foreign as the Waygal, decisiveness and understanding were often at odds with each other: "The more you understand, the more you get to the point where you just don't know what the hell the consequences of anything you're doing up there are."[41]

Both Chris Cavoli's soldiers and Bill Ostlund's after them, Katz felt, were guilty of acting without understanding the consequences, because the consequences took time to play out, more time than American soldiers in Afghanistan had. It wasn't that one unit had behaved well and the next unit behaved badly, even if some locals and interpreters saw it that way. It was that no matter how rosy the friendship might have seemed at the outset, the U.S. Army and the communities of the Waygal were bound to have a falling-out eventually, so different were the two cultures and so many the inevitable friction points.

Night patrols were one small example. These were a basic fact of how the Army operated; an infantry unit that didn't patrol its environs at night was asking to be attacked. But the patrols' use of night-vision equipment was frightening and offensive to villagers who were used to relieving themselves outside at night and felt the soldiers' night-vision equipment was invading their privacy. Just as jarring to Waygalis, if not more so, were military officers' incessant demands that they "get off the fence" and overtly support the government against the insurgency, Katz believed.[42] This was something that Ostlund, for one, never tired of, no matter how evasive the elders he was talking to were; the way the hard-charging colonel

---

* Katz understood things about the Waygal that the troops patrolling it never would. It was easy for the paratroopers to assume, for example, that the Waygal was an implacably hostile place with a hillbilly-type antagonism toward the government and outsiders, like the Korengal. But that wasn't true. As Katz had learned during his fieldwork in the valley, the Waygal had enjoyed an unusually close relationship with the Kabul government for most of the twentieth century; Waygali youths, originally taken as hostages after the 1896 conquest, had risen to high ranks in the army and civil service, and their home communities were still reaping the benefits a century later of having a foothold in the Kabul elite.

saw it, pinning local leaders firmly onto the right side was part of his job.[43] And, of course, no one in the valley—certainly no one in Aranas—had forgotten about the innocent Waygalis who had died at American hands: the family killed by U.S. bombs in October 2003, and more recently a man whom a nervous 10th Mountain guard had shot when he ambled too close to the Ranch House's perimeter one night in January 2007.

Katz's analysis of how wrongs both large and small built up over time squared with what Waygalis told me a decade later. Most of the men who spoke with me had lost at least one close relative to the Americans—either someone killed in an inadvertent air strike or shooting or someone killed fighting against the Americans in battle. "Hate against them grew as they killed goats and sheep and destroyed *bandehs* with their mortars and artillery," observed Mullah Afzal, the *shura* leader who spent a year in Bagram. "That was a turning point," a brother of the man shot on the base perimeter told me of that killing. "They shot him for no reason. They asked for forgiveness, but you cannot repair something like that. They were devils." Both he and another brother joined the Taliban to seek revenge, he said.[44]

A confrontation, in this analysis, had been building since Americans came to Bella and Aranas and put down roots; the militants in the Waygal just took a while to work things out with local communities and Taliban financiers in Pakistan and to stockpile the men and ammunition needed to challenge the heavily armed Americans. The question that loomed as 173rd Airborne Brigade leaders mulled what to do next in the valley was whether the August 22 and November 9 battles had been the main event or merely tremors.

A GAME OF MUSICAL OUTPOSTS

The debate centered on what to do about Bella, the remaining American outpost in the Waygal. Just about everyone in the chain of command agreed that the little base needed to go. It had become superfluous: Chris Cavoli's troops had built it to provide mortar support to the Ranch House, and now the Ranch House was gone. Bella also seemed like a disaster waiting to happen. Sitting at the bottom of a steep "fishbowl," as the paratroopers there invariably described it, the outpost almost seemed to be inviting another Ranch House–style attack.

Bella's vulnerable location and complete reliance on aerial resupply also raised the specter of losing a helicopter in the Waygal. It would be only too easy for an insurgent rocket or heavy machine-gun crew to bring down one of the helicopters that Bella relied on for everything from food and ammunition to medevac and updated radio security codes while it was landing at the outpost. The latter prospect weighed heavily on the mind of Chip Preysler, the brigade commander. As a division staff officer in Afghanistan in 2005, Preysler had watched the whole cascading Red Wings disaster and subsequent recovery mission play out from the Bagram operations center. The loss of a helicopter at or near Bella, he knew, would necessitate a similar recovery mission in terrain even more difficult and dangerous than the Sawtalo Sar.[45]

Ostlund concurred, but where Preysler and Matt Myer both wanted to wash their hands of the Waygal altogether, Ostlund wasn't ready to call it quits in the valley.[46] If Chosen Company left the Waygal completely, the militants the paratroopers had been fighting would undoubtedly claim that they had driven the Americans out, a propaganda opportunity that Ostlund didn't want to give his foe. And he knew that America still had allies in the valley—if not in the high mountain towns like Aranas, then certainly in Want, the tiny town on the valley floor where the Waygal's district center and police station were located and where the Humvee-trafficable portion of the road ended. (Thanks to the decades-long game of telephone that had transliterated place-names from Waygali first into Dari for Afghan government maps, then into Russian for Soviet maps, and then, from those maps, into English for American military ones, The Rock knew Want as Wanat, and pronounced it "Wuh-not."[47])

The district governor and police chief in Want were fence-sitters, in Ostlund's view, but there were vocally pro-American elders there too. If his paratroopers moved in next door, building a new outpost in Want at the same time that they pulled out of Bella, the colonel was sure that the fence-sitters would choose the right side and The Rock would get another shot at getting the "counterinsurgency snowball" rolling in the Waygal.[48]

Ostlund's argument prevailed, but lining up the approvals and resources to build a new outpost was almost as slow a process as closing one, and doing both at the same time was even slower. Helicopters and drones were as scarce as ever, and establishing a new outpost in Afghanistan was no longer as simple as just showing up and starting to fill Hescos and string concertina wire, as U.S. troops had done before in the Pech. To avoid having to dole out compensation payments to landowners after the fact, headquarters had recently begun enforcing long-ignored rules that required potential outpost sites to be vetted by detachments of real-estate specialists from the Army Corps of Engineers. By the time the real-estate team finally came out to Want in early May and got the nine families who owned parts of the site Matt Myer had selected to sign a lease, it was common knowledge that the Americans were planning a new base.

AMONG THOSE WHOM news of the outpost construction plan reached was the militant who had inherited the job of insurgent commander in the valley from the slain Hazrat Omar—Mullah Osman, who had been away in Pakistan over the winter.

The battalion intelligence shop knew the bare bones about Osman. He was from a village in the far north of the valley, where he still lived openly some of the time, confident that he was out of American reach. Like Hazrat Omar before him, he was close to Mawlawi Monibullah, the Aransi cleric who had been one of the first prominent Nuristanis to join the Taliban. Locals later told me that early on he had cooperated with American troops in the Waygal. A native of the poorer side of his town, he had run a small construction business. "Osman was like all of them—ordinary shopkeepers who became leaders of the Taliban in the mountains," one man who knew him told me. In later years, after the Americans left Nuristan, he would become one of the Taliban's commanders in the province and host al-Qaida operatives.[49]

Upon Osman's return to the Waygal in the spring of 2008, elders who had previously voiced support for the Want outpost clammed up,[50] and tips began to come in from informants about what the militant leader was going to do about the impending American game of musical outposts. Throughout April, reports trickled in that

Osman was receiving reinforcements from another guerrilla cell in the town of Gambir, a known militant safe haven ten miles east in the upper Watapur valley whose population was related to that of the Waygal.[51] "They are there in response to hearing that [you] are building a base in Wanat," one informant told his handler late in the month, according to a summary of the conversation that, like all American military documents, used the two-syllable Americanized name for the village.[52]

In the acrimonious aftermath of the battle of Want or Wanat, these reports were grist for criticism: How could Ostlund and his officers not have known that a massive attack was being planned against the new outpost when they were being told explicitly that it was? But the reports The Rock was getting from military intelligence teams and the CIA were sketchy, and it was all but impossible to tease out rumor and deliberate misinformation from solid intelligence. The purported numbers of fighters coming from Gambir varied from twenty to three hundred, and their staging locations from one end of the Waygal to the other. When the tips about the Gambir force subsided for weeks with no sign that there had been any truth to them, only to start bubbling up again in June, it was hard to take the fresh set of reports at face value.[53]

The tips also often directly contradicted one another. Some tipsters said the militants were planning an attack on the new Want outpost, but plenty of others said Osman's intention was to hit Bella hard before Chosen Company left, either with a massed assault or by shooting down a resupply helicopter there. This was the version that Ostlund, Myer, and the battalion intelligence officer were inclined to believe.[54] It was buttressed by a worrying increase in attacks on helicopters flying up the Waygal in the late spring that culminated in the June destruction of a Supreme Air bird at Bella by rocket fire. This, in turn, clogged up the outpost's landing zone for three days until a Chinook could haul away the wreckage.

With the end of The Rock's deployment looming and the first replacement troops already arriving at Jalalabad and Blessing from Fort Hood, Texas, division headquarters finally gave formal approval for the Bella pullout in the first week of July. The last few days at the base were tense. On July 3, a mortar attack seriously wounded a paratrooper, and when Apache attack helicopters reacted to another mortar attack the next day, they shot up both a pickup truck full of insurgents and, mistakenly, a second pickup truck whose passengers included some of the staff of the civilian medical clinic in Bella. The Apaches might have wounded Mullah Osman himself, radio chatter indicated, but they had also killed the clinic's chief doctor, a respected figure in the community who had always been friendly to the Americans.[55] If the relationship between the troops at the base and the people who lived nearby had been going sour before, it was irreparable now, a fact that Mullah Osman's men were quick to take advantage of. At the heavily attended funeral for the Apache strike's victims, Taliban recruiters in the crowd offered the chance for revenge to young men angry about the latest American killing of civilians.[56]

Four days after the Apache strike, with a Predator overhead and two Black Hawks full of reinforcements from a pathfinder platoon standing by at Jalalabad in case something went wrong, a pair of Chinooks plucked Matt Myer and Chosen Company's First Platoon—the same soldiers who had survived the Ranch House battle and the ambush on the Aranas trail—out of the outpost.

Officers watching the Predator feed at Jalalabad and Blessing breathed sighs of relief when the last Chinook lifted off unscathed and Bella was no more. "We dodged a bullet that that place never got overrun," was the assessment of T.W., who had visited the outpost several times during its two-year life.[57] The prevailing view at battalion and brigade headquarters was that the hard part was over: in the opinion of the battalion intelligence officer, Mullah Osman's men had been within twenty-four hours of launching a Ranch House–style massed attack on Bella when the sun came up and revealed an empty base.[58]

ON JULY 9, while militants including Mawlawi Monibullah explored the grounds of the abandoned Bella base,[59] another group of Chosen Company paratroopers got to work fortifying the muddy field that was to be the thirteenth American outpost built in the Pech and its tributaries. Like Restrepo and Vimoto in the Korengal and a base that The Rock had built on the Pech proper called Honaker-Miracle, the outpost was going to be named after a fallen paratrooper: Combat Outpost Kahler, after an NCO killed at Bella over the winter.

Overnight, Second Platoon had crammed their Humvees with all the water and ammunition that would fit and driven up from Blessing to Want, a tiny town centered on a bazaar of shops and stands, a mosque, and a hotel with a blue-railing balcony.[60] When the sun came up, they and some mortarmen and ANA who had been helicoptered in overnight started stringing concertina wire and digging holes to sleep in and shoot from. Their job, over the next ten days or so before they began the trip home to Italy, was to make the site defensible: to fill Hescos and sandbags and build a pair of plywood structures. Some Afghan workers were under contract to start building a stone perimeter wall on July 13.[61] The replacement platoon from Fort Hood would start trickling in two days after that, and it would be up to the newcomers, over the coming weeks and months, to build the base up with guard towers and more permanent buildings.[62]

Myer flew up to Want on his men's fourth day there, July 12. The platoon leader, a laid-back Army brat named Jonathan Brostrom who'd done ROTC at the University of Hawaii, gave his arriving captain a tour. The site was another fishbowl—there was nowhere on the Waygal valley floor that wasn't—but it sat astride a Humvee-capable road.[63] In the middle of the base was the command post: a series of holes in the dirt, shielded on one side by a Humvee and on the other by an unfinished Afghan building, with half-full Hescos protecting other angles. Squads were split up by Humvee and fighting position, and up a few agricultural terraces from the main outpost amid some boulders was a separate, smaller observation post, providing a view of town and a perch for a thermal sight, dubbed OP Topside. It wasn't much of a base yet, but it was what Myer expected.[64]

After dark, Myer and Brostrom strolled over to the home of Haji Juma Gul, the hook-nosed old man who owned the town hotel and had befriended the Army engineers who installed two bridges in Want in 2006. In the months since the chilling of relations in the Waygal, Juma Gul had often been the voice in *shuras* pushing for more cooperation with the Americans, and over a late dinner he tried to make his guests welcome. Jon Brostrom and his NCOs had noticed a worrying absence of women and children in town since they arrived.[65] This was nothing to worry about, Juma Gul explained. Everyone knew that the insurgents were going to start shooting rockets and mortars at the new base soon, maybe tomorrow, so they had sent their families away for a few days; he'd done so himself.[66] That evening, the various thermal and infrared sights at the base spotted a small group of men high up in the mountains to the west—possibly insurgents—but nothing else out of the ordinary: no armed men in town, no clusters of heat signatures in places they shouldn't be.

There *were* insurgents in the mountains above Want, though, dozens of them, moving undetected in the trees and behind folds of terrain. Some were hard-core Taliban members, including the force's commander, the former imam of the Want mosque, Mawlawi Monibullah. Others were angry new recruits who had signed up to fight just a few days earlier at the funeral for the civilians killed in the Bella Apache strike. They included riflemen, machine gunners, RPG gunners, ammunition bearers, radiomen, and, as during the Ranch House attack and the November 9 ambush, several cameramen intent on capturing the coming events from as many angles as possible.[67] And sometime in the early hours of Sunday, July 13, some of them crept into the town itself. Around midnight—probably soon after Myer left Juma Gul's house—an informant in town called his military intelligence handlers, agitated. In a snafu worthy of *Catch-22,* however, the intelligence team's only interpreter with the security clearance required to talk to sources was away sorting out a paperwork issue.

What the informant wanted to report, according to the intelligence NCO who finally talked to him the next day, was that fighting-age men—men he didn't know, who weren't from Want—were quietly going door to door and telling people to leave town before sunup.[68]

THE BATTLE OF WANT

The embryonic outpost's occupants—just under fifty Americans, two dozen ANA, and three interpreters—awoke before four o'clock on Sunday, July 13. With light seeping over the mountains and no clouds in the sky, all seventy-six of them donned their gear for "stand-to," a dawn readiness ritual Chosen Company had adopted after the Ranch House attack.

Scanning the ridges with their long-range sight, the crew of the Humvee-mounted TOW antitank missile at the center of the base called out that they could see two groups of men moving in a distant grove of trees, wearing backpacks and with unidentifiable objects in their hands. They had to be insurgents getting ready to attack, Myer realized, and he told the TOW crew to get ready to fire.[69]

Just then, at 4:20 a.m., before the TOW crew could ready a missile and as paratroopers around the perimeter were removing their night-vision goggles, a burst of machine-gun fire rang out, accompanied by the whoosh of two RPGs and then followed by more bursts from every direction and distance.

The fire focused first on the outpost's most dangerous weapons, the Humvees with their heavy weapons and the mortar pit. As an RPG salvo set the TOW Humvee on fire, Myer jumped into another Humvee to get on the radio with Blessing. With bullets pinging off the truck's armor and the turret gunner pouring machine-gun rounds back, the captain called for immediate artillery fire and reported what was happening: "This is a Ranch House–style attack."[70]

The two senior NCOs at Want were the mortar section leader Erich Phillips, the hero of the Ranch House battle, and Sergeant First Class David Dzwik, who had fought at Phillips's side on August 22 and was now Second Platoon's platoon sergeant. Both men were at the mortar pit, where the raking incoming gunfire killed a private first class named Sergio Abad almost immediately. Dzwik had spent the past several days fuming over the move to Want, which he thought was motivated by hubris on his commanders' parts and feared would lead to exactly what was now happening.

Well, he thought as the shooting started, *here we go.* Standing on his tiptoes in a puddle of rainwater to fire over the Hescos, he could see guerrillas in dark clothes thirty feet away, as if they'd come from nowhere, darting from building to tree to building to loose RPGs. Some were firing down into the base from the roof of the house where Myer had dined with Juma Gul a few hours earlier, others from the branches of trees.[71]

Phillips and his mortar crew managed to get about four mortar shells off before the incoming fire became too intense. RPG after RPG flew right into the pit. One bounced off Phillips's helmet; another sprayed him with shrapnel and ruined his M4, forcing him to switch to hand grenades. When yet another exploded right by the boxes of mortar rounds and one of the metal shell canisters started swelling as if it were about to explode, Phillips led a dash to Myer's location at the command post. There was more cover there, but it was hardly safe. When the burning TOW Humvee exploded, sending unfired TOWs flying, one of them landed among the clustered soldiers, and Phillips had to grab the buzzing, spinning missile with a pair of sandbags and run back out into the machine-gun fire to throw it a safe distance away.[72] On the north side of the perimeter, two Marines urged their ANA advisees to shoot back; many, though not all, did.

ON THE TERRACES above the base, the nine paratroopers manning OP Topside became eight, then seven, then six as RPG blasts and machine-gun fire killed three of them and wounded the rest.[73] Under the cover of heavy fire from the slopes above and from the hotel sixty feet away, enemy fighters climbed from a creek bed up toward the concertina wire surrounding the little bulwark of boulders and sandbags. A Claymore antipersonnel mine killed one blue-robed guerrilla as he tried to climb through the wire—the paratrooper who detonated it saw sparks fly when the spray of ball bearings hit the man—but another Claymore malfunctioned, and a third exploded back toward the OP, as though an insurgent had gotten to it first and turned it around.[74] OP Topside was in danger of being breached, and the surviving soldiers were defending themselves by "cooking off" hand grenades—waiting a few seconds to throw the baseball-sized devices after pulling the pin so that the enemy on the other side of the rocks wouldn't have time to throw them back.

Down at the command post, Jon Brostrom, the platoon leader, grabbed one of his soldiers, Jason Hovater (a specialist known for his pitch-perfect impression of Colonel Ostlund[75]), and headed up the terraces, through the gauntlet of fire, to join his six stranded men. As Brostrom and Hovater helped one of the OP's defenders, Specialist Pruitt Rainey, set up a machine gun, the wounded could hear Brostrom and Rainey shouting to each other about an insurgent who'd climbed over the outer perimeter wire and was letting off bursts from behind one of the big boulders ringing the position. Then, amid explosions that sounded like grenades, Brostrom, Rainey, and Hovater went silent. They were dead. When another paratrooper jumped up to get a better shot at the insurgents firing into the OP from the top of the hotel, he was killed too.[76]

OP Topside was now a lonely place, with just four survivors, all wounded, and few weapons that hadn't either overheated or been destroyed. Unable to see or hear one another, three of the wounded men dashed down toward the main outpost. That left just Sergeant Ryan Pitts, Second Platoon's twenty-two-year-old forward observer.

Hit in both legs, barely mobile, and sure he was about to die, Pitts could hear the agitated voices of insurgents just feet away. Whispering into the radio so that the enemy wouldn't hear him, he told Myer he needed help. There was no one to send, Myer answered. "Roger," Pitts remembered telling the captain. "Well, either you send more people or this place falls."

With nothing more to talk about, Pitts put the radio down and started firing his grenade launcher almost straight into the air, trying to kill any fighters who were right on the other side of the sandbags from him. As soon as help finally came in the form of four more paratroopers who braved the storm of fire to reach the OP, another volley of RPGs wounded all of them.[77]

AMERICAN AIRCRAFT HAD started speeding toward Want almost as soon as Myer called up the attack at 4:23 a.m. Just shy of five o'clock, the first bombs started to fall, delivered by a high-flying B-1. With much of the fighting too close for artillery, the danger-close air strikes were a godsend, but what saved OP Topside from falling and turned the tide of the battle was the arrival of Apaches.

Two Apaches were on the tarmac at Jalalabad, preparing to take off for a twelve-hour shift over Kunar and Nuristan, when word of the attack arrived and sent the birds racing north over the mountains. As the attack helicopters headed up the Waygal just under an hour into the battle, Ostlund's voice came over the radio from Blessing, calmly offering his initials—required to authorize a danger-close gun run—and a succinct indication of the gravity of the situation on the ground: "They're within hand-grenade range at this time." The troops at OP Topside were going to throw a green smoke grenade just outside their position, he said; there was foliage fifty meters from there that the Apaches needed to hit with their 30-millimeter automatic cannon.[78]

"We're going to look for the green smoke, and we're going to put some fucking thirty down fifty meters east," one of the aviators confirmed.[79]

"Any Hedgerow element, Chosen 6," Myer broke in, using the Apaches' call sign as the pilots looked for the smoke. "Be advised, we are in a bad situation and we can't really get spots on rounds." The captain revised Ostlund's estimate: OP Topside needed the rounds just ten meters from their smoke, not fifty.[80] In the helicopters' cockpits, the pilots' and gunners' hearts sank. Normally, the closest they would have put their half-pound explosive shells to friendly troops was eighty meters.[81]

The Apaches swept over once without firing, then again with each bird letting loose two twenty-round bursts. When he relaxed his hand after firing, one pilot started to shake. *Please, God,* he thought, *let us not have hit any good guys.* The next call over the radio was for a medevac, and for a moment the pilot was sure his or the other Apache's shells had struck OP Topside.[82] But they hadn't; they had hit the enemy, creating enough breathing room for Dzwik, Phillips, and nine other paratroopers and Marines to head up the terraces and reinforce the OP.

The scene Phillips saw as he dove through a hole in the sandbags would for years visit him when he closed his eyes to sleep: paratroopers wounded, paratroopers killed, a paratrooper with internal organs exposed, a paratrooper with little left of his face. One of the machine guns lying inside looked as if Superman had bent it in half; it had taken a direct RPG hit. As Phillips was moving one fatally wounded sergeant, an enemy hand grenade plopped down in front of him. Myer, who had followed the relief party up to count the casualties, grabbed it and threw it back.[83]

The Apaches had quieted the fighting down enough for medevac Black Hawks to start braving the simmering gunfire. Then a little after six o'clock, after a hair-raising Humvee drive from Blessing, the first quick-reaction force pulled up—First Platoon. Through a haze of smoke, the arriving reinforcements could see the detritus of the battle: the ruins of *bandehs* that artillery and bombs had destroyed; the burning mortar pit; the TOW Humvee melting down to its chassis.[84]

First Platoon had arrived just in time to help thwart an enemy flanking attack into town, directed from a command post up in the mountains.[85] Exchanges of fire would continue all day and into the night, as platoons from Able and Battle Companies reached the scene and Apaches, fighter jets, a Predator, and an AC-130 struck teams of retreating enemy in the mountains. But the worst was over.

In the space of two hours, twenty-seven Americans had been wounded and nine killed. Helicopter shoot-downs excepted, the July 13 battle of Want had claimed more American lives than any other engagement of the Afghan war.

THE HIGH-WATER MARK

A Black Hawk took Ostlund and Chip Preysler, the brigade commander, to Want that afternoon. Preysler was shaken. He was a friend of the fallen platoon leader Jon Brostrom's father, and at Vicenza before deployment the easygoing lieutenant had been like an older brother to the colonel's own children.[86]

Taking his bosses up to OP Topside, Matt Myer walked them through the morning's events. Then they talked about what should come next: Stay or go?

Go, Myer recommended. The town the outpost was supposed to help had turned on Chosen Company just as Aranas had, he argued; there was no point in building the Want base anymore. He pointed out Haji Juma Gul's house, from which insurgents had fired during the fight. Juma Gul was America's staunchest friend in Want; why, he wondered, had the old man allowed fighters into his home just hours after hosting American officers? He pointed out the district center north of town too, which didn't have a scratch on it. How could the district governor and policemen there not have known that there were dozens of insurgents sneaking around? Myer had thought for months that U.S. resources would be better used in more welcoming places, like Chapa Dara District west of Blessing, than in Want, and now he was sure.[87] "The population proved corrupted or intimidated," he wrote in his recommendation to division headquarters the next day. "The land and human terrain are no longer tenable."[88]

The discipline of the attacking force inevitably led some to speculate that foreign jihadis had been involved—Arabs, Punjabis, Uzbeks, the ever-elusive Chechens. There was no evidence to support these claims, although the presence of some Pakistanis or Arabs couldn't be disproven.[89] What quickly became indisputable, however, was that a large number of local Waygali men had taken part in the attack[90]—probably including members of the Want police force.

On Saturday evening, Chinooks inserted more than a hundred soldiers from the ANA Commandos, a force that was a cut above the rest of the Afghan military and often wound up acting as a mobile reserve. The Commandos scoured the mountains overnight and into the next day, hunting for enemy spotters and stragglers. A small American signals intelligence team had come with the Commandos and their A-team of Green Beret advisers. Along with the Red Ridge eavesdropping plane now overhead, the team started collecting insurgent radio transmissions that provided clues about the composition of the enemy force and the losses it had taken. Some wounded guerrillas were being treated at the medical clinic in Bella, it appeared, and others over the mountains in Gambir. One radio transmission said twenty-one fighters had died; another listed the names, all seemingly Afghan, of fifty-three men who had been killed or seriously wounded.[91]

Then, on Sunday afternoon, the signals intelligence team picked up radio chatter between insurgents and the policemen at the district center. "You are good Muslims for what you did yesterday," the commander of the Green Beret A-team recalled hearing a militant tell the policemen in Pashto.[92] There were usually just a few poorly armed, poorly equipped police at the district center, but when the Commandos arrived to investigate, they found an arsenal: fourteen machine guns, six RPG launchers with a crate of RPGs, seventy-six assault rifles, a video camera. Many of the weapons were dirty and appeared to have been recently used, even though the district center had been spared from attack the day before, and as the Commandos searched the houses around town that the enemy had been firing from during the battle, they found more rifles there of the same Hungarian-built, U.S.-bought model the police had.[93]

The Commandos cuffed the policemen and started to question them. As they did so, the district governor, Zia Rahman, appeared, looking as if he wished he were somewhere else. Consulted by radio, Ostlund gave the order to detain him. The colonel had long suspected Zia Rahman of involvement with the insurgents but had figured him for a fence-sitter who would get on the right side once paratroopers were living next door.[94] No longer.

To Ostlund, the discovery at the district center settled it. It went against his nature to cede ground to the enemy, especially ground that his men had just bled for, but he saw no other good option, and Preysler reluctantly concurred.[95]

The final decision belonged to Major General Jeffrey Schloesser, the division commander at Bagram who had signed off on the move from Bella to Want just ten days earlier. Schloesser's own staff was split, but the general feared that in the aftermath of the battle the Waygal could become a new Korengal, and the Want base the new KOP. One Korengal was plenty.[96] He gave his approval, and on the morning of July 15, Chinooks flew into Want and started taking everyone and everything out—paratroopers, Commandos, unused Hescos, even the skeleton of the melted TOW Humvee.[97] There would be no COP Kahler.

By then the Fort Hood soldiers slated to replace The Rock were arriving at Blessing. The lieutenant whose platoon would have taken over the Want outpost was a friend of Jon Brostrom's from infantry officer training and Ranger School, and after sitting through the memorial ceremony for the nine dead men on his first day at the FOB, he wept for his friend in the base latrine. Besides grief and fear, he felt gratitude. If the enemy had attacked a week later, he guessed, the battle would have gone much worse for him and his platoon of rookies.[98]

TWO WEEKS AFTER THAT, Bill Ostlund and the paratroopers of 2-503 Infantry's Able, Battle, Chosen, and Destined Companies were on their way home to Italy. Collectively, they had been in more than a thousand firefights; 143 of their comrades had been wounded, and 26 had been killed, a death toll that only one other American battalion in Afghanistan would ever surpass.[99]

The Rock had been *the most* at everything during its fifteen months in Kunar and Nuristan. Of all the units in Afghanistan at the time, it had called in the most strikes from jets and helicopters (nearly four thousand) and the most artillery and mortar fire missions (more than five thousand), spent the most development money (80 percent of the brigade's development budget), even handed out the most Beanie Babies (more than ten thousand).[100] The awards its paratroopers earned during the deployment would make The Rock the most heavily decorated battalion since Vietnam: a Presidential Unit Citation, nearly a hundred Bronze Stars for combat valor, twenty-eight Silver Stars, and two Distinguished Service Crosses. After years of review, three Rock paratroopers would be awarded the Medal of Honor: Sal Giunta of Battle Company and Kyle White and Ryan Pitts of Chosen Company, each of whom had battled insurgents alone when everyone around him was dead or wounded.

But Want—both the fight itself and the decision to leave rather than keep building up the base—cast a shadow over the deployment. Two in-depth investigations followed the battle: a routine one, called an Article 15-6 inquiry, that sought to piece together what had happened on July 13, 2008, and then, more than a year later, a CENTCOM inquiry that delved into the lead-up to the fight.

The questions the CENTCOM investigatory team asked were wide-ranging: Why had The Rock sent soldiers to Want at all? Why had it taken so long to start building the outpost? What intelligence indicators had there been of a coming attack? Why hadn't a drone been overhead?[101] Had the soldiers there had enough water, enough construction equipment? Had OP Topside been appropriately sited?

The basic, implied question was this: Whose fault was it that scraggly, lightly armed guerrillas had been able to kill nine American paratroopers in the middle of nowhere?

The investigation's final report, which Ostlund's old mentor David Petraeus approved, blamed Ostlund and Myer for "insufficient oversight" of the base's opening days of construction. Ostlund should have visited the site personally, it found, Myer should have gotten there earlier, and the soldiers at the outpost should have been patrolling into the mountains in search of the enemy instead of relying on devices like thermal sights to scan for suspicious activity. Both officers, the report recommended, should be criminally charged. This put Matt Myer in the odd position of earning both a Silver Star and a formal allegation of dereliction of duty for the same battle: the former for his actions during the fight, and the latter, essentially, for failing to prevent it from happening in the first place.

To some of the family members of the dead, including Jon Brostrom's father, the CENTCOM investigation's findings seemed like a necessary check on arrogant commanders who had thrown away their loved ones' lives. To Ostlund, they were infuriating, unreasonable, and sometimes contradictory,* and he fought back against them hard.[102]

He was not alone. To Schloesser, the CENTCOM investigation seemed like a kangaroo court. "This is not a ship running aground," he objected in frustration to the Marine general in charge of the inquiry. "This is a thinking, living, flexible enemy that knows the area better than we do."[103] The Army, in yet a third investigation in 2010, would side with Schloesser and overturn the CENTCOM findings, sparing Myer, Ostlund, and Preysler from formal punishment. "It is critical that we not mechanically equate U.S. casualties with professional error or misconduct," the Army report warned.

---

* Not all of the investigation's recommendations seemed to follow from the testimony collected. The CENTCOM report recommended, for instance, that a Predator or equivalent surveillance drone be assigned to every brigade in Afghanistan, even though the investigation had found no fault with the allocation of surveillance assets before the battle and even though nine out of the twelve witnesses questioned on the subject said that they did not believe a Predator would have been able to spot signs of the attack before it happened. Under the evergreen trees, fighters were all but invisible even to a drone's infrared cameras; the only thing that usually gave moving enemy personnel away even to experienced sensor operators was the glint of weapons, which insurgents easily countered by stashing their machine guns and RPGs in hidden caches ahead of time. "We could have a full scale TIC and have ISR directly overhead and not pick up a single guy on the ground," testified one officer from The Rock's intelligence section, using the acronyms for firefights and drones. "They knew every crevice and crack."

"In battle, casualties are inevitable. Regrettably, they are often the price of victory."[104]

WANT HAD BEEN a victory in a narrow sense. Paratroopers, Marines, and ANA soldiers had repulsed a larger attacking force while inflicting much greater losses than they suffered. The enemy had never even penetrated the main outpost's perimeter as they had the Ranch House's. This much the investigations firmly established.

None of the investigations evaluated how the battle fit into the larger picture of the war in Afghanistan or America's involvement in Kunar-Nuristan, however. If they had, they might have placed some of the blame for Want with the 10th Mountain Division commanders whose 2006 plunge into the Waygal had left The Rock with the Ranch House and Bella outposts and some of it with the whole way the American-led campaign in Afghanistan was set up.

A catalog of the deeper failings of the war effort had helped bring the fight about and affected its course. The frequent shuffling of top generals in Kabul had made Nuristan a high priority one year and a low one the next. This in turn exacerbated the problems of a unit rotation system that both locked incoming units into the "footprints" of outgoing ones and limited the ability of newly arrived commanders to understand the nuances of their predecessors' approaches. Chronic under-resourcing of the Afghan theater had created a situation where most of the time just two Apache attack helicopters were aloft over a violent, mountainous, three-province region the size of New Jersey. (In Baghdad, meanwhile, four or more Apaches often flew at once over the fifteen-square-mile district of Sadr City.) And the inadvertent killings of local civilians by American aircraft, an issue that top U.S. commanders had been trying and failing to address for years, had also contributed. Even though the assault on the new Want base had been in the works long before the July 4 Apache strike near Bella, Waygal residents later explained to me, the veteran militants who planned and commanded it took the opportunity to swell their force's ranks with angry local men they recruited at the emotional funeral for the victims of the botched helicopter strike.[105]

Viewed in this larger context, Want was no victory.

Ostlund did not mean for the pullout from the outpost site on July 15 to spell the end of American involvement in the Waygal. He was explicit about his hopes that the incoming Fort Hood unit would keep patrolling the Waygal and eventually make another attempt at building a base in Want once the relationship with the valley was repaired.

Others in the chain of command, including Myer, didn't think that was likely, and they were right.

To many people in the valleys around FOB Blessing, the pullout from Want looked like the third step in an American retreat from the Waygal, and this retreat's timing immediately after the July 13 battle made it seem as though the paratroopers had been driven out—exactly the perception Ostlund had hoped to avoid by building a new base in Want in the first place. "When the Americans left Aranas and Want, we hugged each other," Mullah Afzal, the Aranas *shura* leader, recalled. "But what came after them was the Taliban and al-Qaida and Islamic State who were not there before. That was the outcome of the American presence."[106]

Burhan, one of Chosen Company's interpreters, would spend another four years working for American troops in the Pech, and he saw the battle and subsequent pullout as a turning point. "Leaving strengthened the enemy and gave them good propaganda," he told me later when U.S. infantrymen were long gone and militants from both the Taliban and their offshoot, the Afghan affiliate of the Islamic State, lived there openly. "When the Americans left Want, people thought, 'My God, the Americans have run away from the Waygal valley.'"[107]

Hearing it put that way would have frustrated Bill Ostlund. But his own candid take a year after the battle, when he knew that his successors had stayed out of the valley and he had seen the Taliban propaganda videos, was not too different. "I think it was a tactical win and a strategic defeat up there," he told the generals investigating his conduct, "I really do."[108]

By no one's particular intention, the battle of Want was the American high-water mark in the Waygal valley—and, it would turn out, in the broader Pech.

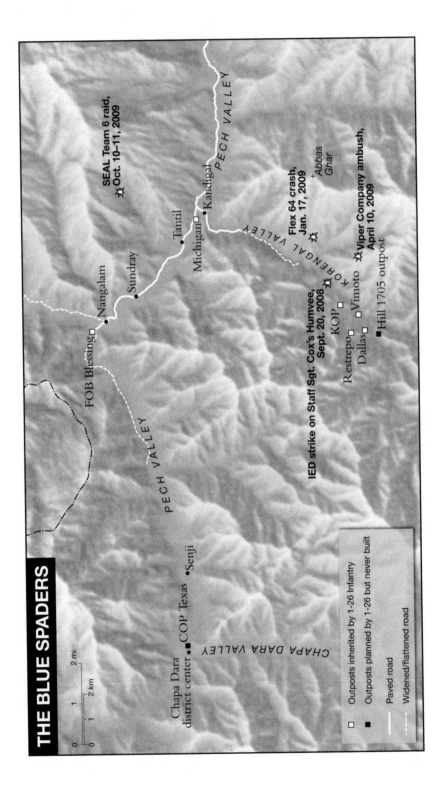

THE BLUE SPADERS

SEAL Team 6 raid,
☆ Oct. 10–11, 2009

PECH VALLEY

Abbas
Ghar

Flex 64 crash,
Jan. 17, 2009 ☆

★ Viper Company ambush,
April 10, 2009

Kandigal

Tantil

Michigan

KORENGAL VALLEY

Sunday

Nangalam

IED strike on Staff Sgt. Cox's Humvee,
Sept. 20, 2008

☆ Vimoto

FOB Blessing

KOP

Restrepo
Dallas

■ Hill 1705 outpost

PECH VALLEY

Chapa Dara
district center ■ • Senji
COP Texas

CHAPA DARA VALLEY

0   1   2 mi
0   1   2 km

□   Outposts inherited by 1-26 Infantry

■   Outposts planned by 1-26 but never built

——   Paved road

– – –   Widened/flattened road

CHAPTER 9

STUCK IN THE VALLEY OF DEATH

2008–2009

THE BLUE SPADERS

To Brett Jenkinson, the lieutenant colonel who succeeded Bill Ostlund in the Pech, it seemed as if there were only one way to really fix the intractable problem he'd inherited in the Korengal valley: build a dam at the Korengal's mouth and fill the valley up with water so that no one could live there anymore, insurgent or civilian.

This was a dark, impossible fantasy, not an actual plan. But Jenkinson was in a dark place. After two months in the Pech, his battalion command in combat—the pinnacle of many infantry officers' careers—was trying him in ways he hadn't expected, racking him with feelings of futility, rage, and guilt.

It had been nearly eight weeks since Ostlund's paratroopers handed the reins over to Jenkinson and his 1-26 Infantry battalion, the Blue Spaders out of Fort Hood, Texas. That was supposed to be enough time for a unit to get in the swing of things, but the tall, bald lieutenant colonel from Indiana felt as though he and his men were treading water. Their mission, as he understood it, was to expand the writ of the Afghan government in the Pech by expanding the American-protected security bubble (the fighting was clearly much too intense for the scrawny, poorly trained, poorly equipped, unmotivated ANA unit they shared their outposts with). Instead, they were fighting just to stay alive, without making any headway or even knowing in what direction they were going.

Jenkinson blamed the Korengal.

He spent as much time as he could out on the road in Humvees, visiting his men at Combat Outposts Michigan, Able Main, and Honaker-Miracle on the Pech. No matter how much he tried to get away from it, though, his deployed life revolved around the battalion operations center at FOB Blessing, a few steps from where he ate and slept and in the same building as his windowless office. And the life of the operations center revolved around the never-ending combat in the Korengal.

On Saturday, September 20, the big screens in the operations center were playing Predator footage of a group of Humvees below, a patrol on the Korengal road north of the KOP. The mission was routine but dangerous: looking for IEDs and hoping to find them the right way instead of the wrong way.

On the screen, Jenkinson could see the Humvees crawling forward. Then he saw the flash of an explosion.

The colonel knew who the senior soldier in the truck was, Staff Sergeant Nathan Cox, and even before the battle-roster number came in over the radio confirming it, he was sure that Cox was gone. The blast had hurled the turret gunner clear, but the obliterated Humvee itself toppled off the road into the ravine below, leaving metal scraps in its wake.

Jenkinson hadn't known Cox well, but his own wife was close friends with the NCO's wife, Annie, and he knew that at thirty-two, with a college degree and sarcastic wit, Cox acted as a role model in a platoon of mostly much younger soldiers. (With Cox and the turret gunner in the Humvee had been an eighteen-year-old private first class named Joseph Gonzales who also died and a fourth young soldier who was badly wounded but survived.)

The Predator feed showed a pair of men scurrying away from the scene and hiding something in a tree. It was obviously the insurgent duo that had triggered and probably also filmed the attack, and Jenkinson, laser focused on killing the men who had killed two Blue Spaders, ordered an orbiting A-10 to track them down. The attack jet dropped a bomb and fired a burst from its cannon but missed, and the pilot reported that he didn't think he'd get another clean shot. Beside himself, Jenkinson called the jet off and tried to get his own mortars to take the shot. Before the mortarmen at the KOP could fire, though, the Predator showed the men disappearing into the safety of a village.

Jenkinson grabbed a chair and hurled it across the operations center. Then he stormed out. Someone had to call Annie Cox, he knew, and that someone was him. He'd made enough of these phone calls by now to dread them; Cox and Gonzales were the eleventh and twelfth soldiers he'd lost in two months.

"There's no worse task in the world than that," he reflected. "To have a warm body bag thrown on your feet and have to fly with it to Bagram is bad, but to have to call a wife or parents is just horrible." Jenkinson called his own wife first and broke down in tears, hardly able to tell her what had happened.[1]

That day and each day afterward that Jenkinson lost a soldier, it felt as if someone were tearing out a piece of his soul. With each loss, he thought about the cool, automaton-like ease with which he'd seen Bill Ostlund manage The Rock's disparate, deadly, complex fights and wondered how he'd done it. He wondered too about the confidence his predecessor had exuded about the prospects for bringing peace and a road to the little side valley that a *Vanity Fair* article had dubbed the "valley of death."[2]

To Jenkinson, the Korengal seemed like a ball and chain, claiming the lives of one of his soldiers after another and tying up resources he could have better used pushing farther up the Pech proper. When the valley came up in conversation, his usually jovial tone turned black. "There's only one way to fix the Korengal," he would say, sometimes to visiting peers, sometimes to subordinates, sometimes to reporters, unknowingly echoing a joke Chris Cavoli had once made, but without much humor. "Build a dam and flood it."[3]

PLAYING ON HIS angular, six-foot-three frame, bald head, and propensity to hop out of his truck and shoot back at the enemy with his M4 as if he were a sergeant instead of a forty-one-year-old battalion commander, some of Brett Jenkinson's soldiers nicknamed him Earthworm Jim. It was meant as a compliment: Earthworm Jim was the protagonist of a 1990s video game whose pointy, bare earth-worm head was attached to a muscular humanoid body (Jenkinson had been on West Point's power-lifting team) and who went around battling evil with a ray gun.[4]

Jenkinson loved his men, and many of them loved him, though some also found him something of a puzzle. His leadership style was cheerful, energetic, even goofy; he joked constantly with his soldiers and sometimes complained to his lieutenants about his own bosses. He did the kinds of morale-boosting things that made people use the word "eccentric" when they talked about him, like pitting a fighting ram whose fur was painted with the Blue Spader crest against another ram that belonged to FOB Blessing's Afghan security guards.

Inside, though, Jenkinson was struggling, and he knew that his 1–26 Infantry battalion was too.

The Blue Spader battalion commander was cut from different cloth from the two hard-charging, ambitious peers who had preceded him in the Pech, both men who seemed marked to be generals. He had wound up in the infantry because he didn't have the grades at West Point to join the Army Corps of Engineers, but had gradually learned to love the infantry life, "doing manly things with other men," as he put it. After two tours in Iraq as a paratroop major, he'd taken a job with the DIA, not expecting the Army to give him another command. But the Army was expanding to meet the demands of two wars, and in 2007 Jenkinson got the call: he'd been tapped to build a new battalion from scratch and take it to war.[5]

The new unit acquired the heritage and heraldry of an old one: the 1st Infantry Division's Blue Spader battalion, so nicknamed for the spade-like blue arrowhead on the regimental insignia, which dated to World War I. To fill out the battalion with new Blue Spaders, the Army sent whole batches of privates straight from basic infantry training; many arrived at Fort Hood before there were rifles and compasses to issue them. For NCOs, the Army scrounged some sergeants from heavy units where their expertise was in fighting from tanklike Bradley fighting vehicles and others from assorted jobs that had previously prevented them from deploying.[6]

To bring in enough recruits for the new units it needed, the Army was lowering enlistment standards and granting unheard-of numbers of enlistment waivers for past criminal activity and medical or psychological problems.[7] That left Jenkinson and his officers to weed out a proportion of their junior soldiers for bad behavior or inability to meet physical fitness standards in the year before deployment.[8] What was left was a motivated but smaller force. Platoons that were supposed to have thirty junior soldiers wound up with twenty-five or twenty-six, and seven or eight NCOs instead of twelve.[9]

Stretched nearly to the breaking point, the service didn't have the luxury of picking which units went to Iraq and Afghanistan's toughest sectors. When one infantry brigade's time in theater was up, the next one in line rotated in, ready or not, and 1-26 Infantry was not nearly as ready as the two battalions before it in the Pech.

T.W. of the Asymmetric Warfare Group dealt with the latest unit in the Pech only briefly before taking a year off from Afghanistan for knee surgery, depriving the incoming battalion of the years of Kunar-specific tactical wisdom he had accumulated since 2005. His uncharitable but truthful judgment was that 1-26 Infantry "was like the opposite of 1-32," the Chosin battalion, which the forty-eight-year-old tactical adviser still saw as the gold standard for a light infantry battalion fighting in the mountains.[10] "We were a jumbled mess that was cobbled together at the last minute," agreed one incoming platoon leader, whose point of comparison was The Rock. "We were proud of being Blue Spaders, but we were a different kind of organization from the 173rd, frankly. We weren't as good."[11] They couldn't have been.

Jenkinson knew that the opening weeks of a deployment were the most dangerous time, but he wasn't prepared for how quickly the losses started. When an IED killed his first soldier, a sergeant from the route-clearance platoon (which had deployed ahead of the rest of the battalion), the colonel hadn't even gotten to Afghanistan yet. When another bomb took four more soldiers from the same platoon the day after the Blue Spader colors were uncased at Blessing, Jenkinson felt as if someone had hit him in the face.

AS IT HAD the previous summer and the summer before that, the Korengal provided the steepest, most lethal learning curve.

Compared with the soldiers who came before them in the Korengal, the men of Viper Company, as 1-26 Infantry's B Company was nicknamed, had a good idea of what they were getting into. Dan Kearney's Battle Company paratroopers had been the subject of article upon news segment upon photo shoot during their fifteen months in the Korengal, which many Blue Spader lieutenants and NCOs studied carefully.[12] Some soldiers had read Marcus Luttrell's bestselling tale of Operation Red Wings, *Lone Survivor*, which was published as the Blue Spaders were training to deploy.

There were also two soldiers in Viper Company who had been to the Korengal before, both of whom shared what they knew about the place with their comrades and showed them shaky videos of ambushes and artillery barrages.

One of the two was Specialist Kieth Jeter, who had hated his time in the valley as a private in Jim McKnight's Attack Company so much that afterward he sought a transfer to Fort Hood, the land of tanks, Bradleys, and Iraq deployments, only to wind up in the one infantry company out of thirty at Hood that was Korengal-bound.

Arriving at COP Vegas, Jeter was pleased to see that living conditions had improved. Generators now supplied power to some of the plywood sheds where the soldiers lived, one of which contained phones, an Xbox video game system, and internet-connected computers where soldiers could check email and Myspace.

Jeter's relief gave way to dread as the firefights began, heavier and more frequent than they'd been when he left. At Vegas that August and September, the insurgents came to fight just about every day, and they came in strength, bold and close enough that the outpost's defenders could see and shoot at their camouflage-clad profiles instead of just their muzzle flashes.[13] A week in, Jeter killed a guerrilla with a well-aimed 40-millimeter grenade.[14] Three weeks in, on August 16, an IED blew up a Humvee as it traversed the Korengal road below Vegas, killing Staff Sergeant Kristopher Rodgers. That same evening, enough insurgents descended on Vegas from the woods of the Abbas Ghar to briefly raise fears of a Want-style attack. Two Apaches and FOB Blessing's relentless howitzers helped fend off the assault, and afterward jets dropped bomb after bomb on the ridge. "The sky lit up for hours," an eighteen-year-old infantryman named

Mikel Drnec wrote of the barrage in his journal that night.[15] Out of some forty or fifty insurgents whose forms or muzzle flashes COP Vegas's defenders had identified, a report on the battle noted, "we estimate that 5 got within 25 meters of the eastern perimeter wire," where some of their bodies were found.[16] At least one soldier had been throwing hand grenades.[17]

Viper Company's other Korengal returnee was its commander, Captain Jimmy Howell. It had been three years since Howell had helped recover the sixteen bodies from the charred wreckage of Turbine 33 as a Ranger platoon leader, and four and a half years since he first set foot in Kunar as a 10th Mountain lieutenant. In the meantime, he'd been back to Afghanistan once more with the Rangers and to Iraq twice

Howell was a calm, collected leader, able to cope with losing men to death and wounds far more steadily than his battalion commander could and better able to keep his cool with the Korengali elders than Dan Kearney or Jim McKnight before him. Like his predecessors, he hoped to push the front line a couple of kilometers farther away from the KOP by building a new outpost deeper in the valley. He was never able to.[18] The fighting was too intense, and Viper Company just too small. Fifteen to twenty soldiers short of a full company to begin with, it kept getting smaller. Four days after the August assault on Vegas, a staff sergeant died of heart failure on patrol. After that, firefights, IED strikes, and a friendly-fire incident killed one soldier after another: two on September 6, two more on September 20, another in October.

At the end of the summer, soldiers started rotating home for midtour leave, meaning the company was always short another dozen or so men. A few soldiers couldn't bring themselves to face the return trip and went AWOL at home. Out of a company of 130 men, 9 would eventually die and 39 more would be wounded badly enough to be evacuated, along with the half a dozen or so soldiers who never came back from leave—losses that were only partially offset by replacement troops from Fort Hood and casualties who returned after treatment.[19]

"As we started taking casualties and guys started going on leave, we really had not much more than a hundred guys, and that isn't very much," said Howell.[20] Just getting two platoons together for a mission at the same time became a struggle, and the front line began to creep backward. The village of Loy Kalay below Restrepo, which had been inside Battle Company's "security bubble," became a battleground again.[21]

Morale in the company plummeted. "It was strange if a guy *wasn't* having nightmares if he was up at Dallas or Restrepo," remembered a platoon leader. Some soldiers self-medicated with marijuana or the opium hash to which the ANA soldiers they lived with were addicted,[22] and combat stress clinicians liberally doled out prescriptions for the antipsychotic Seroquel.[23]

THE KORENGAL ROAD project fell by the wayside. Neither Howell nor Jenkinson had the full story about how the road project had come into being, just the much-expanded version they heard from Dan Kearney and Bill Ostlund. That version wasn't realistic anymore, if it ever had been, and Jenkinson gave Howell his blessing to abandon it. "The Korengal road was explained to me as a governance and development thing," not a counter-IED project, said Jenkinson. "For us it became just about emergency resupply."[24] The road regressed from a vehicle for societal change to what Chris Cavoli had originally conceived of it as: a ground route kept free from IEDs that could keep the KOP supplied when helicopters weren't available.[25] But with more helicopters for resupply runs in 2008 than at any earlier point in the war, the road fell into disuse even for that limited purpose. By the time rainfall washed boulders down onto a long section of the road over the winter and traffic stopped altogether, Viper Company's five outposts in the Korengal—the KOP, Vegas, Restrepo, Vimoto, and Dallas—had effectively been air-centric bases for months.[26]

Air-centric outposts presented their own vulnerabilities, as The Rock had learned in the Waygal. Just a month into Viper Company's deployment, one of the Supreme Air contractor resupply helicopters was taking off from the landing zone at Vegas when everyone heard the pop of an RPG and the big white Mi-17 caught fire, tried to take off, sank back down, and blew up.[27] One of the two civilian pilots made it out, badly burned, but the other was incinerated inside. The soldiers at the outpost (and the stray dog that served as their mascot, who relished the ghastly task more than they did) collected as many scorched pieces of the anonymous man as they could, but they all fit in an ammunition can.[28]

After that, Supreme Air stopped flying to the Korengal, leaving the job to Army Chinooks. The task was no less dangerous for them. The weekly Korengal resupply run used up many of the brigade's helicopters for a day and could take four or five hours as Chinooks hopped back and forth between Blessing and the Korengal outposts and Apaches circled nearby.[29] One helicopter had a close call with an RPG in the fall, and in January 2009 another wasn't so lucky. A Chinook with the call sign Flex 64 had already been in and out of the valley once on January 17 and was leaving Restrepo when the crew saw a flash. A few seconds later, a projectile blew a hole in the port-side fuel tank, fired by an insurgent team that also included cameramen filming the attack from different angles for a propaganda video. With flames blasting out of the helicopter's belly and the crew chiefs chucking out everything they could to drop weight, the pilot banked east and managed to crash-land just outside Vegas. The crew made it out before the downed Chinook exploded in flames, but one of the two passengers aboard, a scout sergeant named Ezra Dawson, didn't.[30] (Soldiers from the ANA platoon in the valley refused to leave their outpost, OP Vimoto, to help secure the crash, further undermining any confidence the Viper Company soldiers had in their Afghan partners.[31])

The other passenger on the Chinook was the Korengal returnee Kieth Jeter, who stumbled into the Vegas concertina wire with his helmet broken in half and his eyebrows singed off and passed out. The crash undid Jeter. At home on leave after a week in the hospital, he drank heavily and returned to Fort Hood late. Judging him unfit for duty, the Army didn't send him back to Afghanistan. Jeter's platoon leader and platoon sergeant told him by email that they understood, and of all the soldiers who didn't come back from leave, Viper Company veterans remembered him as the only one whom no one begrudged.[32] "He always did his job no matter how bad things got," remembered Jeter's platoon mate Mikel Drnec. "Nobody judged him for it."[33] But his departure left Viper Company yet another man short, and guilt over not going back to the Korengal would follow the young veteran for years.[34]

The aviation brigade in eastern Afghanistan responded to the downing of Flex 64 by halting daytime resupply missions altogether in favor of flights in the darkest part of the darkest nights.[35] "First no one wanted to drive to us," the glum joke went in Viper Company, "and now no one wants to fly to us."[36]

It probably wasn't lost on the Korengali insurgents fighting their third U.S. Army rifle company that this was a lot like how The Rock's long departure from the Waygal had played out: first trucks and Humvees had slowed and then ceased their traffic on the road as the ground resupply route gave way to the twin pressures of nature and IEDs; then attacks on helicopters had made aerial resupply more and more dangerous too. And it would not have been lost on the Korengali elders like the mujahidin veteran Haji Zalwar Khan that this was how the only Soviet base to last more than a few weeks in the Pech, Captain Alex Shuvahin's Bar Kanday outpost, had met its end too.*[37]

The Soviet experience was something Americans in Kunar didn't usually hear much about besides triumphantly exaggerated stories of mujahidin victories. Over the winter, though, Zalwar Khan and his cousin Shamshir Khan touched on the subject in a conversation that Jimmy Howell remembered as sobering and uncharacteristically candid. *We talked to them too, you know,* the old men told Howell and the ANA company commander over a meal of rice and goat one day at the KOP. *We know you mean well, but you can't really do anything for us. You say you're going to build a clinic, but then you only build it right by your base. You say you're going to build a road, but you can't build a road. And you won't be here forever. So we talk to you just like we talked to the other companies and like we talked to the Russians.*[38]

WHEN HE VISITED the KOP, Jenkinson reassured Howell and the other soldiers wondering about their purpose in the Korengal that they were the cork in the bottle, defending the good that was hap-

---

* Manned for eighteen months by the soldiers of the 5th Company, 66th Separate Motorized Rifle Brigade, the Soviet Bar Kanday outpost was closed shortly after a Mi-8 transport helicopter was shot down on a resupply run in November 1982, necessitating a risky recovery mission across the Pech River.

pening down on the Pech road. (There were now full-time U.S. government civilians at FOB Blessing helping oversee road-related development projects, like the installation of solar-powered streetlights in Nangalam and other towns.) That was what his own brigade commander was telling him every time he raised doubts about the Korengal.[39]

But Jenkinson didn't really believe the reassurances he was offering. He wouldn't say it in front of anyone from Viper Company, but by the end of 2008 he wanted out of the Korengal, and he was making it known to whoever would listen, from visiting journalists to Major General Jeffrey Schloesser, the division commander. Why, he wondered, couldn't U.S. troops just fly into the Korengal once in a while and hit targets, as they had before the KOP was built and still did in so many other valleys?[40]

"Every time General Schloesser came up, I'd tell him, 'I think we can accomplish what we're doing right now in the Korengal just by flying in and out and shooting some mortars and artillery,'" Jenkinson said. The generals never told Jenkinson they disagreed, but they never gave him any hint that they were taking his suggestions seriously, either.[41]

In fact, Schloesser was thinking hard about many of the things Jenkinson was saying, and fielding pointed queries on the same topics from some of the U.S. military's top officers, including the commander of CENTCOM and the chairman of the Joint Chiefs. On a pre-deployment recon trip that took him to the KOP and the Waygal back in 2007, the two-star general had jotted down the essential question in his green notebook: "Nuristan—Korengal—why?"[42]

A lanky helicopter pilot, Schloesser also spoke Arabic and had held jobs at embassies and in the intelligence community. He had first become aware of the Korengal at the same time most of the military did, during Red Wings, a tragedy that held particular meaning for him: Steve Reich, the air mission commander killed aboard Turbine 33, had been a protégé of the general's, joining the Night Stalkers at Schloesser's urging. Now, much as he had worried that a base in Want would be the next KOP, the general worried that one of the Korengal bases could be the scene of a Red Wings–style fiasco centered on another downed Chinook.[43]

On the other hand, the argument that the fighting in the Koren-gal sucked insurgent resources and attention away from the Pech road was hard to dismiss. But Schloesser detected an emotional component in some of the resistance to reevaluating the usefulness of the Korengal presence too. Leaving the valley "was almost off the table" for some officers in his own headquarters, the division com-mander recalled. "It wasn't something you could mention without somebody saying, 'Sir, we paved this road in blood and we just can't leave.'"[44]

On balance, Schloesser didn't think the time had come to pull out of the Korengal, even though he wasn't sure he would know when it *did* come.[45]

A BRIDGE TOO FAR

With Viper Company making no headway in the Korengal, Brett Jenkinson was alert to anywhere else the Blue Spaders might be able to expand and make a difference—potentially somewhere to build a new outpost and with it a new ink blot or extension of the security bubble.[46]

So Jenkinson looked west. The twenty miles of asphalt on the Pech road stopped just beyond Blessing, but plans and contracts were still on the books to pave forty more miles up to the isolated government enclave in the Parun valley in Nuristan. On the way, nine miles past Blessing before the valley turned north toward the Parun, was a dilapidated district center protected by a small contin-gent of police at the picturesque confluence of the Pech and Chapa Dara valleys. The Chapa Dara district governor was begging for American help, claiming that his district center was effectively be-sieged by a variety of insurgent groups. Kunar's governor, Fazlullah Wahidi, was eager to see American troops there too; with a presi-dential election coming up in 2009, any district center that voters couldn't safely reach, or where an insurgent presence precluded vot-ing, was a black eye to the government and the Afghan democratic process.[47]

Platoons started driving out to Chapa Dara from Blessing two or three times a week.[48] "People were always asking me when we were going to build the base," said the interpreter Burhan, who went along on many of the missions and helped check out different outpost sites. "People wanted the coalition forces to come out because they brought jobs, school supplies, asphalt for the road, and other things."[49] Jenkinson was sold. "That was the one place I was actually making a difference, where I was actually bringing government to the people," he explained.[50] The planned Chapa Dara base was even assigned a tentative name: COP Texas.

As it became obvious what the American patrols to Chapa Dara were up to, the company working west of Blessing started running into ambushes and IEDs with increasing regularity. One soldier received three Purple Hearts for wounds sustained in the attacks, the third for a concussion from an IED blast that triggered a stroke.[51]

Not a single Blue Spader was killed on the road to Chapa Dara, however—a testament, in part, to the vehicles they were making the trip in, a mix of up-armored Humvees and newer, safer, bigger trucks called MRAPs (pronounced "M-Raps").

Based on a three-decade-old design developed for South African troops in the Angolan Bush War, the tall, boxy MRAPs were built around V-shaped hulls that redirected the force of IED explosions and put more room between the soldiers inside and the blast below them. American route-clearance patrols had been using versions of the trucks for years on counter-IED missions, but in 2007, with roadside bomb attacks killing dozens of Americans every month in Iraq, Secretary of Defense Robert Gates had moved mountains to expand production and start fielding various MRAP models to infantry units as replacements for up-armored Humvees.

Fielded first in Iraq, where commanders were clamoring for them, and then in Afghanistan, MRAPs saved many lives. A Blue Spader platoon leader named Carter Cheek was in one of the newly deployed vehicles over the winter, an eight-ton version, when it hit an IED on the way out toward Chapa Dara. The bomb blew the wheels off the MRAP, but no one inside died. In a Humvee, Cheek was sure someone would have.[52]

Paradoxically, though, the coming of the MRAPs helped ensure that COP Texas never moved beyond the planning-and-surveying stage.

In the seesaw balance between giving commanders the freedom

to send troops where they wanted on the battlefield and shielding those troops from roadside bombs, the Army's mass fielding of MRAPs in Afghanistan in 2009 represented the victory of protection over mobility.[53] In Iraq and in flatter areas of Afghanistan, it didn't matter so much that even the lightest MRAP was almost a foot wider than an up-armored Humvee and nearly twice as heavy. On roads in Kunar and Nuristan where Humvees were already scraping by, it mattered a lot—particularly because, in typical fashion, the Army adopted a one-size-fits-all approach to fielding the new vehicles, making their use on all mounted movements a requirement, not a choice left to the lieutenants and captains commanding the patrols. In Kunar, brigade headquarters mandated that an MRAP be the lead vehicle in all patrols as soon as there were enough of them.

Eight or nine feet tall, as heavy as the eight-wheeled armored troop carriers that the Soviets had used in Kunar,[54] and with high centers of gravity, MRAPs were prone to rollovers, and it was all too easy for one to break an axle on a rough stretch of road. One Pech platoon leader complained that an MRAP had "the cross-country mobility of a three-legged drunken elephant."[55] Wherever the new trucks were fielded, there were turns that couldn't be made anymore, stretches of road that were just too narrow, bridges that couldn't be crossed.

One such bridge was located by the village of Senji, three-quarters of the way between Blessing and Chapa Dara. Humvees could cross the Senji Bridge, but to send an MRAP across was to risk breaking the span and sending the truck plunging into the water; instead, MRAPs had to ford the river, which wasn't always possible. Insurgents often planted IEDs and sprang ambushes near the bridge too; the interpreter Farshad was badly wounded by an RPG blast in one such ambush, ending his three years of service with American units in the Pech.[56] When the Afghan construction company that was under contract to pave the road to Chapa Dara built a new, concrete bridge, MRAPs could cross, but only one at a time; there was still no way it could form part of a reliable ground supply route. And building another air-only outpost in Kunar was out of the question: the KOP and its satellites were more than enough. So the plan to build a new base withered. For a military force tied to roads that could support eight- and fifteen-ton armored vehicles, Chapa Dara was a bridge too far.[57]

BY THE SPRING of 2009, the Blue Spaders had left behind many of their early growing pains. In the Korengal, Viper Company was fighting "like water over rocks," as Jenkinson put it—smoothly and with the expertise born not from training but from months of combat.

In early April, an ambush patrol on the lower slopes of the Sawtalo Sar scored a tactical win that any special operations team would have been jealous of—one of the few times American troops ever really got the jump on their enemy in the Korengal. When some of his men spotted footprints and garbage on a trail a third of the way up the mountain, below Chichal, the platoon leader called a halt and had his soldiers nestle into the vegetation, Ranger School–style, as darkness fell. Not long afterward, a column of insurgents approached in single file, oblivious to the American infantrymen's presence.

The soldiers let loose with Claymores, rifles, machine guns, and grenades. Some dead insurgents fell almost at the ambushers' feet, while others tumbled down the mountainside. Apaches and an F-15 killed more as they fled.[58]

The ambush on the Sawtalo Sar, which killed at least fifteen Korengali fighters, seemed to take the wind out of the sails of the valley's insurgency for a few weeks as the Blue Spaders entered the final stretch of their deployment. It was an exceptional event, however. In general, compared with the units before it, 1-26 Infantry didn't go to the insurgent base areas high in the mountains that 1-32, the Chosin battalion, had reached on foot or by pickup truck and that 2-503, The Rock, had reached with its big air-assault operations.[59] It wasn't until the spring, for instance, during a relatively small air-assault mission called Viper Shake, that Howell set foot on the top of the Sawtalo Sar for the first time since he had been there in 2005 and looked down the other side into the Shuryak through icy drizzle.[60]

The difference was partly a result of the Blue Spaders' chronic undermanning, which made it difficult to get enough troops together for anything besides routine patrolling.[61] But it was also Brett Jenkinson's deliberate choice.

The battalion intelligence section, whose office was right across the hall from Jenkinson's in the Blessing operations center building, kept him apprised of the latest tips, rumors, and signals intercepts on the array of insurgent commanders based far back in the various valleys. Jenkinson couldn't muster much enthusiasm for working with his frustratingly unprofessional ANA counterpart, or for checking up on road construction sites with district officials. But he wanted to arrange the deaths of these figures as badly as he wanted almost anything in the world. "We'd want to use CERP [development funds] to put solar lights in Nangalam or something, and Colonel Jenkinson would be like, 'Okay, well, when are we going to kill Abu Ikhlas?'" said one staff officer.[62]

"By the end, I was a killing machine. I was not where I needed to be mentally," the colonel himself said. For Jenkinson, stuck in a stalemate in the Korengal and barred from building a new outpost in Chapa Dara, the hunt for the guerrilla commanders who were killing and wounding his men was the only thing that really felt productive anymore, much more so than checking up on the details of micro-hydro projects or solar-powered streetlights.[63]

But the intelligence was almost never specific or timely enough to plan air-assault operations around, and the alternative—risking men and helicopters on search-and-attack operations *not* based on specific intelligence, like Rock Avalanche and so many other past missions—was unappealing to Jenkinson. The few times he did send companies up into the mountains by helicopter, the results were disappointing. On Viper Shake, when Viper Company landed on the Sawtalo Sar and poked around with a Predator and Apaches overhead, twisted ankles, exhaustion, and falling rocks injured more soldiers than did the enemy, who stayed quiet until Howell and his men were back at the KOP. "I did not like to go up there just trolling for contact," Jenkinson explained.[64]

Instead, he relied on airpower to hit targets out of his soldiers' reach, favoring Apaches with their rockets and Hellfires and jets with their satellite-guided bombs. That risked killing civilians, however, and ran counter to specific guidance from the four-star allied commander in Kabul, who was trying to rein in American units' use of air strikes countrywide. After one Apache strike that he ordered in the Watapur in the spring, Jenkinson wound up with a formal letter of reprimand in his personnel file from the division commander Schloesser. Several insurgents had died in the strike, but it had killed as many as four civilians too, including the young daughter of a militant, and its target had gotten away.[65]

THE NIGHT WAR

What was really needed in the Pech, Jenkinson thought, was a force dedicated to quick, in-and-out raids to kill enemy leaders, with its own intelligence support and its own dedicated helicopters. Such a force existed in theater, of course: the JSOC task force in Afghanistan, which in the spring of 2009 was growing and hitting more targets than it ever had before.

When Jenkinson's rounds took him to the CIA base at FOB Asadabad for intelligence-synchronization meetings, he would cajole the Omega team of SEAL Team 6 operators there for help hitting the targets he couldn't. The Omega operators were eager to get out with the agency's Afghan Mohawks and fight, but strict rules prevented them from joining conventional military operations while working for the CIA unless there was strong evidence of an al-Qaida angle, which there rarely was.[66]

Jenkinson also kept an open invitation for the JSOC personnel at Jalalabad Airfield to use his outposts as staging bases. "Colonel Jenkinson was like, 'You guys just go where you want and kill whoever you want,'" remembered a former Chosin battalion lieutenant who led a Ranger unit at Jalalabad and Asadabad that fighting season.[67] But the Team 6 officers who ran the JSOC show in northeastern Afghanistan were reluctant to risk their men going after what they saw as small-time insurgent commanders, especially in terrain that had a track record of bringing down helicopters. *Hey, dudes, if it was an easy target, my guys would have hit it already,* Jenkinson thought in frustration after each interaction with the SEALs. *That's why you guys are special!*[68] And on the rare occasions when a JSOC strike force did come out to the Pech, the same problems persisted that the Marines had dealt with back in 2005. The special operators were going after different targets from the ones the Blue Spaders wanted to see killed. They shared little information beforehand about what they were doing or even who they were. And they often left brutal messes to clean up in the morning—as when a botched Ranger raid in Kandigal killed the old man who cooked for the ANA at COP Michigan.*[69]

During the later months of the Blue Spaders' deployment, however, Jenkinson received some help from an experienced Pech hand: Bill Ostlund.

AFTER SAYING GOODBYE to the Pech the previous summer, Ostlund had rejoined his beloved Rangers at Fort Benning as the 75th Ranger Regiment's deputy commander at the end of 2008. Within weeks, he was back in Afghanistan, lending a hand as a Ranger headquarters team took over the Bagram JSOC task force from SEAL Team 6.[70]

In the weeks before Ostlund's return to Afghanistan that winter, civilian deaths during JSOC raids had been piling up. During a short period in December 2008, two strike forces in other parts of eastern Afghanistan had killed six policemen, shot several civilians, and allowed a military working dog to bite a child. Special operations raid forces—particularly from Team 6—were acquiring a reputation for unnecessary brutality, often killing people they could have captured rather than see them put into what many operators saw as a dysfunctional catch-and-release detention system.

"There was a snowball effect, a building level of savagery, because we were doing missions so often and had been doing them for so long," one member of Team 6 who was in eastern Afghanistan that winter recalled.[71] Statistics compiled in Kabul showed that JSOC missions accounted for an alarming percentage of the civilian

---

* After the raid, the soldiers at Michigan joked that they'd figured out what the numbers in JSOC's code name at the time, Task Force 373, stood for: one 3 for the three minutes it took the JSOC operators to kill everybody in their target building, a 7 for the seven months of winning hearts and minds that such a raid undid, and another 3 for the three years it would take to smooth things over with the community afterward.

casualties that were steadily undermining President Karzai's trust in the American military.[72]

Concerned and angry, the U.S. ambassador in Kabul summoned the SEAL who had succeeded Stan McChrystal as JSOC's commander, Vice Admiral William McRaven, to the embassy. The message McRaven remembered the ambassador delivering there was blunt: *Afghanistan has been a strategic defeat in 2008 because of you and your men.*[73]

The rebuke made McRaven stew, but after yet more civilians died in another night raid a few weeks later, he put all JSOC missions in Afghanistan on pause.[74] The admiral chose two Army officers to review what the task force was doing wrong and how to fix it: his one-star deputy and Bill Ostlund.[75]

A year earlier, Ostlund had been in the same boat that Jenkinson was in now, equally frustrated with JSOC's unwillingness to go after the insurgent commanders his men were fighting or to share information. Trading on his own Ranger background, he had once brought a group of SEAL leaders out to Blessing to pitch them on helping out in places like the Korengal and Shuryak, but they didn't bite.[76]

The reforms Ostlund and his team recommended in February 2009 were "countercultural," as Ostlund put it,[77] but McRaven accepted them wholesale. The infantry brigade commander in a given area, the admiral ordered, now had to sign off on every JSOC raid, and the task force should prioritize the targets that infantry units wanted hit, even if they seemed like small fry. Afghan commandos and liaisons from the infantry would start tagging along on missions. "It was a sea change," said the CIA officer Ron Moeller, who was back in Afghanistan as the agency's liaison to McRaven, of the changes and the accompanying switch from Team 6 to Ranger leadership at Bagram. "The Rangers were much better at working with the conventional guys than the SEALs, because they all grew up together in the Army. It was a maturing of the task force's outlook."[78]

If Ostlund had struggled at times with the nuance and complexity of counterinsurgency in the Pech, running the special operations night-raiding machine, as he did that spring and again in the fall, was a job he was naturally suited for. He and other senior Rangers focused on turning that machine away from its narrow counter-terrorism mission. "There was resistance, but I thought we should be using our national assets"—JSOC operators and all the technology that backed them up—"to kill IED makers who were killing young American infantrymen," he explained later.[79] What had long been two separate wars—the war of infantry battalions against local guerrillas and JSOC's secret war against al-Qaida terrorists and top-level Taliban commanders—had to become one.[80]

There was little time left for JSOC to help the Blue Spaders before they returned home to Texas. But the next battalion commander coming into the Pech, Lieutenant Colonel Brian Pearl, had been a close friend of Ostlund's since they were lieutenants in infantry school together.[81] Ostlund wanted things to go better for Pearl and his Colorado-based 2-12 Infantry battalion than they had for Jenkinson and the Blue Spaders. The SEAL commander of JSOC's Jalalabad contingent, Task Force East,[82] started coming across the airfield twice a week to sync up his unit's operations with the infantry's and even put his attached Rangers at Asadabad for a while.[83] "It grew into a much better relationship, and the biggest part of that was Bill," said Pearl, who arrived at Blessing in June and soon received a visit from Ostlund. "He laid the foundation."[84]

THE SEVENTY OR SO SEALs and Rangers at Jalalabad lived the "reverse cycle" life of vampires, sleeping during the day and waking up in the evenings to pore over intelligence reports on guerrilla commanders with target code names like Wrigley, Mowgli, Lake James, and Sasquatch. Late at night, the operators would take buses out to the tarmac and board Night Stalker Chinooks for the flight north, usually accompanied by Apaches, an AC-130, a Predator or Reaper, and other aircraft. The most useful of these guardian angels was the plane that the operators knew by the call sign Draco—a small, converted civilian turboprop crammed with sensors.[85]

Instead of landing right at the target site in the mountains (a common tactic earlier in the war that had since been deemed too risky for routine use), the Chinooks would deposit the SEALs and Rangers at the nearest infantry outpost. From there they would head into the mountains, covering as much ground as they could and still get back out before the sun came up.[86]

In a memoir, Matthew Bissonnette, a former chief petty officer in Team 6, recounted an October 2009 Task Force East mission, which soldiers based at nearby COP Michigan at the time also remembered.[87]

The fighting season was winding down when surveillance aircraft started spotting sentries patrolling around a three-building compound on a wooded mountainside several miles north of the Pech, farther up a thin gorge from the valley-floor town of Tantil than the soldiers at nearby COP Michigan had ventured. The battalion intelligence shop at Blessing suspected that the compound was the base of a local commander named Fazil Wahid, code-named Objective Burnside. Fazil Wahid's band of guerrillas had been ambushing and burning supply trucks on the Pech road for months. Eager to hit a juicy target and help out their infantry brothers, Task Force East took the mission.

After dark on October 10, a pair of Chinooks deposited twenty-odd SEALs and some accompanying Rangers and Afghan troops in the field outside Michigan—just in time for one of the long-distance firefights that the infantrymen at the outpost endured a few times a week to erupt around them. As RPGs exploded and Michigan's machine gunners and mortarmen fired back over their heads, the surprised special operators made a dash for the gate, but not before four of them had suffered shrapnel wounds: a Ranger, an Afghan soldier, an interpreter, and the SEALs' attack dog, all of whom had to be evacuated by helicopter.

Once they were inside the wire and the shooting had subsided, the visiting operators prepped their gear in Michigan's cramped weight room while Bissonnette and the other senior frogmen huddled with the outpost's commander over a map to fine-tune their mission plan. Wearing mismatched camouflage, with long hair and beards, the SEALs looked like "Vikings or bikers" compared with the clean-cut soldiers at the outpost, who stared at their sound-suppressed weapons, thermal scopes, and lightweight body armor with envy.[88]

Tagging along behind a late-night infantry patrol, the strike force filed back out of Michigan's gate and headed west. Half a mile up the Pech road, they took a right into the gorge leading up toward their target, three miles back along a switchbacked road and then a foot trail. By the time he and the rest of the strike force moved onto the terraces above the target compound six hours later, Bissonnette was exhausted, and only a couple hours of darkness remained.

The SEALs slipped past the roaming sentries with an orbiting spy plane's help and approached the target buildings silently in three groups. An unlocked door allowed one team to sneak inside. Two men were just waking up and reaching for the weapons at their bedsides when SEALs killed them with sound-suppressed rifles. Stalking from room to room, the operators killed a roomful of guerrillas with a hand grenade, shot another man as he was trying to escape out a window, and then cut down a group of sentries rushing back to the compound—seventeen men in all,[89] including Fazil Wahid and another guerrilla leader who was visiting him. An AC-130 covered their exfiltration back down to the Pech in the early hours of the morning, killing more fighters with its big guns.[90]

The sound of the circling gunship was a telltale sign that the "men with green eyes" were out and about. Five miles away on the south side of the Pech, at a similar mountain compound, a Norwegian journalist was visiting the next commander up in the insurgent hierarchy, Mullah Dawran. "Everyone, just leave your things, just go up in the mountains, we have to hide," Dawran ordered as soon as they heard the AC-130's guns. Among the dead, Dawran learned the next day, was his own second-in-command, who had been visiting Fazil Wahid when the SEALs struck.[91]

Attacks around Tantil subsided for several weeks after that night, no small thing for the infantrymen who patrolled the Pech road every day.[92] But the mission had been a hard and risky one. "Operating in Kunar was tough," Bissonnette wrote in his memoir. "I'd argue it was one of the toughest places to effectively target the enemy in the entire country."[93]

That kept the JSOC commanders responsible for signing off on such missions cautious. One place they would never authorize a raid was the valley where Brett Jenkinson had most wanted their help: the Korengal, where the SEAL commander of Task Force East declined to risk a helicopter insertion even when a fallen Viper Company soldier was briefly feared captured in April.[94]

"DO YOU THINK YOU CAN CHANGE THIS VALLEY?"

Three weeks after Jenkinson and the last Viper Company soldiers headed home to Texas in June 2009, General Stanley McChrystal landed at the KOP for an overnight visit. Selected by President Obama to preside over his Afghan surge and turn the war around, the former JSOC commander had recently arrived at the sprawling International Security Assistance Force headquarters in Kabul to take command of the ninety thousand American and other NATO troops in the country.[95] Now he was visiting ISAF bases in every corner of Afghanistan, getting the lay of the land. A month in, on July 16, his rounds brought him to the valley system he had last seen during Winter Strike in 2003, when the Korengal was almost completely unknown.

A captain was waiting at the KOP landing zone to greet McChrystal and show him around. The general recognized the name on the young officer's gray Velcro name tape: Moretti. McChrystal had had a West Point classmate with that name. This was the classmate's son, Captain Mark Moretti, commander of Baker Company, 2-12 Infantry, the fourth American company commander to preside over the Korengal valley from the KOP. Moretti walked McChrystal around and briefed him on what his men had been up to in the month since they had arrived in the Korengal: how many patrols they were mounting, how many of them ANA soldiers came along for, where the front line was (Aliabad, the same as two years earlier).

"Do you think you can change this valley?" McChrystal asked Moretti.

Yes, the captain answered, as full of optimism as Jim McKnight, Dan Kearney, and Jimmy Howell had all been a month into their deployments. If Baker Company patrolled aggressively, he explained, he thought it could bring Aliabad into the security bubble, and that would be a good start for the rest of the year.[96]

No one had told Moretti yet, but his own battalion and brigade commanders had already decided that his would be the last company in the Korengal and that closing the valley's outposts would be the great accomplishment of their yearlong deployment.

In a paper completed a few days after McChrystal's visit to the KOP, officers from Moretti's parent unit, the 4th Brigade, 4th Infantry Division (4/4 ID), laid out the case for pulling out of two areas: both the Korengal and the Landay Sin valley in eastern Nuristan, where the brigade's cavalry squadron was manning another cluster of outposts built during 10th Mountain's 2006–2007 push into the province.[97]

The paper was based on brigade officers' inevitably incomplete understanding of how the KOP and similar outposts had come into being—origin stories that had become murky after several unit rotations. In places it mischaracterized the history of American involvement in Kunar and Nuristan.[98] It was hard to argue with the paper's main conclusions, however, which were a lot like the ones Brett Jenkinson had reached about the Korengal: that instead of denying sanctuary to the enemy or protecting the population, outposts like the KOP tied down limited U.S. forces "in a grinding attrition battle in which the initiative rests with the insurgents" and "gave the Taliban a rationale for deeper penetration of the region." The brigade argued that U.S. and ANA troops should pull out of the Korengal as soon as possible—by the end of the 2009 fighting season—and shift focus southward to more heavily populated areas near Jalalabad.

McChrystal, whose sign-off would be required to leave the Korengal, was inclined to agree with 4/4 ID's conclusions. They fell in line with his plans to concentrate troops in more densely populated areas countrywide. But as with The Rock's long goodbye to the Waygal valley, deciding that it was a good idea to close a group of outposts and actually mustering the resources to do it were very different things. All the difficulties that had delayed the closure of the Ranch House in 2007 and COP Bella in 2008 were magnified in the Korengal, both because there were so many outposts in the valley—a cluster of five—and because the expanding scope of the war as the surge got under way placed more competing demands on helicopter transport units in Afghanistan than ever before.

One event after another in the summer and fall of 2009 delayed 4/4 ID's pullout plans. When a paratrooper named Bowe Bergdahl abandoned his outpost in southeastern Afghanistan in June, the vain emergency effort to find him before the Taliban did sucked up helicopter support that otherwise could have been used to ferry excess equipment out of the bases slated for closure. Then top Afghan officials persuaded McChrystal to send American troops to reinforce the remote Nuristani district of Barg-e Matal, a stronghold of the terrorist group Lashkar-e-Taiba, in July. The resulting mission prolonged the same resource shortages for the rest of the summer. And then in the fall, when helicopters were available again, the Landay Sin outposts took priority because they were in greater danger—as illustrated by the calamitous, Want-style battle at one of them, COP Keating, during its final days.[99]

By the time Baker Company finally pulled out of Vegas, the most isolated of the Korengal bases, in October, winter weather was about to arrive, ensuring that the soldiers at the KOP, Restrepo, Vimoto, and Dallas would have to wait months longer.[100] It was going to take twenty helicopter flights a day for four days to get everybody and everything—including half a million pounds of equipment—out of the outposts that needed to go. Rangers and a company of ANA Commandos were going to fly in for the evacuation too, to provide extra security.

Before McChrystal finally authorized a full Korengal pullout in April 2010, Baker Company would lose two more soldiers, bringing the total toll in the valley since the establishment of the KOP to twenty-eight (plus the nineteen dead of Red Wings). Just as Mark Moretti was starting to think that Baker Company might make it out with nobody killed, Specialist Robert Donevski was fatally shot during a January 2010 ambush on the rock staircase carved into the mountainside in Aliabad.[101] Four days after that, the staff sergeant leading Donevski's squad, a two-tour Iraq veteran named Thaddeus Montgomery, killed himself. In the days after the younger soldier's death, Montgomery had grown despondent, and Moretti had arranged for the next resupply bird to take him out of the valley for a break. The day the helicopter was supposed to come, the twenty-nine-year-old NCO walked into his barracks room and shot himself with his M4, becoming the last American to die in the Korengal valley.[102]

. . .

THE MONTHS OF deliberations and delays provided plenty of time for word of the impending Korengal pullout to circulate throughout Kunar and throughout the Army, to the soldiers who had fought in the valley and the officers who had made the decisions that put and kept the outposts there.

Many Korengal veterans were happy to hear that the bases would soon be gone. They had been horrible places to spend fifteen months. One of these was Dan Kearney. Back in Afghanistan as a Ranger staff officer, Kearney consulted with 4/4 ID leaders by videoconference as they planned out the Korengal closure. In the year and a half since he and Battle Company had left the Korengal, his thinking on the valley had evolved. The most his company had really accomplished, he now believed, had been to keep some of the fighting away from the Pech proper, buying time for the PRT's road construction project there. If the road and its spin-off development projects were largely done now, he said in the videoconference—if the Pech road had pavement on it (it did, as far as Blessing anyway), if the valley-floor towns had electricity and commerce (they did)—then maybe the fighting in the Korengal had bought enough time. American troops couldn't stay there forever.[103]

Accepting what was coming—and the implications about his own decisions back in 2006—was harder for Chris Cavoli, who was stationed in Germany at the time.

Two things gnawed at Cavoli as he read news articles and heard rumors from friends about 4/4 ID's plans. The first was the notion that the whole Korengal venture had been a mistake. Leaving the valley because the conditions that had led him to build the KOP had changed was one thing. But it was frustrating to read in the newspaper—and even worse to hear from Army peers—that the Korengal was a place of quiet, insular lumber merchants who, had ignorant Americans not stuck their noses into the valley's business, would never have bothered anybody. This, Cavoli felt, was the prevailing narrative, and it infuriated him. "I dispute that absolutely vigorously," he objected in one of my first conversations with him. "It is an ahistorical view of the situation. We went there for a very good reason": Korengal-based insurgents had been coming out of the valley and planting IEDs on the Pech.[104]

It was even harder for him to accept that the whole nature of the war in Kunar had changed—that he had bitten off more than subsequent units like the Blue Spaders had been able to chew. Cavoli had viewed his Chosin battalion as a good unit, even an excellent one, but it hadn't occurred to him that his soldiers were doing things in the mountains in 2006 and 2007 that later units would not be *able* to. He had just been doing what the Army had trained him to do, and so had his soldiers. But then the Pech road construction had dragged on, and the rules about Humvees had come down from Bagram, and then the MRAPs and the rules about them, and all the outposts had turned into little fortresses, cut off from the villages outside them by tall concrete walls, exactly what he had hoped they would never become.

Cavoli might have foreseen this evolution if the Pech hadn't been his first post–September 11 deployment. What happened to the Pech outposts was what eventually happened to almost all outposts American troops built in Iraq and Afghanistan, where the military machine's well-intentioned impulse to protect its people and improve their standard of living proved irrepressible. MRAPs exemplified the same trend. That the richest, most confident army on the planet would deliberately limit itself to these lumbering beasts in terrain where the ideal ride was a pickup truck was still hard for Cavoli to believe years later when he returned to Afghanistan for another tour and saw it himself. "The arrival of the MRAP changed the way we fought and changed our army from mostly to completely road-bound in Afghanistan," he contended.[105]

Pulling out of the Korengal didn't make sense to Bill Ostlund either. He couldn't understand why the Blue Spaders hadn't kept pushing the Korengal road project, and he suspected that if they had, the whole dynamic in the Pech could have changed for the better instead of for the worse during 1-26 Infantry's tour. Unlike Cavoli, however, Ostlund was close friends with the two officers pushing the Korengal pullout plans: Colonel Randy George, who commanded 4/4 ID at Jalalabad, and Lieutenant Colonel Brian Pearl, commanding 2-12 Infantry in the Pech. He considered George his closest friend in the Army officer corps and trusted both men's judgment. Ostlund made his doubts clear when George and Pearl sought his input, as both did. But he knew that they, the commanders on the ground, were basing their pullout plan on changed conditions that he was no longer in a position to appreciate. "Randy and Brian inherited something much different—something I don't completely understand—than what I left a year earlier," Ostlund told me.[106]

FEW PEOPLE HAD a better view of what the war in the Pech had been and what it had become than the Kunar fixture T.W., who returned to the rotation of Asymmetric Warfare Group advisers in the summer of 2009 a year older (he was now forty-nine) and with a refurbished knee. From here on out he would be spending most of his time at Jalalabad Airfield, with only occasional visits to the valleys he'd come to know so well.

During his recuperation, T.W. had visited 4/4 ID in Colorado. What he'd seen there had impressed him. Finally—if only by the luck of the draw—an Army unit bound for the mountains had *trained* in the mountains; Fort Carson sat six thousand feet above sea level, and parts of the nearby Piñon Canyon training site could have passed for the Shuryak.[107] And finally, the Army had managed to outfit a mountain-bound unit with mountain-appropriate gear: $4.4 million worth of everything from antimicrobial socks to stripped-down "plate-carrier" vests that were four pounds lighter than regular body armor and lightweight machine guns that trimmed nine pounds off the standard M240.[108]

The irony was that the Army was finally sending the right tools to the Pech for the war that American soldiers had fought there in 2006 and 2007, but that nimble version of war, as T.W. saw when he returned to Kunar in the summer of 2009, had been replaced by a very different one. The Fort Carson battalion was mounting long-range foot patrols into the mountains above the Pech only occasionally. Trading on JSOC's increased willingness to go after his targets, Pearl, the 2-12 Infantry battalion commander in the Pech, preferred to keep his foot patrols close to the MRAP convoys that could support them with heavy weapons—close to the Pech road.[109]

The road itself was flat and wide now, lined with shops, gas stations, and cell towers that T.W. would never have guessed he would see in the Pech when he first visited in 2004. But American soldiers were looking down onto it from behind the narrow, bulletproof windows of their intimidating-looking new trucks, seated high above everyone outside. Driving through the valley this way, T.W. couldn't help but think of what he'd heard about how many Soviet units had operated in Afghanistan, buttoned up in armored personnel carriers. Like heavily built-up outposts, T.W. believed, MRAPs insulated American troops from the war they were fighting and the local people whose support was necessary to fight it. "You lost contact with the populace that way," he said. "There was just much less ability to talk to folks. You'd drive the whole Pech without ever engaging the populace at all, and that's when you'd see the blank stares."[110]

Chris Cavoli and Bill Ostlund shared a fear about the Korengal withdrawal: that pulling out of the side valley would allow the vicious fighting there to spill down onto the Pech, disrupting the environment of relative security that allowed commerce to thrive along the road.[111] That was already happening, however; more than any previous unit, 4/4 ID's war was down on the Pech road itself.

"We had probably sixty days of hard fighting within three to four kilometers of the road" as guerrilla cells came down from the various side valleys to ambush the new unit's heavily armored convoys, Brian Pearl remembered.[112] Not a single American had been killed on the Pech road since 2006 when the PRT started widening and flattening it and Chris Cavoli started sending his men into the mountains, but in the summer of 2009 Pearl lost four men there: a private first class shot by a sniper, a sergeant killed by a huge IED that flipped an MRAP on its side, and two soldiers killed by close-range RPG barrages fired from the concealment of the thick cornfields that edged up against the road in many places.[113]

T.W. still thought it had made sense to go into the Korengal and build the KOP, but the status quo wasn't working anymore: KOP or no KOP, the Pech security bubble was collapsing on itself. The veteran mountain fighter's prescription sounded like common sense: "Leaders have to stop and think, okay, maybe this made sense six or twelve months ago, but does it make sense today?"[114]

THE LEADER WHO had finally looked at the Korengal and seen something different from his predecessors was Brett Jenkinson, who by the end of his year in the Pech was a changed man, torn up by sorrow and guilt that he did his best to hide even from his company commanders and staff. His coping mechanism was to fight as if he were a rifleman at any opportunity, thereby sharing the dangers to which he was exposing his soldiers; he would hop out of his Humvee at the first sign of contact, sometimes surprising his security detail by sprinting up the road or disappearing down an alley in pursuit of an insurgent before anyone else had even dismounted.

For years afterward, Jenkinson compared himself unfavorably with the commanders who had gone before him. Chris Cavoli and Bill Ostlund had built new outposts and expanded the counterinsurgency security bubble. He had built none, and on his watch the security bubble had shrunk. He had not even been able to leave the outposts he wanted to leave, and he had lost soldiers in the Korengal because of it. He felt that he had failed. The Army would reinforce this notion: while both Cavoli and Ostlund went on to command brigades and Cavoli to join the general officer ranks, the man who had taken the underprepared Blue Spader battalion to war and back did not command again and would retire in 2015 after partially isolating himself from the men he led in Kunar. "I try not to remember my time in Kunar," he would tell me sometimes before interviews where I dredged up painful memories.

Jenkinson had had a greater impact on the course of the war in Kunar than he would ever acknowledge. He had looked at a tiny, isolated valley where his predecessors had overpromised and overcommitted and seen it for what it had become: a place where the American presence was no longer doing much more than protecting itself.

Had he not done this, and had he not made his case to superiors and peers and reporters even when it felt like shouting into a void, the American entanglement in the Korengal might well have lasted even longer than it did, and have cost more lives. It was his vocal objections to anyone who would listen, including his dark, oft-repeated line that the only way to fix the Korengal would be to flood it, that set the stage for the next unit to actually leave the valley. And if not for Jenkinson, what the Korengal pullout presaged might also have been delayed: the long, fraught disengagement from the Pech itself.

The colonel whose lieutenants called him Earthworm Jim never gave himself credit for any of that. Instead, he wondered whether he had been a bad commander, whether his emotions had clouded his judgment, even whether he should have been relieved of command or relinquished it, taking humility to the point of self-flagellation. He tortured himself too over the loss of his men, eighteen of whom died in Kunar.[115] When he was shot during a firefight in May 2009, he felt guilty accepting a Purple Heart, because the non–life-threatening bullet wound seemed like a scratch compared with the fates to which he had committed so many of his men. How, he wondered with each death, did his squad leaders feel, who knew the dead men so much better than he did?[116]

When he went home to Fort Hood in the summer of 2009, with the Korengal closure still an unknown length of time in the future, Brett Jenkinson knew that he would miss the district governor Haji Zalmay and all the Afghans who had fed him like a king when they hardly seemed to have enough to feed themselves. But he never wanted to see the Pech, never mind the Korengal, again.

"Man, was I ready to go. I couldn't take the loss of soldiers anymore," Jenkinson told me four years later, before another Afghanistan deployment, during which he would, unexpectedly, return to Kunar and briefly glimpse the Korengal from a high-flying Black Hawk. "I'd given as much of my soul for that place as I wanted to give."[117]

PART III

THE LONG GOODBYE

2010–2013

The danger exists that in transferring the war to the Vietnamese, we will transfer also our organization, our style of fighting, and our mistakes, thus rendering the Vietnamese incapable of doing anything different from what we have done, and by which we have achieved only limited success.

—*Brian Jenkins,* The Unchangeable War *(1970)*

CHAPTER 10

THE CUL-DE-SAC

2010

A RANGER RETURNS

Three months after Chinooks pulled the last American troops out of the Korengal, Combat Outpost Michigan had replaced the KOP as the most frequently attacked base in eastern Afghanistan. I was on my way there from battalion headquarters, in a convoy that also carried the latest battalion commander for the Pech—Lieutenant Colonel Joe Ryan, who, as a Ranger major, had first visited the valley during Operation Winter Strike. His second visit, almost seven years after the 2003 Ranger surge during which FOB Blessing had been established and its namesake had died, coincided with my first trip to the Pech, reporting on the first summer of President Barack Obama's Afghan surge.

It was a rainy Sunday in the summer of 2010. I had arrived at Blessing and met Ryan on Friday, after nearly a week stuck in the junglelike humidity of Jalalabad Airfield. From Jalalabad, a Black Hawk had taken me up the Kunar valley, past the blimp-like white surveillance balloon that marked FOB Asadabad, and out into the cooler, drizzly territory of the latest U.S. Army battalion in the Pech, the 101st Airborne's 1-327 Infantry. His Bulldog battalion had been in 135 firefights in fifty-seven days, Ryan had explained to me

during a briefing in his office, the same one Chris Cavoli, Bill Ostlund, Brett Jenkinson, and Brian Pearl had occupied before him. So
far, four Bulldog soldiers had been killed.

Sunday's leg of my trip was a short, cramped ride from Blessing
to COP Michigan in the back of an MRAP belonging to Ryan's
sergeant major.

From its humble beginnings as a temporary checkpoint on the
grounds of the lumberyard at the Pech-Korengal junction, Michigan had grown into a formidable complex. The face the outpost
presented to the world around it was a combination of a six-foot-
high stone wall topped with chain-link fence and concertina wire,
dirt-filled Hesco barriers of various heights (many of them sprout-
ing ferns and other greenery), and towering concrete blast barriers—
called T-walls for their shape. The square area these walls enclosed
was about the size of four football fields, spreading from the Pech
road almost to the north bank of the Pech River. Inside, tents had
mostly been replaced by about twenty windowless plywood buildings. More Hescos and T-walls ringed the most important of these
wooden structures, like the barracks and operations center. Green
plastic camouflage netting hung over the only place soldiers were
meant to spend time outdoors, a little wooden deck between two
buildings that was outfitted with a picnic table, some Adirondack
chairs, and a pull-up bar.

Behind all that concrete and earth, in company strength, with
attack helicopters often flitting overhead during the day, Michigan's
hundred or so defenders were safer than their predecessors at more
precarious positions like the Ranch House and the KOP. But life at
the latest fishbowl outpost insurgents had chosen to focus on was
still dangerous and unlike anything I had seen at dozens of other
bases during four reporting trips to Afghanistan and Iraq. The Bulldog battalion soldiers at Michigan had arrived from Fort Campbell,
Kentucky, the 101st Airborne's home, in late May, when the KOP
and its sister bases in the Korengal had been closed for only a few
weeks. They had quickly started absorbing all the attention that Korengali insurgents and their Taliban guests had previously focused on
the Korengal positions. Michigan was now the plug in the bottle,
soaking up everything from heavy machine-gun rounds to recoilless-
rifle rounds, RPGs, and the 30-millimeter shells from a Russian-

made automatic grenade launcher that some hardy guerrillas were lugging around the mountains—probably the same one that had been harassing the KOP until a few weeks earlier. These attacks had killed one Bulldog soldier at Michigan, the forty-year-old mechanic Specialist Carlos Negron, and another at Able Main, the thirty-two-year-old mortarman Staff Sergeant Shaun Mittler. On the Sunday that I arrived, July 25, the soldiers at Michigan had already endured two attacks, fighting them off with their heavy weapons and mortars and the help of Blessing's two howitzers.

After chatting with the company commander and first sergeant in their office, Joe Ryan spoke to Michigan's enlisted soldiers in groups in the chow hall, first the junior soldiers and then the NCOs, giving them a chance to ask questions and air grievances without their officers around. The ruddy-faced battalion commander's demeanor was both restrained and relaxed. The room was sweltering hot, and gunshots snapped occasionally outside. When one infantryman complained about a shortage of dipping tobacco (collateral damage from a new federal law cracking down on shipping tobacco through the mail), Ryan smiled; knowing what he was about to say would fall on deaf ears, he encouraged the young soldier to take the ban as an opportunity to give up dip, as he himself had done a few years earlier.

Later, when a sergeant questioned the ad hoc organization of the garrison at the outpost—a platoon each from the battalion's companies, and the sergeant felt as if his platoon got all the bad jobs—the colonel answered seriously. What the soldiers at the outpost at the mouth of the Korengal were living through was a unique experience, and he wanted a cross section of the battalion to experience it. "Being here at COP Michigan during the surge in Afghanistan in the summer of 2010 is something you'll carry with you for the rest of your lives," he said, looking around the room.[1]

Of all the soldiers in the battalion, he was the only one with more than the most superficial understanding of how the Army's Pech venture had begun.

JOE RYAN HAD spent the years since Winter Strike in the Ranger Regiment, deploying five more times to Afghanistan and Iraq. Ranger deployments lasted only three or four months apiece, and for a Ranger staff officer they took place largely on the confines of JSOC's big airfield bases, helping to plan and supervise the command's night raids. But they came like clockwork, and they added up; since his first Afghanistan tour shortly after September 11, Ryan had spent more than thirty months deployed. He'd been in Baghdad when Iraq burst into flames in 2004, in Mosul when Rangers were chasing the forerunners of the Islamic State around the city in 2005 and 2006, and at Bagram for much of 2007. Now, like all upward-moving Ranger officers, he had returned to the conventional Army for the next rung on the ladder, battalion command.

Ryan was a thoughtful, calculating commander, the kind who spoke his mind but who also, instead of speaking off the cuff, wrote out remarks beforehand, complete with the jokes. He was almost always calm; even when he wasn't, you got the impression that his displays of anger were calibrated for effect. In the Blessing operations center when a firefight was going on somewhere out in the field, he would sit in a chair in the back of the room, watching the machine work. When he wanted to talk to members of the battle staff, he would call them over quietly, in ones and twos, from the computers where they were watching overhead footage or coordinating with aircrews in secure chat rooms. If he got on the radio himself to talk to the soldiers in the fight, it was only briefly; there were no pep talks.[2] Unlike Brett Jenkinson, who had been quick to jump out of his MRAP, rifle in hand, at the first opportunity, Ryan typically remained cool and quiet when he and his convoy took fire out on the Pech road. "When Colonel Ryan is shot at, he doesn't react much," his interpreter told me.[3]

When Ryan described an ambush that had happened a few weeks earlier, on June 25, he did so with such detachment that it wasn't immediately clear to me that he had been present at all, let alone in the middle of it. He and his guard detail had been on their way from Blessing to Asadabad when RPGs and recoilless-rifle shells started slamming into their brand-new MRAPs on a narrow stretch of road across the river from the mouth of the Shuryak.* One of the RPGs

---

* The scene of the ambush was also the former site of Firebase California, the short-lived Chosin battalion outpost established during Mountain Lion in 2006 and dismantled the next year.

punched through the armor of the first truck and killed its driver, Specialist Jared Plunk. More rounds penetrated the hull of Ryan's MRAP. Inside, the colonel was unhurt, but his interpreter and a soldier in the back seat had been peppered with shrapnel, and the turret gunner, Specialist Blair Thompson, slumped down on top of Ryan, bleeding heavily from a large wound to his back. Ryan emptied out his medical pouch so that another soldier could get to work on Thompson. The truck needed to get out of the ambush zone, but the driver was temporarily blinded, so while the driver held his foot on the gas, Ryan leaned over and steered the vehicle out of danger. The medics at nearby COP Able Main did what they could for Thompson, but he did not survive.

"Joe's about as steady as they get" was how a friend and boss from the Rangers described Ryan. "He's measured in his approach to just about everything. And he is not always going to go with the common wisdom."[4]

Ultimately, Ryan would not go with the common wisdom or the cookie-cutter Army approach in the Pech, but it would take him the bulk of an eventful summer to get there.

Ryan was the first commander in five years to arrive in the Pech and not immediately find his attention and resources dominated by the Korengal. Thanks to the long-delayed Korengal pullout, he had nearly a whole battalion of infantrymen in the Pech valley proper—plenty of troops to establish a new outpost somewhere else if he wanted to, as peer battalion commanders were doing in practically every other corner of Afghanistan in this summer of the surge. That was his first impulse, just as it had been Brett Jenkinson's first impulse: keep pushing the Pech road—now paved out to a few kilometers beyond Blessing—and expand the American ink blot to the western Pech district of Chapa Dara. Ryan's memories of his time in the Kantiwa valley in November and December 2003, twenty miles farther up the Pech beyond Chapa Dara, were vivid: living in the medieval-looking fort of the Hizb-e Islami commander Haji Ghafor, patrolling with Rangers through conifer forests and thigh-deep snow, feasting with blond and redheaded Nuristanis at Eid. (He'd been stuck manning the radios in the fort during the game of *buzkashi* that other Ranger veterans remembered so well.) Now the needs of the Army had put him back in the same part of the world, living on a base that friends of his had helped establish and that was named after a fallen fellow Ranger.

"I went in with all these well-intentioned notions," Ryan told me later. "I wanted to be the guy who connected the road to Chapa Dara and made it all the way up to Kusht," the village where the Kantiwa valley joined the Pech, where he'd spent time during Winter Strike. "My personal goal was to get back to Kantiwa just to see it again."[5]

The 101st's bread and butter was air assaults—the big heliborne landings like Mountain Lion and Rock Avalanche that Brett Jenkinson had eschewed—and the Bulldog battalion had rehearsed such missions back at Fort Campbell and in the mountains in northern Georgia. But with sister battalions' missions taking priority, there weren't helicopters available to fly Bulldog troops out to Chapa Dara. So Ryan's soldiers started pushing west by ground.[6] This was dangerous work: the condition of the Pech road beyond Nangalam had deteriorated since the Blue Spaders' time, and the guerrillas based in Chapa Dara had reacted to the ubiquitous use of MRAPs with larger IEDs. One such bomb had killed a 4/4 ID sergeant during a mission to the Chapa Dara district center in February.[7] A month later, a difficult Task Force East mission targeting the guerrilla commander responsible had left a SEAL Team 6 operator dead,*[8] and a month after that, a 4/4 ID sniper had been fatally shot in the village where work on the Chapa Dara road had stalled.

During its first three weeks on the ground, the Bulldog company based at Blessing made three attempts to reach Chapa Dara. None went well.

The first time, the Bulldog troops got a late start and had to turn around for fear of losing attack helicopter support three-quarters of the way to their destination, short of the Senji Bridge, which the battalion's new lighter-weight MRAP model could handle but which was still the biggest physical obstacle on the route. The second time, they made it across the bridge and were just around the last bend in the river from the Chapa Dara district center when one

---

★ Chief Petty Officer Adam Brown was an old hand in Kunar: his first deployment with SEAL Team 6 had been on an Omega team at one of the CIA's Kunar bases, and he'd been back in 2008–2009.

of their MRAPs died. The Bulldog troops were close enough that they could have walked the last stretch, but unable to raise the district police by radio or phone, the captain in charge of the mission again gave the order to turn around.[9]

The third time, on June 10, a column of American MRAPs and a few Humvees full of ANA soldiers was inching up the last stretch of dirt road toward the district center when an IED went off. The blast enveloped one of the ANA Humvees and set off an ambush from the mountains. When the dust settled, the front half of the Humvee was gone, and three of the four Afghan soldiers who'd been inside were dead or dying. The convoy advanced no farther, and just after it turned around and headed back toward Blessing, a second bomb—with a sewing-machine pedal as its trigger—detonated under a Husky, a single-seat mine-detecting truck with ground-penetrating radar and a robotic arm. The blast spared the driver but tore apart the strange-looking vehicle (which was designed to break into three pieces in a blast) and kicked off another hours-long gunfight. In the end, they left the wrecked Husky there. In the weeks to come, occasional drone flights would watch as locals stripped the armored carcass down to almost nothing.[10]

The June mission left two gigantic craters in the road and spelled the end of Joe Ryan's ambition to keep pushing out toward Chapa Dara. When I visited the Pech a few weeks later, his thinking on the district had undergone a sharp reversal. Rather than an opportunity for a counterinsurgency win, Chapa Dara now seemed like a swamp in which insurgents would probably love to see an overambitious American unit become mired, especially so soon after the previous unit had finally extracted itself from the quicksand of the Korengal.

"The time is done for coalition forces to keep spreading out into more places here," Ryan told me in late July. This was the same conclusion that the two commanders before him, Brett Jenkinson and Brian Pearl, had both reached about Chapa Dara.

Ryan wondered out loud about the utility of keeping American troops in the Pech valley at all.

"A lot of people wonder what would happen if we pulled out of here, just left," he mused. "I think life would go on very much the same way it's going on now. There would be violence, yes. That's just the way this place is. But we are interlopers here."[11]

.   .   .

RYAN WAS ECHOING something his former boss and mentor, General McChrystal, had said a few months earlier, during an overnight visit to the KOP shortly before its April closure. "We're not living in their homes, but we're living in their valley," the four-star ISAF commander had told a reporter who accompanied him on the Korengal visit. "There was probably much more fighting here than there would have been" if Americans had never come. "I care deeply about everyone who's been hurt here, but I can't do anything about that," McChrystal had continued. "I can do something about people hurt in the future."[12]

In the intervening weeks, McChrystal himself had been called back to Washington and sacked over insubordinate comments he and members of his staff had made about their higher-ups in the White House in front of a reporter from *Rolling Stone*. But McChrystal's replacement, the counterinsurgency evangelist General David Petraeus, appeared to share McChrystal's priorities for the surge that was taking shape: focus troops and resources on places with large populations, like Kandahar and Jalalabad; get out of remote, sparsely populated areas where there didn't seem to be a return on the investment in blood and treasure.

The Korengal had been one such place. Now Ryan was wondering if the same logic that had driven the Korengal withdrawal might not apply to the Pech too. Was the Pech a detour that had sucked up disproportionate military resources for years and led nowhere—"the ultimate cul-de-sac," as he later put it to an Army historian?[13] He certainly didn't see much evidence that the counterinsurgency approach the Army had been trying to apply in the Pech since before Petraeus popularized it in Iraq was working in the valley.

One sign that seemed like a flashing warning light about the efficacy of six years of American efforts in the Pech was the state of the Afghan military and police there. Unless it planned to occupy a country until the end of time, the eventual end point of any foreign army's counterinsurgency campaign had to be the handover of security from outsiders to local forces—both ANA soldiers capable of fighting and supporting themselves in the mountains and police, who, in theory, were best equipped to keep a lid on a low-grade insurgency in the long run.

When the Chosin battalion had scattered outposts up and down the Pech in 2006, the expectation had been that the ANA would inherit them within a year or two, maybe three at the outside. Four years later, the three hundred or so Afghan soldiers who lived with the Bulldog troops on their bases were a hapless, in some ways help-less, bunch. The latest group, the 2/2 battalion of ANA 201st Corps, had come to the Pech in March and had no idea how long they would stay. The troops they replaced had been there for two years and had lost their battalion commander over the winter when a mortar round exploded near his quarters on Blessing.

Throughout Afghanistan, the relationship between ISAF troops and members of the 160,000-strong Afghan National Army was more need-hate than love-hate. The cultural gulf between well-trained American combat leaders and the ANA soldiers they were supposed to partner with could hardly have been wider. Many of the latter came from the very poorest rural Afghan regions, almost all were illiterate, and many were also innumerate, unable to count high enough to keep track of the bullets they fired in training or combat.[14] There were plenty of brave ANA soldiers, but few who joined for the same kinds of reasons that many American infantry-men did, searching for brotherhood or manhood or a challenge or to serve their country; for most Afghan soldiers, military service was simply about escaping poverty. When Afghan soldiers were caught stealing food or Humvee batteries or foam sleeping mats, or stopped in the middle of firefights to pick up expended brass so they could resell it later, or smoked opium or marijuana on duty, as a huge proportion of them habitually did, they earned American con-tempt.[15] On the flip side, things as simple as the U.S. military's casual profanity earned many American troops their Afghan counterparts' hatred.[16]

For American captains and lieutenants, the unreliability of the ANA under fire was a strong disincentive to working closely with the Afghan troops or giving them important roles to play on mis-sions. Instead—especially after orders came down from ISAF head-quarters in 2008 that Americans could not enter any Afghan homes unless Afghan troops went in before them—the Americans at the Pech outposts tended to use the ANA as add-ons and auxiliaries, dragging a few along to "put an Afghan face" on routine patrols and allotting them bit parts in big operations. This drag-them-along-but-keep-them-in-the-dark approach did nothing to help the ANA develop the planning and fire-support skills they would need when, inevitably, they were eventually left to fight on their own.[17] A Marine combat adviser who lived with the ANA at Michigan in 2009 would typically get a late-night visit from his Army colleagues, saying they needed him and a group of Afghans to be ready to come along on a night patrol in fifteen minutes. Far from being given a say in planning the patrol, the ANA officers and NCOs wouldn't even be told where they were going, lest they leak the information to the enemy, or be provided with night-vision goggles, lest they lose them.[18]

Things were only getting worse. For several years, about a dozen Marines at a time, led by a lieutenant colonel, had acted as mentors, tutors, advocates, and liaisons for the ANA in the valley, living on "their" Afghans' schedules, eating with them, training with them, accompanying them on missions, and trying to bridge the huge cultural divide. Just before the Bulldog soldiers deployed, ISAF's commander, McChrystal, had discontinued the deployment of the adviser teams to ANA units throughout eastern Afghanistan. Without advisers to act as go-betweens, McChrystal's thinking went, American and ANA infantry battalions would be forced to get to know each other better and collaborate more closely. But in the Pech as in many other places, the effect was the opposite.

Ryan tapped a lieutenant who was waiting to lead a platoon, Cale Genenbacher, to fill the Marine advisers' shoes as the only Bulldog battalion officer focused full-time on working with the ANA. Genenbacher discovered right away that the 2/2 ANA battalion commander, a Tajik lieutenant colonel named Ismatullah, who was often away for long, unexplained periods, claimed to have far more soldiers than he really did. (This was a common practice in ANA units where officers skimmed off pay from "ghost soldiers," who allowed the officers to take part of their pay as a bribe for keeping them on the books.) "They were at 90 percent on the books, but probably 50 percent in reality," Genenbacher estimated. There weren't enough living quarters on the ANA part of Blessing even for the part of a battalion that was there; you might find half a dozen soldiers living together in a guard tower and others in bunk beds under the stars if you went over to look, which the Bulldog soldiers mostly didn't do.[19] "It was like living in two separate camps," said Ryan.[20]

Both those camps relied on one logistical system, though—the American one. Ryan had a big abandoned schoolhouse just outside Blessing turned into ANA barracks, bringing in beds and air conditioners through the same U.S. supply chain that brought the Afghan battalion the bulk of their ammunition and even some of their food.[21]

Outside the wire, the ANA relied on the Americans for almost everything. The Afghan troops had a couple of howitzers at Blessing, but they lacked crews trained to fire them. The Afghans felt as though they were getting the short end of the stick driving around the Pech in hand-me-down Humvees while the Americans rode in MRAPs, and they weren't wrong, as the death of a Humvee full of ANA in an IED blast on the road to Chapa Dara showed. "That really took any wind out of the ANA's sails that was in there to begin with," said Genenbacher of the lethal June 10 mission.[22]

In the Pech as in many other places, the U.S. military's efforts to build and professionalize a police force had been even more lackluster than the ANA advising mission. In Nangalam, some two hundred policemen were on the rolls and drawing pay, but only a few dozen were ever around and available for work. The job of training and coaching them fell on a single civilian contractor, a retired Santa Ana narcotics cop who was working at Blessing as part of a Pentagon program that embedded law-enforcement veterans with combat units.[23] So it was no surprise to Ryan or other experienced hands in the battalion that the men manning the police stations outside Blessing and Honaker-Miracle and the three little checkpoints on the road in between, in Tantil, Bar Kanday, and Tarale, were an even sorrier-looking bunch than the ANA—ragged, unmotivated, and often missing.[24]

But as Ryan learned within a couple of weeks, the dysfunction of the police went deeper than that. Five or six police officers in the standard gray-green police fatigues that looked as if they were left over from the Soviet era manned each checkpoint, without helmets or body armor or any weapons heavier than rifles. Some were from Kunar, others from distant parts of the country. Either way, they had much to fear, making them highly susceptible to bribes and threats from the insurgents they were supposed to be standing guard against and gathering information on. Weapons and ammunition issued to police were liable to be found later in insurgent weapons caches, and the guerrillas in the hills included former policemen. One of the cell leaders responsible for the frequent rocket and mortar attacks against Blessing was a former border police commander named Haji Wazir who had spent time in prison on corruption charges.[25]

Other policemen were working for the Taliban while on duty, passing information to friends in the insurgency or just allowing attacks against Americans to happen. The ambush that killed Ryan's driver, Blair Thompson, had been such an attack, the colonel suspected. It had happened right outside the Tarale police checkpoint, and just before his truck rolled into the kill zone, Ryan had noticed through the thick glass of his window that the policemen who were supposed to be on duty there weren't. It seemed likely that the militant commander who laid the ambush had told the police beforehand not to show up to work that day.[26]

There was a police station way out at the Chapa Dara district center too. The fact that it was hanging on at all, when the Taliban could have overrun it handily if they had wanted to, suggested to Ryan that the police at the district center and the militants in the mountains had some sort of understanding with each other. "What do the police do out here? Good question," Ryan said to me. "I think they live and let live. I wouldn't necessarily describe the police or all the members of the government here as people who've chosen our side. Some of these folks are the ultimate fence-sitters." That was disappointing to Ryan, but unlike some of the commanders before him he could understand it and accept it.[27]

Many police officials, as well as some of the district governors who oversaw them, preyed on the civilian population under American noses, demanding bribes at checkpoints or skimming off funds from the government in Kabul or U.S. reconstruction coffers. "The district governors all had one skill: how to bring American officers under their influence and get money from them," the former Pech interpreter Farshad told me. He was thinking in particular of Haji Mohammad Rahman Danish, the polished, English-speaking official who had long been the district governor closest to American commanders at Blessing and had gained the friendship and trust of many of them. Farshad and other interpreters believed that Rahman had been stealing money from both locals and the Americans for years, all the way back to 2007 when he siphoned off a portion of the money paid to the owners of adjacent land when Army engineers expanded FOB Blessing. Rahman had finally been removed from his post shortly before the Bulldog battalion arrived, but rather than being jailed or dismissed from government service, he was shifted to another district elsewhere in Kunar.[28]

The influential Kunari cleric Mawlawi Shahzada Shahid, when I interviewed him in Kabul, was circumspect in his criticism of American troops for their missteps over the years but ferocious when asked about the administrators and police officials in the Pech. "All of them are thieves and there is not a human being among them," he snapped.[29]

Whatever a successful, sustainable counterinsurgency campaign looked like, this wasn't it.

THE SAD BROTHERS

In the years since Ryan had last been in the Pech, the nature of the insurgency there had changed as completely as its scale, partly thanks to the same dynamics that were causing the colonel to question the wisdom of keeping American troops and bases in the valley at all.

The old Hizb commanders Ryan and his fellow Rangers had been hunting during Winter Strike in 2003 were either long gone from the Pech, no longer active in the insurgency, or both. Haji Ghafor, the warlord of the Kantiwa valley in whose castle Ryan had spent a snowy Thanksgiving, was a case in point. As Ryan described the mission targeting Ghafor that had brought him to the Pech the first time, he reached under his desk and pulled out a large, silver bowl—the one he had shaved in during his two cold months in the Kantiwa castle and taken back to Savannah as a souvenir. By now, it was clear that Ghafor was a has-been, living somewhere deep in

Nuristan. Other Hizb figures had reconciled with the Afghan government, and it seemed possible that Ghafor might too. "I want to meet Haji Ghafor," Ryan said, looking at the bowl. "I want him to come down to Nangalam and I want to talk to him. I'll give him his bowl back, if he wants it. I'll give him more than his bowl if he'll support the government." Eventually, Ryan would exchange letters with Ghafor through Afghan intermediaries, a correspondence that briefly raised the colonel's hopes but never resulted in a meeting.

The guerrilla commanders who were actually fighting his men in the Pech, Ryan explained, were a different breed—much younger than Ghafor and mostly affiliated with the Taliban, a movement that most had had nothing to do with before Americans came to their valley and in some cases had opposed. Some Afghan government officials called this brand of militants *naraaz waruna,* meaning the "sad brothers" or "disgruntled brothers," a phrase Ryan had picked up on from his interpreter Nazir.[30]

One such Taliban figure was Haji Mohammad Dawran, a middle-aged Salafist from Sundray, a troublesome town in a bend of the Pech halfway between Nangalam and COP Michigan. Mullah Dawran, as he was widely known, was a sad brother indeed. Not only had Americans killed many of his comrades, but they had, in a 2009 rocket artillery strike aimed at him, killed his wife and children. His story illustrated how the Pech insurgency had developed over the years.

Dawran was a stout man with a wide face, a heavy brow, and a bushy but squarish beard. He was the son of a wealthy family, and as a young man he had joined Jamaat al-Dawa, the other major mujahidin party in Kunar besides Hizb, to fight the Soviets. Like fellow Jamaat figures Haji Ruhullah and Sabar Lal Melma, the future Guantánamo inmates, he had opposed the Taliban when they were in power and, after their ouster, initially supported the new U.S.-backed Afghan transitional government. But in the summer of 2003, with his former comrades Ruhullah and Sabar Lal languishing in Guantánamo, he had taken up arms and headed into the mountains with a group of loyal fighters, becoming a mujahid once again. Eventually, he struck up an alliance with his erstwhile opponents, the Taliban, and his fame and network of subcommanders and guerrilla cells grew.[31]

By the fall of 2009, Dawran was only a "category three" target on the huge list of more than six hundred insurgent figures the military was targeting countrywide (on which he was code-named Objective Viking). For the 4/4 ID battalion fighting in the Pech, however, Dawran was a top target, behind only rare al-Qaida figures like Abu Ikhlas and Taliban shadow government officials like Mawlawi Abdul Rahim. Dawran was linked to almost every other militant leader in the area and tied to many attacks on convoys and outposts.[32]

In October, Dawran had hosted a Western journalist for an embed of sorts. The man he approved for this visit, the Norwegian documentary filmmaker Paul Refsdal, specialized in reporting on guerrilla groups. He and Dawran had met twenty-five years earlier, when Refsdal was covering the anti-Soviet jihad and Dawran was fighting in it. Refsdal's visit provided an unusual firsthand look inside the insurgency just a few weeks before an American strike that would destroy Dawran's family, wound him, and help push him upward in the hierarchy of militant commanders in the Pech.[33]

After meeting a group of masked guerrillas at a prearranged linkup site, Refsdal was escorted up into the forest, where Dawran was waiting, wearing plain brown robes and a *pakol* hat. Dawran took his Norwegian guest higher into the mountains, to a secluded compound above the Pech, where he was living with his wife and three young children. At this compound and other sites Refsdal visited during his stay, Dawran and his men spent their downtime resting, eating, and praying. For entertainment, they would play a shot-put-like game with big rocks.

Dawran observed no separation between family life and his work as a commander, often talking to the radiomen of subordinate insurgent cells by walkie-talkie while his children served him and Refsdal tea. When the time came to lay an ambush above the Pech road, some of the fighters took their young sons along. Dawran brought his oldest, a boy of about twelve who helped carry belts of ammunition. Some fighters had pre-positioned a DShK heavy machine gun on a rotating mount behind a small rock wall high on the mountainside above the Pech, concealed by trees.

"Tell the children to take cover, and take cover yourself," Dawran said in Pashto as he put batteries into his radio and looked down at the road from behind a small tree, with Refsdal filming. "Let the first vehicle pass and then start the attack." Far below, four MRAPs approached along the Pech road. The vehicles' small shapes would be in the DShK gunner's field of view for only a few moments. "God, give victory to the mujahidin!" the gunner prayed, then let off bursts at the second, third, and fourth trucks in the convoy. Fighters nearby were positioned to shoot at the Tantil police checkpoint, which had incurred Dawran's anger by firing back during an earlier firefight, violating a truce he had made with the checkpoint's commander. "Hit the checkpoint hard," Dawran exhorted over the radio.[34]

While Refsdal was with them, Dawran and his men used the same positions two more times to attack the convoy-rich stretch of road. Refsdal's impression of Dawran was of "an honest, plain man" who was completely devoted to fighting the foreigners occupying his homeland.[35] Refsdal captured Dawran giving his men a speech after prayers one day in the woods that linked the two insurgencies in which he had fought: "During the Russian invasion, someone asked, 'When will victory come?' The answer was, 'If the mujahidin are honest and fight only for the sake of God, then victory will come soon. If not, it will take time.'"[36]

In November, just a few weeks after Refsdal's visit, American aircraft tracked Dawran to a three-building compound two miles into the mountains south of the Pech, in the shadow of a peak west of COP Michigan and just over a tall ridge from the Korengal—probably the same compound where Dawran had hosted Refsdal. Brigade headquarters proposed striking the target with a HIMARS long-range rocket launcher, sparing the SEALs and Rangers of JSOC's Task Force East a dangerous infiltration. The impressive precision and destructive power of the GPS-guided rockets made it seem like a sure thing: a HIMARS salvo could flatten every building on the isolated compound without the slightest warning.[37]

The proposal for the rocket strike spent several weeks traveling up the hierarchy of U.S. military headquarters to ISAF in Kabul, where it was approved despite the possibility that it could kill Dawran's wife and small children along with him—a risk judged to be in appropriate proportion to the potential benefit of getting rid of

Dawran. A transport plane delivered the HIMARS detachment to Jalalabad Airfield, forty-three miles from the target, and on the afternoon of Thanksgiving Day 2009, the big rockets roared out of their truck-mounted launchers, leaving bright white contrails. Soldiers and some SEALs visiting from Task Force East, watching a drone's video feed at Blessing, were elated as the mountaintop compound erupted in explosions, but their satisfaction turned to incredulous disappointment as a lone figure appeared amid the clouds of smoke and dust. It was Dawran.

Some of the reports that trickled in from informants over the next few months said that Dawran had lost an eye in the rocket strike; others that he had lost a testicle and was recovering in Pakistan. Regardless, he had survived.[38] His wife and children were not so lucky, a fact that gained him sympathy even among some Afghan government officials. When Refsdal interviewed Kunar's provincial police chief soon after the strike, seeking information about whether Dawran was dead or alive, the police chief said that he wasn't sure, but confirmed the deaths of his family members. The police official "did not speak about Dawran like an enemy, not like someone he hated," Refsdal said. "It sounded like he respected him."[39]

By the time of my visit the next summer, Dawran was back in the field, directing insurgent cells involved in the daily attacks on COP Michigan and convoys on the Pech road, and had formally pledged allegiance to the Taliban. The Bulldog battalion's estimate was that he was fully recovered from his wounds and was "reestablishing his network."[40] His miraculous escape added to his mystique and burnished his image as the latest Taliban field commander in the central Pech.[41]

THE OTHER COMMANDERS the Bulldog battalion was fighting day to day along the Pech were mostly younger men—"local punks," as Ryan called them—up-and-comers who had been babies when Dawran and Haji Ghafor were fighting the Soviets. One was Gul Nabi Bilal, a small-unit leader in his early twenties who lived in the Shuryak valley and was linked to the lethal June 25 attack on Ryan's own convoy. Another was Sayed Shah, a unit leader underneath

Dawran who was believed to be "personally responsible" for an RPG attack in Sundray that had killed a 4/4 ID sergeant over the winter.[42]

Ryan was confident his battalion could kill these men, and possibly some more valuable targets too, especially with the help of airpower and special operations forces. "Gul Nabi Bilal won't make it our rotation. He's too far out front," he told me.[43] He was right; both Gul Nabi Bilal and Sayed Shah would die in a matter of weeks, the former in a barrage of fire from an AC-130 gunship and the latter in a night raid by Task Force East's Ranger platoon.[44] The mid-August Ranger raid in Shamun, the village right across the Pech from Dawran's hometown of Sundray, culminated when Sayed Shah barricaded himself in a rooftop bunker. Before he went down in a hail of machine-gun and sniper fire, Shah or one of the fighters with him managed to kill one of the Rangers, Specialist Christopher Wright.[45]

Ryan was happy to see enemy leaders killed. Sayed Shah's death quieted things down for a while on the stretch of road that passed through Sundray, where a large IED had killed two Bulldog soldiers the day before the Ranger raid. But his experience planning and overseeing such raids as a Ranger staff officer had taught him to be realistic about how much good they did in the long term.[46] After a few days or weeks of calm, the enemy attacks always picked up again; insurgent groups replaced their slain personnel quickly, just as a Western military unit would, and their leadership bench could be surprisingly deep.[47]

What would all these insurgents do with themselves if there weren't any Americans around to fight? The battalion's intelligence files were rife with instances of feuds and infighting among guerrillas in the Pech and its side valleys, often between locals and outsiders. Before the Task Force East SEALs killed him back in March, for instance, the Chapa Dara commander Jan Wali had been on the outs with the Taliban's shadow governor for Watapur, Nur Akbar. He, in turn, was feuding with a rival commander, Dir Alam, possibly over timber revenue, and two small-time cell commanders under Nur Akbar's command were trying to do each other in because each had previously killed a family member of the other.[48]

Paul Refsdal had seen one such feud dangerously close up a few

months earlier. When he returned to the Pech for a second reporting trip, a subordinate of Dawran's named Omar confined the Norwegian journalist for several days at a remote *bandeh* before Dawran
negotiated his release. Refsdal's captors at the *bandeh* were on edge—
not because they were worried about American night raids or air
strikes, they explained to their prisoner, but because they were embroiled in a land dispute with a nearby cell of foreign fighters whom
they described as al-Qaida. If al-Qaida attacked, they told him, they
would give him a rifle and he would have to fight like everyone else,
and he had better do it, because if the foreigners got their hands on
a Western captive, they were as likely to cut his head off during the
upcoming Eid holiday as to keep him for ransom.[49]

Part of the job of really elusive insurgents, Ryan and his intelligence shop believed—figures like Abu Ikhlas and the Taliban shadow
governor Mawlawi Abdul Rahim—was to smooth over disputes between insurgent cells over religion, territory, resources, or personal
grievances. That had the colonel wondering: If the only thing all
these militant factions had in common was that they were fighting
Americans, and if some of them were already at each other's throats
even with four bases full of Americans right under their noses, what
would they do if their common cause was removed?

"There's dissension, and we need to capitalize on that dissension," Ryan mused in August at Blessing. One way to do that might
be to leave.[50]

WHEN REFSDAL HEARD young local men in Dawran's group talk
about why they were fighting the Americans, their complaints were
familiar ones: the occupying soldiers' lack of respect for elders, how
they used metal detectors to search women at checkpoints, how
they broke into homes at night, how their air and artillery strikes
damaged property and hurt civilians. "The complaints were more
about lack of respect for local traditions than actually about the
Americans being there," Refsdal remembered. Unlike the hard-line
al-Qaida fighters who had taken advantage of the conflict to establish a presence higher in the mountains, the men's grievances were
rooted in their experience of foreign involvement in their home,
not in extremism or general hatred of the West.[51]

That years of complicated dealings with Americans had left a sour taste in many local people's mouths was obvious in the summer of 2010. The days when locals would patiently overlook a deadly mistake, as they had when Green Beret A-team 936's commander, Ron Fry, killed a man with a ricochet in 2004, were long gone. Every village had stories about how American actions had cost lives or limbs or property, few more so than Kandigal, the town just outside COP Michigan.

When Michigan was a new outpost and had no walls, just concertina wire, Kandigal had been a peaceful enclave. American soldiers had joined in volleyball games with locals there, swum in the river with local children, and, though they weren't supposed to, sometimes dispensed with their heavy body armor when they strolled through the town's bazaar.[52] That had been just three years earlier. In the meantime, Kandigal's succession of American neighbors had brought the town many useful things—a paved road, a flood-protection wall with a plaque bearing the misspelled caption "Funded by Civil appiars team," a footbridge, a sturdy concrete vehicle bridge with blue-painted railings.

But the American presence had also brought Kandigal a string of needless deaths. There had been the three teenage boys killed in the bazaar when nervous Rock paratroopers opened fire on their red pickup truck in 2007. Four people had died in the summer of 2009 when a mortar round from Michigan fell short and exploded in town,[53] and a Ranger night raid the same year killed the old man who cooked for Michigan's ANA contingent.[54] Just a few months before the latest company of Americans arrived from Fort Campbell, over the winter, word had spread in town that an antitank missile fired from an MRAP during a firefight had killed two children. It wasn't true, but by that point few people in Kandigal were willing to give the foreign soldiers who lived behind concrete walls at the edge of town the benefit of the doubt. A spontaneous protest erupted, with a hundred or so townspeople rolling a boulder into the road, lighting fires, and raising a white Taliban flag. The protesters chanted, "Death to America, death to Bush, death to Obama," outside Michigan's gates until some elders were able to get on a loudspeaker and clear things up.[55] When the Bulldog soldiers from

Michigan walked through town on patrol, schoolboys glowered at them and said things like "Fuck you" and "Taliban good."

Residents' hardened attitudes toward Americans were equally clear in another village, Upper Waradesh, five miles west along the Pech road, on the way from Nangalam to Chapa Dara. The MRAPs carrying the Bulldog soldiers from Blessing rolled to a stop a quarter mile or so from town, halting where a large chunk of the smoothly paved road had already collapsed into the river. Walking past an abandoned U.S.-funded schoolhouse on which someone had painted "Long live the Taliban" in Pashto in huge red letters, the soldiers headed uphill into the center of the little village. They took up outward-facing positions behind walls, rocks, and trees while their interpreter rustled up some local men to meet with the captain in charge of the patrol.

The agenda was derailed almost immediately when a pair of mean-looking village dogs approached the American perimeter and started barking. Just as the captain was yelling for someone to get rid of the dogs by throwing rocks at them, a jumpy private raised his M4 and shot one of the animals.

The village's youngish elder, Sayed Jalal, started bargaining. "This is a shame on your company and your battalion," he told the captain and his interpreter heatedly, standing up to make his point. "Today you shoot my dog. Tomorrow you shoot my children. It would be better for you to shoot me than to shoot my dog." Jalal eventually offered forgiveness for a concession: the captain had to promise not to bring his trucks so close to Upper Waradesh again, because every American visit risked giving the Taliban the idea that the village was on the side of the foreigners.

Joe Ryan's interpreter, Nazir, had seen a lot of this kind of thing in his years working for the Americans at Blessing. He had started out in the battalion aid station in 2007, translating between The Rock's medics and locals who had come in for treatment, usually for sickness and accidental injuries but sometimes for wounds suffered when they'd been caught in the cross fire between the insurgents and the Americans. Much of the goodwill Nazir had seen in Nangalam and other Pech towns when he first started working there had since turned to indifference. He gave the generic example of a man who used to call up an interpreter at Blessing when he heard about IEDs being planted in a culvert near his house, but eventually stopped doing so, preferring to let the Americans take their chances with the bomb rather than risk the Taliban's finding out he was a collaborator. Other people, who had lost relatives or property or livestock to the conflict, actively resented the Americans.

"There was a time when seventy, eighty percent of the people in the Pech were supportive of ISAF and the government, but no longer," Nazir told me. "The people of the area are not grateful anymore. Why? Because of the mistakes. The killings of innocent people based on bad intelligence and wrong reports. Things got out of control."[56]

Much of the harm that had come to the people of the Pech had been at the hands of the Taliban and other insurgents. For every rocket or mortar shell that struck an American outpost, others fell short and landed in villages or fields, like the rocket aimed at Blessing that killed two townspeople in Nangalam on July 6. IEDs meant for American MRAPs wound up detonating under civilian cars instead. And the Taliban were killing people they saw as collaborators, like Blessing's base barber, whom they shot in his home at night in the spring,[57] and the teenage boy they accused in the fall of spying for the NDS and executed in the mountains above Tantil.[58]

That this did not seem to erode support for the insurgency was frustrating to American troops; it hardly seemed fair that resentment over civilian deaths should cut one way but not the other. But in the eyes of many local people, it was the American presence that spurred the "sad brothers" to action, so the Americans were to blame for all of it. Several years later, a report by the Open Society Foundations would use military and UN data on violence and popular opinion in some two hundred villages in embattled parts of Afghanistan to show that this was a common phenomenon. Insurgents killed far more civilians in these villages than ISAF and government troops did, yet over time the only direction that popular support for ISAF and the government went was down, while people's attitudes toward the Taliban changed little. "At some level of accumulation, unique to each conflict," the study claimed, "civilian harm inflicts irreversible damage to the prospects of success."[59]

In the Pech, by the summer of 2010, that threshold had been

crossed. In the eyes of too many people, American forces had brought not security but danger.

"THE BLINDING FLASH OF THE OBVIOUS"

In August, it was already clear that Ryan was leaning toward recommending a pullout from the Pech. But it was a pair of events at the end of the summer, after I was back in the United States, that settled it.

The first came at the beginning of September, when the troops at Blessing made one last push out to Chapa Dara. This time Ryan came along. The purpose of the trip was limited: to get a firsthand look at the district center and the town outside it, which was supposed to house a polling site in the Afghan parliamentary elections that were coming up later in the month. ISAF, and government authorities in Asadabad and Kabul, wanted to know whether the police who were supposed to be garrisoning the district center were actually there and whether they were up to the task of securing the polls.

A pair of Chinooks flew into Blessing from Jalalabad at three in the morning on September 4, picking up Ryan and one of his companies and leapfrogging them over the IED-seeded road right into a field outside the Chapa Dara district center. Moving the full force of more than a hundred soldiers took the helicopters four trips, but everyone was in place by the time the sun came up, revealing gorgeous emerald hillsides to soldiers who had been hearing about Chapa Dara for four months but had never seen it.

When a patrol walked into town a little later in the morning to inspect the schoolhouse where voting was supposed to take place, a teacher warned them that the Taliban were going to attack soon. RPGs started exploding by the American defensive positions less than an hour later, kicking off a long-range firefight that would last all day, on and off. With beautiful weather overhead, a pair of Apaches showed up quickly and started working over the hills with rockets and cannon shells in between shake-and-bake fire missions from the howitzers at Blessing. Soon, Air Force jets were dropping bombs as well.[60]

Ryan took it all in from the district center, a new structure built with U.S. reconstruction dollars less than a year earlier. The slippery district governor wasn't there; the last anyone had heard, he was safe in Kabul. But a few policemen were, among them the police chief, a canny character named Sirajuddin who made no bones about being in touch with local militants. As rockets and bullets flew back and forth between the district center and the mountains, Sirajuddin sat by the window with a walkie-talkie tuned to the same frequency as the Taliban commander overseeing the attack, sometimes yelling at him, sometimes speaking calmly, well aware that the interpreter Nazir was listening to the whole conversation: "Yes, the Americans are still here. No, they don't seem like they're going anywhere." At one point Sirajuddin offered Ryan the radio so he could talk directly to the insurgent leader. Ryan obligingly said something through Nazir and got a defiant response.

At such long ranges, the fight was more "energizing" than frightening, Ryan remembered—until a stray insurgent machine-gun bullet turned things much more serious in the evening. Two Kiowas had replaced the Apaches when the larger attack birds ran low on fuel. Now a round hit the right-side rocket pod on one of the low-flying scout helicopters, starting a fire. Alarmed by the smoke and unsure what other damage there might be, the Kiowa's pilot made an emergency landing in a field by the district center.

Stuck with a downed helicopter and its two pilots, the troops in Chapa Dara settled in for a long night. When news of the crash reached headquarters at Jalalabad and Bagram, it prompted urgent debate about what to do with the damaged aircraft. Bomb it? Wreck it with thermite grenades? Slinging it out underneath the belly of a Chinook in the middle of a battle was out of the question. Finally, at Jalalabad, one of the most experienced Kiowa pilots offered an idea: have somebody drop him off in Chapa Dara, and he thought he might be able to fly the thing out.

The volunteer, Chief Warrant Officer 3 Victor Lezama, was a Marine turned soldier nearing the end of a twenty-year military career, the tail end of which he'd spent flying Kiowas over Mosul, Baghdad, and now northeastern Afghanistan. On the midnight Black Hawk ride out to Chapa Dara with a co-pilot and two enlisted technicians to carry the starter battery, he was already imagining what his wife would say when he Skyped her later and explained what he'd done. Nevertheless, he was reasonably confident; he had done something similar with another damaged Kiowa in Texas before deployment. On the ground, after some Bulldog infantrymen got them oriented, Lezama and his crew ran to the grounded aircraft as fast as they could and got down to business, praying that they could get the Kiowa started before they attracted enemy fire.

It worked. As soon as the two technicians plugged the battery in, Lezama powered the Kiowa on and took off. Flying low so that he could glide down into the river if the engine went out again, he and his co-pilot made it to the landing zone at Blessing, where a Chinook would be able to pick the damaged helicopter up later for transport back to Jalalabad.[61] Thanks to Lezama's successful gambit, Chinooks were able to pull the Bulldog soldiers out of Chapa Dara and return them to Blessing later that same night, not too far behind schedule; they got back in time for those with the energy to watch the second half of a Notre Dame–Purdue football game on the American Forces Network in the chow hall.[62]

Ryan's mind was elsewhere as he ate: he was replaying the final moments of the mission and pondering how badly it could have gone. Hanging on to the red interior webbing in the back of the last Chinook out, jammed in with more soldiers than the transport helicopter was supposed to carry at that altitude, he had seen enemy RPGs arcing up toward the aircraft, missing, and falling back to earth. If just one of those rockets had been as lucky as the machine-gun bullet that brought down the Kiowa, he knew, the mission could have turned into a disaster; a Chinook full of infantry shot down in Chapa Dara would have necessitated a huge recovery operation, à la Red Wings, and who knew what additional losses.

The whole mission had been an unnecessary exercise, Ryan concluded, perhaps an absurd one. There wasn't any fighting in Chapa Dara when Americans weren't around, but almost as soon as he and his soldiers had landed, the place had exploded. Clearly the police force out there had some kind of agreement with the Taliban. That agreement was providing security, which evaporated the moment U.S. troops showed up. Had checking up on those police and a polling site where people might or might not vote at all been worth disrupting that stasis and risking American casualties, potentially quite a lot of them? He didn't think so.

THE SECOND EVENT that solidified Ryan's thinking about the Pech was the parliamentary election itself.[63]

On voting day for Afghanistan's 2009 presidential election, a year before, U.S. troops in the Pech had hung close to the valley's polling sites, helping the ANA and police protect the schoolhouses, checkpoints, and district centers where people were casting their ballots for or against Hamid Karzai. Everywhere they were, the 4/4 ID troops had found themselves fighting all day: by the Tarale police checkpoint, where an MRAP was disabled in a firefight; by the schoolhouse in Qamchi, where a Marine adviser team and their ANA fought through an attack; and on and off all afternoon in Chapa Dara, where a platoon spent the day defending the district center.

Ryan wasn't sure that the 4/4 ID troops had really done much securing; it sounded more as if they had been magnets for militant attacks, making things more dangerous for people lining up to vote, not less. So on the day of the 2010 parliamentary elections, September 18, he had his soldiers keep their distance from polling sites. Maybe the Taliban would leave the sites alone and focus their attacks on his men instead, he reasoned.

The theory panned out. From Blessing in the west to COP Honaker-Miracle in the east, the Bulldog battalion's patrols walked or drove out early in the morning, heading to positions on spurs or stretches of road that would provide good visibility during the gunfights they were expecting. As groups of guerrillas came down from draws or out of side valleys like the Shuryak and Watapur, practically every such position came under attack. In the Waygal, one platoon fought through three attacks. In the second, which started as a close-range RPG ambush and turned into a long-range gunfight across the Waygal River, three of the platoon's four MRAP gunners were wounded, albeit lightly. By evening, the firefight count in the Pech had passed fifty, making it the most violent day the battalion had seen since it got to Afghanistan, but only two of the attacks were directed at polling sites. Excluding Chapa Dara, a respectable six-teen thousand people cast ballots.[64]

"The blinding flash of the obvious that day was, 'They hate us here,'" Ryan said. "They were not against the Afghan government, not against voting or a democratic approach. They were against America, Americans, foreigners."

When Ryan and Nazir discussed the day's events at a *shura* in Nangalam afterward, Ryan remembered some of the assembled elders looking at him as if he were a child finally grasping something he should have learned a long time ago: *You didn't figure this out already, that you guys are the problem here?*

Nazir remembered one of the Pech's most influential elders, Haji Fazil Mohammad of Kandigal, putting it to Ryan simply: "If you leave, things will go back to normal."[65]

Ryan thought it was worth a shot. "For me, the elections were the big turning point in the way I viewed what we could achieve out there," he said. "From that point out, my goal was to hit the enemy hard, and then work out a way to get out."[66]

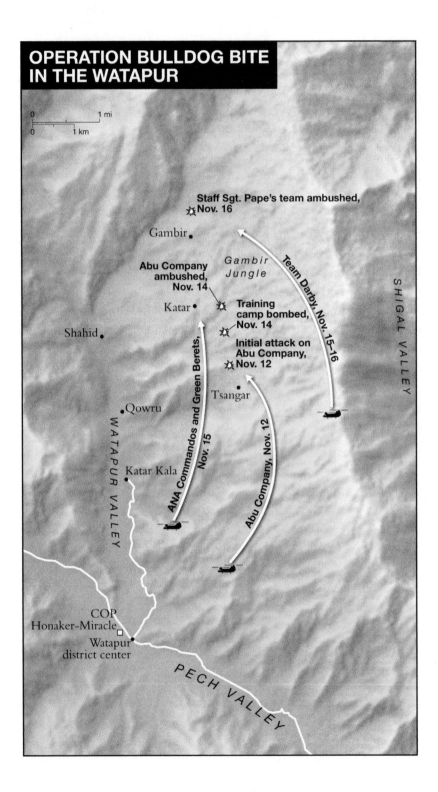

OPERATION BULLDOG BITE IN THE WATAPUR

0   1 mi
0   1 km

Staff Sgt. Pape's team ambushed, Nov. 16

Gambir

Gambir Jungle

Abu Company ambushed, Nov. 14

Katar

Training camp bombed, Nov. 14

Shahid

Initial attack on Abu Company, Nov. 12

Team Darby, Nov. 15-16

SHIGAL VALLEY

Tsangar

Qowru

ANA Commandos and Green Berets, Nov. 15

Abu Company, Nov. 12

WATAPUR VALLEY

Katar Kala

COP Honaker-Miracle

Watapur district center

PECH VALLEY

CHAPTER 11

REALIGNMENT

2010–2011

"A FINAL GUT CHECK"

Joe Ryan had already sold his boss, a colonel of Greek ancestry named Drew Poppas, on the idea that the time was coming to leave FOB Blessing and the Pech outposts. Next Poppas had to convince his own superiors, the 101st Airborne Division generals who ran Regional Command East at Bagram, and they in turn would have to explain to the higher-ranking generals in Kabul why they should sign off on a high-profile, resource-intensive withdrawal operation at the very time that every other brigade in Afghanistan was spreading tentacles into new valleys and districts, building more outposts.

Poppas was a blunt man, but he was proud of one way he hit on of making his argument: with a twist on the old ink-blot metaphor. The ink-blot model of counterinsurgency made sense, Poppas would say, but it worked only on material that ink would soak into, like paper or fabric. More than six years after Green Beret A-team 936's application of the first drop of ink in Nangalam, the Pech seemed more like plastic; it wasn't absorbing the ink.

The division commander, Major General John Campbell, ribbed Poppas the first time he heard him use this metaphor, joking that the plainspoken colonel, who sometimes tripped over his sentences, wasn't smart enough to have come up with it on his own.[1] Nevertheless, it made sense to him as a way of expressing why the counterinsurgency strategy that ISAF was enthusiastically plunging into everywhere from Kandahar in the south to Kunduz in the north was not working in this particular corner of Kunar in the east. By early fall 2010, Campbell too was sold, though his one-star deputy for operations was still on the fence.[2] Neither Poppas nor Ryan nor the generals above them wanted to start closing American bases in the valley without doing one last thing, however: killing as many insurgents as possible in a series of air-assault missions into the Pech's side valleys, the latest in the long succession of such missions since 2003.

Heliborne attacks were the 101st's forte—the unit was officially the 101st Airborne Division (Air Assault), and 101st troops were better trained for such operations than any others in the Army besides the Rangers—and pounding the enemy in the Pech before winter weather set in had been part of Poppas's and Ryan's plans since they left Fort Campbell. Now that withdrawing from the Pech was on the table, hitting the enemy hard before leaving made all the more sense to the two colonels and their bosses at Bagram. Kill enough guerrillas, and (as after Operation Rock Avalanche three falls earlier) there would be a couple of months of quiet over the winter while the Taliban replaced their lost men and supplies. That would be the perfect time for the Bulldog battalion to extricate itself from its outposts, a complex operation that would require constant logistical convoys on the ambush- and IED-prone Pech road.[3] A big offensive might also make the pullout an easier sell in Kabul, where ISAF's commander, Petraeus, had been stressing the importance of staying on the offensive and striking insurgent safe havens. The helicopter raids into the Pech's side valleys would be, as the 101st's intelligence chief put it, "a final gut check before leaving."[4]

Instead of launching one air assault with his whole battalion, à la Rock Avalanche, Ryan wanted to stretch Operation Bulldog Bite, as it was called, out into several smaller missions, spaced apart by several weeks, each sending a company into a different Pech side valley.

No one in the chain of command had any appetite for going into the two deadly side valleys from which previous units had tortuously extricated themselves, the Waygal and the Korengal—not beyond poking into those valleys' mouths, anyway. The valleys Ryan wanted to hit were the ones that had received only sporadic American attention over the years and had never housed American outposts.[5]

The repeated air-assault rehearsals Ryan had put some of his companies through in the Georgia mountains paid off. As one Bulldog company after another headed into the tributaries south of the Pech in October, putting to good use their newly issued brown-green MultiCam camouflage fatigues, they executed their plans to a T. In the narrow valley above Tantil where HIMARS rockets had killed Mullah Dawran's family a year earlier, a platoon got into a sharp gunfight, and one wounded soldier had to be evacuated by helicopter. In the Rechalam valley five miles southwest of Blessing, a pair of Apaches made short work of a group of two dozen guerrillas the pilots spotted clustered around a forest clearing as Chinooks were inbound to deposit infantrymen there. And for four days in the middle of the month, Bulldog troops and an ANA Commando company searched village after village in the Shuryak, one night drawing out a group of militants for an orbiting AC-130 to slaughter. Among the dead, radio intercepts revealed, was Gul Nabi Bilal, the up-and-coming young commander responsible for the June ambush that had killed two members of Ryan's security detail.[6]

It was the same old pattern, to Ryan's disappointment but not his surprise: when the skies were full of aircraft and American troops picked the time and place, only the bravest or stupidest insurgents were willing to come out to fight, limiting the number of them who could be killed. Still, the practiced smoothness with which his companies had executed the opening Bulldog Bite missions—including going into the infamous Shuryak, the scene of the shootdown of Turbine 33, and coming out unscathed—buoyed Ryan's and his officers' confidence. They had a template, and it seemed as though it would work anywhere now.[7]

The next mission fell to the soldiers at the outpost closest to Asadabad, COP Honaker-Miracle, a square base enclosed by a stone wall that bore the names of two Rock paratroopers killed in 2007 on an air assault into a side valley north of the Pech. The mission's target was that same valley: the Watapur.

.   .   .

THE WATAPUR VALLEY, for the U.S. military in the Pech, represented the path not taken, the road and outpost not built.

Stretching eight miles northward from the Pech, the Watapur ran roughly parallel to the Waygal, with a twelve-thousand-foot ridge separating them. The valley floor was wide enough for farming and housed a series of small towns, connected by a bumpy dirt road that caused endless trouble for MRAPs that braved it. Up above, the valley's western wall was sparse, dotted with caves and boulders but few trees. Among the tiny villages up there, out of sight from the valley floor, was one not marked on most U.S. military maps: Kunyak, where twenty-three Soviet infantrymen had been killed in 1985 while chasing down a false tip about U.S.-supplied anti-aircraft missiles.[*]

The valley's eastern face sloped up to the imposing ridge that separated the Watapur from the neighboring Shigal valley, where the CIA had missed bin Laden with a drone strike and JSOC with its first big Kunar raid back in 2002. The ridge dropped off so sharply on the Shigal side that some units called it the Wall.[8] The gentler slope on the Watapur side housed a string of mountainside towns with populations of a few thousand each, running parallel to the valley-floor towns three thousand feet below: Tsangar, Katar, and, five and a half miles back, the biggest one, Gambir. Each town was really a cluster of smaller, separate villages, and specific areas within Tsangar, Katar, and Gambir were marked on the Bulldog battalion's maps as Objectives Patriots, Cowboys, and Packers, respectively.[9] Although they were in Kunar, it was no coincidence that these towns, like those in the Waygal, were built into the side of the mountain in the Nuristani style. Until the forced conversion of Kafiristan into Nuristan at the end of the nineteenth century, Katar

---

[*] In a compilation of accounts by thirty-two survivors of the May 1985 battle of Kunyak, some reported that in the end their wounded company commander shot himself so that they wouldn't have to carry him down the mountain. Like the battle of Want, the Kunyak disaster sparked a criminal investigation into who in the chain of command was to blame.

and Gambir had been Kafir villages, known, like Aranas, for their skilled blacksmiths and silversmiths and for the raids they launched on nearby Pashtun Muslim settlements. A hundred years later, elders from Katar and Gambir still regularly trekked across the mountains to attend Waygali *shuras.*[10]

Above these villages, still mostly untouched by the logging industry in 2010, sprawled twenty square miles of conifer forest, what people called the Gambir Jungle.

It was easy to imagine how, if things had gone a little differently, the U.S. military might have built an outpost somewhere inside the Watapur—a Firebase Tsangar instead of the Ranch House, or a WOP instead of the KOP. Both Chris Cavoli and Bill Ostlund had thought seriously about it.[11] But the first American forays into the valley, by Rangers and the CIA's Afghan surrogates in 2002 and 2003 and by Marines in 2005, had been uneventful, yielding little evidence of the kind of militant sanctuary that would spur the construction of outposts and roads in the Korengal and Waygal.[12] So instead, American involvement in the Watapur had taken the form of heliborne landings on the heights two or three times a year and more frequent patrols up the valley-floor road—first in pickup trucks, which could drive as far back as the valley went and even climb up to Tsangar, then in Humvees, and finally in MRAPs, which could barely make it two miles up the valley without an axle breaking or a wheel getting stuck.[13]

Working from COP Honaker-Miracle way down on the Pech, the succession of junior officers responsible for the Watapur had never gotten to know the place the way their colleagues at the KOP and the Ranch House had gotten to know the Korengal and Waygal. It was common for Honaker-Miracle's Prophet signals intercept team to pick up walkie-talkie chatter from the northern part of the valley around Gambir in what sounded like Waygali, for instance, prompting speculation about what Waygali insurgents might be doing so far from their home turf. Because none of the captains and lieutenants at the outpost were ever able to actually go that far up the Watapur, only a few ever understood the real explanation for much of that radio traffic: while guerrillas and shepherds alike did move freely between the two neighboring valleys, Gambir also had its own language, a Nuristani dialect so closely related to Waygali that Gambiris had served as interpreters for the Afghan army that conquered the Waygal in 1896.[14]

What the successive companies that rotated through Honaker-Miracle did learn was that with each year American troops spent focusing on neighboring valleys, the insurgent presence in the Watapur grew bigger and more deeply rooted. Tsangar, by 2009, housed an active chapter of the Taliban's shadow government, complete with a judge, tax collectors, and a district shadow governor named Nur Akbar who repeatedly evaded air strikes and JSOC night raids meant to kill him.[15] Farther north, the Gambir Jungle offered protection from helicopter raids and aerial surveillance and also a perfect training range for mountain combat—a jihadi version of the swath of northern Georgia mountains where the Bulldog battalion had practiced air assaults before deploying. It was to this sanctuary that some of the militants who attacked The Rock's Chosen Company in Want had retreated with their wounded after the 2008 battle,[16] and every year there were more reports of foreign jihadis running training programs there on how to lay ambushes, build IEDs, or aim rockets and mortars—both occasional visitors like Abu Ikhlas, who was said to have a wife from the Watapur,[17] and younger al-Qaida colleagues who stayed year-round.[18]

The upper Watapur was also a stop on an old, well-known guerrilla infiltration route from militant camps in Pakistan through the mountains north of the Pech, one that the mujahidin had used extensively during the jihad against the Soviets.[19] Running parallel to the route that militants followed from the border through the mountains south of the Pech to the Korengal, this ratline climbed up the Shigal to the heights where it joined the Watapur, then down to Gambir and Tsangar, a trip that took a couple of days. Fighters could then either stay in Gambir or continue on over the mountains toward the Waygal, the next leg of the route.[20] Sometimes reports would come in of fighters driving the whole way in pickup trucks; some 101st intelligence soldiers found that hard to believe until one day a Predator followed a pickup as it did just that, ascending mountain trails that it was almost impossible to believe were drivable.[21]

The Watapur phase of Bulldog Bite fell to the latest occupants of Honaker-Miracle, Ryan's Abu Company. (In 101st Airborne mythology, the Abu, pronounced "A-Boo," is a chimeric monster with the head of a lion, body of a gorilla, tail of an alligator, and antlers of a moose; it has been the mascot of 1–327 Infantry's A Company since the 1950s.) Abu Company's mission was to be a brief one, essentially a repeat of the 2007 operation during which an alarmingly accurate insurgent marksman had killed The Rock paratroopers Christopher Honaker and Joseph Miracle. With a group of about thirty-five ANA tagging along, they would fly up onto the mountain in Chinooks, spend a day searching Tsangar for caches of the rockets and mortar shells that had been hitting Honaker-Miracle recently, sleep there, and then hike back down the next day.

To many of the hundred or so Abu Company soldiers who piled out of helicopters onto terraces around Tsangar before dawn on Friday, November 12, the success of the previous Bulldog Bite missions in other Pech side valleys was not reassuring; it just meant the insurgents in the Watapur were probably expecting them.[22]

"Myself included, we were scared," one of the platoon leaders tasked with clearing Tsangar itself, a thirty-one-year-old former NCO, said. "It's hard to get motivated to walk into an ambush."[23]

ABU COMPANY WAS walking into not just one ambush, as it turned out, but several.[24]

The soldiers in Tsangar had been climbing through town for five hours on Friday morning, negotiating terraces as tall as they were and peering over accompanying ANA soldiers' shoulders as they searched one empty house after another, when explosions and gunfire engulfed an overwatch position the company's smallest platoon had set up on a knoll overlooking the village. Creeping through the boulders and foliage above the knoll to avoid being spotted by spy planes, drones, or attack helicopters, a group of guerrillas had spent the morning getting close enough to unleash a barrage of accurate machine-gun and RPG fire, taking advantage of an uncovered part of the platoon's perimeter. The lieutenant, platoon sergeant, and radioman on the knoll fell wounded right away, and more soldiers were soon hit around them.[25]

Arriving over Tsangar a few minutes into the battle on the knoll, the pilots of two Apaches could see the muzzle flashes out their windows first, and then they could see the insurgents; dressed in a combination of robes and camouflage, they were moving confidently and competently in ones and twos, rushing short distances and covering one another as they spread out around the knoll and closed in to hand-grenade range. Over the radio, the pilot of one attack bird could hear a pinned-down soldier yelling for help and the screams of the wounded around him. The Apache's cannon tore apart one fighter as he looked right up at the helicopter, but not before he'd added the rocket he was carrying to another punishing close-range salvo of RPGs. The next thing the Apache crews heard over the radio was that the RPGs had killed the platoon medic and a pair of Afghan soldiers.[26]

Down in Tsangar itself, the rest of Abu Company spent all day dodging machine-gun fire while negotiating one cliff-like terrace after another, struggling to reach their embattled brothers. By the time the company was reunited after dark and the enemy disappeared, half of the twenty-two Americans on the knoll had been hit, and risky hoist operations were under way to get the wounded and dead out. Guided in by a purple smoke grenade, one HH-60 Pave Hawk rescue bird had taken a DShK round through the right engine, and an Air Force pararescueman aboard had been shot.[27]

That night, Captain Bo Reynolds, the burly Army brat and former West Point wrestler who commanded Abu Company, sat on the cold mountainside, illuminating a laminated map of the valley with the dull red glow from his flashlight, while Ryan gave him new instructions over the radio from down at Honaker-Miracle.

The original plan of coming down from the mountain the next day was off the table now, Ryan said. He and Drew Poppas, the brigade commander back in Jalalabad, had talked it over and agreed that Abu Company needed to get a few hours' sleep and then start heading north toward the next big village, Katar, a mile and a half farther along the mountainside.

It wasn't Ryan's style to give pep talks, but he explained his reasoning to Reynolds, knowing that these were not the instructions the weary captain was hoping to hear. In the operations center at Honaker-Miracle, intelligence soldiers were plotting all the walkie-talkie and cell phone intercepts that spy planes and the base's Prophet team were picking up. It was clear what was happening: the guerrillas who had taken half an American platoon out of commission were retreating toward Katar, where they thought, based on past experience, that they would be safe. Abu Company had found the enemy, and now they had to go after him. Katar—Objective Cowboys—was Bulldog Bite's new target.

THE GAMBIR JUNGLE

Overnight, helicopters dropped off a fresh platoon to round out the company, and the soldiers starting their second day on the mountain used thermite grenades to melt the body-armor plates of their friends who had been killed or evacuated the day before.[28] Then, before sunrise on Saturday, they started hiking north, through the towering pines, firs, and cedars of the lower edge of the Gambir Jungle.

Climbing over fingers and draws and stopping now and again to call in howitzer fire, Abu Company's pace was excruciatingly slow. By nightfall, an ambush on a stretch of trail where the big trees were sparse had killed another ANA soldier and wounded two sergeants in Reynolds's First Platoon, and the column of a hundred or so troops moving north through the forest had covered less than a mile.[29]

The whole thing repeated itself the next morning. Abu Company started moving forty-five minutes before the sun rose on a clear, brisk Sunday. Just a quarter mile on, in a terraced clearing next to a sawmill, the troops up front found a structure that stood out from the modest houses and *bandehs* they had seen so far: a big, rectangular, lodge-like building.

As Afghan and American soldiers entered the building, a colorful character was called forward: Karl Beilby, a middle-aged Anglo-American, born in Cyprus and raised all over Asia, whose varied career had taken him from professional skier to Southern California drug cop to civilian contractor assisting the Bulldog battalion with police matters. With some trepidation about how his forty-seven-year-old body would handle the altitude, he'd joined Abu Company on the Watapur mission to help with evidence collection.[30]

It was obvious to Beilby what he was looking at when he went inside the building. When intelligence reports referred to "training camps" in the Watapur—those mythical sites that surveillance aircraft could never find—this was what they meant. Inside was a spacious room with enough sleeping bags and camouflage fatigues for twenty guerrillas and a box of brand-new Korans, and a smaller room stocked with plasma bags and antibiotics. Nearby, the soldiers found a large cache of small-arms ammunition and RPGs and a single dead body, possibly a casualty of one of the previous day's artillery barrages. Really, the surrounding cliffs and woods were the training camp; this was just the barracks where the trainees slept, and maybe where they recovered from wounds after tangling with Americans down on the Pech.[31]

After a long halt to get an air-strike request going to flatten the place, Abu Company kept moving. They had covered a thousand more feet when Reynolds ordered another pause in a smaller clearing by a little creek. Objective Cowboys was less than half a mile downhill now, at the edge of the forest. While he set up his command post in a farmhouse looking down on the town and got ready to head downhill, the captain sent his Third Platoon uphill, farther into the forest, to a position from which they would be able to watch as he and the rest of the company moved into Katar and started searching houses.[32]

Two Apaches, a Predator, a larger Reaper, and a manned spy plane crammed with eavesdropping equipment were all circling above the Watapur that afternoon. That was more air support than some previous battalions in the Pech had seen for weeks at a time, but it still did not constitute an all-seeing eye. The Predator was stuck watching the enemy barracks Abu had found in the morning, making sure that no civilians went near it before the air strike that was working its way through the approval process, and the Reaper was staring down into Katar itself. The only warning sign came a little before three o'clock, when some Americans and ANA on a ledge at Third Platoon's position spotted three men moving near them in the forest, but through the vegetation the pilot of the closest Apache couldn't make out any weapons and declined to open fire.[33]

The Apaches had moved away when, at 3:07 p.m., all hell broke loose at both of Abu Company's positions: machine-gun rounds skipping in from multiple directions and distances, volleys of RPGs from the woods, fighters with rifles emerging from nowhere and maneuvering with the same quick, practiced bounds as the guerrillas who had surrounded the overwatch position above Tsangar on Friday.

IN THE CHAOS of the fight, it was not immediately clear to Reynolds which of the two attacks was the more serious, and even less so to Ryan and his staff listening to the radios in the Honaker-Miracle operations center. The first reports of contact, and the first report of a soldier wounded, came from First Platoon at the farmhouse, so it was to the farmhouse that attack helicopters rushed and toward the clearing around the farmhouse that the orbiting Reaper's sensor operator (sitting in a stateside control trailer) tilted its camera. On computer monitors at Honaker-Miracle, the Reaper's video feed showed First Platoon's defense in agonizing detail: hand grenades and RPGs exploding, a soldier moving backward toward cover firing his M4 with one hand. As the drone's camera zoomed out, someone spotted an enemy fighting position, and Ryan approved a strike. With a push of the red button that the drone crews called the pickle, a Hellfire missile blasted off one of the rails under the Reaper's wings, followed by a second missile when someone emerged alive from the first explosion.[34]

Then the reports started coming in by radio from Third Platoon's position: multiple casualties. The Reaper's camera tilted to look a few hundred feet up the mountain, where Third Platoon was spread out in a circular perimeter amid huge trees on either side of the creek. In forest that thick, the drone's camera could show only what was happening on one tiny patch of earth directly below it, perhaps sixty by sixty feet. Everything else was obscured by the branches and needles of the huge conifers.

Beneath the canopy, Third Platoon was fighting a desperate battle as a disciplined force of militants tried to overrun its position. The insurgent scouts spotted fifteen minutes earlier had done their work well; the first volley of RPGs exploded around the hasty command post in the middle of the position where the platoon leader, platoon sergeant, and their radiomen were all gathered, knocking radios out of commission and forcing everyone to dive for cover in the creek bed or behind tree trunks and roots. One RPG blast knocked the civilian contractor Karl Beilby down the mountainside, briefly deafening him. Third Platoon was well and truly pinned down. When Beilby tried to crawl over to a wounded soldier near him, he was shot too. The bullet entered Beilby's back and exited his stomach, dragging some of his intestines out with it.[35]

On the perimeter, Sergeant Sean Outman, a stocky Marine veteran who had joined the Army after September 11 and become a fire team leader in Third Platoon, was amazed by what he was seeing. It was the best-executed support-by-fire position he had ever seen, the incoming suppressive fire shifting from the command post to the platoon's machine-gun positions as riflemen with long hair and scraggly beards emerged from the trees and closed in, taking careful shots like trained infantrymen. A team of attackers had gotten within fifty or sixty feet of Outman and started throwing grenades when he caught a long enough glimpse of a beardless guerrilla with an RPG to shoot him with his M4; then Outman ran back to the creek bed, where he was promptly shot in the back as he flopped down next to Karl Beilby.[36] A radioman, Specialist Jesse Snow, had been trying to cram Beilby's guts back inside him, and now he climbed on top of both wounded men to try to protect them and start treating Outman too. Snow had just started to get to work when he was shot; Outman felt the twenty-five-year-old from Ohio go limp on top of him as a bullet struck the back of his head and killed him.

Despite the din, Outman could hear reports coming in from other parts of the platoon of more dead and wounded. At a machine-gun position facing downhill, one soldier was killed, then a second, then two more wounded.[37] It seemed as though there had to be fifty or sixty insurgents around them, some of them inside the platoon's perimeter. For a moment, people were screaming about a suicide bomber—an interpreter said he heard some of the enemy shouting to bring one forward—but if there really was a bomber, he either retreated or was cut down by machine-gun fire before he could blow himself up.[38]

Apaches and Kiowas arrived an hour in and started shooting rockets and Hellfires, followed a few minutes later by a pair of Pave

Hawks. The gray Air Force rescue helicopters' crews had stripped the armor from their cabins because of the altitude, but from the doors the crewmen were firing heavy machine guns and M4s at any enemy muzzle flashes they saw. As one bird lowered its pararescuemen between the trees, bullets struck the metal cable they were descending on and punched through the cabin floor and windshield. From the creek bed, Outman watched with concern as an RPG sailed past the helicopter. The blast of another RPG knocked the two pararescuemen flat as soon as they got on the ground, but with rockets, cannon fire, and a danger-close bomb strike from a jet beating back the insurgent force and the sun setting, the tide had turned and the airmen were able to start preparing the wounded for evacuation.[39]

As the wounded started to disappear up into the sky on the Pave Hawks' hoists, Outman felt as if he were living in a Vietnam movie, being winched out of the jungle. The stretcher carrying Karl Beilby flipped over in the air partway up, suspending him upside down, and he threw up what felt like all the bodily fluids still left inside him. The last thing the retired cop remembered seeing of the Watapur was the forest spinning around and around below him.[40]

WHEN THE EXHAUSTED, angry soldiers of Abu Company went through Katar house by house the next morning, assisted by ANA Commandos who had been flown in overnight, they found as little as they had in Tsangar: some recoilless-rifle rounds under a rock, and, on the wall of a house with a balcony overlooking the valley, a child's detailed drawing of a rifle firing bullets at a twin-rotor helicopter.[41]

Five miles away at Honaker-Miracle, a color-coded map in the operations center displayed the radio and cell phone intercepts coming in. *We're moving north now,* the guerrillas who had attacked Abu Company in Katar were saying to each other. *We're out of ammunition and it's time to go.*[42] The retreating militants' destination was the cluster of small villages that made up the town of Gambir. That was the end of the line in the Watapur; to the north, there wasn't much besides fields of boulders and expanses of forest that grew sparser the higher you climbed. Americans hadn't set foot in Gambir since a brief 2008 Green Beret mission that had been cut short by a blizzard. This rugged sanctuary, Ryan was sure, was the real prize.[43]

But the steeply sloped part of Gambir on which the enemy seemed to be converging was nearly a mile and a half farther north along the mountain, through treacherous terrain and dense forest. Even with the ANA Commandos and their Green Beret advisers, Abu Company was too depleted and worn out to get there. Someone else would have to go, and the one command with the resources and flexibility to drop into Gambir midoperation was JSOC.

Watching aerial footage of the previous day's battle at Bagram, the Ranger colonel in charge of JSOC's Afghanistan task force—a friend of Ryan's who had been in Kunar during Winter Strike—had already reached out to the 101st to ask if they needed help. On a secure conference call, Drew Poppas laid out a case to the Ranger task force commander and the top JSOC officer in the country, Brigadier General Tony Thomas, who had been Ryan's battalion commander during their first Afghanistan deployment back in 2002.[44]

Committing a heliborne assault force to a place like the Gambir Jungle was not an easy call, especially on short notice, and Thomas was skeptical. Too many such operations had cost more than they were worth, he knew—going back to the 2002 battle of Takur Ghar, where he and Ryan had lost the first Rangers killed in the war on terror and insurgents had shot down their first Chinook. But helping conventional forces had become part of JSOC's charter in Afghanistan, and the case Ryan and Poppas made was convincing. The enemy had just given American forces their worst bloodying in the Pech since the 2008 battle of Want. But in past air-assault operations in Kunar, even large enemy forces operating on their home turf had tended to lose steam and start falling apart around the five-day mark. It was day four in the Watapur now, and on their radios the guerrillas were complaining that they were tired and running low on food, ammunition, and batteries. Someone needed to keep pushing north and hit them where they thought they were safe.[45]

Thomas and the task force commander offered a unit called Team Darby—eighty-plus Rangers whose role in the Afghan surge was to rove around the country, hitting targets that were too big or heavily defended for a single SEAL or Delta Force troop or Ranger platoon. Once again, Rangers would be leading the way, this time into one of the historic sanctuary areas from which insurgents had waged their war in the Pech.[46]

AS THE BLACKED-OUT Night Stalker Chinooks approached their landing zone before dawn on Tuesday, November 16, the Ranger officers and fire-support specialists on board used video handsets to watch in real time as ordnance pummeled the surrounding woods. It took two trips to get the whole force of Rangers and fifteen or so Afghan troops onto the terrace. The enemy walkie-talkie chatter reporting the party's landing started almost immediately.

Between the clouds, the waning crescent moon, and the patchy forest canopy above the troops' heads, there was almost no ambient light—just the way the Rangers liked it. They intended to do all their work before sunrise and then spend the day holed up in a compound somewhere, the opposite of the way Abu Company had been fighting.

It was hard enough to negotiate the boulders, cliffs, and huge tree roots of the Gambir Jungle walking laterally during the day; doing it uphill and downhill through the green fog of night vision was even slower going. By the time the Rangers reached the first of the houses they were supposed to clear, on Gambir's upper edge, it was three in the morning. Some dogs were waiting around to bark at them, but otherwise the place seemed almost abandoned. The men had left to go fight, some terrified women in one house told the lead platoon's interpreter. The women were afraid their husbands and sons were all dead.

In fact, there were plenty of men very close at hand, and the turboprop spy plane and AC-130 gunship circling above Team Darby had spotted some of them with their sensors. As the lead platoon left the first cluster of buildings on its target list and headed for the next, one of the planes reported that two groups of people had left a house and were heading for the woods—two men in one group, about five in the other. They had to be insurgents. Infrared tracking beams shone down from the planes, one following the larger group and the other tracking the pair until they disappeared behind a formation of boulders.

Team Darby was prepared for this. Part of the lead platoon had the job of chasing down "squirters": a squad plus a highly trained attack dog with a camera strapped to his head—a Belgian Malinois named Jari. Descending as quickly as the terrain and the darkness allowed, this chase team hurried toward the boulders where the men had disappeared from the planes' view.

Leading the way was Staff Sergeant Kevin Pape (pronounced "Poppy"), a thirty-year-old squad leader. Pape, who was nicknamed GQ for his photogenic looks, was typical of a generation of Ranger NCOs who had enlisted in the years after September 11. Growing up in Indiana, he had spent his childhood playing with G.I. Joes and making tanks out of cardboard boxes. In the Rangers, with their endless cycle of short, intense combat rotations, he had found his calling; although he had a new baby back at home in Savannah, he'd delayed a surgery he needed in order to accompany his squad on this latest deployment, his sixth in five years.[47]

The distance Pape and his Rangers had to cover was only a few hundred feet, but much of it was nearly straight down—one cliff face after another, with plenty of big tree roots to break one's fall or one's bones. Almost at once, the chase team and its dog disappeared from the rest of the platoon's view. As they approached the rock formation where the pair of squirters had last been seen, one of the planes overhead spotted the pair of men again and illuminated them with its infrared beam. The chase team was almost on top of them, but between the Rangers and the two guerrillas was a tall cliff. Kevin Pape and two other NCOs slipped over the edge into the darkness and clambered down. They had just reached the bottom of the cliff when the two squirters spotted them and started shooting. Raising his sound-suppressed M4, Pape shot both men and threw a grenade in their direction.

Then a burst of gunfire leaped out of the rocks to Pape's right. He had walked into the field of fire of a machine gunner lying inside the hidden mouth of a cave, his eyes adjusted to the dark, waiting patiently for the silhouette of an American to appear. Pape fell to the ground, shot in the side. Just behind him, the two sergeants who had followed him down the cliff opened fire on the cave mouth, a car-door-sized opening at the end of a rock formation that protruded from the mountain like the entrance to an igloo. That kept the machine gun inside quiet long enough for them to reach their wounded squad leader and drag him to cover, shooting two more fighters who spilled from the mouth of the cave as they did so.

The sun was rising and the AC-130 was striking other guerrillas on the mountain as more Rangers arrived on the scene. Pape was talking a bit, but the medic treating him could tell that he was bleeding internally. If he wasn't evacuated soon, he would die.[48] Guided through the woods by the surveillance planes toward a terrace just big enough to fit a Black Hawk or Pave Hawk, the platoon leader and another squad set out to secure a landing zone.

As half the platoon fanned out around the terrace and half kept up the fire on the cave, it seemed as if the whole valley were erupting; rifle and machine-gun bursts were coming from positions nearby on the mountainside and from many more positions across a creek bed. The platoon leader's guess was that Pape had stumbled onto the entrance to an enemy command post, maybe the one that a Taliban or al-Qaida commander had been using to oversee the fight against Abu Company for the past few days. Now groups of fighters from all around were rallying to protect it.[49]

At the cave, where Pape had gone gray and stopped talking, fresh fighters kept firing from inside the rock opening, even after the Rangers got up on top of the rock formation surrounding it and threw special cave-clearing grenades inside. From the trees farther down the slope toward the creek bed, other insurgents were yelling to each other in the dawn gloom.[50]

It was almost unheard of for AC-130s to stay out in daylight, but two of them did so now, trying to obliterate the cave with their side-mounted cannon as the Rangers withdrew toward the medevac landing zone. The company medic could do nothing more for the dying Pape, but a sniper and an interpreter had both been shot by now as well and needed to be lifted out.

Finally, as the gunships brought their fire precariously close to the Rangers' positions and a pair of Kiowas skimmed the treetops, a rescue helicopter settled down onto the terrace just long enough to get the three casualties aboard—the sniper, the interpreter, and the litter with Kevin Pape's body strapped to it.

Team Darby spent the rest of Tuesday maintaining a strongpoint in a house higher uphill, hitting everything that moved around them with air strikes and the bazooka-like Carl Gustaf recoilless rifles that a few of the Rangers had lugged along. After dark that night, while planes and artillery pummeled every ridge, helicopters came for all the troops on the mountain—the Rangers in the Gambir Jungle, and then Abu Company and the ANA Commandos outside Katar.

When they got back down to Honaker-Miracle, some of the Abu platoons memorialized the ordeal they'd been through by posing for group pictures, their MultiCam fatigues a uniform dirt brown and stubble on their faces. Abu Company's commander, Bo Reynolds, had been on the last lift out, and when he walked into his command post, disheveled and exhausted, Joe Ryan was there to shake his hand. Ryan greeted the Rangers too, cigar in hand, thanking them for doing exactly what he had needed them to: show the enemy that even in the Gambir Jungle, they were not safe.[51]

"BLOOD AND SWEAT AND TEARS AND MONEY"

The Bulldog battalion commemorated the soldiers killed on the mountain four days afterward, in a ceremony at Honaker-Miracle. Big photographs of the six Abu Company soldiers who had died stood on easels in the gravel courtyard, and the 101st Airborne Division commander, Major General John Campbell, was there, visiting from Bagram.

While Apaches prowled above, ready to pummel any insurgents who tried to interrupt the ceremony, officers and friends spoke about each man: about the medic Shannon Chihuahua, and how, when he'd taken some shrapnel to the face earlier in the tour, he wouldn't let anyone treat the wound until he'd gotten a picture for Facebook; about Christian "Kade" Warriner, a "crazy redneck hick," as the friend who spoke about him put it with affection, who had been shot in the forehead in the livestock pen of the farmhouse outside Katar; about Jesse Snow, who loved Patrón tequila and was also a neat freak; about Shane Ahmed and how the Pashto language course the Army had sent him to didn't seem to have stuck; about Scott Nagorski and the purple PT Cruiser that he didn't mind other soldiers' laughing at; and about how it was weird that Nathan Lillard, a die-hard Dallas Cowboys fan who had been wounded at the same position Nagorski and Ahmed were manning and bled to death before the pararescuemen could get him on a Pave Hawk, had lost his life fighting for an objective named after his team.[52]

In the November days following the mission in the Watapur, some Abu Company soldiers had pointed questions for their commanders. Many were angry with Ryan for deviating from the plan and sending them north into the forest, where the advantages of airpower and artillery were blunted and the worst had happened. Others wondered why they hadn't slept during the day and moved at night, like the Rangers.[53] The colonel entertained some what-ifs himself. Might the company's death toll have been lower if it had taken more troops north? If more drones or attack helicopters had been overhead, could they have spotted the force that attacked Third Platoon in the forest? If he had been up on the mountain with his men, would that have made any difference? These were unanswerable questions, but Ryan would still be wondering about them years afterward.[54]

He was sure, however, that he had made the right call in sending Abu Company north after the initial fight in Tsangar. "There's a myth, I think, amongst us coalition forces and ISAF that there are some places we can't go," Ryan said shortly after the operation. "That is absolutely and unequivocally untrue. We can go anywhere we want to go."[55] Going all the way to Katar and Gambir, where the enemy felt safe enough to keep command posts like the one Kevin Pape had stumbled on, was what had made the mission worthwhile. They had hurt the enemy badly there; the battalion's official estimate, based on signals intercepts and reports from informants, was that the operation had killed somewhere north of a hundred guerrillas and wounded another forty.[56]

That only went so far, as Ryan well knew. Gambir was still just as far away after the operation as before; the enemy could have gathered up all their dead afterward and thrown their own memorial ceremony in the middle of town without anyone at Blessing or Honaker-Miracle knowing about it. And every militant killed would be replaced. But not immediately—for a period of a few weeks, until fresh fighters arrived from the Waygal and Pakistan and ammunition stores were replenished, there would be some quiet down in the eastern Pech around Honaker-Miracle. That quiet could be used to begin the Pech withdrawal.

With division headquarters on board, logistics convoys from Jalalabad began making frequent runs to Blessing and the other Pech bases late in the fall, taking away excess cargo like spare treadmills and containers full of disused old rifle sights so that when the order to actually pull out of the bases came down, there would be less to do.

THE NAME THE 101st Airborne came up with for the withdrawal it was planning was Operation Pech Realignment. The euphemism occasioned laughs among soldiers working on the plan at Blessing. Some of them wholeheartedly supported the idea of leaving the Pech, but for others it was as hard a pill to swallow as leaving the Korengal had been for some of the soldiers who served there.

One skeptic was Captain Jonathan "J.J." Springer, Ryan's brightly earnest fire-support officer, who had met me at the Blessing landing zone when I visited over the summer. Springer looked up to his colonel and took most of what Ryan said as gospel, but the idea of pulling out left him uneasy and, privately, dejected. Framed photos of the thirteen Bulldog battalion soldiers killed in action so far during the deployment hung in the hallway of the operations center where Springer worked, and every day on his way to the chow hall he walked past five gray marble plaques—beneath the waving American, Afghan, and U.S. Army flags—onto which were etched the names of sixty-five more Americans who had died in the Pech.[*] As he and the rest of the staff planned the "realignment," Springer couldn't help but look at those names and wonder what they had died for.[57]

"I was mad, at the Army and at my leaders, because I knew the sacrifice, the blood and sweat and tears and money, we'd put into this valley over the years," Springer told me. "It was very deflating

---

[*] The names of another twenty-nine American troops were not on the plaques at Blessing, including those of the nineteen SEALs and Night Stalkers killed during Operation Red Wings.

and it made me wonder a lot about why we went into the Pech in the first place. Some guys won't say it, but a lot of us were pissed."[58]

Ryan was anticipating that kind of unhappiness. He picked Jon Peterson, the captain who had been in charge of the repeated Chapa Dara missions over the summer, to help him write up a memo to distribute within the battalion explaining why the time had come to leave and arguing that the deployment had not been a waste of time or lives. It was a subject Peterson had been thinking about already. The first 10th Mountain platoon leader killed in the Pech, Forrest Ewens, had been a friend of his, and he'd gone to middle school with a Rock lieutenant killed in the nearby Chowkay valley, Ben Hall.[59]

The document Peterson produced, which Ryan expanded on before emailing it to the company commanders to distribute to their soldiers, offered an analogy, comparing the Pech to remote World War II battlefields. That war hadn't been won in the Alps or on Pacific islands that Army and Marine troops had fought for and then left, but moving on from them hadn't signified defeat, just shifting priorities on the way to victory. Another bullet point explained that the reasons for which the Pech outposts had been built didn't necessarily still apply: Blessing had started as a "helicopter staging base" for a long-ago counterterrorism mission (the name Winter Strike wasn't mentioned), and Michigan had been built to support the bases inside the Korengal, which had now been vacant for the better part of a year.

"The enemy is constantly evolving," the memo stated. "So should we."[60]

The formal proposal that Ryan and his staff submitted up the chain of command in December included a set of options for division, corps, and ISAF headquarters to consider for the Pech.

One was to make no change: let the Bulldog battalion finish its tour and be replaced at Blessing by the next unit in the deployment chute, a Hawaii-based battalion that was busily preparing for the task. A second option was to double down, adding even more U.S. forces to the Pech. That one was a straw man, which Ryan knew the generals weighing the various options would not seriously consider. The other option, the one the plan clearly favored, was to close down the U.S. bases in the valley and withdraw.[61]

As Ryan began the trip home to Fort Campbell for his midtour leave in late December, he was bullish about the chances of approval. The division commander, Campbell, needed no convincing, and it seemed likely that the three-star corps commander in Kabul wouldn't either. That just left ISAF, the multinational headquarters of all 146,000 foreign troops in Afghanistan that General David Petraeus headed up.

When Ryan returned to Blessing in mid-January 2011 after two weeks at home, however, there was still no go-ahead order. He didn't know for sure what was holding things up, but he had a guess. Generals in Kabul, he imagined, were struggling to answer a basic question about the years of American involvement and loss in the Pech: What was it all worth?[62]

RYAN WAS RIGHT. The particular general who was grappling with that question was Mick Nicholson, the lanky alumnus of Georgetown, West Point, and the Ranger Regiment who, as a colonel commanding a 10th Mountain brigade five years earlier, had presided over the creation of the whole network of outposts in Kunar and Nuristan that his successors had spent the intervening years pruning down. Nicholson had recently deployed to Kabul as the two-star operations chief at ISAF, screening any major proposals before they reached Petraeus. When the Pech Realignment plan crossed his desk, he hit the brakes.

Since his eventful sixteen-month deployment back in 2006 and 2007, Nicholson had spent a year helping run the Pentagon's high-tech national military command center and been promoted to brigadier general and then major general. A year and a half earlier, while based in Kandahar on his second Afghanistan deployment, he had visited Jalalabad Airfield as the Korengal withdrawal was being litigated. Briefed on 4/4 ID's view that the KOP and other bases he had helped establish had outlived their usefulness, he had found it hard to contain himself, raising objections that some 4/4 ID officers had found unseemly coming from someone outside the relevant chain of command. In retrospect, Nicholson realized that he had been straying outside his lane. The Korengal wasn't his fight anymore, and he didn't have the full picture of how things had evolved there since his departure in the summer of 2007. "I made my opinions known, but then I backed away from it," he recalled.[63]

Newly arrived in Kabul for his third Afghan tour in early 2011, Nicholson was back in the chain of command now, and he wasn't going to sign off on the Pech Realignment without getting that full picture.

The argument coming out of the 101st, from Joe Ryan up through the division commander, Campbell, was that counterinsurgency didn't work in the Pech—that the U.S. presence was the problem. That didn't make sense to Nicholson. He couldn't square the picture the 101st was painting of an intrusive, unwanted foreign presence with his memories of how much villagers and elders had seemed to love some of the junior officers he charged with making inroads in Kunari and Nuristani communities, like Mike Harrison and the late Doug Sloan. Nor did he agree that the Pech and its side valleys lacked strategic value. It seemed as if no one remembered the original counterterrorism-through-counterinsurgency rationale that had drawn him and Cavoli there in 2006, or the guidance they had received from the CIA that the side valleys were safe havens for international terrorist groups like al-Qaida and Lashkar-e-Taiba.[64] If anything, the hive of militants that Bulldog Bite had run into in the upper Watapur in November—including a bona fide training facility—seemed, to Nicholson, to reinforce the importance of the Pech in the counterterrorism fight. And in reporting from JSOC and the CIA, the name of a charismatic young Arab al-Qaida operative, Farouq al-Qahtani, was popping up more and more in the area, often appearing in the Waygal just like the figures Nicholson had been tracking back in 2006.

That some 101st officers seemed to dismiss his concerns as angst over 10th Mountain's losses or legacy, or an inability to identify a sunk cost, frustrated Nicholson. He had specific questions: Planners were promising that they could still hit the enemy in the side valleys with Bulldog Bite–style operations and JSOC raids even after the Pech bases were gone, but how would a big air assault or a night raid somewhere like Aranas or Gambir be viable without the support of Blessing's howitzers? Would SEAL or Ranger missions in the Pech still be feasible without conventional forces in the area to help them find the best infiltration routes and bail them out if a strike force got pinned down or a helicopter crashed? Why were there discrepancies between ISAF's estimate of the number of al-Qaida operatives active in Kunar and Nuristan and the civilian intelligence community's?[65]

To address Nicholson's questions, in January 2011 a joint planning team assembled at ISAF headquarters. Meeting every morning in one of the container-style two-story prefabricated offices that dotted the walled base complex, the team, which included corps and division officers and a major who had recently moved to Kabul after six months as Ryan's executive officer at Blessing, war-gamed every in and out of the Pech plan they could think of.[66]

There were layers of myth and misunderstanding surrounding the valley, as well as voids of information. Bill Ostlund was now working in Kabul as JSOC's liaison to his old mentor Petraeus, and he joined the planning team as the counterterrorism task force's representative. Ostlund tried to explain the developments that had gotten the Pech to where it was now.[67] Personally, Ostlund was skeptical of the withdrawal plan and hated the thought of all his paratroopers' toil and blood going to waste.[68] But just as he had held back his private thoughts about the Korengal withdrawal from his friends Randy George and Brian Pearl of 4/4 ID a year earlier out of professional respect, Ostlund stuck to the JSOC perspective once he had given his history lesson.

In the counterterrorism task force's view, Nicholson's worry about losing an offensive lily pad was misplaced; pulling out of Blessing would have little effect on their ability to strike serious al-Qaida targets up in the mountains when required, though doing so would always be risky.[69] After taking casualties the last three times it had gone into Pech side valleys, JSOC was losing interest in such missions anyway and looking at lower-risk alternatives. Some in the task force saw drones as the way forward in Kunar and Nuristan; if intelligence pinpointed Farouq al-Qahtani in the Waygal in the months to come, for instance, JSOC's confidence in its ability to kill him with a Hellfire missile launched from a Predator or Reaper was higher than it had ever been before.

Fortuitously, just as the merits of the Pech bases as counterterrorism platforms were being debated in Kabul, American interrogators were prying loose the secrets held by the Egyptian al-Qaida commander who had bedeviled a succession of American units in the Pech and helped suck them into the Korengal, all the way back to the first JSOC teams to inhabit FOB Asadabad. One night in December, an Afghan police patrol in Jalalabad had gotten a tip that an Arab insurgent commander was at an address in the city. A Green Beret team that worked with the police jumped into pickup trucks and went along on the raid.[70] The balding, bearded, fiftyish man they captured turned out to be none other than Abu Ikhlas al-Masri, the Egyptian national who had come to Afghanistan during the jihad against the Soviets and never left.

Joe Ryan had been aware of Abu Ikhlas for years, since his stints as a staff officer with the JSOC task force at Bagram, but he had never expected to see him captured or killed on his watch. "I'd love to get him, and we've been trying to get him for nine years, but he's not going anywhere, because he's too smart," Ryan had told me over the summer.[71] The veteran guerrilla's surprising capture in Jalalabad, fifty miles from the mountainous security of his usual haunts, did not alter the calculus surrounding the Pech Realignment or change anyone's mind about it. Farouq al-Qahtani was doubtless already picking up where Abu Ikhlas had left off. Nevertheless, it was a satisfying win—a loose end tied up just in time.

The planning team briefed Petraeus in his office on February 15. The Bulldog battalion should proceed with the withdrawal plan, they recommended, with the modification that COP Honaker-Miracle, the easternmost Pech outpost, should remain for the time being as a buffer between Asadabad and the valley's insurgent groups. Petraeus had heard out Mick Nicholson's questions, and now he had heard their answers. After a brief closed-door discussion with the corps commander, he gave Operation Pech Realignment the go-ahead.

GOODBYE TO BLESSING

A week after the order came down from ISAF to start pulling out, the Bulldog battalion was well on its way to closing up shop at Blessing; trucks and helicopters were taking more bits and pieces away each day. But one big question remained unanswered: whether the understrength ANA battalion the Americans shared the base with would be coming with them or staying behind.[72]

For months, Afghan commanders at Blessing and Jalalabad had been telling their American counterparts one thing about the withdrawal plans: *If you leave, we leave, because we can't handle this place on our own.*[73] But as on the American side, the decision had to be made in Kabul, and, typically for a war in which the United States and the Afghan government were so often out of sync, the Americans and the Afghans were making their decisions separately, on different timelines and based on different criteria.

Abdul Rahim Wardak, Afghanistan's heavyset, bespectacled minister of defense, delivered his government's decision at his ministerial offices in Kabul at the end of February. As a soldier, he understood why ISAF wanted to leave the Pech, Wardak told the two- and three-star American generals, breaking the news in English. He had spent time in Kunar while fighting against the Soviets and knew how tactically difficult counterinsurgency operations were there. But Nangalam was a district center, so from the Afghan standpoint, leaving it was not a tactical matter but a political one, and President Karzai himself had directed the ANA to stay. Stripping any district center of military protection was bad enough, but Nangalam was the only gateway to several other district centers and a provincial seat. Pulling the ANA out of Nangalam would mean that many of the fifteen thousand people in the Pech who had been able to vote in September wouldn't be able to do so again in the next election, and that was something the Afghan president simply wouldn't accept.[74]

Petraeus discussed the decision with both Karzai and Wardak at that weekend's meeting of the Afghan National Security Council at the Arg.[75] "For us, Blessing didn't make sense anymore. As you're starting to get ready for the post-surge drawdown, you just can't stay out there," Petraeus said, recalling the meeting. "But the Afghans wanted to hold on to it. To them it had value. President Karzai, Minister Wardak, the chief of staff General Karimi, they were all determined to hang on to it."[76]

The order from Kabul hit the 2/2 ANA battalion at Blessing like a mortar shell. The battalion commander, Ismatullah, who was not especially enthusiastic about his duties even with American forces there to back him up, lodged a protest with his chain of command that at least two or three battalions would be required for the ANA to hold the Pech on their own; then he disappeared, as he often did for weeks at a time.[77]

Ryan hadn't planned on leaving the Pech without the ANA, especially with a missing Afghan battalion commander. But he didn't think there would ever be a better time—just worse ones. Another week, another month, or another year with an American infantry battalion in the Pech wasn't going to make things better there. It would just cost more lives and make it that much harder to leave the next time someone wanted to try.[78]

The Bulldog battalion's final week at Blessing was a hard one, driving that point home. Convoys were coming and going daily, pulling matériel out of Blessing and Michigan and Able Main, but the Bulldog soldiers were still out in their sectors patrolling—sometimes with reluctance, because everyone knew they were about to leave. On February 27, a platoon was checking out a tip about a roadside bomb in Bar Kanday when it was ambushed. A recoilless-rifle shell punched through the armor of one of the platoon's MRAPs and left the vehicle smoking. Before the patrol, the platoon's medic, Specialist Brian Tabada, had asked his platoon leader a question the lieutenant had heard a few times lately: "Sir, do we really have to do this?" When the lieutenant got to the stricken truck and pulled its door open, smoke poured out. Inside, Tabada was dead—the 15th soldier the Bulldog battalion had lost in combat, and the 112th American to die in the Pech since 2003. All the platoon leader could hope as he and his platoon sergeant sat with their medic's body waiting for a helicopter was that Tabada would be the last.[79]

That was Sunday. On Tuesday morning, a confused handoff between one of Blessing's surveillance cameras and a pair of Apaches produced one of the worst civilian casualty incidents since Americans had first come to Kunar. A well-aimed rocket had just exploded inside the wire at Blessing, wounding an Afghan worker, when a camera mounted on one of the perimeter towers spotted a group of five men in the mountains, climbing toward a ridge in the same area where walkie-talkie chatter had been intercepted just before the rocket attack.

When another rocket struck the base two hours later, a pair of Apaches was on station, their gunsights locked onto what they thought was the same group of men the tower camera had spotted earlier. The figures were twenty-three hundred feet above Blessing, cutting branches from a stand of trees. When the Blessing operations center called up saying that the company commander thought these were the rocketeers, just posing as woodcutters, and that he wanted them killed, the senior Apache pilot raked through the group methodically, first with his cannon and then with rockets. He counted nine bodies.

All of them, it turned out, were children, boys between the ages of nine and fifteen who really were out gathering firewood for their families. "Everybody was crying and running in different directions. They were screaming, 'Mother! Father!' All I could think was, 'I wish I could go home. I just want to go home,'" the one boy who survived later told a journalist who tracked him down, an Army combat veteran named Elliott Woods. The boy, an eleven-year-old named Hemad, told Woods about how two of his friends who had died on the mountain used to argue about whether they wanted to join the ANA or the Taliban when they were old enough. As for himself, after what he had gone through, Hemad wanted to do both: first join the ANA and learn how to fire rifles and machine guns, then run away and use his new skills to kill Americans.[80]

In Kabul, Petraeus apologized to Karzai for the incident; at a Wednesday *shura* in the district center, American and ANA officers did the same to assembled Nangalam residents and district officials and did their best to explain that high-tech cameras hadn't been able to tell the difference between insurgents and children. When the Americans had said their piece, the father of one of the slain boys said his. He appreciated that the Afghan officers and officials felt bad, he said, but he believed that the strike had been deliberate, and he wanted the pilot responsible to go to jail for life. Then he expressed exactly the sentiments that had convinced Joe Ryan that he and his soldiers shouldn't be in the Pech anymore. "We don't want the Americans here," the grieving man said. "If they leave, then we will have peace."[81]

.   .   .

THREE DAYS AFTER the botched Apache strike, on Friday, March 4, 2011, Ryan presided over a transfer ceremony on the Blessing parade ground. His troops lowered and folded the American flag, leaving the Afghan one flying. The blue parapet behind them had already been stripped of the marble plaques commemorating the U.S. fallen.

"The soldiers of the 2nd Kandak are our brothers," Ryan said in his speech, using the Dari and Pashto word for a battalion. "We've fought alongside them for the last ten months and they've proven they're ready to assume this great responsibility." The ANA battalion commander Ismatullah was notably absent—nobody had heard from him since he left, and he had switched his cell phones off[82]—but his senior NCO, Sergeant Major Mohammad Afzal, was there to offer the obligatory expression of confidence: "We are more than ready to take over this area. . . . We have trained and fought for this day and finally it has come."[83] Jonathan Springer, the artillery captain who was having trouble coming to terms with the withdrawal, wrote those quotations up for a public affairs story about the transfer ceremony, but he had a hard time mustering much of the optimism he affected in the press release. *Maybe these guys are ready,* he told himself. *Maybe this will work out.* But it didn't seem far-fetched to him that the two small D-30 howitzers the ANA had at Blessing might be in Taliban hands in a few months, the base overrun or abandoned.[84]

As the last Bulldog troops lined up to board their MRAPs and leave late Saturday night, Afghan soldiers were already going into the buildings the Americans had just vacated, coming out carrying sellable items of every description: light fixtures torn from the ceilings, electrical wires pulled out of the walls or even out of Humvees, boxes of sugary cereal from the chow hall—all things that American troops took for granted but that were luxury goods for the Afghan soldiers.[85] "One guy was running with a mattress," a junior soldier recalled. "That's my memory of closing Blessing—just the ANA taking everything."[86]

MICHIGAN, WHERE NO ANA were staying behind, was next, three weeks later. It was with evident joy that the soldiers there spent their final day, March 26, laying into everything standing with sledge-hammers. When the engineers started blowing buildings with plastic explosive and Bangalore torpedoes, "everyone was ecstatic and videotaping everything on their helmet cams," a participant remembered.[87] The final step was to pull the plug on OP Pride Rock, the observation post above the base that looked south into the Korengal. When the charges there blew, a huge dust plume rose into the sky and then settled, eerily, on the town and rubbled base below.[88] When Ryan left with one of the last groups that night, relocating nine miles down the road to Honaker-Miracle, where U.S. troops were going to stay for now, the plot of ground where the most frequently attacked outpost in eastern Afghanistan had stood looked like the surface of the moon.[89]

The transfer of Able Main ten days after that was quieter—there were no bulldozers or explosions—but it left a sour taste in the mouths of both the departing Americans and the ANA who were staying there. Terrified of what would happen to them without American firepower, some of the Afghan troops at the base disappeared as the hour of departure approached, one making off with his M16 and two pairs of American night-vision goggles.[90] The Bulldog soldiers had cleaned out their living areas and latrines so that the ANA could start using them, but as the Americans were waiting by their MRAPs for the word to leave, they caught one of the Afghan troops trying to steal something from a U.S. soldier while he wasn't looking—cigarettes or sunglasses, one sergeant remembered.

It was a small thing, but it still felt like a stab in the back. Angry, some of the Bulldog troops returned to the rooms they'd cleaned and broke the air conditioners and relieved themselves on the mattresses.[91]

For a hastily pulled-together post-withdrawal strategy predicated on a working partnership between Afghan soldiers in the Pech and Americans outside the valley, it was an inauspicious start.

CHAPTER 12

REDUX

2011

A BATTALION ON ITS OWN

The two-hundred-odd Afghan soldiers at Blessing had been on their own for more than a month when the Afghan National Army got around to sending out a new commander to replace the one who had deserted. The man the ANA generals selected was an unlikely fit for one of the toughest postings in the country: not a charismatic combat commander, but a thoughtful, bookish staff officer named Haji Rahmdel Haidarzai. A veteran of the communist-era Afghan army who had served in the post-2001 ANA nearly since its inception, Rahmdel had spent his career in intelligence billets at various headquarters. But he was a Safi Pashtun who had grown up in the Pech, which the ANA commander responsible for northeastern Afghanistan, Major General Mohammad Afzal, thought would make him a good fit.[1]

Rahmdel disagreed; he didn't want the job, and said so when General Afzal called him into his office to deliver the news that he would be taking over the isolated 2/2 battalion of the 201st ANA Corps in the post-realignment Pech. "I told him I will go anywhere except the Pech, because I am from there and it would create problems for my family," Rahmdel remembered protesting. With his short graying beard and reading glasses, Rahmdel looked more like an administrator or schoolhouse instructor than a battlefield leader. In addition to his fears for his family, who still owned a farm outside Nangalam, Rahmdel had never commanded a combat unit, and he didn't want to start now by taking over one of the only ANA battalions in the whole country that could no longer count on American airpower, artillery, medevac, or resupply.[2]

But General Afzal insisted, and that same night in mid-April 2011, Rahmdel found himself on a U.S. Army Black Hawk headed up the Pech. "Keep fighting, improve morale," the ANA's top general, Sher Mohammad Karimi, exhorted Rahmdel by phone before he boarded the helicopter in Jalalabad. The ANA and American officers who flew with him to Nangalam said the same thing when they saw him off at Blessing's disused landing zone. Then they got back on the Black Hawk and were gone.[3]

What Rahmdel learned from the battalion operations officer who greeted him, a major with whom he had served on a previous Kunar tour named Mahboob Khan, left him in even worse spirits. In the weeks after the Americans left, Mahboob explained, the other major in the battalion, the executive officer, had opened negotiations with the Taliban. He had also given orders that no one was to fire on the Taliban fighters who were now walking around Nangalam openly, strolling within a hundred meters of Blessing's gates and parking their machine-gun-equipped pickup trucks in town. On top of that the base had no electricity, no extra stores of ammunition, and no one with the training to use the two small D-30 howitzers that sat near the landing zone for anything other than shooting directly at targets visible to the gunners on the mountainside.

The soldiers Rahmdel inspected in their barracks that morning were afraid that the executive officer, who was away, was scheming to sell them out to the Taliban, a fear Rahmdel thought was well founded. "The soldiers had lost their morale. You could see it in their faces, their eyes, their posture," he told me of that first encounter. "All they were thinking was 'How will we die?'"[4]

. . .

THE SOLDIERS OF the 2/2 ANA battalion had already been in the Pech for a year when their Bulldog battalion counterparts pulled out in March and the only road out of the valley fell into insurgent hands. On a hardship tour with no set end date—the battalion before them had stayed at Blessing for two years—they had already lost eleven soldiers in combat, most recently four men killed during a January firefight in the Kandigal lumberyard. "We knew it would be hard when we went to the Pech, and it was very hard," said the battalion sergeant major.[5]

Living conditions, though somewhat better than in years past, were not good and seemed likely to get worse. Despite the 2010 conversion of an abandoned schoolhouse on the base perimeter into new barracks, the downhill portion of the base where the ANA lived was cramped. Bunk beds were crowded into guard towers or sat under the stars, some of them next to an open sewage line.[6] Six hundred men were on the rolls, but only between three and four hundred were actually present for duty at any given time. Incapable of running their own logistics patrols with any regularity, the Afghan troops had come to rely entirely on their American counterparts, until they left, for ammunition, spare Humvee and weapon parts, and anything else that couldn't be bought in the Nangalam bazaar. There, many of the soldiers felt almost as much like foreign occupiers as Americans did, because the majority of the battalion spoke either Dari or the southern Kandahari dialect of Pashto, not the eastern one spoken in Kunar.

There were dedicated leaders among the ANA's officer ranks, but there were also many risk-averse beneficiaries of the Afghan military bureaucracy's endemic nepotism and corruption—men who had bought their commissions or commands and did not see fighting in the field as part of their job description, which made them difficult for hard-charging American officers to respect. The partnerships over the years between the American battalion commanders at Blessing and a succession of ANA counterparts had ranged from good to miserable. Brett Jenkinson had found his counterpart maddening and had mostly ignored him, an attitude that filtered down to Jenkinson's men. Bill Ostlund emphasized to his paratroopers what he called "true partnership" with the ANA, and

he liked to think that he had been a good partner to the ANA battalion commander he worked with longest.[7] Despite Ostlund's good
intentions, though, dislike and distrust had permeated The Rock's
relationship with the ANA, especially after Afghan troops fled under
fire during both the battle of the Ranch House and the deadly November 2007 ambush near Aranas. "They are worthless, they really
are," one Rock first sergeant had scoffed of the ANA his company
worked with.[8] His counterpart at Able Main so despised the ANA
that when the Afghans set up a desk in the company operations
center, he built himself a new office in another building rather than
share the space with them.[9]

Deploying just after the last Marine adviser team left the Pech,
Joe Ryan's soldiers had easily formed the habit of taking small ANA
contingents along as afterthoughts on U.S.-planned missions. That
was how the 2/2 battalion had taken most of its casualties during the
year preceding the realignment: four soldiers killed in an IED blast
when they were dragged along on one of the early Bulldog missions
to Chapa Dara; three more killed in the Watapur during Bulldog
Bite, a mission in which ANA commanders hadn't wanted to participate at all.[10]

Ryan's low opinion of the 2/2 battalion commander, Ismatullah,
had contributed to his lack of concern when the lieutenant colonel
left Blessing shortly before the March 4 American pullout. Ismatullah spent much of his time away "on leave" anyway, so it seemed
possible that he would come back, although the fact that he had
turned all his cell phones off so no one could reach him was not a
promising sign. Even if he was gone for good, Ryan didn't consider
his desertion disastrous; the battalion's two majors seemed to be
doing most of the work of running the unit.[11] The operations officer Major Mahboob, who had been with the battalion since its
founding five years earlier, was a hard worker who had swallowed
his private doubts about the American departure,[12] while the executive officer Major Zulfiqar, a Safi Pashtun from Kunar's Chowkay
valley who had recently joined the battalion, exuded a cocky confidence that was rare in an ANA officer: he wore his standard-issue
beret neatly and with apparent pride, along with hiking boots,
wraparound sunglasses like those American troops always wore, and
a nice watch.[13]

Before leaving the Pech, Ryan and the Nangalam district governor had hosted a *shura* at which many of the Pech's top elders, including ones like Haji Fazil Mohammad of Kandigal and Haji Zalwar Khan of the Korengal who had close ties to insurgent leaders, had signed or stamped with their thumbprints a document pledging their support to the ANA and police in the post-realignment Pech. "All the members of our Islamic government are Muslims," the agreement pointed out, "so no harm against them is considered to be permissible unless they show signs of being infidels."[14]

A week or two later, it was Major Zulfiqar who represented the ANA at another big *shura,* this time with no Americans present. The message the major offered was not inconsistent with the one put to paper earlier in the month. It even included some of the same talking points. But with the Americans gone, the emphasis was different. "We are all Muslims" was how one elder in attendance remembered the thrust of Zulfiqar's speech, "so if you're going to fight the Americans, just leave us out of it."[15]

FOR WEEKS, TALIBAN commanders had been building local support by delivering gifts of freshly cut pine, fir, and spruce to villages in the mountains above the Pech and in protected side valleys like the Shuryak. It was wood that chain-saw teams had cut along with more valuable cedar during a major clear-cutting operation the Taliban's high command in Pakistan had ordered over the winter in Kunar.

The irony of this development was apparent only in retrospect. False alarms about just this sort of clear-cutting had led to Kabul's misguided 2002 ban on the lumber trade, which in turn helped ensnare American troops in the Pech and brought in the Taliban. Only now, as American troops were leaving, were the Taliban actually doing to Kunar's timber reserves what outsiders had long *believed* them to be doing. After taking a drubbing in 2010 in its poppy-growing southern heartland at the hands of U.S. and allied surge troops, the Taliban needed money, and orders had arrived in Kunar to liquidate as much timber as possible, as quickly as possible. While the cedar went to Pakistan to be sold, less valuable types of wood were distributed to build goodwill in places like Chapa Dara and the Shuryak, where helicopter overflights in the opening weeks of 2011 spotted piles of freshly cut lumber and conspicuous new construction.[16]

The same day that American combat engineers turned COP Michigan into rubble, March 27, groups of guerrillas came down from the mountains to the more heavily populated valley floor to make a show of both force and benevolence, demonstrating to locals in towns that had once been part of the American security bubble that there was a new pecking order while also allaying fears about what was coming. One band of fighters showed up outside the district center in Chapa Dara, demanding and receiving the surrender of the fiftyish policemen there but freeing most of them within hours.[17] Another group did the same in Want. The group that walked into Sundray included Mullah Dawran, the Salafi turned Taliban commander who had been fighting the Americans in the Pech for eight years and whose wife and children had died in a Thanksgiving 2009 HIMARS strike.

Showing himself openly in his hometown for the first time in years, Dawran made a statement for Afghan newspapers and Taliban propaganda to print. On behalf of the Taliban, he claimed, he had assembled a twelve-member *shura* to administer the Pech, and his two hundred fighters were ready to act as police. "We have decided to keep open all the schools and health institutions," he added, including girls' schools and clinics built with American money, and he promised to be fair to those who had collaborated with the Americans by working on their bases. Like the timber distribution, it was an obvious attempt to make the pill of Taliban occupation go down more easily at a time when people were both fed up with Americans and afraid of what life would be like without them.[18]

The next day an Al Jazeera cameraman accompanied a fourth unit of a dozen or so fighters as they came down to Kandigal from a mountain hideout and examined the ruins of COP Michigan. Some wearing camouflage, others civilian clothes, the guerrillas strolled around the haphazardly scattered sandbags and T-wall rubble with rifles and RPGs slung on their backs, then prayed with some of the same Kandigal elders who had attended the recent government *shuras* in Nangalam.

"The infidels failed to hold this outpost. Our jihad against American troops will continue, and one day we will reach the gates of America," a young cleric in white robes gloated to the camera, his face unmasked to show a thin beard. An older fighter identified as Commander Intiqam was less belligerent. "The whole area is secure and sharia is being applied here and all the people are very happy," he said, adding that he and his men had "no links with al-Qaida."[19]

The Al Jazeera video angered some Bulldog battalion soldiers who saw it online at the bases outside the Pech where they were spending the last few weeks of their deployment. Why hadn't Apaches or a Predator been able to kill these insurgents as they brazenly strolled around a site where Americans had lived and shed blood? From where Ryan sat, however, such videos were inevitable and nothing to worry about; all they showed was Taliban posturing. The skinny Taliban cleric making the bombastic threats in the video wasn't really coming to attack America, and Dawran wasn't really about to impose an orderly system of Taliban governance on the Pech. That the Taliban had taken the Chapa Dara and Want district centers was no shock. They'd controlled all of Chapa Dara and the Waygal valley *except* the district centers for years, and many of the policemen who surrendered to them had probably already been on the Taliban payroll.[20]

Nor was Ryan overly troubled by the patchy reports coming out of Nangalam, which suggested that insurgent rocket and mortar attacks against Blessing had plunged almost to zero but also that the terms of the deal the elders, Americans, and Afghan security forces had agreed to in March were being renegotiated now that the Americans were gone. The document stipulated that the "mujahidin" were to stay away from the road and only come into Nangalam unarmed. But no Taliban commanders had put their thumbprints to it, of course, and when armed Taliban fighters made their first appearance in Nangalam shortly after the American departure, the leaderless 2/2 ANA battalion did not try to stop them. The militants drove machine-gun-equipped pickup trucks right into town and parked them by the traffic circle. But they made no move to attack the ANA base or exact retribution against collaborators, other than to collect fines from former base workers. By one account, their first day in town they handed out oranges.[21]

In the absence of a commander, the ANA officer who opened up negotiations with the militants was Major Zulfiqar, the executive officer. By early April, through intermediaries and directly by phone and radio (in calls that U.S. signals intelligence was listening in on), Zulfiqar was talking to three local Taliban leaders. One was Dawran. The second was Gul Zaman, a commander operating west of Blessing whose brother had died in a SEAL Team 6 raid a year earlier. The third was Qadir Mohammad, a Nangalam native and longtime district government employee who had taken over a Taliban unit after his brother died in a firefight with American troops.[22]

There were unverifiable rumors that Zulfiqar went so far as to bring Dawran onto the grounds of the base and talk with him over tea in the vacant battalion commander's office.[23] Regardless of whether that was true, an agreement was reached: Zulfiqar gave orders that no patrols were to go into town and troops on guard were not to fire on the trucks full of Taliban they could see from their posts. In return, Dawran and the other commanders agreed not to attack the base. According to the operations officer Mahboob, who went along with the orders, when one sergeant disobeyed and fired on a group of fighters from his guard tower, Zulfiqar had him locked in a dark room as punishment.[24]

Ryan had expected that the ANA would try to reach some kind of understanding with the insurgency once he was gone. He had seen the same kinds of negotiations taking place between the Taliban and the isolated police station in Chapa Dara, even getting on the radio with the police chief's Taliban contact himself during the big September 2010 air assault out west. If that was what it took to achieve the kind of quiet that had descended on Nangalam, he figured—which he saw for himself during two brief visits to Blessing before heading home to Fort Campbell—that was what it took. It wasn't as though Zulfiqar were talking to high-level Taliban commanders or al-Qaida operatives. All three of the men Zulfiqar was dealing with were Pech natives. Americans had killed close relatives of each. It didn't seem outlandish that some of them might eventually reconcile with the government now that the Americans weren't around. Dawran had been independent of the Taliban for years and had opposed them before Americans came to Kunar. The same argument could be made about Qadir Mohammad, who had been working in the district center just outside Blessing printing identification cards until his brother's death at American hands. That sort of local arrangement, possible only once Americans were out of the picture, was the kind of thing Ryan hoped the realignment might spur, and it could not happen without the two sides talking to each other.[25]

"I know it's only been a month (please knock on wood with me)," Ryan wrote in the last newsletter he emailed to friends and family of the Bulldog battalion in early April as the first groups of their loved ones were coming home to Fort Campbell. He offered a cautiously optimistic assessment, noting the plunge in insurgent attacks against Blessing since he and his soldiers had left and going so far as to suggest that the "realignment" might turn out to be a model for future disengagement elsewhere in Afghanistan.

"While certainly there's the potential for this to be the 'calm before the storm,'" he wrote, "every day that passes with peace bodes well for the future."[26]

"THE ANA DID NOT TAKE THE BATON . . . THEY THREW IT SOMEWHERE ELSE"

The hapless Rahmdel, who arrived in Nangalam to take command of the stranded 2/2 battalion just as Ryan himself was heading home two weeks later, disagreed.

"Everything on the base had been stolen, and as far as electricity and sewage we had to start over at the beginning," Rahmdel remembered of the ruinous situation he inherited at Blessing. "The Taliban were a hundred meters away walking with their weapons." Rahmdel didn't believe that Zulfiqar was trying to bring reconcilable insurgent leaders into the fold; he was sure his executive officer was trying to arrange the surrender of the base and the battalion to the Taliban, possibly for profit.[27]

With Zulfiqar away at Able Main, Rahmdel reversed the major's orders, telling the troops on guard to shoot at any Taliban they saw, and he started sending patrols out into town, supporting them with mortar and recoilless-rifle fire when they came under attack. "This showed the soldiers of the battalion that the base was not going to be surrendered," he explained. His own confidence in the battalion's ability to fend off a militant assault was low, however. He needed help, if not from his own faraway superiors, then from the latest American unit to deploy to Kunar, headquartered not in the Pech but twenty miles away at FOB Joyce* in the province's southeast.[28]

Rahmdel's new long-distance American partner was a forty-year-old battalion commander in the Hawaii-based 25th Infantry Division with weathered features and graying hair, Lieutenant Colonel Colin Tuley. The son of a Citadel graduate, a Citadel graduate himself, and the father of a teenage daughter who would also attend the Citadel, Tuley had only recently joined the Aloha Army, as people sometimes called the division for the ways Hawaii's relaxed culture rubbed off on it. Before moving to Oahu to command the division's 2-35 Infantry battalion, the Cacti, he had spent nearly six years with the Ranger Regiment.

Tuley was a leader with two sides. Gregarious and charming, he could drink his lieutenants under the table. "Tuley was a bro," one platoon leader remembered with affection.[29] "Good guy—maybe not the most thoughtful leader, but we really liked him," said another.[30] Tuley's own brigade commander leaned heavily on him. When his platoons and companies were in combat, he was skillful and supportive, a leadership style honed in JSOC operations centers. Within his battalion headquarters, though, Tuley was widely disliked, with many staff officers and NCOs remembering him as a yeller and micromanager who easily blew up at subordinates over trivial matters. Staff meetings were tense affairs.[31] "Everyone in the Army yells from time to time," said one captain. "This was all the time. Someone was always going to get yelled at, and everyone was working to make sure it wasn't them."[32]

Tuley's Ranger deployments had given him little experience coaching Afghan or Iraqi troops. Thrown into that task in Kunar, he and the other leaders of the Cacti battalion were about to spend a year grappling with the problem that would bedevil American commanders and advisers all over Afghanistan in the years to come: With your local allies crying out that they were drowning, how much help was it appropriate to offer when everyone knew they would eventually have to sink or swim on their own?

---

* Named after Kevin Joyce, a nineteen-year-old Marine lance corporal who drowned in the Pech three days before Operation Red Wings in 2005.

As counterparts in 1st and 2nd Ranger Battalions, Joe Ryan and Colin Tuley had often switched off with each other in Iraq and Afghanistan, Tuley arriving as Ryan was heading home. Replacing Ryan again in April 2011, Tuley felt his friend had done him a favor, setting him up for a deployment that wouldn't be monopolized by the Pech and its war of built-up outposts. That had been Ryan's intent, and he underlined it in his parting advice. No matter how bad things get in the Pech, he urged Tuley, resist the impulse to throw Rahmdel a life preserver in the form of American help.[33]

That made sense to Tuley, but the Pech, as one of his officers would sourly put it after the deployment, proved to share some key qualities with the tar baby from the old stories of Br'er Rabbit and Br'er Fox, sucking Americans in against their better judgment.[34] As April turned into May, Rahmdel was calling the interpreters at the Cacti battalion's headquarters at FOB Joyce every week, sometimes almost every night, urgently reporting that Blessing was about to be attacked and perhaps overrun—only for Nangalam to appear calm and quiet when a Predator arrived overhead to check things out.

Tuley wanted to know what was really going on. With Rahmdel reporting that neither he nor any of his men could drive to Asadabad because of the Taliban checkpoints and IEDs that were proliferating along the Pech road, that meant heading back out to Blessing again, at least for a few days.[35]

ON A SUNDAY night at the beginning of May, a pair of heavily modified Black Hawks from a JSOC aviation unit took off from Jalalabad Airfield and headed north into Kunar, following the same flight path that all American helicopters flying into the province did. But instead of banking left into the Pech, where some of the embarked SEAL Team 6 operators had seen the toughest missions of their careers, the stealth helicopters turned right and crossed the Pakistani border. They were heading for the compound where the CIA had finally located the target who had first brought American troops to Afghanistan and to Kunar—Osama bin Laden.[36]

The Cacti troops at the remaining U.S. outpost in the lower Pech, COP Honaker-Miracle, had other things on their minds when news of the Abbottabad raid broke. The base had been taking fire most of the day Sunday. Then, in the evening, with regular military helicopter flights in the area canceled to clear the airspace for the top secret mission, a ground patrol had left for Asadabad to pick up the coming week's radio codes.

The patrol barely made it a kilometer before one of the MRAPs hit an IED. Air-traffic controllers made an exception and cleared a pair of medevacs to enter the airspace reserved for the stealth Black Hawks' mission. But a badly wounded soldier, Corporal Kevin White, still died late that night, right around the same time the SEALs were killing bin Laden 135 miles away. "Any greater context about what happened that night meant nothing to us," an NCO who was at Honaker-Miracle remembered. "We remember that Sunday and Monday as when we lost Kevin."[37]

Two weeks later, with the attacks on Honaker-Miracle getting worse and the reports from Blessing more alarming, a flight of Chinooks took off from the same airfield, stopping at an outpost in southern Kunar before taking the left turn up the Pech for yet another air assault. None of the Cacti infantrymen aboard knew how intertwined the early stages of the long search for bin Laden had been with the origins of the campaign they were inheriting in the Pech, and their war chugged on unaffected by the al-Qaida leader's death. The Chinooks disgorged Cacti's Bastard Company on the ridge opposite the mouth of the Korengal, overlooking the ruins of COP Michigan.

Landing within sight of the Korengal was an eerie, intimidating, exhilarating feeling for soldiers who had been in middle school or high school on September 11, many of whom had recently seen the documentary *Restrepo* back in Hawaii or read *Lone Survivor.* The place lived up to the hype: Bastard Company spent the next few days in long-distance firefights just like the ones that had consumed the deployments of their predecessors in the Pech and Korengal. With low-flying Kiowas bouncing from one fight to the next, firing rockets until they had none left, the whole valley often seemed as if it were full of smoke, and when Chinooks came to extract them at the end of the operation, the soldiers were amazed to see the trails of not one but several RPGs arcing up toward the big helicopters and missing.[38]

Bastard Company's mission on the mountain had been to suck

up and suppress enemy fire along the most dangerous stretch of the Pech road while a second group of Cacti battalion soldiers escorted trucks full of ammunition and other supplies from Honaker-Miracle out to Rahmdel's beleaguered base. For the troops who drove through the ambushes on the road below and reached Blessing, including Colin Tuley, it was hard to believe that the place had been an American forward operating base only two months earlier. Blessing was a husk of the base Tuley had seen when he visited on a predeployment recon in the fall. Metal roofs were missing, floors torn up, doors ripped off. Garbage and rotting food were everywhere, and with the septic tanks and attached latrines overflowing, the Afghan soldiers had started defecating in shower stalls and buildings, including the old American chow hall. Oddly, the ANA had kept their radio operators in the old U.S. battalion operations center; the soldiers still sat in the same corner, with the same equipment, facing the same wall with the same map on it. Otherwise the building was empty, and its halls stank of urine.[39]

To Tuley, it seemed clear during the few days he spent at Blessing that Rahmdel's battalion was collapsing as surely as the base itself was. "When I saw the way it was out there, feces on the walls, everything torn off and broken down, everything a mess, I had a hard time getting past that," he recalled. "The ANA did not take the baton after the realignment out there. They took the baton and they threw it somewhere else."[40]

He could hardly blame Rahmdel. If the ANA were going to keep troops in the Pech, Tuley thought, the command slot there should be a second-time-around job, reserved for an experienced colonel who had already led a battalion in combat somewhere else, the model the U.S. Army's Ranger battalions used.[41] Instead, the ANA had dumped an intelligence officer with little leadership experience into the job, and as soon as the operation was over, despite Rahmdel's assurances during it that he would start using the road, the ANA at Blessing hunkered down again.[42] "We are prisoners here," Rahmdel told Tuley and other Cacti officers in one meeting before they left.[43]

The reports coming out of the Pech became more alarming after the mid-May mission out to Blessing. The Taliban were stopping beardless men at checkpoints, shaking them down, and beating them.[44] In the toughest part of the valley, between the mouths of the Korengal and Shuryak, insurgents were melting the road surface with burning tar, then digging in IEDs as big as a hundred pounds.[45]

High on the list of concerns was the continuing stream of reports about the battalion executive officer Zulfiqar's contacts with the Taliban commanders Dawran and Qadir Mohammad. Still, Tuley remained cautious, taking the return of American troops to Blessing in small steps—one of which, late in the spring, seemed to confirm the lingering suspicions about Zulfiqar's motives.

Late at night on June 10, the Cacti battalion scout platoon flew into Blessing for a daylong visit. Before catching a few hours' sleep, the platoon leader and a captain acting as an adviser shared a meal of greasy chicken with Zulfiqar. In the morning, while half the platoon stayed below with the adviser captain, the other half climbed up to OP Avalanche, the little observation post on the ridge just above Blessing looking down into the lower Waygal, planning to check up on the small ANA contingent there. The scouts had been at Avalanche a couple of hours when insurgents attacked them from a ridge higher up. The attack began with accurate RPG fire: one grenade exploded against an exterior wall of the concrete observation post building and sprayed shrapnel among a group of scouts who were conducting weapons training with the ANA outside, hitting one Cacti soldier in the face and chest, another in the arm, a third in the foot, and mangling the leg of a fourth. All four wounded Americans had to be hoisted off the mountain by a medevac Black Hawk.[46]

That guerrillas could freely roam the ridges just above Blessing was bad news, and worse followed when battalion headquarters received a summary of a phone call U.S. signals intelligence had intercepted between Zulfiqar and Qadir Mohammad. Qadir Mohammad had led the Avalanche attack, the call revealed, and he was giving the ANA major a report on how it had gone, complete with an estimate of American casualties. Zulfiqar, in return, was passing along information about the previous day's American visit.[47]

The next time Zulfiqar visited Able Main, a few days later, the ANA brigade commander Afzal was waiting with a guard detail to arrest him and put him on a helicopter to Kabul, where he would stand trial and be imprisoned.[48]

For Tuley, this latest development was too much. For weeks, his own superiors had been stressing to him that the ANA could not be allowed to collapse in the Pech, no matter what it took. The 2/2 ANA battalion seemed to be on the brink, and Tuley had an idea of what reversing it would take: a team of American advisers and infantry living back out at Blessing, eventually full-time, focusing all their efforts on improving the ANA and doing nothing without them.

With troop levels about to start shrinking by tens of thousands as the surge ended,* the writing was on the wall throughout Afghanistan: the mission was shifting. "As Afghan security forces move into the lead," President Obama said in a June White House speech announcing the end of the surge, "our mission will change from combat to support."[49] Units would have to wind down big U.S.-led combat operations and focus instead on what some had been suggesting they put ahead of everything else all along: training, advising, and supporting the ANA in a serious way, not as an afterthought, so that when Americans inevitably left them, they didn't collapse as the 2/2 battalion had at Blessing.

But what the Cacti battalion did next exemplified the old approach, not the new one. When Obama's speech aired on the morning of June 23, Afghan time, the battalion was deep into preparations for what was, to many of Tuley's officers and NCOs, a puzzling, frustrating, and dangerous throwback to the type of campaign that was supposed to be ending.

THE WATAPUR PILGRIMAGE

The battalion flew up the Watapur valley in waves on the night of Friday, June 24, Chinooks ferrying one group of troops after another into two clearings in the Gambir Jungle: first the scout platoon that had been ambushed above Blessing earlier in the month; then Apache, Bastard, and Gundog Companies, half of them above Gambir and half of them above Tsangar, their objectives. A group

---

* U.S. troop levels would fall from their peak of a hundred thousand to ninety thousand by the end of the year and then below seventy thousand in 2012.

of ANA tagged along with each American company. At the more northerly of the two landing zones, code-named Honey-Eater, soldiers from Bastard Company could see huge trees swaying in the Chinooks' rotor wash and feel weirdly soft ground underfoot, grassy and lush with small ferns. Their GPS units told them they had landed nearly ten thousand feet above sea level, just below the sharp ridge separating the Watapur from the neighboring Shigal valley.[50]

The operation was a far larger affair than Joe Ryan's Bulldog Bite mission that had targeted the same towns seven months earlier. With nearly five hundred American and Afghan troops on the ground by morning, it was the biggest air assault in a Pech side valley in more than three years.[51]

Even before the firefights began later that day and casualties started to mount, many of the troops on the mountain had questions about the mission. Why were they doing it at all—a scaled-up version of the Watapur air assaults so many other battalions had done before? The overarching plan for the rest of the deployment, Tuley had made clear to his subordinates, was to reestablish a small American presence at Blessing—an adviser team and a couple of platoons—who could get the ANA there back on their feet. The battalion-scale attack into the Watapur didn't seem connected to that task. Although 179 Afghan soldiers, an unusually large group, would be flying in with the Americans, they came from an ANA unit in eastern Kunar, not Rahmdel's 2/2 battalion. And the mission was decidedly U.S. planned and U.S. led. In a typical case of "putting an Afghan face" on the operation, ANA officers were told nothing about the plan or targets for the mission practically until they boarded helicopters.[52]

"It was like an annual pilgrimage going up the Watapur," said Tuley's intelligence officer, expressing a sentiment that many members of the Cacti battalion staff echoed in interviews about the mission. "We, the battalion, were not the ones who wanted to go up there."[53]

The officer insisting on the Watapur operation was the brigade commander, Richard Kim, a colonel with a reputation for being prickly and aggressive, who was flying over the valley in a command-and-control Black Hawk on the night of the insertion.

In early June, Kim had directed the Cacti battalion to start planning an air assault into the mountains somewhere north of the Pech. When the battalion operations officer, Major Marcus Wright, briefed Kim on a tentative plan to send a company into the mountains north of Able Main, where signals intercepts suggested there might be an enemy command post of some sort, the brigade commander was unhappy. Shaking his head faster and faster the longer Wright talked, Kim explained what he had in mind instead: a bigger mission into the Watapur to find the rest of the training camps in the Gambir Jungle that Bulldog Bite had missed the previous fall.[54]

The officers briefing Kim returned to FOB Joyce frustrated. "Our analysis was that previous units had done a whole bunch of these Watapur operations and all they netted was some dead bad guys," said Wright.[55] Wright's planner, Captain Loren Crowe, was incensed. Crowe had deployed to Kunar before, as a Blue Spader platoon leader, and had sought out another Kunar-bound unit with the hope of passing along some of what he'd learned the first time. Nothing about the mission made sense to him, starting with Kim's insistence on a battalion air assault. Those were tried-and-untrue tactics as far as Crowe was concerned from his previous time in Kunar. Every day spent out on an air assault in a side valley somewhere, it seemed to him, was a day *not* spent getting the ANA in the Pech itself ready to stand on their own.

Nor did Crowe understand the brigade commander's focus on the Watapur. "There was nothing remarkable about the enemy situation in the Watapur to justify singling it out—no justification or concrete intelligence," he said. "There was just brigade saying, 'Do Tsangar and Gambir.' That isn't supposed to be how you do operations."[56]

But Kim was dead set on a battalion air assault, and signals intercepts showed a lot of enemy fighters in the upper Watapur—maybe, the brigade commander hoped, evidence of training camps like the one Joe Ryan's troops had stumbled on during Bulldog Bite. On a pre-deployment recon trip in the fall, Kim had been on the ground for Bulldog Bite's Shuryak phase and had been impressed by it. His basic explanation of the plan echoed how 101st officers had talked about their fall forays into the side valleys. "We were looking at where we could go in and make our first impact on the enemy where they thought we weren't able to come after them," he said.[57]

Kim could rattle off a series of objectives he wanted the big Watapur mission to accomplish. Besides locating undiscovered training camps, he thought that a fresh offensive into the valley would quiet the mortar and rocket attacks against Honaker-Miracle, which had been rising since U.S. troops left the other Pech bases. Kim also cited an analysis done by division intelligence back at Bagram claiming that the well-known Shigal-Watapur-Waygal ratline was part of a much longer insurgent movement and supply route stretching all the way through Nuristan and neighboring Laghman to the outskirts of Kabul, more than a hundred miles distant. By attacking this route, Kim argued, the mission would contribute to the strategically important defense of the capital from terrorist attacks.[58]

All of this strained the credulity of some officers on the brigade and battalion staffs. An al-Qaida operative called Falik Naz was said to run a training program for local fighters somewhere in the Watapur, but drone flights couldn't find any evidence of a camp, and probably wouldn't, if it was being run in the forest. "We'd had reporting about training facilities near Gambir and Tsangar, but they were not pinpoint targets," remembered the brigade intelligence chief. "It just became a big circle on the map."[59] The idea that Taliban units were reaching Kabul via a mountain ratline passing through the Watapur raised even more hackles, given the ease with which insurgents routinely used lowland highways to move men and weapons from the Pakistani border to the capital. One skeptic of this theory on the brigade staff compared it to smuggling drugs from Florida to New York via the Appalachian Trail instead of I-95.[60]

Tuley later acknowledged having some of the same doubts. "It almost seemed like an old wives' tale," he said of the idea of a ratline to Kabul. "Same with the training camps. You're not going to go up there and find an obstacle course and monkey bars."[61] But the Cacti commander was being told by his bosses that they wanted a battalion-sized air assault, and while he knew such an operation wouldn't fix the Pech, he thought it could help. "They're not the ace card that will solve everything, but they have an impact," he said, thinking back on all the smaller raids he'd seen damage insurgent networks during his Ranger deployments. "That impact is just hard to measure." He declined to say whether, behind closed doors, he pushed back against Kim on those points.[62]

Nobody on the battalion staff was happy about what they were being ordered to do. Kim and Tuley didn't remember hearing objections at the time, however, and objections or no objections the mission was happening. Loren Crowe proposed a name: Operation Hammer Down. The name stuck. He didn't bring up the proverb he'd been thinking of when it came to him, a saying that seemed applicable to how the Army was still choosing to fight in Kunar after all this time: "When all you have is a hammer, every problem looks like a nail."[63]

Hammer Down would be Bulldog Bite in reverse: killing insurgents in the Watapur not as troops were coming out of the Pech but as they were getting ready to go back in.[64]

HAMMER DOWN'S UNGAINLY, complex plan—involving the insertion of nearly the whole battalion into four landing zones, followed by clearances of both Gambir and Tsangar—started to veer off course before the first troops even landed on the mountain.

Worried about tipping off the enemy with scout flights, the aviation unit flying the Cacti soldiers in had used terrain-analysis software to pick the landing zones from satellite photos. The software's weakness (a glaring one in a place like Kunar) was in estimating slopes. The experienced Chinook pilots supporting the operation dropped Bastard Company off as planned at Landing Zone Honey-Eater, the ninety-eight-hundred-footer on the ridge above Gambir. But when the aviators saw the other clearings for the first time through their night-vision goggles, they blanched, judging them too small or blocked with trees. The helicopters couldn't get the scout platoon into its primary landing zone, or Apache Company into its, or Gundog Company into its, instead putting them into backup sites farther from their destinations on the ground.[65]

Files of men in MultiCam were spreading out in every direction on the mountainside as the sun rose on Saturday, June 25. Some troops were heading uphill, dragging heavy weapons to set up on tripods in six sandbagged strongpoints on the ridge, others downhill, disappearing from the view of orbiting helicopters and surveillance aircraft into the towering conifers of the Gambir Jungle. Down in the Honaker-Miracle operations center, where Tuley was monitoring the operation, blue digital map icons representing the nine Cacti platoons on the mountain showed the plan heading off track. The scouts were across the valley from where they were supposed to be. Gundog Company was too far from Tsangar to be able to reach it that day. And instead of advancing down toward Gambir in orderly files under the watchful scopes of the scouts opposite them, Bastard Company's three platoons were spreading farther and farther apart from one another, channeled by terrain that was steeper and more difficult than their maps indicated.[66]

An Army combat photographer captured eerie photos of Bastard Company descending the mountain, picking their way down trails and cliffs, the lush greens of the forest vegetation brilliantly illuminated where there were breaks in the canopy and in shadow where there weren't. The ground was jagged with boulders and hidden gorges and worse for walking than any volcanic rock they'd trained on in the Hawaiian hills. Very quickly a machine gunner broke his ankle and had to be hoisted out—the daylight medevac mission broadcasting his platoon's position in the forest—and soon other soldiers had sprained or hurt their ankles or legs as well, including the company commander, who tore tendons in both ankles but kept trudging downhill, taped up. Step by step, the three Bastard Company platoons fell out of one another's sight, each descending toward Gambir along its own draw or finger, each expecting to search a designated set of houses in the town when they got there.[67]

All the aircraft that headquarters in Kabul and Bagram could offer were flying over the valley, but that was no more a guarantee of early warning of an attack now than it had been during Bulldog Bite. First Platoon was still eight hundred very steep feet above Gambir, negotiating thinner pine forest and prickly, knee-high bushes just above the terrace where Kevin Pape and the other Team Darby Rangers had landed in November, when radio traffic indicated insurgents were close at hand, and just then militants sprang an ambush on the platoon's lead squad. The fire was precise and came from many directions and ranges: riflemen hidden in the vegetation all around, taking careful shots at heads and necks; machine gunners delivering long bursts from concealed positions across the gorge.[68]

The lieutenant in charge of First Platoon, Dimitri del Castillo, had turned twenty-four just a few days earlier; his wife, Katie, a

West Point classmate who worked at brigade headquarters, had managed to visit him at FOB Joyce for the occasion, bringing a celebratory cupcake.[69] Del, as friends called him, got on the radio. "They're shooting at us. They're laying down underneath blankets and they pop up and start shooting," the Army photographer recorded the lieutenant saying, attempting to guide in a pair of attack helicopters whose pilots were eager to help but couldn't tell where the fire was coming from because of the vegetation.[70] Then a bullet struck del Castillo just above the front plate of his body armor, killing him. The platoon interpreter fell dead as well. The wounded began to pile up: an ANA soldier shot in the leg, a squad leader shot in the arm, an engineer NCO shot in the hip as he tried to reach the fallen interpreter, and two more Americans shot in the face.[71]

As the remains of First Platoon consolidated around a mountainside farmhouse and started filling sandbags, the rest of Bastard Company struggled through its own gunfights to reach them, mostly at ranges too close for artillery to be helpful. The combat continued after dark, as medevac Black Hawks hoisted out the dead, the wounded, and the men who had incurred leg injuries from the hike down the mountain (including, to Bastard Company's chagrin, their company commander). Equipped with thermal sights, the Americans picked off some militants who were able to use the concealment of tall grass and shrubs to get within fifty meters of First Platoon's farmhouse. Other infiltrators went undetected but came close enough to a sister platoon that on intercepted walkie-talkie traffic they could be heard reporting the green glow of the Americans' night-vision goggles.[72]

TO TRY TO get Hammer Down back on track, that night Tuley and the brigade commander, Kim, sent in the first of three backup forces available to them. Team Havoc, as it was called, was a two-platoon reserve, just some sixty Americans and fifteen ANA cobbled together from different companies, but it was led by the most experienced captain in the battalion, Chris Bluhm, an 82nd Airborne veteran with a relaxed attitude who had already commanded a Cacti company in Iraq. Tuley and Kim judged that under Bluhm's steady leadership Team Havoc would be enough to get the Bastard Company troops pinned down outside Gambir back on their feet, after landing and making the same trek down the mountain, and then lead the way into Gambir.[73]

Despite bursts of rain and lightning overnight, a Chinook managed to get the first Team Havoc platoon into Landing Zone Honey-Eater, the same ninety-eight-hundred-foot clearing where Bastard Company had landed twenty-four hours earlier, without a hitch. Inside the second Chinook as it made its approach, though, Chris Bluhm had just taken off the radio headset connecting him to the pilots when he heard, felt, and saw an explosion. Then two of his soldiers were floating above him inside the cabin as the Chinook with the ill-fated call sign Extortion 17 plummeted the rest of the way down to the rocky earth.[74] Watching a drone's video feed of the mountaintop, Rich Kim's heart sank as he saw the helicopter drop: Had Bluhm and a whole platoon of his men just been killed?

They hadn't; the wrecked Chinook settled upright in the clearing and did not explode, its tail pointing toward the steep, rocky hillside where the forest began. On the aerial video feed, small figures emerged from the wrecked helicopter. Amazingly, no one aboard had died, even when one of the huge spinning rotors sliced into the fuselage. What had happened to Extortion 17 wasn't clear, even to its pilot—whether it had struck a tree, as many people assumed at the time, or fallen victim to a "vortex ring state" created by its own downward rotor wash, or been struck in a sensitive spot by a very lucky bullet, as the flight engineer and others aboard who saw tracers flying outside just before the crash believed. But the cause of the crash didn't matter much to the troops aboard at the time, or to the Bastard Company soldiers twenty-five hundred feet below who could hear the "Fallen Angel" call that went out over the radio net, the code phrase for a downed helicopter, and see a glow from the ridge through their night-vision goggles. No one would be coming down to reinforce them that night.[75]

Once Extortion 17's crew and eleven soldiers injured in the landing had been evacuated, barely sixty American and ANA troops were left to form a perimeter around the clearing and prepare by the light of the burning aircraft for the inevitable insurgent assault from the surrounding forest—positioning machine guns and Claymores and digging fighting holes at the bases of boulders. Team Havoc's commander, Bluhm, was still dazed from the concussion he'd suffered in the crash when the attack came, RPGs arcing out of the morning fog followed by machine-gun fire targeting the heavy-weapons positions along the perimeter. With the clouds too thick for Apaches or Kiowas to help, and the fighting too close for artillery, it was bomb strikes from Air Force jets—eleven two-thousand-pounders, many of them dropped danger close—that blunted the dawn attack, the first of two that Team Havoc would endure that day.[76]

One enemy fighter Bluhm saw through his rifle scope seemed to be outfitted for travel, not combat: he had bedding and some big metal pots hanging from him. Unknowingly, Bluhm and his men had crash-landed right on a crossing point where insurgents using the Shigal-Watapur-Waygal ratline hiked from one valley over into the next. Walkie-talkie traffic was coming from all around them in the forest, some of it in Pashto, some of it in Waygali or Gambiri: reinforcements were being contacted along the route in the Waygal and the Shigal, and Team Havoc was going to have to fight them off, one group after another. Someone else would have to reinforce Bastard Company.[77]

The whole concept of the operation had changed now, with Team Havoc stranded and embattled at another position atop the mountain. Down at Honaker-Miracle, Tuley could see that his plan had been far too ambitious. There was no way he would have had the resources to support major fights both in Gambir and in Tsangar, and now he canceled the already-delayed clearance of the second town. From here on out, the goal was to kill as many insurgents as possible from the positions where the Cacti troops were effectively stuck. At their landing zone, Bluhm and his Air Force targeting specialist were calling in dozens of bombs each day, and intercepted radio traffic confirmed that they were killing somebody, even if there were never any insurgent bodies around to see when the sun came up.[78]

FIREFIGHTS RIPPLED UP and down the chain of seven sandbagged strongpoints on the mountain on Monday and Tuesday, days three and four of Hammer Down. At Strongpoint Indus, nestled among giant boulders looking down into the Shigal, the tenacity of the enemy coming up from the other side shocked the scout platoon. Initiating their attacks with RPGs, the militants scaled a cliff-like slope over and over under withering fire, their walkie-talkie traffic revealing that they were hoping to overrun the position and take a soldier prisoner.[79] Another fight cost the life of a SAW gunner, Specialist Kevin Hilaman, when his platoon was ordered to reoccupy a hilltop position it had just left, Strongpoint Cat.[80] Soldiers at the farmhouse Bastard Company had fortified outside Gambir worried that they might be overrun. Three times on Monday the fighting was close enough for hand grenades, and twice for Claymores.[81]

The Americans got fleeting glimpses of their opponents through their scopes, but after one fight a platoon got its hands on two dead enemy bodies. Both men wore robes, canvas ammunition rigs, and sneakers, and both were clean, as though they had been bathing regularly. One fighter was carrying a rifle, some grenades, and a journal full of Taliban recruiters' phone numbers. A Pakistani religious-school ID card showed his age: sixteen.[82]

As clouds hung around the strongpoints, delaying extraction, the toughest fighting was at Landing Zone Honey-Eater, the clearing in the clouds where fewer than fifty Americans and some ANA were defending the wrecked Chinook. Every day, Team Havoc's mortarmen shot through all the rounds that helicopters had dropped off overnight. When they weren't being shot at, the troops dug more and deeper holes to fight from. When they were being shot at, the fighting was almost all with rifles and grenades. At night, Bluhm had his men lend some of the ANA night-vision goggles; equipped with the tools they needed, the Afghan soldiers maintained watch as diligently as the Americans next to them.[83]

On Wednesday, fresh ANA Commando reinforcements and their Green Beret advisers finally searched the original target houses in Gambir, finding little of note. It was day five of Hammer Down now, and on the radio militants were complaining of exhaustion and lack of ammunition and fielding complaints from village elders who thought the fighting had gone on long enough and that they should leave.[84] After days of hanging on thanks to helicopter and parachute deliveries, Tuley's troops were running low on supplies too, and that afternoon down at Honaker-Miracle the colonel gave the order for the Chinooks to head back up the mountain and start pulling the Cacti battalion out.[85]

Rainstorms and lightning made the extraction a two-night task, to the frustration of tired infantrymen who emptied their sandbags and filled their fighting holes before heading to their pickup zones, only to be told, after hours of waiting in the rain, to go build their strongpoints back up and try again the next night. Before the helicopters finally came for them Thursday night, the troops at Honey-Eater rigged the remains of Extortion 17 with incendiary grenades, and after the last of them were out, F-15s bombed the Chinook for good measure, hoping to melt away any propaganda value a Taliban camera crew might find at the mountaintop landing zone.[86]

AT FORT CAMPBELL, the news that more Americans had died in the Watapur valley just a few months after their own costly mission there was deflating for some Bulldog battalion veterans, who had hoped not to hear about the Pech and its side valleys anymore.

"Hearing about Hammer Down felt like being a little kid with a sandcastle that someone kicks over," remembered Jon Springer, the Bulldog fire-support officer who had struggled to come to grips with his own unit's departure from the Pech just three months earlier.[87]

To Joe Ryan, it seemed as if Kim and Tuley were squandering the opportunity he had given them to minimize their role in the Pech. "I personally wouldn't have done it," he said of Hammer Down. But he also wasn't surprised, knowing Kim from his time in the Rangers and thinking back on the keen interest he had shown in the Shuryak phase of Bulldog Bite during his pre-deployment visit in the fall. "I know Rich Kim too well," he said. "He wanted to get back out and get after it in the Pech. He was going to use the McChrystal doctrine: when in doubt, do something."[88]

No troops had wound up reaching Tsangar. Whatever disruption the operation caused to the Gambir ratline would be temporary. And the phantom Watapur training camps had not turned up. "We weren't able to pinpoint an actual training camp," Kim admitted, "but we had enough SIGINT reporting to indicate the enemy lost quite a bit, including some leaders."[89] Intelligence estimates put the enemy's losses at between 108 and 150 fighters killed[90]—about par for a big Watapur air assault—but the three leaders known to be among the dead were small-time commanders, none of them active outside the Watapur itself. The bigger fish, like the al-Qaida adviser Falik Naz, had all gotten away.[91]

Responses within the Cacti battalion ran the gamut. The Team Havoc soldiers who had held Landing Zone Honey-Eater were "ecstatic" and justifiably proud of their performance, killing dozens of Taliban without losing a single defender.[92] But others who took part in Hammer Down or its planning judged their commanders harshly.[93]

"Do I think we accomplished anything? We got a kill count, and that seemed to be the flavor of the deployment," said one Bastard Company soldier. "I guess it was a target that we knew was ripe: we go in there; we know we're going to get some."[94] But what, many Cacti troops wondered, was killing 100 or 150 fighters accomplishing? To Loren Crowe, the staff captain on his second Kunar tour, Tuley's willingness to undertake the battalion-wide air assault stood in stark contrast to how his previous battalion commander, Brett Jenkinson, had comported himself—avoiding what he called "trolling for contact" missions, and tirelessly advocating for a Korengal pullout even to bosses who clearly didn't want to hear it. Hammer Down had been "unconscionably risky and pointless," Crowe thought—a reversion to old, unsuccessful tactics—and he couldn't understand why Tuley hadn't resisted Kim's insistence on it, especially if the battalion commander had private reservations.[95]

In retrospect, Tuley would acknowledge some mistakes in the Hammer Down plan but maintain that the operation itself was "the right call." He had underestimated the terrain, he knew, and his expectation of clearing both Tsangar and Gambir had been unrealistic; the whole force should have concentrated on Gambir. "We were like a fly landing on that terrain; we were such a small element relative to it," he said. "That terrain just consumes you." He also wondered whether he could have done a better job explaining to his men the rationale behind the operation.[96]

And mistakes or no mistakes, he knew, the effect on the enemy of all those casualties would be fleeting. He had sent more American and ANA troops into the Watapur than had ever gone into the valley before, and the effect had still been, as he put it to some of his staff, like putting your finger in a glass of water and then pulling it out.[97]

BACK TO BLESSING

Later, Tuley would credit Hammer Down with helping get U.S. advisers reestablished at Blessing. That was the next step he'd settled on for getting the ANA back on their feet in the Pech, and he would claim that the operation had created some calm for the move by temporarily "degrading" the Pech insurgency.

That was debatable at best, because few of the fighters in the Watapur were likely ever to have anything to do with attacks on Blessing. And another large operation—a major push by both the Cacti battalion and Afghan troops—would be required to finally bring the beleaguered Rahmdel's ordeal to an end a month after Hammer Down.

At the end of July, hundreds of American and Afghan troops flooded back into the Pech, this time pushing out to Blessing and beyond. After leaving Rahmdel and his 2/2 battalion stranded for months, ANA headquarters in Kabul had announced a massive resupply mission, not just to the long-suffering battalion in Nangalam but all the way up the Pech to the Parun valley, where Nuristan's provincial seat was as isolated and precarious as ever. Escorted by Afghan troops and paramilitary Civil Order Police, convoys of government pickup trucks spent two weeks winding their way up to Parun and back not once but twice, filled with hundreds of tons of rice, flour, gasoline, and cooking oil. Another ANA battalion came up from Kabul equipped with M113s, boxlike Vietnam-era armored personnel carriers that made an impression when they showed up in Nangalam; it had been twenty-five years since anyone had seen "tanks," as Afghans called the tracked vehicles, in the Pech. The valley was seeing a side of the government that had rarely been in evidence there before.[98]

Five years after construction began on it, the American-funded road the convoys drove along had already begun to deteriorate badly. The pavement was pockmarked with craters from IEDs, and in some places eroding riverbanks had narrowed the road by several feet. Torrential rainstorms during the operation washed away the PRT-financed bridge just outside Honaker-Miracle; engineers had to replace it with a portable Bailey bridge. Out in Chapa Dara, the same storms washed huge boulders and what seemed like whole chunks of the mountain down onto the dirt road, undoing all the road-widening work that contractors had done in previous years.[99]

No Cacti battalion troops went as far as Parun, although one company did fly ten miles beyond Blessing to man a strongpoint overlooking the road where it turned north on the other side of Chapa Dara. For Tuley and his officers, the ANA's big resupply mission to Nuristan presented an opportunity to accomplish a more modest goal: to install a group of fifty to sixty soldiers back at Blessing, a twenty-strong ad hoc adviser team led by a major with an infantry platoon to protect them. These troops' task would be to reoccupy the old U.S. operations center at the base, clearing out all the garbage and human waste that had accumulated there since the Bulldog battalion's departure back in March and turning it into a command post and barracks. Then, as the resupply mission wound down, they were to oversee the ANA battalion transition that Tuley saw as integral to getting the Pech headed back in the right direction: Rahmdel and his 2/2 battalion would leave the valley, and a fresh, more capable unit, the 6/2 battalion, whose commander had all the charisma, confidence, and command experience that Rahmdel lacked, would replace them.

There was little evidence of any serious effect from Hammer Down as four of the Cacti battalion's five companies, backed by a cavalry troop and ANA Commandos, drove or flew out into the Pech and fought to defend the Afghan resupply columns at the end of July and into the second week of August. Some of the toughest fighting was on the road outside the Korengal, whose veteran insurgents had, of course, not been affected by the Watapur operation at all.

The detritus of a nine-year-old war was everywhere. On their way out to the Senji Bridge near Chapa Dara, one company passed by the stripped-down remains of the Husky mine-clearing vehicle that an IED had destroyed during one of the Bulldog battalion's abortive attempts to reach the district center a year earlier. In Kandigal, Hesco barriers and sandbags from COP Michigan had worked their way into local construction, and troops fighting from the outpost's ruins used the rubble as cover for mortar and missile teams. Children who had grown up with the routine of near-daily firefights strolled nonchalantly between the American MRAPs, collecting brass shell casings to melt or sell. Jets dropped dozens of bombs, howitzers were airlifted back out to Blessing, and an IED killed an engineer sergeant. For two hot, rainy weeks, it was almost as if U.S. troops had never left the Pech at all.[100]

The most anxious moment came on the first night of the operation, when Tuley was waiting to fly into Blessing to join a small adviser team that had already gone out and started setting up a command post. A Chinook with the call sign Big Apple 10 was approaching Nangalam with a load of passengers and cargo from battalion headquarters when the soldiers aboard heard a pop, then saw sparks fly by their feet: fired from almost directly beneath them, an RPG had pierced the helicopter's belly and exploded inside—miraculously detonating against a little Gator utility vehicle that shielded the seven Cacti passengers aboard from the shrapnel.[101]

With the Gator on fire and leaking fuel, a burning SAW cooking off rounds, and boxes of ammunition and a Javelin missile also stacked in the cabin, Big Apple 10's pilot knew the whole aircraft could go up in flames. So he aimed the bird at an open spot between the base and the river—a graveyard, as it turned out—and put it down as quickly and gently as he could. Clambering out and running toward the nearest wall of the ANA base, everyone aboard managed to get clear before the fire spread and burned the crashed helicopter down to its skeleton.[102]

THE SHOOT-DOWN of Big Apple 10 wound up being just a wrinkle in the plan for Operation Diamond Head and the big Pech resupply mission, neither killing nor seriously injuring anybody. But it was a very close call, nearly diverting the whole mission into disastrous territory.

To Tuley, who had been waiting to board another Blessing-bound helicopter when Big Apple 10 was hit, it seemed like a reminder of the stakes in the Pech, a place that had now claimed two

Chinooks in as many months. His men had been aboard both aircraft, and only luck had kept them all alive. Less than two weeks later, another lucky RPG shot elsewhere in the east would bring down another Chinook,* killing the crew and a whole strike force of SEALs and other special operators, for thirty-eight total dead, the worst combat loss of the whole war. That could all too easily have been the fate of the Chinooks downed above Gambir and outside Blessing.[103]

To some of the Cacti soldiers trickling into Blessing who would be staying there for the rest of their deployment as advisers to the ANA, the shoot-down seemed like a message from the Taliban: "Welcome back."

---

* An aircraft from the same unit as the Chinook that crashed during Hammer Down, coincidentally bearing the same call sign, Extortion 17.

CHAPTER 13

AFGHANIZATION

2011–2013

FIRE ROCK

To lead the Cacti battalion's contingent in the Pech for the rest of the deployment, Colin Tuley tapped Loren Crowe, the staff captain who had fought in Kunar before as a lieutenant in Brett Jenkinson's Blue Spader battalion. It wasn't obvious at the time, and it wasn't by design, but Crowe's arrival as the American commander at the reoccupied FOB Blessing marked a shift to a new phase of the campaign in the Pech: one in which a succession of captains, rather than colonels or generals, would set the tone there. He was the first of three young officers who, over the next two years, would tap into past experience on the ground in a way that would help address one of the persistent problems American efforts in Afghanistan had suffered from: the lack of continuity and institutional knowledge.

Crowe, who had seethed at what he saw as the needless risk and waste of lives of Operation Hammer Down, had been lobbying Tuley to put him in command of Gundog Company and send him to the Pech. His previous tour in Kunar in 2008 and 2009 had left Crowe with a conviction that living and fighting in small groups with the ANA, not flying into the mountains to search for phantom training camps, was the only way for American forces to get the

Afghan troops to the point where they could fight the war on their own. With his previous experience in the valley, Crowe had ideas about how best to build up the confidence and competence of the ANA at Blessing and was pitching a different version of what the Cacti battalion could accomplish in the Pech to his superiors.

"It was very simple," he explained later. "We were never going to get out of the Pech and stay out if that ANA battalion wasn't successful." Not a day of the deployment went by when Crowe didn't think about Brandon Farley, a Blue Spader sergeant who'd died in the same firefight that had earned Crowe his valor award and a lifetime of survivor's guilt, and his black gravestone in Oklahoma. "I felt like every inch we withdrew was preventing another family from losing their son. I wanted to get all the way out," he recalled, and fighting a small-unit advisory war at the Afghans' side a little longer seemed like the only way to get there.[1]

Crowe was a divisive figure at battalion headquarters at FOB Joyce, undeniably abrasive and seen by some of his peers as arrogant and unnecessarily argumentative. But Tuley saw the promise in what the captain was selling, and in September he agreed to send Crowe out to the Pech, where he would take command of Gundog Company and split his time between Blessing and Honaker-Miracle. "Loren had the people skills and he had the combat experience," the Cacti battalion commander recalled. "I had a lot of confidence in him for that mission."[2]

When the first Gundog Company platoon reoccupied the old operations center in August, it had been in disgusting condition, with rats and human feces everywhere, forcing the troops to sleep under the stars while they started getting the place in shape to be a company command post and makeshift barracks.[3] In early September, while Crowe was finishing up his staff time at Joyce, two fresh platoons from the company drove out to get the full-time advisory mission going and start patrolling with the ANA. The trip took hours as engineers painstakingly cleared IEDs from the Pech road and the two platoons' MRAPs stopped periodically to trade fire with insurgents in the hills. Arriving at Blessing, the Gundog troops circled their trucks by the landing zone, unsure how safe to feel around their Afghan cohabitants at the base.[4]

One of the platoons had fought in the Watapur during Hammer Down, and whatever the dangers of living at a base where they were outnumbered by Afghan soldiers with whom they could speak only through interpreters, arriving at Blessing felt like the start of something new. "My platoon got really good at killing radicalized teenagers in the mountains, but I'm not sure that's really something we needed to be doing," the platoon's lieutenant joked bleakly of the June air assault, during which one of his SAW gunners had died retaking a hill the platoon had been ordered to give up earlier in the day.[5] The small-unit advisory mission seemed like a more sensible approach. It wasn't hard to conclude that this version of the war was the one American units should have been waging all along—more similar to the experience of small groups of Green Berets and Marines in the Pech back in 2004 and 2005 than to the war of infantry patrols and air assaults that had unfolded since, but now with a sizable force of Afghan troops to work with.

As ever, though, the U.S. military in eastern Afghanistan was not of one mind. Before Crowe joined his platoons at Blessing, the Cacti battalion was diverted by orders from above for yet another large-scale air assault. This time, for reasons that were even more opaque to battalion planners than the ones that had spurred the Watapur mission, the Hawaii-based troops were going back to the place where the American project in the Pech had seen its deadly highwater mark: the village of Want in the Waygal valley.

AMERICAN TROOPS HADN'T set foot in Want since Bill Ostlund's shaken paratroopers left the district center after nine of their comrades died there on July 13, 2008. Regional Command East headquarters had barred subsequent units at Blessing from visiting the town, even after militants set the new U.S.-funded district center building on fire in the spring of 2009 and an ambush south of town in early 2010 turned up evidence that a group of Arab al-Qaida fighters had arrived in the area from the Watapur.[6] Three weeks after the Bulldog battalion's pullout from Blessing in March 2011, sketchy reports had come in of a Taliban takeover: a large militant force had descended on the district center, driving out the police and government workers and raising the Taliban flag.[7] Nearly six months later, it was unclear what was going on in Want, but it was certainly under Taliban control.

The first time officers at Cacti battalion headquarters heard of a Want mission was from a towering, rangy brigadier general named Gary Volesky, the deputy commander of the 1st Cavalry Division, the latest unit to run Regional Command East at Bagram. A Silver Star recipient from a tour in Baghdad years earlier, Volesky was known for his irrepressible aggressiveness. The high enemy death toll from Operation Hammer Down had impressed him, both as he watched aerial video of the operation during its opening night and when he flew into Landing Zone Honey-Eater to shake the hands and slap the backs of the Team Havoc soldiers fighting there.[8] Visiting Cacti headquarters at Joyce at the end of the summer, Volesky told the battalion to get ready to replicate their Watapur mission in the Waygal and retake the Want district center for the Afghan government.[9]

"The words that came out of General Volesky's mouth were 'I want to show those motherfuckers we can fly the flag up there in Wanat,'" a Cacti officer remembered, using the Americanized version of the town's name.[10]

All the units involved in the Want mission met for a final walkthrough of the plan at FOB Joyce in late September. Cacti battalion planners had named it Operation Fire Rock, and unlike any other mission in the Pech since Operation Red Wings it involved all three of the U.S. military's tribes in Afghanistan from the get-go—conventional troops, Green Berets from the "white" special operations task force, and SEAL Team 6 operators from the JSOC task force. Representatives from each were there for the rehearsal drill. Colin Tuley and two of his company commanders walked through how they were going to fly into clearings on the mountain that loomed east of town and dig in with sandbags and heavy weapons, setting up strongpoints for the enemy to come impale themselves against as they had at Landing Zone Honey-Eater. A Green Beret described how the ANA Commando company that his A-team advised would do the actual clearance of the town, searching it building by building and showing the flag for the Afghan government when the sun came up. Another team of special operators didn't identify their unit or say much about what they would be doing; there were just three or four of them, sporting beards and the tan digital camouflage of SEALs. They were the JSOC operators of the Omega team attached to the CIA at FOB Asadabad, and they planned on tagging along with the Cacti battalion's scout platoon for reasons they didn't describe.[11]

A patchwork of reports from informants and radio and cell phone intercepts suggested that somewhere between twenty and forty militants stayed in Want at any given time. Some reports said that a group of al-Qaida Arabs had taken up residence in the town's vacant police station, and the Taliban's provincial shadow governor and other insurgent leaders sometimes visited and held meetings at a restaurant or an old French-built medical clinic building.[12] "I wouldn't say we had conclusive evidence that they had a camp or C2 [command-and-control] node there," Rich Kim, the brigade commander, said.[13] To some at both brigade and battalion headquarters, the intelligence seemed thin for a large-scale offensive operation.[14]

Among those to whom it all didn't quite add up was Tuley, who would be flying in along with his men this time. "Why go up there?" he wondered aloud later. "Just to rattle people's feathers and say you went up there?" That was how Volesky was framing it, but it felt to Tuley and some of his officers as though something were being left out of the rationale they were hearing as they planned their risky follow-up to Hammer Down. Maybe something hadn't been communicated down to battalion level, something they didn't need to know. "There may have been other intel that we weren't seeing," Tuley speculated.[15]

THERE WAS, IN FACT, a backstory behind Operation Fire Rock that hadn't trickled down to the soldiers actually carrying it out. It consisted of two parts—one involving JSOC, the other involving the American military's old partner in Nuristan, Governor Tamim Nuristani—and both had contributed to an order from the latest ISAF commander in Kabul to put boots on the ground in the province again.

One night in May, intelligence had reached the JSOC task force at Bagram that top commanders in the Nuristani Taliban were gathering in Want for a meeting. Among them seemed to be the Taliban's top official in the province, its shadow governor, Dost Mohammad—a figure high on the task force's targeting list both because he'd overseen the Want-style attack on COP Keating in eastern Nuristan in 2009 that killed eight Americans and because he was believed to host al-Qaida Arabs.[16] The shadow governor and his foreign guests tended to spend their time farther up the Waygal, in mountainside villages like Amshuz that were inaccessible by helicopter, so a meeting on the valley floor in Want presented an opportunity. Bill Ostlund had just begun another stint commanding the Bagram task force, and he was all for it, eager to take down a high-profile Taliban commander with links to Arabs and American blood on his hands. But after a long discussion, the JSOC chain of command above Ostlund shut the mission down. Flying a two-platoon force in daylight into a place where both the enemy and the terrain had a track record of downing helicopters was just too risky. Dan Kearney—back in Afghanistan leading Team Darby, the Ranger unit Ostlund had alerted for the mission—got the stand-down call as he was briefing the plan to his Rangers and as a quick-reaction force was already on the way to Asadabad.[17]

In July, a new ISAF commander took over in Kabul, General John Allen of the Marine Corps. During his early days in command, Allen met with officers from the CIA's Kabul station, who described their understanding of the al-Qaida presence in Nuristan to him: how many of the terrorist group's operatives there were (the estimate was somewhere between fifty and a hundred), where they were, and which Taliban officials, like Dost Mohammad, were harboring them. "They were in the process of identifying specific locations of al-Qaida and Arab terrorists, supported by Nuristani insurgents who protected them," Allen remembered. "That defined my interest in Nuristan."[18]

For more information, Allen and Mick Nicholson, still in Kabul as ISAF's two-star director of operations, turned to Tamim Nuristani, the former California pizza franchise owner who, as governor of his home province in the middle of the decade, had helped draw Nicholson's 10th Mountain troops into Nuristan for their program of outpost and road building. Fired in a corruption scandal in 2008,

Tamim had been waiting in the wings ever since, and in August, in the weeks preceding Fire Rock, his old patron Karzai had reinstated him as governor.

Tamim told Allen and Nicholson what he knew: six out of Nuristan's eight district centers were under Taliban control, and Arab militants moved freely among them, including a rising al-Qaida star in whom the CIA was interested called Farouq al-Qahtani.[19] Nicholson was as impressed as ever by his old friend's energy and ambition. Tamim wanted help kicking the enemy out of the district centers they had taken over, like Want, and he wanted renewed assistance paving the long road from Nangalam up the Pech to Parun.[20]

But there was only so much that Allen and Nicholson were willing to offer Tamim. No one at ISAF had an appetite for road building in Nuristan anymore; the days when the U.S. military had poured millions of dollars into infrastructure projects to connect remote districts were over, the experiment largely viewed now as a dead end. During the ambitious expansion into the northeast a few years earlier when those road projects had begun, "we grossly overestimated what the government could bring to the table in terms of connecting to the people," Nicholson acknowledged later.[21] So for roads, Tamim would have to make his case to his own government in Kabul. "They told me, 'Not anymore, everything goes through the government now,'" Tamim remembered.[22]

As far as taking back Nuristan's fallen district centers, what the American generals could offer was one or two big offensive missions to kick the Taliban out of a couple of them and raise the Afghan flag, with ANA Commandos playing a starring role. The results of Hammer Down in the Watapur had impressed Nicholson, just as they had Volesky, and he knew that the window for similar operations was closing fast. Since President Obama's declaration of the end of the surge earlier in the summer, U.S. troop levels had already begun to drop from their peak of a hundred thousand, and as part of the drawdown the next brigade to deploy to northeastern Afghanistan in early 2012 would be a smaller organization, manned for a slimmed-down advisory mission, not for air assaults into insurgent strongholds. "We were looking at where the first ten thousand troops were going to come out of and where we needed to hit before we leave, and as part of this we decided to put pressure on the enemy in Nuristan," Nicholson remembered.[23]

This was how Operation Fire Rock had come about—the backstory that no one told Colin Tuley or his officers. The instructions went down from Allen through Nicholson and the corps commander to Regional Command East, and not long after the meeting with Tamim in Kabul, Gary Volesky was at Jalalabad Airfield telling Rich Kim and his staff to start planning Fire Rock. Tamim became a familiar face at brigade headquarters too, meeting with planners and intelligence officers to draw maps of Want on scrap paper and rattle off things he'd heard from his own informant network about who was doing what in town, just as he'd done with Nicholson and Cavoli as their forces pushed into Nuristan in 2006.[24]

Allen also told JSOC to start figuring out how to address the al-Qaida presence in the province.[25] For the counterterrorism task force, the big mission conventional troops were planning presented an opportunity for a few operators to piggyback along and try to pick up some information about the presence of Arabs in an enemy-controlled town where they couldn't normally put boots on the ground, as the May episode with Kearney and Team Darby had demonstrated. That was how the shaggy-looking SEAL Team 6 operators from the Asadabad Omega team wound up at the final Fire Rock rehearsal at FOB Joyce.[26]

As the Cacti troops, Green Berets, and frogmen boarded helicopters and headed up the Pech on the night of September 20, almost all of them were expecting a tough fight. Everyone knew how hard the enemy had fought to kick American troops out of Want three years earlier, how nine paratroopers had died there. Some officers, considering the whole thing ill-advised, dreaded what was coming. Other troops were thrilled. "It was exciting," said an infantryman who flew in on the same Chinook as the Omega team. "It felt like we were going to get revenge."[27]

NO MASSED FORCE of insurgents confronted the Americans and ANA when they landed; for the Cacti battalion, Operation Fire Rock was an anticlimax. But for the residents of Want, it was a tragedy, resulting in three separate instances of harm to civilians—one involving each of the three U.S. military tribes that participated in the mission.[28]

The operation began with a rare pre-assault bombardment, authorized up at Allen's ISAF headquarters in Kabul: hoping to stun any fighters who might have shot at the incoming transport helicopters, jets pounded the mountainside clearings where the Chinooks were going to land with satellite-guided bombs. In a step whose irony wasn't lost on Tuley, the jets dropped more bombs on the road north of town—the one American reconstruction funds had built and previous units had fought to protect—in an effort to keep militant leaders from escaping Want by pickup truck.[29] Then Apaches moved in, picking off small groups of fighters with the help of Predators and other surveillance aircraft prowling above.

There was some shooting from down below as the Chinooks approached, but when the first Cacti soldiers hit the ground, the only noise came from dying cows at the main landing zone—a herd of cattle that had been ripped apart by the exploding bombs. While an officer put the wounded animals out of their misery, the Cacti troops spread out to their strongpoints and started filling sandbags and setting up heavy weapons: Tuley and Bastard Company at a position overlooking Want, Gundog Company higher up the slope where they could fight off any enemy reinforcements coming over the mountains from the Watapur, and the scout platoon and Omega team SEALs farther downhill, on a spur with a better view down into town.

The next wave of troops to hit the cattle-littered clearing was the ANA Commando company and its team of Special Forces advisers. Waiting at the landing zone while the Commandos and part of the A-team hiked down toward town, the captain in charge of the Green Berets could hear sporadic gunfire and the explosions of one or two grenades as the force approached Want through a cornfield, killing some defending militants as they went, and then moved into town.[30] Apaches circled overhead, in one case firing at a machine-gun nest up on the mountain, and the SEALs took some shots at figures on the periphery of town with their sniper rifles.[31] Moving past the clearing the Rock paratroopers had defended three years earlier, the Commandos entered the town and started searching buildings. Just after sunrise, a mortar shell exploded in town; Kiowas that had joined the Apaches overhead spotted a plume of smoke in the woods that they thought must be the firing point and struck it with rockets and Hellfires.[32]

Up on the mountain at the Cacti strongpoints, the morning brought silence and a sense of relief: Fire Rock clearly wasn't going to be another Hammer Down, let alone another battle of Want. Besides the small number of militants the Commandos had encountered in town overnight, "the enemy just weren't there. They were gone," said one platoon leader.[33] The only force that approached the upper strongpoint—the one bracing for an onslaught from the Watapur—was a herd of countless goats and sheep, remembered Burhan, the interpreter who had worked for the Chosin and Rock battalions at their outposts in the Waygal and now found himself back in his family's home valley with Cacti.[34]

The Commandos didn't find much in town, either; the most interesting discoveries were a sniper rifle and a well-cared-for RPG launcher. As was their standard practice, imparted by the Green Berets who trained them, the Afghan troops had corralled everyone they had found during their house searches in a roped-off area, to be questioned later. Sorting through the villagers in the morning, the A-team's interpreters didn't find any wanted Taliban leaders.[35] In the afternoon, as the American and Afghan special operators boarded helicopters to head home after what from their perspective had been a flop, they handed responsibility for the holding area over to another force from the Cacti battalion: Team Havoc, the two-platoon force that had fended off enemy assaults day after day at Landing Zone Honey-Eater earlier in the summer.

While Team Havoc's commander, Chris Bluhm, got to work paying village elders for the cows killed during the night, another soldier who had flown in with him, Sergeant Don Nicholas, began talking to the seventy-odd corralled villagers. A fifty-nine-year-old former podiatrist, Nicholas was far older than any other American on the mission; as a young Marine embassy guard, he'd been on the second-to-last helicopter out of Saigon in 1975, then enlisted in the Army Reserve in 2004 after decades away from military life. His work as a civil affairs soldier—a rare specialist in dealing with local civilians—had taken him to the Pech once before, attached to the Marines there in 2005.[36]

As Nicholas talked with the villagers through an interpreter, he heard repeated complaints that a family had been killed by airpower in the mountains overnight. Patting them down and handing them a digital camera, Nicholas sent a small group of older men off with instructions to bring back photographic evidence, and Bluhm informed Bastard Company and the scouts at their strongpoints above town that they should expect to see the men heading into the woods. Ten or fifteen minutes passed before Bluhm and Nicholas heard a shot ring out, the only one they'd heard since landing. Then the group of men appeared again—two of them carrying a third, who was bleeding from a gunshot wound to his right leg above the knee. While Nicholas dressed the wound, the men told him the gunshots had come without warning and that the final member of their party had taken off running when the third collapsed wounded.[37]

The shots had come from the Cacti battalion scout platoon's strongpoint on a finger overlooking Want, but they hadn't come from any of the scouts. "It was one shot, maybe two," a scout remembered. "It was a SEAL sniper, on a sniper rifle with very good optics." Another scout ran over to the Omega team's part of the strongpoint perimeter and found the SEAL who'd taken the shot still sitting behind his rifle, ready to explain: he'd seen a man at the edge of the village running suspiciously between the trees and shot him. The SEALs said they hadn't heard the call over the radio saying to expect unarmed men in their field of vision.[38] The Cacti scouts were taken aback, but not wholly surprised. During the night, the SEALs had fired several shots without explaining to anyone over the radio whom they were shooting at. Looking out over the same vista just a few meters away from the SEALs, the scouts had seen some men outside town but no one who appeared to be armed or to pose a threat.[39] "They were in their own world, doing whatever they wanted," one scout said of the frogmen. "They were trigger-happy."[40]

Next Nicholas sent two other, younger men up the mountain. Although they were scared they'd be shot too, they came back an hour later with photos and then led Nicholas, Bluhm, and a platoon northwest to the place they'd taken them—a house sitting amid a cornfield on a hillside terrace. What the soldiers found there was horrific, even to an old hand like Nicholas: the mangled corpses of two small boys who Nicholas thought looked about ten years old, a teenage boy and girl, and an adult woman, all covered with blankets. There was also a mass of mangled human tissue that the two guides said was a baby but that Nicholas thought might be part of the woman. Nearby, a big tree had been split in half by an explosion, and the unmistakable fragments of a U.S. munition lay around it, along with what seemed like a piece of a skull. Nicholas took pictures of all of it. It wasn't clear which of the various aircraft at work overnight had done the damage, but Bluhm's best guess was that whatever it was, it had killed the family after they ran out of their home and huddled for cover at the edge of the woods.[41]

When Gary Volesky, the 1st Cavalry Division brigadier general, flew in the next day, he brought along a military representative who doled out a compensation payment to surviving members of the family.[42] To the Cacti infantrymen, he handed out mementos that seemed off-key given how the operation had turned out and reminded some of the troops who received them of Robert Duvall's 1st Cav character in *Apocalypse Now*. They were playing cards with the division's black-and-yellow insignia emblazoned on the back, intended for the soldiers to leave behind just as 1st Cav troopers had done in Vietnam and in the 1979 film's iconic air-assault scene.[43]

Tuley recommended ending the mission and going home. "I remember being on the mountaintop above Wanat, talking to Rich Kim and division, and they were asking me, and I was saying, 'I'll stay here another week if you want, but we're not getting anything,'" he recalled.[44]

IT WAS ONLY after all the American troops had flown away that reports of the third civilian casualty incident emerged, when Want residents discovered a body underneath the town's hotel.[45] It was the corpse of the hotel's elderly owner, Haji Juma Gul, the dealer of antiquities who had befriended American troops when they lived in the Waygal and hosted Jon Brostrom late on the night before the battle that took the Chosen Company platoon leader's life. Juma Gul had died of an apparent knife wound, and suspicion among locals, and among Nuristanis in Kabul, quickly fell on the ANA Commandos and the Green Berets who had carried out the search of the town.

After the 2008 battle, some American troops and their interpreters had accused Juma Gul of complicity with the insurgents who launched the attack, some of whom used his house as a fighting position just hours after he met with Brostrom. "He had an oily tongue," the former Chosen Company interpreter Farshad told me of him. "He was always friendly during the *shuras,* but he was working both sides." One rumor had it that after American troops pulled out of their nascent outpost, Juma Gul welcomed the Taliban into town with fruit juice and congratulated them on their victory.[46] But in the three years since then, Juma Gul had persistently encouraged the Americans to return; when he visited Blessing on his way through Nangalam, he would sit down with U.S. officers, including Joe Ryan, offering them apricots he'd brought down from Want, and urge them to resume their abandoned road project in the valley.[47]

Tamim Nuristani, for one, trusted Juma Gul, who also sat on the government's High Peace Council, a body of elders and clerics charged with trying to bring militants from the Taliban and other groups into low-level peace talks. The old man's loyalty lay with Kabul, Tamim believed, and his dealings with the Taliban didn't go beyond what his position in that body required and what any prominent person needed to do to survive on the perilous border between government and militant control. On the eve of Fire Rock, Tamim later told me, he had advised Afghan security officials working with the Americans to talk to Juma Gul when they reached Want, only to receive a call after the operation from an irate President Karzai, who knew Juma Gul from their days fighting for the same minor mujahidin party in the 1980s, reporting his death and demanding answers about it.[48]

Karzai convened an investigatory team of security officials and parliamentarians to look into the civilian deaths during Fire Rock, but with Want already back under Taliban influence, if not outright control as before the operation, its members couldn't visit the town and had to rely on what they could learn by phone, from Waygalis who visited them in Jalalabad and Parun, and from the Commandos. In their report, the government investigators accused the Green Beret A-team of murdering Juma Gul: after the Commandos rounded up residents, they wrote, the team's interpreter had been heard calling Juma Gul's name, and after finding him, he and two American soldiers had taken him to a nearby shop from which he didn't emerge alive.[49]

All the Americans I interviewed about the mission denied the Afghan government investigation's allegation. Chris Bluhm, Don Nicholas, and the Green Beret captain who oversaw the A-team's part of the mission all said they didn't hear anything about Juma Gul during the mission.[50] The Special Forces battalion commander who dealt with the fallout in Kabul didn't believe any of the Commandos had done it either, and other American officers who spoke with the investigators suggested the Taliban killed the old man after the mission because they suspected he was an informant for U.S. intelligence and had helped prompt the mission.[51] Some Waygalis I spoke to proposed another theory: that a member of a family with whom Juma Gul was engaged in a dispute—perhaps over land, perhaps over a marriage—took advantage of the chaos during Fire Rock to settle a score.[52]

The truth of what happened to Juma Gul will probably remain a mystery. The story that gained currency in the Waygal and among Nuristanis in Kabul, though, was that Americans had either killed the hotel owner in retaliation for his perceived betrayal of Chosen Company in 2008 or had a Commando do their dirty work for them.[53] Paired with the two other instances of civilian casualties during the Want mission, that perception was enough to outweigh any benefit of the operation, judged the brigade's intelligence chief.[54] Gary Volesky and Rich Kim disagreed, citing reports that when the Taliban moved back into Want after the mission, locals persuaded them not to immediately reoccupy the government's district center building, lest doing so spur another operation with all its accompanying dangers.[55]

FIRE ROCK WAS the last gasp of the long era of big, blunt air assaults in the Pech's tributary valleys, underlining the damage they could do to local communities and the reputations of the American military and Afghan government. Years of such operations had shown that errant killings of innocents by aircrews seeking to protect the troops on the ground—and the ensuing fallout—were tragically common side effects of them.

But the SEAL sniper's puzzling shooting of one old man and the unsolved stabbing death of another fell into a different, murkier category of violence attributable directly or indirectly to American operations. It didn't help that they weren't the only mysterious incidents in that category to occur during the month of September 2011, nor even the only ones in which SEAL Team 6 operators were implicated. Eighteen days before the mission to Want, in a mission that likewise sparked the ire of Karzai and allegations of an illegal execution, Team 6 operators from JSOC's Task Force East had raided a house in an upscale Jalalabad neighborhood and killed another High Peace Council member who had a fraught history with the American military: Sabar Lal, the Salafi militia commander from the Pech who had spent five years confined at Guantánamo Bay Naval Base after his detention in Asadabad back during American troops' first summer in Afghanistan.

Since his release from Guantánamo in 2007, Sabar Lal had settled in Jalalabad, where he started a real-estate business and leveraged his ties to his home valley to deal gems and his time as an inmate at the island prison to assume a spot on the High Peace Council. In August 2010, I had met one of his grown sons, Zaid, when a Bulldog battalion platoon I was tagging along with visited the family home in the lower Waygal. Over tea, Zaid explained that his father was afraid he would be detained again if he came home, prompting the platoon leader to assure him that Sabar Lal was a free man, of no interest to the battalion intelligence section at FOB Blessing.

Unknown to the platoon leader, Sabar Lal had remained a subject of scrutiny for the CIA ever since his return from Guantánamo. Tracking his movements and listening to his calls, intelligence officers were trying to discern how much of his contact with militant leaders in Kunar stemmed from his role on the peace council (the insurgent leader Qadir Mohammad was a cousin) and how much represented a secret embrace of the Taliban, the movement he had fought against before the American intervention, or al-Qaida, whose operatives he had supposedly helped escape from Tora Bora in 2001. When the Taliban took over Want in March 2011, he had secured the release of some of the police officers captured at the district center, but at the same time, according to a later news account, U.S. and British intelligence had turned up evidence that he was acting as an insurgent financier.[56]

One day in August, operatives of the NDS, the CIA-backed Afghan intelligence service, showed up at Sabar Lal's door and hauled him away. After nine days of pressure from the High Peace Council—including from his fellow Kunari Guantánamo releasee, Haji Ruhullah—Karzai had ordered the NDS to release him, but the reprieve proved short-lived. On the night of September 2, SEALs from Task Force East came calling, this time at night, scaling the walls of the compound with ladders.[57]

What happened next is disputed. In a statement about the raid that accused Sabar Lal of financing attacks in the Pech and being in touch with unnamed al-Qaida figures, ISAF claimed that a member of the strike force shot Sabar Lal as he brandished a rifle, a surefire way to be killed by special operators during a night raid.[58] But the compound's night watchman later told a *New York Times* reporter that the foreign troops—who neither the watchman nor the reporter knew were SEALs—handcuffed Sabar Lal before taking him out onto the house's porch, away from other men they had detained. Only after that, the watchman said, did shots ring out.[59] The implication was that it had been a battlefield execution—a crime that SEAL Team 6 had been accused of before in Afghanistan and would be accused of again, including by an American doctor whom SEALs would rescue from Taliban captivity in another Task Force East mission fifteen months later.[60]

CLOSING THE PECH GAP

Down where the Waygal met the Pech at Blessing, Loren Crowe and his company didn't see any positive effects from Fire Rock; it just seemed as if it had been another waste of time, a distraction from the small-unit advisory war that was everyone's ticket home.[61]

Arriving in the Pech just after the big Want operation, Crowe was in command of about two hundred soldiers—a little more than half of them at Honaker-Miracle and the rest at Blessing.* The latter included two infantry platoons, a mortar section, a handful of full-time advisers, and assorted cooks, mechanics, radiomen, and fire-support specialists. They all slept in the old operations center building, Crowe on a cot in the room that had been the well-appointed office of a succession of U.S. Army battalion commanders. His goal was to get American troops back out of Blessing again—not by pulling out precipitously, as the Bulldog battalion had done, but "the right way," with the ANA battalion there ready to stand on its own two feet, because the Kabul government had made clear that it intended to keep troops in the Pech come hell or high water and no matter what their American partners thought of the place's strategic value. "For years, U.S. units have gone into Kunar just expecting to kill some motherfuckers on offensive operations," the battalion operations officer recalled. "Loren knew that if we kept operating that way, we'd keep going back."[62]

Crowe and the advisers at Blessing would be working with a new Afghan battalion that had rotated into the Pech during the big resupply operation at the end of the summer, 6/2 ANA. Where the outgoing 2/2 ANA had been a ragged husk of a battalion after years on end in the Pech and the trauma of the Bulldog battalion's withdrawal, the incoming unit was fully manned, and at its helm was an energetic, confident officer with previous Pech experience from 2008 and 2009, Lieutenant Colonel Turab Khan.

A short-statured Pashtun from Khost with a dark beard and sharp features, Turab had gained his position through hard work and competence, rather than buying it with cash or Kabul connections the way many ANA officers did. In February, ahead of the American pullout from Blessing, he'd told a *New York Times* reporter that keeping the ANA at the base on their own would be "absolutely impractical"—a prediction that had proven accurate.[63] Taking over there himself while Gundog Company was settling back in, he was grateful to have American advisers with him, but he understood well they could not stay forever and eventually his 6/2 battalion

---

* Orders had come down from battalion to call the camp Nangalam Base, because it belonged to the ANA now, but Crowe couldn't bring himself to, and even the Afghan troops there mostly still used its old American name.

would be on its own just as 2/2 had been. The necessity of being better prepared when that time came lent an urgency to his actions that Crowe and other Cacti officers admired and that seemed to rub off on his officers in the same way that Major Rahmdel's passivity and helplessness had pervaded the 2/2 battalion.[64] With Turab at Blessing and Crowe there supporting him, it was the first time during the deployment that Colin Tuley had felt good about the Pech's security prospects.[65]

It seemed to the Americans at Blessing that Turab did more in his first month there than Rahmdel had been able to during his whole time in command. "He was an actual partner, someone you felt like you were dealing with who was on the same page as you," Crowe said of the soft-spoken ANA officer.[66] Holding frequent *shuras* at the district center, he would berate elders for failing to keep the Taliban out of their communities, and he wasted no time in sending troops out on regular patrols to show a daily presence at least out to the distance from which insurgents were firing rockets and mortars. When one of the patrols got into a firefight, the advisers would step outside and listen to the crackle of gunfire and wait for Turab to tell them whether his men had the situation in hand or needed air support from American Kiowas or Apaches. "He was not going to put up with being shot at all the time and sitting there as a target," the leader of the small adviser team that worked with the colonel and his staff said.[67]

Turab had no interest in big offensive operations, which he knew his battalion would never be in a position to conduct on their own. "He'd never say, 'We need to go do a giant operation up in that valley.' He'd say, 'Well, if we could kill this one guy in that valley, that would be good,'" remembered Crowe, who was impressed by the network of local informants and nuanced attitude that allowed Turab to focus on particular militants in a Taliban-controlled village rather than painting the whole place as hostile.[68] Instead, Turab's version of counterinsurgency resembled the ink-blot approach that American units had pursued early in the campaign in Pech—a war of daily patrols and incremental progress, only now with Afghan troops, not Americans, doing most of the work.

.   .   .

The Pech valley, looking southeast, in the direction of Asadabad. Nangalam is in the lower middle. The mouth of the Waygal valley, where it joins the Pech, is at the lower left, while the Korengal valley is on the far side of the easternmost of the three spurs visible on the right.

PHOTOGRAPH BY BILL OSTLUND

FOB Blessing in 2004.
PHOTOGRAPH BY RON FRY

FOB Blessing in 2010.
AUTHOR'S PHOTOGRAPH

A CH-47 Chinook lands near Aranas in the Waygal valley during Operation Mountain Resolve in November 2003.
U.S. ARMY PHOTOGRAPH BY SGT. GREG HEATH

Rangers patrol through a valley in Nuristan during Operation Winter Strike in November 2003, when the Army's 1st and 2nd Ranger Battalions deployed on short notice to the Pech and its tributaries.
PHOTOGRAPH COURTESY OF BRIAN GARGANTA

Captain Ron Fry (in T-shirt) of Special Forces A-team 936 eats with teammates and district officials, 2004. PHOTOGRAPH BY SCOTT JENNINGS

The May 2004 ceremony at which the base established during Winter Strike was named in honor of slain Ranger Sergeant Jay Blessing. A-team 936's "indig" militiamen are at left, in tiger-stripe camouflage. PHOTOGRAPH BY ERIC ELIASON

An aviator from the 160th Special Operations Aviation Regiment speaks at the Bagram Airfield memorial ceremony for the eight Night Stalkers killed when the MH-47 Chinook Turbine 33 was shot down during Operation Red Wings on June 28, 2005. PHOTOGRAPH COURTESY OF BRIAN GARGANTA

Lieutenant Colonel Chris Cavoli, 1–32 Infantry battalion commander (left), promotes Bravo Company commander Doug Sloan (right) from captain to major during the company's push into the Waygal valley in June 2006.
PHOTOGRAPH COURTESY OF CHRIS CAVOLI

The view south from a machine-gun bunker at Firebase Phoenix in the Korengal valley.
U.S. ARMY PHOTOGRAPH BY SPC. JASON MACE

Lieutenant Colonel Bill Ostlund, 2-503 Infantry battalion commander (right), speaks to the elders of Yakha China during Operation Rock Avalanche in October 2007. Captain Dan Kearney of Battle Company stands in the background.

PHOTOGRAPH BY BALAZS GARDI

Paratroopers from Battle Company, 2-503 Infantry, near COP Vegas in the Korengal, early 2008.

PHOTOGRAPH COURTESY OF IAN MACGREGOR

Specialist Kyle White stands on the trail outside Aranas minutes before insurgents ambushed his platoon of Chosen Company, 2-503 Infantry, on November 9, 2007, killing five paratroopers and a Marine.

U.S. ARMY PHOTOGRAPH

Left: COP Bella in the Waygal valley, established in the summer of 2006 and closed two years later. PHOTOGRAPH BY BILL OSTLUND. *Right:* Want (known to American troops as Wanat), the town where nine paratroopers were killed on July 13, 2008. The field where Chosen Company would establish its short-lived outpost is in the lower middle right, bounded on the left by the road, opposite the terraces where the paratroopers built OP Topside. U.S. ARMY PHOTOGRAPH

The view from COP Vegas after the Chinook Flex 64 crash-landed in the Korengal, killing Sergeant Ezra Dawson, in January 2009. PHOTOGRAPH BY MIKEL DRNEC

Lieutenant Colonel Brett Jenkinson, the 1-26 Infantry battalion commander who advocated pulling out of the Korengal in 2008–2009, during a visit to the main outpost there, the KOP. PHOTOGRAPH BY CLIFF PEDERSON

Lieutenant Colonel Joe Ryan, 1-327 Infantry battalion commander, in the operations center at COP Michigan, July 2010.
AUTHOR'S PHOTOGRAPH

A mural in a Kandigal home depicting a Chinook helicopter and air strikes by U.S. fighter jets, February 2010. PHOTOGRAPH COURTESY OF GABE DEARMAN

A Chinook removes a howitzer from FOB Blessing during the Pech "realignment" in late February or early March 2011. PHOTOGRAPH BY JONATHAN SPRINGER

The Watapur valley, scene of Operations Bulldog Bite in November 2010 and Hammer Down in June 2011.

AUTHOR'S PHOTOGRAPH

ANA advisor Captain Hugh Miller of 2-12 Infantry stands with a group of Afghan soldiers from the 6/2 battalion during his second Pech deployment, in 2012.

PHOTOGRAPH COURTESY OF HUGH MILLER

General John "Mick" Nicholson (left) poses with General Joseph Votel (middle) and Colonel Bill Ostlund (right) at Jalalabad Airfield in 2016. All three officers had previous experience in Kunar and Nuristan—Nicholson in 2006–2007, when he oversaw the U.S. military expansion in the provinces, and the other two in 2007–2008, when Ostlund commanded 2-503 Infantry in the Pech and Votel was the deputy Regional Command East commander at Bagram. Votel and Ostlund both oversaw later JSOC targeting in the region.

PHOTOGRAPH BY DAVE HODNE

IF JOB NUMBER one was pushing the Taliban out of Blessing's immediate environs, the bigger task—the one Turab knew he had to accomplish before American support went away again—was reestablishing a ground supply route between Nangalam and Asadabad on the Pech road. The farthest his troops could patrol from Blessing and count on mortar support was Sundray; coming the other direction from Able Main, where two ANA companies remained without advisers, they could go as far as Tarale. In between was a four-mile red zone, centered on the mouths of the Korengal and Shuryak valleys, that neither American nor ANA convoys could drive through without being hit by IEDs and ambushes. The first time Crowe made the trip through what he and the other advisers called "the gap," he was shocked to see that erosion and neglect had left the road a good six feet narrower than when he'd last driven on it in 2009 and that IED craters were everywhere; for routine moves between his company's two outposts, Blessing and Honaker-Miracle, he had to take a helicopter.[69] Some of the bombs were huge, larger than had been seen in the Pech in years; without routine patrols and convoys to disturb them in the gap, militants were able to take their time, pouring tar onto the road and lighting it on fire to melt through the pavement and create a hole that would fit enough explosives to obliterate a Humvee.[70] But where Rahmdel had simply given up on venturing into the danger zone, Turab had barely been in command a month when he sent a convoy out to brave the Pech gap's bombs and ambushes under the protection of American helicopters—an initial step whose boldness encouraged the advisers.[71]

On base, Crowe paired his platoons up with Turab's companies and tried to match the daily tasks of soldiering that the troops were performing so that the Americans were doing maintenance on their MRAPs at the same time that the Afghans were working on their Humvees, for instance, to model good maintenance habits. For Thanksgiving, Turab brought a live turkey up to the American part of the base as a gift and shared a meal with the advisers.[72] But from Crowe's perspective, the most important work of advising was that done outside the wire, on joint patrols and other missions where his troops initially accompanied the Afghans at a one-to-one ratio and then gradually decreased their own numbers as the ANA grew more assertive and proficient. "We weren't sitting inside the wire running ranges for the ANA," the Gundog Company commander said. "It was learning by doing. If you don't patrol, you're nowhere."[73]

That work remained dangerous for the American troops doing it; advising Afghan troops in the Pech was still a combat mission, even as more frequent patrolling cut down the number and size of IEDs on the road and drew firefights away from Blessing and Honaker-Miracle. When Gundog Company convoys traversed the gap, they would pick off Taliban machine-gun positions on the slopes above them with the antitank missiles mounted on some of their vehicles, just as Chosin battalion troops in the Pech had done five years earlier. Soldiers were wounded during the continued rocket attacks on Blessing, including a platoon leader who had to be medevaced from Blessing, and they were wounded out on patrol. Crowe was willing to accept risk in the small-unit, ink-blot fighting because that seemed like the only way for the war to *end*. Crowe himself was shot and medevaced out during a routine patrol in February. He was out with an American platoon and an Afghan platoon when a Taliban fighter started firing from the road, and although he was standing behind an ANA Humvee, a bullet ricocheted off a rock and struck his lower leg, breaking both bones. The wound would require seven surgeries to repair between the field hospital at FOB Asadabad and Fort Sam Houston in Texas, and more later.

A month after Crowe was shot, another Gundog Company officer was wounded, this time fatally. On March 15, as the Cacti battalion's deployment was entering its final days, Second Lieutenant Clovis Ray got out of his MRAP during a routine security patrol a few kilometers up the Waygal to guide his driver through the precarious process of turning the hulking truck around on the narrow mountain road. Whether he stepped on an IED or was sprayed with shrapnel from an incoming RPG wasn't clear to the soldiers still inside their MRAPs, but they managed to get their badly wounded platoon leader back to Blessing and onto a medevac Black Hawk.

A thirty-four-year-old former San Antonio investment banker, Ray had taken his family by surprise when he enlisted and went to Officer Candidate School, and ever since joining the battalion in Kunar in December, he'd been itching for a chance to get out to the Pech and lead infantrymen in combat. He died in surgery at FOB

Asadabad, leaving behind a wife and a five-year-old son—the sixth American death in the Pech and its tributaries since the Bulldog battalion's short-lived departure from Blessing a year earlier.[74]

BY THE TIME of Clovis Ray's death, a new infantry company and team of advisers were starting to arrive in the Pech to replace the Cacti troops in the small-unit war.

To Loren Crowe and many others who fought in Kunar and the Pech over the years, the story of American involvement there was a story about the Army's inability to retain knowledge—about how it had to keep learning the same lessons over and over as new units rotated through, like the lesson that big air-assault missions were more trouble than they were worth. The closest the service got to solving this problem was when it sent officers or units back to the same place for multiple tours. This tended to happen only by co-incidence or through the individual initiative of soldiers like Crowe who pulled strings to get back to a battlefield that had been forma-tive to them. But by 2012, the war had dragged on for so long that it was happening more and more. By the luck of the draw, the new unit that took over at Blessing and Honaker-Miracle that April had been in the Pech before: Dagger Company, 2-12 Infantry, from the 4th Brigade, 4th Infantry Division, which had spent a year there in 2009 and 2010, some of its platoons living at COP Michigan and one of them in the Korengal as the long entanglement there came to an end.

The company commander and platoon leaders hadn't been on that deployment, but many of the NCOs had, and by chance one platoon sergeant had even been in the Pech back when Blessing was first established in November 2003. To many of these soldiers, as it had to Crowe, the scaled-down advisory approach made intuitive sense as the way to get out of the Pech for good.[75]

Among the 4/4 ID troops arriving at Blessing was another cap-tain who, like Crowe, had been there as a lieutenant and finagled a way to return, this time as an ANA adviser attached to Dagger Company. A former lacrosse player from outside Baltimore, Hugh Miller had gone to the U.S. Air Force Academy in Colorado Springs, only to commission into the Army infantry after graduation, drawn by a desire to see ground combat at the height of the post–September 11 wars. Leading infantrymen in the Pech as a 4/4 ID platoon leader in 2009 and 2010 had enthralled Miller, and he fell hard for Kunar's wild beauty, intense gunfights, and edge-of-the-empire feel.[76] On the deployment's most exciting day, he and his platoon had ventured a little farther up the Waygal than they were supposed to and wound up in a firefight with a group of Arabs, including one whose fingerprints, collected postmortem, matched a military database showing he'd previously fought in Iraq.[77]

Back at Fort Carson afterward in a dull staff job, Miller had persuaded his superiors to put him on a newly formed four-soldier adviser team, remembering the independence the Marine ANA advisers at Blessing had enjoyed in 2009 and seeing in the news that advising, not U.S.-led combat operations, was the future of the mission in Afghanistan. He'd harbored hopes of seeing the Pech again, and to find himself back there in the spring of 2012 on an adviser team with a more senior officer and two NCOs was a dream come true.[78]

During his last stint at Blessing, Miller had sometimes been awed by the sheer incompetence of the ANA contingent there; he remembered watching in amazement as Afghan troops stuffed rocks down the barrels of their newly issued grenade launchers. The soldiers of the 6/2 battalion were operating at a much higher speed, able to organize and mount patrols on short notice and hold their own in small firefights. Miller found he and his team didn't need to spend time teaching the ANA basic infantry skills or supervising them on patrol, leaving that work to the four Dagger Company platoons split between Blessing and Honaker-Miracle. Nor did Turab need any help with the kinds of counterinsurgency tasks that American officers often struggled with, like dealing with elders and the police force; those came more naturally to him than to any U.S. commander Miller had worked with last time around. Instead, the adviser team worked with Turab to integrate the work of his platoons into a more cohesive whole that, they hoped, would be able to impose control on the Pech gap by the end of the year. Turab would wake Miller and the other advisers early each morning at their quarters in what had been the base's USAID building in the Pech's road-building heyday, then huddle with them for a ten o'clock meeting to go over the day's training and patrol schedules.[79]

The skills the advisers wanted to imprint on Turab's troops before they left included logistics, vehicle maintenance, bomb disposal, and the ability to fire their D-30 howitzers to support patrols out in the valley. Some of these nuts proved harder to crack than others.

Miller scored a win, over months of effort, with the D-30s—small, Soviet-made artillery pieces that the advisers were surprised to find sitting in disuse by the Blessing landing zone with weeds growing around them and no trained operators in the ANA battalion. Miller didn't know much about howitzers either, but he threw himself into learning, with help from a 4/4 ID field artillery sergeant who visited Blessing now and again to dole out technical expertise. Every day, the Afghan troops Miller was trying to turn into artillerymen would practice firing the guns at the big mountain north of base, and then he and an NCO would help a pair of sergeants with their map-reading skills. Eventually, the crews not only learned to fire beyond their line of sight but grew confident enough at it that the ANA preferred calling for fire from their own howitzers over Dagger Company's mortars. Every time the D-30s fired, the Afghan troops watching would dance and cheer.[80]

Bomb disposal was tougher. The American approach to finding and destroying IEDs was high-tech—mine detectors with ground-penetrating radar, backpack jammers to block the signals that triggered many of the bombs, and robots to dismantle the deadly devices. None of that was going to be available to Afghan troops once the Americans were gone, so Miller had an American combat engineer fly out to teach "land-mine detection techniques from fucking World War I," using unsophisticated tools the Afghans could rely on. Miller's heart would sink before a patrol as he watched a Dagger Company infantryman strap a high-tech IED jammer onto his back while the painfully courageous Afghan bomb technician he'd trained went out with nothing but a bare-bones metal detector and a utility knife. The bomb-disposal training ended a month later after a patrol a couple of miles from Blessing. Someone spotted a bomb, and the young ANA bomb tech crawled over to it through a ditch and started inspecting the device, but before he could cut a wire in the hopes of rendering it inert, a triggerman somewhere nearby detonated it, killing the Afghan soldier. "After that, we just trained the officers in detection and basically told them, 'If you see an IED, just fucking shoot it with anything you have, grenades, RPGs, .50-cal, whatever,'" Miller remembered with frustration.[81]

TO START CLOSING the gap and open the Pech as a reliable ground supply route, Turab knew, he first had to bring Shamun and Sundray into the ink blot. The pair of Taliban-controlled villages across the river from each other just east of Blessing, where the Green Berets and Marines had gone to get in scraps back in 2004 and 2005, were still Mullah Dawran's home turf, and they represented the edge of the gap. After taking a conciliatory approach to the bumbling 2/2 battalion, Dawran was telling his men to be ruthless in fighting Turab's more effective unit. "I want to tell all mujahidin to prioritize the local traitors because these soldiers are the eyes of the foreigners. Their damage is more," Dawran told an Al Jazeera correspondent that spring, referring to Turab's troops. He compared the ANA to young trees, suggesting they had to be killed before they grew more powerful. "When the Americans leave, they leave us these saplings," he said. "We want to uproot them so they dry out."[82]

Every couple of months, Turab would gather as many of his platoons as he could and push into either Shamun or Sundray to raid houses Dawran was thought to use, but it was a dangerous endeavor. One day in August, Miller was tagging along with one of Turab's companies on a mission in Shamun when an IED pulverized an ANA Humvee, and insurgents waiting in the high corn on the side of the road gunned down one of the Afghan soldiers who ran into the open to try to check for survivors in the burning hulk. Six Afghan soldiers died that day in Shamun, half the total the battalion would lose during Miller's deployment, and he remembered thinking, as he tried to comfort the devastated ANA company commander, that if they had been Americans, the deaths would have made the newspaper. Because they were Afghans, the incident went unnoticed outside the Pech and the villages around the country from which the six soldiers had hailed.[83]

To drive the whole Pech road and reach Asadabad for a resupply run was called shooting the gap. Massing as many men and vehicles as he could for safety in numbers, and relying on the advisers to arrange overhead cover from Kiowas and Apaches, Turab had shot the gap once in the spring as Dagger Company and the 4/4 ID advisers were arriving, and the battalion did it again in June, running the gauntlet with more than a hundred Humvees and other trucks. In September, after a summer of practice using their own artillery to support patrols, the ANA did another run, and this one "they did 95 percent on their own. They didn't need a lot and we really just sat back," remembered a more senior adviser who monitored the operation from the ANA brigade commander's headquarters outside the valley, where Afghan staff officers were receiving progress updates from the convoy in the field by cell phone and the American advisers were watching its progress via drone feed.

With the ANA howitzers firing from Blessing, Asadabad, and Honaker-Miracle, the big convoy made not just one or two round-trips this time but six or seven, because they weren't just bringing out supplies; the mission was bringing reinforcements into the Pech, a whole second battalion of them. The new unit, Lieutenant Colonel Asef Naseri's 6/1 ANA battalion, drove as far as Honaker-Miracle, relieving half of the 6/2 battalion of its duties there so that Turab's troops could consolidate deeper in the valley at Blessing.

With twice as many Afghan troops in the Pech and Turab's men confidently firing their howitzers and patrolling ever more frequently to the edge of the gap, the Dagger Company officers and advisers at Blessing started to get ready to leave. Every time Ben Walker, the company commander, talked to Turab or the 6/2 company commanders, he asked about the progress of their artillery crews, mentally checking what he heard against his own company's tentative withdrawal timeline.[84] Compared with the big pullout in 2011, this one would be quicker, because the troops occupying Blessing for the scaled-down advisory mission had been living without most of the creature comforts earlier units had enjoyed there. But it would have to stick this time: no one was going to send American troops to live at Nangalam again, no matter what happened to the ANA there.

. . .

AS DAGGER COMPANY was getting ready to leave, Turab and his counterpart on the far side of the gap, the 6/1 battalion commander, Naseri, were planning their next move, and it wasn't one that all of their advisers were eager to see. With more than a thousand Afghan troops in the valley, Turab, Naseri, and their brigade commander wanted to close the gap for good, and they wanted to keep it closed by scattering small, fortified outposts and checkpoints the whole length of the Pech road, far more of them than the Americans had ever manned in the valley.

Hugh Miller and his superior on the adviser team, Major Jay Bullock, were skeptical. By tying their troops down on roadside outposts, they worried, the newly reinforced ANA in the Pech would lose any ability to go after the enemy in the side valleys. Worse, any outpost in the Pech was necessarily surrounded by high ground and vulnerable both to the kind of constant harassing fire that I'd witnessed during my first visit to COP Michigan in 2010 and to massed assaults from the heights like those at Blessing in 2004, Combat Main in 2006, the Ranch House in 2007, and Want and COP Vegas in 2008. American troops had been able to fend off those attacks with the help of their umbrella of jets, drones, attack helicopters, and artillery. ANA outposts, in the same positions, would have their D-30 howitzers and little else.[85] "We had two long conversations with them, like, 'Can you do this? Are you really sure?'" remembered Miller. "Right before they started putting the bases in, we had the second one, saying, 'It's not too late,' and reminding them that they had lost twelve guys in the past few months just around Nangalam and they wouldn't have air support anymore."[86]

But for Turab, Naseri, and their brigade commander at FOB Joyce, the way to secure the Pech road was to keep every inch of it under continuous observation, and without drones, attack helicopters, or surveillance-camera towers the only way to do that was by building one outpost after another between Blessing and Honaker-Miracle, close enough to each other that each little garrison could see its neighbors to the east and west with the naked eye.

The speed with which it all happened took Miller and the other advisers by surprise. "Tomorrow we're going to go out and test the enemy," Turab told Miller's teammate Bullock one day soon after the September resupply mission. The next day half the ANA at Blessing drove out into Sundray and Tantil and fought the Taliban for six hours. That evening, Turab, heartened by his men's performance during the day's gunfights, walked into the advisers' quarters and announced that the battalion was going back out again the next day, and this time staying out.[87]

In the morning, while Turab watched from one of the OPs above Blessing with Bullock arranging limited American air support at his side, nearly the whole battalion ventured out of Blessing in Humvees. As the big convoy crept east, it left some troops in Shamun, others in Tantil, and came to a halt in Kandigal at the mouth of the Korengal, the dangerous middle of the gap. At each site, the Afghan troops staked out perimeters with their Humvees and started filling Hesco barriers and digging in.[88]

Over the next couple of weeks, Hugh Miller would drive out and watch as the Afghan troops built up their new outposts, sometimes staying a night or two before returning to the safety of Blessing while the Afghans braced themselves for the inevitable Taliban response. After building up their base in Shamun, they pushed across the river into Sundray and repeated the procedure, fortifying a pair of houses owned by a pro-government resident whose son was an ANA officer elsewhere in the country. For Tantil, they built an observation post looking down into town first, then a larger base in the town itself. Miller and the Dagger Company soldiers didn't accompany the 6/2 troops farther than that; if they had, they would have seen that in Kandigal, the ANA were building a new outpost right on top of where the old American one, COP Michigan, had been, and that the construction even included lumber, marked "KOP," that had somehow made its way from the grounds of the old Korengal Outpost.[89]

Dagger Company's mortarmen joined the ANA artillery crews in quieting enemy machine-gun positions that harassed the outpost builders the first few nights, and the company's air controller arranged for A-10s to fly low over the valley; if the jets were available for a couple of hours in the evening, Turab would have his men carry out their most dangerous construction tasks during that window. But by the time the new walls of the Kandigal base were rising in the second week of October, it was time for the Americans to go, this time for good, as they took a second shot at executing the re-traction in the Pech that Joe Ryan had initiated two years earlier.

The scouts and mortarmen left by helicopter after dark on the night of October 10, and then it was just sixty infantrymen and advisers left in a circle of sixteen MRAPs around the landing zone. With most of the Afghan troops out at the new outposts in the Pech, the base was quiet. Around midnight, the adviser team leader, Bullock, walked around the base and gave Turab the keys to the buildings the Americans had been using before parting with a hug. Then the Americans climbed aboard their MRAPs and left, driving past the new ANA outposts in the dark as they passed Sundray and the mouth of the Korengal, where one truck rolled over in a big IED crater and the convoy had to make a tense stop to recover it. Then they were on their way again, relocating to Honaker-Miracle, where U.S. troops would remain for the time being.[90]

THE CALL OF THE WAYGAL

The Pech would remain one of the most violent places in Afghani-stan in 2013.[91] But when I visited Asef Naseri's 6/1 ANA battalion for a brief embed that March, the valley seemed quiet, at least in comparison to the last time I'd been there, with Joe Ryan's troops in 2010. Driving out to 6/1 battalion headquarters at Honaker-Miracle from Asadabad in an ANA pickup truck, my interpreter, Farshad, and I passed one bunker-like strongpoint after another, all built as part of the big push since the fall, and when we joined the Afghan troops on foot patrols into what had been the gap, we quickly hit the next outpost after a brief, uneventful walk. ANA convoys were driving between Blessing and Asadabad as a matter of routine.

While Turab had been building outposts eastward from Blessing, Naseri had been building westward; his unit's greatest accomplish-ment had been wresting control of Matin, the village at the mouth of the Shuryak, from the Taliban and putting a base there. But my introduction to him at his headquarters illustrated that just as with U.S. Army battalions the personality and approach of the com-manders could create a world of difference between two otherwise identical units. In a war of village conflicts and local grievances, Naseri lacked Turab's nuanced understanding and sensitive touch.

Tall, mustached, and with eyes that darted quickly around him, Naseri seemed unpredictable and hotheaded. As Farshad and I arrived at Honaker-Miracle, we could hear gunfire across the river, and when Naseri sat down with us a little later, he explained that one of his soldiers had been shot in the stomach during a raid. "Fucking Taliban," he complained to me in English, before adding, "The Taliban, they should all be killed. If they have a long beard, we should kill them." At his direction, a soldier produced the weapons they'd captured during the raid for me to photograph: a pistol, an assault rifle, and two bolt-action rifles.

Then the religious officer of the district police force arrived—the police station's chaplain, essentially, a uniformed mullah named Sayed Rahman Rahman—and began to argue with Naseri in Pashto before turning to me and Farshad and conveying a different version of what had just happened. The house the ANA had targeted had belonged to a family that was loyal to the government, he said, and during the raid they'd killed an off-duty policeman who was home on leave from his post in another dangerous part of the country. The soldiers had also raided Rahman's own house, he explained, and confiscated his family's self-defense weapons, which had been sitting in plain sight, over a discrepancy in their registration paperwork. These were the weapons on the table that Naseri had presented to me as captured from the enemy, and Rahman wanted them back.

"You guys pick up weapons from a fellow government person's house and then show it off to a foreigner as a good achievement," Rahman scoffed. "If I were defense minister, I'd promote you to general!"

As Rahman stormed off, Naseri disparaged him to me. "How do we know if he is a policeman during the day and an insurgent at night?" he asked. "He has a beard like an insurgent; it's a meter long." After Farshad and I went across the road to talk to the district governor, Haji Zalmay—the towering official who had worked with every American commander in the Pech since Chris Cavoli in 2006—Naseri accused Zalmay of being "fucking Taliban" too. It was without apparent irony that he added, during a patrol I tagged along on later in the day, that he was proud of maintaining good relations with the locals.

Although ISAF headquarters in Kabul had disapproved my request to embed with them, the 101st Airborne Division advisers at Honaker-Miracle allowed me to stop by the smaller, more heavily fortified compound they'd occupied since relieving Dagger Company in December. This inner compound was centered on a flagpole and a series of plaques commemorating the Americans who had died in the Pech just like the memorial I'd seen at Blessing three years before. The eighty soldiers there came mostly from Alligator Company of 2-327 Infantry, a sister 101st Airborne unit that had spent its last deployment in eastern Kunar while 1-327, the Bulldog battalion, was in the Pech.*

Alligator Company's commander was yet another Kunar veteran, a former West Point football player named Brandon Newkirk who had led a Viper Company platoon at COP Vegas in the Korengal while his fellow Blue Spader lieutenant, Loren Crowe, had been in the east of the province and then at Blessing. Like Hugh Miller, Newkirk had found the violent deployment to be a dream come true, exactly the kind of fighting he'd hoped to see when he branched infantry. When he moved to the 101st and learned that his new company was headed back to Kunar, he'd both wanted to wind up at Honaker-Miracle, the closest remaining outpost to his old haunts, and felt guilty for wanting it.[92]

Like Crowe and Miller, Newkirk enjoyed working directly with the ANA, seeing it as a more complex and probably more useful evolution of the type of soldiering he'd done last time around. Along with a small team of dedicated advisers from the brigade's cavalry squadron, he spent the bulk of his time on base, helping the Afghan troops sort out issues like maintenance and resupply requests. Firewood and Hesco barriers were the items in greatest demand, and

---

* The brigade commander—a 2nd Ranger Battalion veteran who had known Jay Blessing—opted for Alligator Company because he feared that ill will and bad memories from the last Pech deployment would outweigh the benefits of institutional knowledge if he sent one of the Bulldog battalion's companies back to the valley. "There was no way I was sending guys from 1st Battalion back to the Pech," he told me. "The withdrawal from the Pech had been a very emotional event for them."

Newkirk and the advisers tried to help Naseri and his officers master the paperwork required to get them from brigade or corps headquarters. (American troops were not supposed to give the ANA any supplies directly, but after Newkirk learned that some of the Afghan Humvee gunners were lubricating their .50-caliber machine guns with diesel, he broke the rule and gave them some U.S. Army–issued lubricant.)[93]

When Newkirk and his infantrymen did go out on patrol, about every other day, they trailed behind Naseri's soldiers and focused mainly on trying to keep track of where all the Afghan troops and their outposts were, because the ANA had a tendency to "just kind of wind up everywhere" outside the wire. The number of little bases, checkpoints, and observation posts in the valley kept growing; it was up to seventeen at the beginning of March, by Newkirk's count, a number it had taken him several weeks to ascertain after arriving. Although there were gunfights somewhere in the eastern Pech on a daily basis, Alligator Company rarely found itself involved in them; outside the wire, Newkirk preferred that only his snipers fire their weapons, for fear of mistakenly shooting an Afghan soldier or policeman who popped up somewhere unexpected.[94]

Newkirk often wondered what the enemy was doing instead of fighting. "I think a kind of a symbiotic relationship has developed between them and the Taliban," he told me of the ANA. The Taliban acknowledged that with their string of outposts Turab's and Naseri's battalions controlled the Pech road and didn't contest it except with occasional probing attacks. But venture beyond certain invisible lines in the Shuryak or the Watapur, and things would get ugly fast, so the ANA didn't go up the side valleys at all unless specifically ordered to do so by their brigade commander back at FOB Joyce. That obviously wasn't how American troops had approached the side valleys when they were in the Pech, but it seemed like a reasonable approach to Newkirk, especially because he knew JSOC's Task Force East was launching its own strikes against al-Qaida figures up in the tributaries. "They know where the red lines are, and they just don't cross them," he told me of the ANA. "I think that's what success is going to look like in the end for them."[95]

But Newkirk worried that people higher in the Afghan chain of command would disturb the balance the ANA were working out with the Taliban on the ground, forcing them into new missions they weren't ready for. "You've got politicians in Kabul who've got really different priorities from the ANA," he observed.[96]

NEWKIRK WAS RIGHT. The side valley that would soon draw the ANA in against their will was, yet again, the Waygal, where the last foray by government troops had been the ill-fated Operation Fire Rock.

The Afghan government's insistence on not only keeping troops in the Pech but adding another battalion and cramming the valley with outposts had puzzled some Americans, who wished that the ANA would just pull out of the valley the way the United States had. "I never could really get a solid answer on why they felt they needed to be out there, other than that the government wanted them out there," remembered an adviser of his conversations with Turab and other ANA commanders about the Pech during this period. "We'd ask why it was important, and they'd just say it *was* important and that they needed to secure it for the people. Since they were there and they weren't going anywhere, we'd leave it at that and focus on how to make them successful."[97] But when orders started coming down from Kabul for the ANA to get ready for a fresh offensive up the Waygal to Want—which had fallen back under Taliban control within months of Fire Rock—some Americans who remembered the difficulties and tragedies of their involvement there over the years tried to head the operation off.

In the weeks after my March visit to the Pech, orders reached the ANA brigade commander for Kunar and Nuristan at FOB Joyce, Colonel Hayatullah Aqtash, telling him to prepare for a mission to retake Want—an ANA version of Fire Rock, but this time leaving behind soldiers and policemen and a string of outposts like the ones Turab and Naseri had built in the Pech over the past six months. Hayatullah argued against the idea, telling corps headquarters that such an operation would be dangerous and of limited value, but as with Fire Rock two years earlier, the impetus for the mission was coming from the top.[98] Nuristan's on-and-off governor, Tamim Nuristani, was out of a job again, fired over another corruption scandal, but the pressure on Karzai and his defense ministry from the new governor and Nuristan's parliamentarians remained strong: the province was full of district centers that had effectively been ceded to the enemy, including Want, and the Nuristani officials wanted them retaken. "There would be these phone calls from the chief of staff of the army and the minister of defense to the 201st Corps commander saying, 'We want you in Nuristan tomorrow.' It was ridiculous," remembered an adviser to the ANA corps responsible for the northeast.[99]

But with Karzai himself telling his top generals they needed to retake Want, a plan for an operation began to take shape, involving Turab's 6/2 ANA battalion as well as a battalion of the well-regarded paramilitary Civil Order Police because no ANA Commandos were available.

In Kabul, the American corps commander in charge of advisory operations was no stranger to the difficulties of operating in places like the Waygal, and he argued against the mission. Lieutenant General Mark Milley, the gruff, Princeton-educated future chairman of the Joint Chiefs, had first come to Afghanistan in 2003 as a colonel advising the ANA in its infancy. He'd been back as a one-star with Regional Command East at the time of the deadly 2008 battle, flying up to Blessing that morning while the fighting was still raging to offer any support he could. The battle of Want had burned into Milley's mind the risks of overextension in the narrow side valleys of Kunar and Nuristan. "It is hard-pressed for me to argue that forces should be up there," he told CENTCOM investigators afterward. "When we do put forces up in all of those valleys, they get fixed by the enemy in these little COPs."[100]

Milley made his case just a couple of days before the operation was scheduled to launch in a meeting with Minister of Defense Bismillah Khan Mohammadi and his uniformed counterpart, General Sher Mohammad Karimi. "I talked to them at length about the cost and benefit of putting a *kandak* [battalion] up there, and they said, 'Thank you very much for your advice, but we're going to do it anyway,' and they asked for attack helicopters and other support," Milley remembered of the meeting. "In some ways it seemed to come down to pride: 'We don't want to yield one piece of territory to the enemy.'"[101] Karimi had just gone before parliament and told the lawmakers that his troops were ready to go. "I gave my promise to parliament that we would do the operation," he explained. "The only person who could stop this operation is President Karzai—no one else."[102]

Milley asked his civilian political adviser—a lawyer named Matt Sherman who had been working as a de facto diplomat for American commanders in Afghanistan since 2009—to explain what his Afghan counterparts and their president were thinking. The paper Sherman wrote about what was pulling the Afghan government back to the Waygal in the face of so many practical military obstacles read as if it could have been written in 2011 or 2006. "For two years, Waygal and its district center have been under enemy control. As a result, Waygal has become a symbol of the [Karzai] regime's weakness," Sherman wrote. "The Waygal operation is all about psychology," he quoted the political opposition leader and future president Ashraf Ghani saying.[103]

Turab had recently been suspended from command, to the frustration of the American advisers who'd come to admire him, but in his absence his 6/2 ANA battalion and the Civil Order Police headed up the Waygal in Humvees and pickup trucks on June 6.* A team of 101st Airborne advisers, including Bryan Laske, a Green Beret lieutenant colonel I'd met in Kunar in March, flew out to Blessing with Hayatullah, the ANA brigade commander, to monitor the operation from 6/2 battalion headquarters. As reports came in by radio and drones watched from overhead, Laske was impressed: the Afghan troops fought through barrages from DShK heavy machine guns in the mountains without stopping and made it halfway to Want by the end of the day. The only American support came in the form of surveillance footage that helped guide the fire of the ANA's own howitzers, a couple of low passes by fighter jets to intimidate the enemy, and a drone strike deeper in the valley—coordinated by the SEALs of JSOC's Task Force East—that killed a local Taliban commander and seemed to cause the defending mili-

---

* Turab's suspension, from which he would not end up returning, was punishment for something that had happened as a direct result of the Afghan strategy of relying on small, fixed-site outposts: Taliban fighters had gotten inside the wire of one of the new strongpoints in the Pech and made off with some mortars and machine guns, an embarrassment for which someone in the chain of command had to take the fall.

tants to disperse. "The ANA were ecstatic about that," remembered Laske. "It gave them a big confidence boost."[104]

Moving into Want itself on the afternoon of June 7 after ANA engineers cleared rockfall and erosion from the road outside town, the government troops reoccupied the district center and police station. The reception in town, Hayatullah reported back to Laske after heading up himself for a visit, was neither hostile nor cordial. The elders at a *shura* offered the same kinds of assurances of support for the government that they always did when the government was around.[105]

After a week, the bulk of the two-battalion force pulled out of the Waygal. But a company of ANA stayed, building new outposts on hilltops along the mountainside road between Nangalam and Want, while the Civil Order Police built fighting positions at the town's intersections and the exiled district police chief moved back in with his men.[106]

Some American officers had been expecting the Taliban to put up a tougher fight for Want up front, just as the planners of Fire Rock had, and were similarly surprised by the anticlimax. "We all collectively thought it was a fucking bad idea, but they went and did it and did a pretty darn good job of doing it," said the U.S. brigade commander for the northeast at the time, who watched by drone at Jalalabad in the days that followed as the Afghan troops strung concertina wire and stacked sandbags at the new positions, extending the ink blot with the same tactics they'd used in the Pech.[107]

Drew Poppas, the 101st Airborne officer who had overseen the Pech "realignment" as Joe Ryan's brigade commander, was back in eastern Afghanistan as a one-star, in the same deputy division commander job that Mark Milley had held during the battle of Want and Gary Volesky had held during Fire Rock. Poppas was impressed with the government troops' ability to pull the operation off, but he knew that the hard part would be what came afterward, when insurgents starting testing the little chain of outposts. "Well, once you're up there, that's when you're isolated," Poppas remembered objecting to the Civil Order Police commander's confident, and accurate, prediction that the move into town would go smoothly.[108]

"The real reasons for the ease of the operation remain a matter of speculation," wrote Matt Sherman, Milley's political adviser, in an internal paper in the immediate aftermath. "It may be that the ANSF [Afghan National Security Forces] have reached some sort of local accommodation with the insurgents, or it may be that the enemy is waiting to see and assess the situation before taking action"[109]—the approach militants in the Waygal had taken after Mick Nicholson and Chris Cavoli first sent American troops to establish outposts in the valley in 2006, watching quietly for a while before starting to fight back.

IN A RAND paper at the height of Vietnam, the same Green Beret captain who compared the war of endless short deployments to "a recording tape that is erased every twelve months" had worried that American advisers were building a South Vietnamese army in their own military's image, complete with their own military's problems: the focus on body counts, the irrepressible drive for big-unit offensives. "The danger exists that in transferring the war to the Vietnamese, we will transfer also our organization, our style of fighting, and our mistakes," he wrote, "thus rendering the Vietnamese incapable of doing anything different from what we have done, and by which we have achieved only limited success."[110]

The same fear was common among American troops who spent time advising the ANA and other Afghan security forces, and the ANA's insistence on doubling down in the Pech and reviving the war in the Waygal seemed like prime examples. The ink of American ink-blot counterinsurgency had not soaked into the Pech, to use Poppas's analogy from 2010, and there seemed little reason to think the Waygal would prove a more absorbent surface—a valley where U.S. and Afghan government involvement had caused the needless deaths of civilians in one incident after another, from the CIA-directed air strike outside Aranas back in October 2003 that killed the family members of Mawlawi Ghulam Rabbani up through Fire Rock in 2011. This time around, the counterinsurgents on the ground were all Afghans, but the Afghan government had been there all along with the Americans, inextricably linked to their mistakes. Many Waygalis placed equal responsibility for the botched 2003 strike on the United States and on the former communists of the NDS, who they believed had caused the tragedy by giving the CIA false intelligence, and few Want residents drew much distinction between the ANA Commandos and the Green Berets who'd accompanied them when they talked about who was to blame for the mysterious death of Haji Juma Gul during Fire Rock. Why, experienced advisers wondered with frustration, would the ANA recommit to the same battlefields where American units with all their firepower and high-tech advantages had not succeeded?

The mirror-image problem was undeniable—that the U.S. military's unproductive big-unit approach had rubbed off on the ANA and taught Afghan officers bad habits and tactics—and it might have been part of that question's answer. But another part was almost the inverse. Controlling the towns and district centers of the Pech, and the more remote Nuristani district centers like Want to which the Pech provided access, had always been of deep importance to Afghan governors, parliamentarians, and presidents, no matter the American experience fighting for them and no matter the military difficulties involved. Indeed, it was partly for those reasons that they had encouraged American colonels and generals to extend roads and networks of outposts into the Pech and its side valleys in the first place. That American commanders felt burned by those efforts after the losses they'd suffered during them didn't lessen the Karzai government's political need to exert its reach even into places where, from an American viewpoint, it didn't seem militarily feasible or worth the risk.

With the U.S. military role receding from counterinsurgency and battlefield advising to more limited headquarters advising and occasional air strikes, the political adviser Sherman concluded in his paper about the June 2013 Waygal operation, Afghan commanders and security officials were likely to weight the cautionary tactical advice of American officers less heavily than the demands of vocal, unified political constituencies like the Nuristani political leaders who had sold Karzai on sending troops back to Want. American commanders' "definition of success, refined by the years of experience we gained while we led security operations . . . may not be applicable to this or future Afghan-led operations," because for the Karzai government just the initial "perception of success" after moving into a place like Want with relative ease might well satisfy the political goals that had spurred the mission.

"For better or worse," the paper concluded, "the operations in Waygal illustrate how security operations may be carried out in the future."[111]

PART IV

THE NEW COUNTERTERRORISM

2011–2017

Al-Qaida and its affiliates try to gain footholds in some of the most distant and unforgiving places on Earth. . . . [I]t is in this context that the United States has taken lethal, targeted action against al-Qaida and its associated forces, including with remotely piloted aircraft commonly referred to as drones. As was true in previous armed conflicts, this new technology raises profound questions—about who is targeted, and why; about civilian casualties, and the risk of creating new enemies.

—*Barack Obama, May 23, 2013*

Those whose attitude towards the war is most nearly rational are the subject peoples of the disputed territories. To these people the war is simply a continuous calamity which sweeps to and fro over their bodies like a tidal wave. Which side is winning is a matter of complete indifference to them.

—*George Orwell, 1984 (1949)*

CHAPTER 14

HAYMAKER

2011–2013

"WE HAVE A GOOD BATTALION THERE LED BY BROTHER FAROUQ"

During a stint at Bagram as the JSOC task force commander in 2011, Bill Ostlund came face-to-face with the Egyptian al-Qaida operative Abu Ikhlas al-Masri. During his fifteen months in the Pech a few years earlier, Ostlund had known Abu Ikhlas as a tantalizingly elusive adversary whose presence in some village deep in the Korengal or Watapur informants would report only after the fact. Now Abu Ikhlas was sitting on a couch, playing a video game—an inmate in JSOC's wing of the sprawling military prison at Bagram, housed in a comfortable cell reserved for cooperative detainees.

For years before his December 2010 capture, Abu Ikhlas had been the main al-Qaida figure American troops and intelligence officers were chasing in Afghanistan, and now that he was in custody, Ostlund couldn't resist going over to get a look at him up close. "I wanted to see what he looked like, and he just looked like a fifty-year-old Afghan guy," he remembered: a man of average height with a black beard, receding hairline, narrow face, and widely separated eyes.[1]

Because he was chatty and polite—cagey about his own role in the insurgency but happy to talk about the history of the war in Kunar—JSOC interpreters enjoyed speaking with Abu Ikhlas, and Ostlund gave them a few questions to ask him. After a quarter century living in Afghanistan, he could no longer even speak the Egyptian dialect of Arabic; instead, the conversations played out in Pashto, the language of his adopted home.[2] "He was fairly cooperative, he wasn't blustery, and helped lay out the [insurgent] network," recalled Ostlund of his brush with the al-Qaida operative who had helped kill his paratroopers in places like the Korengal and Watapur.[3]

Over time, Abu Ikhlas gave up valuable information about both his old allies in the Taliban and his fellow al-Qaida operatives who were embedded among them as advisers and trainers. "Pakistan knows everything. They control everything. I can't piss on a tree in Kunar without them watching," he complained during one session of questioning, grumbling that Pakistani ISI operatives now controlled the Taliban cells he'd spent so many years working alongside. In another session, dispirited by his experiences with the insurgency and by what his new hosts were telling him about the popular uprisings rocking Middle Eastern countries that year, including his native Egypt, he disavowed his own organization. "Al-Qaida is no longer the answer," he said. "They have lost the faith."[4]

Yet as American conventional forces drew down in Kunar, U.S. intelligence was finding more al-Qaida operatives in the province than ever before. An air strike in the Korengal in September 2010 had killed three of them at once—a Kuwaiti IED expert, a young Saudi whose brother had spent time in Guantánamo, and a veteran Saudi jihadi.[5] JSOC had tracked them to a mountainside camp after Joe Ryan's troops at COP Michigan started hearing fragments of Arabic walkie-talkie chatter from inside the Korengal and references to people called "the Saudi" and "the Kuwaiti."[6] Then, in the spring of 2011, as Abu Ikhlas was undergoing his early months of interrogation, JSOC targeted an even more important al-Qaida leader with a drone strike followed by a rare daylight SEAL Team 6 raid: Abu Hafs al-Najdi, a senior Saudi commander overseeing al-Qaida operatives both in Kunar and across the Pakistani border in Bajaur. Abu Hafs had been number two on the counterterrorism command's overall target list in Afghanistan.[7]

Al-Qaida was expanding in Kunar and Nuristan as America left, Abu Ikhlas explained: just as the twin pressures of CIA drone strikes and Pakistani military offensives were pushing them out of Bajaur and Waziristan in Pakistan's tribal areas, the withdrawal of U.S. troops from their remote outposts in and around the Pech was opening up new sanctuaries for them to move into. That made sense. The Arabs had revealed themselves in the Korengal shortly after the closure of the U.S. bases there, and the SEALs had found Abu Hafs not far from the Pakistani border, in a valley he had moved into along with Pakistani Taliban* militants with whom he had been living in Bajaur before Pakistani troops pushed them west.[8]

The standard role for Arabs in Kunar and Nuristan was the one Abu Ikhlas had himself always played: that of an adviser to local guerrillas, a kind of al-Qaida version of a Green Beret. But when another group of SEAL Team 6 operators killed Osama bin Laden in Abbottabad less than three weeks after the Abu Hafs strike, in May 2011, files recovered from the slain al-Qaida sheikh's hard drives cast the group's expanding activities in the mountains north of the Pech in a different light—one that caught the attention of top CIA and military leaders and would be the genesis of a lethal JSOC air campaign there.

ONE OF THE few people in touch with the secluded bin Laden had been his chief of operations, a Libyan called Atiyah Abd al-Rahman, essentially al-Qaida's number three leader. Based in Waziristan in Pakistan's Federally Administered Tribal Areas with much of the group's senior leadership, Atiyah had exchanged letters with bin Laden through couriers, which CIA analysts combed through in the weeks after the SEALs' Abbottabad raid. In one 2010 letter, Atiyah had described the toll the agency's intensifying drone campaign was taking on al-Qaida's core cadre in Waziristan. On a recent day when the CIA killed al-Qaida's top financier, Atiyah explained, everyone

---

* Shorthand for the Tehrik-e-Taliban Pakistan, an amalgamation of Pakistani militant groups that merged into one in late 2007 and formed close ties with al-Qaida.

had known to expect a strike when the drones that were always overhead started making distinctive loops that the militants and their families had come to associate with an impending attack.

The priority in Waziristan now was not planning attacks abroad, he explained, but "persevering and survival." He asked for bin Laden's advice on a backup option if the pressure worsened.[9]

"We might go to Nuristan, some of us, and some may stay," Atiyah suggested in another letter. He was referring to members of some of al-Qaida's core support and oversight cells that had for years been in Waziristan, like its media wing and religious law council, he explained. "As I have reported before, we have a good battalion over there led by brother Farouq al-Qatari."[10]

Farouq al-Qatari and Farouq al-Qahtani were the noms de guerre of an Arab al-Qaida operative in his early thirties. Known to JSOC by a series of code names, including Objective Elizabeth, he was about to become the focus of American counterterrorism activity in Afghanistan.

American troops in the Pech had occasionally heard rumors about him. When Hugh Miller, the two-time Pech veteran advising the ANA at Blessing in 2012, heard a group of Nangalam policemen trading stories about a Waygal-based militant called Farouq al-Qahtani who traveled with foreign bodyguards, he didn't put much trust in the story and didn't bother sending up a report about it.[11] Intelligence officials who were familiar with Farouq didn't know much about him. His real name was Nayef al-Hababi, and he had been born in Saudi Arabia but raised in Qatar, where he spent six months in prison in 2005 and 2006, in his twenties, after becoming involved with jihadis. Upon releasing him, the Qatari government— eager for its homegrown militants to be somewhere else rather than undermining the state at home—issued him a fresh passport, which he used to travel to Pakistan and join al-Qaida.[12] It's not clear whether the intelligence community had a photo of him at the time, but a later one posted to a jihadi social media page shows a man with large, dark eyes, thick eyebrows, and a mustache and chin patch that just barely connected with his beard.[13]

By 2009, he had adopted the name Farouq and was embedded with the Taliban in Kunar, proving himself in attacks on American outposts. "He wanted to fight Americans, and Kunar-Nuristan was the best place to go for that at the time," said the CIA officer Douglas London, who oversaw arms and finance at the agency's Counterterrorism Center at the time. "When he first got there in 2008 or 2009, he was a nobody. He was from the Gulf, he had money and contacts, but he made a name for himself through the experience he got on the ground and the process of elimination of everybody else."[14] In 2010, when Atiyah and bin Laden were discussing him, Farouq was known to have taken part in at least two ambushes on U.S. convoys and to have distributed weapons like RPGs to Taliban fighters.[15] From his early days of militancy in Qatar, he knew one of al-Qaida's top Gulf financiers, who still lived openly in Doha. Some of al-Qaida's new Saudi and Qatari recruits would go on to join Farouq in Kunar and Nuristan as his fame grew back home.[16]

This all fit the profile for an up-and-coming commander among the hundred or so Arabs the CIA and the military believed were in eastern Afghanistan advising the Taliban. But Atiyah singled Farouq out and suggested his role had another dimension.

"He is the best of a good crew," Atiyah wrote of Farouq to bin Laden. "He recently sent us a message telling us that he has arranged everything to receive us; he said the locations are good, there are supporters and everything."[17]

"I am leaning toward getting most of the brothers out" of Waziristan, bin Laden replied in the fall of 2010 as the CIA was closing in on him. "Whoever can keep a low profile and take the necessary precautions should stay in the area, and those who cannot do so, their first option is to go to Nuristan, Kunar, Ghazni, or Zabul." Likely thinking back to the months he had spent hiding in the Shigal valley after Tora Bora, a few steps ahead of his JSOC pursuers, bin Laden weighed in in favor of Farouq's foothold in Kunar and Nuristan, saying its wooded heights would provide the best natural defenses against the kind of surveillance and strikes that were hounding al-Qaida in Waziristan. Due to its "rougher terrain and the many mountains, rivers, and trees," the area where Farouq was operating could "accommodate hundreds of the brothers without being spotted by the enemy," bin Laden wrote.[18]

The CIA's acting director at the time, Michael Morell, read his agency's initial analysis of the Abbottabad letters in August 2011, around the same time he made a visit to Afghanistan during which he stressed Farouq's importance to his military counterparts.[19] Eventually, Morell, a longtime terrorism analyst, would come to believe that Farouq was a possible heir to the whole al-Qaida enterprise. But that summer his concern was the prospect of Farouq's offering safe haven in the mountains to more senior terrorist leaders fleeing from the CIA's Pakistan drone campaign.

"He was sent there by bin Laden," Morell told me of Farouq. "He was sent there because al-Qaida was under such intense pressure in Pakistan that they felt they needed a fallback position, and he was sent there to prepare that."[20] How far along this plan had gotten before bin Laden's death, or whether it was still under way, was not clear.

In a speech that summer announcing the end of the military surge in Afghanistan and the beginning of a long drawdown from a hundred thousand troops to just a few thousand, President Obama had laid out a clear goal for the ongoing, smaller military and intelligence mission in the country: "No safe haven from which al-Qaida or its affiliates can launch attacks against our homeland or allies."[21] But in Nuristan, a "small safe haven" was exactly what Farouq and his al-Qaida "battalion" had, according to a late 2011 JSOC analysis, as guests of local Nuristani Taliban commanders. Farouq moved from village to village in valleys like the Waygal, where Hugh Miller heard about his popping up, with a small retinue of Pakistani Taliban militants and fellow al-Qaida Arabs.[22]

The military, which ran the counterterrorism show on the Afghan side of the border, needed to pick up Farouq's trail and get rid of him and his group, or at least make life difficult enough for them that they couldn't host new arrivals from Waziristan. The latest four-star ISAF commander, John Allen, remembered CIA officers laying out their renewed interest in Kunar and particularly Nuristan for him shortly after he arrived in Kabul that summer.[23]

With the drawdown of conventional troops in the northeast well under way, Allen turned for help to JSOC. The answer the counterterrorism command came back with in the fall, soon after Bill Ostlund had given up command of the Bagram task force, was an aerial man-hunting campaign that would use drones and other aircraft to find and strike remote al-Qaida targets. Operation Haymaker, as the program was code-named, would soon rival in scale the CIA's more heavily classified but (paradoxically) better-known drone war in Pakistan.

FIND, FIX, FINISH

In other theaters, like Yemen and Somalia, the unwillingness of the Obama administration to put American boots on the ground was increasingly pushing JSOC to rely on drone strikes instead of commando raids that would have posed greater political risks to the local host governments. In Kunar and Nuristan, it was the terrain, as well as the emotional scar tissue that nearly a decade of risky missions and heavy losses had built up in the counterterrorism command's senior leaders.

Just as interest in Farouq al-Qahtani was intensifying in the summer of 2011, an Army special operations officer with long experience in eastern Afghanistan had taken charge of JSOC, Lieutenant General Joseph Votel.

Votel was a reserved, cerebral West Point graduate from Minnesota. His time in Afghanistan stretched back to a Friday less than six weeks after the September 11 attacks when he had parachuted into the southern desert as commander of the 75th Ranger Regiment. Since then, Votel had visited the most remote Korengal and Waygal bases during a year as Chris Cavoli's and Bill Ostlund's one-star boss at ISAF's Regional Command East in 2007 and 2008. He had advocated for pulling out of the Waygal outposts after insurgents burst through the wire at the Ranch House and killed six Americans in the Aranas trail ambush.[24] Along with Ostlund, he'd helped overhaul the way JSOC did business in Afghanistan in 2009.[25]

In the fall of 2010, seven months before taking the helm at JSOC, Votel had headed an investigation into a botched SEAL Team 6 mission in Kunar. It had taken place in the shadow of a peak ten miles south of Chapa Dara. Taliban fighters had kidnapped a British aid worker, Linda Norgrove, and the Team 6 squadron that was deployed to Jalalabad Airfield as JSOC's Task Force East had scrambled to find her before she disappeared into the Korengal, where no general would authorize a rescue mission. After two dozen SEALs fast-roped into the village where Norgrove was being held, the most inexperienced operator in the strike force wound up killing the hostage with a hand grenade that he had been told not to bring on the mission.[26]

When Votel interviewed them for the investigation, the Task Force East SEALs painted a vivid picture of the difficulties inherent in operating in Kunar. When troops arrived, villagers would start shooting in the air to warn militants that Americans were in the area, the Team 6 squadron commander explained.[27] In this case the target village had been eight thousand feet up, nestled among conifers and cliffs, with no landing zones anywhere nearby except the terraces surrounding the target itself; the slain hostage's body had had to be hoisted up to a hovering helicopter afterward.

"The terrain was unreal," a SEAL with eleven combat tours under his belt told Votel.[28]

"I've done missions up in Kunar and I mean, it's like being on a different planet," agreed the squadron's senior enlisted SEAL, a master chief also on his eleventh deployment.[29]

The Norgrove mission "was a watershed, and it highlighted just how significant the risk was that we were taking up there," Votel explained to me. "What we asked those SEALs to do was unbelievable. In that terrain, the margins for safety and success are really narrow." He worried especially about the risk of losing a helicopter in some Kunari gorge.[30] (His predecessor, Bill McRaven, had once said succinctly of Kunar when disapproving a proposed raid, "I've parked enough helicopters up there."[31])

"As I looked back in 2011 on what we had done in the past, it was hard to define a circumstance where we'd accept that risk," Votel recalled.[32] The ever-growing fleet of Predator and Reaper drones over Afghanistan looked like an attractive, low-risk way to go after Farouq al-Qahtani's associates in places that Votel and other JSOC leaders saw as too dangerous for ground operations. An armed drone had fired the opening shot of the American campaign in Kunar in May 2002. Now, after years of costly ground fighting, armed drones would close the campaign out, or carry it on forever.

. . .

MUCH LIKE THE first special operators to enter Kunar back in 2002, the JSOC personnel who got Haymaker under way at Jalalabad and Bagram in late 2011 and early 2012 were looking for any indicators of a foreign presence—anything that could zero them in on where Farouq and a handful of other known al-Qaida operatives might be holed up. But these were people who didn't stay in one place long and were careful about communications security. The counter-terrorism command would have to cast a wide net, striking not just foreign fighters but locals associated with them, from district-level Taliban commanders who hosted al-Qaida advisers to guides who helped the Arabs get from valley to valley and recruiters for their training programs.

One of the first Haymaker strikes, as winter set in, targeted a local Taliban commander called Ahmad Shah.* Based in the Shuryak, "he was like this negotiator who could make peace with the local elders and let foreign fighters come in," including members of the Pakistani Taliban and their al-Qaida allies, remembered one intelligence officer.[33] There were reports that he was trying to orchestrate suicide bombings, a tactic insurgents had rarely used in Kunar and that intelligence analysts worried he might be doing at the behest of his foreign guests.[34]

Aerial footage and communications intercepts pinpointed where Ahmad Shah was living—at a compound deep in the Shuryak with his family, not far from where a different Ahmad Shah had brought Operation Red Wings to grief and where any ground raid would have been exceedingly dangerous. Predators, Reapers, and other aircraft watched the compound for the better part of a week. Finally, Ahmad Shah ventured into a nearby field alone, without any of his family members, and the drone on station released a Hellfire. The missile hit its mark.[35]

This was the future of American involvement in Afghanistan's northeast. "We know these guys are there, the intel is driving us

---

* There was some confusion among troops involved in the strike as to whether the Ahmad Shah of 2011 was the same Ahmad Shah whose men had shot down Turbine 33 during Operation Red Wings. It wasn't—*that* Ahmad Shah had been killed in a firefight in Pakistan in 2008—but the new Ahmad Shah was operating in the same area and likely trying to benefit from his predecessor's notoriety.

there, but how do we get at them at a reasonable risk level?" said an officer involved in Haymaker's conception. "And drone strikes were the way."[36]

JOE RYAN DEPLOYED to Afghanistan for the seventh time in the spring of 2012, just as Haymaker was hitting its stride. This deployment would be a short one, spanning just the summer months; back in the Ranger Regiment, he was bridging a gap between two other Ranger colonels as commander of JSOC's thirty-five-hundred-person Afghanistan task force. Though Ryan would spend almost all this deployment behind the high walls of JSOC's Bagram headquarters compound, his role overseeing Haymaker meant that his career was intersecting with the story of the war in the Pech for the third time, albeit through a classified air campaign that he still can't talk about.[37]

Ryan had been there to watch as the counterterrorism command's aerial capabilities evolved and grew. He'd been in Kantiwa during Winter Strike in 2003 when a Predator crew mistook blurry footage of children playing soccer for Osama bin Laden and his bodyguards, showing the immaturity of both the technology and the tactics of drone surveillance. He'd been at JSOC's Iraq headquarters the next summer, when the command first learned to use a combination of Predators, souped-up old turboprops, and fighter jets to find and bomb targets in Fallujah, an insurgent-controlled city deemed too dangerous for ground raids.[38] And during his year leading the Bulldog battalion in the Pech, the only confirmed killing of Arab al-Qaida operatives had come from the September 2010 JSOC drone strike in a similarly inaccessible place, the Korengal.

Although it wasn't within Ryan's purview as an infantry battalion commander to suggest it, he had hoped, when his troops came out of Blessing and the other Pech bases in 2011, that a precision air-strike campaign would follow, a special operations equivalent to the CIA's drone program in Pakistan. Such an effort, Ryan had thought, could exploit the same fissures and tensions within the Pech insurgency that he'd hoped the pullout of American troops would intensify.[39]

Now Ryan was deployed to Bagram as the JSOC task force

commander approving the strikes, and the early results of Haymaker suggested that what he'd wished for a year before was starting to happen. The killing of Ahmad Shah in the Shuryak had prompted exactly the kind of infighting and suspicion he'd imagined a drone campaign might provoke. A few weeks after the strike, Pakistani Taliban members staying in the Watapur detained a local Afghan Taliban fighter on suspicion of spying. Not long after that, a group of Pakistani Taliban militants was eating at a restaurant in Kandigal when local insurgents surrounded the place, gunned some of them down, and dragged others back into the Korengal. Before long, for reasons that weren't clear to U.S. analysts but seemed to have something to do with the budding turf war, the Peshawar *shura* had removed the Korengali elder Abdul Rahim from the post he had long held as the Taliban's shadow governor for Kunar.

"When Ahmad Shah was removed from the picture, people started getting really upset that foreign fighters were in the valley and there were these strikes occurring," said an intelligence officer involved.[40] "They were kidnapping each other, holding each other for ransom. It picked up steam" in the early months of 2012 as the pace of drone strikes increased, agreed another.[41] It was "the power struggle that Bulldog predicted when they left," said a third officer.[42]

AS HAYMAKER WAS getting under way, JSOC had six Predators at Jalalabad, enough to keep two drones aloft 24/7—two "orbits," in military lingo.[43] The Air Force allocated more aircraft to Haymaker over time, including Reapers, the scaled-up Predator cousins that flew up from Kandahar carrying both Hellfire missiles and five-hundred-pound bombs. The cameras in the drones' ball-shaped sensor turrets had evolved in leaps and bounds since 2002, shrinking in size while gaining in definition just like cell phone cameras back home. Even a couple of years earlier, during the surge, "you would see a group of fighters, but you would struggle to identify things like weapons," said a soldier involved in Haymaker. "By 2012, 2013, we weren't struggling with that anymore. The technology just keeps getting better and better."[44] Reapers with the newest high-definition cameras produced crisp imagery that allowed viewers to tell whether a person was holding a cell phone, the color of his vest, and physical characteristics like a limp or unusual stride.[45] Even the black-and-white night-vision footage was eerily crisp and clear, allowing viewers to make out some features on human beings.[46]

Kunar and Nuristan's steep slopes and thick woods still posed challenges, even at night, when the heat emitted by the trees could swallow up that emitted by the human beings a drone was trying to track in the forest.[47] JSOC tried to make up for this with persistence—keeping drones over the valleys it was interested in day and night and supplementing them with manned surveillance planes flying shorter shifts out of Bagram. Predators and Reapers carried their own limited signals intelligence tools, allowing them to pinpoint the locations of targets' phones, but the manned turboprops from Bagram carried more sophisticated eavesdropping gear, along with analysts who could listen to it in real time.

Although Ranger commanders like Ryan oversaw Haymaker from Bagram, the operation's nerve center was at Jalalabad Airfield, where a rotation of SEAL Team 6 squadrons still ran JSOC's Task Force East. One of several nondescript plywood buildings inside JSOC's fenced-off compound on the far side of the airfield was the SEALs' operations center. Inside, the SEAL squadron's staff and about three dozen intelligence personnel planned, orchestrated, and monitored the secret air campaign, working busily but quietly at plywood desks organized into stadium-like tiers to find targets, monitor them, and set up the strikes.[48]

The SEAL leaders in charge of Task Force East sat at a desk in the middle tier, facing the wall full of sixty-inch monitors where footage from the drones and planes over Kunar and Nuristan played at all hours. As the mission rotated every four months among Team 6's squadrons, it passed from one set of old eastern Afghanistan hands to another—SEAL commanders and master chiefs who had been on missions in Kunar going back a decade, working on Omega teams out of Asadabad and participating in risky raids out of Jalalabad like the botched hostage rescue south of Chapa Dara that Votel investigated and the mission on the other side of the Pech that killed Chief Adam Brown earlier in 2010. Some had been around for Operation Red Wings and the recovery effort afterward. All understood the risks of operating on the ground or in helicopters in Kunar and welcomed a new approach that minimized them.

To help the Navy special operators find targets to strike and manage the expanding fleet of aircraft at their disposal, JSOC beefed up Task Force East with extra personnel who sat at desks above, below, and beside the SEAL leaders: Ranger staff officers; DIA, NSA, and National Geospatial-Intelligence Agency representatives; Air Force intelligence analysts tasked with watching the drone feeds at all hours of the day and night; and a separate set of Air Force strike specialists who would run the show when the time came to attack, talking on the phone with the pilots and sensor operators on the other side of the world.

Every Haymaker killing was a worldwide collaboration. Air Force and civilian pilots and intelligence specialists were aloft over Kunar in their turboprop spy planes whenever the weather permitted, flying five- or six-hour shifts out of Bagram. During twelve or fifteen hours on station, a Predator flying out of Jalalabad or a Reaper out of Kandahar might bounce from the control of a pilot in Nevada or New Mexico to another in Missouri.[49] NSA analysts in Georgia and Maryland monitored cell phone communications in whatever valley was Haymaker's highest priority, providing backup to other signals intelligence personnel doing similar work in Afghanistan. (The NSA, by now, was recording every cell phone call made in Afghanistan.[50]) A secret military cyber-operations unit outside Washington looked for ways into targets' phones and computers—whatever militant commanders were using to connect to the internet and communicate over email and messaging apps. And after a strike, military intelligence analysts in Florida and at JSOC's Fort Bragg headquarters would go over all the footage and intercepted communications again, looking for clues that could help lead to the next target. CIA analysts in Virginia helped out as needed, while CIA and DIA officers in the field in Afghanistan were scrambling to recruit more informants on the ground.[51]

The other key node for Haymaker was Dam Neck, SEAL Team 6's home base near Virginia Beach. Haymaker was just one of several air campaigns JSOC was running, along with missions the Obama administration had authorized in Yemen and Somalia.[52] While one Team 6 squadron was in Jalalabad running Haymaker, another was always hard at work running the Somalia and Yemen strike campaigns from a base in the East African nation of Djibouti, answering not to Rangers but to their own SEAL leadership. As Haymaker got under way in 2012, lessons gleaned from those missions filtered from Djibouti back to the state-of-the-art operations center at Dam Neck, and from there to Jalalabad.[53]

JSOC'S METHODOLOGY IN all theaters, developed during its night-raid campaign in Iraq and now being refined as new surveillance technology came online, was called Find, Fix, Finish—as in *find* a target, *fix* him in the crosshairs while getting approval to attack, and then *finish* him off with a raid or air strike.

First, either a tip from a CIA or DIA source or a trick of the NSA's technological wizardry would locate the targeted militant somewhere in whatever city or desert or mountain range he operated from. In Haymaker, more so than Team 6's Yemen and Somalia missions, information from informants—human intelligence—played an increasingly key role as the CIA, DIA, and their Afghan NDS counterparts recruited more sources in places like the Waygal and the Watapur. "The beauty of Haymaker for the task force was this body of HUMINT," one special operations officer said of Haymaker's first year. "I was surprised by it."[54] Drones and turboprops would then stick to the target like glue, with Air Force intelligence specialists in the Jalalabad operations center watching his suspected location at all hours while the aircrews used their onboard signals intelligence tools to "register" and then "lock" the target's phone, locating it with enough confidence for a strike—the "fix."[55] If the target went into a building or a forest where the drones' cameras couldn't see him anymore, the whole process might have to start over.

Once Task Force East was sure it had its man, the staff in the Jalalabad operations center would develop a plan for how to kill him. In the rare instances when the destruction of a building was on the table, the task force might use the HIMARS rocket launcher it kept on hand, which could flatten a structure with stunning destructiveness and precision but would almost certainly kill anyone inside, including any civilians the overhead surveillance might have missed. In other cases, one of the Air Force F-15s and F-16s that the task force had on call might be the best tool for the job; the five-hundred- and two-thousand-pound satellite-guided bombs they carried were the weapons of choice in thick forest, for example. If the target was a cave complex far away from any civilians—as with an unsuccessful 2013 strike based on an informant's tip that Farouq al-Qahtani himself was inside—the task force might call in a B-1 with its massive load of bombs.[56]

Most often, though, drones executed the Haymaker strikes, typically with Hellfire missiles. The Air Force strike specialists at Jalalabad would get on the phone with the stateside drone crews to decide exactly how to conduct the attack—at what range, from what angle, with what model of Hellfire, with a warhead fused to strike on impact or detonate in the air, and so on. Along with the SEAL leaders sitting in the middle of the room, they would then submit a packet with information about the target and the latest intelligence on his location up to the Rangers at Bagram, who in turn might send it on to Kabul for final approval. The SEALs, meanwhile, checked with the infantry brigade commander across the runway to make sure he was all right with the strike.[57]

While the drone that had found the target backed off and flew in a wider circle, lowering its noise signature, more of the unmanned planes would converge on the area—ideally Reapers with their heavier weapons loads, as many as the task force could muster. Two or more of the aircraft would move into "strike posture," shining their infrared laser designators, invisible on the ground, on the man they meant to kill, in order to guide the missiles in; others would scan the surrounding area, watching for people or vehicles approaching the target. In the operations center, approval would arrive over speakerphone from Bagram, and a SEAL leader would give the nod to the Air Force strike specialist, who in turn would tell the drone crews. The Reapers' sensor operators in their stateside trailers would launch their first Hellfires, then more, working off the assumption that one missile wasn't enough to be sure of a kill. This was the "finish." Twenty to thirty seconds after launch, the incoming Hellfires would appear for a moment on the big screens in Jalalabad and Bagram, and then there would be a flash and a plume of smoke.[58]

After zooming in for the strike, the attacking Reapers' cameras would now zoom out to assess the damage; one drone might be waiting to do "squirter control," killing with more Hellfires any survivors it spotted running away from the scene. Then the drones and planes would return to surveillance mode, watching and listening for clues from the scene about whom to target next, and the cycle would begin again.[59]

DURING THE SUMMER months of 2012 when Ryan was signing off on Task Force East's targets, Haymaker began to rack up promising kills.

Much as JSOC and the CIA had searched high and low for Gulbuddin Hekmatyar and the Hizb-e Islami commanders thought to be bin Laden's hosts back when they first came to Kunar, the task force prioritized the Taliban's top officials in Nuristan, the provincial shadow governor Dost Mohammad—a stout, red-bearded, Arabic-speaking cleric from Kantiwa known for his stirring sermons[60]— and his deputy, Jamil ur-Rahman bin Saadullah. In May, not long after Ryan took over at Bagram, JSOC found Jamil ur-Rahman in his hometown of Amshuz, the village high on a Waygal mountainside that had always been tantalizingly out of reach for the Chosin and Rock troops who had lived two map miles away at the Ranch House outpost in 2006 and 2007. Known to U.S. intelligence as Objective Lead Hill, he was believed to host Farouq and other Arabs in Amshuz regularly, and while Dost Mohammad himself also sometimes visited the Waygal, it was Jamil ur-Rahman who was really the Taliban's point man in his native valley. The missile, two Waygali sources later told me, killed the Taliban deputy governor when he was out working in a cornfield, harming no one else—an ideal strike.[61]

Four days later, a strike in the Watapur killed an important al-Qaida Arab—a Saudi called Sakhr al-Taifi. Objective Vilonia, as the task force knew Taifi, was a big fish: U.S. intelligence understood him to be Farouq's deputy, the second-ranking al-Qaida commander in Afghanistan, who often visited even more senior figures across the border.[62]

This was the first of a string of strikes in the Watapur, a place Ryan remembered well from his battalion's Bulldog Bite experience, which killed subordinates of Farouq's. Five weeks after killing Sakhr al-Taifi, Task Force East successfully struck another Saudi, an

IED specialist called Hanzallah, in a different part of the side valley, killing him and several of his colleagues.[63] A month after that, at the beginning of August, a pair of strikes killed two Pakistani nationals thought to be the al-Qaida commanders specifically responsible for Kunar and his deputy.[64] And a Watapur strike at the end of August, after Ryan had finished his deployment and handed the Bagram task force over to another Ranger colonel, killed yet another Saudi along with three Pakistanis. Among the dead in that strike was a courier whom al-Qaida leaders in Pakistan and Afghanistan used to carry messages back and forth across the border and who JSOC believed had been helping move members of al-Qaida's propaganda branch from Pakistan into Afghanistan, suggesting that the shift in personnel that bin Laden had approved before his death was still under way.[65]

Now and again, Farouq al-Qahtani himself would appear in a Reaper's crosshairs, and while senior commanders at Bagram, Kabul, and Fort Bragg tuned in, Task Force East would take its shot. More than once during his nineteen months in Kabul, ISAF's commander, John Allen, watched in high definition and in real time as JSOC lined up a strike against a person it was confident was Farouq, only for the al-Qaida commander to reappear somewhere else later, or even walk away unscathed as the Americans, unable to launch a follow-up strike for one reason or another, watched in frustration. "The rule of squirters is, if one person gets off the target, it's invariably going to be the guy you were going to kill," Allen joked. In one Haymaker strike he remembered approving, "we killed everybody but him. . . . We thought we got him, but then a couple people came off the target alive," one of whom proved to be Farouq.[66]

Farouq fought back with a lethal tactic: suicide bombings. Although they were a preferred tool of al-Qaida commanders around the world, the Taliban had only rarely carried out suicide bombings in Kunar, and they had been almost unheard of in the Pech.[67] But in 2012, such attacks began to add up in the province as, according to reports that reached American intelligence, Farouq and his subordinates outfitted operatives from local Taliban cells with explosive vests and sent them off to strike the dwindling American troop presence in Kunar.[68] An April suicide bombing near the Watapur district center killed the Kunari cleric in charge of the province's High

Peace Council, the body of elders responsible for local peace negotiations with the insurgency. In another attack nearby, just outside
Honaker-Miracle, an old man wearing an explosive vest attacked
American troops working on repairing a disintegrating U.S.-built
bridge, wounding a platoon leader and his forward observer.[69]

Worse, on August 8, a pair of bombers struck a group of visiting
senior American officers as they were walking from the Asadabad
PRT compound into the city to meet the governor, blowing themselves up as the party crossed a small bridge. Captain Flo Groberg, a
second-tour Kunar veteran who was in charge of security for the
patrol, spotted one of the bombers and tackled him, absorbing part
of the explosion and saving the top two American officers in the
party—the 4/4 ID brigade commander, Colonel Jim Mingus, and
the ANA adviser Colonel Dan Walrath, both Ranger veterans who
had spent time in Kunar back at the start of the war. "I thought to
myself, 'He looks like a suicide bomber,' and as the thought went
through my head, the detonation occurred," remembered Walrath,
whose wounded leg was salvaged through repeated surgeries. Groberg's heroic act earned him a Medal of Honor, but he lost his own
leg in the process. Four Americans died in the attack: Major Thomas
Kennedy and Command Sergeant Major Kevin Griffin of 4/4 ID, as
well as the brigade's Air Force liaison Major Walter Gray and a
USAID representative named Ragaei Abdelfattah.[70]

The four men were the last Americans to lose their lives in the
Pech valley. Task Force East's response came five weeks later, when
a Haymaker strike outside the city killed an Afghan al-Qaida "facilitator" named Asadullah, who U.S. intelligence believed worked
with Farouq's Arab operatives in the Watapur and had sent the
bombers into the city.[71]

"HAYMAKER WAS A CROWD-PLEASER"

Communications intercepts and occasional interrogations of detainees captured in Kunar's safer lowlands showed that Haymaker was
making a splash, changing the calculus of militant leaders who had
long thought of places like Amshuz and the Gambir Jungle as safe.
The most worrying thing "at any level, from fighter to senior Tali-

ban leadership, is anything to do with drones or aerial bombings," a captured Nuristani Taliban commander told interrogators—more so than night raids on the ground—because the group "has no way to defend against them and they are certain to end in absolute destruction of whatever their target is."[72]

What did that psychological effect translate to in practical terms, though? In March 2013, a few weeks after Allen handed over command of ISAF to another Marine four-star, JSOC graded itself in an internal assessment of the air campaign's effectiveness, later published by the news site *The Intercept*.[73]

Over the course of fourteen months, Task Force East had launched an average of one Haymaker strike a week—about the same pace the CIA's covert drone campaign was achieving in Pakistan during the same period.[74] Roughly half of the Haymaker strikes had been in the Pech or its tributaries. The SEALs and their helpers had killed their intended targets a little over 60 percent of the time; in 56 strikes, they had gotten their man 35 times. Some of the remaining 184 people killed in the strikes were other known insurgent figures with documented relationships with the targets, but most were not; they were just men, often but not always armed, who were in the company of a target and met the task force's criteria for being judged combatants.

Since the summer, the operation's focus had shifted from the Watapur to the Waygal. A stateside NSA team was helping Task Force East track a dozen militants, some of them Arabs, as they moved among three Waygali villages: Amshuz; Waygal, the village at the far northern end of the valley that American troops had hardly ever visited; and Muldesh, a tiny settlement that sat below the peak of the mountain that separated Aranas and Bella, the old American outpost sites, and just over a ridge from the even smaller settlement that the military had destroyed with bombs and AC-130 shells while hunting for Gulbuddin Hekmatyar in October 2003. The targets in the Waygal were "not only senior-level Taliban facilitators and hosts, but Arabs themselves," the documents reported, adding that Farouq al-Qahtani was known to frequent the valley with his entourage. When I visited Jalalabad the month the classified study was circulated, an intelligence analyst there told me the same thing, saying that Farouq bounced between Waygali settlements north of Want and that Task Force East had recently struck a "no-shit training camp" where Arab fighters were thought to be training for operations overseas.[75] Later, a well-connected Nangalam resident who ran informants for a wealthy Kunari timber family would tell me more about how the Waygali Taliban hosted Farouq. In Waygal village, he would stay as a guest of Mullah Osman, the Taliban commander whose troops had attacked Chosen Company in Want in July 2008. In two other villages, Kownd Kalay and Kalaygal, he would stay with other militants who fought in the 2008 battle, and wherever he went, "he was famous for organizing and giving money and making bombs."[76]

Haymaker had allowed JSOC to kill more al-Qaida Arabs in a shorter period of time than it ever had before in Afghanistan, according to the internal report card, and U.S. intelligence had collected "sporadic reports" of concern within al-Qaida about the continued viability of Kunar-Nuristan as a sanctuary, given the increased pressure. But the air campaign had not yet prompted an exodus of al-Qaida personnel back to Pakistan, as some intelligence officials had hoped it might. Instead, Farouq and his followers were just shifting from one remote valley to another, trying to stay a step ahead of the Americans and their intelligence sources—from the Watapur to the Waygal, then back to the Watapur, then to the Shigal, then farther north to the Helgal, and so on.

Compared with the summer months when it had been killing Arabs at an unprecedented pace, it seemed, Haymaker was yielding diminishing returns, possibly because of the trade-off inherent in relying on air strikes rather than ground missions. Unlike a night raid that exposed Rangers or SEALs to danger, a Hellfire strike produced no prisoners to interrogate, just corpses, and it destroyed whatever documents, phones, thumb drives, or other evidence the target had on his person. "Kill operations significantly reduce the intelligence available from detainees and captured material," warned a separate Pentagon study of SEAL Team 6's air campaigns in Somalia and Yemen, conducted at the same time as the Haymaker assessment and likewise published by *The Intercept*.[77] Where air strikes were the preferred "finish" method—whether because of the tactical risk, as in Kunar and Nuristan, or the political risk, as in Yemen and Somalia—JSOC was playing catch-up intelligence-wise. The counterterrorism task force knew the names of Farouq and a few other Arabs, but not of the people who answered to them, including most of the militants charged with explosives training and other specialist tasks at al-Qaida's mountain training sites. "We don't know anything about who the guys are who are doing the actual training," the intelligence analyst I spoke to at Jalalabad in March 2013 explained.[78]

AS THE 2013 fighting season began, Task Force East was killing fewer Arabs and senior Taliban commanders than in 2012, even as its tempo of strikes accelerated. "By the summer of 2013, it was about double what it was in the summer of 2012, and we'd been busy in 2012," a JSOC officer said of the tempo of Haymaker missions.[79] This meant the task force was increasingly going after insurgent figures at lower levels in the Taliban hierarchy. Most of the people it targeted were smaller-time insurgent figures whom al-Qaida advisers relied on in some way—district-level commanders or local hosts, guides, or recruiters, people JSOC called facilitators.

"They wound up going after the targets they could find. You'd get intelligence on a particular cell, and they'd go and dismantle it that week" with drone strikes, said an intelligence analyst. "It was a pretty efficient killing machine, but it grew to be more about quantity than quality."[80]

Such strikes could hamper the ability of the al-Qaida figures who were Haymaker's real targets to do their work by killing Afghan militants they depended on. "Local fighters understand what we can see and what we can't see [with drones], and they can walk an al-Qaida guy from the Korengal to the Waygal while keeping him out of our line of sight," explained another JSOC officer involved in Haymaker, "so if you kill those guides off, the foreigners are more exposed."[81] And it could yield payoffs that were more visible to ANA troops and their American advisers on the ground in the Pech than the death of an Arab far up a remote side valley. Once, for example, Haymaker surveillance stumbled on a gathering of low-level militant leaders out west toward Chapa Dara, with machine-gun-equipped pickup trucks pulled over by the side of the Pech road while fighters walked around openly—the kinds of people who weren't major targets for JSOC but who spent their days making life difficult for the ANA in the Pech. Aircraft of various types converged and killed as many of them as they could, including the Taliban's Chapa Dara district governor and several of his subordinates.

Hugh Miller, the ANA adviser on the ground at Blessing, was impressed by the effect that strike seemed to have on Taliban activity west of Nangalam, at least for a while; less a targeted killing than a target-of-opportunity attack against enemy troops in the open, it killed sixty fighters, according to reports that reached Miller.[82] The strike prompted a more senior Taliban commander to "order a temporary halt to movement of fighters into Afghanistan," JSOC assessed, although it wasn't clear if that was because of the district commander's death, the deaths of so many rank-and-file fighters, or both.[83] A Chapa Dara resident who was critical of other strikes cited that one to me as a success, saying that the targeted militants were on their way back from a meeting of commanders when they stopped for a rest and were hit. "That is the kind of strike that is good, that the people accept," he said. "They killed a lot of Taliban and no one else."[84]

But as Task Force East's target list expanded, some of the strikes seemed to veer in the direction of revenge killings, or at least so it appeared to many Kunaris. "Drone attacks used to be against high-level people only. Not now," said Mawlawi Shahzada Shahid, the Asadabad cleric who, at the dawn of American involvement in Kunar eleven years earlier, had been amused to see American Green Berets' and intelligence operatives' cautious approach to eating Afghan food that they feared would make them sick. "There are people who used to fight against the Americans but now are tired of the fighting. But they are still targeted."[85]

In April 2013, a Haymaker strike killed Haji Matin, the timber baron turned Taliban commander who had fought against every American unit in the Korengal from A-team 361 in 2004 to Mark Moretti's Baker Company in 2010 and on whose sawmill the KOP had been built. What exactly prompted the strike on Matin remains classified. A military press release afterward described him as the "highest-ranking Taliban official" in the district that included the

Korengal and Nangalam,[86] but the intelligence officers of the conventional units advising the ANA in 2012 and 2013 saw Matin as a has-been.[87] Matin had even "split with the Arabs" he had hosted in previous years, an intelligence analyst contended[88]—a suggestion supported by the rarity of Haymaker strikes in the Korengal compared with side valleys like the Watapur and the Waygal.

At COP Honaker-Miracle, Brandon Newkirk—the company commander on his second Kunar tour whom I'd met a month earlier when I visited the outpost—had mixed feelings about Matin's death, which the outpost's intelligence officer alerted him to shortly after the strike. At first, he wasn't sure whether to believe it. But then he saw old friends on a Facebook page for Korengal veterans talking about it, sharing links to news stories and the military press release announcing that Matin was dead. "Overall, I was definitely very happy" as a Korengal veteran who had fought Matin and his men, Newkirk told me. But the captain was also "almost sympathetic to him, to a degree," he said. "Essentially we made him what he was by taking over his lumberyards and land without really compensating him." Newkirk had grown up on a farm and could see himself taking up arms if foreign troops came and requisitioned it for use as an outpost, as Marines and 10th Mountain troops had turned Matin's sawmill into the KOP where he had served as a lieutenant.[89]

Then there was Mullah Dawran, the stocky Salafi commander from Sundray. He had been fighting the Americans in the Pech since almost the beginning but hadn't formally joined the Taliban until after American raids and strikes had killed countless friends and subordinates as well as some of his children and wives. SEALs and Rangers had hunted Dawran and his associates in the hills at the height of Task Force East's efforts to help out the infantry battalions in the Pech, sometimes at great risk. But during the first year and a half or so of Haymaker, the task force wasn't interested in him; he wasn't an Arab, nor was he known to work closely with Arabs, and he didn't seem to hold a formal position in the Taliban's district shadow government for the Pech. Although he was "the bane of 6/2's existence, almost taunting the battalion" with videos showing him and his men relaxing in Pech towns the government had once controlled, remembered an ANA adviser who shared intelligence with the Jalalabad SEALs, he wasn't someone the task force talked or asked about.[90]

"He seemed locally important and you heard his name a lot, but he definitely wasn't high on East's target list," agreed another of the advisers working at Blessing in 2012. "I think we almost forgot why we were hunting him other than that we'd just been hunting him for so long. He was just like a cockroach that refused to die."[91]

During the 2013 fighting season, as JSOC delved lower in the Taliban ranks to rack up more strikes, Dawran wound up on the Haymaker kill list. The end finally came for him on October 21, nearly four years after he had limped from the wreckage of his mountain compound after the Thanksgiving 2009 HIMARS strike that killed his wife and children. Drones circled over Kalaygal, one of the villages in the Waygal that had supplied many of the fighters during the 2008 battle of Want, and then struck, killing four people, according to reports that reached the Nangalam district center. Dawran and his brother Qais were both among the dead, the district governor told a local media outlet.[92]

Drew Poppas, the former 101st brigade commander who had authorized Joe Ryan's 2011 Pech Realignment plan, was back at Bagram at the time of Dawran's death, now the one-star deputy commander of ISAF's Regional Command East. The senior JSOC officer at Bagram, a one-star general who kept a big map of Kunar and the latest Haymaker strikes on the wall of his office, was an old friend of Poppas's from West Point, and now they traveled around the east together, holding joint check-ins with conventional adviser units and JSOC units like those on opposite sides of the airfield at Jalalabad. Poppas defended the strike, which his conventional division headquarters had signed off on when the special operators proposed it. "Dawran was not just a threat to U.S. forces. He had a destabilizing effect on the long-term stability of the region. Haji Matin too," he insisted to me. "You have to kill these senior guys. You're not just mowing the grass."[93]

That was exactly what some other participants and observers thought Haymaker was devolving into as 2014 approached, though. "Every militant killed in a leadership position was replaced within two or three weeks," said an intelligence analyst, referring to a still-classified RAND report on Haymaker that he said reached that conclusion based on 2013 data. "It was mowing the lawn—keeping the foreign guys up there off balance enough and paranoid enough that they couldn't get their shit together" for overseas terrorist attacks by killing just about any local fighter who came into their orbit. Put another way, he said, it was "running to stay in place."[94]

But "Haymaker was a crowd-pleaser," the analyst said, especially at the main special operations headquarters in the country at Kabul Airport, where some senior officers saw that process as value enough. "People in the headquarters loved to see the red Xs through the targets' headshots," because it appeared to show progress.[95] The top commander there, presiding over all the various "tribes" of U.S. and allied special operators in Afghanistan, was the Delta Force veteran Major General Tony Thomas, another officer with built-up emotional scar tissue from risky missions in the Afghan mountains. It was Thomas who, as Joe Ryan's battalion commander in 2002, had lost the first Rangers in combat of the war on terror, and it was Thomas who had reluctantly signed off on the 2010 mission into the Gambir Jungle that killed Kevin Pape, the Ranger squad leader.[96]

"General Thomas just loved it," the intelligence analyst said of the regular Haymaker briefings. "It made his day looking at those things and seeing who was being killed"—all without putting American boots on the ground.[97]

THE REALITY OF whom JSOC was killing in Kunar and Nuristan clashed with the picture President Obama had painted for the nation and the world in a May speech explaining his administration's increasing reliance on drone strikes from Afghanistan and Pakistan to Somalia and Yemen. Echoing the logic that had birthed Operation Haymaker, he spoke of "rugged mountains" and the risk of "more Black Hawks down" and said that it was "not possible for America to simply deploy a team of special [operations] forces to capture every terrorist." And it was terrorists that his counterterrorism forces were after, Obama emphasized. "America does not take strikes to punish individuals," he said, referring broadly to the CIA's and JSOC's drone operations but characterizing them in a way that simply wasn't true of Haymaker. "We act against terrorists who pose a continuing and imminent threat to the American people."[98]

Farouq al-Qahtani, Haymaker's ultimate, elusive target, met that bar. But it was impossible to say the same about Haji Matin, Mullah Dawran, or many other Pech insurgent leaders killed in Haymaker.

THE CIVCAS PROBLEM

In the same May 2013 speech, Obama reassured Americans that "before any strike is taken, there must be near-certainty that no civilians will be killed or injured—the highest standard we can set." But innocents did die in some strikes, the president acknowledged, in spite of everything the targeters did to spare them; he and those below him in the chain of command, he said, had to weigh the risks against the threat the terrorists would pose to civilians if allowed to live.[99]

The military, inevitably, had developed an abbreviation by which to refer to civilian casualties: CIVCAS. The JSOC task force's ability to use its advancing technology and tactics to kill militant targets without harming civilians impressed ISAF's commander, John Allen, for whom preventing CIVCAS, and thereby preserving a badly damaged relationship with the Afghan president, Hamid Karzai, was a top priority. Allen would visit Bagram periodically for briefings about Haymaker from Joe Ryan or the other Ranger commanders who preceded and followed him. On other occasions, a task force representative would come to Allen at his Kabul headquarters when the four-star general's sign-off was required for a particularly difficult strike or one where there was a risk of civilian casualties. "Sometimes they really had to thread the needle with a Hellfire in these mountainside villages," Allen remembered, describing the footage from the Reapers' high-resolution cameras. "They'd lay out the geometry of the shot to me, how it had to fly past these houses to kill the target and nobody else."[100] In one strike that Allen's successor as ISAF commander, General Joseph Dunford, recalled as a particularly impressive feat of "weaponeering," the task force was able to use a missile to collapse the struts under one of the elevated verandas that extended from many Nuristani homes, killing the militant leader sitting on the porch without damaging the rest of the house or harming anybody inside.[101]

Compared with the dense villages of southern Afghanistan, Kunar and Nuristan's sparse mountainsides offered a lot of chances, once Task Force East was tracking someone, to kill him when he was away from any buildings or bystanders. One typical Haymaker strike, detailed in the leaked JSOC briefing, took place on a sparsely wooded mountainside two and a half miles north of the Pech on the Sunday before the November 2012 presidential election in the United States. The target was a low-level guerrilla commander named Qari Munib who was known to be in touch with Haji Matin and Dawran and who had recently led an attack on the ANA base that had once been COP Able Main. One after another, the SEALs and their intelligence personnel checked the boxes: concurrence with the conventional brigade across the runway, a match between a voice on the phone they had been tracking and Munib's previously recorded voice, a lock on the location of that phone, video footage of the people at that location, identification of Munib among them, and a chance to strike with a low probability of harming any civilians.[102]

Early in the morning, a surveillance plane pinpointed Munib's phone at a mountain compound two-thirds of the way up the Kurbagh Sar mountain, far out of sight of the valley floor and higher up than American patrols had ventured since the ambitious days of 2006 and 2007. Zooming in with its cameras, the aircraft watched as five men left the compound and walked down the mountain, past a cluster of trees, then halted, as if to wait for someone. If that was what they were doing, they waited a long time—more than four hours, until noon, when three of the men hiked back up a ridge to the compound. In the meantime, a Reaper arrived overhead. Checking the location of the phone against an "imagery intelligence signature," the sensor operators and analysts thought they could tell which of the three men was Munib, and watched as he and the other two emerged from the compound again.

The two men were unknowns and didn't appear to be armed. If the target had been an Arab or a Taliban district governor, the task force might have accepted the risk of killing them along with their quarry, but not in the case of a small fish like Munib. Just past one o'clock in the afternoon, when Munib was far enough away from his two anonymous companions that the blast likely wouldn't kill them, the Reaper launched a Hellfire. Everyone watching the drone footage in their various operations centers saw a blurry gray figure with a white hat disappear in smoke, and then watched as the two men who had been walking with Munib, both unharmed, picked up his remains and carried them away.

"When you can track guys walking for miles on trails, you're not going to kill anyone else," a special operations officer involved in Haymaker explained.[103] Sometimes, the moment to strike was "when a target wandered away from a meeting to take a piss," added an intelligence analyst.[104]

Nevertheless, Haymaker did kill civilians—some directly, some indirectly.

"HAYMAKER SCARED THE shit out of everybody," a different special operations officer said of the Taliban's leadership in Kunar. "You get dudes getting blown off the sides of mountains in the middle of the day in places where they thought they were safe."[105] Taliban officials reacted to this fear by lashing out at anyone they could—not at the Americans, who were barely there anymore, but at the people they guessed must be spying for them (even though many strikes were lined up solely on the basis of technical intelligence and video footage). After trying their suspects in courts that tended to produce guilty verdicts regardless of whether there was any evidence, the militants tortured and shot suspected spies. Sometimes they killed other guerrillas, and sometimes they might really have ferreted out informants for the CIA, DIA, or NDS. But more often, they just wound up killing villagers who, stuck between the two competing governments in their districts, had done nothing wrong beyond having had some type of contact with officials at the district center.

"With what the task force guys were doing, the insurgents were paranoid, and they would take that out on the locals," said Brandon Newkirk, who sometimes heard reports of militants getting into gun battles with each other in the mountains after strikes but more often heard of "spy hunters" executing locals or cutting off beards to send a message.[106]

The Taliban spy-hunting campaign in Kunar picked up steam in the fall of 2012. In October, a Taliban court executed three people suspected of spying in a village in the Watapur. A month later, around the time of the strike that killed Qari Munib, militants kidnapped and killed a man they suspected of spying in a valley east of Asadabad. Two weeks after that, in the Watapur again, camouflage-clad militants came to a different village and abducted the nephew of an elder, returning four days later to take the elder himself and three other villagers.[107]

"We found the corpses of my father and cousin in the mountains near our village," the elder's son told a UN representative later. "While we were washing their dead bodies before the funeral ceremony we found they had been severely tortured," he added, with bruises on their legs and shoulders and burn scars—seemingly from hot metal rods—around their waists. In a video released a few days later, the Taliban claimed that all five men had confessed to being spies. "After this incident fifteen families decided to leave the village to [go to] Asadabad and other more secure areas," the son said.[108]

Even people who lived outside the areas in the mountains that the Taliban actually controlled felt compelled to answer summonses to the Taliban's courts deep in the side valleys, not wanting to get on the wrong side of a group that might well gain broader power in the years to come. One elder told a UN representative that even though he participated in the government's *shuras* at the Watapur district center next door to COP Honaker-Miracle, he still felt obligated to go when the Taliban summoned him to their own district court inside the valley. "I do not support the Taliban. However, if they call me I go," he said. Elsewhere in the Pech, the Taliban took, tried, and executed two more elders in January 2013; that October, in the Watapur again, they tried and executed a pair of boys, ages eight and ten.[109]

THEN THERE WERE the cases where the strikes themselves went wrong and killed or wounded innocents.

Between 2006 and 2010, when American troops had been living at outposts in the Pech's side valleys, verifying claims that an air strike had killed civilians had been a fraught but more straightforward matter. A patrol could hike up to the scene, sometimes within hours of the strike, and photograph what they found and talk through an interpreter to the family members of the dead in the village. That had been the procedure when the Marine platoon commander Jesse Wolfe confirmed the deaths of children in a Korengal AC-130 strike during Operation Mountain Lion in 2006, when Dan Kearney and his paratroopers confronted the aftermath of a strike they called in during Rock Avalanche in 2007, and when Colin Tuley's troops documented the gruesome results of a strike during the ill-fated 2011 mission back to Want. But once American advisers were restricted to Blessing and Honaker-Miracle in 2012, and then just Honaker-Miracle in 2013, getting to the bottom of what had happened in a strike on a mountainside above the Watapur or Waygal became a more difficult proposition, one that rarely ended in something approaching a satisfying resolution for any party involved.

The JSOC strikes "weren't in areas that we would've been able to go out and do collateral damage assessments," explained Tommy Ryan, the penultimate company commander at Blessing in 2012, who oversaw just Hugh Miller and his advisers and two trimmed-down infantry platoons for basic security. Instead, Haji Zalmay— the district governor who had enjoyed showing successive waves of American officers the machine pistol he claimed to have taken off a dead Soviet pilot—would handle whatever accusations people from a Taliban-controlled village like Amshuz or Tsangar might bring to the district center, armed with a list of whom Task Force East believed it had killed. "Zalmay would confirm they were the same names, and then he'd go and talk to people and basically say, 'Yeah, those were bad guys; too bad they died,'" the company commander remembered.[110]

The UN's small mission in Afghanistan did its best to look into disputed incidents as well, comparing the claims of the American military headquarters in Kabul and those of officials like Zalmay with the accounts of whatever villagers they could reach by phone or persuade to visit their compound in Jalalabad. Twice in the fall of 2012, the UN team deemed allegations of civilian deaths in Haymaker strikes credible: a September strike north of Asadabad that killed two insurgents also wounded a girl working in a nearby field, who then died en route to a hospital in the city, the investigators concluded, and a December strike in the Waygal that killed three members of the same family, including a child.[111] The UN team didn't simply rubber-stamp any claim of civilian deaths that they came across, as some in the military wrongly believed. After the Taliban alleged civilian deaths in a Helgal valley drone strike in February 2013, for example, the UN's investigation concluded that the Taliban claim was false and only militants had died.[112]

IN THE SECOND week of June 2013, with about sixty thousand American troops left in Afghanistan, Brandon Newkirk and the 101st Airborne contingent at COP Honaker-Miracle packed up all their gear into MRAPs and drove out of the Pech, leaving the base in the hands of the ANA. They had already sent home the marble plaques around the flagpole bearing the names of Americans who had been killed in the valley and painted over any murals or artwork left behind by previous units, although there was no way to get rid of the three-dimensional friezes of 173rd Airborne Brigade insignia that projected from some of the buildings' walls.[113]

The departure from Honaker-Miracle brought an end to the American military's day-to-day presence on the ground in the Pech. From now on, the only American troops to venture into the valley would be advisers making rare short-term visits to support the increasingly aggressive ANA as they mounted offensive operations and built new outposts—sometimes in places where the Americans had never built bases, even in the heyday of the Pech "security bubble." When hundreds of Afghan troops pushed up the valley to establish control over the Chapa Dara district center in early September, a small team of 10th Mountain Division advisers flew out to Nangalam to help but wound up watching the action entirely via drone footage.

As the ANA troops reached Senji Bridge—the crossing of the Pech that had stymied Brett Jenkinson's efforts to build a Chapa Dara outpost in 2009—they encountered stiff Taliban resistance. The advisers watched the battle play out silently from above.[114] "It was like something from a World War II movie—guys crawling across a bridge that's booby-trapped with IEDs," one of the 10th

Mountain officers who'd flown out to Nangalam remembered. "If U.S. soldiers were doing that, clearing that bridge dismounted under DShK fire, that's the kind of thing we'd be handing out Medals of Honor for."[115] Using the same aerial surveillance and strike tools that Task Force East used for Haymaker, the advisers did what little they could, dropping bombs on the mountainside machine-gun position that was keeping the advancing ANA soldiers pinned down.

It was during the same week the ANA's Chapa Dara operation kicked off—with the on-the-ground link between American advisers and Afghan officials like Zalmay gone—that the most controversial civilian casualty allegations to emerge from Haymaker reached Kabul. The strike would cause a firestorm and anger Afghanistan's embittered, increasingly anti-American president, Hamid Karzai.[116]

On the afternoon of Saturday, September 7, a Reaper circling above the northern Watapur launched a Hellfire at a pickup truck on a mountainside trail—by some accounts a red one, by others blue.[117] Watched by sensor operators, analysts, and commanders from the United States to Bagram and Jalalabad, the pickup, packed with people, had been winding its way up a mountain trail on the Watapur's east side from the valley mouth toward Gambir, the Taliban-controlled settlement where the Rangers' Team Darby and the Cacti battalion's Bastard Company had run into fierce resistance in 2010 and 2011 and where al-Qaida trainers were often reported, sometimes including Farouq.[118] Inside the truck, JSOC personnel believed, was a "mid-level facilitator" to the terrorist group, a militant named Sulayman al-Hamdan, "who maintained courier networks back into Pakistan."[119]

The first Hellfire was followed by a second, then three more, obliterating the truck and engulfing the roughly fifteen people crammed into its bed and cab in flames and shell fragments.[120]

ISAF, the main allied headquarters in Kabul, often issued carefully worded press releases about strikes on JSOC's behalf, obfuscating the involvement of the counterterrorism command and never mentioning Haymaker by name. Contacted by journalists about the Gambir strike, ISAF put out a statement the next day claiming that it had killed ten militants and that there had been "no signs of civilians in the vicinity."[121]

Behind the scenes, JSOC and the other parts of the Haymaker

apparatus already knew that something had gone wrong. Conflicting reports were coming in from Kunar; the NDS office in Asadabad said in two different reports to Kabul that the strike had killed the Taliban's district governor for Watapur and an Arab al-Qaida fighter. But dozens of elders were trekking down from the Watapur to the governor's palace to report that women and children had died too.[122] The district governor Zalmay—usually not one to credit reports of civilian casualties from towns like Gambir that he deemed sympathetic to the Taliban and al-Qaida—told Afghan journalists the same.[123]

Donning his neatly pressed service uniform as he always did for presidential visits, ISAF's commander, Joe Dunford, ventured over to the Arg and told Karzai that the reports were likely true:[124] while Task Force East believed it had killed its target, somehow there had been women and children in the truck too. In the days that followed, JSOC and ISAF would acknowledge initially that two civilians, and then three—a child and two women—had died in the strike.[125] The UN's own investigation offered a much different death toll: six militants and ten civilians, including four women and four children.[126]

One passenger had survived the strike, badly wounded, and that passenger was indisputably an innocent; she was a four-year-old girl named Aisha, whose parents, grandmother, and baby brother had all been killed. Aisha was horribly burned and mangled, her eyes still there but sightless, much of her face gone. "God left her alive as proof," a relative would later tell an American journalist.[127]

Transported for treatment to Kabul, Aisha caught the attention of Karzai, who, in the last year of his presidency, visited her in the French-run hospital where she stayed before moving on for more specialized care in the United States. "It was one of the most painful moments of my presidency and my life," Karzai told me later, recalling how the girl's face was completely masked with bandages. "I asked why," he recalled. "The doctor said it was because she had no face. I was shocked. I didn't want her to know, but I wondered, 'God, why have you kept her alive?' It caused a deep anger in me that lingers today."[128]

Karzai appointed the Kunari cleric Mawlawi Shahzada Shahid to investigate the strike on his government's behalf. Shahzada remained a political moderate, willing to interact with ISAF officers, although they sometimes wrongly saw him as a radical because he maintained communications with Taliban figures in the mountains. I had met him a few months earlier, in Kabul, and interviewed him about his experiences with the succession of American units that fought in the Pech and other parts of Kunar. "Some American commanders loved the Afghan people, and when they were here, civilian killings were fewer," Shahzada told me of his experience with American ground units. "The problem is that one commander is replaced by another so quickly."[129]

Now, with foreign ground troops gone but with drones killing ever more people in the mountains, Shahzada was watching American involvement in the Pech move into a new phase in which civilians died not because they were caught in the cross fire of infantry firefights and artillery barrages but because they were targeted based on information of mysterious provenance. In a way, this was a return to the beginning, when Kunaris targeted in special operations raids had puzzled over who among their neighbors might have told the Americans what about them and why.

"We went to the Watapur district center, and our investigation showed 100 percent that there were civilian casualties," Shahzada told me of the Gambir incident the next time we met, in 2017, adding that he didn't believe the strike had even killed a wanted militant as ISAF claimed. "We met with the Americans, and they said they attacked militants. But there was no high-ranking Talib there. Whoever the target was, they didn't hit him." Back in Kabul, he said, American and British officers urged him not to make waves with his investigation; there could be political trouble with Karzai.[130] In the end, despite his rage over the Gambir incident, the Afghan president didn't impose any new restrictions on American counterterrorism strikes afterward.[131]

What had happened? People in Gambir—remembering the early days of American involvement in Kunar when such occurrences had been common—figured an informant for the Americans or the NDS had provided faulty information in order to settle a grievance against one of the passengers in the car, most of whom had been members of two extended families.[132] Karzai, embittered and suspicious to the point of paranoia, became convinced that murderous Americans had done it deliberately, either to terrorize the people in the valley or as part of some kind of weapons test.[133]

Mawlawi Shahzada Shahid's guess was vaguer but more charitable. "The Americans plan the drone attacks well now, but the chance for mistakes is still high," he said, noting that an armed shepherd in the mountains looked no different from the sky than an armed guerrilla did.[134]

Colin Tuley was back in Afghanistan at the time, signing off on Haymaker strikes as commander of the Bagram JSOC task force, the job Joe Ryan had held a year earlier. The Watapur was an area Tuley was more familiar with than most in the task force, because that was where his Cacti battalion troops had fought during Operation Hammer Down in 2011, and he oversaw an investigation into the 2013 strike in his old hunting grounds, but he declined to comment on the episode, or Haymaker in general, citing classification. The only official explanation from the military was in another statement from the Kabul headquarters on behalf of the counterterrorism task force. "In spite of persistent observation, unknown to ISAF there were at least three civilians located in the vehicle with the target," the statement said, seeming to acknowledge with the "at least" that the count of innocent deaths could be too low.[135]

Any number of errors in execution or misunderstandings of the intelligence underpinning the strike might have been to blame for the killing of innocents on the mountain outside Gambir that Saturday four days before the twelfth anniversary of September 11. But a later Pentagon study of other civilian deaths in air strikes in Afghanistan pointed to something basic as the common flaw: misplaced American confidence in their cameras in the sky at a time when there were no longer ground troops around to maintain relationships with local people. Examining twenty-one strikes that the military had declared civilian-casualty-free based on its aerial footage, the study team found that in nineteen of the cases later investigations on the ground had discovered civilian casualties that the high-flying cameras and the people watching them around the world had missed—whether because the noncombatants had stayed inside vehicle cabs during the whole period of surveillance or had been behind some feature of the terrain where the cameras couldn't see them, or a shell fragment had struck them outside the expected blast radius.[136]

The point of Haymaker was that it kept Americans off the ground in places like Gambir, capitalizing on drone technology and tactics that had evolved vastly in the decade since the fuzzy, mistake-riddled days of 2002 and 2003. But a Reaper's high-definition camera was still not an all-seeing eye, and a Hellfire warhead was not a scalpel.

TWO YEARS INTO Haymaker, Farouq al-Qahtani, the al-Qaida operative whose presence in the valleys north of the Pech had prompted the JSOC air campaign, remained at large. A new generation of special operations and intelligence personnel spoke of him in the same terms that an older one had used for Abu Ikhlas al-Masri: "elusive," "like a ghost," "a phantom." Hopes kept rising that a strike had killed him, only to be dashed. "We declared that guy dead any number of times," remembered Joe Votel, the JSOC commander.[137]

If it wasn't killing Farouq, and if the returns were diminishing, what was Haymaker accomplishing?

It was keeping a lid on Farouq and his associates, American generals and intelligence officials argued; just because it wasn't killing its number one target didn't mean it wasn't hemming him in and preventing him from planning the next September 11. The U.S. government's official estimate was that there were fewer than a hundred al-Qaida operatives in Kunar and Nuristan, and they were occupied with trying to survive the drone campaign, not planning attacks overseas.[138] "Today, the core of al-Qaida in Afghanistan and Pakistan is on the path to defeat," President Obama asserted in his 2013 drone policy speech. "Their remaining operatives spend more time thinking about their own safety than plotting against us."[139]

But for this effect to persist, the pressure would have to be kept up, and on this point the White House and the military were in tension.

In the same drone speech, Obama had reiterated his pledge that American combat troops would withdraw from Afghanistan by the end of 2014 and predicted that after that the need for counterterrorism strikes in the country would wane too, even though a few thousand special operations and support troops would remain behind to conduct them for a couple more years. This did not match how the military saw the issue. Although the number of al-Qaida operatives in Kunar and Nuristan was only "in the dozens," according to military analysis produced later in the year, "their presence continues to demonstrate their intent to maintain the region as an alternate safe haven to their sanctuaries in Pakistan"—the mission that bin Laden had charged Farouq with before his death.[140] Al-Qaida leaders knew what the administration had promised about the end of the combat mission, and they were likely waiting it out, the internal JSOC assessment of Haymaker produced in March had suggested. All of the operation's effects were "temporary," and to keep them up would require "a long-term, persistent campaign," lasting beyond the scheduled December 2014 mission change.[141]

The implication was that Haymaker, or something like it, would have to last longer than Obama was suggesting the U.S. presence would, and probably longer than he would be in office. To some who had seen the misguided infantry war in Kunar and Nuristan with its high costs, this seemed reasonable—even a bargain, compared with what had come before, the era of air-centric outposts and road building and combat in the mountains with a tenacious enemy. "The question is, can you tolerate those guys hiding up there, and perhaps coming out?" said a former brigade commander in the counterinsurgency fight in the northeast, now back in Kabul with a headquarters job that gave him glimpses of Haymaker. "I don't know. But maybe if you're going to do whack-a-mole, you do it with drones rather than rifle companies."[142]

There was an inevitable flip side to taking American infantrymen and special operators out of harm's way, however—especially when what was billed as a counterterrorism campaign was actually mostly killing young local militants. "The militants' sons and nephews replace them, and the drone attacks have created new enemies in these places" was how Mawlawi Shahzada Shahid put it. "People will still remember these strikes in a hundred years."[143]

CHAPTER 15

THE WAR THAT NEVER ENDS

2014–2017

THE LAST OUTPOST

The first base that Americans had established in Kunar back in the spring of 2002 was also the last one they closed on their way out: Asadabad. More than one of the Green Berets who turned off the lights there in late October 2014 had spent time at the base on previous Afghan deployments.

The rectangular base a mile south of Kunar's main city had gone by a number of names since SEAL Team 6 operators first dubbed it Firebase Puchi Ghar in the spring of 2002. It had been Firebase Asadabad, then FOB Asadabad, and then FOB Wright, in honor of a Green Beret sergeant, Jeremy Wright, who had become the fourth American to die in the province when an IED hit his pickup truck in 2005 on the then-unpaved Kunar valley road. Most of the time, the American troops and intelligence personnel deployed there had simply called it A-Bad. To Kunaris it was still Topchi Base, the artillery base, the same as it had been when Soviet troops lived there.

In the twelve and a half years the Americans had spent at Asadabad, tents had been replaced by plywood huts and then concrete buildings; new walls had gone up around a roomier outer compound for artillery, helicopter pads, an ammunition dump, and big bladders of fuel; and the ten-acre interior compound's population had risen toward a thousand and then shrunk again. Just three hundred or so Americans were left at Asadabad in the summer of 2014 as the soldiers there prepared to leave the base and its other tenant, the CIA, reluctantly packed up alongside them. There was an A-team from the 3rd Special Forces Group, the latest of nearly two dozen such teams to pass through the base since Jim Gant's days there at the start of the war. Living with the Green Berets was a platoon of infantrymen who helped with security and crewed their MRAPs. The provincial reconstruction team was gone, but there was still a detachment of about two hundred conventional infantrymen and cavalrymen from the 101st Airborne, led by a lieutenant colonel, who advised the ANA brigade in Kunar, traveling back and forth between Asadabad and an Afghan base across the river but rarely going farther into the field than that. And as always, there was the CIA's group of case officers, analysts, contractors, and support personnel.

Some of the Green Beret sergeants on the team had been in Kunar on their last deployment, working with a village militia elsewhere in the province. Their captain was a Kunar veteran too: as an engineer platoon leader attached to Brett Jenkinson's Blue Spader battalion, he'd spent countless hours clearing IEDs from the Pech road and its side-valley offshoots in 2008 and 2009, driving up and down the Korengal and Watapur and taking part in the battalion's attempted westward expansion to Chapa Dara.[1]

It was the Green Berets' impression that the ANA and the Taliban were in a stalemate in the Pech over the summer of 2014. But generals and their staffs in Kabul were uninterested in letting the Special Forces team make any trips to the Pech to see for themselves, where the rules said they could venture only if medevac Black Hawks—a scarce resource again in post-surge Afghanistan— flew up to stage at FOB Asadabad in case something went wrong. The most detailed information they had about anything happening out west consisted of intelligence readouts regarding the ongoing Haymaker strikes. The most the A-team could do for the Afghan security forces out in the Pech was to scrounge up some Hesco barriers, sandbags, and plywood to send out to a new government militia force that was standing up in Chapa Dara. "As much as we wanted to go out in the Pech and get in gunfights, it wasn't happening," the team captain remembered. "There was no stomach for us to go out there" at headquarters in Kabul. "They saw that valley as a place where a lot of Americans had died."[2]

Nevertheless, chasing combat just like Jim Gant and his team back at the beginning in Kunar, the Green Berets found their way into firefights. On the A-team's patrols into the Kunar valley's smaller tributaries—like the Marawara and Shonkrai valleys, which were within range of medevac helicopters at Jalalabad—several of the young infantrymen working with the Green Berets earned Purple Hearts for shrapnel wounds and minor bullet wounds suffered in brief firefights.[3] It was more combat than most American troops were seeing in Afghanistan as the clock ticked down to January 1, 2015. That was the date when the Obama administration and NATO were declaring a formal end to their "combat mission" in Afghanistan and a transition to something new—a smaller and more restricted presence of ten thousand American and six thousand allied troops for training and counterterrorism, which the White House hoped would also wind down after two more years, by the time Obama left office.

HOW LONG AMERICANS would remain at FOB Asadabad was a subject of debate stretching from Bagram and Kabul back to the Pentagon, the White House, and CIA headquarters at Langley. Senior intelligence officials wanted their little corner of Kunar to remain open as long as possible, but the agency wasn't capable of running its own bases in the rugged Afghan east without the military either colocated or very close by. The departure of nearby military units had already forced the early closure of one of the CIA's oldest bases in the country, at Shkin in the southeast—the one that a Delta Force team had set up around the same time SEALs were setting up shop at Asadabad—catching agency officials in Kabul unprepared. "The station chief was like 'How can you guys do this to us? You can't leave!'" remembered Ron Moeller, who had retired from the CIA after twelve Afghan deployments but was back in Afghanistan at the time, in 2013, as a civilian adviser to ISAF. "It was like the agency was totally disconnected from what was going on. The military was downsizing rapidly."[4]

In debates that stretched back to the National Security Council staff at the White House, the CIA argued for Asadabad to stay open even after the January 1 change of mission that would carry the war into 2015. "CIA was pretty adamant that they wanted Asadabad to stay open, but it had to close," said a senior military officer in the country at the time.[5] The number of American infantry brigades in Afghanistan was falling over the course of 2014 from six to two, helicopter battalions from thirteen to five, Special Forces A-teams from forty to eighteen. Whenever it happened, the military pullout from Asadabad was going to put a damper on both of the main areas of CIA activity in Kunar: paramilitary night raids and running informants, including some who were feeding valuable intelligence into Operation Haymaker.

Part of what the agency used Asadabad for was raids with its Kunari surrogate force, the unit known back in the early days of the war as the Mohawks. Now called Unit 04, the Asadabad force was formally part of the NDS, the Afghan intelligence service that the CIA worked closely with, and it was the only combat force still launching night raids against militant leaders on the ground in Kunar. But it leaned heavily on the U.S. military for support in the field, as a mission one night in April 2013 had illustrated. Seventy-five Unit 04 commandos and four Americans—a mix of agency officers and contractors—had driven in pickup trucks from Asadabad up the Kunar valley, across the river, and into a side valley that led up toward the Pakistani border. Raiding a compound where they were hoping to capture a militant commander, the Afghan commandos and CIA personnel found only women, children, and an old man, but as they searched the place, insurgents started shooting at them from the hills. The enemy force was large, and as dawn approached, the paramilitary operatives and their Afghan surrogates were pinned down, unable to move.[6]

The nearest military unit available to bail out the CIA raid force was a Green Beret A-team—like the one at FOB Asadabad the next year, a detachment from Fort Bragg's Afghanistan-focused 3rd Special Forces Group. The special operations soldiers drove as far up the valley as they could in MRAPs, then hiked the last few miles toward the sound of the firefight until they too were embroiled in it, defending a building a few hundred yards from the raid force's position while machine-gun fire and RPGs poured in from the mountains on either side. As Unit 04 commandos braved the incoming fire and tried to move toward the Green Beret reinforcements, one of the CIA contractors was fatally shot. The A-team's Air Force air controller spent the rest of the morning talking drones, A-10s, and an AC-130 onto targets around the valley, standing exposed while the Green Berets fought their way to the stranded CIA team and retrieved the slain contractor's body. The contractor was the last American known to have died in Kunar. The CIA has never revealed his name and has yet to acknowledge his death except as one of four nameless stars added to its memorial wall at Langley the next month in an annual remembrance ceremony. But the mission that claimed his life clearly illustrated the degree to which the province's conditions required the agency to lean on the military for support both on the ground and from the air.*

After paramilitary operations, the other role Asadabad served for the CIA was as a platform for the agency's traditional role—the collection of intelligence, in this case the collection of intelligence on al-Qaida figures in Kunar and Nuristan like Farouq al-Qahtani.

Brett Jenkinson was back in Afghanistan for his third Afghanistan deployment at the time, working as the operations director of the main U.S. military headquarters overseeing the withdrawal—including from Asadabad. Jenkinson was still reeling internally from the pain of his deployment leading the Blue Spader battalion in the Pech, the hardest year of his life; when he'd left Blessing in 2009, he'd hoped never to see Kunar again. But in 2014, hitching a ride with the colonel commanding the aviation brigade at Bagram, Jenkinson headed into the province once again. Flying high over the Korengal, he could see just the faintest outlines of what had been

---

* After the raid force withdrew, the building where they had been pinned down collapsed, killing at least thirteen women and children whom the Unit 04 commandos had corralled into a room. Whether the collapse was due to shock waves from the nearby U.S. air strikes or to structural damage from the pounding the building had taken from incoming Taliban RPGs wasn't clear even after U.S., UN, and Afghan government investigations.

the KOP and Vegas, the outposts he'd lost so much sleep over. Jenkinson tried to take a picture with his iPhone, but he was too high up and there was too little left to see: "You couldn't tell they'd ever been bases. No Hescos, no HLZs."[7]

FOB Asadabad looked the same to Jenkinson as the last time he'd seen it, back in 2009, when he made weekly visits there to check in with its CIA base chief. Thanks to his time working for the DIA as well as his collaboration with the Asadabad intelligence personnel as a battalion commander, he had a better grasp than most infantry colonels would have of the challenges the CIA and its NDS partners were looking at in maintaining their informant networks once the base was gone. "What hurts you most from closing Asadabad Base was, they had sources who could come to talk there," he remembered. "Once that base closes, some of those human sources will have a much harder time making it down to report" to the remaining military-protected CIA hub in Jalalabad, fifty miles to the south, through both government and Taliban checkpoints. By necessity, intelligence efforts in Kunar and Nuristan—the underpinnings of Operation Haymaker—would have to rely more on signals intercepts from here on out.[8]

THE FINAL CALL about Asadabad belonged to ISAF's four-star commander, Joe Dunford. Visiting Asadabad, the Marine general heard out the Green Berets, the 101st Airborne advisers and ANA commanders they worked with, and the CIA. "I remember leaving those visits convinced that we should keep Asadabad Base open as long as we could," he told me. Back in Kabul, a joint team of conventional and special operations officers put together planning options for Dunford that included keeping the base beyond 2014, as the military was planning to do for a pair of CIA bases in the south and southeast that the agency deemed essential for monitoring al-Qaida activity across the border. But Dunford had to draw the line somewhere, and Asadabad didn't make the cut. The base, he decided, would remain open through one last fighting season, but then it would close in October as the U.S.-led military mission in Afghanistan shrank down to Kabul, Bagram, Jalalabad, Kandahar, airfield hubs in the north and west for NATO's German and Italian contingents, and the two military-supported CIA bases in Helmand and Khost.[9]

As the clock ticked down toward FOB Asadabad's closure date, the Americans remaining there spent less time planning and executing missions and more time inside the wire packing up everything they could and blowing up or handing over to the Afghans what they couldn't. "We shot a huge amount of ammunition" on the range just to get rid of it, the Green Beret team captain said, and threw "cases and cases of hand grenades; the boys got really good at throwing hand grenades."[10]

The final convoy headed out in the third week of October: the Green Beret A-team in their MRAPs and the last of the 101st Airborne advisers in theirs, escorted by dozens if not hundreds of armed pickup trucks belonging to the hodgepodge of Afghan National Army, police, militia, and NDS forces they had worked with, seeing the departing Americans safely to Jalalabad.

Among the last things to go had been the items commemorating Jeremy Wright, the Green Beret in whose memory the base had been formally renamed FOB Wright. "We brought as much of the Sergeant Wright stuff out as we could," said the team captain: a big vinyl banner that had hung at the main gate, and a plaque that the departing special operators hacked off its concrete pedestal, hoping to deliver it to the fallen soldier's parents.[11]

FREEDOM'S SENTINEL

With the closure of FOB Asadabad and the departure of the special operators and intelligence personnel there, air strikes went from the military's main counterterrorism tool in the Pech and its tributaries to its *only* tool there.

As part of the troop reduction, the JSOC task force in Afghanistan shrank in the months leading up to January 1, 2015. SEAL Team 6 was closing down Task Force East in Jalalabad and leaving the country after thirteen years of continuous involvement. Counterterrorism missions throughout Afghanistan, including Operation Haymaker, would now be the responsibility of the Rangers, working out of a two-story building in the same old JSOC compound at

Bagram: two big operations centers stacked on top of each other, battalion headquarters on the first floor and regimental headquarters above it, both full of giant screens that showed feeds from drones and surveillance planes around Afghanistan.[12]

Because the Ranger Regiment was the home of many of the Army's best light infantry officers, and so many of the Army's light infantry units had passed through Kunar and Nuristan over the years, the unit's leadership was seeded with men who had spent time on the ground in the two provinces in the years leading up to the Haymaker air campaign. "After I walked down those valleys in '03, I remember thinking it was going to be like a needle in a haystack if we ever went targeting up there," said one Winter Strike veteran who found himself signing off on Haymaker strikes in 2015. "Twelve years later, there I am trying to do that."[13] Then there were the Ranger captains and majors who had fought in Kunar as lieutenants. "I wanted to get on Haymaker, because I knew who all those assholes were and had been in a bunch of the villages we were targeting," a Ranger captain told me.[14]

One of these officers was Dan Kearney, now a major, who was working on the first floor of the task force headquarters building during the weeks leading up to and following the transition. As a Ranger company commander and staff officer, Kearney had gone back to Afghanistan over and over again since his time in the Korengal, overseeing raids in the southeast on one tour, in the south on another, and now focusing on the northeast again. Lining up and planning strikes there was the responsibility of a small group of soldiers and contractors within the Ranger headquarters called the Haymaker desk—a Ranger captain and NCO running a handful of intelligence analysts—but Kearney oversaw them as 1st Ranger Battalion's operations officer, vetting their proposed attacks and passing them on to the task force commander and generals in Kabul for approval.[15]

AS PART OF the January 1 transition, the international military missions in Afghanistan were being renamed: the Pentagon's Operation Enduring Freedom, after thirteen years, was giving way to Operation Freedom's Sentinel, and NATO's ISAF command was being renamed Resolute Support. For JSOC's Haymaker desk, the transition didn't mean much materially. Under the new post-2014 rules that accompanied the name changes, the Rangers could no longer strike Taliban targets unless they either posed an imminent threat to American, NATO, or Afghan government forces or were affiliated with al-Qaida, but the latter was exactly the kind of target Haymaker was going after anyway. The closure of the CIA's Asadabad outstation had already downgraded the amount and quality of human intelligence tips coming out of the Pech; for the most part, what remained was signals intelligence, and the pace of strikes had already fallen accordingly.[16] "In 2015, the focused operation that was Haymaker kind of goes away," recalled Joe Votel, then back in the United States as the military's four-star top special operations commander.

Haymaker continued on a smaller scale, however; the first strike of the new year in the Pech came on January 6.[17] Kearney leaned on his Korengal experience as he watched the Haymaker video feeds and weighed whether and when to pass strikes up to his bosses for approval. "It absolutely was useful," he said. "Understanding how the people up there go about their everyday lives, up in the mountains in the trees or down in the valleys, I was able to take my fifteen months in the Korengal and apply that lens while watching people go about their normal business and also do things that were out of the ordinary."[18] In a headquarters full of younger troops and contractors who'd never been in Kunar or Nuristan, Kearney and others with similar experiences served as conduits introducing on-the-ground knowledge into JSOC's air war.

Just maintaining an understanding of what was happening between the ANA and the Taliban was difficult from the air and with reduced intelligence coming in. "You get these reports once in a while that an outpost had fallen or a bunch of ANA were being burned at the stake or whatever, and you fly ISR [surveillance aircraft] up there and there's not much going on; it's like one vehicle burning at the end of a short battle or something," said another Ranger officer. "It was rarely anything close to what was being reported."[19] But sometimes, there really had been a battlefield disaster. When American aircraft arrived over an observation post in northern Kunar one winter night, for example, the place had been over-run, and the carnage was worse than anything Americans had experienced during their own desperate outpost battles at Want and the Ranch House: twenty-one Afghan soldiers were dead and five more were missing after traitors within the ANA garrison helped the Taliban get inside the wire.[20]

KEARNEY EXPECTED, and hoped, to be arranging drone strikes in his old stomping grounds, the Korengal, but he was disappointed. "It was all around the Korengal, to the north, just to the south, just to the east, but never really *in* the Korengal like he seemed to expect," remembered one Ranger who worked for him.[21] Al-Qaida targets—what had first drawn American attention to the Korengal at the start of the war—just weren't popping up there. As Brett Jenkinson had seen when he flew over the valley a few months earlier, what had been the KOP was again being used as a timber mill, not a Taliban command post or training camp, while OP Restrepo had been so thoroughly dismantled for its parts that it might as well not have been there at all. The Korengal road was free from Taliban check-points;[22] without Americans or Afghan government troops bother-ing them, the Korengalis seemed to be shedding some of their ties to outside militant groups.

A valley that did draw persistent Haymaker attention was the Waygal, where Kearney's fellow Rock paratroopers from Chosen Company had fought in 2007 and 2008.

Since the ANA's big 2013 push up the Waygal, Afghan troops and policemen had been hanging on to a collection of precarious outposts ringing the Want district center where Chosen Company paratroopers had fought and died during the July 2008 battle. One of the first Waygalis to join the Taliban after September 11, Maw-lawi Monibullah of Aranas, now sat on the Peshawar *shura,* and a relative of his served as the Taliban's district governor in the valley.[23] "A few dozen Taliban control the whole district through fear," a Waygali government official living in Kabul explained. "What is the need for the base in Want if the police there can't even come out of it? You're only controlling a hundred families and supporting the base by helicopter, while thousands of other families are left to the Taliban's mercy, and just to show that you are holding the district center."[24]

Outside Want, the Taliban controlled the valley outright, collecting taxes, holding courts, and punishing those who had worked with U.S. troops. "The Taliban are searching for people who had good relationships with the Americans, and I can't live there," a middle-aged Waygali man told me.[25] In an effort to spur desertions among Nuristanis serving elsewhere in the country in the ANA and the police, the Taliban issued a warning for their relatives to pass along to them: "Come back or we will marry your wives."[26] But returning was not wise. "If you work for the government and you go back, you will be beaten and tortured," said a Waygali cleric who was in contact with the Taliban in his home valley as a member of the High Peace Council.[27]

The Afghan government was determined to hold on to Want, whatever the cost, and the Taliban were intent on periodically showing their strength by attacking it. In December, just before the transition, Kearney and his boss signed off on three strikes in the Waygal, one that killed six militants, another that killed eight, and a third, between Christmas and New Year's, that killed a local Taliban commander called Sayed Izam.[28] In June 2015, a group of militants—Waygali Taliban reinforced by comrades who had marched over the mountains from Gambir and Katar in the Watapur—descended on Want, overrunning several police checkpoints, killing about a dozen policemen, and looting and partially destroying the district center. When an ANA force came up from Nangalam to take Want back, supported by at least one U.S. air strike, the Taliban melted away again.[29] This pattern would play out repeatedly in the Waygal as the Taliban stormed into Want and then left again when pressed, content with having shown that they could reach the district center, however briefly. The week of Thanksgiving, frantic reports started coming in from Want again, and the task force had to fly a drone up to see how much truth there was to claims of a major Taliban offensive and surrenders by scores of ANA, police, and government workers.[30]

Most of the insurgent leaders from Kearney's time in the Korengal were dead or in detention: Abu Ikhlas, Haji Matin, Dawran. The militants the Rangers and their supporting airmen and intelligence personnel were killing now in places like the Waygal were ones the former Battle Company commander had never heard of before—often, with al-Qaida targets few and far between, fairly low-level ones a degree or more removed from the terrorist group, the local fighters who acted as "facilitators" to the Arab and Pakistani militants in one role or another. Kearney relished the targets' deaths all the same. "Putting warheads on foreheads!" he would exult when the explosion of a bomb or Hellfire bloomed on the screens in the operations center, to the amusement of younger Rangers working there.[31]

Some other Rangers who worked on Haymaker wondered how much of the killing they were doing really accomplished anything. "What effect is it having on the network? Are we just hitting whoever we can with Hellfires? You'll never run out of people to kill there," said one.[32] "If a radioman or a machine gunner is the only guy we can find this month, we'll call him Objective Box Cutter," for example, "and try to kill him," acknowledged another.[33]

Later, after Haymaker strikes had largely ceased in the Waygal, I interviewed residents who either had been forced out of the valley or were visiting Kabul with the permission of the Taliban about how the air campaign had affected their communities and their perceptions of who was being killed. The refrain I heard was that while no women or children had died of drone strikes in the Waygal in recent years, many young men with only loose connections to the Taliban had, and the deaths of Taliban commanders had sometimes made life more difficult in towns they controlled like Aranas and Amshuz. In one strike in 2014 or 2015 that several Waygalis recalled, but which I couldn't match to a particular strike reported in news outlets or confirmed by special operations sources, Reapers attacked a group of men in the north of the valley on their way to an intervillage meeting that Taliban officials were to preside over, a *jirga*. Nine men died, an elder named Haji Abdul Qudus told me, including his elderly uncle. "There was a land dispute between families, and they had solved the dispute and were going to meet with each other when a drone attacked them," Abdul Qudus said. "I don't deny that there were Taliban there, but they were low-ranking people, and they were just involved in settling the dispute."[34] A government worker who lost a cousin in the strike agreed: "They were targeting a local Taliban commander who was at the *jirga,* but of course he was there. They control the area."[35]

A member of the government worker's family who visited for the funerals after the strike told me that the gradual culling of Taliban officials in the valley in air strikes had eliminated the more educated and reasonable men among them—the Taliban's top picks for the jobs—and left in their place new officials who were illiterate and more violent and paranoid. "The better Taliban have been killed by drones, and only the bad ones are remaining," he said.[36] As successive militants imposed stricter counterintelligence measures, cell phones had been banned in most villages; risking execution if they were caught and accused of being spies, residents had to hike into the mountains to make calls.[37]

EXTERNAL OPERATIONS

No matter how far down the kill list they ventured, Rangers working at Bagram were reminded each day when they entered the task force headquarters of the core counterterrorism purpose that kept them in Afghanistan: in the building's main hallway, impossible to miss as one entered the ground-floor operations center, hung a print of *The Falling Man,* the iconic photo of an unidentified man plunging headfirst from the World Trade Center's doomed North Tower. Fifteen years after September 11, 2001, the Haymaker target who most closely personified that mission was Farouq al-Qahtani, who senior national security hands in the Obama administration feared harbored something between a desire and a plan to strike the West with terror attacks.

For years, the war in Kunar had been on autopilot, fought by small units on the ground many echelons below a Pentagon, CIA, and White House interested only in the big picture of the Afghan conflict, not what was happening in any one remote corner of the country. But Farouq, and the Haymaker campaign targeting him and his associates, had changed that. Where previously the highest-ranking officials paying attention to the Pech and its tributaries had been generals in Kabul, the presence of a high-profile al-Qaida

leader in the mountains had the attention of some of the government's top counterterrorism officials, who received updates whenever the intelligence agencies thought they had a lead on him. The
last time officials back in Washington had been so interested in
Kunar and Nuristan had been during the hunt for bin Laden in
2002 and 2003.

The official most vocally concerned about him was Michael
Morell, the career terrorism analyst who, as the CIA's acting director, had rung alarm bells about him in 2011 after the Abbottabad
documents shined new light on his ties to senior al-Qaida leaders.

Since bin Laden's death in Abbottabad, al-Qaida's top leader had
been Ayman al-Zawahiri, the Egyptian who had hidden with Osama
in Kunar's Shigal valley after Tora Bora. But Zawahiri was in his
mid-sixties, had grown frail, and lacked bin Laden's magnetism. It
seemed all but certain that the next tier of al-Qaida leaders were
considering who would eventually replace him, and Morell thought
it could well be Farouq. "Smart and operationally sophisticated"
after years of evading raids and air strikes and "a charismatic leader,"
he was a "counterterrorism expert's worst nightmare," Morell wrote
from retirement in 2015. He had already proven himself in combat
and earned enough trust from his superiors that bin Laden charged
him with the critical task of developing a backup sanctuary in case
the CIA drone campaign drove al-Qaida leaders out of Pakistan. As
the Taliban gained more ground in the years ahead, Farouq's star as
al-Qaida's top liaison to the Afghan insurgent movement in the land
where bin Laden founded the group would only rise, Morell worried, positioning him to inherit al-Qaida's top position. "He is one
of the few al Qa'ida leaders I worry might have what it takes to replace Bin Laden" after Zawahiri's eventual death, Morell wrote.[38]
Lieutenant General Mike Flynn, then director of the DIA, agreed
when I asked him about Farouq in 2015, saying that al-Qaida might
turn to him "when they look for leaders who can replace the UBLs
[Osama bin Ladens] and the Zawahiris."[39]

The CIA, DIA, and military intelligence all officially maintained
that the number of al-Qaida operatives in Afghanistan was about a
hundred,[40] but that was little more than a guess, and it was clear to
almost no one what exactly the number counted—just Arab
al-Qaida fighters, or Pakistani and Afghan militants who had sworn

allegiance to the terrorist groups as well? Morell's understanding was that it was an estimate of the number of Arab fighters, largely, although not entirely, excluding Afghan and Pakistani militants who sometimes played key roles in Farouq's group.[41] From the Ranger headquarters at Bagram, the numbers could seem as if they had been pulled from thin air. "There was good intel work that pieced together that there were something like ten, fifteen actual Arabs sitting up there in those valleys with him," said a Ranger officer of Farouq's group.[42] A June 2015 military assessment suggested the one hundred number referred to the size of al-Qaida's "sustained" presence in Afghanistan—the operatives, "concentrated largely in Kunar and Nuristan," who remained in the country year-round, rather than staying only for the warm months as some fighters did in other eastern provinces.[43]

The bigger question than how many al-Qaida operatives were with Farouq in Kunar and Nuristan was what they were doing there. Were they plotting the next September 11? Hanging on for dear life under the constant shadow of drone strikes in relative isolation from the rest of their organization? Or something in between? U.S. intelligence believed that Farouq was al-Qaida's top commander, or emir, for eastern Afghanistan, overseeing the work of trainers and advisers to the Taliban across most of the provinces where they operated, but also that he was in charge of planning "external operations," the euphemism for international terrorist attacks.[44] The question was whether this was a concrete responsibility, with plots under way, or more of an aspirational one. "Nobody really cared about the emir part" of Farouq's role, a JSOC officer explained, "but they cared a lot about the external ops part."[45]

AS THE 2015 fighting season got under way, the military's official assessment was that Farouq and his men were "more focused on survival" than on planning international attacks.[46] "What he's up there doing is not planning external operations; he's up there planning for a role in the Taliban takeover of the Afghan government, if he's still alive then," Mike Flynn told me.[47] "We never saw a lot of operational planning out of al-Qaida up there," said another senior special operations officer, who added that of the occasional communications from Farouq back to Pakistan that they intercepted, many were not operational messages but requests that some of his wives or children be sent to join him in his hideout. "That's about the only way we ever saw his communications; he would say to bring some of his family over the border to link up with him," the officer said. The risk-reward calculus seemed simple nevertheless. "From a national security perspective, is it worth taking the risk?" the officer asked, referring to the possibility of halting routine surveillance flights and drone strikes over Kunar. "That's an easy answer. It's worth flying some freaking Reapers up there to make sure it doesn't turn into something worse."[48]

There were some in the intelligence agencies who saw Farouq as a bigger threat than that. When he stepped down as the CIA's deputy director in 2013, Mike Morell told me, he and other intelligence officials were "deeply concerned" about Farouq, not only because of the original role bin Laden had assigned to him and his men—as "a fallback and a vanguard should the Pakistan senior leadership disappear"—but because they appeared intent on conducting overseas attacks. Of the terrorist threats around the world that worried Morell the most at the time, when Haymaker was at its height, "number three was Qahtani in Kunar," he said—the first and second being al-Qaida's senior leadership council in the Pakistani tribal areas and an al-Qaida branch in Yemen that was plotting to blow up commercial airliners.[49]

Morell compared Farouq to a notorious al-Qaida figure in Yemen: a bomb maker named Ibrahim al-Asiri.[50] None of Asiri's plots had ever succeeded; when he sent his younger brother on a suicide mission with a bomb in his rectum to kill a Saudi prince, the target lived, and an "underwear bomb" he built for detonation on a transatlantic flight failed to explode. Asiri's interest in attacking commercial aviation and his creative tactics—the intelligence agencies believed he was experimenting with metal-free bombs to sneak into airports and with surgically implanting bombs into living subjects—made him a white whale to officials on the White House's National Security Council staff.

At the CIA's Counterterrorism Center, the agency veteran Douglas London didn't think Farouq was in the same league as Asiri when it came to involvement in international attack plotting.

"There was always intelligence suggesting he aspired to conduct external operations, and there were some plots that were attributed to him, but you can't compare him to Asiri; that's apples and oranges," said London, who in 2015 and 2016 was in charge of the Counterterrorism Center's collaboration with the military and other organizations. One of the most worrying strains of information about Farouq suggested that he was hosting dual-national Pakistani recruits with British passports whom al-Qaida had selected for their clean records, professional credentials, and ability to travel to Europe or the United States.[51] London saw that as "evidence of his continued interest and tangible efforts in the past." But "most of his effort was toward representing al-Qaida's interests in northeastern Afghanistan and providing aid and support to the Taliban," said London, whereas for Asiri external plots had been a full-time job.[52]

Nevertheless, Farouq's apparent interest in overseas attacks led officials on the White House's NSC staff to treat him similarly. "Farouq al-Qahtani generated a level of celebrity interest in the national security community akin to that of Asiri," explained a counterterrorism official who acted as the liaison between JSOC and the NSC staff. "He was someone with tactical chops and religious and operational credibility, and he had an easy-to-remember name and was difficult to find. He was sort of seen as almost like a supernatural character, and he attracted senior-level attention automatically."[53]

At the NSC staff's counterterrorism desk, a dozen analysts spent their days triaging intelligence about different al-Qaida branches and affiliates so that Obama's top national security aides could discuss them in NSC meetings with defense and intelligence officials. But the information tended to be vague enough that an official working on the NSC staff at the time wondered about various possible explanations for it: Was Farouq actively directing overseas attack plots? Was he trying to but failing because of the pressure from Haymaker? Were informants hyping him up because they could tell that their CIA handlers wanted to hear about him? Or was Farouq's cell a red herring, a successful effort to get the American military and intelligence agencies to waste precious resources like Reapers and spy planes chasing him around an isolated region? "To this day, I couldn't tell you with confidence which of those it was," the official said. "But as long as you were hearing his name in ways that couldn't be run down and found to be totally bogus, it made sense to take it as seriously as Mike Morell did."[54]

The NSC's Afghanistan-Pakistan desk, down the hall, was headed up by a recently retired Navy commander, Jeff Eggers. A SEAL who'd deployed to Iraq and Afghanistan, Eggers had spent time as Erik Kristensen's roommate in San Diego, and he'd been hearing about the Korengal, the Pech, and Kunar since June 28, 2005—the day Kristensen died trying to rescue his stranded recon team on the Sawtalo Sar. As an adviser to Stan McChrystal during the surge, Eggers had seen the place for himself, visiting COP Michigan and accompanying infantry patrols into town, where he noticed that villagers had pilfered the batteries from U.S.-funded solar panels. What did it mean for al-Qaida to be in a place like the Waygal valley, isolated from resources and compatriots? Eggers wondered. He respected Morell's analysis of Farouq, viewing him as a sober analyst not prone to hyperbole. But he still worried that the U.S. government's counterterrorism apparatus, from the intelligence agencies to military task forces, was exaggerating the danger Farouq and his men posed, or at least lacked a way to ensure that the resources arrayed against him were commensurate with the highly subjective scale of the threat.

"There's the operational threat al-Qaida poses, but al-Qaida's presence in [Afghanistan] also has psychological and emotional significance to us, and I think there's a gulf between the two," Eggers said. But "that's difficult to talk about. Because of what we went through on 9/11, it sounds blasphemous to a lot of people to suggest that we exaggerate the importance of al-Qaida in that region." In a campaign of "perpetual targeting to keep them in hiding," and amid competing demands for surveillance aircraft in Iraq, Syria, Yemen, and various parts of Africa, where did you draw the line? How many Reapers, signals intelligence planes, and intelligence analysts could JSOC and the spy agencies commit to hunting a small, hard-to-find group like Farouq's in perpetuity? That question would have been easy for generals and Pentagon and CIA officials to answer if they understood both Farouq's future intentions and his ability to carry them out. But those were things no one in the U.S. government knew for sure, and short of placing an agent inside his band of fighters—or capturing a member of the group, a possibility that Haymaker's air-only approach precluded—they wouldn't. "Someone might say the leader of al-Qaida in Afghanistan has the intent but not the capability right up until the day when he unleashes a tragedy in the West," said Eggers.[55]

One of the most senior and experienced counterterrorism hands in uniform was Lieutenant General Mike Nagata, who had spent much of the post-2001 era hunting terrorists in Iraq, Somalia, and Yemen with a top secret JSOC reconnaissance unit. Nagata first read reports about Farouq and heard discussion of him as the senior special operations officer on the Pentagon's Joint Staff in 2012 and 2013, and then again starting in the spring of 2016 as a top official at the National Counterterrorism Center, the agency in northern Virginia that had been established after September 11 to coordinate the counterterrorism efforts of the CIA, NSA, FBI, DIA, JSOC, and so on. "Certainly it was the view of some of my peers that Qahtani was an operational-level threat at most," one who might not have warranted the kind of top-level attention in Washington that he was receiving. But "what that didn't take into account was how much the administration had staked on counterterrorism success in Afghanistan" as Obama's second term waned, said Nagata.[56]

This was true. For Obama and his national security team at the White House, getting out of Afghanistan before a new president took office in January 2017—withdrawing all but roughly a thousand troops who would guard the embassy and CIA station in Kabul—was a cherished second-term goal, and al-Qaida's continuing presence in the country was getting in the way of it.

JSOC GROUND OPERATIONS in Afghanistan were a rarity now; only half a Ranger battalion was deploying to Bagram at a time anymore, and most platoons would go a whole four-month rotation without seeing combat. But after a July 2015 air strike in Bermel, a border district 160 miles to Kunar's south, Rangers who landed to comb through the rubble turned up information that suggested al-Qaida operatives were venturing into parts of the country far from Kunar and Nuristan—into places where the group hadn't maintained a regular presence since before September 11. The question, as with

Farouq in Kunar, was what they were doing there, and that question had implications for the Obama administration's plan to mostly pull out of Afghanistan by the time the president left office.

The July air strike, the JSOC task force confirmed, had killed an even more senior al-Qaida figure than Farouq, Abu Khalil al-Sudani. The intelligence agencies believed that besides being a member of al-Qaida's Pakistan-based leadership *shura*, Abu Khalil oversaw the group's bomb-making program and suicide operations in the Afghanistan-Pakistan theater and was involved in planning overseas terrorist attacks. That he had felt safe enough to venture across the border took intelligence analysts by surprise.[57] Even more surprising was where the intelligence from the Bermel raid led the task force next: to a vast desert complex where al-Qaida operatives were training militants from other groups the way they had at their Afghan camps before September 11 and producing propaganda footage as part of a new regional branch the group had recently established, al-Qaida in the Indian Subcontinent, or AQIS.[58]

The Rangers dubbed the AQIS propaganda cell Objective Thanos Lobo, after a pair of comic-book villains. Working with the CIA, they located it in Afghanistan's far southern corner, four hundred miles from Kunar—among rocky, arid hills in Kandahar's desert district of Shorabak. "Soaking" the area with drones for two weeks, intelligence analysts identified more than fifty compounds and cave entrances that militants seemed to be using across a thirty-square-mile expanse close to the Pakistani border. Who exactly the fighters living there were wasn't clear, but the place was big enough that raiding it would require more manpower than JSOC had at Bagram. Orders went back to Savannah for a fresh company from 1st Ranger Battalion to head downrange, and the task force enlisted the help of a Green Beret team and the company of ANA Commandos they advised.

Hitting the ground in Shorabak after two waves of air strikes, two hundred Rangers started combing through some of the buildings and caves while the ANA Commandos and Green Berets took the rest. It was the biggest mission JSOC had launched in Afghanistan since the surge, and after scattered gunfights with surviving fighters and more drone strikes the special operators flew off, leaving behind the bodies of more than 150 slain militants.

Most of the dead, intelligence analysts guessed, had been Taliban fighters who were at the Shorabak site receiving training from a small cadre of operatives from al-Qaida's new regional branch, AQIS. That group's presence at the camp was confirmed by the haul of papers, hard drives, and cell phones the Rangers brought back to Bagram. "We didn't find any key HVIs [high-value individuals], but we found Thanos Lobo, this AQIS social media and comms detachment," said an officer involved in the mission. "It was a bunch of cameras and a bunch of digital and printed documents and publications describing the training and everything they were doing there and the growth of AQIS." Passports showed that among the dead had been at least a few foreigners, with nations of origin ranging from North Africa to Southeast Asia, the officer recalled.[59]

THE THANOS LOBO raid demonstrated that al-Qaida's presence in Afghanistan was growing, and it contributed to a decision President Obama announced just four days after the mission. Walking back a plan to have almost all American troops out of the country by the end of his presidency, Obama was slowing the pullout down so that thousands would remain at several major bases when he left office—enough to continue JSOC's counterterrorism mission. Speaking from the West Wing's Roosevelt Room, the president made no mention of the Shorabak mission. "Our troops are not engaged in major ground combat against the Taliban," he said instead, reiterating the artificial distinction his administration had tried to draw between the counterterrorism activities of special operations troops and the conventional "combat mission" that had supposedly ended at the start of the year. But "pressure from Pakistan has resulted in more al-Qaida coming into Afghanistan," he acknowledged, referring to a theory in the intelligence community that the establishment of the Shorabak camp and Abu Khalil's presence in Bermel were side effects of a recent Pakistani military offensive.[60]

What the big October mission didn't turn up evidence of was external attack planning by the new al-Qaida branch, whose focus appeared to be training and advising the Taliban. As far as al-Qaida in Afghanistan went, the intelligence community believed, overseas planning remained the responsibility of Farouq and his crew of veterans, and so drone strikes in the east remained the main focus for the Ranger battalions rotating through Bagram as the Obama presidency waned.

At least once a deployment, intelligence would come into the task force headquarters building from the CIA, DIA, or NSA about the terrorist commander's location in the mountains north of the Pech. A company of eager Rangers would "spin up" for a possible high-risk raid like those their leaders had executed in Kunar in years past, going over which squads would land where, what to do if Farouq surrendered, what to do if he tried to blow himself up. But every time, the word would come to stand down; the task force was handling it remotely instead, staying on the right side of the risk calculus that had spawned Operation Haymaker.

"It was like a react-to-contact drill: somebody farted in D.C. and thought it smelled like Farouq; better fly some ISR [surveillance aircraft] up there," remembered a Ranger officer of the Farouq spin-ups during his Bagram deployments, referring to a type of movement that infantry units trained for so often that it effectively became muscle memory. "It happened a lot."[61]

"HOLY SHIT, THEY FINALLY GOT HIM"

JSOC finally killed Farouq al-Qahtani on a Sunday in October 2016, after five years of trying. The presidential election that would put Donald Trump in office was sixteen days away, and ten thousand American troops remained in the country, overseen by a man who'd already served in Afghanistan through two presidential administrations and three surges: Mick Nicholson, now a four-star general.

It had been more than a decade since Nicholson landed in Kunar during Operation Mountain Lion, and that night in April 2006 remained one of his most vivid memories of his years in Afghanistan: listening on the radio as Chinooks disgorged Marine and 10th Mountain platoons onto the ridges on either side of the valley, and then landing and stepping out onto the snowy Sawtalo Sar summit himself. Nicholson had more time in Afghanistan under his belt than almost any other American general—just shy of four years when word came in from the Rangers that they again believed they had their top target in their sights.

Since taking over the top military job in Kabul in March, Nicholson had been surprised by the situation in Kunar that briefers described to him. On the one hand, government troops—ANA battalions, police, and local militias—controlled the main valley floors, manning a density of outposts in the Pech and even the lower Waygal that would have been unimaginable during his first Afghan deployment, when there were hardly any ANA in the northeast to speak of. On the other hand, side valleys like the Watapur remained as inaccessible to those same Afghan troops as ever, so Farouq and his small al-Qaida group were able to live unmolested by anything but the patient JSOC drone campaign the Rangers were orchestrating from Bagram. Intelligence analysts told Nicholson that Farouq presented a real threat to the United States and that he and his comrades had dug into their remote sanctuaries like ticks. They were going to be there for the long haul, and JSOC's efforts to find and kill them remained the central mission of the American military in Afghanistan. This was an evolution of the same counterterrorism purpose that had underpinned Nicholson's plunge into Kunar and Nuristan as a counterinsurgency-minded 10th Mountain brigade commander and that he hadn't imagined would last this long: punishing al-Qaida and preventing it from attacking the United States from Afghan soil as it had on September 11, when Nicholson had survived the Pentagon attack only by the luck of being out of the office.

When Nicholson had to sign off on a JSOC strike, he and some of his staff would walk down the hall from their usual office space to an annex equipped for classified videoconferences with JSOC's commander at Fort Bragg, CENTCOM headquarters at Tampa, and the CIA at Langley. That was where Nicholson went on the night of October 23. The Reaper footage on the screens in the annex showed a cluster of mountainside buildings not in the Korengal, Waygal, or Watapur but in a different valley that had escaped the attention of Nicholson's 10th Mountain troops during their big push into Kunar and Nuristan ten years earlier: the Helgal.

.   .   .

TWENTY MILES NORTH of the Pech, the Helgal valley dropped down from the far side of the barren heights to which the Watapur and the Shigal rose. Like the Korengal and the Waygal, it was a tight gorge with steep walls and few flat spots where helicopters could land—a canyon "so deep and narrow that a well-placed cloud could constitute a sky," as one aviator who flew there put it.[62] During the years when American soldiers had been fighting on the ground in the northeast, the Helgal had been a kind of no-man's-land, located on the border between the sectors of the infantry battalion in the Pech and the cavalry squadron in northern Kunar and eastern Nuristan and a priority for neither.

Instead, the valley had drawn the occasional attention of counter-terrorism forces—often the CIA with its Kunari surrogates and the Omega team SEALs who worked with them, attracted by hints of an al-Qaida presence among the insurgents who camped out there, away from the outposts and patrols of conventional troops.* More than one soldier who dealt with the Helgal came away thinking that if American forces had chosen to hang their hats there by building an outpost, the Helgal might well have wound up in magazines and newspapers as the "valley of death" instead of the Korengal.

By mid-2015, Farouq's relationships in the Waygal had soured, perhaps because the local Taliban saw him as a magnet for the air strikes that kept killing them. "There were twenty Arab families living in the Waygal valley, but their relations with the people became bad and they started fighting and the people asked them to leave," a Waygali government official recounted.[63] The al-Qaida emir moved on to the Helgal. Much as Haji Matin had once harbored Abu Ikhlas and a series of Taliban officials had hosted Farouq in the Waygal, he settled in this latest valley as a guest of a local insurgent com-

---

* In one dramatic 2008 episode, a Chinook called Mastodon 34 was trying to land in a ninety-four-hundred-foot clearing in the Helgal on a CIA reconnaissance mission when it clipped a massive pine tree, crash-landed, and slid into a ravine. A tense night followed as JSOC troops flew in from Bagram to defend the site from approaching militants until a general made the call to destroy the stranded helicopter.

mander and sawmill owner.[64] In his new home, he stayed farther from populated areas than he had in the Waygal.

Farouq's host wound up on JSOC's Haymaker target list just as Haji Matin had, and the Helgal began to dominate the attention of battalion and task force headquarters.[65] Drone attacks became so common that residents kept their children indoors when they could see or hear the aircraft and often mistook lightning for strikes, a local official told a journalist that July.[66]

WHEN IT HAPPENED in October 2016, it happened quickly. Farouq had been on the move in the Helgal in recent days, a Ranger remembered, "bouncing around between several different places," including a hideout in a village where he was effectively untouchable. But then he returned to a more isolated site in the valley, and Reapers and signals intelligence planes followed him.[67] "It was a set of compounds just like you'd see in any valley in Kunar—spread-out compounds on a mountainside that are kind of connected to each other," said a soldier working in the task force headquarters at the time.[68] Besides Farouq, there seemed to be about a dozen foreign al-Qaida fighters there,[69] including his deputy Bilal al-Utaybi.

"It was good intelligence that led us to the location, and then we used all means of collection and reconnaissance to fix the location," said Doug London, who was in charge of collaboration with the military at the CIA Counterterrorism Center at the time. Analysts zeroed in on two compounds—one where Farouq and his wife were staying, and another that housed his deputy Bilal al-Utaybi and other members of the group. Among the Arab militants at the second compound, intelligence revealed, was a senior al-Qaida bomb maker whom the intelligence community hadn't expected to find there, Abd al-Wahid al-Junabi. "Farouq was in one compound, and Bilal and Junabi were in the other," remembered London.[70]

The contractors and staff officers on the Rangers' Haymaker desk put together and pored over PowerPoint slide decks presenting different ways of striking Farouq. One option was to flatten the place—obliterate the relevant buildings with HIMARS long-range missiles—but that approach was abandoned due to worries that the rockets might damage other compounds in the village. "It was a challenging one to thread the needle of when he wasn't going to be around civilians," the soldier working in the task force headquarters remembered. It would have to be an air strike—either missiles and bombs from the Reapers patiently "soaking" the mountainside, or larger munitions from a fighter jet while the drones filmed the proceedings. Rather than waiting for Farouq to venture out of the building as was the norm for Haymaker strikes, the task force settled on an option seen as likeliest to hit all three Arab commanders— bombing the two compounds where they expected to kill Farouq, Bilal, and Junabi while leaving alone other structures on the mountainside that also housed some of their retinue.[71]

With Nicholson's sign-off, the plan went back to CENTCOM and then the Pentagon for final discussion. In each combat theater, the military maintained a maximum number of expected civilian deaths that top generals could sign off on. Formally called the "noncombatant casualty value," the classified number varied by theater. In Iraq, where government troops and their American advisers were gearing up for the massive urban battle of Mosul, the number was ten, meaning that CENTCOM's commander, Joe Votel, could authorize a strike knowing it would likely kill as many as ten women or children if he deemed it important enough.[72] In Afghanistan, the number had varied over the years, but by 2016, after years of tension between American commanders and the Kabul government over civilian deaths, it was zero. That meant that if there was any expectation of a civilian dying—as there was in this case, because Farouq's wife and perhaps other relatives were in the compound with him— the task force needed approval from very high up in its chain of command, higher even than Nicholson or Votel. The plan would have to go all the way back to the Pentagon office of Secretary of Defense Ash Carter, who would in turn notify Obama's national security aides at the White House.

No one I interviewed would describe the final consultations about the strike between the Pentagon and the White House or even confirm that such consultations occurred. Two former NSC officials told me that they didn't remember any, and the CIA wasn't part of them. "Any discussion concerning the possible presence of Farouq's family members was addressed between the Pentagon and the NSC," Doug London told me.[73]

At whatever echelon it was approved, authorization came back down the chain of command on the night of October 23. As the Reaper crew prepared for the final order to hit their red launch buttons, the eerily sharp night-vision image from the Reapers' camera balls played on giant television screens in secure rooms around the world: upstairs and downstairs in the Ranger operations center at Bagram; in the special operations headquarters at Kabul's airport; in the headquarters annex where Nicholson was watching; and in operations centers at Fort Bragg, CENTCOM headquarters in Tampa, Langley, and the Pentagon. The aircraft launched their weapons at two compounds on the mountainside a few hundred meters apart, striking them nearly simultaneously. The buildings exploded in black-and-white blooms. "It was executed superbly and had exactly the intended effect," an officer who was watching remembered.[74]

Initial reports that trickled out of the Helgal put the number of people killed at between eight and fifteen, including Farouq, another Arab, and four of the Pakistani Taliban fighters who were part of their entourage. The news prompted celebration all the way from the Ranger battalion operations center at Bagram up to the White House. *Holy shit, they finally got him after all this time,* an official working for the NSC at the time remembered thinking when the news came in.[75] It would take several weeks for the U.S. military and intelligence community to confirm for sure, but the missiles had killed Farouq, Bilal, and Junabi. "These individuals were directly involved in planning threats against the United States in the last year," Nicholson said in a briefing to reporters.[76]

IN A STATEMENT acknowledging Farouq's death, al-Qaida's "general command" in Pakistan praised him for "vexing the Americans and their allies" and claimed his family had died with him, just as some special operations planners had worried they might. "The Americans tried to target brother Farouq many times, and God saved him," the al-Qaida statement said, "but this time they resorted to killing him with his wife, his sons, and his supporters."[77]

Whether the al-Qaida claim was true or false may not be known until JSOC files relating to the strike are eventually declassified. No one I interviewed on the American side recalled evidence or allegations that Farouq's family or other civilians died with him, including Joe Dunford (by then serving as chairman of the Joint Chiefs at the Pentagon), the CENTCOM commander, Joe Votel, and NSC and Pentagon officials who learned of the strike the night it happened. Nicholson and the trio of Ranger officers most directly involved wouldn't answer my questions about the October 23 mission, citing classification, and while Doug London confirmed the presence of Farouq's wife before the strike, he wouldn't confirm whether it killed her.

No Afghan government officials came forward publicly with information supporting the al-Qaida claim, but the Helgal was inaccessible to them, and they might not have cared. Farouq and his family were outsiders who had lived secluded from local people in Taliban-controlled mountains; no one was likely to show up at the district center demanding answers about their fate. And besides, after the years–long standoff between Karzai and the Americans over civilian deaths, the government of President Ashraf Ghani was trying to smooth over any controversy around U.S. counterterrorism strikes, mindful of the Obama administration's eagerness to draw down troop levels and that the next American president, whether Clinton or Trump, might well be inclined toward troop cuts or a pullout.

Mike Nagata, the three-star Green Beret then working at the National Counterterrorism Center, told me that whatever the truth of the matter, the U.S. government would have looked into civilian casualty allegations after the fact only if they had come "through U.S. intelligence channels or other reliable intelligence channels like the British" or perhaps if the strike had missed Farouq. "It may be that because the strike was successful, nobody cared about the details," he said. "If it hadn't been successful, the narrative from the U.S. government afterward might have been quite different."[78]

"THERE WILL ALWAYS BE DRAGONS TO SLAY UP THERE"

No other al-Qaida figure of similar stature immediately emerged to replace Farouq al-Qahtani. Nine months later, during a summer

2017 visit to Afghanistan, most Kunaris and Nuristanis I spoke to described the al-Qaida branch that still wandered remote areas of their home provinces as a spent force, one that didn't seem to be recovering from the killing of its longtime leader. "Since the death of Farouq, there has been less information about Arabs. If there were new figures who were as active, we would have heard about it," said a Nangalam native who was in charge of security and intelligence for a wealthy Kunari timber family.[79] "Al-Qaida used to bring money. Now the Arabs are stuck and can't go anywhere else," agreed a government official from a prominent Nuristani family.[80]

In part, this might have been because JSOC had killed Farouq and his deputy with the same blow—in keeping with the man-hunting "best practices" the command had learned over the years for maximizing disruption to a militant group. But there were other factors at play as well.

When Farouq rose to prominence and received marching orders from top al-Qaida leaders to prepare a backup sanctuary for them, his corner of Kunar and Nuristan had represented one of just a few viable safe havens for a group whose top echelons were under devastating pressure from the CIA's drone campaign in Pakistan. But in the final months of his life, the importance of that safe haven had diminished. Five years into the Syrian civil war, the catastrophic conflict had given al-Qaida a new home. Rather than hiding in the mountains of the Hindu Kush, under the shadow of JSOC drones, members of the group were living in the ruins of an urban center forty miles from the Mediterranean, the Syrian city of Idlib. The pocket of territory that al-Qaida and its local allies held around Idlib had become battlefield destination number one for al-Qaida's Arab recruits, and some of al-Qaida's most senior leaders had begun showing up there too, traveling from Pakistan and Iran to a new base where the presence of Russian and Syrian government aircraft complicated the ability of JSOC and the CIA to strike them.[81] According to one later report, Farouq had even trained and sent local recruits to fight in Syria before his death.[82] Echoes of this shifting calculus reached Kunaris in contact with the Taliban fighters who hosted al-Qaida, including the Asadabad cleric Mawlawi Shahzada Shahid. "There are very few Arabs in the mountains now. They are just trapped there. They go to Syria and Libya and Iraq now instead," he told me when I caught up with him in Kabul that summer.[83]

The few Arabs who remained in old haunts like the Waygal and the Watapur faced a new threat—an offensive mounted not by American special operators or by Afghan government troops but by a group of mostly Afghan and Pakistani militants that was emerging in eastern Afghanistan as a bold and combative rival to al-Qaida and the Taliban. Afghans called the group Daesh.

DAESH WAS AN acronym for the Islamic State—the equivalent in Arabic, Dari, and Pashto of the Western abbreviation ISIS, as Americans called the Salafi jihadist movement that had stormed across Iraq, Syria, and Libya in 2014 and 2015. By the time they killed Farouq, JSOC and the Rangers at Bagram had already shifted much of their focus from al-Qaida to the Afghan branch of the Islamic State's self-declared caliphate, which was launching dramatic terror attacks in Jalalabad and Kabul. Daesh's Afghan franchise—which the group referred to as Khorasan Province, using a medieval name for the lands between Persia and India—had burrowed into villages and tunnel complexes in several districts near Tora Bora in Nangarhar. As Daesh extended tentacles northward into the caves, forests, and *bandehs* of Kunar, its presence seamlessly occasioned the indefinite extension of the task force's drone campaign in the same Pech side valleys where JSOC had been on the prowl on and off since the spring of 2002.

The Obama administration had initially been dismissive of the Islamic State, viewing it as a locally focused offshoot of al-Qaida that was incapable of the kinds of international terror attacks figures like Farouq al-Qahtani and Ibrahim al-Asiri were believed to be plotting. But the collapse of government security forces in major Iraqi cities like Mosul and Ramadi, followed by a string of deadly terror attacks, including a sophisticated November 2015 assault in Paris that killed 130 people, shocked the administration into action. In early 2016, as a ferocious American-led air campaign pummeled Islamic State strongholds in Iraq and Syria, the White House let JSOC off the leash against the group's Afghan branch, adding Daesh to the task force's al-Qaida-focused targeting list.

The Rangers at Bagram took to the task with relish. Even as the Haymaker desk was searching for Farouq in the Helgal, the lion's share of the task force's drones started spending their days and nights flying over the rural districts south of Jalalabad in Nangarhar, where Daesh was in full control. "It was a target-rich environment" compared with the hunt for al-Qaida in Kunar, a Ranger officer explained. "With al-Qaida, it was a lot of long-term development and surveillance—very labor-intensive." With Daesh in Nangarhar, "you'd put up a drone, see some activity, and strike."[84] The strikes accompanied offensives by ANA Commandos and their Green Beret advisers on the ground, and they racked up kills quickly. Treading into the body-count territory that the military usually kept behind closed doors, Nicholson estimated publicly that by the end of 2016, Operation Green Sword, as the effort was called, had killed as many as a third of Daesh's fighters in Afghanistan.[85]

The natural place to retreat to was Kunar, for all the same reasons that bin Laden had retreated there after Tora Bora. As the group took a beating in Nangarhar, "there was a definite effort to move up to Kunar because they knew it was harder for us to target up there with the weather and the trees and everything," remembered the same Ranger officer.[86] Speaking to an Afghan researcher for the Italian scholar Antonio Giustozzi, a Daesh commander who relocated northward in the spring of 2016 agreed. "Here the drones cannot target us," he said, citing Kunar's forest cover. "From every point of view Kunar is a great place for us."[87] The first JSOC strike against Daesh in the Pech came that May, killing a former Taliban commander who had changed allegiances.[88]

As Daesh appeared in the same areas whose topography and vegetation had always made them difficult for American forces to reach, it pushed out those al-Qaida and Taliban fighters who wouldn't join it. After a spree of Daesh offensives into new villages and districts in and around the Pech at the end of 2016, just after Farouq's death in the Helgal, the top Daesh official to have traveled to Afghanistan from the Islamic State's core in Iraq and Syria gave the Arabs in the mountains an ultimatum to switch sides or leave.[89]

The result was an exodus of the remaining Arab al-Qaida fighters from the valleys north of the Pech deeper into Nuristan and across the border into Pakistan. It was a more complete and more immediate reversal than years of JSOC drone strikes had been able to inflict on the group, but one that was likely assisted by the disarray of the al-Qaida operatives after the death of Farouq. By the time I was interviewing Kunaris and Nuristanis about the arrival of Daesh in the summer of 2017, the newcomers had displaced al-Qaida from some of the key sites where the terrorist group had maintained a persistent presence for a decade. In some places they fought the Taliban openly, in firefights and with IEDs; in others, like Aranas, the two groups coexisted uneasily as some Taliban fighters raised the Daesh flag and others refused to.[90] "Now Daesh is in the Pech valley too," Mawlawi Shahzada Shahid told me, listing the places where he had heard of the group rearing its head: Chapa Dara, Watapur, Waygal, Dewagal, Nurgal, Shigal. "The Taliban in Kunar were not attacking clinics and schools, but Daesh is totally different. They want no schools or anything."[91]

It wasn't just the terrain that was favorable. That the Pech and the Waygal were among the first valleys outside Nangarhar where Daesh started recruiting was no coincidence. At the core of the group's ideology was an extreme, violent brand of Salafism, the Islamic movement that sought to re-create the days of the Prophet Muhammad, and the most significant populations of Salafis in Afghanistan were in Kunar, Nuristan, and Nangarhar. For some Kunari Salafis who had opposed the Taliban regime before the American intervention drove them to ally with it, the theology of the Islamic State represented a more comfortable fit than the Taliban—a product of a completely different school of Islamic thought—ever had.

One such figure was Haji Hayatullah, a commander from Nangalam in his fifties who was one of the first to join Daesh after its fighters started showing up in the Pech in 2015. Hayatullah had fought for years alongside Dawran as his deputy, under the auspices first of Jamaat, the Kunar-based Salafi party, and then, after Dawran finally joined it in 2010, of the Taliban. At the same time that other members of Dawran's group were telling reporters that they had nothing to do with al-Qaida, in 2011, Hayatullah had been providing unspecified "support" to Farouq al-Qahtani and his men, U.S. intelligence believed. When Daesh fighters arrived in the Pech two years after Dawran's death, Hayatullah helped them get their footing, allowing them to recruit and run training programs at religious schools he controlled. He even purportedly sent one of his men on the long journey to the Islamic State's center in Iraq.[92]

On the American side, the skeptical view was that for most Kunari fighters and commanders who joined Daesh, the change of allegiance was motivated not by a desire to join the caliphate's vicious international jihad but by the high wages it paid, the promise of advancement, or just a pragmatic instinct to go with the prevailing wind. That was what Waygalis told me of the first Taliban commander to join Daesh in Aranas; he had been a low-level figure in the Taliban's Waygal hierarchy, they said, and jumped ship in the hopes of getting in on the ground floor of the Islamic State's competing militant government in the valley.[93] For figures like these, the move was "just a flag change," as one intelligence analyst put it[94]— from the white flag of the Taliban to the black flag of Daesh.

Sometimes this "flag change" could play out literally. "I remember one vivid shot at an HVT [high-value target] up there who was physically flying both the Taliban flag and the ISIS flag at the same time," remembered a Ranger officer. "He just wanted his damn valley. It was all the same guys," including some who, when he first visited Kunar during Winter Strike, had been older than he was now.[95]

Several years later, the U.S. government would allege the involvement with Daesh of another old Salafi whom Americans had encountered before: Haji Ruhullah, the wealthy Pech native who had spent six years in Guantánamo after special operators detained him during their first summer in Kunar and whose uncle had founded Jamaat and brought Saudi-style Salafism to the province in the first place during the 1970s.

What Ruhullah had and hadn't really done to help Arab militants escape Tora Bora into Pakistan back at the dawn of American involvement never became any less murky. Speaking regularly to Western reporters in Kabul, including me, he maintained his innocence and denied any association with al-Qaida. He also denied any association with the CIA or Pakistan's ISI, but he was widely known to have worked with both intelligence agencies in Peshawar during the 2001 American intervention—all at the same time that he was allegedly helping Arabs flee the American bombing and that the ISI was quietly supporting his Taliban foes. His association with the

Islamic State proved little more clear-cut. He sat on the leadership council of a Salafi charity in Kabul, the Nejaat Social Welfare Organization. That charity, the United States contended, was a cover organization used to raise and launder money for Daesh, and a Daesh recruiter worked out of its Kabul office with Ruhullah's approval, recruiting young men in the capital to go and fight against the Taliban, the government, and the Americans in Nangarhar. In late 2016, Ruhullah had hosted a meeting of Nejaat's leaders that Daesh leaders also attended, running their own planning meetings on the sidelines, according to a Treasury Department announcement of sanctions against him and the charity.[96]

The extent of Ruhullah's involvement with Daesh wasn't clear, nor was the reason for it. Was he supporting the group because of its anti-American agenda or because it was a Salafi group fighting against the Taliban, as his own party, Jamaat, had been in the 1990s, when he helped raise funds in the Gulf for its fight against the Taliban in Kunar? Either way, it attracted the attention not only of the U.S. government but of the NDS, the CIA's main partner and proxy in Afghanistan. During my 2017 visit to Kabul, Ruhullah—previously enthusiastically accessible to journalists—was making himself scarce. At the beginning of the summer, an Afghan government official told me, commandos from one of the NDS's CIA-backed paramilitary units raided Ruhullah's convoy as he was traveling through Kabul but wound up releasing him. "He was in a member of parliament's car; otherwise I think the same thing would have happened to him that happened to Sabar Lal," the official told me, referring to the suspicious 2011 killing of Ruhullah's fellow Guantánamo inmate during a SEAL Team 6 raid in Jalalabad.[97]

JSOC'S AIR CAMPAIGN against the Islamic State shifted to Kunar in earnest in the summer of 2017, picking up where Operation Haymaker had left off.

Speculation was rife that President Donald Trump would soon forge a new path for the United States in Afghanistan, either doubling down with a new troop surge, ordering a pullout as he had hinted on the campaign trail that he would, or handing the combat advisory effort over to private security contractors. But so far, the new administration's only major change had been to delegate the decision to launch air strikes lower in the chain of command. The Ranger battalion commander on the ground floor of the Bagram headquarters building was ordering most JSOC strikes on his own now, where previously they had had to go back to Kabul for approval. In Kabul, Nicholson was signing off on decisions that would previously have had to go back to the Pentagon.[98]

In April, Rangers and Afghan special operators landed at a site in Nangarhar, attacking a Daesh command post in a raid that cost the lives of two Ranger sergeants on one side and three dozen militants on the other. Among the insurgents killed was the governor of the Islamic State's Khorasan Province, an Afghan veteran of the war in Syria whom the Pentagon saw as the group's top leader in Afghanistan.[99] The killing precipitated a succession crisis within Daesh's Afghan branch, which the JSOC task force took advantage of, searching out and killing as many likely candidates for the governorship as it could as quickly as it could.[100]

The trail led JSOC's surveillance and strike aircraft to the Watapur valley, where Rangers had been the first American troops to venture back in 2002 and where twelve Americans had died on successive battalions' pilgrimage-like air-assault missions into the wooded heights. Two nights after the lethal raid in Nangarhar, the task force's Reapers struck a compound near Qowru on the valley floor, hitting a group of Daesh commanders who appeared to have assembled in an area they viewed as relatively safe, perhaps to discuss the succession.[101] Further strikes in the Watapur made the news every couple of weeks for the rest of the summer. The drones killed a Daesh recruiter and financier somewhere in the valley at the beginning of July.[102] Nine days after that, they struck another group of Daesh leaders who had assembled near Katar, the village on the edge of the Gambir Jungle where well-trained militants had tried to overrun one of Joe Ryan's platoons during Operation Bulldog Bite in 2010. The Katar strike, the Pentagon announced at the end of the week, had killed Daesh's latest governor, a compromise candidate with credentials as a commander in the Pakistani Taliban, along with the group's top religious adviser in the country and other members of its leadership council.[103]

As the summer wore on, more strikes killed Daesh fighters in

Gambir, the Shigal, and Chapa Dara, where Nicholson's aide-de-camp had fought as a Blue Spader company commander.[104] On August 11, working its way down the Islamic State hierarchy more quickly than the group could appoint new governors, a strike in the central Pech killed four more of its leadership figures—including one U.S. intelligence believed was in the running to fill the vacant governorship. "He found out just like those before him that there are no safe havens in Afghanistan," Mick Nicholson said of that killing in a public statement.[105]

But as with Operation Haymaker, the air campaign the Rangers were overseeing against the Islamic State in Kunar faced a troubling calculus. It was killing Daesh leaders just a bit faster than the group could replace them. But was it also pushing different militants into the caliphate's fold in the process—ones with whom the Afghan government might otherwise have negotiated? And if so, was the trade-off worth it?

At the same time that the Islamic State was moving into Kunar and bringing JSOC air strikes in its wake, the old mujahidin party whose leaders had harbored bin Laden when he came to the province, Hizb-e Islami, was at a crossroads. After the initial spurt of interest JSOC had shown in them in 2002 and 2003, Gulbuddin Hekmatyar and his Hizb lieutenants had largely fallen off the counterterrorism command's radar, fading into the background of the Taliban-led insurgency to play bit parts while their followers fought under the larger group's banner.

In September 2016, Hekmatyar, the survivor of the first American drone strike in Kunar, announced that he was putting down his arms to join the political process in Kabul. The move caused a split within Hizb.[106] When Hekmatyar entered the capital in the spring of 2017, the old Hizb commander in charge in the Shigal valley—where it had all begun for JSOC and the CIA in Kunar—stayed put. A fellow veteran of the 1980s jihad, Haji Amanullah declared that he would be taking a different path—breaking off from Hizb along with other party members who were unwilling to recognize the U.S.-backed government.

Amanullah had already offered sanctuary to a group of Daesh fighters who arrived in his valley fleeing American airpower.[107] Their presence drew the JSOC task force's attention to the Shigal as it ramped up Kunar strikes that summer. One air strike killed members of Amanullah's extended family, according to Mawlawi Shahzada Shahid, who was in touch with him.[108] Another strike, or perhaps the same one, nearly killed Amanullah himself. He later said that he had heard the drones following him for days before two missiles exploded next to him as he was walking on a mountainside, slightly injuring him and killing two of his men. When an Afghan journalist visited him in the Shigal toward the end of the year, after the strike, he had welcomed more Daesh fighters into the valley, and he was allowing them to enforce bans on smoking, music, shaving, and the common practice of using hand grenades to fish in the river. He was also considering formally declaring for the group himself. "I tell people here that the rules and laws of Daesh were the rules of Hizb," Amanullah told the journalist. "First they were adopted by the Taliban, now they are adopted by Daesh." Rather than deterring Amanullah from harboring the Islamic State in the Shigal, the strikes there had pushed him closer to the group.[109]

WHEN I INTERVIEWED residents and former residents of the Pech and its side valleys about the legacy of American involvement, two subjects came up over and over again. The first was the unfulfilled promise of infrastructure: disappointment with the roads and bridges that the provincial reconstruction team in Asadabad had initiated and extended into ever-more-inaccessible valleys, only for them to fall into disrepair as the Afghan government proved incapable of the kind of regular maintenance that an environment like the Pech required for infrastructure to survive. "We had a hard time understanding the Russians. They were godless and all their views were wrong, but they made roads and bridges that lasted" was how a Waygali cleric, Mawlawi Shafiullah Nuristani, put it. "What did the Americans do? They built temporary bases that we can't do anything with, they didn't invest in wise ways, and their roads and bridges don't last."[110]

The other was the arrival of militant groups that had not been present before September 11. To some, the coming of Daesh to the Pech and its environs represented just the latest step in a process that had begun when the activity of American troops drew the Taliban into places like the Korengal, and continued with the arrival of al-Qaida figures like Farouq al-Qahtani who came to fight the invaders at the height of the insurgency. "The Americans left behind the Taliban and al-Qaida and Daesh. Did they leave them to torture us?" a young Waygali man asked me rhetorically.[111]

The role American intervention played in bringing to the Pech the very groups that the United States was at war with wasn't lost on American veterans, either, but to some the presence of such groups in places whose terrain presented such self-evident challenges to military power seemed as timeless as it did endless. The Americans I came back to again and again for their perspectives, and to offer updates on the places they had once fought, were the ones who deployed to the area repeatedly, participating in different stages of the long war there: men like Joe Ryan and the Asymmetric Warfare Group contractor T.W. Among these was Loren Crowe, the abrasive former infantry officer who went to Kunar first as a Blue Spader lieutenant and then again as a captain with the Cacti battalion.

Crowe had seen pieces of the war as a platoon leader in and around the Shigal, where he'd heard locals say bin Laden had sheltered after Tora Bora but hadn't known whether to believe them, then at Blessing as a staff officer when Brett Jenkinson was struggling to pitch a pullout from the Korengal. He'd been back as a staff officer again at the time of Operations Hammer Down and Fire Rock in the Watapur and Waygal, and finally as the company commander advising the ANA at Blessing in late 2011 and early 2012, until he was shot on patrol.

The most frustrating experience during Crowe's time in the Army had been watching as his battalion launched big heliborne assault missions, losing and taking lives, in valleys that he thought the United States should already have washed its hands of. Operation Haymaker, which had been getting under way in those same valleys during his second stint in the Pech, seemed like a better alternative. But that JSOC was still striking away with its drones more than five years after his departure, now targeting a group that hadn't even existed in Afghanistan during his deployments, seemed to him like yet another case of a hammer seeking nails to pound—a new version of the phenomenon that he believed had led to the Cacti battalion's costly air-assault adventures in the summer of 2011.

People hiding out from the Kabul government, and hiding out from an American military that in many ways had met its match in the brutal terrain surrounding the Pech, would always find their way to places like the Gambir Jungle, Amshuz, and the Korengal, Crowe guessed. But their mere presence there, in a place that loomed so large for a generation of Army leaders, seemed to him as if it might magnify their importance and tip the scales toward using military tools to search for them and strike them.

For as long as the soldiers, intelligence officers, and contractors charged with America's counterterrorism missions went looking for people to kill there, that is, they would keep on finding them.

"There will always be dragons to slay up there," he said.[112]

EPILOGUE

2018–2020

When Joe Ryan deployed to the Pech as the Bulldog battalion commander in 2010, the fighting in the valley had been at a stalemate. The same could be said of the war as a whole when Ryan returned to Afghanistan for his seventh tour there at the end of 2018, this time as a brigadier general with the 4th Infantry Division. "As much as things change around the world and in Afghanistan, Kunar kind of remains the same, this mosaic of groups and alliances," he told me by phone a few weeks after he arrived at FOB Gamberi, the Afghan National Army base in a deforested desert north of Jalalabad where he would spend the coming winter commanding a task force of advisers and other troops.[1]

This time around, Ryan didn't expect to set foot in the Pech, or in Kunar at all; his duties were those of a headquarters adviser, the top American officer assigned to the Afghan 201st Corps, the command that oversaw ANA operations in that province and its three neighbors. But thanks to an expansion of the U.S. advisory mission and air campaign that President Donald Trump had reluctantly authorized, small numbers of American soldiers were still making trips into the province where Ryan had first set foot as a Ranger staff officer in 2003. Staying behind the walls of an ANA base twenty miles south of Asadabad, conventional Army adviser teams and howitzer crews had returned to Kunar over the summer to help the ANA fight their daytime war in the same old side valleys of the Pech. After dark, the nighttime counterterrorism war ground on as well, with a team of seasoned Ranger NCOs accompanying CIA personnel and their Afghan surrogates on dangerous nocturnal raids, hunting the latest generation of al-Qaida and Islamic State leaders to take refuge in the menacing terrain that had sheltered Osama bin Laden after Tora Bora and Farouq al-Qahtani during the U.S. government's long hunt for him.

Although few Americans were fighting and dying in it any longer, the war in Afghanistan was the deadliest conflict in the world in 2018 as the Taliban and the Afghan government took and retook villages, outposts, and checkpoints from one another. The government "controlled or influenced" barely half of the country's districts, according to U.S. estimates, and the government forces were hemorrhaging casualties, losing more than ten times as many soldiers and policemen in an average month—somewhere north of five hundred—as the U.S. military's monthly toll during its costliest year of combat operations in the country. The White House had authorized a miniature surge, boosting U.S. troop numbers from eleven thousand to fifteen thousand. The extra troops' role was to bring to bear artillery and airpower in an effort to inflict enough casualties on the Taliban to bring its envoys to the negotiating table with U.S. representatives in Doha, Qatar.[2] What kind of agreement might emerge from the Doha talks wasn't yet clear, but the two parties' ultimate aims were. Both the Taliban and the Trump administration hoped to get American troops out of Afghanistan. The Taliban wanted recognition as a government, which Washington was loath to offer; the United States wanted guarantees that the Taliban would prevent the planning of international terrorist attacks from Afghan soil—either by the group's al-Qaida allies or its Islamic State foes.

The war in Kunar, where al-Qaida and Daesh both remained active, offered a glimpse of what might lie on the other side of a deal: an outsourcing of what had once been a core American mission in Afghanistan—counterterrorism—to the uneasily coordinated forces of the Afghan government and the Taliban. On the ground in valleys such as the Watapur and the Korengal, Taliban and government troops who had long fought against each other were already quietly cooperating against their mutual enemy, the Islamic State. As its strongholds to the south in Nangarhar collapsed, Daesh had doubled down in Kunar, consolidating control over the Shuryak and the Chalas Ghar heights where it converged with the other side valleys ten miles south of the Pech. "That's where they've put down the deepest roots and become entrenched and have a supportive population," Ryan told me, then rattled off a list of other places in his old area of operations where Daesh had established smaller footholds by pushing down from the heights: the Rechalam valley, the Korengal, the Chowkay. Like the Taliban before it, the militant group was digging in where it would make money: it had secured the biggest remaining timber reserves in the province and seemed poised to seize Chapa Dara and its gem mines come spring.[3]

The Afghan brigade responsible for Kunar contained some 40 percent of the ANA troops in the northeast, more than two dozen companies' worth.[4] Over the summer, American drones, warplanes, artillery, and advisers had helped the ANA push into the Nurgal, Chowkay, Shuryak, and Korengal—valleys in which the Kabul government had been content to let the Taliban govern for several years but was unwilling to tolerate Daesh. On the heels of a brief countrywide ceasefire between the Taliban and the government in June, and with Taliban operatives now supplying ANA intelligence officers with information about Daesh's positions, the ANA brigade commander had asked for limited American support, making it clear that to preserve his troops' image of independence from foreign help, he didn't want or expect any American advisers to come along on the missions.[5] Instead, the advisers and a howitzer crew would do their work coordinating air strikes and firing their big 155-millimeter gun from a disused base on the far side of the Kunar river, just within artillery range of the Korengal's upper reaches.[6] "They appreciated our support but they liked us to stay inside," explained an adviser captain—fifty or sixty Americans safely out of sight behind the base's walls during visits that lasted only the few days that the operations did.[7]

When the ANA went up a valley, usually with a battalion or two, Reapers roamed above, watching for Daesh movements farther back where the government troops couldn't see. At their base, the advisers would watch the drone feed and pass along coordinates for strikes to the artillerymen and sometimes to fighter jets and Apaches, pummeling Daesh observation posts and reinforcements when they moved forward to lay ambushes for the ANA. The sound of the artillery pounding targets beyond the next ridgeline heartened the Afghan troops on the ground, their commanders reported back. The ANA didn't say so explicitly to the American advisers, because they knew the U.S. still viewed the Taliban as a hostile force, but it seemed clear that they were using local Taliban as guides and auxiliaries. Sometimes, the Afghan troops would bring in heavily bearded locals and ask the U.S. medics to treat them, saying they were civilians when they obviously were not; the medics obliged, not asking too many questions. Afterward, they'd give the American advisers black Islamic State flags they'd captured; at least one made its way back to an Army museum stateside.[8]

Two back-to-back missions targeted the Shuryak and the Korengal. In the Shuryak, in the middle of the summer, an ANA force made it about two miles in before Daesh resistance, along with storm clouds that kept American Reapers and Apaches grounded, halted the mission.[9] Next up was the Korengal in late July. When two ANA battalions crossed the Kandigal bridge near what had once been COP Michigan and headed up the valley, the aim was to penetrate deeper, up toward the Chalas Ghar. While some of the troops drove Humvees up what was left of the road on the west side of the valley, others hiked along the slopes across the river. As the operation began, one of the tiny Afghan Air Force's A-29 turboprop attack planes flew a rare mission, dropping bombs on preplanned targets. But when the Afghan troops started taking contact, losing two soldiers killed and several wounded, it was American artillery fire that tried to silence the heavy machine-gun positions pinning them down from deep in the valley, working from Reaper footage and grid coordinates passed along from an ANA officer on the ground. "As soon as they got into the valley, they started taking contact and it got heavier as they went in," remembered a major who worked remotely on the Korengal mission from the base across the Kunar river. "We laid down quite a bit of [artillery] fire trying to get them up the valley, but we just weren't able to get them a clean break."[10] Within thirty-six hours, the government troops were out again, having penetrated less than a mile, not even as far as what had been COP Vegas, the northernmost of the former American outposts in the Korengal.[11]

The U.S.-backed ANA offensives hadn't made much of a dent—much like most of the American air-assault missions into the same valleys over the years. "It's not like they ever found a hundred ISIS guys or destroyed a huge weapons cache," the adviser major said.[12] The government troops never got anywhere close to Daesh's Chalas Ghar base area. But the twin ANA and Taliban operations provided an early look at the shape that collaboration between the two groups against their mutual opponent might take if the Trump administration's Doha negotiations bore fruit. As Ryan was deploying at the end of the fall, a semiofficial ceasefire had just been declared in several districts surrounding Asadabad, including Watapur, and the State Department's new special representative for Afghanistan, the Afghan-American diplomat Zalmay Khalilzad, was beginning direct talks with Taliban emissaries in Doha and Abu Dhabi.

It seemed that the war in the Pech might again be offering a preview of things to come elsewhere in Afghanistan—as it had in 2003 with the first stirrings of the Pech insurgency, in 2006 with the commitment to a counterinsurgency strategy of building outposts and roads, and in 2011 with both the withdrawal of American troops and their return in a more limited role. But the on-and-off understandings between government forces and the Taliban and the infighting and changing of allegiances among militants also reminded Ryan of what he'd seen in the Pech eight years earlier, when police and the insurgents had coexisted in Chapa Dara and different militant cells had been at one another's throats in the Watapur over timber-revenue disputes and other grievances. "It's Kunar," he said. "People and groups are going to waffle and flip-flop and trade sides and do what they need to do in the short term, but not much is going to change in the long term."[13]

THE LONGER AMERICAN troops had been involved in any given Afghan valley, district, or province, the more veterans of the place there were rising through the Army's ranks—and the Army had been in Kunar since almost the beginning. When Ryan took over as the top adviser at FOB Gamberi in December 2018, the 101st Airborne Division officer he took the reins from was John Brennan, another brigadier general who had been there in the early days after September 11.

"Same drunks, same bar," Brennan said with a laugh when I pointed out to him the way the U.S. campaign in northeastern Afghanistan seemed to recycle characters as it dragged on toward the end of its second decade. "I was one of the first Americans into Kunar."

Brennan had spent much of his career in Delta Force, and it was as the commander of twenty or so Delta operators that he had arrived at FOB Asadabad in the late spring of 2002, taking over for the smaller SEAL recon team that had claimed the compound as the first American outpost in the province. If someone had told him back then that he and other American soldiers would still be spending time there sixteen years later, he wouldn't have believed it. But there he'd found himself during a Kunar trip a few months earlier in 2018, checking on conditions because the JSOC task force sometimes used the same old compound to refuel helicopters and stage a surgical team on nights when it had Rangers in the field. Now a heavily fortified Afghan government installation, where Interior Ministry and NDS paramilitaries lived in barracks built over the years for American units, it was a far cry from the dusty compound in which Brennan had slept in a tent and used a windowless, mud-walled building for an operations center as his men started poking around in the Pech and Kunar's other valleys for the first time.[14]

Many other veterans of Kunar and the Pech had risen in the ranks alongside Ryan and Brennan. Several of the Ranger company commanders of Operation Winter Strike were brigade commanders. Chris Cavoli, who had overseen the establishment of most of the Pech outposts as the Chosin battalion's commander back in 2006, was a general, the Army's top commander in Europe. As of mid-2019, the aides-de-camp to both the secretary of defense and the chairman of the Joint Chiefs were officers who had fought in the Pech, one as a company commander in the Bulldog battalion and the other as The Rock's fire-support officer. Jim McKnight, the commander of the first company to live the brutal Korengal Outpost life, had left active duty but stayed in the military part-time; as a lieutenant colonel, he would help oversee the National Guard response to the COVID-19 pandemic in the state of Georgia, splicing his infantry battalion into teams of medics and sanitization workers to send into hospitals. Dan Kearney, McKnight's successor in the Korengal, became the 82nd Airborne Division's chief of staff as a colonel, while Colin Tuley, the former Cacti battalion commander who had launched his troops back into the Pech and its tributaries after the Bulldog battalion's pullout, returned to the special operations world as JSOC's chief of staff before being selected for promotion to brigadier general. As the Army they served in worked to reinvent itself for high-tech conflicts with Russia or China, they carried with them the memories of a place where technology had come up against hard limits in the form of terrain, vegetation, and weather, leaving young soldiers to fight tenacious guerrillas with old-fashioned tools: rifles, machine guns, mortars, and a walkie-talkie with a good interpreter if they were lucky.

Others had left the Army behind. Bill Ostlund and Brett Jenkinson had both retired as colonels, their careers capped out before the general officer ranks because of investigations into deaths on the battlefield during their deployments—in Ostlund's case, the investigations into the battle of Want, and in Jenkinson's, the reprimand he received over an Apache strike that killed an insurgent commander's daughter. For Jenkinson, hanging up his uniform had been a release; although he had loved being an infantryman, the weight of the deaths of his Blue Spaders in Kunar had nearly crushed him, and it was with relief that he began a new career working in civil engineering in Minnesota.

Ostlund's last role before retiring and taking a private-sector job was as the director of military instruction at West Point, responsible for schooling cadets on tactics and leadership. The tour at the gray campus on the Hudson gave him time to think about his experiences in Afghanistan in a way that he hadn't during his years deploying there. "I never shed a tear in Kunar," Ostlund told me; that came only years later. "Now I have time to reflect, to wonder if I made the right decisions." When fall came to West Point, the cool weather transported him back to Rock Avalanche, the 2007 operation during which three of his soldiers had died in close combat on the cold slopes of the Abbas Ghar and air strikes during the insertion had killed five women and children in Yakha China. The lunar phases, which had dictated when helicopters could launch air-assault missions during Ostlund's deployments, could be a similar trigger: full moons took him back to the "green-illum" nights when Black Hawks and Chinooks had ferried his paratroopers into the Korengal, Shuryak, Watapur, and other side valleys to search for the enemy, while new moons reminded him of the completely black nights on which the Night Stalkers had preferred to launch their riskiest insertions of Rangers and SEALs during his stints leading the Bagram JSOC task force. "Practically every night feels like an air-assault night," he told me one day in the fall during his time at the military academy. "The cool weather—it's just that time of year."[15]

When Ostlund had been stateside between Afghanistan deployments, civilian acquaintances or family members often thanked him for his service, and sometimes expressed guilt at their own lack of involvement in the conflict that defined so much of his life—how they went about their daily lives without thinking about it. Ostlund had worked out a standard reply early on and stuck with it. *That's where you need to be,* he would say. *That's why I'm over there. That's why I'm fighting the away game*—so that life at home could continue uninterrupted.[16]

It was a canned response, but it was one that Ostlund believed. It also suggested the essential question that still hung over the future of the U.S. military enterprise in Afghanistan. It was the same question the United States had faced when the Bush administration chose to keep troops there after the initial intervention and when the Obama administration opted against a full withdrawal: How much of a threat did terrorist groups in Afghanistan pose to the United States and the West? How likely were al-Qaida, and now the Islamic State, to orchestrate their next international attack from Afghan soil?

BACK IN NORTHEASTERN Afghanistan in the opening months of 2019, Joe Ryan's duties centered on the war waged by the ANA 201st Corps and the conventional Army advisers, artillerymen, and attack helicopter pilots who supported them. But as ever, the daytime counterinsurgency war of the conventional troops and the nighttime counterterrorism campaign of American and Afghan special operators and intelligence operatives were linked—not least because both now focused on Daesh, an insurgent group that was made up mostly of locals like the Taliban but which U.S. commanders and intelligence officials worried might pose an international terrorist threat like al-Qaida.

In his typical reserved fashion, Ryan let on little about his past experiences in Kunar and Nuristan during his day-to-day work at FOB Gamberi. An aide remembered him speaking more often about books he was reading—a tome about the CIA's post–September 11 involvement in Afghanistan and Pakistan, a biography of the frontiersman Kit Carson—and retirement investments than about his time as a Ranger in Kantiwa or as the Bulldog battalion commander in the Pech. Stories from Kunar came out only occasionally, and focused on the bright days, not the dark ones: Ryan reminisced to the aide about Christmas 2010, when he and the battalion chaplain had handed out donated iPads to soldiers at the four Pech outposts, but never told the young officer about the day an RPG exploded inside his truck and killed his gunner. Ryan's views would come out, though, when the subject of ANA offensives to secure remote district centers came up. "If we're talking about Kunar in an intel brief, he'll be like, 'We've seen this before—we tried it ten years ago and it doesn't work,'" the aide remembered.[17] On Ryan's watch, which lasted until he took a staff job in Kabul in March, some of his men returned to the same base on the east side of the Kunar river that advisers had visited over the summer, but didn't go farther than that.[18]

Ryan's role in the night war was limited to email coordination and occasional phone calls with acquaintances from the Ranger Regiment, which by now had been running the Bagram JSOC task force continuously for a decade. The task force's war was still being waged largely from the air, with drone strikes, but its Rangers were going outside the wire more on night raids again too—sometimes a company flying out from Bagram to hit Daesh targets, but more often small teams of senior Ranger NCOs who had inherited the old Omega mission of providing military backup to the CIA and its surrogate troops from the Afghan intelligence agency, the NDS.[19]

Working under a Trump administration mandate to more aggressively pursue Taliban and Daesh leaders as well as their traditional al-Qaida targets, the CIA's small teams of paramilitary officers and contractors were launching more missions in Afghanistan than they had in years.[20] The troops kicking in doors on these raids were Afghans, members of the NDS commando units that had evolved from the Mohawks and other surrogate units that the agency had established back in the war's early days. But teams of about seven handpicked senior Rangers tagged along just as SEAL Team 6's Omega teams had earlier in the war—providing tactical advice to the NDS troops and acting as the link to military drones, gunships, and medevac helicopters.[21] The Rangers called them ANSOF teams, a bland acronym standing for "Afghan National Special Operations Forces," and their missions could be risky: in July 2018, a Ranger sergeant first class on one of the teams, thirty-two-year-old Christopher Celiz, was killed helping evacuate wounded NDS troops in Paktya in southeastern Afghanistan.

The most active of the Ranger teams in late 2018 and early 2019 was the Jalalabad-based ANSOF 20—the seven Rangers who, along with a handful of CIA personnel, ran missions with Unit 02 and Unit 04, the pair of NDS outfits working in Nangarhar and Kunar.[22] "They were doing what we called deep-valley penetrations, mostly going after ISIS, with a couple Taliban missions here and there," usually flying in on American Black Hawks and Chinooks, a special operator explained of the ANSOF 20 team's Kunar raids.*[23] Because of the missions' secretive nature, only trace evidence of the missions appears in unclassified U.S. military documents and Afghan media coverage: a mid-September article alleging that "foreign" advisers had been on the ground during a raid that killed three Daesh fighters in the Pech, an October ground mission that the U.S. military acknowledged had killed three civilians.[24]

Al-Qaida targets—long the CIA's bread and butter—were few and far between, appearing more often now in areas south of Kabul than in their old haunts north of the Pech.[25] "They exist. They're probably not going anywhere," Ryan said of the al-Qaida presence in the northeast that he was briefed on during his 2018–2019 de-

---

* Green Berets and British special operators were making occasional trips to Kunar with their partners too, supporting an ANA Commando mission in the Chowkay valley and an air assault by an Interior Ministry paramilitary over the winter into Kandigal in the Pech.

ployment. "But they don't seem very active right now."[26] Reports about one al-Qaida figure in particular, though, dripped in now and again from different parts of Kunar and Nuristan[27]: Hamza bin Laden, Osama bin Laden's oldest living son. Hamza had been about twelve when he last saw his father, during the fall 2001 air campaign, and had spent most of the ensuing decade as something between a guest and a prisoner in Iran. Ensconced in Waziristan with al-Qaida's senior leadership council starting in 2010, he had long since become accustomed to the constant presence of CIA Predators and Reapers, going outside only for time at the rifle range.[28] The U.S. intelligence agencies didn't view Hamza as a top-level target, according to Douglas London, the longtime official at the agency's Counterterrorism Center, but by virtue of his name, Hamza drew the attention of the White House—including the attention of Trump himself. The president "regularly demanded updates on Hamza and insisted we accelerate our efforts to go after him," explained London, and the CIA obliged.[29]

With orders to catch Hamza coming from the very top, tips that he or his associates were in Kunar prompted swift action. "Who's going to get Hamza or Z-man [Zawahiri], those were the jokes," a special operator told me.[30] In mid-December, just as Brennan and Ryan were switching out, helicopters flew the whole package of Rangers, NDS troops, and CIA personnel up from Jalalabad for a raid in Kunar, on the eastern end of the old ratline that fed from the Pakistani border over to the Shigal valley and then the Watapur. Who exactly the target was remains unclear, but the raid was part of the agency's hunt for Hamza; Kunari journalist Bilal Sarwary heard afterward that bin Laden had been there himself shortly before the raid, visiting Arab and local fighters, while a special operations source told me the strike force was going after one of Hamza's couriers. Either way, the mission ran into heavy resistance, requiring the Rangers on the ground to call in Apaches and other aircraft to help the raid force fight its way out—firing at buildings where the defending militants were holed up alongside their families. Locals would later tell UN representatives that NDS operatives executed four local men during the mission; whether that was true or not, the U.S. military would conclude that the air strikes during the firefight killed eight civilians and wounded seventeen more.

Operations such as the one on the night of December 13—ones that put American soldiers in harm's way and killed civilians—were a far cry from the version of the Afghan war that the Pentagon preferred to present to the public by 2018. The nighttime man-hunting mission and its fallout wouldn't have seemed out of place in any earlier stage of the war in Kunar, even its opening days when JSOC and the CIA had been chasing Hamza's father there—back when the Ranger NCOs of the ANSOF 20 team, some of the most experienced in their battalion, had been in middle and high school.[31]

TRUMP WOULD EVENTUALLY announce Hamza bin Laden's death in September 2019, without saying when he had been killed or specifying where, just that it was in the "Afghanistan/Pakistan region."[32] No U.S. government assessment suggested that his removal from the battlefield substantially affected the threat al-Qaida itself posed from Afghanistan, but the group's role in the conflict seemed to be changing anyway. More and more of al-Qaida's fighters, in the military's view, were not planners of attacks abroad but battlefield operatives working with their Taliban hosts at the front—combat advisers assisting in the war of attrition in the south and southeast. Al-Qaida posed a "limited, indirect threat" to American troops, said one report; the threat had "decreased," said another; and the latest CENTCOM commander, General Kenneth McKenzie, called international attacks "a long-term, aspirational goal" for the group, not a short-term focus.[33]

The need to keep al-Qaida on the run and under pressure so that it couldn't plot more attacks overseas the way it had in 2001 had long been the core rationale for keeping appreciable numbers of American forces in Afghanistan. Now, though, with al-Qaida's Afghan presence morphing and shifting its focus, the familiar debates about whether a terrorist group had the capability to strike overseas from the country were swirling around the Islamic State. Military officials assumed that any withdrawal agreement resulting from the Doha talks would include a Taliban pledge to keep al-Qaida under control and prevent it from using Taliban-controlled territory to launch overseas attacks. This was an optimistic assumption, given that the Taliban hadn't known about al-Qaida's plans for September 11 beforehand and that even in 2019, a top Taliban spokesman refused to acknowledge that al-Qaida had been responsible for the attacks on New York and Washington. (The public text of the Doha agreement signed in February 2020 would require that the Taliban prevent such attacks as a condition of a 2021 U.S. military pullout, but whether the group would or even could make good on this pledge seemed uncertain at best. U.S.-backed Afghan troops continued to find and kill al-Qaida operatives working alongside the Taliban in the months after the deal, and in October 2020—as U.S. troop levels in Afghanistan fell below 5,000 for the first time since 2002—a top UN counterterrorism official would allege that the Taliban had offered al-Qaida "informal guarantees that they would honor their historic ties.") But it was an assumption that brought similar questions into focus about Daesh, which the Taliban was not in a position to make any promises about at all.[34]

Was the Islamic State's Khorasan Province, now concentrated mainly in Kunar, an upstart group focused on local and regional power? Or would the caliphate, as its last urban strongholds in Syria crumbled in 2019, turn to its Afghan branch to plot international operations such as its deadly 2015 attacks in Paris? The question was made more complicated by the Islamic State's operating model, which focused less on centralized planning of attacks—the al-Qaida approach—than on using propaganda and internet communications to inspire homegrown terrorists already living in the United States and Europe. The language that top generals used to describe the threat they saw from Daesh in Afghanistan could be tortured: "They pose a direct threat to the United States by aspiration," McKenzie, the incoming CENTCOM commander, said in December 2018, but "right now, they're severely constricted."[35]

Joe Ryan left the advisory job at FOB Gamberi in the spring of 2019 and took a position on the staff of General Scott Miller, who had succeeded Mick Nicholson in the fall at the helm of the Resolute Support mission in Kabul. Miller, a veteran of Delta Force's long campaign in Iraq who had also spent time as the top special operations commander in Afghanistan, was concerned that the intelligence agencies were underestimating the Daesh threat.[36] Ryan wasn't convinced. Nine years earlier, at FOB Blessing, he'd suggested to me that the U.S. government counterterrorism machine's intense focus on Arabs in Kunar might have led military intelligence to overstate their importance.[37] He worried that the same thing might be happening now, with the counterterrorism task force and its military intelligence analysts so singularly focused on the Islamic State that they unintentionally overplayed the group's significance to the broader Afghan conflict and the importance that its northeastern safe haven might hold for external attack plans. To him, the Daesh presence in Kunar looked less like an international terrorist branch and more like reshuffling of the same old groups of local militants—Hizb-e Islami loyalists and Salafis who had joined the Taliban-led insurgency only out of convenience.

"We're not seeing foreign fighters up there. These are localized folks," Ryan told me in mid-2019, after returning to Fort Carson from his seventh Afghanistan deployment.[38] "I'm not saying there aren't worrying indicators, but I don't believe that a transnational terrorist attack is going to emanate from Kunar anytime soon."[39]

In an interview arranged by Resolute Support commander Miller's spokesman, a Kabul-based intelligence analyst gave me the opposing viewpoint, the one that had the general worrying that Daesh could strike out from northeastern Afghanistan at targets abroad. "ISIS-K has the intent and the capability to attack the homeland. The threat is real and the threat is high," the analyst told me confidently, noting that the caliphate's dwindling core leadership in Syria had encouraged all its far-flung branches to take up the mission of attacks on the West and citing the increasing frequency and lethality of Daesh's terrorist attacks against crowded civilian targets in Kabul. But he acknowledged that no Islamic State attack plots in Europe or the United States had yet been linked back to Afghanistan and that he was more concerned about members of the group inspiring attacks by homegrown "lone wolves" than actually planning or materially assisting them. "They've claimed attacks in India and Pakistan," he said. "Through online forums where they're inciting and inspiring, ISIS-K maintains the capability to reach the homeland, through these social media spaces."[40]

The question was whether that type of threat—which could just as easily emanate from Libya, Nigeria, or anywhere else that Daesh propagandists had reliable internet access and were paying attention to the core caliphate's orders—warranted maintaining a military counterterrorism force in Afghanistan in the aftermath of whatever U.S.-Taliban deal came out of the Doha talks. If the answer was no, the solution for the United States would have to rest on outsourcing the battle against Daesh, in part to the Afghan government but also in part to the Taliban.

That put the U.S. military in Afghanistan in a strange position in the final months of 2019 and the early months of 2020, as the diplomats in Doha hashed out the terms of the deal: that of helping one enemy, the Taliban, push another, Daesh, out of the very valleys in Kunar where American troops had fought for so many years against the former.

AT FOB GAMBERI earlier in 2019, Ryan had watched developments in Washington and Doha with curiosity. I spoke to him by phone the day before the State of the Union address that February, amid rampant speculation that Trump would order a rapid pullout from Afghanistan. "We're going to be watching like everybody else," he said with a chuckle when I asked whether he expected any major strategy changes to come from it. When Ryan and his aide tuned in from his office early in the morning Afghan time, the president's speech passed without any surprises—just a brief reference to the talks in Qatar.

When Ryan left the northeast for the Kabul headquarters job a few weeks later, in March 2019, he gave his successor roughly the same advice about Kunar that he'd given Colin Tuley eight years earlier: *Don't read too much into the reports about district centers falling; it's usually not going to be true. It's often a bit of a cry for attention. Even if it is true, it may not matter much.* The district he was thinking of was the same one that Rangers from his battalion had driven through in Hiluxes during Winter Strike and that his Bulldog troops had struggled to reach during the summer of the surge: Chapa Dara. Ryan suspected that Daesh was looking to supplement its Korengali timber income with revenue from Chapa Dara's gem mines, and he was right.[41] Daesh fighters had consolidated their hold over the Korengal in January, and at the end of March, some of them hiked down from the valley to Chapa Dara, taking over a smattering of villages around the district center before government and Taliban reinforcements arrived to push them back.[42]

Both Daesh and the Taliban busily posted videos and photos of their clashes in Kunar in the spring and summer of 2019 to online propaganda channels—some from Chapa Dara and more from the Korengal after the Taliban sent a large force over the mountains from the neighboring province of Laghman in June to try to dislodge the Islamic State from its stronghold. On the Taliban's side, the photos showed men in U.S. Marine–style camouflage—one of many American patterns that were now ubiquitous among Afghan insurgents—arriving in the valley, sporting long hair and red headbands, the insignia of the group's "Red Units," which were geared toward offensive operations. For its part, Daesh took the body-count approach, issuing press releases with headings such as "Battle of Attrition" that gave detailed rundowns of how many Taliban fighters their men had killed that week—three here in an ambush in Omar, two there in an attack on Yakha China—sometimes with grisly photos as proof.

The Taliban sometimes suggested, in their Kunar videos that summer, that the U.S. military and Afghan government forces were helping Daesh. The claims had no basis in reality, and in fact, something closer to the opposite was true. Informal local ceasefires between government troops and the Taliban continued, intended to give the Taliban space to fight the mutual foe, and the Taliban, at times, would come to the government's aid. When presidential elections came around at the end of the summer, government forces in Chapa Dara were few and far between—and, in a development that would have seemed bizarre a few years earlier, it was Taliban fighters who patrolled the outlying villages on election day, burning the houses of suspected Daesh members and encouraging residents to come out to their polling places and vote.[43]

Even more bizarre, especially for the troops involved, was the American role in supporting the Taliban from the air in the second half of 2019 and early months of 2020. Ranger ground missions into Kunar had mostly ceased now. In the air, though, the JSOC task force's fleet of Reapers and surveillance planes remained active over Kunar—but with a twist. "All the shooting we're doing is in Kunar now, probably a strike a day, and it's all against ISIS, not the Taliban," a special operator told me. "What we're doing with the strikes against ISIS is helping the Taliban move, supporting their movements with our air strikes."[44]

There wasn't any direct contact between the U.S. military and its longtime foes—that would have been too controversial, and top generals like CENTCOM commander McKenzie needed to be able to reassure congressmen and other worried parties that his troops were providing only "very limited support" to the insurgency responsible for the deaths of so many Americans over the years.[45] So the two forces relied on other cues. After years of using signals intelligence to pinpoint Taliban positions for air strikes, the Rangers and intelligence personnel of the task force's Team East adapted the radio and cell phone intercepts for a different purpose: identifying Taliban troops so that drone crews could spare them and focus on the Daesh militants they were fighting. Taliban units on the ground, meanwhile, appeared willing to take the help they were getting, waiting to assault Daesh positions until they heard and saw the explosions of bombs and Hellfires.[46]

In the task force operations center, Rangers gave Team East and the drones and other aircraft that it coordinated a nickname: the Taliban Air Force. The captain in charge of the team, some would joke, was doing the work of a Taliban Red Unit commander. "Yeah, it raised eyebrows," the special operator told me. "Everyone in the task force would rather be out there fighting the war themselves. But I think everyone understands that it's time to try something different."[47]

FOR AMERICAN VETERANS who had fought in the Pech and its tributaries, the latest developments were strange to see, and could spark anything from anger and bitterness to nostalgia.

Sergeant First Class Steve Frye was in Kabul that summer when he learned that the Taliban and the Islamic State were killing each other in the Korengal. That was the valley where Frye had spent the first of his five Afghan tours, as a private first class and corporal in the Chosin battalion's Attack Company—the company that Chris Cavoli had agonized over keeping in the Korengal when the unit's deployment was extended in January 2007.[48]

Since then, Frye had seen combat in other tough corners of the country, but nothing had ever compared to those sixteen months in Kunar, when the KOP and Vegas had seemed like the edge of the world and the Korengali Taliban came out to fight just about every day. Back then, he'd hated the place, and he'd seen how their time there had tortured some of his friends in the years since; one of his squadmates had been Kieth Jeter, the young soldier who wound up back at Vegas for a second deployment, during which he survived a Chinook crash and suffered a breakdown while home on midtour leave.

But the Korengal had gotten Frye hooked on Afghanistan. He'd volunteered for this latest deployment, as an ANA adviser, not because he saw adviser duty as the soundest way forward in Afghanistan but because the Army was billing it internally as *combat* adviser duty—a chance to get back to the front lines, or near them. In practice, the job had turned out to be a boring one: headquarters advising, far from the battlefield. During a particularly dull stretch, he took to logging on to Blue Eye, a secure military portal that showed drone feeds from every corner of America's wars, and looking at the footage coming out of the Korengal, where Reapers were monitoring the "red-on-red" skirmishes between the Taliban and Daesh.

Then, looking at a public mapping site that linked to the latest militant propaganda content, he got the guerrilla's-eye view of trails he remembered hiking until it seemed like he knew every rock and branch. One photo showed a small campsite, and he thought of the big black wildcats that he'd seen poking around a similar campsite during a patrol into the deep forest in the fall of 2006. "It was a bunch of ISIS fighters in this area above Landigal, one of the shittier places," Frye told me, "and it's this little camp—fires, empty water bottles, just like the one with the dang black panthers."

Frye kept checking back on the footage and the mapping site for more photos; it was the most exciting thing he had going on. "It brought a lot of memories back," he told me. "If I could go back and do one deployment again, the Korengal would be it, no doubt."

He remembered the friends with whom he'd slept shivering in the same sleeping bag for warmth, the bond they'd built that he'd never found in another unit or on another deployment. He also remembered the exhilaration and the satisfaction of fighting the enemy directly, in the mountains, with overwhelming firepower.

Knowing that no one in his adviser unit would appreciate the weirdness, Frye posted a pair of screenshots to Facebook, where friends from Attack Company would see them: a still from a Taliban video and a Daesh press release, showing how both were fighting in the Korengal. "I'd give my left nut," he wrote, suggesting he wished he could go back to the valley where he'd begun his Afghan adventures and fight the guerrillas once again.

Fellow Korengal veterans chimed in. "Wait what? Bro I'm getting the pig," a former machine gunner typed, referring to the belt-fed M240 he'd once lugged around the same mountainside shown in the video.

"Did someone say troops in the open?" another chimed in.

"Something about fire for effect, perhaps?"

"My only regret is there is only so much WP [white phosphorous]."

It was the "Kunar syndrome" that other veterans of the Pech and its side valleys had talked to me about, the one that had drawn some troops to finagle their way onto repeat tours in the area. Thirteen years earlier, the Korengal had been a place of misery for Frye and the veterans who commented on his post. Now, all adopted the same half-joking tone of nostalgia about the place that had changed their lives, sometimes for the better, sometimes very much for the worse.

ACKNOWLEDGMENTS

During the nearly ten years it took to report and write, this book benefited from the time and candor that hundreds of people spared for it as they sat for interviews, shared photographs and documents, and read drafts. Space doesn't permit me to thank all the interview subjects individually, but every one of them has my gratitude, and I'd like to name some of those whose assistance opened the door to that of others. I'm especially grateful to the military leaders who allowed me to accompany their troops' patrols in Afghanistan and took the time to speak with me while deployed in combat zones, including Joe Ryan, Drew Poppas, Dakota Steedsman, George Ehlschide, Jon Peterson, William Stanton, Alex Pruden, Tom Kunnman, Bryan Laske, Brandon Newkirk, Tom Feltey, Ian MacGregor, Joey Paolilli, Cliff Pederson, and Sean Outman of the U.S. Army, and Hayatullah Aqtash, Rahmdel Haidarzai, Asef Naseri, Mahboob Khan, and Mohammad Afzal of the Afghan National Army.

The commanders who oversaw American operations in the Pech acted as gatekeepers to practically everyone else I interviewed: Chris Cavoli, Mick Nicholson, Jim McKnight, Joe Evans, Rob Stanton, Burke Garrett, Joseph Dichairo, David Paschal, Chris Downey, and James DeOre of the 10th Mountain Division; Bill Ostlund, Lou

Frketic, Dan Kearney, and Matt Myer of the 173rd Airborne Brigade; John Spiszer, Brett Jenkinson, Nick Bilotta, James Howell, and James Stultz of the 1st Infantry Division; Randy George, Brian Pearl, Kevin Hutcheson, Mark Moretti, Shaun Conlin, Ben Walker, and Tommy Ryan of the 4th Infantry Division; Jeffrey Schloesser, John Campbell, J. P. McGee, Tim Leone, Bo Reynolds, John Lynch, and Jimmy Blackmon of the 101st Airborne Division; Colin Tuley, Jake Hughes, Jon Cheatwood, Loren Crowe, and Christopher Bluhm of the 25th Infantry Division; Tom Von Eschenbach of the 3rd Combat Aviation Brigade; Dale Alford, Norm Cooling, James Donnellan, James Bierman, and Patrick Byron of the Marine Corps; Ryan Scholl, Larry Legree, and Sam Paparo of the Navy; and Karl Eikenberry, David McKiernan, David Petraeus, John Allen, and Joseph Dunford of the U.S.-led military headquarters in Kabul.

These officers introduced me to the hundreds of their former subordinates, from privates to staff officers, whose memories, journals, and hard drives were the real prize. Of particular help were the Pech returnees who fell in love with the place over the course of multiple deployments there, including Jim Gant, Andrew Glenn, Michael Harrison, Hugh Miller, and Don Nicholas, and the military and civilian veterans of the Asymmetric Warfare Group, especially George Sterling and the contractor referred to in this book as T.W., a hero in a bleak story whose name younger veterans mentioned with awe. Military public affairs officers facilitated many of the interviews as well, including the staff of the New York branch of the Army's Office of the Chief of Public Affairs and the spokespeople of many brigades, divisions, and other commands. Most of the veterans of the special operations community I interviewed cannot be named here, but I owe a tremendous amount to the men who spoke to me about their experiences in Kunar and Nuristan with the 75th Ranger Regiment; the 3rd, 7th, 19th, and 20th Special Forces Groups; the 160th Special Operations Aviation Regiment; and SEAL Teams 6 and 10. Douglas London, Ron Moeller, Michael Morell, and Gary Berntsen lent the CIA perspective, as did other agency veterans who asked not to be identified. Harry Bader was crucial to my understanding of Kunar's timber trade, and David Sedney, Dante Paradiso, and Tim Standaert shared useful perspectives on the military from the State Department's standpoint.

Although I can't use their full names, Farshad, Musawer, Ruhullah, and Shaheer made this book possible by serving as my interpreters during reporting trips to Kabul and Kunar. Arash, Arian, Burhan, Nazir, and Samim, as interpreters to U.S. military commanders, offered some of the most valuable insights of anyone I spoke with. Among the other Afghans who helped me understand what the war looked like from outside the walls of American outposts were Haji Zalmay Yusufzai, Mawlawi Shahzada Shahid, Haji Salih Mohammad Salih, Anayat Rahman Safi, Zabiullah Rabbani, Fazlullah Wahidi, Asadullah Wafa, Jamaluddin Badr, Tamim Nuristani, Obaidullah Nuristani, and Haji Abdul Qudus Nuristani.

I'm indebted to those who rose to the painful task of sharing memories of loved ones who died in the Pech and its tributaries, including Marc Pape, Oaken Ewens, Dave Brostrom, Frankie Gay, and Ray Fuller Sr.

Among those who improved this book by reading portions of it in draft form were David Katz, Hyder Akbar, Evan Wright, Chris Sands, Ross Ritchell, R.M. Schneidermann, and Ed Darack; others did the same but preferred not to be named. I cite the work of many journalists who spent time reporting from Kunar and Nuristan, but Bilal Sarwary, Sebastian Junger, Tim Hetherington, Paul Refsdal, Elliott Woods, Elizabeth Rubin, Franz Marty, Kate Clark, and May Jeong all wrote stories or filmed documentaries that provided key glimpses into periods before and after my own experience in eastern Afghanistan. Michael Gordon gave me world-class on-the-job training in finding and interviewing sources and assembling material for a book. Alissa Rubin and Rod Nordland kindly gave me a place to live and work in Kabul, while the U.S. Institute of Peace generously offered research funding; there, I thank Shahmahmood Miakhel, Colin Cookman, Scott Smith, and Jim Marshall. Sami Nuristani helped with translations from both Pashto and the Nuristani languages, and Nelly Lahoud and another person who can't be named here helped with Arabic translations. Asfandyar Mir and Tom Joscelyn were always willing to lend an ear as I struggled to understand al-Qaida and the other militant groups whose presence drew the attention of the U.S. government to the Pech.

Bonnie Nadell patiently shepherded this project through the publishing process, and I am thankful to her and Austen Rachlis at the Hill Nadell Literary Agency. At Random House, David Ebershoff took a chance on this book and gave it shape before turning it over to Sam Nicholson and then Molly Turpin, who saw it through as my second and third editors; and Craig Adams, Katie Zilberman, Elizabeth Rendfleisch, Carlos Beltran, Ingrid Sterner, Judy Kiviat, Frieda Duggan, David Goehring, and Ayelet Gruenspecht took it across the finish line. My college professors Michael Reynolds and Robert Finn also deserve thanks for overseeing the senior thesis that was the germ of this project in the months after my first visit to the Pech, and so does John McPhee for encouraging me to pursue turning it into a book.

Thanks also to my brother Owen and to the friends and partners who tolerated years of my chatter about road building, cedar prices, and the cultures of various military units; to my grandfather, Don Tucker, who fed my fascination with military history; and, most of all, to my parents, Kerry and Hal, who raised me to love reading and writing and never wavered in encouraging me to pursue it professionally, even when doing so took me out of college and into places of which they knew little except that they were dangerous. Without their love, support, and shadow editing, this book would not exist.

GLOSSARY

A-10   Air Force attack jet equipped with bombs and a 30-millimeter antitank cannon

AC-130   Air Force gunship equipped with a 105-millimeter howitzer and other weaponry

ANA   Afghan National Army

ANSOF TEAM   small team of Rangers charged with assisting the CIA and its Afghan surrogate forces on the battlefield in Afghanistan; successor to the Omega teams

APACHE   AH-64 attack helicopter

A-TEAM   detachment of a dozen Green Berets and other attached special operations troops

AWG   Asymmetric Warfare Group, an Army unit of soldiers and contractors established to spread tactical lessons in Afghanistan and Iraq

B-1   Air Force bomber equipped with satellite-guided bombs

BANDEH mountainside structure used by shepherds

BLACK HAWK medium transport helicopter, in Army (UH-60), Air Force (HH-60), and special operations (MH-60) variants

BUD/S Basic Underwater Demolition/SEAL training, the course sailors must complete to become SEALs

C-17 Air Force heavy transport jet

C-130 Air Force medium transport plane

CENTCOM Central Command, the U.S. military headquarters responsible for operations in Afghanistan and the Middle East

CHINOOK twin-rotor heavy transport helicopter, in Army (CH-47) and special operations (MH-47) variants

CIA Central Intelligence Agency

CLAYMORE M18 antipersonnel mine

COP combat outpost (pronounced "cop")

CTPT Counterterrorism Pursuit Teams, the CIA's Afghan surrogate forces

DAESH nickname for the Islamic State or ISIS

DIA Defense Intelligence Agency

DSHK Soviet bloc heavy machine gun (pronounced "dushka")

F-15 Air Force fighter jet equipped with satellite-guided bombs

F-16 Air Force fighter jet equipped with satellite-guided bombs

FOB forward operating base (pronounced "fob")

GREEN BERET member of the Army's Special Forces

HELLFIRE   laser-guided missile fired by Predator and Reaper drones and Apache and Kiowa helicopters

HESCO   collapsible structure of wire mesh that, when filled with dirt, forms a wall to protect against incoming fire

HILUX   Toyota pickup truck common in Afghanistan

HIMARS   M142 High-Mobility Artillery Rocket System, a truck-mounted launcher of long-range guided missiles

HIZB-E ISLAMI   militant group led by Gulbuddin Hekmatyar; founded as an anticommunist mujahidin party

HOWITZER   artillery piece that fires explosive shells (of 105-millimeter or 155-millimeter caliber in the U.S. military) in a high arc

IED   improvised explosive device

ISAF   International Security Assistance Force, the U.S.-led NATO military headquarters in Kabul (pronounced "eye-saff")

ISI   Inter-Services Intelligence, Pakistan's intelligence agency

JAMAAT AL-DAWA   Salafi militant group founded as an anticommunist mujahidin party

JAVELIN   guided antitank missile used by infantry units

JSOC   Joint Special Operations Command, the counterterrorism headquarters responsible for overseeing operations by SEAL Team 6, Delta Force, and the 75th Ranger Regiment (pronounced "jay-sock")

KIOWA   OH-58 light attack helicopter

KOP   Korengal Outpost (pronounced "kop")

M4   standard U.S. military infantry rifle

MAWLAWI   title for an Afghan cleric

MI-8/MI-17 Russian-built transport helicopter used by civilian transportation companies in Afghanistan

MOHAWK member of the CIA's Asadabad-based CTPT surrogate force

MORTAR bipod-mounted weapon used by U.S. infantry units to fire 60-millimeter, 81-millimeter, or 120-millimeter explosive shells in a high arc

MRAP mine-resistant, ambush-protected armored truck used to replace the Humvee (pronounced "em-rap")

NCO noncommissioned officer (an enlisted leader such as a corporal or sergeant)

NDS National Directorate of Security, Afghanistan's intelligence agency

NIGHT STALKER member of the 160th Special Operations Aviation Regiment

NSA National Security Agency

NSC National Security Council

OMEGA TEAM small team of JSOC operators, often members of SEAL Team 6, charged with assisting the CIA and its Afghan surrogate forces on the battlefield in Afghanistan

OP observation post

PAKOL common Afghan hat

PESHAWAR SHURA northern leadership council of the Taliban, based in the Pakistani city of Peshawar and responsible for overseeing the insurgency in northeastern Afghanistan

PREDATOR Air Force drone armed with Hellfire missiles

PRT provincial reconstruction team

RANGER   member of the Army's 75th Ranger Regiment

REAPER   Air Force drone armed with Hellfire missiles; larger successor to the Predator

ROTC   Reserve Officer Training Corps

RPG   rocket-propelled grenade

SAW   M249 light machine gun (pronounced "saw")

SEAL   member of one of the Navy's sea-air-land special operations teams (pronounced "seal")

SHURA   meeting or council

SPETSNAZ   Soviet special operations forces

TASK FORCE EAST   Jalalabad-based JSOC unit led by SEAL Team 6

TOW   wire-guided antitank missile often mounted on Humvees or MRAPs (pronounced "toe")

USAID   U.S. Agency for International Development

NOTES

PROLOGUE: 2010

1. Except where otherwise specified, this prologue is based on my notes, recordings, and photos from a July–August 2010 embed with 1-327 Infantry.
2. Carter Cheek, interview with author.
3. Capt. Antonio Salinas, interview with author.
4. Alex Pruden, interview with author.
5. Gen. (Ret.) David McKiernan, interview with author.
6. Nazir Shahid, interview with author.
7. Men from Khaliqlam, group interview with author.

CHAPTER 1: AMERICA COMES TO KUNAR, 2002–2003

1. Author correspondence and interview with Tom Greer, whose name I use with permission of his widow, Deidre. Greer was in charge of the three teams of a reconnaissance task force called Northern Advanced Force Operations (NAFO), answering to the Joint Special Operations Command's Advanced Force Operations cell at Bagram. The team that went to Kunar was called NAFO-3. Three other former Delta Force members and a former JSOC officer also described the broad outlines of how AFO teams were dispatched and bases established in eastern Afghanistan that spring on condition of anonymity.
2. Greer, interview.
3. U.S. embassy, Kabul, "PRT Asadabad: Semi-annual Report on Security, Political, Economic, and Social Conditions in Kunar Province," cable to Department of State, Feb. 21, 2007.
4. Former Delta Force operator, interview.

5. Greer, interview.

6. It is not clear what Soviet units were actually based at Topchi Base. Maps and photographs from the 1980s make clear that the main Soviet base in Asadabad was farther north, adjacent to the city itself on a triangular peninsula jutting into the Kunar River. The major units based there included an infantry battalion of the 66th Separate Motorized Rifle Brigade, which arrived in Kunar in the early months of 1980 and stayed on and off until the spring of 1988, and a special operations unit called the 334th Separate Spetsnaz Detachment, which deployed in the spring of 1985.

7. Steve Coll, *Directorate S: The CIA and America's Secret Wars in Afghanistan and Pakistan, 2001–2016* (New York: Penguin Press, 2017), 123.

8. Greer, interview.

9. For a detailed description of this incident from the perspective of Hekmatyar, who had arrived in the Shigal over the winter and departed shortly after the May 6 strike, which came very close to killing both him and bin Laden, see Chris Sands and Fazelminallah Qazizai, *Night Letters: Gulbuddin Hekmatyar and the Afghan Islamists Who Changed the World* (London: Hurst, 2019), 419–20.

10. The strike was first reported by *The New York Times* three days after it took place. The *Times* report identified Hekmatyar as the target and a CIA-operated, Hellfire-equipped Predator as the aircraft used (Thom Shanker and Carlotta Gall, "U.S. Attack on Warlord Aims to Help Interim Leader," *New York Times,* May 9, 2002). But "the real target was bin Laden; it wasn't Hekmatyar," a U.S. government source who was involved in the approval and reporting of the strike told me. "People were aware that every time you tried to kill bin Laden and failed, that increased his image as being invulnerable. So what happened was there was an effort to camouflage what actually happened, and *The New York Times* got part of the story."

11. Toby Harnden, "Bin Laden Is Wanted: Dead or Alive, Says Bush," *Telegraph,* Sept. 18, 2001.

12. Yaniv Barzilai, *102 Days of War: How Osama bin Laden, al-Qaeda, and the Taliban Survived 2001* (Washington, D.C.: Potomac Books, 2014), 43–52. Bush's own pugnacious defense secretary, Donald Rumsfeld, remained unconvinced that the military should be in the man-hunting business even as JSOC was diving into it. "The more I think about it, the more DoD [Department of Defense] is being looked to as the entity responsible for finding UBL and [the Taliban emir Mullah Mohammad] Omar," he wrote in a memo to his senior subordinates in April 2002, as JSOC's recon teams were spreading out and establishing outposts like FOB Asadabad. "It seems to me that these are not DoD primary responsibilities. Rather, they are law enforcement and intelligence responsibilities, with DoD in a supporting role."

13. Robert Grenier, *88 Days to Kandahar: A CIA Diary* (New York: Simon & Schuster, 2015), 4–5.

14. According to Cathy Scott-Clark and Adrian Levy in *The Exile: The Stunning Inside Story of Osama bin Laden and Al Qaeda in Flight* (New York: Bloomsbury, 2017), 96–97, bin Laden broadcast this message from a loca-

tion near Jalalabad several hours after he had already fled Tora Bora. Different perspectives on his escape are described in Dalton Fury, *Kill Bin Laden: A Delta Force Commander's Account of the Hunt for the World's Most Wanted Man* (New York: St. Martin's Press, 2008); Gary Berntsen, *Jawbreaker: The Attack on bin Laden and al-Qaeda* (New York: Crown, 2005); and analytical accounts including Barzilai, *102 Days of War;* Senate Foreign Relations Committee, *Tora Bora Revisited: How We Failed to Get bin Laden and Why It Matters Today* (Washington, D.C.: U.S. Government Printing Office, 2009); and U.S. Special Operations Command History and Research Office, *USSOCOM History, 1987–2007* (Tampa, 2007), 93–98.

15. Grenier, in *88 Days to Kandahar,* describes an exception in early 2002, when one of the JSOC reconnaissance teams was permitted to embed with the Tochi Scouts of the Frontier Corps but was unable to get along with its Pakistani hosts.

16. JSOC's evolution since September 11 from a niche unit focused on hostage rescue and counter-proliferation to a major command fighting multiple wars is chronicled in detail in Sean Naylor, *Relentless Strike: The Secret History of Joint Special Operations Command* (New York: St. Martin's Press, 2015). The first JSOC units into Afghanistan in 2001–2002 were code-named Task Force Sword and then Task Force 11, designations succeeded over the years by Task Force 121, Task Force 6-26, Task Force 714, Task Force 373, Task Force 3-10, Task Force 7, and so on.

17. Scott-Clark and Levy, *Exile,* 85–87.

18. Grenier, *88 Days to Kandahar,* 295–97.

19. Gary Berntsen, interview with author; Coll, *Directorate S,* 110–11.

20. At various times in the decade before September 11, 2001, al-Qaida operated at least fifteen camps and other sites in Afghanistan, according to documentary evidence and accounts by al-Qaida associates, most of them clustered around Jalalabad, Khost, and Kandahar, but never that many all at once, and never one in Kunar. By the time of the U.S. intervention, al-Qaida's main Jalalabad camp, Derunta, had been closed for about a year and the group's main training facilities were a set of camps in Kandahar Province and the Mes Aynak and Murad Beg camps in Logar and Parwan, along with some safe houses in Kabul and Kandahar city. The only foreign jihadi group known to have maintained a camp in Kunar during the 1990s was the Pakistani group Lashkar-e-Taiba, which would not develop a close relationship with al-Qaida until after the U.S.-led intervention; the camps belonging to other Arab militant groups besides al-Qaida were concentrated in the same regions as the al-Qaida sites, where the Taliban could monitor them. Mustafa Hamid and Leah Farrall, *The Arabs at War in Afghanistan* (London: Hurst, 2015), 248–72; Anne Stenersen, *Al-Qaida in Afghanistan* (Cambridge, U.K.: Cambridge University Press, 2017), 119–26, 135–42.

21. Former senior intelligence officer, interview with author.

22. Ibid.

23. The figure of more than ten thousand is from Thomas Hegghammer, "The

Rise of Muslim Foreign Fighters," *International Security* 35, no. 3 (Winter 2010/2011).

24. Brian Fishman, *The Master Plan: ISIS, al-Qaeda, and the Jihadi Strategy for Final Victory* (New Haven, Conn.: Yale University Press, 2016), 12; Stenersen, *Al-Qaida in Afghanistan,* 127–47. Of the fourteen Arab jihadi groups operating in the country as guests of the Taliban, only five had joined al-Qaida in its 1998 declaration of war against America, the "far enemy," and even most al-Qaida members were focused on assisting the Taliban on the battlefield, with only a handful involved in planning for international terrorist plots.

25. Hamid and Farrall, *Arabs at War in Afghanistan,* 248.

26. Greer, interview; Delta Force and JSOC sources, interviews with author; Stenersen, *Al-Qaida in Afghanistan,* 176. Bases established in this manner included Asadabad in Kunar and Firebase Camelot near Shkin in Paktika (later renamed FOB Lilley).

27. Joint Task Force Guantánamo detainee assessment of Abd al-Hamid Abd al-Salaam al-Ghazawi, Jan. 22, 2008.

28. Joint Task Force Guantánamo detainee assessment of Riyad Nasir Muhammad Atahar, Sept. 15, 2008.

29. Joint Task Force Guantánamo detainee assessment of Ahmed al-Hikimi, June 2, 2008. Hamza al-Qaiti later returned to Yemen to help revitalize al-Qaida's branch there and was killed in a raid by U.S.-supported Yemeni counterterrorism forces in 2008.

30. News reports had placed bin Laden in Kunar a year earlier too; see Kathy Gannon, "Afghans Feel They're in U.S. Crosshairs," Associated Press, Nov. 14, 2000.

31. Abdel Bari Atwan, quoted in Peter Bergen, *The Osama Bin Laden I Know: An Oral History of Al Qaeda's Leader* (New York: Free Press, 2005), 171, and in Stenersen, *Al-Qaida in Afghanistan,* 55.

32. Osama bin Laden to Atiyah Abd al-Rahman, Oct. 21, 2010, www.ctc.usma .edu/v2/wp-content/uploads/2013/10/Letter-from-UBL-to-Atiyatullah -Al-Libi-3-Translation1.pdf.

33. Greer, interview.

34. Brig. Gen. John Brennan, interview with author.

35. Special operations and CIA sources, interviews; Naylor, *Relentless Strike,* 353.

36. The first Rangers to arrive at the Asadabad base were two platoons of B Company, 2nd Ranger Battalion, who drove up in May and spent three weeks at the base, according to the memoir of a Ranger veteran who was a member of the company, Nicholas Moore, *Run to the Sound of the Guns: The True Story of an American Ranger at War in Afghanistan and Iraq,* with Mir Bahmanyar (Oxford: Osprey, 2018), 40–41.

37. Berntsen, *Jawbreaker,* 277, 290–91, 305–14; Naylor, *Relentless Strike,* 181. "The biggest and most important failure of CENTCOM leadership came at Tora Bora when they turned down my request for a battalion of U.S.

Rangers to block bin Laden's escape," Berntsen writes, referring to U.S. Central Command.

38. Moore, *Run to the Sound of the Guns,* 41.

39. Both Soviet and American soldiers who served in Kunar displayed a weakness for pet monkeys (evidenced in their many photos posing with the animals) to which local merchants were happy to cater. Curiously, in his account of his 1840 expedition to Kunar, the East India Company naturalist William Griffith meticulously described wildlife ranging from swallows and kingfishers to leopards and jackal-like creatures that he could not identify, but no monkeys.

40. Ranger sources, interviews with author. Joe Kapacziewski, who was at Asadabad that summer as a junior Ranger with 3rd Battalion, describes life at the base in the summer of 2002 in his memoir, written with Charles Sasser, *Back in the Fight: The Explosive Memoir of a Special Operator Who Never Gave Up* (New York: St. Martin's Press, 2013), 55–60.

41. Ranger source, interview with author.

42. Ibid. Elements of 3rd Ranger Battalion's A and C Companies hiked up the Shigal in August 2002 along with their battalion commander.

43. This account of JSOC's fall 2002 Shigal raid is pieced together from special operations and intelligence sources who mostly prefer to remain anonymous and whose memories, more than a decade later, are sometimes fuzzy (they do not provide a date for the mission, for example). Two separate Ranger companies, both from 1st Ranger Battalion, took part in the mission.

44. This quotation comes from an interview with the intelligence officer of JSOC Task Force East's Team Logar later in the war, during the CENTCOM investigation into the shoot-down of Extortion 17, a CH-47 Chinook carrying a troop of SEAL Team 6 operators and their support personnel, www2.centcom.mil/sites/foia/rr/CENTCOM%20Regulation%20CCR%2025210/Wardak%20CH-47%20Investigation/r_EX%2022.pdf.

45. Special operations sources, interviews with author.

46. Ranger source, interview with author. "I about froze to death that night," another former Ranger who was on the mission added.

47. Col. John Rafferty, interview with author.

48. Special operations sources, interviews with author.

49. 160th Special Operations Aviation Regiment source, interview with author.

50. Ranger source, interview with author.

51. Sands and Qazizai, *Night Letters,* 423; Chris Sands, interview with author.

52. Different versions of the story of bin Laden's escape from Tora Bora to the Shigal and then on to Pakistan have been published, but they agree on the key point that a local commander—either Mawlawi Nur Mohammad or Awal Gul, who later wound up in detention at Guantánamo—smuggled him into the Shigal, stopping in Jalalabad on the way, and then handed him over to Kashmir Khan for safekeeping that lasted until some time after the May 6 drone strike.

According to the account the captured courier, Qari Harun al-Afghani, gave to interrogators after being detained in 2007 and sent to Guantánamo, he had been working for a senior al-Qaida commander named Abd al-Hadi al-Iraqi in the fall of 2002 when he helped Mawlawi Nur Mohammad process a claim for $7,000 from al-Qaida, which Nur Mohammad told him was reimbursement for money he had given to bin Laden while smuggling the sheikh from Tora Bora to the Shigal (Joint Task Force Guantánamo detainee assessment of Harun al-Afghani, Aug. 2, 2007; Joint Task Force Guantánamo detainee assessment of Haji Awal Gul, Feb. 15, 2008). Zawahiri himself would confirm a key detail of this account in an August 2015 video in which he stated that it was Nur Mohammad who guided bin Laden out of Tora Bora (Ayman al-Zawahiri, *Days with the Imam,* episode 7, Aug. 15, 2015, translation by SITE Intelligence Group, news.site intelgroup.com/Jihadist-News/zawahiri-recalls-siege-escape-from-tora -bora-advises-jihadi-media-to-stop-promoting-discord-between-fighters .html).

According to Harun's account, bin Laden stayed in the Shigal for about ten months—that is, until about August 2002, not long before the big JSOC raid. But a source with more direct knowledge—a militant who traveled with bin Laden when he left Tora Bora—told the British journalists Cathy Scott-Clark and Adrian Levy much later that bin Laden moved on from the Shigal to a tiny village in Pakistan in July; he also said that Zawahiri parted ways with bin Laden before he reached the Shigal, heading straight into Pakistan after their stop in Jalalabad while bin Laden entered Kunar on horseback, just as the CIA's information at the time described (Scott-Clark and Levy, *Exile,* 85–87, 158–60, 282, 512).

But based on interviews with Kashmir Khan himself and other militants, the British and Afghan journalists Chris Sands and Fazelminallah Qazizai write in the most detailed account of the terrorist leaders' movements that both bin Laden and Zawahiri arrived in the Shigal in mid-December 2001, staying at a house with an electrical generator in Khwarr and occasionally visiting Kashmir Khan's nearby home village of Derai, where the May 6 air strike occurred (Sands and Qazizai, *Night Letters,* 404–8, 416–21).

A former Army infantry officer who spent time in the Shigal later in the war, Loren Crowe, said in an interview that people sometimes talked about how bin Laden had stayed with this person or that one in their valley in 2002. At the time, he dismissed it as idle talk and assumed other units were hearing similar stories all over Afghanistan.

53. Special operations source, interview with author.
54. "What Does the Death of Usama bin Laden Mean?," *SIDtoday* (internal NSA newsletter), May 17, 2011, item released by *The Intercept.* "Zawahiri has *never* been seen in SIGINT," the classified item notes. According to Stenersen, when the Taliban took over bin Laden's security from his own people in February 1999, six months after the embassy attacks and subsequent cruise-missile strikes, they also took his satellite communications equipment from him (Stenersen, *Al-Qaida in Afghanistan,* 88).

55. Sands and Qazizai, *Night Letters,* 419–20.

56. In *A Nightmare's Prayer: A Marine Harrier Pilot's War in Afghanistan* (New York: Threshold, 2010), 120–22, Michael Franzak, a former pilot of AV-8B Harrier attack jets, describes using this tactic in support of Task Force 5 (as the SEAL-led JSOC task force at Bagram was then calling itself) in the Pech valley one night in January or February 2003. Franzak's role in the mission was to zoom loudly past the mouth of the Korengal while a signals intelligence plane flew overhead and helicopters full of special operators stood by.

57. Moeller, interview with author.

58. Author correspondence with Schuyler Jones, a former Oxford scholar who was given this estimate at a Nangalam teahouse by the Norwegian linguist Georg Morgenstierne.

59. Lt. Col. John Paganini, interview with author. The Russian maps, according to a declassified Army Intelligence and Security Command history, were pulled together in late 2001 in a joint effort by the National Ground Intelligence Center and the CIA, initially just to help U.S. troops avoid old minefields as they entered Afghanistan.

60. The unit defeated in the May 25, 1985, battle at Kunyak was the 4th Company, 2nd Battalion, 149th Guards Motorized Rifle Regiment. The battle is mentioned in many descriptions of Soviet military activity in Kunar, including General Valentin Varennikov's memoir *Nepovtorimoe* (Moscow: Sovetskii Pisatel, 2001), 5:200–202, but the most detailed description is the one accessible at artofwar.ru/s/shennikow_w_w/text_0130.shtml.

61. Jim Gant, interview with author. When a British officer, Colonel H. C. Tanner, visited a community in what is now southern Kunar in 1879, he had a similar experience, with a village first describing itself by one name and then by another, apparently more private name.

   Make enough of these visits, and a particularly astute soldier might figure out what few ever did: that most villages did not really have set decision-making councils at all, even if that was the way the elders made it seem. Village *shuras* had varying membership and traditionally existed to deal with mundane matters of daily agrarian life; only the arrival of aid workers and other foreigners in recent decades had thrust the loose councils into the role of negotiating with outsiders. David Katz, a Foreign Service officer who spent time in Nuristan later in the war and had done anthropology fieldwork there in the 1970s, viewed this as one of the most widespread and basic misunderstandings that American troops, as well as aid workers and journalists and others, were guilty of.

62. Moeller, interview.

63. Former U.S. government official, interview with author.

64. Coll, *Directorate S,* 164.

65. CIA source, interview with author.

66. The unit massacred in the April 20, 1985, battle at Daridam in the Marawara valley was a company of the 334th Separate Spetsnaz Detachment, which had arrived in Afghanistan only a month before. Valentin Varennikov

describes the event in *Nepovtorimoe,* 5:142–55, as well as the meeting afterward with an informant in Kabul, which left him convinced that disinformation had led the commandos to their deaths. The event is also the subject of a book by Petr Tkachenko, *Особая рота: Подвиг в Мароварском ущелье* (Moscow: Eksmo Press, 2005).

67. Haji Ruhullah Wakil, interview with author.
68. Malik Ayoub Zarin, interview with author.
69. Ian Fisher and John Burns, "U.S. Troops Focus on Border's Caves to Seek Bin Laden," *New York Times,* Aug. 28, 2002; Ruhullah, interview.
70. Ruhullah, interview.
71. The importance of Guantánamo detentions in squandering goodwill in the war's first couple of years is explored in two of the most thorough books on Western missteps in Afghanistan, Anand Gopal's *No Good Men Among the Living: America, the Taliban, and the War Through Afghan Eyes* (New York: Metropolitan Books, 2014), which cites the story of Ruhullah and Sabar Lal, and Mike Martin's *Intimate War: An Oral History of the Helmand Conflict* (London: C. Hurst, 2014), which covers the British experience in the south.
72. "Jamaat al-Dawa" is shorthand for the different longer names that Kunar's Salafi party has gone by over the years: Jamaat al-Dawa ila al-Quran wa Ahl al-Hadith, Jamaat al-Dawa al-Salafiya wal-Qital, Jamaat al-Dawa ila al-Quran wal-Sunna, and so on. The group should not be confused with Jamaat ud-Dawa, the Pakistani political party associated with the terrorist group Lashkar-e-Taiba.
73. Sworn statement of Haji Ruhullah Wakil to the Combatant Status Review Tribunal, n.d., www.dod.gov/pubs/foi/Reading_Room/Detainee_Related/Set_30_2048-2144.pdf.
74. Joint Task Force Guantánamo detainee assessment of Haji Ruhullah Wakil, June 17, 2005; Joint Task Force Guantánamo detainee assessment of Sabar Lal Melma, June 3, 2005.
75. Shahmahmood Miakhel, interview with author.
76. Ayoub Zarin, interview with author.
77. Ibid.
78. Ibid.
79. Relative of Matiullah Khan, interview with author.
80. Barnett Rubin, interview with author.
81. Tom Lasseter, "Guantanamo Inmate Database: Sabar Lal," McClatchy News Service, June 15, 2008.
82. Joint Task Force Guantánamo Administrative Review Board hearing transcripts for Haji Ruhullah Wakil and Sabar Lal Melma.
83. CW3 (Ret.) Brian Halstead, interview with author.
84. Ibid.
85. Hyder Akbar, interview with author.
86. This account of Jim Gant's 2003 Kunar deployment is based on my interviews with Gant, Halstead, and Hyder Akbar; on the reports on missions in Kunar that Gant wrote at the time; and on the book that Gant's wife, the

former *Washington Post* reporter Ann Scott Tyson, wrote after his return to Kunar in 2010–2012 and ensuing dismissal from the Special Forces in scandal, *American Spartan: The Promise, the Mission, and the Betrayal of Special Forces Major Jim Gant* (New York: William Morrow, 2014).

87. Gant, interview.
88. Halstead, interview.
89. Hyder Akbar, *Come Back to Afghanistan: A California Teenager's Story* (New York: Bloomsbury, 2005), 284.
90. Gant and Halstead, interviews.
91. Gant, interview. The same quotation is in Tyson, *American Spartan,* 96.
92. Tyson, *American Spartan,* 65.
93. Ibid., 98–100.
94. Gant, interview.
95. Halstead, interview.
96. Gant, interview; Jim Gant, "Trip Report for CONOP 310-05," May 24, 2003; Halstead, interview.
97. Halstead, interview.
98. Gant, interview.
99. Lt. Col. Rich Garey, interview with author.
100. Akbar, *Come Back to Afghanistan,* 58.
101. Halstead, interview.
102. Moeller, interview. In his memoir *88 Days to Kandahar,* the station chief in Islamabad at the time, Robert Grenier, complains that "inexperienced graduates of the Farm were being issued carbines and rushed, on their first assignments, into Afghanistan."
103. Halstead, interview. The 2014 Senate Intelligence Committee report on CIA detention programs confirms that in the early years after September 11, analysts were stationed alongside case officers at forward bases in Afghanistan.
104. This account of the detention and death of Abdul Wali is based on my interview with Halstead, Passaro's sentencing recommendation (U.S. District Court for the Eastern District of North Carolina, Western Division, "United States of America v. David A. Passaro: Government's Sentencing Memorandum," Feb. 12, 2007, www.humanrightsfirst.org/wp-content/uploads/pdf/pmc-passaromemo.pdf), and Hyder Akbar's account in *Come Back to Afghanistan.*
105. See Senate Select Committee on Intelligence, Executive Summary, *Committee Study of the Central Intelligence Agency's Detention and Interrogation Program,* released Dec. 9, 2014.
106. Clyde Haberman, "A Singular Conviction amid the Debate on Torture and Terrorism," *New York Times,* April 19, 2015.
107. Akbar to the Honorable Terrence W. Boyle, Feb. 8, 2007 (Attachment A of Passaro sentencing memorandum).
108. Halstead, interview.
109. An extensive retrospective report by the Open Society Foundations on the effects of civilian casualties and other damage to civilian lives quotes an

Afghanistan analyst who made a similar observation, telling the report's authors that the detention of Haji Ruhullah "was more damaging than all the civilian casualty cases that came after." Christopher Kolenda et al., *The Strategic Costs of Civilian Harm: Applying Lessons from Afghanistan to Current and Future Conflicts,* Open Society Foundations, June 2016, 24.

110. Mawlawi Shahzada Shahid, interview with author.
111. For descriptions of the April 1979 massacre and the role Soviet advisers played in it, see David Edwards, *Before Taliban: Genealogies of the Afghan Jihad* (Berkeley: University of California Press, 2002), 145; Edward Girardet, *Killing the Cranes: A Reporter's Journey Through Three Decades of War in Afghanistan* (White River Junction, Vt.: Chelsea Green, 2011), 90–96; and, for the massacre's use in mujahidin propaganda, "The Heartbreaking Massacre of Karhala," *Jihad Rays* 3, no. 7–8 (Nov.–Dec. 1984): 18–19. In October 2015, after a years-long investigation that took them all the way to Kunar, Dutch police arrested a former officer in the Soviet-advised Afghan unit responsible for the massacre, the 444th Commandos, Sadeq Alamyar, and charged him for his role in it.
112. Shugrullah Motakil, interview with author.
113. Gant, interview.

CHAPTER 2: WINTER STRIKE, 2003

1. Special operations sources, interviews with author; Anthony Shaffer, *Operation Dark Heart: Spycraft and Special Ops on the Frontlines of Afghanistan and the Path to Victory* (New York: Thomas Dunne Books, 2010), 195–96.
2. This description of the October 30, 2003, air strike in the Waygal valley is based on interviews with Zabiullah Rabbani, Obaidullah Nuristani, Mawlawi Shafiullah Nuristani, Mawlawi Mohammad Afzal, Haji Abdul Qudus Nuristani, President Hamid Karzai, two other Rabbani family members who asked not to be identified, Lt. Gen. (Ret.) Robert Elder Jr., David Sedney, Lt. Col. (Ret.) Anthony Shaffer, and a former senior U.S. intelligence official, three former senior special operations officers, and another former senior U.S. government official who all asked not to be identified. The strike is also described in Shaffer, *Operation Dark Heart,* 206–9, and was noted at the time in news reports, which generally identified the target as Mawlawi Faqirullah, a Hizb-e Islami commander based in Aranas at the time.
3. Milton Bearden and James Risen, *The Main Enemy: The Inside Story of the CIA's Final Showdown with the KGB* (New York: Random House, 2003), 275. In one of several books he wrote about the jihad, Hekmatyar elaborated on his belief that not only the KGB-backed Afghan intelligence service but also his CIA partners were trying to have him killed in the 1980s. Sometime after a May 1984 visit to Pakistan's North-West Frontier Province by the then vice president (and former CIA director) George H. W. Bush, Hekmatyar claims, he met with the provincial governor, who had hosted Bush during the visit. The governor supposedly claimed to Hekmatyar that Bush had asked him to "eliminate this fanatic," referring to Hek-

matyar. Gulbuddin Hekmatyar, *Secret Plans Open Faces: From the Withdrawal of Russians to the Fall of the Coalition Government,* ed. S. Fida Yunas, trans. Sher Zaman Taizi (Peshawar: University of Peshawar, 2004), 81.

4. Former senior intelligence officer, two former senior special operations officers, and Shaffer, interviews. Most sources were reluctant to speak directly about the CIA's role in the event. When I asked another senior government official who ordered the strike, he would not answer, saying only, "You'd need to interview George Tenet," then the director of central intelligence. The senior U.S. military officer in Afghanistan at the time, Lieutenant General David Barno (who was not in the chain of command for either JSOC or CIA operations), declined to speak about the air strike at all. At the time, however, Tenet had the authority to order lethal strikes against top counterterrorism targets without consulting the National Security Council or President Bush. The Monday after September 11, President Bush had signed a classified finding authorizing CIA covert action to kill or capture top al-Qaida terrorists and their associates and had then issued another finding on a similar issue in October. "George could decide, even on killings," an official told *The Washington Post,* referring to Tenet. "That was pushed down to him. George had the authority on who was going to get it"—an authority that he sometimes delegated to senior subordinates at CTC, the agency's Counterterrorist Center operational headquarters. Dana Priest, "Covert CIA Program Withstands New Furor," *Washington Post,* Dec. 30, 2005.

5. Former senior special operations officer, interview.

6. Former senior intelligence officer, interview.

7. Different sources have different recollections about what aircraft conducted the October 30 strike, with Sedney remembering "gun tape" that looked to him as if it had come from an A-10 attack jet, the senior intelligence official recalling the involvement of F-16 fighters, and Zabiullah reporting that he heard helicopters during the raid as well as two types of planes, one of which dropped bombs and the second of which matched the characteristics of an AC-130. Elder and two of the former senior special operations officers remembered it as a B-1 followed by an AC-130.

8. Zabiullah, interview.

9. Former senior intelligence official and former senior special operations officer, interviews.

10. Zabiullah, interview.

11. Ibid.

12. Report captured at Osama bin Laden's Abbottabad compound, "Lessons Following the Fall of the Islamic Emirate" (n.d. but likely written sometime in 2002), www.dni.gov/files/documents/ubl/english/Lessons%20Learned %20Following%20the%20Fall%20of%20the%20Islamic%20Emirate.pdf.

13. Elder, interview. The air operations center had lent the CIA the use of the bomber that dropped the opening munitions on the buildings, but the headquarters didn't control the special operations gunship.

14. Shafiullah, interview. "It was a big deal how long the thing went on," agreed Elder.

15. Zabiullah, interview.

16. Shafiullah, interview.

17. See Carlotta Gall, "6 Afghans Die in U.S. Raid, Report Says," *New York Times,* Nov. 11, 2003; Carlotta Gall, "Afghan Villagers Torn by Grief After U.S. Raid Kills 9 Children," *New York Times,* Dec. 8, 2003. The latter is an article about a different civilian casualty incident that also mentions the October 30 Waygal strike and ascribes a death toll of eight to it.

18. Elder, interview.

19. See "New Purported bin Laden Tape Raises Fears of New Attacks," CNN, Sept. 11, 2003.

20. "We haven't found Osama bin Laden. And every day, Americans live at risk because of this failure. Instead of ferreting out al-Qaida, the administration focused its energy and resources on Iraq," General (Ret.) Wesley Clark said in New Hampshire on November 12. "It's been a world-class bait-and-switch." Later that month, Senator Bob Graham, seemingly alluding to JSOC, correctly asserted that starting in 2002, "important military units, including those that were most appropriate for fighting the war against Osama bin Laden, were relocated out of Afghanistan to begin the war on Iraq, as were intelligence assets."

21. Donald Rumsfeld, "The Lack of Clarity as to Who the Enemies Are, and What the Problems Are from an Intelligence Standpoint in Afghanistan and Iraq," memo to Steven Cambone, Sept. 8, 2003.

22. This account of the origins of Operation Winter Strike is based on interviews with Gen. (Ret.) John Abizaid, Brig. Gen. (Ret.) Brian Keller, Brig. Gen. (Ret.) Craig Nixon, Col. (Ret.) Walter Herd, Col. Joe Ryan, Col. John Rafferty, and other special operations and intelligence sources who preferred not to be named, as well as on Stanley McChrystal, *My Share of the Task: A Memoir* (New York: Portfolio, 2013), 108–9, and correspondence with McChrystal. Aspects of Winter Strike are also described in Naylor, *Relentless Strike,* 235, and in Shaffer, *Operation Dark Heart,* 189–98, 206–38.

23. Fayz Muhammad Katib Hazarah, *The Reign of Amir 'Abd al-Rahman Khan,* trans. and notes by R. D. McChesney and M. Mehdi Khorrami, vol. 3 of *The History of Afghanistan: Fayz Muhammad Katib Hazarah's Siraj al-tawarikh* (Leiden: Brill, 2013), 714.

24. A nineteenth-century Briton who drank some wine from Kafiristan shortly before it became Nuristan, Colonel T. H. Holdich, compared it to "badly corked Chablis" (T. H. Holdich, "The Origin of the Kafir of the Hindu Kush," *Geographical Journal* 7, no. 1 [Jan. 1896]: 49). The best brief history of the conquest of Nuristan is in Karl Jettmar, ed., *The Religion of the Kafirs,* vol. 1 of *The Religions of the Hindukush,* trans. Adam Nayyar (Warminster: Aris & Phillips, 1986).

25. Alexander Gardner, *Soldier and Traveller: Memoirs of Alexander Gardner, Colonel of Artillery in the Service of Maharaja Ranjit Singh,* ed. Hugh Pearse (Edinburgh: W. Blackwood and Sons, 1898), 89. The Pech was then called the Kama or Kaimeh, as Gardner rendered it, and was still part of Kafiristan.

26. David Edwards, in *Before Taliban*, 225–52, provides a detailed description of Hekmatyar's background and the origins and evolution of Hizb, his party.

27. This description of the relationships between Hekmatyar and the CIA and between Hekmatyar and bin Laden draws on declassified CIA documents; the 9/11 Commission Report; Sands and Qazizai, *Night Letters;* Bearden and Risen, *Main Enemy;* Steve Coll, *Ghost Wars: The Secret History of the CIA, Afghanistan, and Bin Laden, from the Soviet Invasion to September 10, 2001* (New York: Penguin, 2004); Alex Strick van Linschoten and Felix Kuehn, *An Enemy We Created: The Myth of the Taliban–al Qaeda Merger in Afghanistan* (Oxford: Oxford University Press, 2012); and Farrall and Hamid, *Arabs at War in Afghanistan*. Postmortem accounts by CIA hands, like Milton Bearden's, tend to emphasize the skeptical pragmatism with which the agency viewed Hekmatyar during the 1980s. As Coll relates, however, at the time the CIA was adamant in fending off efforts by the State Department and others to question the relationship. After a State Department envoy questioned the agency's support for Hekmatyar in a high-level cable in 1988—the same year that Director of Central Intelligence William Webster met personally with Hekmatyar—the diplomat in question found himself under investigation for mishandling classified material and for alleged misconduct in his personal life (Coll, *Ghost Wars,* 119–21, 181–84). The still-classified records of the American intelligence community's response to September 11 almost certainly contain more material about both real and perceived links between bin Laden and Hekmatyar. In response to a Freedom of Information Act request, CENTCOM released a set of files in 2013 titled "Gulbuddin Hekmatyar of Hezbe-Islami and Osama Bin Laden," but nearly the entire text of the files was redacted, including all references to Hekmatyar. One small clue is the word "Dragonfire," in the unredacted title of a redacted intelligence report apparently relating to bin Laden's pre–September 11 movements. Various press accounts in the early months after September 11 described "Dragonfire" as a code name associated with a DIA or CIA human intelligence source responsible for an October 2001 false alarm about the supposed infiltration of a nuclear weapon by al-Qaida into New York City.

28. Sands and Qazizai, *Night Letters,* 216–17.

29. Bearden and Risen, *Main Enemy,* 251.

30. Ibid., photo insert.

31. Hekmatyar, *Secret Plans Open Faces,* 81, 139–40.

32. Sands and Qazizai, *Night Letters,* 217–18.

33. "After Jaji, [bin Laden] shifted his trust . . . to Hekmatyar," Mustafa Hamid, who was friends with bin Laden at the time, says in Farrall and Hamid, *Arabs at War in Afghanistan,* 100. For the battle of Jaji, see Jamal Khashoggi, "Arab Youths Fight Shoulder to Shoulder with Mujahedeen," *Arab News,* May 4, 1988.

34. Coll, *Ghost Wars,* 211–19; Farrall and Hamid, *Arabs at War in Afghanistan,* 113; Stenersen, *Al-Qaida in Afghanistan,* 19, 35. The site that al-Qaida rented from Hekmatyar was the Jihadwal camp in Khost, according to

Hamid, established in 1989 and operated through most of the ensuing decade. According to Coll, bin Laden helped finance a failed coup attempt by Hekmatyar in 1990 and also acted as a personal interlocutor between Hekmatyar and Ahmad Shah Massoud during the early civil war years.

35. 9/11 Commission Report, 95; Strick van Linschoten and Kuehn, *Enemy We Created,* 134–36; Sands and Qazizai, *Night Letters,* 371.

36. Strick van Linschoten and Kuehn, *Enemy We Created,* 136–44; Farrall and Hamid, *Arabs at War in Afghanistan,* 218–20.

37. Central Intelligence Agency, "Afghanistan: An Incubator for International Terrorism," March 27, 2001. The other warlord the 2001 CIA report singled out was Abdul Rasul Sayyaf, one of the mujahidin commanders who had a long personal relationship with bin Laden and, along with Hekmatyar and Mohammad Yunus Khalis, welcomed him in Jalalabad in 1996.

38. Sands and Qazizai, *Night Letters,* 395–97.

39. Ryan Crocker, interview with author; Sands and Qazizai, *Night Letters,* 6–9, 414–16; Fishman, *Master Plan,* 20–22.

40. Crocker, interview.

41. Sands and Qazizai, *Night Letters,* 420–21.

42. Special operations and intelligence sources, interviews with author; Shaffer, *Operation Dark Heart,* 191–94.

43. CIA source, interview with author.

44. In *A Nightmare's Prayer,* 75–77, the Marine pilot Franzak describes witnessing one such unsuccessful JSOC mission from above during the winter of 2002–2003. "Sparkling" the objective with the infrared laser on his targeting pod, Franzak watched from his Harrier attack jet as Night Stalker Chinooks deposited a team from what was then called Task Force 5 into a snowy ten-thousand-foot landing zone near a village in western Nuristan. After an hour-long search, the Task Force 5 operators declared the target a dry hole and called for extraction.

45. Former senior special operations officer, interview.

46. Lt. Gen. William "Burke" Garrett, interview and correspondence with author. Confusingly, Operations Winter Strike and Mountain Resolve occurred simultaneously in roughly the same area with intertwined missions but with separate chains of command.

47. The battalion that made this movement was 2-87 Infantry, and this description of it is based on interviews with the battalion's former commander, Col. (Ret.) David Paschal, and his former subordinates Lt. Col. Rich Garey, Newton Grant, and Sgt. 1st Class Brent Fetters.

48. According to one estimate made five years before Mountain Resolve and Winter Strike, as much as half of the Pech's prewar population remained in Pakistan. Agency Coordinating Body for Afghan Relief, "Baseline Survey of Pech District, Kunar Province," June 1998.

49. Grant, interview.

50. Юра Токарь, quoted in Igor Kotov, "After Khara," afganistana.net/cms/posle-hary. . . . php. See also Nikolai Yusupov, 66brigada.ucoz.org/publ/vspomnim_rebjata/11_maja_1980_khara/6-1-0-39. In Edwards, *Before*

Taliban, 159–61, the Pech gem baron Matiullah Khan's brother Samiullah, who was a mujahidin commander at the time, describes watching the heliborne insertion in Bar Kanday on May 11 as well as the landing of reinforcements near Nangalam two or three days later by an even larger force of helicopters. "Really," he told Edwards, "I myself had never seen such a huge force and such modern military equipment and such tactics for scattering the mujahidin," an apparent reference to the two-pronged movement into the Pech on May 11, which initially confused the guerrillas. Samiullah and other mujahidin mistakenly believed that some of the troops inserted were Cubans, whose presence in Afghanistan was rumored at the time.

51. Kotov, "After Khara." The Soviet column wound up fighting its way into Nangalam on May 14, three days into the operation, and then spending five more days pushing west as far as the mouth of the Digal west of Nangalam. By the end of May 1980, Soviet troops were re-clearing towns they had passed through on their way up the Pech, like Bar Kanday. According to the officer who commanded the 66th Brigade at the time, the battle of Khara and the twenty days of tough fighting in and around the Pech that followed it were a shock that forced the brigade to reevaluate its tactics. Oleg Smirnov, "We Walked Under the Roar of the Cannonade and Looked Death in the Face," n.d., 66brigada.ucoz.org/publ/history/my_shli_pod _grokhot_kanonady_i_smerti_smotreli_v_lico/1-1-0-61.

52. Edwards, *Before Taliban,* 128.

53. Troy Carter, interview with author.

54. Fetters, interview.

55. This description of 2-22 Infantry's insertion into Nangalam, ground movement up the Waygal valley to Objective Winchester, and subsequent air assault into Aranas is based on interviews with Garrett, Col. John King, Col. (Ret.) Joseph Dichairo, Lt. Col. Tobin Moore, Lt. Col. Jorge Cordeiro, Maj. James Howell, and Command Sgt. Maj. Carl Ashmead, and on Ann Scott Tyson, "Uphill Pursuit for Afghan Warlord," *Christian Science Monitor,* Dec. 22, 2003.

56. Howell, interview.

57. The satellite settlement south of Aranas where the air strike took place, marked as Objective Winchester, is called Ataza.

58. Albert Herrlich, *Land des Lichtes: Deutsche Kundfahrt zu unbekannten Völkern im Hindukusch* (Munich: Knorr and Hirth, 1938), quoted in translation in Thomas Ruttig, "The Hunt for the Holy Wheat Grail: A Not So 'Botanical' Expedition in 1935," Afghanistan Analysts Network, July 20, 2015, www.afghanistan-analysts.org/the-hunt-for-the-holy-wheat-grail-a-not -so-botanical-expedition-in-1935/.

59. Howell, interview.

60. Moore, interview.

61. Ashmead, interview.

62. Howell, interview.

63. Ashmead, interview.

64. It's not clear exactly how many people died in the October 30 strike. Locals

I talked to gave figures of eight and nine, and news accounts cited eight, six of them members of the Rabbani family (see Gall, "Afghan Villagers Torn by Grief After U.S. Raid Kills 9 Children"). These included Ahmad Rabbani, the son of Ghulam Rabbani who was sleeping in the mosque when the first bomb struck it; Zahida, who Ghulam Rabbani told *The New York Times* was twenty-one and Zabiullah told me was sixteen and who was killed by the subsequent gunship fire; the elderly aunt Sayimid and the three young children Hamida, Bibi Shirini, and Zaki Ahmad Shah with her, who Ghulam Rabbani said were killed by the gunship and Zabiullah told me were killed in the second bomb strike. Other accounts mention two students from the religious school and the local holy man, but do not name them.

65. Dichairo and Moore, interviews.
66. Rabbani family members, interviews with author. A mujahidin newsletter published in 1991, when the victors of the jihad were squabbling for control of Kunar and Mawlawi Rabbani was serving as the governor of Kunar in Asadabad, includes a biography of him. Born in Aranas in the mid-1940s, Ghulam Rabbani studied at Kabul University in the 1960s and then undertook further religious studies in Pakistan to become a *mawlawi* before returning to Afghanistan to teach at a school in Shigal north of Asadabad. When war came to Kunar in 1978, he was again in Pakistan, preparing to make the pilgrimage to Mecca, but he canceled his trip to return to his homeland and join the initial antigovernment uprising in the Pech. In the years that followed, he was viewed as a well-connected moderate who could help mediate disputes among the bickering mujahidin factions, culminating in his yearlong tenure as Kunar's consensus governor from 1989 to 1990, when the last Afghan communist troops were being pushed out of the province and the Salafi Jamaat party and Hekmatyar's Hizb were at loggerheads. "The recent clashes between the supporters of Mawlawi Jamilur Rahman, known locally as Wahabis, and Hezb Islami of Hikmatyar clearly demonstrates the need for moderate people like Ghulam Rabbani to deal with the complicated situation in Kunar," the mujahidin newsletter reported. "Who Is Who in the Mujahideen: Mawlawi Ghulam Rabbani," *AFGHANews,* June 15, 1991.
67. Former senior intelligence official, interview.
68. Zabiullah, interview. Various family members suggested that it would have made more sense for Hekmatyar to stay with Mawlawi Faqirullah, a Hizb commander who lived nearby in Aranas. Indeed, some early news accounts of the strike based on anonymous accounts from American and Afghan officials said the strike had been aimed at Faqirullah, leading some to wonder whether the air strike had hit a different settlement than it had been intended for—either inadvertently or due to misinformation.
69. Sands and Qazizai, *Night Letters,* 425.
70. Karzai, interview.
71. David Sedney, interview with author.
72. Ibid.

73. Karzai, interview.

74. Abdul Rahman, interview.

75. Engineer Arif had known Ghulam Rabbani since the jihad, when Ghulam Rabbani's Nuristan logistical channel had been a key conduit for weapons and other matériel headed to the area where Arif was fighting the Soviets, the Panjshir valley.

76. Zabiullah, Abdul Qudus, and Abdul Rahman, interviews. Shaffer, in *Operation Dark Heart,* corroborates that the CIA had two main Afghan sources working for them in Nuristan, a pair of men whom the DIA's informants encountered at FOB Asadabad during Winter Strike.

77. Provincial Reconstruction Team Nuristan file on biographical details of Afghan government officials, n.d.

78. Abdul Qudus, interview.

79. "This was the CIA's inheritance," Steve Coll writes of the NDS during those early years after September 11 in *Directorate S,* 126: "a workforce of opaque subgroups that had operated torture chambers and prisons, intimidated citizens across the land, and owed its professional culture mainly to the K.G.B."

80. PRT Nuristan file on Afghan officials.

81. Rabbani family members describe an unsuccessful air strike by Soviet or Afghan communist forces against their same home settlement near Aranas, and Hekmatyar describes an unsuccessful communist air strike in the early 1990s that he believed was orchestrated by the communist intelligence service KHAD after it intercepted communications between him and his brother. Hekmatyar, *Secret Plans Open Faces,* 136–37.

82. CIA source, interview with author. Both the CIA's contracted interpreters and its NDS partners "often tried to use their billet to settle personal or family feuds and advance their families' fortunes," agreed Ron Moeller, who was also in Afghanistan at the time of the strike.

83. PRT Nuristan file on Afghan officials.

84. Former senior government official, interview.

85. Sedney, interview.

86. Special operations sources, interviews with author; McChrystal, *My Share of the Task,* 92–100; Naylor, *Relentless Strike,* 232–35.

87. While the 75th Ranger Regiment formally answers to U.S. Army Special Operations Command (USASOC), a different subcomponent of U.S. Special Operations Command through which it is also funded, and USASOC retains "administrative control" of the regiment, Ranger units are under the "operational control" of JSOC while deployed and, in the post–September 11 era, have often led JSOC's subordinate task forces. The evolution of the Rangers' role within JSOC is described in Naylor, *Relentless Strike,* 351–66, and was described to me by special operations sources.

88. Ryan, interview.

89. Ibid.

90. Girardet, *Killing the Cranes,* 190.

91. Notes of interview with Nuristani journalist by PRT officers. The three

valleys the interviewee identified as places bin Laden visited in 1996 were all targeted during Winter Strike, perhaps coincidentally: the Kantiwa and Parun valleys by 1st and 2nd Ranger Battalions, respectively, and Barg-e Matal by SEALs, according to McChrystal, who writes in *My Share of the Task,* 331, that he visited the Navy special operators there in December.

92. Taliban propaganda about the "defeat" of this raid or reconnaissance mission places it on March 1, 2003.

93. None of the Rangers interviewed for this book recalled the date of the Kantiwa air assault, and several pointed out that standard operating procedure on JSOC operations was for them not to take photos and to turn over any handwritten notes at the end of the operation to be burned. But the moon was half-full or more for the entire first half of November, the period during which the mission certainly occurred, and almost completely full during the November 7–12 period, the most likely dates based on cross-referencing with the chronology of Operation Mountain Resolve.

94. Rafferty, interview.

95. Ranger source, interview with author.

96. Some special operations sources, but not others, recall that a similar air strike occurred in the Kantiwa around the same time, unsuccessfully targeting Haji Ghafor and tipping the hand of the Rangers who were getting ready to fly into the valley.

97. Ranger source, interview with author.

98. Ryan, interview.

99. Ibid.

100. Edwards, in *Before Taliban,* 167–69, relays an account by a fellow mujahid of how Haji Ghafor earned this reputation early in the jihad: by throwing the first rock in the stoning death of a young woman convicted of having traveled alone with a male cousin in disobedience of her husband.

101. Tamim Nuristani, interview with author.

102. Ryan, interview.

103. Ranger sources, interviews with author; Moore, *Run to the Sound of the Guns,* 78–87.

104. Ranger source, interview.

105. Rafferty, interview.

106. For the wildlife of the Pech, see "Wildlife Surveys and Wildlife Conservation in Nuristan, Afghanistan," Wildlife Conservation Society and U.S. Agency for International Development, Aug. 2008, pdf.usaid.gov/pdf_docs/PA00K5PJ.pdf; and Kara Stevens et al., "Large Mammals Surviving Conflict in the Eastern Forests of Afghanistan," *Oryx* 45, no. 2 (April 2011): 265–71.

107. Ranger source, interview with author.

108. Nixon described this incident at the 2012 Aspen Ideas Festival; video of his remarks is accessible at www.youtube.com/watch?v=kB-pnOLfGCw #t=11.

109. This description of the limitations of unmanned aerial surveillance early in the war draws on accounts including Richard Whittle, *Predator: The Secret*

Origins of the Drone Revolution (New York: Henry Holt, 2014), Chris Woods, *Sudden Justice: America's Secret Drone Wars* (Oxford: Oxford University Press, 2015), and Andrew Cockburn, *Kill Chain: The Rise of the High-Tech Assassins* (New York: Henry Holt, 2015), which describe the Predator program's early years; Sean Naylor, *Not a Good Day to Die: The Untold Story of Operation Anaconda* (New York: Berkley, 2005), and Pete Blaber, *The Mission, the Men, and Me: Lessons from a Former Delta Force Commander* (New York: Berkley, 2008), which describe the difficulties the armed Predator had during its first engagement in support of ground troops, the March 2002 battle of Takur Ghar; and T. Mark McCurley, *Hunter Killer: Inside America's Unmanned Air War,* with Kevin Maurer (New York: Dutton, 2015), which describes the specific difficulties of Kunar from a longtime Predator pilot's viewpoint.

110. McCurley, *Hunter Killer,* 199.
111. Naylor, *Not a Good Day to Die,* 139, 177.
112. McCurley, *Hunter Killer,* 119.
113. Blaber, *The Mission, the Men, and Me,* 283–88; Whittle, *Predator,* 195–96.
114. Moeller, interview.
115. A similar mistake had led to tragedy a year and a half before the Kantiwa episode, soon after Operation Anaconda, when U.S. personnel watching a Predator feed in another eastern border province spotted a tall, white-robed man and a group of smaller people get into SUVs and head for Pakistan. F-16s bombed the convoy, and only after everyone on the ground was already dead did SEALs land and discover that the "tall man" had only been tall in comparison to the many children in the traveling party, all of whom the strike had killed (Naylor, *Relentless Strike,* 376–77).
116. JSOC and Ranger sources, interviews with author; Moore, *Run to the Sound of the Guns,* 85–86.
117. Rafferty, interview.
118. Ryan, interview.
119. Jeff Struecker, interview with author.
120. After moving from the Shigal to the border district of Dangam, bin Laden had crossed into Pakistan sometime in the second half of 2002, staying in the Swat valley for a while before relocating to the Pakistani city of Haripur after the March 2003 capture of the September 11 attack planner Khalid Sheikh Mohammad and then to Abbottabad in 2005. Scott-Clark and Levy, *Exile,* 194–95, 227; Sands and Qazizai, *Night Letters,* 425.
121. This description of Sergeant Jay Blessing is based on the service biography that U.S. Army Special Operations Command released after his death, on local news articles about him, and on interviews with friends who knew him in 2nd Ranger Battalion, including Ray Fuller Sr., 1st Sgt. Ray Fuller Jr., Sgt. 1st Class (Ret.) Rick Swain, Neal Boissonneault, and James Mabry.
122. Boissonneault, interview.
123. Boissonneault and Mabry, interviews.
124. Swain, interview.
125. Fuller senior, interview. Fuller was replaced as the battalion armorer by

Gary Toombs, a retired Green Beret senior NCO; Blessing became Toombs's assistant.

126. This account of Sergeant Jay Blessing's death is based on interviews with Matt Work, Maj. (Ret.) Robert Kinder, 1st Sgt. Ray Fuller Jr., and others; the time and location marked on a topographic map used during Winter Strike/Mountain Resolve; Moore, *Run to the Sound of the Guns,* 79–80; and a reference to the event in a Ranger newsletter. A 2nd Battalion Ranger is also quoted describing the event in Jon Krakauer, *Where Men Win Glory: The Odyssey of Pat Tillman* (New York: Doubleday, 2009), 279–80.

127. Work, interview.

128. Carter, interview.

129. Work, interview.

130. Fuller junior, interview.

131. Fuller senior, interview.

132. Kinder, Struecker, and Fuller junior, interviews.

133. Gen. (Ret.) Stanley McChrystal, correspondence with author.

134. Sedney, interview.

135. Alex Shuvahin, "Bar Kanday: Memoirs of a Company Commander," n.d., 66brigada.ucoz.org/publ/vspomnim_rebjata/bar_kandaj_vospominanija _komandira_roty/6-1-0-24. Shuvahin, who was a company commander in the 2nd Battalion, 66th Motorized Rifle Brigade, describes the June 1981 operation in which his own 5th Company established an outpost in Bar Kanday while Captain Slava Kondratyev's 4th Company continued on to Nangalam.

136. Photograph in author's possession.

137. Ron Fry, interview with author.

CHAPTER 3: THE A-CAMP, 2004

1. The main sources for Operational Detachment Alpha (ODA) 936's deployment are my interviews with Fry, Maj. John Trent, Lt. Col. Robert Nesbit, Chaplain Eric Eliason, Lt. Col. Marcus Custer, and Col. (Ret.) Walter Herd, and Fry's memoir, written with Tad Tuleja, *Hammerhead Six: How Green Berets Waged an Unconventional War Against the Taliban to Win in Afghanistan's Deadly Pech Valley* (New York: Hachette, 2016). Walter Herd's book *Unconventional Warrior: Memoir of a Special Operations Commander in Afghanistan* (Jefferson, N.C.: McFarland, 2013) was also helpful, and the May 16, 2004, Camp Blessing dedication ceremony is described in a press release by Combined Joint Special Operations Task Force—Afghanistan, "Special Forces Camp Named for Fallen Ranger," May 19, 2004.

2. Fry, interview.

3. Photos of Camp Blessing.

4. Fry, *Hammerhead Six,* 119.

5. Fry, interview.

6. Ibid.

7. Custer and Herd, interviews.

8. Fry, Custer, and Nesbit, interviews.

9. Fry, interview.

10. Fry, *Hammerhead Six,* 229.

11. Ibid., 164.

12. Just as they had during the jihad against the Soviets, insurgents sometimes used Americans' fondness for alcohol for points in the propaganda war. "As for alcohol, they do not consider it as a drug. It is widespread like water," the al-Qaida figure Abd al-Hadi al-Iraqi told an interviewer for a jihadi propaganda arm. Appellate Exhibit 38, *USA v. Abd al-Hadi al-Iraqi.*

13. Fry, interview.

14. See Michael P. M. Finch, *A Progressive Occupation? The Gallieni-Lyautey Method and Colonial Pacification in Tonkin and Madagascar, 1885–1900* (Oxford: Oxford University Press, 2013), 60; and Thomas Rid, "The Nineteenth Century Origins of Counterinsurgency Doctrine," *Journal of Strategic Studies* 33, no. 5 (2010): 727–58. Modern American practitioners of ink-blot counterinsurgency and its derivatives often cite Lieutenant Colonel David Galula, a French army officer who fought in Algeria in the 1950s and wrote the English-language book *Counterinsurgency Warfare: Theory and Practice* (New York: Praeger, 1964, republished 2006), as an inspiration for their tactics. As Rid explains, though, Galula—while undoubtedly a heavy influence on first one generation of American counterinsurgents, in the 1960s, and then another, in the first decade of the twenty-first century—borrowed heavily from a pair of his much more prominent and successful predecessors in earlier pacification campaigns, the French generals Joseph Simon Gallieni and Louis Hubert Lyautey, who first served together in mid-1890s Indochina—where Lyautey coined the "oil spot" phrase—and then refined their tactics in Madagascar.

15. See Andrew Birtle, *U.S. Army Counterinsurgency and Contingency Operations Doctrine, 1942–1976* (Washington, D.C.: U.S. Army Center of Military History, 2006), 477–95.

16. Lyautey, in 1903 letter to Gallieni, quoted in Ian F. W. Beckett, *Modern Insurgencies and Counter-insurgencies: Guerrillas and Their Opponents Since 1750* (London: Routledge, 2001), 40.

17. Troops involved in pacification should maintain "close contact with the population, to try to understand their behavior, their mind-set, and to attempt to satisfy their needs and tie them to the new institutions through persuasion," Gallieni wrote in his 1908 memoir, *Neuf ans à Madagascar,* 47.

18. Fry, interview; Fry, *Hammerhead Six,* 321–35, 349–52.

19. Fry, interview.

20. Fry, quoted in "The Green Berets: Lara Logan Follows U.S. Special Forces in Afghanistan," *60 Minutes II,* CBS, May 19, 2004, www.cbsnews.com/news/the-green-berets/.

21. Ryan, interview.

22. Lincoln Keiser, a student of the Pashai cultures that dot the uplands between Kabul and Nuristan, hiked into the Korengal one day in the mid-1960s, hoping to arrange a field visit. When he reached the first Korengali-speaking village in the valley, the reception was chilly, and the elders' answer was a

firm no. "They didn't want anything to do with non-Muslims, even back then," before Saudi-style Salafism came to the Korengal, Keiser remembered.

23. A chronology on a Russian-language Afghanistan veterans' site notes that Soviet patrols ventured into the Korengal to a distance of twelve kilometers and a height of 1,582 meters on May 13–14, 1980, in the days immediately following the disaster at Khara when the 66th Separate Motorized Rifle Brigade was slowly advanced up the Pech toward Nangalam. (The chronology, accessible at www.vko.ru/voyny-i-konflikty/afganskaya-kampaniya -nevostrebovannyy-opyt-17, indicates that three Soviet soldiers were killed in Kunar on each of these two days, but does not make clear whether any of these losses were in the Korengal.) Igor Kalmykov, who took part in many operations in Kunar as a member of the 66th Brigade's Jalalabad-based air-assault battalion five years later, told me that his unit was inserted by helicopter onto the mountains above the Korengal after an infantry unit was ambushed on the valley floor in May 1985, during the largest operation that the Soviets ever mounted into the Pech and other parts of Kunar.

24. Joint Task Force Guantánamo detainee assessment of Haji Ruhullah Wakil, June 17, 2005. One of the allegations listed as a reason for Ruhullah's continued detention was an intelligence report linking him to Arabs who had supposedly moved into the Korengal in the weeks after Tora Bora. "As of mid-February 2002, a group of almost 40 Arabs were resettled in various houses with Afghans in a valley approximately 16 kilometers west of the city of Asadabad," the Guantánamo document states. "The Arabs were resettled with the assistance of detainee [Ruhullah] and Maulawi Abdul Rahim Koresh. Detainee provided funds and material assistance to Koresh and paid to have a radio antenna installed in the valley to facilitate the Arabs [sic] communication." Mawlawi Abdul Rahim was one of the most influential elders of the Korengal, and the sixteen-kilometer mark from Asadabad lies on the mountain separating the Korengal from the neighboring Shuryak valley.

25. See Franzak, *Nightmare's Prayer*, 120–22, for one instance of JSOC activity at the mouth of the Korengal in January or February 2003.

26. This description of A-team 316's visit to the Korengal is based on interviews with Gant and Halstead; Jim Gant, "Trip Report for CONOP 316-13: Korangal Area Assessment"; Akbar, *Come Back to Afghanistan*, 204–14; Hyder Akbar, "Teenage Embed, Part Two," *This American Life*, episode 254, Chicago Public Media, Dec. 12, 2003, www.thisamericanlife.org/254/ transcript.

27. Halstead, interview.

28. Not much is known about the history of the Korengal valley or its residents. The Korengalis consider themselves a subset of the Safi Pashtun tribe, even though their ancestors were not Pashtuns at all and Pashto is not their first language, and some Nuristanis tell a story that has the Korengalis being expelled from a more northerly valley in what is now Nuristan before settling in the Korengal. The first English-language reference I was able to find is by the East India Company botanist William Griffith in his book *Journals*

of Travels in Assam, Burma, Bhootan, Affghanistan, and the Neighbouring Countries (Calcutta: Bishop's College Press, 1847), 464, where he notes that during an 1840 visit to the Pech he "met a Khungurlye slave, of the caste Krungurlye, the headquarters of which are at a mountain village. . . . The chief of Koorungul is Ahmed Khan, he is independent: his village having 400 men, well armed."

Korengali is part of the Pashai group of Dardic languages, which a few centuries ago were spoken across a large highland area sandwiched between the Pashto-speaking lowlands around Kabul and mountainous Kafiristan. Many Pashai communities converted to Islam during the couple of centuries before the better-known Kafirs of what would become Nuristan, apparently including the Korengalis, as Griffith notes that they had converted to Islam "long ago." There is scholarly debate about where these two groups of people, Pashai and Nuristani, came from. Two academics who have studied the Pashai, the Danish and American anthropologists Jan Ovesen and Lincoln Keiser, have argued that both the Pashai and the Nuristani are indigenous populations who have inhabited the mountains of northeastern Afghanistan for thousands of years. The Norwegian linguist Georg Morgenstierne disagreed, arguing that the Pashai are remnants of an ancient Hindu-Buddhist civilization who moved into the mountains when they were displaced from lowlands closer to Kabul by invading Pashtuns. See Jan Ovesen, "The Construction of Ethnic Identities: The Nuristani and the Pashai of Eastern Afghanistan," in *Identity: Personal and Socio-cultural,* ed. Anita Jacobson-Widding (Uppsala: Academiae Upsaliensis, 1983).

29. Akbar, *Come Back to Afghanistan,* 204–14; Akbar, "Teenage Embed, Part Two."

30. Gant and Halstead, interviews.

31. Garey and Ranger sources, interviews.

32. Matt Trevithick and Daniel Seckman, "Heart of Darkness: Into Afghanistan's Taliban Valley," *Daily Beast,* Nov. 15, 2014.

33. Gant and Halstead, interviews; Akbar, *Come Back to Afghanistan,* 207–14.

34. Etienne Delattre and Haqiq Rahmani, "A Preliminary Assessment of Forest Cover and Change in the Eastern Forest Complex of Afghanistan," Wildlife Conservation Society Afghanistan draft report submitted to the U.S. Agency for International Development, 2007.

35. Former interpreters who asked to be identified only as Farshad and Burhan, interviews with author; Almuth Degener, "Hunters' Lore in Nuristan," *Asian Folklore Studies* 60, no. 2 (2001): 331–33.

36. Griffith, *Journals of Travels,* 436–38, 460–61, 473. The place-names in nineteenth-century British accounts of travels in Kunar can be hard to decipher: Griffith, who tagged along with the January 1840 British military expedition to seize the fortress at Pashat and then stayed four more months to describe the plant life of the area, rendered Kunar as "Kooner," Korengal as "Koorungul," Watapur as "Otipore," and so on.

37. Harry Bader, interview with author.

38. Ibid.

39. Ibid.

40. Akbar, "Teenage Embed, Part Two."

41. Ranger source, interview.

42. Afghan Interim Administration Decree No. 405, Feb. 6, 2002, ronna.apan .org/Lists/Submitted%20Content/Attachments/60/Presidential%20 Decree.pdf.

43. United Nations Environment Programme, "Afghanistan: Post-conflict Environmental Assessment," Jan. 2003, postconflict.unep.ch/publications /afghanistanpcajanuary2003.pdf.

44. Bader, interview. See also Harry R. Bader et al., "Illegal Timber Exploita-tion and Counterinsurgency Operations in Kunar Province of Afghanistan: A Case Study Describing the Nexus Among Insurgents, Criminal Cartels, and Communities Within the Forest Sector," *Journal of Sustainable Forestry* 32, no. 4 (2013): 329–53; and Delattre and Rahmani, "Preliminary Assessment of Forest Cover and Change in the Eastern Forest Complex of Afghanistan."

45. Bader, interview.

46. The ban reads, "In order to protect and conserve the national wealth (for-ests) of our country, all the security organizations and authorities at the provincial level are kindly instructed to strictly prevent cutting of natural and artificial forests and such acts that cause damage and harm to the forests and the violators be prosecuted accordingly."

47. Fry, interview.

48. Special Forces NCO who asked to be identified as Sgt. 1st Class Luke, in-terview with author.

49. Fry, interview.

50. Gallieni, quoted in Finch, *Progressive Occupation?,* 65.

51. Luke, interview.

52. Ibid.

53. Maj. Steve Ray and 1st Sgt. (Ret.) William Bodette, interviews with au-thor.

54. Luke, Bodette, and Ray, interviews.

55. Bodette, interview.

56. Anayat Rahman, interview.

57. Bodette, interview.

58. Luke, Bodette, and Ray, interviews.

59. Luke, interview.

60. Ibid.

61. Provincial Reconstruction Team Asadabad, "Timber in Kunar" (July 2006 version).

62. Luke, interview.

63. Kate Clark, correspondence with author.

64. See Muhammad al-Shafii, "News of the Death of al-Qaeda Explosives Ex-pert Abu Ikhlas al-Masri in Eastern Afghanistan," *Asharq al-Awsat,* Jan. 9, 2003, archive.aawsat.com/details.asp?issueno=8800&article=146003#.WB dlEuErLoA. Various U.S. military intelligence reports also mention a vague connection between Abu Ikhlas and the 1981 assassination plot against the

Egyptian president Anwar Sadat, over which hundreds of Egyptian Islamists, including Zawahiri, were arrested.

65. Malik Ayoub Zarin, interview.

66. Accounts differ as to where Abu Ikhlas's Kunari wife was from, ranging from the Korengal to Qowru in the Watapur valley to Asadabad; he might have had several.

67. Former Kunari government official, interview with author.

68. Joint Task Force Guantánamo detainee assessment of Amir Mohammad, Jan. 27, 2008.

69. Malik Ayoub Zarin, interview.

70. Notes of U.S. government official's interview with Kunari cleric.

71. Stenersen, *Al-Qaida in Afghanistan,* 127–47.

72. An intelligence report on Abu Ikhlas, its contents still classified, is dated September 16, 2002.

73. Intelligence summary, Feb. 18, 2005.

74. Fry, *Hammerhead Six,* 255–62.

75. Fry, interview.

76. "Pech: Locals Told Not to Deal with ISAF," NATO military intelligence threat report, Feb. 26, 2008.

77. Fry, *Hammerhead Six,* 216.

78. Moeller, interview.

79. Former CIA officer, interview.

80. Mark Mazzetti, "Qaeda Is Seen as Restoring Leadership," *New York Times,* April 2, 2007.

81. Untitled, undated al-Qaida document accessible at www.cia.gov/library /abbottabad-compound/0F/0FFC7FA486132AC35343515071ADCD64 _%D9%85%D9%86_%D8%AA%D9%88%D9%81%D9%8A%D9%82.doc .pdf. Abu Ubaydah apparently answered to Abd al-Hadi al-Iraqi, an Iraqi army veteran who had run al-Qaida's Kabul guesthouse before September 11 and who acted as its emir for operations inside Afghanistan between 2002 and 2005. Abd al-Hadi had a hand in insurgent activities from Jalalabad to Shkin in the southeast and even in Kabul, overseeing senior regional emirs like Abu Ubaydah who in turn oversaw more locally focused figures like Abu Ikhlas. But Abd al-Hadi worked out of al-Qaida's Shakai valley headquarters in Waziristan, making only occasional trips into Afghanistan.

82. Former Kunari government official, interview with author.

83. "Full transcript of bin Laden's speech," Al Jazeera, Nov. 1, 2004, www .aljazeera.com/archive/2004/11/200849163336457223.html.

84. Luke, interview.

85. 3/6 Marines, "3rd Battalion, 6th Marine Regiment Combat Engagements in Operation Enduring Freedom from May to November 2004," entry dated June 7, 2004.

86. Luke, interview; 3/6 Marines, "Combat Engagements in Operation Enduring Freedom," entry dated July 3, 2004; Sgt. Maj. Dwight Utley, "Personal Experience Paper: Operation Enduring Freedom, Konar Valley, Afghanistan, May 15–December 1, 2004," Aug. 20, 2006.

87. Lt. Col. Chris O'Connor, interview with author.

88. See Elizabeth Rubin, "Battle Company Is Out There," *New York Times Magazine,* Feb. 24, 2008; Sebastian Junger, *War* (New York: Twelve, 2010), 49; Bing West, *The Wrong War: Grit, Strategy, and the Way out of Afghanistan* (New York: Random House, 2011), 36; and Ryan Devereaux, "Manhunting in the Hindu Kush," *Intercept,* Oct. 15, 2015. No account that notes the alleged bombing of Haji Matin's compound and family cites a specific date or even year for the event, but the story was in circulation by early 2006, when Captain Dave Mayfield, the intelligence officer of 1–32 Infantry, heard it from the Marine officers he was replacing.

89. Provincial Reconstruction Team Asadabad, "Timber in Kunar" (July 2006 version).

90. Luke, interview.

91. Ibid.

92. Ibid.

93. Anayat Rahman, interview.

94. Alford and Luke, interviews; 3/6 Marines, "Combat Engagements in Operation Enduring Freedom," entry dated Sept. 23, 2004.

95. Alford, interview.

96. Luke, interview.

97. Ibid.

98. Chapa Dara resident serving in the Kabul government, interview with author. "He came and booked a hotel near the district office in Chapa Dara, and he started warning all the people, especially the businessmen of stones and gems, 'I am supported by American troops, and if you pay me $1,000, okay, but otherwise I will say to the Americans that you are with al-Qaida or the Talibs and they will come to your house and capture you,'" the resident told me, noting that the incident took place in 2004 and adding that he and the Chapa Dara District's governor had gone to discuss it with an American at Blessing whom he knew as the base commander. "His response was that [the militiaman] is our representative and whoever is not working with him is not working with us. I was not expecting this. A year after that, except for the district building, Chapa Dara was completely controlled by Taliban because of this."

99. Luke, interview.

100. Capt. Justin Bellman, interview with author.

101. Ibid.

102. Brian Jenkins, *The Unchangeable War,* RM-6278–2-ARPA (Santa Monica, Calif.: Rand, 1970), 8.

103. Fry, interview.

104. Bellman, interview.

CHAPTER 4: RED WINGS, 2005

1. Kroll Election Team, "Nuristan SITREP," May 22, 2005.

2. Antonio Giustozzi describes the 2005 foundation of the Peshawar *shura* in his chapter "The Arab Gulf Connections of the Taliban," in *Pan-Islamic*

Connections: Transnational Networks Between South Asia and the Gulf, ed. Christophe Jaffrelot and Laurence Louer (Oxford: Oxford University Press, 2018), 141–54. "Pakistan and the Arabs did not support the Shamshatoo Shura, because all the people in this shura were Hizb-i-Islami," Giustozzi quotes a senior insurgent commander as telling him, referring to an early insurgent command council based at the Hizb-controlled Shamshatoo refugee camp. "Therefore, Pakistan and the Arabs . . . were telling the Shamshatoo Shura that we should join the Ijraya Shura of the Peshawar Shura [of the Taliban] and after this they would help us, so this was the reason why we joined the Ijraya Shura."

3. Robert O'Neill, *The Operator: Firing the Shots That Killed Osama bin Laden and My Years as a SEAL Team Warrior* (New York: Scribner, 2017), 145.

4. Maj. Scott Westerfield, interview with author; Fry, *Hammerhead Six,* 226–36.

5. Two internal NSA newsletter items dating from the period of Operation Red Wings, and later released by *The Intercept,* illustrate the degree to which both the conventional military and special operations forces had come to rely on NSA signals intelligence support. In one, a member of the NSA's Bagram-based Cryptologic Support Group describes how "80 percent of the actionable intelligence for CJTF-76 Forces" like the Marines and SEALs involved in Red Wings came from the NSA, and adds that "no matter what INT [intelligence type] they had on a target, the decision makers almost always held out for SIGINT corroboration" before authorizing a raid. "Having the (SIGINT) Time of My Life," *SID Today,* April 12, 2005.

6. Westerfield, interview; Ed Darack, *Victory Point: Operations Red Wings and Whalers* (New York: Berkley Books, 2009), 84–87.

7. Intelligence source, interview with author.

8. Jeffrey Eggers, interview with author.

9. Dr. David Townsend, interview with author.

10. John Ismay, interview with author.

11. SEAL sources and other special operations sources, interviews with author. Kristensen's element, which consisted of a SEAL assault platoon from Team 10 along with attached personnel from SEAL Delivery Vehicle Teams 1 and 2, was formally known as Naval Special Warfare Task Unit—Afghanistan (NSWTU-A), and the Special Forces–led headquarters it answered to was Combined Joint Special Operations Task Force—Afghanistan (CJSOTF-A).

12. SEAL, Special Forces, and Marine sources, interviews with author.

13. Special operations source, interview with author.

14. Wood, Westerfield, and a SEAL source, interviews. According to another source who was at Bagram with the JSOC task force at the time, Kristensen first approached the counterterrorism task force's Ranger contingent with the proposal for a mission targeting Ahmad Shah, turning to the Marines after the major in charge of the Rangers declined to participate.

15. This account of Operation Red Wings and its aftermath is based on interviews with more than two dozen sources from conventional and special

operations units and the intelligence community who were involved in the events; on news reports and military journal articles; on military documents, including Army and Navy award citations, the enemy action reports filed by CJSOTF-A on the event, and debriefs of the pilots of the A-10 with call sign Grip 21 and Black Hawk with call sign Skill 47; and on the many books, of widely varying scope and quality, that along with the fictionalized portrayal in the 2013 movie *Lone Survivor* constitute something of an Operation Red Wings cottage industry.

The books include the former SEAL Marcus Luttrell's two first-person books, *Lone Survivor: The Eyewitness Account of Operation Redwing and the Lost Heroes of SEAL Team 10* (New York: Little, Brown, 2007), written with the thriller novelist Patrick Robinson, and *Service: A Navy SEAL at War* (New York: Little, Brown, 2012), written with the naval historian James Hornfischer; Ed Darack's *Victory Point,* by far the soberest and most thoroughly researched of the third-person accounts; two memoirs by former members of SEAL Team 6's Red Squadron who were involved in the recovery effort, Robert O'Neill's *Operator* and James Hatch's *Touching the Dragon and Other Techniques for Surviving Life's Wars,* written with Christian D'Andrea (New York: Knopf, 2018); Moore, *Run to the Sound of the Guns;* Peter Nealen, *Operation Red Wings: The Rescue Story Behind Lone Survivor* (New York: St. Martin's Press, 2013); Gary Williams, *SEAL of Honor: Operation Red Wings and the Life of Lt. Michael P. Murphy, USN* (Annapolis, Md.: Naval Institute Press, 2010); and Patrick Robinson, *The Lion of Sabray: The Afghani Warrior Who Defied the Taliban and Saved the Life of Navy SEAL Marcus Luttrell* (New York: Touchstone, 2015). McChrystal's *My Share of the Task* and McCurley's *Hunter Killer* also include helpful details.

News reports, journal articles, and first-person blog entries that deal with various aspects of the saga include R. M. Schneiderman, "Marcus Luttrell's Savior, Mohammad Gulab, Claims 'Lone Survivor' Got It Wrong," *Newsweek,* May 11, 2016, www.newsweek.com/2016/05/20/mohammad-gulab -marcus-luttrell-navy-seal-lone-survivor-operation-red-wings-458139 .html; Leo Banks, "Navy SEAL Down: A Tucson Helicopter Crew Looks Back on an Unforgettable Rescue in the Mountains of Afghanistan," *Tucson Weekly,* Nov. 12, 2009, www.tucsonweekly.com/tucson/navy-seal-down /Content?oid=1539548; Ed Darack, "Operation Red Wings: What Really Happened?," *Marine Corps Gazette,* Jan. 2011; Iassen Donov, "Operation Red Wings II: Lone Survivor Recovery," SOFREP, Jan. 1 and 2, 2013, sofrep.com/15734/operation-red-wings-ii-the-recovery-part-i/ and sofrep .com/15748/operation-red-wings-ii-the-recovery-part-ii/; John Ismay, "Seeing My Friend Depicted in Lone Survivor," At War (blog), *New York Times,* Jan. 24, 2014, atwar.blogs.nytimes.com/2014/01/24/seeing-my -friend-depicted-in-lone-survivor; Leo Jenkins, "*Lone Survivor* and Truth," Hit the Woodline, March 23, 2014, havokjournal.com/culture/lone -survivor-and-truth/; Andrew MacMannis and Robert Scott, "Operation Red Wings: A Joint Failure in Unity of Command," *Marine Corps Gazette,* Dec. 2006; James Gordon Meek, "Afghanistan Reports Posted on WikiLeaks

Include Details of L.I. Navy SEAL Michael Murphy's Death," *New York Daily News,* July 27, 2010, www.nydailynews.com/news/world/afghanistan -reports-posted-wikileaks-include-details-navy-seal-michael-murphy -death-article-1.200328; James Gordon Meek, "An Overlooked Hero of Navy SEALs' Operation Red Wings," ABC News, July 1, 2015, abcnews .go.com/International/overlooked-hero-navy-seals-operation-red-wings /story?id=32136944; James Gordon Meek, "Reporter's Notebook: Re- membering Fateful SEAL Rescue Operation," ABC News, June 28, 2013, abcnews.go.com/blogs/headlines/2013/06/reporters-notebook -remembering-fateful-seal-rescue-operation/; Lisa Myers and NBC Inves- tigative Unit, "An Interview with a Taliban Commander," NBC News, Dec. 27, 2005, www.nbcnews.com/id/10619502/ns/nbc_nightly_news _with_brian_williams-nbc_news_investigates/t/interview-taliban -commander; and Robert Scott, "A Battalion's Employment of the Ele- ments of National Power," *Small Wars Journal,* Feb. 5, 2008.

16. Lt. Col. Tom Wood, interview with author.
17. Wood, Lt. Col. Robert Scott, Westerfield, and 160th Special Operations Aviation Regiment and SEAL sources, interviews with author. While 160th SOAR crews mostly supported JSOC missions by this point in the war, according to a SEAL source, some of the particular Chinook pilots involved in Operation Red Wings had worked closely with SEAL Team 1 during an earlier deployment to southern Afghanistan.
18. The plan for Operation Red Wings went through various tweaks, as Da- rack details in *Victory Point,* 101–9, 121–23: at different times, Marine pla- toons were slotted either to fly in with the SEAL Team 10 assault force or to fly into lower-altitude landing zones after the SEALs had landed and then march up to meet them.
19. Special operations source, interview with author.
20. Luttrell, *Lone Survivor,* 179–84; SEAL source, interview. According to the SEAL source, the next iteration of the plan called for as many as three small SEAL recon teams to infiltrate the area, but during the back-and-forth planning with CJSOTF-A, the plan shifted again to its final version, involv- ing just the one SEAL recon team.
21. Sgt. 1st Class Hank Adames, Sgt. 1st Class Brett Lang, Joel Love, Dan Pro- vitola, James Rothenberg, Staff Sgt. Roberto Tavarez, and Carl Witkowski, interviews with author.
22. Special operations sources, interviews with author. One SEAL also remem- bered one conversation at Bagram in which a Green Beret leader visiting the SEAL operations center "expressed disbelief" that they were planning a mission in the Korengal and another in which a SEAL Team 6 officer warned about the area when some of Kristensen's frogmen were visiting the Team 6 squadron's compound.
23. Intelligence source, interview with author. In *The Operator,* 145–46, the former Team 6 member O'Neill describes the plan receiving a similar re- ception at the CIA safe house in Jalalabad. When he and some other envi- ous Team 6 operators asked on the morning of June 28 for permission to go

along on Kristensen's raid that night, the "outstation chief" there denied their request, citing the risky nature of the mission. "He knew something bad was going to happen," O'Neill writes, referring to the outstation chief. "We had the intelligence but SEAL Team Ten didn't listen."

24. Michael Breen, interview with author.
25. Wood and Col. Andrew Rohling, interviews with author; Maj. Keller Durkin, interview with Operational Leadership Experiences Project.
26. Wood, interview.
27. Rohling, interview.
28. Darack, *Victory Point,* 108, 121.
29. SEAL source, interview. Murphy, Axelson, and Luttrell were members of the Pearl Harbor–based SEAL Delivery Vehicle Team 1, while Dietz was from SEAL Delivery Vehicle Team 2 out of Virginia.
30. SEAL source, interview.
31. Details on the equipment the Spartan recon team carried come from Luttrell, *Lone Survivor,* 186–87; Darack, *Victory Point,* 126–27; and video shot by an insurgent videographer accompanying Ahmad Shah's men that was released by the al-Qaida-affiliated propaganda outfit As-Sahab Media under the title *The War of the Oppressed* and first broadcast on Al-Arabiya in early August 2005, vimeo.com/56327972.
32. Luttrell, *Lone Survivor,* 188.
33. 160th SOAR source, interview.
34. There are discrepancies in the various accounts as to how many transmissions Spartan 01 made on June 28, when, and by what means. In *Lone Survivor,* Luttrell reports that the team made a "soft compromise" call shortly after releasing the three goatherds before a later "hard compromise" one, which Luttrell describes as the call the team made when the enemy attacked them.
35. Intelligence source, interview.
36. Wood, interview; Darack, *Victory Point,* 130.
37. MacMannis and Scott, "Operation Red Wings."
38. Peter Capuzzi, interview with author; Darack, *Victory Point,* 129–33.
39. Rohling, interview. Darack, in *Victory Point,* 132–33, ascribes the delay to the special operations chain of command but does not specify whether on the JSOC side that supervised the 160th SOAR helicopters or the "white" CJSOTF-A side that supervised Kristensen's task unit.
40. Williams, *SEAL of Honor,* 153.
41. Charles Briscoe, "Everyone Can Take Pride in This Fight: ODA 163 in Afghanistan," *Veritas: Journal of Army Special Operations History* 2, no. 3 (2006): 60–61; SEAL source and Special Forces source, interviews.
42. 160th SOAR source, interview.
43. Most accounts agree on these call signs, but some documents from the mission—including a "knee-card" from one of the crew members—list the call signs as Turbine 43 and 44 instead. The discrepancy likely stems from the ad hoc nature of the rescue mission. According to Night Stalker convention, the Chinooks would have flown under the call signs 33 and 34 if

they had been flying a typical JSOC quick-reaction force mission; on the raid scheduled for that night, they would have flown under 43 and 44. The improvised mission that Reich led on June 28 was a combination of those two mission profiles.

44. Maj. Gen. (Ret.) Jeffrey Schloesser, Brig. Gen. Wally Rugen, and Lt. Col. David Borowicz, interviews with author.

45. 160th SOAR source, interview.

46. Ibid.

47. Ranger source, interview.

48. 160th SOAR source, interview.

49. Rohling, interview. "When we found out Turbine 33 had gone down, we were surprised it was even there," said Rohling, who was on duty in the Combined Joint Task Force 76 operations center at Bagram on the afternoon of June 28 as the division's chief of current operations. "The SEALs launched without getting approval from division because they were using 160th aircraft."

50. SEAL source, interview.

51. Source who was aboard Turbine 34, interview with author.

52. Hatch, *Touching the Dragon,* 306.

53. Although most accounts agree that the projectile fired was a rocket-propelled grenade, O'Neill writes in *The Operator,* 148, that some SEALs aboard Turbine 34 told him that afternoon that they had seen the projectile's smoke-trail turn, as a heat-seeking anti-aircraft missile like a Stinger, Blowpipe, or SA-7 would. O'Neill's squadron mate and fellow member of the recovery party, Hatch, dismissed that in an interview. "I don't know why you'd waste a MANPADS. It was daylight and they were coming into the same spot," Hatch said. "At the spot where they got shot down, there was a little bit of an incline not far from it, so you could actually have been above it when you shot. I bet the guy with the RPG was like, 'Man, I hope the thing has time to arm.'"

54. Debrief of pilot of Black Hawk with call sign Skill 47.

55. Unnamed chief warrant officer quoted in Elizabeth Collins, "Honoring the U.S. Army Heroes of Operation Red Wings," *Soldiers: The Official U.S. Army Magazine,* Feb. 2014.

56. The eight Night Stalkers killed in the crash of Turbine 33 were Reich; Chief Warrant Officer 4 Chris Scherkenbach, forty; Chief Warrant Officer 3 Corey Goodnature, thirty-five; Master Sgt. James "Trey" Ponder III, thirty-six; Sgt. 1st Class Marcus Muralles, thirty-three; Sgt. 1st Class Michael Russell, thirty-one; Staff Sgt. Shamus Goare, twenty-nine; and Sgt. Kip Jacoby, twenty-one. The eight SEALs killed in the crash were Kristensen; Lieutenant Michael McGreevy, thirty; Senior Chief Petty Officer Daniel Healy, thirty-six; Chief Petty Officer Jacques Fontan, thirty-six; Petty Officer 1 Jeffrey Taylor, thirty; Petty Officer 1 Jeffery Lucas, thirty-three; Petty Officer 2 Eric Shane Patton, twenty-two; and Petty Officer 2 James Suh, twenty-eight.

57. Special operations source, interview with author.

58. McCurley, *Hunter Killer*, 138–49.

59. Special operations source, interview with author; Luttrell, *Service*, 235.

60. U.S. Air Forces Central Command Public Affairs, "Second Anniversary of Largest Successful Search and Rescue Operation Since Vietnam," Aug. 13, 2007.

61. Luttrell, *Service*, 233–34.

62. Special operations source, interview with author.

63. 160th SOAR source, interview.

64. MacMannis and Scott, "Operation Red Wings."

65. O'Neill, *Operator*, 149–50.

66. Intelligence source, interview; O'Neill, *Operator*, 149–52.

67. Ranger sources and Senior Chief Petty Officer (Ret.) James Hatch, interviews; Elizabeth Bumiller, "4 Afghan War Veterans Look Back, and Ahead," *New York Times*, Jan. 3, 2010.

68. Ranger and Night Stalker sources, interviews; Moore, *Run to the Sound of the Guns*, 119–23; Hatch, interview; Hatch, *Touching the Dragon*, 305–6; Valorous Unit Award citation, C Company, Headquarters and Headquarters Company (elements), and B Company (elements), 2nd Ranger Battalion.

69. Hatch, interview.

70. Ranger sources, interviews; Moore, *Run to the Sound of the Guns*, 123–25; Hatch, interview; Hatch, *Touching the Dragon*, 306.

71. Hatch, interview; Hatch, *Touching the Dragon*, 305–7.

72. Ranger sources, interviews; Bumiller, "4 Afghan War Veterans Look Back, and Ahead"; Moore, *Run to the Sound of the Guns*, 125; Hatch, interview; Hatch, *Touching the Dragon*, 306–7.

73. Ranger source, interview with author.

74. Maj. Jody Shouse, interview with author.

75. Westerfield, interview; Luttrell, *Service*, 238.

76. When First Lieutenant Patrick Kinser's Marine platoon took over from the Rangers in Chichal, locals told them that the air strike had killed a dozen or more members of one family—possibly true, or possibly false information meant to spur compensation money or conceal the presence of insurgents.

77. Bellman and Maj. Matthew Bartels, interviews with author.

78. Bartels, interview.

79. Ibid. O'Neill, in *The Operator*, 153, writes that Luttrell had also scrawled out his Social Security number.

80. Marcus Luttrell was not the first lone survivor of a botched commando mission in Kunar. After the destruction of a company of the 334th Separate Spetsnaz Detachment in the village of Daridam in April 1985, General Valentin Varennikov flew to the Soviet base in Asadabad to oversee the response operation. While there, he met with the one commando who had made it out of Daridam alive, a sergeant named Vladimir Turchin who was in his barracks, mute, his whole body shaking and his teeth chattering. Only later was Turchin able to explain that he had survived by submerging himself in the reed-clogged creek on the edge of the village when the mu-

jahidin brought in local teenagers to finish off the wounded. Varennikov, *Nepovtorimoe,* 5:145–47.

81. Bartels, interview.

82. Intelligence source, interview.

83. O'Neill, *Operator,* 154.

84. Ranger sources, interviews; Moore, *Run to the Sound of the Guns,* 126–28; Hatch, *Touching the Dragon,* 308–9.

85. "NSA Tipoff Leads to Rescue of Serviceman in Afghanistan," *SID Today,* July 11, 2005.

86. O'Neill, *Operator,* 154–56; Luttrell, *Service,* 238.

87. Luttrell, *Lone Survivor,* 348.

88. Luttrell, *Service,* 248–58; Banks, "Navy SEAL Down."

89. The site on the northeastern spur where the team regrouped was in fact their original hide site, which they had abandoned earlier in the morning for a second site on the Abbas Ghar because fog and trees had interfered with their view of Chichal.

90. Schneiderman, "Marcus Luttrell's Savior, Mohammad Gulab, Claims 'Lone Survivor' Got It Wrong." A detail that two of the Rangers who fast-roped in on June 29 recounted supports Mohammad Gulab's version. In an abandoned fighting position above the crash site, the two Rangers told me, amid wrappers and other detritus showing insurgents had been there recently, a Ranger patrol found the nylon rope the SEALs had hastily buried when they inserted—probably after it had been found and dug up by militants out searching for the SEALs on the morning of June 28.

91. Quoted in "Murphy's Heroism," *Eye to Eye with Katie Couric,* CBS News, Oct. 22, 2007, www.youtube.com/watch?v=yIx0YPejzE4.

92. "Ignoring his own wounds and demonstrating exceptional composure, Lieutenant Murphy continued to lead and encourage his men," reads the citation for Murphy's Medal of Honor. "When the primary communicator [Dietz] fell mortally wounded, Lieutenant Murphy repeatedly attempted to call for assistance for his beleaguered teammates. Realizing the impossibility of communicating in the extreme terrain, and in the face of almost certain death, he fought his way into open terrain to gain a better position to transmit a call. This deliberate, heroic act deprived him of cover, exposing him to direct enemy fire. Finally achieving contact with his headquarters, Lieutenant Murphy maintained his exposed position while he provided his location and requested immediate support for his team. In his final act of bravery, he continued to engage the enemy until he was mortally wounded, gallantly giving his life for his country and for the cause of freedom."

93. Quoted in "Survivor, Part One," *60 Minutes,* CBS News, Dec. 7, 2013, www.dailymotion.com/video/x186afy.

94. As-Sahab, *War of the Oppressed;* Darack, *Victory Point,* 165.

95. Luttrell, *Service,* 235.

96. In both *Lone Survivor* and *Service,* Luttrell reports that Axelson was fatally shot during the battle and then buried by locals. The official Navy account corroborates this, putting Axelson's date of death as June 28, as do the ac-

counts of soldiers involved in the recovery effort that eventually found Axelson's body on July 10. In April 2008, though, after the publication of *Lone Survivor,* Luttrell contradicted himself and all other accounts of the battle when he said to an audience at the Army and Navy Club in Washington, D.C., "When they found Danny and Mikey, their bodies were decomposing, rigor mortis had set in, the whole nine yards, you can only imagine. When they found Matt—people don't know about this—he didn't have that. There wasn't any larva or anything like that. He survived for two weeks out there. . . . That SOB lived for two more weeks out there with those injuries, and when they found him, he was in a clearing—someone had laid him there, you know." After *Stars and Stripes* quoted him on these remarks, Luttrell backtracked, saying he did not know when Axelson died.

97. Luttrell, *Service,* 275–76; Donov, "Operation Red Wings II."

98. This number includes four military personnel who were killed by an ordnance cache that by some reports was booby-trapped, and three CIA personnel.

99. Department of the Navy, "SECNAV Instruction 1650.1H: Navy and Marine Corps Awards Manual," Aug. 22, 2006.

100. Luttrell, *Lone Survivor,* 179.

101. Ibid., 230. In the foreword to Brandon Webb, *The Red Circle: My Life in the Navy SEAL Sniper Corps and How I Trained America's Deadliest Marksmen* (New York: St. Martin's Press, 2012), xii, Luttrell would push the figure further to "a couple hundred."

102. Moore, *Run to the Sound of the Guns,* 135.

103. Navy officer, interview with author. The unclassified citation accompanying Murphy's Medal of Honor estimates "between 30 and 40 enemy fighters."

104. Navy officer, interview with author.

105. Four Air Force Crosses (the equivalent of the Navy Cross) were awarded to crew members of CH-53 and HH-53 special operations helicopters for their actions on May 15, 1975, during the *Mayaguez* incident. A few other post-Vietnam battles had come close to, but had not matched, the valor award tally of the Sawtalo Sar ambush. The military awarded special operators two Medals of Honor and one Air Force Cross for the October 3, 1993, battle of Mogadishu, and a Navy Cross and two Air Force Crosses for the March 3–4, 2002, battle of Takur Ghar. (A decade and a half later, two of those awards would be upgraded to Medals of Honor.) Two Navy Crosses and two Distinguished Service Crosses were awarded for the first battle of Fallujah in April 2004, and nine Navy Crosses (and eventually, in 2019, a Medal of Honor) for the second battle of Fallujah in November–December 2004, but in those cases the awards were for separate actions spread out over the course of several weeks.

106. Myers and NBC Investigative Unit, "Interview with a Taliban Commander."

107. Scott, interview.

108. Hatch, interview.

109. Luttrell, *Service,* 233–34: "Part of the reason things got so confused was that nearly everyone from my command who had all the details about Operation Redwing [*sic*] was on board Turbine 33 when it went down. The secrecy of our mission meant that we hadn't filed an evasion plan with the Air Force. . . . Special operations forces sometimes work in that independent way, but when things go wrong it can complicate and slow a response, and in this case overlapping and conflicting command responsibilities definitely made life difficult for our rescuers."
110. Intelligence source, interview.
111. Lt. Gen. (Ret.) Karl Eikenberry, interview with author.
112. Ibid.
113. 160th SOAR source, interview.
114. Eggers, Hatch, and another SEAL source, interviews with author.
115. Hatch, interview.
116. Hatch, *Touching the Dragon,* 312.
117. Bartels and Patrick Kinser, interviews with author.
118. Col. (Ret.) James Donnellan, Westerfield, Wood, and Scott, interviews with author.
119. Westerfield, interview. The alleged role of Islamist militants from the Russian republic of Chechnya is one of the enduring puzzles of the post–September 11 war in Afghanistan. A host of officers with extensive Afghanistan experience confidently told me that their troops had fought Chechens in the Pech, and al-Qaida documents show that some Chechens (or at least militants al-Qaida described as Chechens, which might have included some from neighboring countries in the Caucasus like Georgia) were training alongside Uzbeks at al-Qaida's al-Faruq Camp in Khost in the mid-1990s (Stenersen, *Al-Qaida in Afghanistan,* 46–50). The journalist Joanna Paraszczuk's website dedicated to tracking reports in militant propaganda of Chechen participation in foreign insurgencies, From Chechnya to Syria, includes a small number of references to Chechens purported to have spent time in Afghanistan, like one killed in Aleppo in 2014 who supposedly spent a year in Afghanistan earlier in his jihadi career (Joanna Paraszczuk, "Sayfullah Shishani 'Fought in Chechnya, Afghanistan,'" From Chechnya to Syria, June 20, 2014, www.chechensinsyria.com/?p=22189). But skeptics argue that there has never been an appreciable number of Chechen militants in Afghanistan in the post-2001 period. Instead, for many Afghans on whom the U.S. military relied for information—like human intelligence sources and the interpreters who listened to walkie-talkie traffic—"Chechen" was a catchall term for militants of many different nationalities, from Uzbek to Russian, that caught on because it was an easy way of categorizing foreign fighters who looked or sounded different from Pakistanis or Arabs and because American ears invariably perked up when the word "Chechen" was mentioned.

In his book on the March 2002 battle of Shah-e Kot, *Not a Good Day to Die,* Sean Naylor uses this theory to explain that the "Chechens" reported to have participated in the battle (including, repeatedly, by the

CENTCOM commander, General Tommy Franks, and the 10th Mountain Division commander, Major General Buster Hagenback) were probably actually Uzbeks. Another account of the battle describes how JSOC operators believed they were fighting both Chechens and Uzbeks at one point, citing as evidence the discovery of "Cyrillic documents confirming the fighters' Chechen ethnicity" (Dan Schilling and Lori Chapman Longfritz, *Alone at Dawn: Medal of Honor Recipient John Chapman and the Untold Story of the World's Deadliest Special Operations Force* [New York: Grand Central Publishing, 2019], 171). A translated al-Qaida account the book quotes from includes references to Arabs of various nationalities, a Somali, and Uzbeks, but no Chechens. Similarly, an Arab al-Qaida commander who fought in the battle, Abd al-Hadi al-Iraqi, told a jihadi propagandist in an interview that "the Uzbeks in particular had heroic triumphs" at Shah-e Kot but made no mention of Chechens (Appellate Exhibit 38, *USA v. Abd al-Hadi al-Iraqi*). Not a single Chechen is known to have been detained by U.S. forces in Afghanistan, and in a June 2010 letter to Osama bin Laden recovered from bin Laden's Abbottabad compound, a senior al-Qaida figure listed among the nationalities of fighters with him in North Waziristan "Uzbeks, Turks, Azerbaijanis and the like, Turkistanis, Germans, Bulgarians, and others," but not Chechens.

In a pair of pieces for the Afghanistan Analysts Network, "A Battlefield Myth That Will Not Die" and "How to Identify a Chechen," Christian Bleuer suggests that the Chechens-in-Afghanistan meme manifests itself in the form of two logical fallacies that U.S. troops fell into: that because Chechen fighters were light-skinned and spoke a Russian-sounding language, any light-skinned fighters spotted on propaganda videos or fighters overheard speaking Russian-sounding languages on the radio had to be Chechens; and that because Chechen fighters were supposed to be courageous and particularly skilled or competent, any courageous and particularly skilled or competent fighters encountered on the battlefield were likely Chechens.

I found no actual evidence of Chechen fighters' presence in Kunar or Nuristan but plenty of instances where interpreters, officials, elders, or informants told Americans that Chechens were present, and most of them fit into Bleuer's two categories. When an interpreter overheard what sounded like Russian in radio chatter in the mountains north of the Pech in April 2006, for instance, a brief military report indicated the presence of Chechens, and at a *shura* in August 2007 one of the senior elders of the Korengal *shura*—who had a vested interest in painting a picture to his American interlocutors of a foreign-based insurgency rather than a local one—told American officers that "Pakistani, Chechen, and Iranian" fighters were massing deep in the valley. During one of my visits to Kunar, in 2013, both Afghan National Army officers and a local official made similar assertions to me in reference to the Watapur valley.

"If someone was shooting at us and they got close, they were foreign fighters—we figured it was Chechens," a company first sergeant who spent more than a year in the Korengal told me. "I had a really experienced interpreter who was great at IDing other languages, and he confirmed on separate occasions that he heard Arabic and Chechen," an officer who served in the same company in the Korengal said; at the time, he didn't question how the interpreter, who spoke neither Russian nor Chechen, could tell the difference.

"People would tell us there were Chechens, but I'd ask how they knew and they'd just say they were speaking Russian," the Marine lieutenant Justin Bellman told me, referring to his 2005 deployment to FOB Blessing. The most experienced Kunar hand I interviewed, a former Delta Force operator who worked in the Pech on and off from 2005 to 2010 as a contractor with the Army's Asymmetric Warfare Group, said that he "personally never saw anyone, dead or alive, that was proved to be a Chechen. There was lots of subjective arguments made by [military intelligence] analysts about a significant Chechen presence. As for me, no definitive proof or evidence."

120. Donnellan, interview.
121. As-Sahab Media, *War of the Oppressed*. In place of the actual MH-47 shootdown, the video's editors added shots of conventional Army CH-47s flying around, misleadingly implying that one of them was the aircraft about to meet its end. Coincidentally, the movie *Lone Survivor* also substitutes regular CH-47s for MH-47s in its shoot-down scene.
122. Westerfield, interview.
123. Moeller, interview.
124. Wood, interview.
125. Donnellan, interview.
126. Ibid.
127. Wood, interview.
128. The Marines who died in the Pech in 2005, all lance corporals, were Kevin Joyce, nineteen, who drowned in the Pech River two days before Operation Red Wings; Phillip George, twenty-two, killed in an ambush in the Korengal during 2/3 Marines' Operation Whalers in mid-August; Steven Valdez, twenty, killed by indirect fire on FOB Blessing in September; and Ryan Nass, twenty-one, who committed suicide at Blessing in September.

CHAPTER 5: THE PLUNGE, 2006

1. This scene is reconstructed from interviews with Brig. Gen. Chris Cavoli, Maj. Andy Knight, and Ray McPadden and from an unpublished manuscript by Cavoli titled "Guns and Tea."
2. Maj. Gen. John "Mick" Nicholson, interview with author.
3. Jim Maceda, *NBC Nightly News* segment.
4. Col. (Ret.) Bart Howard, interview with author.
5. Howard and Nicholson, interviews.
6. Nicholson, interview.
7. Col. Tom Gukeisen, interview with author. In fact, as captured al-Qaida documents and questioning of detained al-Qaida members show, the facil-

ity where al-Qaida members who were "read in" on its closely guarded plans for international terrorism operations worked was the group's Abu Ubaydah Camp, located at Kandahar Airfield. Stenersen, *Al-Qaida in Afghanistan,* 103–7.

8. Portions of the report that Cavoli and a research partner co-authored were published, with their permission, in the then chairman General Richard Myers's memoir, *Eyes on the Horizon: Serving on the Front Lines of National Security,* with Malcolm McConnell (New York: Threshold, 2009), 285–94. "Local struggles provide the global insurgents [that is, al-Qaida operatives] extremely useful points of entry," the paper posited. Combating this problem, according to Cavoli and his co-author, would "require simultaneous efforts to defeat the global insurgents and to defeat, suppress, defuse, or prevent local insurgencies"—counterterrorism through counterinsurgency.

9. As-Sahab Media, "Winds of Paradise, Part 5," Oct. 2010, archive.org /details/windsofparadisepart5.

10. Nicholson, interview.

11. Former senior intelligence officer, interview with author.

12. Mazzetti, "Qaeda Is Seen as Restoring Leadership"; Joint Task Force Guantánamo detainee assessment of Harun al-Afghani, Aug. 2, 2007; untitled, undated al-Qaida document accessible at www.cia.gov/library/abbottabad -compound/0F/0FFC7FA486132AC35343515071ADCD64_%D9%85 %D9%86_%D8%AA%D9%88%D9%81%D9%8A%D9%82.doc.pdf.

13. 10th Mountain Division sources, interviews with author. According to Scott-Clark and Levy, *Exile,* 225–27, Zawahiri moved to Demadola in Bajaur in the summer of 2004 after a Pakistani government raid displaced him from the Shakai valley.

14. Mazzetti, *Way of the Knife,* 115–17; Naylor, *Relentless Strike,* 387.

15. Former senior intelligence officer, interview with author.

16. Moeller, interview.

17. Former CIA officer, interview.

18. Former military intelligence officer, interview with author.

19. 1st Sgt. (Ret.) David Roels, interview with author.

20. Col. (Ret.) Mike Kershaw, interview with author.

21. Command Sgt. Maj. James Carabello, interview with author.

22. These quotations come from 1-32 Infantry's pre-deployment preparation documents, including a memo with the subject "Standards," dated June 27, 2005, and a PowerPoint presentation titled "Fighting in Afghanistan," dated Feb. 2006.

23. Former Asymmetric Warfare Group operator who asked to be identified only as T.W., interview with author.

24. Ibid.

25. This was the assessment of Task Force Paladin, the countrywide counter-IED headquarters, as of January 2006. Robert Stanton, "Company Continuity for the Pech Valley," Jan. 23, 2007.

26. A spate of helicopter crashes plagued the international coalition in Afghanistan in the late summer and early fall of 2005. Among the helicopters lost

was another Night Stalker MH-47 identical to Turbine 33 that clipped a rotor and made a "hard landing" between FOB Blessing and the Korengal while extracting a Special Forces A-team on October 7. No one was killed in the crash, but the aircraft was disabled and had to be destroyed by an orbiting AC-130.

27. Col. James "Chip" Bierman, Lt. Col. Sean "Rush" Filson, and Don Nicholas, interviews with author.

28. The other soldiers killed were Sgt. Kevin Akins, twenty-nine; Sgt. Anton Hiett, twenty-five; and Spc. Joshua Hill, twenty-four.

29. T.W., interview.

30. Ibid.

31. Bierman and Filson, interviews.

32. This account of Operation Mountain Lion is based on interviews with Brig. Gen. (Ret.) Anthony Tata, Nicholson, Cavoli, Bierman, Filson, Knight, McPadden, Lt. Col. Paul Garcia, Maj. David Mayfield, James McKnight, Maj. Michael Harrison, Erik Malmstrom, Maj. Sean McQuade, Matt O'Donnell, Jason Crawford, and John Garner; Cavoli's "Guns and Tea" manuscript; accounts by embedded reporters; and the daily journal entries of two participants.

33. Participant journal notes.

34. Knight, McPadden, McQuade, and O'Donnell, interviews.

35. Wolfe, interview; Christian Lowe, "Killer Platoon: USMC Distributed Ops Experiment Succeeds in Afghanistan," *Marine Corps Times,* May 2006.

36. Journal entries of participants and SALTUR and enemy action reports of 1/3 Marines and 1-32 Infantry.

37. Garner, interview.

38. Cavoli, interview.

39. Filson, interview.

40. Wolfe, interview.

41. Filson, interview.

42. Bierman, Filson, Nicholson, and Wolfe, interviews; participant journal notes.

43. Wolfe, interview.

44. Ibid.

45. Nicholson, interview.

46. Cavoli and Knight, interviews.

47. Nicholson, interview.

48. Cavoli, "Guns and Tea"; Jake Tapper, *The Outpost: An Untold Story of American Valor* (New York: Little, Brown, 2012), 79–80.

49. McQuade, interview; Sgt. 1st Class Michael Pintagro, "Chosin Infantry Platoon Climbs to Victory in Korengal," Aug. 17, 2006.

50. Nicholson, interview.

51. Cavoli, interview.

52. Tata and Moeller, interviews.

53. Cavoli, "Guns and Tea."

54. Erik Malmstrom, "Waigul Valley Debrief 22 May 2006–27 May 2006."

55. The collaboration between al-Qaida and Lashkar-e-Taiba fighters in Kandahar is described in Farrall and Hamid, *Arabs at War in Afghanistan,* 288. The former CIA Islamabad station chief Robert Grenier, in his book *88 Days to Kandahar,* 318, describes how joint CIA-FBI-ISI teams operating in Pakistan in early 2002 would often find al-Qaida and Lashkar-e-Taiba suspects together in militant safe houses; while the CIA took custody of the al-Qaida suspects, according to Grenier, the Lashkar-e-Taiba suspects would be handed back to their ISI sponsors.

56. A captured al-Qaida report for Osama bin Laden on lessons learned during the group's expulsion from Afghanistan suggests that collaboration between the two groups was not always smooth, however: the report's anonymous author attributes the detention of al-Qaida figures Abu Zubaydah and Abu Yasir (in CIA-FBI-ISI raids in Pakistan) to either signals intelligence or "our opening up so much to Lashkar-e-Tayyiba" and the group's "treachery" ("Lessons Following the Fall of the Islamic Emirate," n.d., www.odni.gov /files/documents/ubl/english/Lessons%20Learned%20Following %20the%20Fall%20of%20the%20Islamic%20Emirate.pdf).

57. Joint Task Force Guantánamo detainee assessment of Harun al-Afghani, Aug. 2, 2007.

58. Bilal Sarwary and Mohammad Issa Wardak, interviews with author; Provincial Reconstruction Team Asadabad documents.

59. Garcia, interview.

60. Cavoli and Garcia, interviews.

61. Lt. Col. (Ret.) Jack Rich, interview with author. The rules restricting U.S. troops from traveling in nonstandard vehicles, and mandating that all mounted patrols contain a certain minimum number of Humvees, were instituted in 2005 by the same Italy-based division headquarters that barred the Marines from entering the Korengal during the later part of its tour at the Joint Task Force headquarters at Bagram.

62. Cavoli, interview.

63. Crawford, interview.

64. O'Donnell, interview.

65. Malmstrom and Crawford, interviews.

66. Cavoli, "Guns and Tea."

67. This description of 1-32 Infantry's arrival in Aranas is based on interviews with Cavoli, Garcia, Malmstrom, O'Donnell, Carabello, and Capt. Ryan Scholl, and on Cavoli, "Guns and Tea."

68. Malmstrom, interview; Cavoli, "Guns and Tea"; narratives accompanying award of the Silver Star to Spc. Andrew Small and the Army Commendation Medal with "V" device to Pfc. Andrew Sousa.

69. Crawford, interview.

70. PRT Asadabad document.

71. Malmstrom, interview.

72. Cavoli, "Guns and Tea."

73. DIA report, Aug. 7, 2006.

74. Cavoli, newsletter to 1-32 Infantry families, Aug. 24, 2006.

CHAPTER 6: WHERE THE ROAD ENDS . . . , 2006–2007

1. This account of the October 6, 2006, battle of Combat Main is based on my interviews with Maj. Robert Stanton, Maj. Michael Harrison, Maj. Sean McQuade, and Sgt. Maj. John Mangels; on a January 10, 2012, interview with Stanton by Jenna Fike of the U.S. Army Combat Studies Institute's Operational Leadership Experiences project; and on audio recordings of some of the radio traffic during the battle from the perspective of the platoon sergeant of First Platoon, Combat Company, 1-32 Infantry, who was nearby at Firebase California when the battle began.

2. Stanton, author interview.

3. Stanton, OLE interview.

4. Stanton, author and OLE interviews.

5. Stanton, author interview.

6. Stanton, OLE interview.

7. Cavoli, interview.

8. McQuade, interview.

9. Ibid.

10. Audio of Combat Company radio traffic during the battle.

11. McQuade, interview.

12. Stanton and Mangels, interviews.

13. Eikenberry does not remember when, why, or in reference to what he first said this, but throughout 2006 he was using the phrase often.

14. William Griffith, the East India Company naturalist who accompanied the 1840 expedition, wrote that the Pech road was "execrable" and "not passable for guns." Griffith, *Journals of Travels,* 457–58.

15. Katib Hazarah, *Reign of Amir ʿAbd al-Rahman Khan,* 1590.

16. Ibid., 1448–57.

17. Stenersen, *Al-Qaida in Afghanistan,* 60.

18. James Michener, *Caravans* (New York: Random House, 1963), 102–5.

19. Government Accountability Office, "Afghanistan Reconstruction: Progress Made in Constructing Roads, but Assessment for Determining Impact and a Sustainable Maintenance Program Are Needed," GAO 08-689, July 2008.

20. Agency Coordinating Body for Afghan Relief, "NGO Programs in Kunar, 1990–1992," Dec. 1992. As of 1992, four different international aid organizations were working in the Pech. Work on at least one of these projects, the French aid group MADERA's road project from Wama in the western Pech to the Parun valley, was still under way five years later.

21. Eikenberry, interview.

22. Ibid.

23. Cavoli and Capt. Ryan "Doc" Scholl, interviews with author.

24. Quoted in Peter Apps, *Churchill in the Trenches* (Amazon Digital Services, 2015), loc. 921.

25. Scholl, interview.

26. Timothy Standaert, interview with author.

27. Scholl, interview.

28. Cavoli, "Guns and Tea."

29. Scholl, interview; Maj. J. P. Guerin, interview with author. "If locals built a bridge, they could leave their equipment out there and no one would mess with it," Scholl remarked. "Put a Bailey bridge in"—a prefabricated U.S. military bridge—"and the locals will steal the rivets right out of it."

30. Stanton, interview.

31. Stanton, Harrison, Mangels, and Capt. Darren Riley, interviews with author.

32. Igor Kalmykov, who participated in some of these missions as a member of the 66th Separate Motorized Rifle Brigade's air-assault battalion, told me that his unit sometimes patrolled as high up as fourteen thousand feet in Kunar.

33. Stanton, Harrison, Riley, and McQuade, interviews.

34. 1st Lt. Michael Harrison, "Central Pech Valley Platoon Leader's Assessment," May 24, 2007.

35. Knight, interview.

36. Capt. Rob Stanton, "Pech Valley Company Commander's Assessment," Jan. 23, 2007.

37. Shuvahin, "Bar Kanday: Memoirs of a Company Commander." The unit that occupied the Bar Kanday outpost was 5th Company, 2nd Battalion, 66th Separate Motorized Rifle Brigade.

38. Stanton and Nicholson, interviews.

39. Cavoli and Maj. Joseph Evans, interviews with author; Gregg Zoroya, *The Chosen Few: A Company of Paratroopers and Its Heroic Struggle to Survive in the Mountains of Afghanistan* (Boston: Da Capo Press, 2017), 47.

40. Lt. Col. Christopher Cavoli, report on Nov. 2006 meetings with Governor Tamim Nuristani, n.d.

41. Tamim, interview.

42. U.S. embassy, Kabul, "Situation in Nuristan," cable to Department of State, date not available, 2005.

43. Maria Karlstetter, "Wildlife Surveys and Wildlife Conservation in Nuristan, Afghanistan," Wildlife Conservation Society and U.S. Agency for International Development, n.d.

44. Cavoli, interview.

45. Cavoli, report on Nov. 2006 meetings with Governor Tamim Nuristani, n.d.

46. Tamim, interview.

47. Maj. Andrew Glenn, interview with author.

48. Farshad, interview.

49. Glenn, interview.

50. T.W. and Evans, interviews.

51. T.W., interview.

52. Crawford, interview. Some intelligence indicated the attack on Sloan was a targeted killing ordered by Mawlawi Monibullah, akin to U.S. efforts to strike guerrilla commanders. But Andrew Glenn believed it was a target of opportunity and that there was no way for the insurgents to have known which truck Sloan was in.

53. Evans, interview.

54. Ryan, interview.

55. Nicholson and Cavoli, interviews.

56. Cavoli, interview.

57. Eikenberry and Moeller, interviews. Eikenberry and his civilian counterpart, Ambassador Ronald Neumann, also wanted thirty more adviser teams for the Afghan National Army and police. Ronald Neumann, *The Other War: Winning and Losing in Afghanistan* (Washington, D.C.: Potomac Books, 2009).

58. George W. Bush, *Decision Points* (New York: Crown, 2010), 212.

59. T.W., interview.

60. McPadden, interview.

61. McKnight, Sgt. 1st Class (Ret.) Paul Zuzzio, Sgt. 1st Class Steve Frye, and Kieth Jeter, interviews with author; James Christ, *Yakah China: The 3rd Platoon, A/1/32 in the Korengal Valley, September 2006* (Venice, Fla.: Battlefield, 2011).

62. McKnight and McPadden, interviews.

63. Zuzzio, interview.

64. Participant notebook.

65. Cavoli, Knight, and McKnight, interviews; 1-32 Infantry, "Operation Ghat Sha-maal Hawa (Big North Wind) CONOP Brief," Aug. 27, 2006.

66. Frye, interview.

67. Cavoli, interview.

68. Cavoli, Knight, McKnight, and McPadden, interviews.

69. McPadden, interview.

70. Cavoli, interview.

71. Cavoli and Knight, interviews. I asked Harry Bader, the forester who studied Kunar's timber trade for the military in 2010 and 2011, what the effects of such a forest fire would have been like. Ecologically speaking, he told me, it would not have been disastrous, but economically and psychologically it could have been for the Korengalis. "It's not because they only cared about the money," he added. "It's because the timber is tied to every single aspect of daily life. I don't know, culturally, what would bring us to our knees in the same way."

72. Zuzzio and former interpreter who asked to be identified as Samim, interviews with author; Christ, *Yakah China.* The quotation from Cavoli's speech is as Zuzzio recalls it. Christ, in *Yakah China,* quotes Cavoli similarly but not in exactly the same words.

73. McPadden, interview.

74. Knight, interview.

75. Farshad and Burhan, interviews.

76. Cavoli, interview; Cavoli, "Guns and Tea"; McKnight, interview.

77. Cavoli, "Guns and Tea."

78. Cavoli, Knight, and McKnight, interviews.

79. McKnight, McPadden, Frye, Jeter, and Zuzzio, interviews.

80. Entry by Capt. Jim McKnight in 3rd Brigade Combat Team, 10th Mountain Division, "Afghan Commander AAR Book (OEF-7)," March 2007.

81. McKnight, interview.

82. Capt. Joseph Paolilli, interview with author.

83. Cavoli, interview.

84. Stanton and Guerin, interviews.

85. U.S. embassy, Kabul, "PRT Asadabad: Semi-annual Report on Security, Political, Economic and Social Conditions in Kunar Province," cable to Department of State, Feb. 21, 2007.

86. 2-503 Infantry, "AO Rock Fragmentary Kit #5 Mission Analysis and Recommendation," June 22, 2007.

87. Moeller, interview.

88. Cavoli, interview.

89. Mangels, interview.

90. Harrison and Col. Frederick O'Donnell, interviews with author.

91. Paolilli, interview.

92. Cavoli, "Guns & Tea."

93. Cavoli, interview.

CHAPTER 7: ROCK AVALANCHE, 2007

1. Col. Bill Ostlund, interview and correspondence with author.

2. Maj. (Ret.) Lance Manske, interview with author.

3. Lady Emma Sky, interview with author. To Sky's amusement, when Ostlund wrote her a performance review, he described her as in "the top tier of civilians" he'd ever come across, a very Ostlundian compliment.

4. Lt. Col. (Ret.) John Nagl, interview with author.

5. Ostlund, interview.

6. The words here are as the paratrooper Ryan Pitts remembers them. Ostlund did not write out his remarks beforehand, but he referred to what he had said in them in another speech that he wrote a year and a half later when he gave up command of The Rock back in Italy: "I told you all before we left, there would be times in our shared future that I would care more for you than I do for my own sons—that occurred on more occasions than I care to remember."

7. 1st Sgt. (Ret.) David Roels, interview with author.

8. Ostlund, correspondence.

9. Haji Zalmay Yusufzai, interview with author.

10. Farshad, interview.

11. Samim, interview.

12. Burhan, interview.

13. T.W., interview.

14. 2-503 Infantry incident report, "D11 111208Z TF Rock Reports Escalation of Force Incident IVO FOB Michigan," June 11, 2007; UN Assistance Mission to Afghanistan report on civilian casualty incident.

15. UNAMA report on civilian casualty incident.

16. PRT Asadabad, "Kunar Province: Province of Opportunities," July 26, 2008.

17. Capt. Larry LeGree, interview with author.

18. Lt. Col. Tom Gukeisen, interview with author.

19. Cavoli, interview.

20. LeGree, interview. Cavoli does not recall saying this.

21. Ostlund, correspondence.

22. A February 21, 2007, cable from the PRT's State Department representative estimated that while road workers could make $3–$5 per day, insurgent groups paid more like $12, plus "signing bonuses and large rewards for verifiably killing an [American] soldier." Five months later, another cable reported, "Insurgent organizers in Kunar are having difficulty recruiting locals, because the $160 monthly wage they offer Taliban foot soldiers compares unfavorably with the wages and security offered on ISAF-funded projects."

23. This account of Battle Company, 2-503 Infantry's time in the Korengal is based on interviews with the Battle Company veterans Maj. Daniel Kearney, Command Sgt. Maj. LaMonta Caldwell, Maj. Joseph Wells, Capts. Ian MacGregor, Michael Moad, and Rudy Varner, 1st Sgt. Mark Patterson, and Brendan O'Byrne and with the Asymmetric Warfare Group advisers T.W. and Dave Roels and the 173rd Airborne Brigade psychologist Maj. (Dr.) Brian O'Leary; on published material, including Junger, *War,* and Rubin, "Battle Company Is Out There"; and on the documentaries *Restrepo,* directed by Junger and the late Tim Hetherington (National Geographic Entertainment, Outpost Films, 2010), and *Korengal,* directed by Junger using Hetherington's footage (Gold Crest Films, Outpost Films, 2014).

24. Ostlund, interview.

25. Maj. Lou Frketic, interview with author.

26. Darren Shadix, *To Quell the Korengal* (CreateSpace Independent Publishing Platform, 2016), 10, 24.

27. McKnight, "Afghan Commander AAR Book."

28. Kearney and Maj. Jeffrey Pickler, interviews with author.

29. Junger, *War,* 12; Hetherington and Junger, *Restrepo.*

30. O'Byrne, interview.

31. Kearney, interview.

32. Patterson, interview.

33. Hetherington and Junger, *Restrepo.*

34. Kearney, Patterson, and O'Byrne, interviews; Junger, *War,* 62–66.

35. Kearney, interview; Rubin, "Battle Company Is Out There."

36. Emailed memo from Lt. Col. Bill Ostlund to Gen. David Petraeus, "Kunar—AO ROCK COIN Thoughts," July 12, 2008.

37. Gen. Daniel McNeill, "COMISAF Tactical Directive," June 2007.

38. 2-503 Infantry PowerPoint presentation, "AA6/B6 ROE Discussion," Oct. 8, 2007. Ostlund was referring to a provision in the U.S. military's standing rules of engagement, or SROE, that often seemed to be in direct conflict with the guidance that generals in Afghanistan gave encouraging restraint. The SROE, which unlike ISAF commanders' tactical directives carry the force of law, not only enshrined U.S. troops' right to self-defense but stated that U.S. forces had an *obligation* to attack positively identified enemy forces. The murky part was "positive identification," or PID.

39. T.W., interview.
40. Varner, interview.
41. O'Byrne, interview.
42. Kearney and Varner, interviews; Hetherington and Junger, *Restrepo.*
43. T.W., interview.
44. Kearney, interview.
45. 2-503 Infantry meeting report, "31 MAR 08 TF Rock KLE Nangalam District Governor," March 31, 2008.
46. Moad, interview.
47. Ostlund, interview.
48. DIA Joint Intelligence Task Force—Combating Terrorism, "Dynamic Threat Assessment," Nov. 2007.
49. Seckman, email correspondence.
50. Cavoli, interview.
51. In a 2015 interview with the Pakistani edition of *Newsweek* about his five years with the Taliban, a militant from northwestern Pakistan calling himself Qari Mohammad described an experience that matched this theory. Recruited at age sixteen, Mohammad underwent several months of training at a camp on the Pakistani side of the border; then he and fourteen other trainees were sent to Kunar, where they watched more experienced militants lay mountain ambushes for American troops and sometimes were sent on their own to plant IEDs. After this trial tour in Kunar, Mohammad and his training group were sent to fight British troops in Helmand on their first tour as full-fledged fighters.
52. Kearney, interview.
53. Ibid.
54. Ostlund and Rich, interviews.
55. Himes, interview.
56. Hetherington and Junger, *Restrepo;* Salvatore Giunta, *Living with Honor: A Memoir,* with Joe Layden (New York: Threshold, 2012), 231–32.
57. Shadix, *To Quell the Korengal,* 153.
58. 2-503 Infantry, "Operation Rock Avalanche Level II CONOP," Oct. 19, 2007. A Level II CONOP—the highest level—was an operation that, because of the resources required or the risks entailed, required approval by ISAF's two-star deputy chief of staff for operations in Kabul.
59. Frketic, interview.
60. T.W., interview; Col. Brian Mennes, interview with author.
61. Giunta, *Living with Honor,* 233–34.
62. Kearney, interview; Rubin, "Battle Company Is Out There"; Junger, *War,* 94–96; 2-503 Infantry enemy action report, "N1 191751Z TF Rock TIC IVO OBJ Clark (Rock Avalanche)," Oct. 19–21, 2007.
63. Rubin, "Battle Company Is Out There."
64. Battle Company initially reported three dead civilians, but other accounts agree on five.
65. Hetherington and Junger, *Restrepo;* Junger, *War,* 96–100.
66. Junger, *War,* 101–3.

67. Salvatore Giunta, interviewed by Maj. Jake Miraldi, "A Medal of Honor Recipient's Story," *The Spear*, podcast by the Modern War Institute, U.S. Military Academy, March 26, 2019.
68. Kearney, interview; Junger, *War*, 103–13.
69. O'Leary, interview.
70. Incident report made public by WikiLeaks.
71. Giunta, MWI interview.
72. Narrative accompanying the award of the Medal of Honor to Sgt. Salvatore Giunta; Giunta, *Living with Honor*, 243–52; Rubin, "Battle Company Is Out There"; Junger, *War*, 117–19.
73. Giunta, *Living with Honor*, 25–26, 182.
74. Ostlund, correspondence.
75. 2-503 Infantry meeting report, "06 2210Z TF Rock KLE Korengal Valley Elders," March 6, 2008.
76. 2-503 Infantry meeting report, "06 FEB 2008 TF Rock KLE (Kunar Governor)," Feb. 6, 2008.
77. 2-503 Infantry meeting report, "05 FEB 2008 TF Rock KLE (Managai Governor)," Feb. 5, 2008.
78. Himes, interview.
79. T.W., interview.
80. Col. George Sterling, interview with author.
81. Ostlund, correspondence.
82. Kearney, interview.
83. Ibid.

CHAPTER 8: A VALLEY TOO FAR, 2007–2008

1. Maj. Matthew Myer and Evans, interviews with author.
2. Testimony of Maj. John Thyng to the CENTCOM investigatory team led by Lt. Gen. Richard Natonski, Nov. 4, 2009. A redacted version of General Natonski's investigation and supporting exhibits and enclosures including interviews with members of Chosen Company, The Rock, and the 173rd Airborne Brigade staff are accessible at www2.centcom.mil/sites/foia/rr /CENTCOM%20Regulation%20CCR%2025210/Forms/AllItems.aspx ?RootFolder=%2Fsites%2Ffoia%2Frr%2FCENTCOM%20Regulation %20CCR%2025210%2FWANAT%20-%20Re-Investigation%20into%20 the%20Combat%20Action%20at%20Wanat%20Village%2C%20Wygal %20District%2C%20Nuristan%20Province%2C%20Afgh%2E%20on%20 13%20July%202008&FolderCTID=0x012000BDB53322B36BD84DA 24AF0C8F8BCD011&View={7AED4B57-43F2-4B7D-A38E-4BDDC 5BB9BD6}.
3. Myer, interview.
4. David Katz, Capt. Sam Paparo, Cavoli, and Gukeisen, interviews with author. According to Cavoli, "We looked at ideas like compostable toilets and micro-hydro generators and a reverse-osmosis water purification unit. . . . [But] the 'system' only knew one way to make a FOB—bulldoze it, Hesco it, gravel it, install Chigos [big air conditioners] and port-a-johns every-

where, and put in generators, which was clearly not feasible up there. We require a big logistical footprint for a simple task."

"Had I known what was coming [from the 173rd], I would've just moved us up there with what we had, like Cortés burning his ships," said Sam Paparo, the Navy PRT commander who would have occupied the site.

5. Rich, interview; sworn statement of Col. Charles Preysler for CENTCOM investigation into the battle of Want, Dec. 10, 2009.

6. Ostlund, interview.

7. By 2007, neither Haji Ghafor nor his superior Gulbuddin Hekmatyar was a high-priority target for JSOC or the intelligence community, but he remained on U.S. target lists. In the spring of 2008, Green Berets and ANA Commandos would find themselves locked in a ferocious battle during Operation Commando Wrath, an ill-fated attempt to target Hekmatyar and Ghafor in the Shok valley far away in western Nuristan.

8. Ostlund, interview and correspondence. Myer and brigade headquarters shared Ostlund's skeptical view of the Waygal bases' intelligence value. Predictably, some 1-32 Infantry officers disagreed. "There was a lot of valuable information that was gained by being in Aranas—assets who had a good idea of who was coming and going and hiding in southern Nuristan," 1-32's former intelligence officer, Major Dave Mayfield, insisted. Another 1-32 officer who asked not to be named made the same argument about Bella: "Bella is the only settlement on the valley floor of the Waygal until you get to Want. There was a restaurant, a clinic, and a little hotel. Anyone transiting through the Waygal has to stop there. What do transient populations have in common? They know shit about faraway places. You put a couple of THTs [intelligence-collection soldiers] there and guys from other organizations, and you've got a HUMINT gold mine."

9. Ostlund, interview.

10. Testimony of Sgt. 1st Class David Dzwik to Lt. Gen. Richard Natonski, Oct. 6, 2009.

11. This account of the August 22, 2007, battle of the Ranch House is based on interviews with Myer, Gregory Rauwolf, and former Sgt. Kyle White; Dzwik's testimony to the CENTCOM investigation; Command Sgt. Maj. Shane Stockard's description in a podcast interview by Jake Miraldi, "An Infantry Company's War in Afghanistan," *The Spear*, Oct. 10, 2018, mwi .usma.edu/podcast-spear-infantry-companys-war-afghanistan/; the blow-by-blow reconstruction in Zoroya, *Chosen Few*, 70–108; John McGrath, "The Attack on the Ranch House, August 2007," in *16 Cases of Mission Command*, ed. Donald Wright (Fort Leavenworth, Kans.: Combat Studies Institute Press, 2013); the citations and narratives for the award of the Distinguished Service Cross to Staff Sgt. Erich Phillips and the Silver Star to 1st Lt. Matt Ferrara and Spc. Jason Baldwin; and the 2-503 Infantry medevac report, "N7 220142Z TF Rock MM(E)08-22B Ranchhouse 11x US WIA, 1x ANA KIA, 1x ANA WIA, 1x ASG KIA," Aug. 22, 2007.

12. Rauwolf, interview.

13. Mark Bowden, "Echoes from a Distant Battlefield," *Vanity Fair*, Dec. 2011.

14. Stockard in "Infantry Company's War in Afghanistan."
15. Myer, interview.
16. Ferrara, Phillips, and Baldwin citations and narratives; Zoroya, *Chosen Few,* 100.
17. Ferrara citation and narrative.
18. Al-Fajr Media Center, "Destroying the Cross," May 20, 2008.
19. Zoroya, *Chosen Few,* 39.
20. Col. Mark Johnstone, "AR 15-6 Investigation Findings and Recommendations—Vehicle Patrol Base (VPB) Wanat Complex Attack and Casualties," Aug. 13, 2008.
21. 2-503 Infantry meeting report, "250900Z TF Rock KLE," Aug. 25, 2007.
22. 2-503 Infantry meeting report, "220900Z TF Rock KLE," Sept. 22, 2007.
23. Kyle White, interview with author.
24. White, Farshad, and Burhan, interviews.
25. This account of the events of November 9, 2007, is based on my interviews with White, Myer, and Maj. Eric Carlson; correspondence with Carlson; a briefing titled "TF Rock, 2-503 IN, Attack Waygul Valley, 09 NOV 07"; the citations and narratives for the award of the Medal of Honor to Kyle White, the Distinguished Service Cross to Staff Sgt. James Takes, and the Silver Star to Staff Sgts. Conrad Begaye and Peter Rohrs; a first-person narrative of the battle written by the participant Kain Schilling for the 2-503 Infantry–focused blog From Cow Pastures to Kosovo, April 15, 2014, from cowpasturestokosovo.blogspot.com/2014/04/sgt-r-kyle-white-to-receive-medal-of.html; a narrative of the medevac mission in the newsletter of the DUSTOFF Association, "Charley Company 3/82 GSAB: 2008 DUSTOFF Rescue of the Year," *DUSTOFFer* (Spring/Summer 2009); video of the medevac mission shot by an Apache and released in January 2008, www.youtube.com/watch?v=cVYgsYiE2yU; and the 2-503 Infantry enemy action report, "D7 091124Z TF Rock Reports TIC IVO COP Bella 6xUS KIA, 7xUS MIL WIA, 3xANA KIA and 11xANA WIA," and medevac report, "D7 091200Z TF Rock 9-Line MEDEVAC Request MM(E)11-09D IVO COP Bella 9x US WIA, 1x ANA WIA," Nov. 9, 2007.
26. Schilling, blog post.
27. Army public affairs interview with Sgt. Kyle White, army.mil/medalof honor/white/.
28. White, interview.
29. This is according to White's Medal of Honor narrative; he himself does not remember calling for fire in the blur of events.
30. Carlson, interview.
31. 305th Military History Detachment interview with 1st Sgt. Scott Beeson, May 2, 2008.
32. CENTCOM investigation testimony of 1st Lt. Aaron Thurman, Oct. 14, 2009.
33. Thurman, CENTCOM testimony.
34. Myer, interview; 2-503 Infantry meeting report, "03 DEC 2007 TF Rock KLE (Ameshuza Shura)," Dec. 3, 2007.

35. Myer, correspondence. "Over time, it takes deliberate and active mental energy to fight a general bitterness towards Iraqis and Afghans," Myer explained.

36. When the Aranas elders visited Bella over the winter, after months of quiet, all the wounds still felt so fresh that the *shura* devolved into a shouting match, with the Aransis denying they'd had anything to do with either November 9 or the death of Doug Sloan and the lieutenant who'd replaced Matt Ferrara insisting they had.

37. Beeson, 305th MHD interview.

38. Burhan and Farshad, interviews.

39. Farshad, interview.

40. Men from Aranas, group interview with author.

41. Katz, interview.

42. Ibid.; David Katz, "Community and Social Control in Cima-Nisei Kalasa Society," MS, Dec. 9, 2013.

43. A *shura* a few weeks after the November 9 ambush was typical of Ostlund's interactions with Waygali elders and officials. The Waygal's district governor, an Aransi, had quit after the battle, and in the *shura* the colonel came down hard on his replacement for failing, in a few short weeks, to get Waygali communities to turn in the militants among them. Ostlund "stated that they must pick a side," a soldier recorded in notes of the *shura,* "the [insurgency's] side or the Government."

44. Waygali men, group interview with author.

45. Rich, interview; CENTCOM investigation testimony of Col. Mark Johnstone, Oct. 20, 2009, and of Lt. Col. Peter Benchoff, Oct. 21, 2009. According to Benchoff, when Preysler held a brigade planning session in March, figuring out how to leave Bella was number one on a list of sixty-eight tasks that the brigade commander wanted accomplished in the weeks ahead.

46. Myer and Rich, interviews; CENTCOM investigation testimony of Capt. Matt Myer, Oct. 29, 2009; Maj. Gen. Jeffrey Schloesser, interview with author. Myer wanted to use the platoon that had been stuck in the Waygal to increase patrolling west of Blessing along the Pech road, toward the neglected Chapa Dara district center, which actually seemed to want what his paratroopers and the PRT had to offer.

47. CENTCOM investigation testimony of Col. Bill Ostlund, Nov. 20, 2009.

48. Ostlund, CENTCOM testimony.

49. Abdul Qudus, Abdul Rahman, Inayat Rahman, interviews with author.

50. CENTCOM investigation testimony of Capt. Benjamin Pry, Oct. 20, 2009.

51. Task Force Bayonet daily intelligence summaries, April 11 and 23, 2008.

52. Task Force Bayonet daily intelligence summary, April 23, 2008.

53. Capt. Benjamin Pry, interview with the Combat Studies Institute historian Douglas Cubbison, May 6, 2009.

54. Ostlund, Myer, and Pry, CENTCOM testimony.

55. Schloesser, Johnstone, Ostlund, Myer, Himes, and Pry, CENTCOM testi-

mony; Schloesser, Myer, Farshad, and Burhan, interviews; Article 15-6 investigation.

56. Aransi men, group interview with author.

57. T.W., interview.

58. Pry, CENTCOM testimony.

59. Video footage of insurgents strolling around the Bella outpost was released by a Taliban propaganda arm interspersed with footage taken during the battle of Want of a few days later; the footage was first aired in the United States by ABC's *World News with Charles Gibson* on November 12, 2009.

60. CENTCOM investigation testimony of Sgt. 1st Class David Dzwik, Oct. 6, 2009.

61. In the original plan that 2-503 submitted for approval, these Afghan workers were supposed to arrive on July 10, but they changed their timeline before Second Platoon headed up on the night of the eighth. According to Scott Himes, he, Ostlund, and Myer all discussed this delay in Ostlund's office and concluded that it shouldn't be a problem.

62. Himes, CENTCOM sworn statement.

63. The bowl that Want sat at the bottom of was wider and less steep than Bella's. An alternative would have been to put the base above the town on the mountainside, but that would only have put the higher ground a little farther away, and it would have taken away what Ostlund and Myer saw as the key advantages to having an outpost in Want in the first place: being next door to the local government, and being accessible by road. "The fact is, over there, there's always higher ground," Ostlund told CENTCOM investigators. "The enemy will always be able to get the higher ground until you're on top of the Hindu Kush mountain ridge line."

64. Myer, CENTCOM testimony and sworn statement for 15-6 investigation, July 16, 2008.

65. Dzwik, CENTCOM testimony; CENTCOM investigation testimony of unidentified Second Platoon specialist, Oct. 28, 2009.

66. Myer, CENTCOM testimony.

67. As with many engagements in Kunar-Nuristan, U.S. estimates of the size of the insurgent force that attacked Want varied widely, were based on slim evidence, and tended to rise over time. The first estimate that Matt Myer provided soon after the battle was 40 to 50 attackers, but later he guessed 100, citing the likely presence of ammunition bearers, litter bearers, and other enemy personnel who wouldn't have been showing themselves with muzzle flashes. The battalion intelligence shop initially estimated 115 but later revised the guess upward, after learning that some fighters had joined the battle partway in, according to Ben Pry. The division intelligence shop's estimate was lower—50 to 75 fighters. Ostlund consistently told investigators he thought there were 200 attackers, and that was the number that went into the 15-6 investigation's report, which stated, "Assuming 2-3 AAF per position with an average of 6 supporting AAF per fighter, 200 is a reasonable number."

68. CENTCOM testimony of brigade intelligence sergeant first class identified

in the redacted version as "JULIET," Oct. 13, 2009. For all the scrutiny Want has received, this episode has not been included in other accounts of the battle. I shared the brigade intelligence NCO's testimony on the subject with Ostlund and Myer, neither of whom knew about it. Both were agnostic about whether the source really did have more detailed information the night before the battle and whether, even if he did, it could have made any difference. "If the source would have been deemed credible at the time"—the HUMINT team deemed him very credible—"and we were able to pull back assets, we may have detected something," Ostlund wrote to me. "Maybe not." "Sources were smart, and knew how to build credibility," added Myer. "It would be natural for a source, after the fact, to adjust his information and make it line up with what occurred. There is no way to know for sure in this case."

69. Myer, 15-6 testimony.
70. Myer told the Combat Studies Institute historian that he said, "This is a Ranch House–style attack and they're in close range with the intent to overrun." Bowden's account has him saying, "Whatever you can give me, I'm going to need. . . . This is a Ranch House–style attack."
71. Dzwik, CSI interview.
72. CENTCOM testimony of Sgt. 1st Class Erich Phillips, Oct. 14, 2009.
73. Specialists Matthew Phillips, Jonathan Ayers, and Gunnar Zwilling (all posthumously promoted to corporal) were the first three defenders of OP Topside to die. Phillips was fatally struck as he stood to throw a grenade; Ayers died manning an M240 machine gun; and Zwilling, who had gotten up to urinate just before the shooting started, was probably killed immediately by the opening wave of RPGs, according to Ryan Pitts.
74. Combat Studies Institute, *Wanat: Combat Action in Afghanistan, 2008*, 152–56; Zoroya, *Chosen Few*, 283.
75. Zoroya, *Chosen Few*, 124.
76. No survivors actually saw Rainey, Hovater, Bogar (all promoted posthumously to corporal), or Brostrom die, but Specialists Tyler Stafford and Christopher McKaig could both hear Brostrom and Rainey in their final moments and agree that the insurgent they were yelling about, who seems to have gotten through the OP's concertina wire, likely killed them. "I heard him [Brostrom] talking with Pitts, and then—I heard they were up there, I guess setting up a machine-gun position from what I know, and I heard Rainey yell that the enemy had gotten in the wire. I very vividly remember him screaming, 'He's right behind the rock, he's right behind the fucking sandbag. He's right behind the fucking sandbag,'" Stafford told Rainey's father, Frankie Gay, in a videotaped interview. Stafford described the event almost identically to a Combat Studies Institute interviewer: "Him and Rainey were yelling back and forth together, and I don't remember who said it, but they said, 'They're inside the wire.' I distinctly remember hearing Rainey's voice saying, 'He's right behind that fucking sandbag.' Then I just heard a whole bunch of fire and explosions which I am sure were grenades. I didn't hear them after that." McKaig recalled that the boul-

der the insurgent was hiding behind was near the OP's sleeping area, and the memories he shared with Gay in another videotaped interview closely match Stafford's account: "Rainey tried to warn them. He tried to warn them that there was an insurgent right behind this big boulder. It was five meters away from us. He was shooting up in our OP, he was raking—bullets were hitting everywhere. And we couldn't kill him. He only exposed his arm and an AK-47. And Rainey tried to warn them that there was insurgents down there. And I think—I don't know, I didn't see it happen, but I didn't hear Rainey's voice again. I think he got him. I think that one guy killed a lot of people that day."

In contrast to the Ranch House battle, during which insurgents breached the perimeter and advanced well inside the base, this incident at the OP is the only reported instance of an enemy fighter actually crossing U.S. concertina wire during the battle of Want. Matt Myer stressed this difference when I asked him about Stafford's and McKaig's accounts, saying that he worried readers could interpret the phrase "inside the wire" to imply a larger, Ranch House–like penetration and conjure up images of Vietcong sappers. "I think the enemy did cross an outer layer of wire [at OP Topside], but I still would hesitate to use that term, because of what people would assume by use of it (i.e., Keating, RH, FB Mary Ann)," he wrote to me, citing the Combat Outpost Keating and Ranch House battles in 2007 and 2009, where insurgents fully penetrated U.S. outposts, and the 1971 battle of Fire Support Base Mary Ann, a disastrous Vietnam War incident that historians have often blamed on poor discipline on the part of the defending U.S. unit.

77. Pitts, author interview, Medal of Honor interview, and Medal of Honor narrative.
78. Townsend, interview; Apache gun-tape footage.
79. Apache gun-tape footage.
80. Ibid.
81. Townsend, interview.
82. Ibid.
83. Phillips, CENTCOM testimony.
84. Green, interview.
85. According to Myer's sworn statement for the 15-6 investigation, a Red Ridge signals intelligence plane had just arrived overhead when the flanking attack began; the plane's radio intercepts located the apparent command post.
86. Preysler and Milley, CENTCOM testimony.
87. Myer, correspondence and CENTCOM testimony.
88. Quoted by Schloesser to Cubbison in his CSI interview.
89. The attackers left only one man behind, a body found near OP Topside wearing woodland camouflage under civilian robes. An ANA Commando officer told his Special Forces advisers that the dead man's face looked Arab, but that was only a guess. Nevertheless, Sebastian Junger, in "Return to the Valley of Death," *Vanity Fair,* Oct. 2008, described the attacking force as

"composed of Arabs, Chechens, and Uzbeks who acted as a complement to local fighters."

The battalion intelligence officer Ben Pry told CENTCOM investigators that he recalled the Red Ridge signals intelligence plane picking up a very small number of Uzbek-language transmissions, one or two, but could not recall any details. The division intelligence officer, Lieutenant Colonel Pierre Gervais, didn't remember such communications. "From an intel perspective, I didn't have any communications that would lead me to believe that there were foreign fighters. I cut that [speculation] right off," Gervais told a Combat Studies Institute historian. "Right from the beginning in the first reports that came out, there was discussion of foreign fighters, but when we did our look back on it, I didn't have any comms that would lead me to believe that there were. There wasn't any Arabic language, Uzbek language, Turk language, or Uighur that would lead me to believe there was a foreign fighter presence."

90. Insurgent footage of the battle supported this. Several cameramen had filmed teams of insurgents firing their weapons from different positions in the mountains, in town, and near the OP, shouting "God is great" and "Long live the Taliban" and passing back and forth the same kind of informational chatter that might be expected of soldiers in a firefight anywhere: *Be careful with your ammunition. Keep aiming at the black thing moving down there. I'm hit.* Most of the recorded dialogue was in Waygali and the rest in Pashto, and the accents, according to Waygalis who watched the video, were mostly those of Aranas and Amshuz. The interpreter Burhan heard that most of the attackers were from Aranas, Amshuz, and two other Waygal towns closer to Want, Kownd Kalay and Kalaygal.

91. Ostlund, CENTCOM testimony; Article 15-6 investigation report.

92. Special Forces officer who asked to be identified as Steve, interview with author.

93. Ibid.; Article 15-6 investigation report; C. J. Chivers, "Arms Sent by U.S. May Be Falling into Taliban Hands," *New York Times,* May 19, 2009.

The interpreter Farshad later heard more about the police's role from Want residents. Before dawn on July 13, according to the story he was told, policemen had spotted some of the insurgents as they infiltrated town through an area behind the mosque that couldn't be seen from the outpost. A policeman who hailed from the Watapur valley approached the insurgents but, after talking with them, allowed them to continue on their way to Haji Juma Gul's house.

94. The platoon leader Jon Brostrom had raised concerns about Zia Rahman over the winter, writing after a meeting with him at Bella that he believed him to be "ACM or an ACM supporter." That might have been correct, or the district governor might have been in the kind of impossible situation that it was hard for American soldiers on fifteen-month deployments to appreciate. He hailed from Amshuz, a religiously conservative town in the northern Waygal, and according to the interpreter Burhan his lifelong

neighbor there was the well-known militant Jamil Rahman, who would be killed by a JSOC drone strike in 2012 while acting as the Taliban's deputy shadow governor for Nuristan.

95. Ostlund, CENTCOM testimony. Many in the battalion felt the same way. "If there was a good enough reason for us to go in the first place, there should be a good enough reason for us to stay there," one junior paratrooper who'd fought in the battle said simply. The operations officer Scott Himes later came around to the decision Ostlund made, but at the time and for some time after he felt differently. "To go through all that and just leave, in my mind that was fucked up," he said in a Combat Studies Institute interview, and he said much the same thing to the Marine general who headed the CENTCOM investigation: "We should have stayed, sir. We should have stayed."

96. Schloesser, interview.

97. Himes, CENTCOM sworn statement.

98. Cheek, interview with author.

99. This figure includes a Marine and a Navy corpsman who were attached to The Rock as combat advisers to the ANA. The only U.S. battalion whose single-deployment death toll in Afghanistan was higher was the 3/5 Marines, during an infamous 2010–2011 deployment, although several other Marine and British battalions took losses proportionally in line with The Rock's during the course of shorter six- and seven-month deployments.

100. 2-503 final O&I brief, July 2008; Ostlund, correspondence.

101. Three types of surveillance aircraft provided significant coverage of the Want area in the days leading up to the battle—Predator and Warrior-A drones (which collectively provided fifty-nine hours of video surveillance to The Rock between July 8 and July 12) and a Red Ridge signals intelligence plane (which provided thirty-two hours of signals coverage)—but all had moved on to other parts of the country by the end of Saturday, July 12, after picking up no signs of the coming attack. (Separately, one of the Air Force's huge Persian Gulf–based RQ-4 Global Hawk drones flew over the Pech AO in the week before the battle, but it's unclear whether any of its coverage was focused on the Waygal or Want.)

Why, Lieutenant General Richard Natonski and Major General David Perkins asked during the CENTCOM inquiry, hadn't the surveillance aircraft stayed a day longer? And if they had, could they have provided advance notice of what was coming?

The answer to the first question was that the drones and the Red Ridge plane were scarce assets in a combat theater where Want was just one of many surveillance priorities. Compared with more than two dozen orbits of Predator and Predator-like drones supporting the surge in Iraq at the time, just four orbits were available to conventional forces in Afghanistan in July 2008, and only two of those worked the eastern part of the country. Both of these two available orbits (a Predator line and a Warrior-A line) were allocated to The Rock to cover the closure of Bella and establishment of the

Want outpost, but with high demand for their services elsewhere they had to leave eventually, despite repeated requests from battalion staff officers that they stay longer; the Predator was pulled away on Friday to cover another combat hot spot in the east, the Tangi valley in Wardak, and heavy winds grounded the Warrior-A on Saturday.

The answer to the second question was more subjective. Natonski wound up recommending, based on what he learned, that a Predator orbit be permanently assigned to every infantry brigade in Afghanistan, but at times in his questioning of witnesses Natonski seemed unclear about what the capabilities of the Predator really were in the mountainous, wooded terrain typical of Kunar-Nuristan. Plenty of his interviewees knew all about that subject, however, and went into it at length, sometimes with obvious frustration.

Of the twelve witnesses Natonski posed the question to, only two, the battalion operations and intelligence officers Major Scott Himes and Captain Ben Pry, said they thought it was likely that a Predator would have spotted the enemy as they moved into position in Want overnight, and one other didn't hazard a guess. All nine others, including Ostlund and the brigade and division intelligence officers and both lieutenants who acted as Pry's assistants, thought it was very unlikely. They explained that the forest often masked infrared signatures altogether and that even in daytime, teams of three, four, or five armed men could move through the mountains right under a Predator's camera and only be spotted if the metal on one of their weapons happened to catch the sunlight—and even then, with the quality of video that Predator cameras produced in 2008, only the most experienced, well-trained analyst could hope to guess whether he was looking at a rifle, a machine gun, or an RPG with any accuracy. (Ostlund cited the example of the ambush on Honcho Hill that had killed Josh Brennan and Hugo Mendoza back in October; a Shadow drone was staring directly down at the Battle Company patrol when it was attacked, he noted, and had completely missed the waiting ambush force because of the vegetation.)

The most emphatic skeptic was the division commander, Major General Jeffrey Schloesser, who had plenty of experience with surveillance footage, having spent several years as a senior official in the intelligence community. "That is incorrect. That just means that people don't have a clue about how to fight, I mean, or haven't fought, that's all," he stewed when Natonski suggested to him that a Predator might have thwarted the enemy attack. "You might get lucky, but probably not," agreed Schloesser's deputy, Brigadier General Mark Milley. "That technique of dismounted light infantry-type infiltration is extraordinarily difficult to pick up through something like a Predator."

As for why the Red Ridge signals intelligence plane didn't intercept any communications indicating the presence of a large enemy assault force, it seemed likely that the enemy had simply maintained radio silence in the days before the attack, but it was also possible that insurgent team leaders had coordinated their movements using cell or satellite phones that the Red Ridge didn't have the capability to pick up. This possibility was implied during the investigation by a senior CENTCOM military intelligence analyst who had focused on Afghanistan and Pakistan for years and briefed CENTCOM's acting commander on the intelligence aspects of the battle right after it happened. "There just was just not any SIGINT," the analyst told the investigators. In his written statement, he elaborated: "We had the capability at the National level [that is, via NSA systems] to collect SIGINT that we could not collect on the tactical [level] that the enemy could have used. Were they using devices and maybe we did not see that particular chain of intelligence? Quite possibly."

102. Bowden, "Echoes from a Distant Battlefield."

103. Schloesser, CENTCOM investigation testimony.

104. Gen. Charles Campbell, "Army Action on the Reinvestigation into the Combat Action at Wanat Village, Wygal District, Nuristan Province, Afghanistan on 13 July 2008," May 13, 2010.

105. The CENTCOM investigation delved into the possibility of a causal link between the deaths of civilians in the July 4 Bella Apache strike and the July 13 assault on COP Kahler, which press reports had speculatively linked at the time, but the members of 2-503 whom the investigators interviewed dismissed that possibility, accurately noting that preparations for the attack had been going on for weeks if not months and that it would have taken much longer than nine days to stockpile all the necessary weapons in the hills above town. The Chosen Company interpreters Farshad and Burhan, on the other hand, insisted to me in later interviews that revenge had been a major motivating factor in the attack. An interview with a group of men from Aranas, including some whose relatives had participated in the battle, who said that the Taliban had recruited Aransis at the funeral following the Apache strike, allowed me to reconcile these two seemingly opposing notions in a way that Bill Ostlund, for one, found convincing when I shared it with him: while the attack would have happened with or without the Apache strike, the strike provided an opportunity for the core group of attackers to quickly grow their force by recruiting at the funeral.

106. Waygali men, group interview with author.

107. Burhan, interview.

108. Ostlund, CENTCOM testimony. The Rock's executive officer, Brian Beckno, made a similar remark to the CENTCOM investigators: "Strategically, did the enemy probably win? Yes, because we pulled out of that area." So did the Marine who was the chief ANA adviser in the Pech at the time, Lieutenant Colonel Kevin Anderson. "They won again," he remembered thinking as he walked out of a briefing on the decision to leave Want. "I mean, if you look at it, they attacked us at Aranas, right? We withdrew out of there. They attacked us at Bella, and they did that on a regular basis, but we withdrew out of there." Command Sergeant Major Bradley Meyer was blunter: "The thing with not staying—we are the last superpower in the world and we get pushed out by the Taliban?"

CHAPTER 9: STUCK IN THE VALLEY OF DEATH, 2008–2009

1. Col. (Ret.) Brett Jenkinson, interview with author; some details from Capt. Cliff Pederson, interview with author, and from C. J. Chivers, *The Fighters: Americans in Combat in Afghanistan and Iraq* (New York: Simon & Schuster, 2018), 209–10.

2. Jenkinson, interview.

3. Many people who interacted with Jenkinson during 1-26 Infantry's deployment remember hearing him make some version of this remark, including at least two of his platoon leaders, a Marine combat adviser, a journalist, and two officers from the aviation task force that supported Jenkinson's troops. "If I could dam the mouth of the Korengal and fill it with rats, that's what I'd do," the aviation task force intelligence officer Captain Jillian Wisniewski remembered hearing Jenkinson say when she visited FOB Blessing on a pre-deployment recon. Jenkinson told me that he was parroting Kunar's provincial police chief, at least when it came to the rats.

4. Pederson and Tom Gearhart, interviews with author.

5. Jenkinson, interview.

6. Jenkinson, Gearhart, Maj. James Howell, John Rodriguez, and Maj. James Stultz, interviews with author.

7. The number of "moral waivers" the Army granted to recruits with past criminal histories rose steeply in 2005, 2006, and 2007 as the Army built ten new infantry brigades: the proportion of recruits enlisting on such waivers grew from 4.6 percent in 2003 to 11.2 percent in 2007. Between moral waivers, medical fitness waivers, and others, nearly one-third of recruits in 2007 entered the Army on a waiver of some sort. (By 2012, that proportion would fall to one-tenth.) See Russell Carollo, "Suspect Soldiers: Did Crimes in U.S. Foretell Violence in Iraq?," McClatchy News Service, July 11, 2008.

8. Gearhart, interview.

9. Gearhart, Steve Benedetti, Jenkinson, Pederson, Cheek, Col. (Ret.) John Spiszer, Lt. Col. Keith Rautter, Lt. Col. Tito Villanueva, and Lt. Col. Kendall Clarke, interviews with author. According to the brigade commander Spiszer, 3/1 ID deployed with 97 percent of the soldiers it was supposed to have (later boosted by replacements and late deployers), when the Army's minimum threshold for deployment was 95 percent. That was in contrast to the 173rd, which not only deployed at 107 percent strength but was bigger to begin with, because airborne brigades included a unit of about ninety parachute riggers who on deployment filled odd jobs and acted as replacements and augmentees.

10. T.W., interview.

11. Pederson, interview.

12. Rodriguez, interview.

13. Rodriguez, Jeter, and Mikel Drnec, interviews with author.

14. Mikel Drnec, journal entry.

15. Ibid.

16. Viper Company SALTUR and enemy action report, Aug. 16, 2008.

17. Chivers, *Fighters,* 204.

18. Howell and Rodriguez, interviews.

19. West, *Wrong War,* 42; Rodriguez, interview.

20. Howell, interview.

21. Gearhart, interview. The enemy action reports filed by Viper Company after its firefights also show Loy Kalay becoming an area of frequent contact.

22. Drnec, interview.

23. Pederson, interview.

24. Jenkinson, interview.

25. Jenkinson, Howell, and Rautter, interviews.

26. Jenkinson, Howell, and Rodriguez, interviews.

27. Rodriguez, interview.

28. Drnec, interview.

29. Jimmy Blackmon, *Pale Horse: Hunting Terrorists and Commanding Heroes with the 101st Airborne Division* (New York: St. Martin's Press, 2016), 90.

30. Jeter and Blackmon, interviews; Blackmon, *Pale Horse,* 91–97. Members of the Jalalabad-based aviation task force believed the projectile was an RPG, but some Viper Company soldiers who saw the Taliban video of the attack said the weapon looked like something much more unusual—a shoulder-fired surface-to-air missile or antitank missile.

31. Chivers, *Fighters,* 212–13.

32. Jeter, Howell, Rodriguez, Drnec, and Capt. Brandon Newkirk, interviews with author.

33. Drnec, interview.

34. Jeter, interview.

35. Blackmon, *Pale Horse,* 97–100.

36. Howell, interview.

37. Captain Alex Shuvahin, who both established and closed the Bar Kanday outpost, described what happened in a blog post a quarter of a century later (Shuvahin, "Bar Kanday: Memoirs of a Company Commander"). Helicopter crews were already reluctant to fly to the far-flung base when a Mi-8 transport was shot down on a resupply run in November 1982, necessitating a risky recovery mission across the Pech River. A month after that, headquarters decided to close the outpost.

38. Rodriguez and Pederson, interviews; Howell, correspondence.

39. Spiszer and Jenkinson, interviews.

40. Jenkinson, interview.

41. Ibid.

42. Schloesser, interview. "I frankly didn't know everything I needed to know coming in about how we got into the Korengal in the first place and how those decisions were made," said Schloesser.

43. Ibid.

44. Ibid.

45. Ibid.

46. In the opening weeks of 2009, 3rd Brigade, 10th Mountain Division re-

turned to Afghanistan for another tour, the first part of a large wave of re-inforcements that commanders in Kabul had been begging for and that would become the first of President Barack Obama's two Afghan surges. Most of the reinforcements went to locations south of Kabul, but 1-32 In-fantry, the Chosin battalion—after a year and a half at home—went back to Kunar, this time to the province's southeast. That freed a Blue Spader com-pany that had been working in the area to move up to COP Michigan in the Pech.

47. Jenkinson and Stultz, interviews.
48. Stultz and Cheek, interviews.
49. Burhan, interview.
50. Jenkinson interview.
51. Stultz, interview.
52. Cheek, interview.
53. The protective power of the MRAP against IEDs is not in dispute, and some Kunar veterans staunchly defend their use for that reason. Loren Crowe, for instance, who led a Blue Spader platoon and later came back to Kunar to command a company, was dismissive of MRAPs during his first deployment, when the IED threat was slight in the sector he patrolled, but relied on them heavily and gratefully during his second, 2011–2012 deploy-ment, when the Pech road was again heavily mined with IEDs. "I probably did complain once or twice about them, but I didn't feel hindered in the Pech on deployment number two by having to drive around in MRAPs," Crowe told me.

The majority of the interview subjects whom I asked about MRAPs, however, decried the Army's inflexibility in mandating their use in the Pech. Especially vociferous in their criticism were several Asymmetric War-fare Group advisers, including T.W. and Colonel George Sterling. "It was very noble of America to want to field those things, but the bottom line was that we wound up relegated to the roads," said Sterling, who came back to Kunar in the 2010–2011 period after his time there with 2-503 in 2007–2008.

54. A BTR-80 armored troop carrier (one of two common models of wheeled armored vehicle the Soviets used in Kunar) weighed some fifteen tons, compared with weights ranging from fourteen to seventeen tons for a MaxxPro Dash MRAP.
55. Salinas, interview.
56. Farshad, interview.
57. Stultz, Jenkinson, Rautter, and Spiszer, interviews.
58. Howell, Pederson, and Rodriguez, interviews; Chivers, *Fighters*, 214–27; Scott J. Gaitley, "Ambushing the Taliban: A US Platoon in the Korengal Valley," in *Vanguard of Valor: Small Unit Actions in Afghanistan,* ed. Donald Wright (Fort Leavenworth, Kans.: Combat Studies Institute Press, 2011), 27–44.
59. Some Blue Spader platoons conducted more air-assault operations than others. Carter Cheek, whose platoon was involved in several, remembered

them fondly. "If I were to say I missed anything about warfare, it would be conducting air assaults in the predawn hours in the mountains of Afghanistan," he wrote in a Facebook post on Veterans Day 2016, referring to his Pech deployment. "The darkness during flight was oddly peaceful. . . . As the rotor wash faded with the departure of the helicopter, suddenly you are nearly alone in the middle of nowhere, and it felt briefly overwhelming."

60. Howell and Newkirk, interviews; C. J. Chivers, "The Long Walk," *Esquire,* Aug. 2009.

61. In part, too, it was another symptom, like the fielding of MRAPs, of the army's decreasing appetite for risk in small-unit operations by conventional infantry. With six Apaches and sixteen smaller Kiowas now based at Jalalabad, attack helicopter support that had been a rare luxury in 1-32 Infantry's time had become not only routine but a headquarters-mandated requirement for nearly all operations in the Pech. If no Apaches or Kiowas were available on a given day because of a crisis or planned operation in some other unit's sector—which was often—troops in the most dangerous areas, like the Korengal, would curtail their patrolling down to a one-kilometer radius from their outposts.

62. Clarke, interview.

63. Jenkinson, interview.

64. Ibid.

65. Jenkinson, Spiszer, and Schloesser, interviews.

66. Special operations and intelligence sources, interviews with author.

67. McPadden, interview.

68. Jenkinson, interview.

69. Cheek, interview; 1-26 Infantry source, interview with author.

70. A declassified military email relating to the death of a detainee captured by a special operations strike force in Paktika proves the widely known fact that by mid-2009 the leadership of Task Force 373 was provided by the 75th Ranger Regiment. Buried in declassified email traffic between General David Petraeus (then the commander of CENTCOM), General Stanley McChrystal (then in command of ISAF), and the JSOC commander, McRaven, is the text of a previous email to McRaven from an individual whose signature block reads "373 / TF Red CDR," followed by redacted contact information for offices at both Bagram and Fort Benning, Georgia, home of the Ranger Regiment. Ranger units are always color-coded red in declassified JSOC documents, and Ranger-led task forces are often referred to as Task Force Red (with Delta Force, SEAL Team 6, and 160th SOAR elements as Task Force Green, Task Force Blue, and Task Force Brown). See "RE: Update: RE: Pics of Deceased Detainee," email from Gen. David Petraeus to Gen. Stanley McChrystal, July 4, 2009, www.documentcloud .org/documents/3233625-07-Email-RE-Update-RE-Pics-of-Deceased -Detainee.html#document/p2/a330722.

71. SEAL Team 6 source, interview with author.

72. Mark Mazzetti and Eric Schmitt, "U.S. Halted Some Raids in Afghanistan," *New York Times,* March 9, 2009.

73. Adm. (Ret.) William McRaven, correspondence with author.

74. Ibid.; William Ostlund, "Irregular Warfare: Counterterrorism Forces in Support of Counterinsurgency Operations," Institute of Land Warfare, *Land Warfare Papers,* no. 91, Sept. 2012, www.ausa.org/file/1064/download?token =qK05bu5C.

75. McRaven, correspondence.

76. Himes and Sterling, interviews. In Iraq, Stan McChrystal had successfully pushed his JSOC operators to cooperate closely with regular infantry units and go after low- and mid-level guerrilla commanders, targets they would previously have ignored. But the same evolution hadn't yet happened in Afghanistan.

77. Ostlund, "Irregular Warfare."

78. Moeller, interview.

79. Ostlund, interview.

80. Ranger source, interview with author.

81. Ostlund, interview.

82. The same declassified email thread that shows that Rangers were in charge of JSOC's Task Force 373 in July 2009 also shows that at the same time an individual whose signature block reads "RED SQDN CDR" was the commander of Task Force East, Task Force 373's Jalalabad-based subordinate unit. Although SEAL Team 6 is often referred to as Task Force Blue, its subordinate squadrons are color-coded blue, red, gold, silver, and black, and Red Squadron, formally DEVRON 2, has been widely reported as the unit whose members killed Osama bin Laden in May 2011. See "RE: Update: RE: Pics of Deceased Detainee," email from Petraeus to McChrystal.

83. Brig. Gen. Randy George, interview with author.

84. Col. Brian Pearl, interview with author.

85. Ranger source, interview with author.

86. SEAL Team 6, Ranger, 1-26 Infantry, and 2-12 Infantry sources, interviews with author.

87. This description is based mainly on the account by Mark Owen, in *No Easy Day: The Firsthand Account of the Mission That Killed Osama bin Laden,* with Kevin Maurer (New York: Dutton, 2012), 117–37. Owen does not identify the location, date, or specific target of the mission except to say that it was in Kunar during a summer–fall 2009 deployment. Interviews with members of 2-12 Infantry, an interview with the Norwegian journalist Paul Refsdal (who was visiting the insurgent commander Haji Mohammad Dawran on the opposite side of the Pech at the time), and the 2-12 Infantry SALTUR and enemy action report fill in the gaps.

88. Owen, *No Easy Day,* 123.

89. Ibid., 136.

90. Refsdal, interview.

91. Refsdal, "Behind the Mask."

92. Maj. Chris Owen, interview with author.

93. Owen, *No Easy Day,* 121.

94. McPadden, 1-26 Infantry sources, and 2-12 Infantry sources, interviews.

95. This figure includes sixty-five thousand ISAF troops (thirty thousand of them American) and twenty-seven thousand U.S. forces who answered to McChrystal under the separate Operation Enduring Freedom mandate.

96. Capt. Mark Moretti, interview with author.

97. 4th Brigade Combat Team, 4th Infantry Division, "Towards the Tipping Point," draft paper, July 22, 2009; Brig. Gen. Randy George and Dante Paradiso, interviews with author.

98. "For the past three years," the paper asserted, for example, "coalition forces in N2KL have focused on fixing and destroying enemy forces in remote areas." It was true that all three battalions before 2-12 had spent significant energy and resources targeting enemy leaders and sanctuaries, but they had had to, and it hadn't been their singular focus, not even under Brett Jenkinson (from whose personal focus on targeting insurgent commanders the paper might have been generalizing).

99. The soldiers sent to Barg-e Matal, coincidentally, were those of Attack Company, 1-32 Infantry, many of them Korengal veterans from Jim McKnight's time and now led by Mike Harrison.

100. Moretti, George, Pearl, Ukiah Senti, Ryan Wempe, and Owen, interviews with author. Colonel Randy George's 4th Brigade, 4th Infantry Division deployed to northeastern Afghanistan in June 2009, having previously "socialized" the idea of coming out of the Korengal and Landay Sin bases with the 82nd Airborne Division headquarters that deployed to Bagram shortly ahead of them, and took the reins from 3rd Brigade, 1st Infantry Division on June 26. At that point, according to supporting documents declassified with the military investigation into the October 3, 2009, battle of COP Keating in the Landay Sin (which killed eight soldiers from 2-12 Infantry's sister cavalry squadron), 4th Brigade's plan was to close both COP Keating and nearby COP Lowell by the end of September, if not earlier, followed by the KOP and its satellites in October.

    General Stanley McChrystal had taken command of ISAF in mid-June, and he mentioned the possibility of coming out of the Korengal in one of his first media interviews thereafter, which 4th Brigade took to be an encouraging sign. When 4th Brigade briefed McChrystal on its pullout concept shortly after his mid-July visit to the KOP, however, his response was lukewarm; according to the battalion operations officer (later executive officer) Ukiah Senti, the general suggested even then that coming out of the Korengal might have to wait until the end of 4th Brigade's deployment.

    What definitively precluded the possibility of a summer pullout from the Landay Sin outposts and a fall pullout from the Korengal was the series of events that occurred next. First, on June 30, Private First Class Bowe Bergdahl walked off his outpost in a sister brigade's area of operations in southeastern Afghanistan, initiating a weeks-long search effort that drew heavily on Bagram- and Jalalabad-based Chinooks (to insert units involved in the search on air-assault missions), Predator and Reaper drones and various manned spy planes, and JSOC strike forces and their transport and reconnaissance assets, including Task Force East.

Then, on July 7, reports reached U.S. troops that the Afghan police contingent in Barg-e Matal was in danger of collapse under Taliban pressure. 4th Brigade was prepared to ignore these reports, but at ISAF headquarters McChrystal received what he called in his memoir *My Share of the Task* a "passionate request" from Nuristan's governor (himself a Barg-e Matal native) and Minister of the Interior Hanif Atmar to send American troops to retake the Barg-e Matal district center. (Why exactly McChrystal granted this request at a time when his own handpicked campaign planners were advising getting out of remote areas like Nuristan remains one of the war's mysteries; McChrystal explains his decision in *My Share of the Task* only by noting that he had visited Barg-e Matal with a group of SEALs in December 2003, during Winter Strike, and that he "remembered the faces of children who'd gathered to investigate the strangers" and the picturesque mountains.)

Despite 4th Brigade's objections, Mike Harrison and 1-32 Infantry's Attack Company were uprooted from southern Kunar and sent on a long-range air-assault mission to reinforce Barg-e Matal, Operation Dragon Fire, which had no end date attached. "During July CJTF [division] priorities shifted, largely driven by the intensity of operations in support of ANSF [Afghan forces] in the Barg-e Matal area and the personnel recovery efforts to find missing PFC Bergdahl," the COP Keating investigation specifies. The U.S. presence in the district wound up being maintained through mid-September, creating a massive drain on helicopter transport and aerial surveillance resources, and in the meantime all U.S. units in the country were also tasked with helping provide security for the August presidential elections that reelected the incumbent president, Karzai.

SEAL Team 6 operators from one of the Omega teams attached to the CIA accompanied Attack Company to Barg-e Matal and would visit again as operations to "Barg" became something of an annual pilgrimage. That hinted at the district's significance in counterterrorism operations, probably related to the persistent presence of Lashkar-e-Taiba operatives there, as did the deployment of case officers from the CIA's Asadabad and Falcon Base teams.

For a more detailed description of the Barg-e Matal episode and its role in the dance of conflicting priorities that delayed the various bases' closure, and for the October 3, 2009, battle in the Landay Sin that resulted from the delays, see Jake Tapper's account of the life and death of COP Keating, *Outpost*.

101. Moretti, interview; narrative accompanying the award of the Silver Star to Spc. Robert Donevski.
102. Moretti, interview; Greg Jaffe, "Honoring the Service of Soldiers Who Commit Suicide," *Washington Post*, July 18, 2010.
103. Kearney and George, interviews.

104. Cavoli, interview.
105. Ibid. Cavoli drew a parallel to a phenomenon described in T. R. Fehrenbach's classic book on the U.S. Army's early failings in Korea, *This Kind of War: A Study in Unpreparedness* (New York: Macmillan, 1963). "Korea is a land cut by multiple hills and valleys, lacking roads. It is no terrain for a mechanized army," Fehrenbach wrote. "But American troops, physically unhardened for foot marches, were road-bound. They defended on roads, attacked on roads, retreated on roads. If their vehicles couldn't go, they did not go either." North Korean troops, meanwhile, scurried all over the hills, where American units could not bother them and American airpower didn't.
106. Ostlund, interview and correspondence.
107. T.W., interview.
108. Paradoxically, when I asked two dozen Pech veterans from different units to estimate their typical individual loads for mountain patrols, the troops issued the new lightweight gear reported some of the heaviest weights: eighty to ninety pounds was a common answer among 4/4 ID's Pech veterans, while veterans of The Rock were more likely to report loads of sixty to eighty pounds. (In both cases, radiomen, machine gunners, mortarmen, and medics carried heavier loads.) Possibly the new lightweight equipment encouraged leaders to go heavier on batteries.
109. Pearl, interview.
110. T.W., interview.
111. Ostlund, interview and correspondence.
112. Pearl, interview.
113. These soldiers were Pfc. Steven Drees, Sgt. Matthew Ingram, Spc. Gregory Missman, and Sgt. Youvert Loney.
114. T.W., interview.
115. The soldiers 1-26 Infantry and its attached engineer route-clearance units lost were: Staff Sgt. Kristopher Rodgers, Spc. Marques Knight, Pfc. Michael Dinterman, Staff Sgt. Nathan Cox, Pfc. Joseph Gonzales, Sgt. John Penich, Sgt. Ezra Dawson, and Pfc. Richard Dewater, all killed in the Korengal; Staff Sgt. David Paquet, who died of natural causes; Staff Sgt. Brandon Farley, killed near Asmar in eastern Kunar; and Sgt. Douglas Bull, 2nd Lt. Michael Girdano, Spc. David Badie, Spc. William Mulvihill, Pvt. Jair Garcia, Sgt. Preston Medley, Spc. Stephen Fortunato, and Spc. Corey Bertrand, all killed in the Chowkay valley south of the Pech.
116. Jenkinson, interview.
117. Ibid.

CHAPTER 10: THE CUL-DE-SAC, 2010

1. This scene is based on notes of my July–August 2010 visit to the Pech, during which I spent time at FOB Blessing and COP Michigan, accompanied Bushmaster Company's Third Platoon, Coldsteel Company's Third Platoon, and Maddog Company's First Platoon on patrols, and interviewed various Bulldog battalion leaders, including Lt. Col. Joe Ryan, Maj. Timo-

thy Lindsay, Command Sgt. Maj. Antoine Cannon, Capt. Chris Muller, Capt. Jon Peterson, Capt. Dakota Steedsman, 1st Sgt. William Stanton, and 1st Sgt. George Ehlschide.

2. Capt. Adam Alexander, interview with author.
3. Nazir, interview.
4. Maj. Gen. Richard Clarke, interview with author.
5. Ryan, interview.
6. The Bulldog battalion had barely arrived at its outposts when the resource suck that had helped delay the Korengal closure a year earlier was repeated: word came down from Kabul that President Karzai wanted U.S. troops to get on the ground in the remotest of Nuristan's far-flung district centers, Barg-e Matal. The result was the immediate diversion of helicopters and surveillance aircraft—which was compounded a few weeks later when Ryan's best company was stripped away and sent to the battalion in eastern Kunar for a mission there. As during the long 2009 Barg-e Matal adventure, many senior commanders tasked with overseeing the May–July 2010 operations had little idea what logic underpinned them. When I asked the division commander in the east, Major General John Campbell, about the Barg-e Matal mission in his office at Bagram that summer, he made no effort to hide his own confusion about the mission to which he had been ordered to commit troops and helicopters, telling me, "I'm going back to [corps commander] General Rod and General Petraeus saying 'Why are we up here?'"

   Matt Sherman, a senior civilian adviser at ISAF headquarters who was involved in the Barg-e Matal affair, explained to me later that he thought both McChrystal (in 2009) and Petraeus (in 2010) felt compelled to accede to Hamid Karzai when he personally requested American help, even though doing so went against their stated priorities of getting out of remote, low-density districts. In the 2010 case, he believed that Karzai had played up the presence of an al-Qaida cell in Barg-e Matal, knowing that the terrorist group was like a magnet for American commanders. "Petraeus got played to send units up there," said Sherman, who spent ten days in Barg-e Matal as Petraeus's eyes and ears. "There was genuinely a small al-Qaida cell up there, and Karzai played that card and Petraeus fell for it hook, line, and sinker. . . . What Karzai did repeatedly, anytime there was a new COMISAF, was play the Barg-e Matal card."

   The CIA station chief fell prey to the same manipulation by Karzai over Barg-e Matal, added Ron Moeller. "The small al-Qaida presence Matt refers to didn't really mean much in the larger scheme of things, and most senior ANA officers agreed with us in private, yet we repeatedly allowed ourselves and our finite resources to be directed to this zero-impact area," he told me.

7. Maj. Kevin Hutcheson, interview with author.
8. The life and death of Chief Brown are chronicled in Eric Blehm, *Fearless: The Undaunted Courage and Ultimate Sacrifice of Navy SEAL Team SIX Op-*

erator Adam Brown (Colorado Springs: WaterBrook Press, 2012). The raid, one of several Task Force East conducted in support of 2-12 Infantry's operations in Chapa Dara in the late winter of 2010, involved a grueling trek from an insertion site near the village of Gulsalak to a compound in the Digal valley, where the SEALs succeeded in killing their target, Gul Zaman.

9. Peterson, interview.

10. Peterson, Stanton, Lindsay, and Karl Beilby, interviews with author.

11. Ryan, interview.

12. Matthew Rosenberg, "U.S. Forces Leave Afghan 'Valley of Death,'" *Wall Street Journal,* April 15, 2010.

13. Lt. Col. Joseph Ryan and Capt. Robert "Bo" Reynolds, interview by Ryan Wadle, Combat Studies Institute, March 21, 2012.

14. Antonio Giustozzi, *The Army of Afghanistan: A Political History of a Fragile Institution* (London: Hurst, 2015), 151, 159–60.

15. For a litany of the common complaints of American troops about their counterparts' laziness, cowardice, drug abuse, and general unsoldierliness, see Jeffrey Bordin, "A Crisis of Trust and Cultural Incompatibility: A Red Team Study of Mutual Perceptions of Afghan National Security Force Personnel and U.S. Soldiers in Understanding and Mitigating the Phenomena of ANSF-Committed Fratricide-Murders," N2KL Red Team report, May 12, 2011, 63–70.

16. Farshad and an interpreter who asked to be identified only as Arian, interviews; Bordin, "Crisis of Trust and Cultural Incompatibility," 34–35.

17. Matt O'Donnell, Col. Patrick Byron, Maj. Jonathan Bossie, Capt. Brian Buland, John Farris, Staff Sgt. Luis Repreza, and Sgt. Rodrigo Roman, interviews with author.

18. Roman, interview.

19. Capt. Cale Genenbacher, interview with author.

20. Ryan, interview.

21. Ryan and Genenbacher, interviews.

22. Genenbacher, interview.

23. Beilby, interview.

24. Ryan, Peterson, Beilby, Genenbacher, and Stanton, interviews.

25. Pruden, interview.

26. Ryan, interview.

27. Ibid.

28. Farshad, interview; former U.S. government official, interview with author. See 2-12 Infantry, "TF Lethal Civil Affairs Bulk Funds," Dec. 2009, projects.propublica.org/cerp/projects/6E0693E2-A5B8-7E49-B56594F1 F9AA1D8A, for records of $25,000 of U.S. Commander's Emergency Response Program money disbursed to Rahman's office shortly before he was removed from his post.

29. Shahzada Shahid, interview.

30. Ryan, interview.

31. It is not clear exactly when Dawran formally pledged allegiance to the

Taliban, but one of his close associates, the Nangalam native Haji Hayatul-lah Ghulam Mohammad, did so in January 2010, while Dawran was recovering from wounds.

32. 4th BCT, 4th ID, "TF Mountain Warrior Graphic Intelligence Summary (GRINTSUM) 200500DSEPTEMBER2009-210500DSEPTEMBER 2009," Sept. 21, 2009; ISAF, Joint Prioritized Effects List, Aug. 2010. The declassified 4/4 ID intelligence summary places Objective Viking (Dawran) atop its list of "active objectives" in the Pech, that is, targeted individuals on whom usable intelligence was being collected. (Below him on this short list were Objectives Burnside, Kilty, Copycat, Wrigley, Mowgli, and Hotdate, of whom Objective Wrigley would be killed three weeks later in the Task Force East raid described by the SEAL Team 6 operator Matt Bissonnette in *No Easy Day*.) On ISAF's much more comprehensive JPEL list, as of August 2010, Dawran was one of thirty-five category-three targets in Kunar; the only category-two targets were Haji Matin (a.k.a. Objective Ronin) and someone known as Objective Flathead, and the only category-one target was a Korengali dubbed Objective Kalispell, possibly Mawlawi Abdul Rahim, the former *shura* chief who had become the Taliban's shadow governor for Kunar.

33. This description of Refsdal's stay with Dawran in October 2009 is based on an interview with Refsdal and on his documentary *Taliban: Behind the Masks* (Journeyman Pictures, 2010), www.youtube.com/watch?v=5OI8Y0jjM0k&app=desktop.

34. As the fighters packed up the DShK's key pieces and ammunition afterward, they joked and laughed. "The patrol has been stopped, a vehicle is destroyed, and the people inside have been sent to hell," Dawran enthused into his walkie-talkie. He was exaggerating. U.S. records corroborate the attack but indicate none of the MRAPs were seriously damaged and no one inside them was hurt.

35. Refsdal, interview.

36. Refsdal, *Taliban: Behind the Masks*.

37. This account of the November 26, 2009, HIMARS rocket attack in the Lagham valley is based on interviews with several officers from 4th BCT, 4th ID who were involved in its planning and execution, including Pearl, Owen, Wempe, and Ted Preister.

38. In a press release a month after the strike, ISAF's Regional Command East erroneously described Dawran as having died as a result of the November 26 attack, as some informants initially reported he had (Bagram Media Center, "Key Militants Out of Action," press release, Jan. 6, 2010, www.dvidshub.net/news/43487/key-militants-out-action). Dawran was not the only insurgent commander whose death in Kunar ISAF was announced prematurely. At the time of my 2010 visit, the Taliban shadow governor for the Pech's Watapur district was a militant named Nur Akbar, whom ISAF had erroneously declared dead the previous December after a JSOC-directed air strike targeted him near Tsangar.

39. Refsdal, interview.

40. 1-327 Infantry, "Target Summaries."
41. In January 2010, while Dawran was recovering, the Salafi insurgent group under whose banner he had been fighting, a descendant of the old Jamaat mujahidin party called Jamaat al-Dawa ila al-Sunna, formally merged with the Taliban by pledging allegiance to Mullah Mohammad Omar, the Taliban's Pakistan-based emir. See Thomas Ruttig, "On Kunar's Salafi Insurgents," Afghanistan Analysts Network, Jan. 14, 2010, www.afghanistan -analysts.org/on-kunars-salafi-insurgents/.
42. Ryan, interview; 1-327 Infantry, "Target Summaries."
43. Ryan, interview.
44. 1-327 Infantry, "TF Bulldog Historical Report."
45. ISAF issued a press release after the Rangers' mission in Shamun, typical of those released after successful JSOC night raids, that described its results but identified the strike force only as "an Afghan and coalition security force" (ISAF Joint Command, "ISAF Confirms Jama'at ul Dawa al-Qu'ran Commander," press release, Aug. 20, 2010, www.dvidshub.net/news /54895/update-isaf-confirms-jamaat-ul-dawa-al-quran-commander). The Army later released an account of the mission in the form of the narrative accompanying the award of the Silver Star to the squad leader Staff Sergeant Trevor Tow, however, and a Ranger NCO on the mission, Grant McGarry, described it in more detail in an independently published 2016 book, *A Night in the Pech Valley: A Memoir of a Member of the 75th Ranger Regiment in the Global War on Terrorism*, 247–304.
46. Ryan, interview.
47. The effectiveness of operations against insurgent leaders is the subject of lively and inconclusive debate both in the military and intelligence communities and in academia. A 2009 CIA assessment drawing on various case studies (Central Intelligence Agency, "Best Practices in Counterinsurgency: Making High-Value Targeting Operations an Effective Counterinsurgency Tool," July 7, 2009) reached several of the same conclusions as various scholarly articles that have tackled the issue in recent years: "high-value targeting" operations against insurgent leaders could erode and weaken insurgent groups in the short term, especially if they were carefully integrated into a broader counterinsurgency strategy, but they could also inadvertently increase local support for insurgents or radicalize surviving insurgent leaders, and the operations' effectiveness depended heavily on local conditions that varied from conflict to conflict and from region to region within a conflict. In Afghanistan, the CIA assessment warned, "the Taliban has a high overall ability to replace lost leaders, a centralized but flexible command and control [structure] overlaid with egalitarian Pashtun structures, and good succession planning and bench strength, especially at the middle levels."

A 2012 report by the intelligence staff of the Bagram JSOC task force based on interrogations of some four thousand detainees would reach similar conclusions, reporting, "When a Taliban district commander is captured or killed, he is replaced within hours by his deputy. If ISAF can quickly remove the deputy, a senior commander from the district typically takes his place and a new deputy must be chosen. . . . When that replacement commander is killed or captured, insurgent operations in the area often cease, at least temporarily, in order to reshuffle the chain of command and resolve any perceived operational security issues." Only through sustained targeting, successfully killing or capturing a leader, his replacement, *his* replacement, and so on in quick succession, especially "in the spring or early summer, at the beginning of the fighting season," could JSOC "disable a Taliban district command for weeks or months" (Task Force 3-10, "State of the Taliban," Jan. 6, 2012).

Operations in the Pech bore out these cautionary assessments even though the valley, with its mix of Pashtun, Nuristani, Pashai, and foreign fighters, many of them linked to other groups like Hizb and Jamaat, was not a typical Taliban operating area. When an air strike killed an al-Qaida commander named Qari Masiullah in the Watapur in December 2009, for instance (according to the unclassified "Target Summaries" document that 1-327's intelligence shop provided me with during my visit), a higher-ranking al-Qaida figure based across the Pakistani border, Abu Hafs al-Najdi, had dispatched a temporary replacement from Bajaur almost as soon as the dead man was in the ground, followed a few weeks later by a more permanent successor named Falik Naz. Al-Qaida's work training local fighters in the Watapur had hardly missed a beat.

48. 1-327 Infantry, "Target Summaries."
49. Refsdal, interview.
50. Ryan, interview.
51. Refsdal, interview.
52. Cavoli and Glenn, interviews.
53. Mark Zambarda, interview with author; Maj. Louis Gianoulakis, interview with Angie Slattery, Operational Leadership Experiences Project, Oct. 12, 2010.
54. Cheek, interview; another 1-26 Infantry source, interview with author.
55. 2-12 Infantry incident report, "(Non-combat Event) Demonstration RPT TF Lethal Warrior: 0 INJ/DAM," Dec. 5, 2009.
56. Nazir, interview.
57. Salinas, interview.
58. United Nations Assistance Mission in Afghanistan, "Afghanistan Annual Report 2010: Protection of Civilians in Armed Conflict," March 2011, unama.unmissions.org/sites/default/files/engi_version_of_poc_annual_report_2011.pdf, 14.
59. Kolenda et al., *Strategic Costs of Civilian Harm,* 5.
60. Jonathan Springer and Ryan, interviews with author.
61. CW3 (Ret.) Victor Lezama, CW2 Alek Jadkowski, and Lt. Col. Thomas von Eschenbach, interviews with author.
62. Springer, interview.
63. Ryan, interview.

64. Ryan, Pruden, Peterson, Steedsman, and Lincoln Kaffenberger, interviews with author; 1-327 Infantry, "TF Bulldog Historical Report," Feb. 19, 2011.
65. Ryan and Nazir, interviews.
66. Ryan, interview.

CHAPTER 11: REALIGNMENT, 2010–2011

1. Brig. Gen. Andrew Poppas, interview with author.
2. Gen. (Ret.) John Campbell, interview with author.
3. Ryan and Poppas, interviews. The purpose of Operation Bulldog Bite "was to kill the enemy," Ryan later told an Army historian simply. "We were going to go where the enemy was, to engage with and destroy the enemy."
4. Col. Michele Bredenkamp and Douglas Ollivant, interviews with author.
5. Ryan, interview.
6. Ryan, Peterson, Pruden, von Eschenbach, Chris Zeitz, Sgt. Daniel Sabedra, and a former 20th Special Forces Group officer, interviews with author; 1-327 Infantry, "TF Bulldog Historical Report."
7. Ryan, interview.
8. Maj. Nick Bilotta, interview with author.
9. Gambir, Katar, and a smaller village across a ravine from Gambir, Dewuz, were collectively known to locals as the Tregam, a term the U.S. military did not use. On U.S. military maps, Katar was marked as Katar Darya-ye and Dewuz as Zawardiwuz, if they were marked at all, and a portion of Gambir was sometimes separately marked as Sero Kalay.
10. When the East India Company botanist William Griffith hiked up the Watapur in 1840, he reported meeting Kafirs who carried bows and arrows and wore skins and silver jewelry (Griffith, *Journals of Travels,* 458–60). For Gambir's reputation as a place whose silversmiths had magical powers, see Max Klimburg, *The Kafirs of the Hindu-Kush: Art and Society of the Waigal and Ashkun Kafirs* (Stuttgart: Steiner, 1999), 71. Fayz Muhammad Katib Hazarah's multivolume *History of Afghanistan* notes raids back and forth between Gambir and Katar, on the one hand, and nearby Muslim settlements, on the other, in 1884, 1885, and 1886, with the towns apparently subjugated by 1893, a few years ahead of the Waygal, though pockets of Kafir holdouts would cause trouble for government troops for several years to come (Katib Hazarah, *Reign of Amir 'Abd al-Rahman Khan,* 111, 200–205, 257–58, 1051).
11. Cavoli, Ostlund, and Himes, interviews.
12. Former members of 1st Ranger Battalion's Charlie Company describe venturing up the Watapur road (which they knew only as Route Orange) in pickup trucks during the fall of 2002 and again during 2003's Operation Winter Strike, and encountering an IED on the road during one of the two missions. In October 2005, two companies of the Hawaii-based 2/3 Marine battalion landed by helicopter on either side of the valley in Operation Pil, one of the big air assaults that followed Operation Red Wings; veterans of

the mission remember uneventful visits to Tsangar and Gambir, with the only action being some artillery fire based on suspicious traffic picked up by an attached signals intelligence team.

13. Evans, Stanton, McPadden, Frketic, Bilotta, Reynolds, Salinas, Capt. Brandon Kennedy, Capt. Jason LeVay, Capt. Steve Benedetti, Maj. Shaun Conlin, Capt. Florent Groberg, and Capt. Tom Goodman, interviews with author. In 2-503 Infantry's time, the "red line," where patrols could reliably expect to get in a firefight, was the village of Qowru, a little more than three miles up the valley, where the Asadabad PRT was financing the construction of a medical clinic. As subsequent companies rotated through Honaker-Miracle, militants from Tsangar destroyed the clinic, and the red line crept south: first from Qowru down to the 71 grid line on U.S. maps, and then by early 2010 a kilometer farther south to the 70 grid line outside Katar Kala, the first large village on the valley floor. The day-to-day reports on U.S. missions in Kunar from 2009 and 2010 show frequent MRAP breakdowns in the Watapur, usually resulting in long firefights while soldiers waited for their stranded trucks to be repaired or towed out of the valley: a broken MRAP axle prolonged a particularly intense firefight around Katar Kala by hours on June 17, 2009, for example, and less than a month later, on July 7, an MRAP breakdown forced a patrol to stay in the valley overnight. "I was more stressed out by the idea of having to drive an MRAP on the Watapur road than I ever was in any firefight," said one former platoon leader involved in that incident, Captain Antonio Salinas.

14. Katib Hazarah, *Reign of Amir 'Abd al-Rahman Khan,* 1623. The upper Watapur valley was once home to several languages besides Pashto, according to scholars like Richard Strand who have studied the languages of Kunar and Nuristan: not just the relative of Waygali spoken around Gambir (sometimes called Gambiri or Tregami), but also Watapuri and Katar Kala'i, which were spoken in towns on the valley floor well into the twentieth century, Strand told me, and were likely remnants of a larger group of languages once spoken more widely in the Pech.

15. Stanton, Conlin, and Pearl, interviews. Nur Akbar was suspected killed during an hours-long battle between Kiowa helicopter pilots and insurgent DShK gunners in October 2009, and his death was actually announced by ISAF two months later after a series of JSOC-directed air strikes around Tsangar. In both cases he survived.

One officer who had driven up to Tsangar in pickup trucks as a member of the Chosin battalion was amazed, when he returned to Afghanistan in 2009 as a Ranger platoon leader, to find that the village had become a hard target; the SEALs he answered to at JSOC's Task Force East would go there only if they had rock-solid intelligence and support from his Rangers and at least one AC-130 gunship.

16. Ostlund, CENTCOM testimony; Wanat Article 15-6 investigation report.

17. Frketic, interview.

18. As of the summer of 2010, according to 1-327 Infantry's "Target Summaries" packet, the main al-Qaida figure in the Watapur was an operative of

unknown nationality named Ayoub, whom the Bajaur-based Saudi al-Qaida commander Abu Hafs al-Najdi had dispatched from Pakistan over the winter to replace Qari Masiullah after he was killed in a December 2009 air strike. Other al-Qaida visitors to the Watapur included Falik Naz, whom Abu Hafs had sent as a temporary replacement for Masiullah before Ayoub arrived, and Abu Hafs himself, who was occasionally reported to pass through the valley during circulations through different militant safe havens in Kunar, like Abu Ikhlas.

19. Miakhel and Mohammad Salih, interviews; Klimburg, *Kafirs of the Hindu Kush*, 38. During the jihad, Gambir and the upper Waygal were stops on a much longer and more heavily trafficked route that took men and arms from Bajaur all the way to the strategic Panjshir valley north of Kabul.

20. Stanton, Mayfield, Frketic, Pickler, and Bilotta, interviews.

21. Joseph Holliday, interview with author.

22. Alexander, Beilby, Kaffenberger, and Capt. David Broyles, interviews with author. According to Adam Alexander, who conducted the battalion's Article 15-6 investigation into the circumstances surrounding the deaths of its soldiers in the Watapur afterward, there were intelligence reports that insurgent leaders in Tsangar knew roughly when Abu Company was coming and told their subordinates to stay awake and near their walkie-talkies on the night of November 11–12.

23. Broyles, interview.

24. This account of Abu Company's November 12–16, 2010, mission in the Watapur, Bulldog Bite 2C East, is based on interviews with Ryan, Reynolds, Broyles, Beilby, Sabedra, Kaffenberger, Alexander, Sgt. 1st Class Ryan Krause, Staff Sgt. Sean Outman, Chief Warrant Officer 3 Aaron Simbro; the Combat Studies Institute interview with Reynolds and Ryan; notes and photos supplied by 1-327 Infantry veterans; 1-327 Infantry, "TF Bulldog Historical Report"; the citation and narrative for the posthumous award of the Silver Star to Spc. Jesse Snow; Greg Jaffe, "Fighting to Get out of the Way," *Washington Post*, Dec. 27, 2010; Jimmy Settle, *Never Quit: From Alaskan Wilderness Rescues to Afghanistan Firefights as an Elite Special Ops PJ* (New York: St. Martin's Press, 2017), 269–97; and two articles by Mike Dunham, "Alaska Squadron Rescues Troops in Fierce Battle," *Anchorage Daily News*, Aug. 20, 2011, and "The Teeth of Bulldog Bite," *Air Force Magazine*, Nov. 2011.

25. Reynolds, interview.

26. Simbro, interview.

27. Reynolds, Broyles, Krause, and Outman, interviews; Dunham, "Alaska Squadron Rescues Troops in Fierce Battle"; Dunham, "Teeth of Bulldog Bite"; Settle, *Never Quit*, 269–70.

28. Jaffe, "Fighting to Get out of the Way."

29. Reynolds, Broyles, Outman, and Krause, interviews.

30. Beilby, interview.

31. Reynolds, Broyles, Beilby, and Krause, interviews. This might have been the training site an al-Qaida operative named Ayoub had reportedly been

sent from Bajaur to establish somewhere in the upper Watapur over the winter.

32. Reynolds, interview.
33. Alexander and Beilby, interviews.
34. Alexander and Ryan, interviews.
35. Beilby, interview.
36. Outman, interview.
37. Outman and Beilby, interviews; Snow citation and narrative.
38. Beilby, interview.
39. Dunham, "Alaska Squadron Rescues Troops in Fierce Battle"; Dunham, "Teeth of Bulldog Bite"; Settle, *Never Quit,* 179–96. In their Voice of Jihad update for November 14, the Taliban claimed they had shot down a helicopter near Katar and killed nine Americans.
40. Outman and Beilby, interviews.
41. Broyles, interview; Jaffe, "Fighting to Get out of the Way."
42. Ryan, Kaffenberger, and Alexander, interviews.
43. Poppas and Ryan, interviews.
44. Ryan, Poppas, and special operations sources, interviews. Thomas led the Bagram headquarters of JSOC's big multitheater counterterrorism headquarters, known at the time as Task Force 5-35, while Colonel Chris Vanek of the Rangers led Task Force 3-10, the countrywide tactical headquarters to which the SEALs' Task Force East, the Rangers' Task Force South and Task Force Central, Delta Force's Task Force North, and Team Darby all answered.
45. Poppas and Ryan, interviews.
46. Team Darby was built around 1st Ranger Battalion's Charlie Company— the same company that had hiked into both the Korengal and the Watapur during Winter Strike. The company moved from Iraq to Afghanistan in the fall of 2010 as part of a "Ranger surge" that ISAF's commander, Petraeus, requested JSOC implement to increase its pace of night raids in support of conventional forces. This account of Team Darby's November 16, 2010, Gambir mission is based on interviews with Capt. Craig Nelson, Luis Aponte, and several Team Darby Rangers who asked to remain anonymous; the portion of Nelson's personal experience monograph published in *The Maneuver Force in Battle, 2005–2012,* ed. Joanie Horton (Fort Benning, Ga.: Maneuver Center of Excellence, 2015), 166–70; and the Silver Star citations and narratives for Staff Sgts. Dylan Maynard and Todd Mark.
47. Marc Pape, interview with author.
48. Aponte, interview.
49. Nelson, interview.
50. Ranger source, interview with author.
51. Nelson and Ryan, interviews.
52. These details come from a script of the memorial ceremony prepared by Chaplain Ted Randall, including the prepared remarks of the soldiers who spoke about each of the Bulldog troopers killed; Staff Sgt. Mark Burrell,

"TF Bulldog Remembers 6 Fallen Comrades," Regional Command East news release, Nov. 21, 2010, www.dvidshub.net/news/60686/tf-bulldog -remembers-6-fallen-comrades; and Jaffe, "Fighting to Get out of the Way."

The Rangers of Team Darby memorialized Kevin Pape separately at their base, and his picture joined the long line of photographs of fallen task force members in the hallway leading into JSOC's headquarters at Bagram. Shortly after the photo was hung, a group of congressmen stopped by during a visit to Bagram, among them Mike Pence, the future vice president, whose district in Indiana was just north of Pape's hometown. "I snapped a quick photograph of the wall of tribute for his family and marveled at the hushed tone of respect from senior officers as they described how he fought and how he died," Pence wrote afterward in a Facebook post.

53. Reynolds and Broyles, interviews.
54. Ryan, interview; Ryan and Reynolds, Combat Studies Institute interview.
55. Staff Sgt. Mark Burrell, "'Bulldog Bite' Clears Pech River Valley," Task Force Bastogne press release, Nov. 30, 2010.
56. 1-327 unit historical report. Local estimates were lower, with Kunar's governor, Fazlullah Wahidi, telling *Pajhwok Afghan News* that seventy-five militants had been killed, including some low-level commanders he identified and an unspecified number of Arabs. For their part, the Taliban told *Pajhwok*'s reporter that only four of their men had died. Khal Wali Salarzai, "75 Militants Killed in Kunar Offensive: Governor," *Pajhwok Afghan News,* Nov. 8, 2010, archive.pajhwok.com/en/2010/11/18/75-militants-killed -kunar-offensive-governor.
57. Springer, interview.
58. Ibid.
59. Ryan and Peterson, interviews.
60. 1-327 Infantry, "Pech Realignment Discussion Points," n.d.
61. Ryan and Springer, interviews.
62. Ryan, interview.
63. Nicholson and Stanton, interviews.
64. Nicholson, interview.
65. Ibid.
66. Lindsay and Lt. Col. Thomas Feltey, interviews with author.
67. Lindsay and Feltey, interviews.
68. Ostlund and Sterling, interviews.
69. Lindsay and Feltey, interviews.
70. Special operations source, interview with author.
71. Ryan, interview.
72. The battalion intelligence officer Captain Lincoln Kaffenberger wrote in his journal on February 22, a week after the order, that whether the ANA would stay was "still up in the air."
73. Ryan and Poppas, interviews.
74. Feltey, interview.
75. Nicholson, interview.

76. Petraeus, interview.

77. Lt. Col. Rahmdel Haidarzai, interview with author.

78. Ryan, interview.

79. Genenbacher, interview with author.

80. Elliott Woods, "The Kunar Nine," *Prairie Schooner* 87, no. 4 (2013): 13–28; Alissa Rubin and Sangar Rahimi, "Nine Afghan Boys Collecting Firewood Killed by NATO Helicopters," *New York Times,* March 2, 2011; Combined Joint Task Force 101, "AR 15-6 Investigation into an [redacted] Engagement near FOB Blessing, Darah-ye Pech District, Konar Province, on 1 March 2011, That Allegedly Resulted in the Death of Nine Civilians."

81. Quoted in summary of March 3, 2011, meeting proceedings included in supporting materials of CJTF-101 Article 15-6 investigation.

82. Rahmdel, interview.

83. Capt. Jonathan Springer, "ANA Assumes Responsibility of FOB Blessing," Regional Command East news release, March 10, 2011.

84. Springer, interview.

85. Burhan and Capt. Tim Leone, interviews with author.

86. Sergio Diaz, interview with author.

87. Genenbacher, interview.

88. Diaz, interview.

89. Ryan, interview.

90. Capt. Duncan Walker and Brett Barrett, interviews with author.

91. Barrett, interview.

CHAPTER 12: REDUX, 2011

1. Rahmdel, interview; Michael Phillips, "Afghan Base Tests U.S. Exit Plans," *Wall Street Journal,* Nov. 8, 2011.

2. Rahmdel, interview.

3. Ibid.

4. Ibid.

5. Sgt. Maj. Mohammad Afzal Afzali, interview with author.

6. Genenbacher, interview.

7. Ostlund, interview.

8. Beeson, 305th MHD interview.

9. Frketic, interview.

10. Ryan, Genenbacher, Peterson, and Reynolds, interviews.

11. Ryan, interview.

12. Mahboob, interview.

13. 1st Lt. Trey Van Wyhe, interview with author.

14. "Safi Tribe's Letter of Resolution, Manogai District," dated 23 Kab 1389 (March 14, 2011).

15. Mahboob, Rahmdel, Burhan, and Farshad, interviews; Phillips, "Afghan Base Tests U.S. Exit Plans." What Zulfiqar said at the Nangalam *shura* is from a relative of Farshad's.

16. Bader, interview; Bader et al., "Illegal Timber Exploitation and Counterinsurgency Operations in Kunar Province of Afghanistan."

17. Khan Wali Salarzai, "Taliban Set Free 19 of 50 Abducted Policemen," *Pajhwok Afghan News,* March 28, 2011.

18. Anonymous, "Taliban Claim Launching of Administration in Pech Valley," *Frontier Post,* March 28, 2011.

19. Hashem Ahelbarra segment, Al Jazeera English, April 9, 2011, www.youtube.com/watch?v=NovWSBJUlCg.

20. Ryan, interview.

21. Burhan, interview.

22. Rahmdel, interview. Qadir Mohammad was known to American troops as Objective Dewey Beach. According to Hugh Miller, he had briefly been detained on suspicion of insurgent activity back in late 2009 or early 2010, then released.

23. Burhan, interview.

24. Mahboob and Afzal, interviews. Dawran alluded to this agreement in his March 27 statement, saying that he would not try to take Blessing so long as the ANA there stayed within the base's confines.

25. Ryan, interview.

26. Ryan, email newsletter, April 4, 2011.

27. Rahmdel, interview.

28. Ibid.

29. Simmons, interview.

30. Former 2–35 Infantry platoon leader, interview with author.

31. Crowe and four other 2–35 Infantry sources, interviews.

32. Crowe, interview.

33. Ryan and Tuley, interviews.

34. Former 2–35 Infantry staff officer, interview with author.

35. Tuley, Rahmdel, and Lt. Col. Glenn Kozelka, interviews with author.

36. O'Neill, *Operator,* 301.

37. German de la Roche, interview with author. White, twenty-two, was posthumously promoted to sergeant.

38. Van Wyhe, Capt. Tyler Martin, Capt. Colin Brodmerkel, Capt. David Hoffmaster, Capt. Patrick Kerins, and Staff Sgt. Travis Watson, interviews with author.

39. Tuley, Maj. Marcus Wright, and 1st Lt. A. W. Simmons, interviews with author.

40. Rahmdel, interview.

41. Tuley, interview.

42. Kozelka, interview.

43. Notes of meeting participant.

44. Burhan, interview.

45. Joe Laws, interview with author.

46. Kerins, interview.

47. Tuley, Wright, Kozelka, Maj. Jared Crain, Capt. Casey Brown, and Maj. Travis Rudge, interviews with author.

48. Tuley, Rahmdel, Wright, Kozelka, Crain, Burhan, Brown, Rudge, and Van Wyhe, interviews.

49. "Text of President Obama's Speech on Afghanistan," *New York Times,* June 22, 2011, www.nytimes.com/2011/06/23/world/asia/23obama -afghanistan-speech-text.html.

50. Watson, interview.

51. This description of Operation Hammer Down and its origins is based on my interviews with Tuley, Wright, Kozelka, Crain, Brown, Hughes, Hoffmaster, Brodmerkel, Van Wyhe, Kerins, Crowe, Simbro, Watson, Maj. Gen. Gary Volesky, Brig. Gen. Richard Kim, Col. Daniel Beatty, Col. David Pendall, Lt. Col. Christopher Downey, Lt. Col. Patrick Stich, Lt. Col. Christopher Rankin, Maj. Christopher Bluhm, Capt. Tyler Martin, 1st Lt. Chris Gaulin, Don Nicholas, Buddy Lee, and Daniel Lennox-Choate; photos and video shot by the combat cameraman Sgt. Elwyn Lovelace; 2-35 Infantry, "Operation Hammer Down Executive Summary," draft memo, n.d.; Anna Mulrine's five-part *Christian Science Monitor* series, published between September 6 and September 10, 2011; Tony Dokoupil and John Ryan, "In Afghanistan's 'Valley of Death,' a Medevac Team's Miracle Rescue," *Newsweek,* Nov. 5, 2012; Staff Sgt. John Wright, "Air Force Provides Critical Close Air Support During Operation Hammer Down II," 455th Air Expeditionary Wing news release, July 12, 2011; and Ryan Wadle, *Hammer Down: The Battle for the Watapur Valley, 2011* (Fort Leavenworth, Kans.: Combat Studies Institute Press, 2014).

52. Beatty, interview.

53. Brown, interview. "It just seemed arbitrary to us. It was the annual Watapur pilgrimage," echoed one of Richard Kim's own staff officers.

54. Wright, interview.

55. Ibid.

56. Crowe, interview.

57. Kim, interview.

58. Kim, Stich, Rankin, and Crain, interviews. "We were able to convince higher headquarters that there were multiple effects," said the brigade operations officer Stich. "That was what Colonel Kim believed—reasons, not just one reason."

   By some credible accounts, the Watapur had formed a stop on just such a major supply route from Pakistan to the Panjshir at the height of the anti-Soviet jihad, when the volume of men and matériel flowing across was far greater. In the spring of 2011, a "geospatial intelligence," or GEOINT, team at 1st Cavalry Division headquarters at Bagram was arguing, like Kim, that this route might still be in use. The division intelligence chief, Colonel David Pendall, who oversaw the GEOINT team, was among the many skeptics. "To be honest, it's probably easier to get in a cab and come across the border than it is to walk across that terrain," let alone smuggle heavy weapons or ammunition across it, Pendall told me, making the same argument that intelligence officers at both brigade and battalion levels did against the existence of this "line of drift," as it was termed.

59. Rankin, interview.

60. Crain, interview.

61. Tuley, interview. Tuley also repeated the rationale, which members of his staff derided, that Hammer Down was intended to relieve pressure not just on Honaker-Miracle but on Nangalam and Blessing. "It was really to create a condition where we can push back the insurgency and degrade it to such a manner that we can get back into Nangalam Base and start building the capacity and partnership," he told me.

62. Tuley, interview.

63. Crowe, interview.

64. Tuley, interview.

65. Tuley, Downey, Crowe, and Wright, interviews.

66. Tuley and Wright, interviews. Bastard Company's objective was the section of Gambir marked as Sero Kalay on military maps.

67. Hughes, Hoffmaster, Brodmerkel, Van Wyhe, Nicholas, and Watson, interviews.

68. Hughes and Hoffmaster, interviews; Wadle, *Hammer Down,* 47.

69. Brodmerkel, interview.

70. Combat camera video by Lovelace, June 25, 2011.

71. Hughes and Hoffmaster, interviews; Wadle, *Hammer Down,* 47–50.

72. Anna Mulrine, "Battle for Afghanistan's Gambir Jungle: A Race Against Daybreak," *Christian Science Monitor,* Sept. 9, 2011.

73. Tuley, interview. Team Havoc, also called the Focused Targeting Force, or FTF, consisted of a platoon from 2-35 Infantry, a platoon from sister battalion 2-27 Infantry, a signals intercept team, a mortar team, and the company headquarters element of 2-35 Infantry's headquarters and headquarters company.

74. Bluhm, interview.

75. Bluhm, Lee, Downey, and Lennox-Choate, interviews; Ed Darack, *The Final Mission of Extortion 17: Special Ops, Helicopter Support, SEAL Team Six, and the Deadliest Day of the U.S. War in Afghanistan* (Washington, D.C.: Smithsonian Books, 2017). As Darack describes in his comprehensive account of both the Honey-Eater crash and the lethal shoot-down, six weeks later in the Tangi valley in Wardak, of the Chinook that inherited the Extortion 17 call sign, the aviation unit conducted a "safety investigation" into the cause of the crash at HLZ Honey-Eater, but with inconclusive results, in large part because by that time the aircraft no longer existed and Honey-Eater was not accessible to investigators. The aviation task force commander, Lieutenant Colonel Christopher Downey, to whose 6-6 Cavalry squadron the National Guard crew of Extortion 17 was attached for Hammer Down, told me that he believed a tree strike or "power-management issue" associated with settling downward into its own rotor wash at such a high altitude with a heavy load was most likely, and had never heard that hostile fire was a possibility. The surviving pilot Buddy Lee (whose co-pilot Chief Warrant Officer Bryan Nichols would die in the second Extortion 17 crash six weeks later) told me he did not believe there was enough evidence to warrant ruling out any theory, including the hostile-fire theory that his trusted flight engineer espoused and that Darack concludes is most likely.

76. Bluhm and Lennox-Choate, interviews; Wadle, *Hammer Down,* 63–65.

77. Bluhm, Lennox-Choate, Rankin, Brown, and Rudge, interviews.

78. Tuley, interview.

79. Kerins, interview.

80. Simmons, interview.

81. Van Wyhe, Hoffmaster, and Brodmerkel, interviews; Wadle, *Hammer Down,* 74–76.

82. Simmons, interview.

83. Bluhm and Lennox-Choate, interviews.

84. 2-35 Infantry, "Hammer Down Executive Summary."

85. Tuley, interview.

86. Bluhm, interview.

87. Springer, interview.

88. Ryan, interview.

89. Kim, interview.

90. 2-35 Infantry, "Hammer Down Executive Summary." Governor Fazlullah Wahidi put the figure at 103, saying that Arabs were among the dead, while a Taliban spokesman claimed that only nineteen militants had died along with more than thirty Americans. Khan Wali Zalarzai, "103 Militants Killed in Kunar Offensive: Governor," *Pajhwok Afghan News,* July 2, 2011, www .pajhwok.com/en/2011/07/02/103-militants-killed-kunar-offensive -governor.

91. 2-35 Infantry, "Hammer Down Executive Summary"; Brown, Rudge, and Jones, interviews with author.

92. Bluhm and Lennox-Choate, interviews.

93. Hughes, Hoffmaster, Brodmerkel, Van Wyhe, and Watson, interviews.

94. Bastard Company soldier, interview with author.

95. Crowe, interview.

96. Tuley, interview.

97. Tuley and Brown, interviews.

98. Tuley, Beatty, Stich, and Lt. Col. Guillermo Guillen, interviews with author.

99. Van Wyhe, Bluhm, and Crowe, interviews.

100. Tuley, Bluhm, Hughes, Guillen, Jones, Capt. Ryan Occhiuzzo, and Capt. Adam McComb, interviews with author.

101. Derek Price, interview with author.

102. Price, interview.

103. Tuley, interview.

CHAPTER 13: AFGHANIZATION, 2011–2013

1. Crowe, interview.

2. Tuley, interview.

3. Van Wyhe, interview.

4. Simmons, interview.

5. Ibid.

6. Jenkinson and Hugh Miller, interviews with author.

7. Amir Shah, "Afghan Police: Taliban Overrun Remote District," Associated Press, March 29, 2011.

8. Volesky, Pendall, and Bluhm, interviews.

9. Volesky, interview. "We told them, 'You're going to Wanat,'" Volesky told me by way of acknowledging that division headquarters pushed the operation on brigade and battalion. "In Wanat, they were talking about how Americans could never come back up."

10. Wright, interview.

11. Stich, Hughes, Wright, and 2-35 Infantry sources, interviews. Officers from 2-35 were reluctant to say much about the visiting special operations team beyond that they were SEALs, but members of the scout platoon remembered them acknowledging that they were the Omega team.

12. Pendall, Rankin, Wright, and Rudge, interviews; 2-35 Infantry veteran, interview with author.

13. Kim, interview.

14. Stich and Brown, interviews. It was a subjective thing, but in the battalion intelligence officer Casey Brown's opinion, what this group of both local and outside militants was setting up in Want seemed like "a logistical node, not a planning headquarters"—a more westerly stop on the same Pakistan-Shigal-Watapur supply ratline that the Cacti battalion had targeted during Hammer Down.

15. Tuley, interview. Tuley thought the whole thing would have made more sense if part of the force could have driven up to Want and brought along a police force to leave behind, but the Waygal road was in no condition for that.

16. After the Keating battle, the Taliban distributed a propaganda video that showed Dost Mohammad sitting on an exercise bike at the outpost's abandoned gym while his men picked through other supplies left at the base. On JSOC target lists Dost Mohammad was labeled Objective Dakota.

17. Ostlund and Ranger sources, interviews. A few weeks later, while the Cacti battalion was immersed in the planning for Hammer Down, according to Ostlund, JSOC had a firmer shot at Dost Mohammad and again didn't take it—this time because of concern over civilian casualties, not American ones. Filming a cluster of mountainside homes north of Want for hundreds of hours at the end of June and into July, the task force's drones found the shadow governor holed up in a house at the upper end of the settlement, whose roof he paced for part of every day. There were no landing zones near this site, so it would have to be a Hellfire strike from one of the drones, and it seemed as if such a strike would be possible without harming civilians, because the women and children in the settlement seemed to stay in the houses at its lower end. Ostlund took the plan to ISAF's commander, Petraeus, but Petraeus wanted an ironclad guarantee that the strike wouldn't harm any civilians, and Ostlund couldn't offer that. Even if no civilians were killed, insurgents might well put out false accusations that they had been, which ISAF and JSOC would be in no position to dispute because they couldn't put troops on the ground. Petraeus was already in hot water with

Karzai over a series of inadvertent killings of civilians by American air-power, and he demurred.

18. Gen. (Ret.) John Allen, interview with author.

19. Nicholson and Tamim, interviews. Tamim was saying the same things publicly. Abdul Moeed Hashmi, "Taliban in Control of Six Districts in Nuristan, Says New Governor," *Pajhwok Afghan News*, Sept. 4, 2011.

20. Allen, Nicholson, and Tamim, interviews.

21. Nicholson, interview.

22. Tamim, interview.

23. Nicholson, interview. "The one in the Watapur in June, I was like, 'Holy shit,'" Nicholson said of Hammer Down, referring to the surprisingly large and active hive of insurgent activity that the Cacti battalion encountered.

24. Beatty, interview.

25. "Now he's asking the Task Force to take a look at Nuristan," the operations director of the higher-level JSOC task force at Bagram said of Allen on August 15, during a briefing about JSOC activities with a CENTCOM team that was investigating the shoot-down of Extortion 17, the Chinook full of SEAL Team 6 operators. Officer identified as "TF [redacted] J3," quoted in interview by CENTCOM investigation team of leaders and senior staff from the two echelons of JSOC task force at Bagram and the special operations aviation unit there, Aug. 15, 2011, www3.centcom.mil /FOIA_RR_Files/5%20USC%20552(a)(2)(D)Records/Wardak%20CH -47%20Investigation/r_EX%2001.pdf.

26. Special operations and intelligence sources, interviews. Although the Asadabad Omega team is not known to have participated in previous conventional offensives in the Pech, it had tagged along in similar fashion on at least two other large air assaults elsewhere in Kunar in 2010 and 2011, according to 101st Airborne veterans who participated in the missions—2-327 Infantry's Operation Strong Eagle II in Marawara in July 2010, when the Omega team similarly attached itself to the conventional battalion scout platoon (and inadvertently called in an air strike on another of the battalion's platoons), and 1-32 Cavalry's Operation Northern Avalanche in Ghaziabad in February 2011. Some conventional and special operations officers who had experience working alongside SEAL Team 6 were skeptical that the reason for the Omega team's presence was as thoroughly thought through as the intelligence mission that other special operations and intelligence sources described; they suggested that the Omega operators were looking for excuses to leave Asadabad and see combat.

27. Hughes and a member of Cacti scout platoon, interviews with author.

28. This account of Operation Fire Rock is based on interviews with Volesky, Kim, Beatty, Stich, Rankin, Crain, Tuley, Hughes, Bluhm, Nicholas, Downey, Simbro, Laws, Van Wyhe, Burhan, a Green Beret officer who asked to be identified only as the Special Forces ground force commander, and members of the scout platoon who asked not to be named because of the sensitivity of speaking about their experience with the SEALs of the

Omega team. It also draws on Staff Sgt. Luke Graziani, "Tropic Lightning Stay Vigilant Above Wanat," 7th Mobile Public Affairs Detachment press release, Sept. 25, 2011, www.dvidshub.net/news/77561/tropic-lightning -stay-vigilant-above-wanat.

29. Tuley and Stich, interviews.
30. Special Forces ground force commander, interview.
31. Special Forces ground force commander, Simbro, and Cacti battalion scout platoon veterans, interviews.
32. Special Forces ground force commander and Simbro, interviews.
33. Van Wyhe, interview.
34. Burhan and Laws, interviews.
35. Special Forces ground force commander, interview.
36. Nicholas, interview.
37. Bluhm and Nicholas, interviews. Bluhm remembered the group consisting of only two old men, while Nicholas put it at four—the number he recorded in his journal at the time. "We sent four guys out to find the bodies and one of them was shot by our own people, actually the SEALs," Nicholas wrote.
38. 2-35 Infantry scout platoon veterans, interviews.
39. 2-35 Infantry scout platoon veterans and Special Forces ground force commander, interviews. Other Cacti troops who were slightly higher on the mountain at Bastard Company's strongpoint didn't recall these shots, but they were also noted in a military public affairs write-up of Fire Rock, in which Staff Sergeant Luke Graziani wrote that some Cacti troops heard "intermittent shots from a distant sniper rifle" after the brief firefight between the ANA Commandos and the insurgents had ended (Graziani, "Tropic Lightning Stay Vigilant Above Wanat"). According to the former scout platoon veterans, no one in their platoon—which included all of the battalion's snipers—fired their weapons that night.
40. 2-35 Infantry scout platoon veteran, interview. At Bastard Company's strongpoint higher up, Colin Tuley was furious that the SEALs were taking shots without clearing them over the battalion radio net, according to the Bastard Company commander, Jake Hughes, and told Hughes to make sure the frogmen didn't do it again. "It was unsettling," Tuley acknowledged to me later, although he cautioned against attributing carelessness or a nefarious motive to the special operators.
41. Bluhm and Nicholas, interviews.
42. Bluhm, interview.
43. Volesky, Hughes, and 2-35 Infantry sources, interviews.
44. Tuley, interview.
45. Kim, Beatty, Tuley, Brown, and Special Forces ground force commander, interviews.
46. Farshad, interview.
47. Ryan and Burhan, interviews.
48. Tamim, interview.

49. Mohammad Tahir Safi et al., "Delegation Report on Civilian Casualties in Want Village, Nuristan Province, During Cordon and Search Operation," n.d., translated by Sami Nuristani.

50. Bluhm, Nicholas, and Special Forces ground force commander, interviews. The A-team's commander was home on leave during Operation Fire Rock, leaving the officer I interviewed, who was not part of the team, to fill in as ground force commander during the mission. The Special Forces team sergeant who oversaw the clearance of the town that night wouldn't speak to me about Fire Rock when I contacted him through a former teammate and through U.S. Army Special Forces headquarters at Fort Bragg.

51. Wilson, Volesky, Kim, Pendall, Beatty, Tuley, and Brown, interviews.

52. Waygali serving in the Kabul government, interview.

53. Tamim, Abdul Qudus Nuristani, Sami Nuristani, Jamaluddin Badr, and Burhan, interviews.

54. Rankin, interview.

55. Volesky and Kim, interviews; Fabrizio Foschini, "Nuristan in Fall," Afghanistan Analysts Network, Oct. 11, 2011, www.afghanistan-analysts.org/nuristan-in-fall/.

56. Miles Amoore, "Murky Death of MI6 Ally Who Paid Linda's Abductor," *Sunday Times,* Dec. 4, 2011, www.thetimes.co.uk/article/murky-death-of-mi6-ally-who-paid-lindas-abductor-hlrzcffqvgl.

57. Special operations and 3rd Brigade, 25th Infantry Division sources confirmed to me that the September 2, 2011, raid in Jalalabad was carried out by Task Force East.

58. ISAF Joint Command, "Combined Forces Kill, Detain Several Insurgents," Sept. 7, 2011, www.army.mil/article/65010/combined_forces_kill_detain_several_insurgents. "The security force located Sabar Lal at a compound in the Jalalabad district thanks to a tip from local residents. The insurgent emerged from the building with an assault rifle and was killed," said the ISAF statement, which described Sabar Lal as "a key affiliate of the al-Qaida network."

59. Ray Rivera, "Troops Kill Man Linked to Al Qaeda and Attacks," *New York Times,* Sept. 3, 2011; Ray Rivera, "Anger After a Raid Kills a Wealthy Afghan with a Murky Past," *New York Times,* Sept. 4, 2011. An elderly gatekeeper who let the SEALs into the compound's main building later gave a less clear-cut version to a British journalist, Miles Amoore of *The Sunday Times.* Sabar Lal was not among a group of men the special operators initially handcuffed and lined up on the street, the gatekeeper told Amoore, because he did not come down from his upstairs quarters when everyone else did. The gatekeeper had then gone upstairs to fetch him, and Sabar Lal had said he would come down when he finished washing, and the gatekeeper had seen him start to come downstairs, but by the time the shots rang out, the old man was outside with the other detainees.

60. Mark Mazzetti et al., "SEAL Team 6: A Secret History of Quiet Killings and Blurred Lines," *New York Times,* June 6, 2015, www.nytimes.com/2015/06/07/world/asia/the-secret-history-of-seal-team-6.html.

61. Crowe, interview. This account of Gundog Company's experience in the Pech in late 2011 and early 2012 is based on interviews with Crowe, Guillen, Gaulin, Laws, Van Wyhe, Simmons, and Jon Cheatwood.
62. Crain, interview.
63. Rubin, Chivers, and Morgan, "U.S. Pulling Back in Afghan Valley It Called Vital to War."
64. Guillen, interview.
65. Tuley, interview.
66. Crowe, interview.
67. Guillen, interview.
68. Crowe, interview.
69. Ibid.
70. Gaulin, interview.
71. Guillen, interview.
72. Ibid.
73. Crowe, interview.
74. Cheatwood, Ken Rowe, and Crain, interviews with author.
75. This description of Dagger Company, 2-12 Infantry's 2012 Pech deployment is based on interviews with Lt. Col. Jay Bullock, Lt. Col. Joe Power, Miller, Rowe, Ben Bain, Ben Walker, Tommy Ryan, and Brent Fetters.
76. Miller, interview.
77. Ibid.
78. Ibid.
79. Miller, Bullock, Bain, and Walker, interviews.
80. Miller and Bullock, interviews.
81. Miller, interview.
82. Qais Azimy and Mujib Mashal, "Commander's Words Shed Light on Taliban Views," Al Jazeera English, April 4, 2012, www.aljazeera.com/indepth/ features/2012/04/201243135956894735.html.
83. Miller, interview.
84. Walker, interview.
85. Power, Bullock, and Miller, interviews.
86. Miller, interview.
87. Bullock, interview.
88. Power, Bullock, Miller, and Walker, interviews,
89. Power, Bullock, Miller, Walker, and Lt. Col. Dave Sentell, interviews.
90. Bullock and Walker, interviews.
91. Department of Defense, "Report on Progress Toward Security and Stability in Afghanistan," Nov. 2013, www.globalsecurity.org/military/library/report /2013/afghanistan-security-stability_201311.pdf. The top four most violent districts were in Helmand; the Pech district centered on Nangalam ranked number ten.
92. Newkirk, interview.
93. Ibid.
94. Ibid.
95. Ibid.

96. Ibid.

97. Power, interview.

98. Matt Sherman, interview with author.

99. Col. Dan Walrath, interview with author.

100. Milley, CENTCOM testimony.

101. Milley, interview.

102. Matt Sherman, "Politics and the Perception of Force," June 2013.

103. Ibid.

104. Lt. Col. Bryan Laske, interview with author.

105. Ibid.

106. Ibid.

107. Col. J. P. McGee, interview with author.

108. Poppas, interview.

109. Sherman, "Politics and the Perception of Force."

110. Jenkins, *Unchangeable War.*

111. Sherman, "Politics and the Perception of Force."

CHAPTER 14: HAYMAKER, 2011–2013

1. Ostlund, interview.

2. Intelligence source, interview.

3. Ostlund, interview.

4. Task Force 3-10, "State of the Taliban." Far from torturing or abusing their captives, JSOC interrogators had learned to use "rapport-based approaches," acknowledging to detainees that American troops had made mistakes in Afghanistan, for example. To Abu Ikhlas, they played up the unfolding events of the Arab Spring, which had kicked off just a few weeks after his capture in Jalalabad: how Arabs from Tunisia to the Persian Gulf were already seeing more success standing up to their repressive regimes peacefully than al-Qaida and other militants had during decades of violent jihad, including (or so it seemed at the time) in his home country of Egypt. It worked. "I was taught that this was never possible, that the only way to change anything was violence. Tunisia and Egypt have changed all that," Abu Ikhlas told interrogators. "Nothing is the same."

5. ISAF Joint Command, "UPDATE: Force Confirms Al Qaeda Senior Commander Killed," Sept. 29, 2010, www.dvidshub.net/news/57157/update -force-confirms-al-qaeda-senior-commander-killed.

6. Ryan, Genenbacher, and intelligence source, interviews. "We got a little more than we actually bargained for," an intelligence officer involved in the strike remembered.

7. Intelligence source, interview; ISAF Joint Command, "ISAF Confirms Number 2 Insurgent Killed in Coalition Airstrike," April 13, 2011, www .dvidshub.net/news/69345/isaf-confirms-number-2-insurgent-killed -coalition-airstrike.

8. Special operations and intelligence sources, interviews.

9. Rahman to bin Laden, June 19, 2010. The letters between bin Laden and Rahman, which come from the trove of documents SEAL Team 6 col-

lected from Abbottabad, are from the collection of original letters and English translations first released by the Combating Terrorism Center at West Point and accessible at ctc.usma.edu/letters-from-abbottabad-bin-ladin -sidelined/.

10. Rahman to bin Laden, July 17, 2010.

11. Miller, interview.

12. David Andrew Weinberg, "Catch and Release: Did Qatar Free a Future al-Qaeda Emir?," *Huffington Post,* May 18, 2017, www.huffpost.com/entry /catch-and-release-did-qatar-free-a-future-al-qaeda_b_591e3b27e4b07617 ae4cbabe.

13. Shabab al-Ummah Facebook post commemorating the death of Farouq al-Qahtani.

14. Douglas London, interview with author.

15. Department of the Treasury, "Treasury Designates Senior al-Qaida Leader in Afghanistan," Feb. 10, 2016, www.treasury.gov/press-center/press -releases/Pages/jl0346.aspx.

16. London, interview.

17. Rahman to bin Laden, July 17, 2010.

18. bin Laden to Rahman, Oct. 2010.

19. Michael Morell, *The Great War of Our Time: The CIA's Fight Against Terrorism—from al Qa'ida to ISIS,* with Bill Harlow (New York: Twelve, 2015), 175–76.

20. Michael Morell, interview with author.

21. Barack Obama, "President Obama on the Way Forward in Afghanistan," June 22, 2011, obamawhitehouse.archives.gov/blog/2011/06/22/president -obama-way-forward-afghanistan.

22. Task Force 3-10, "State of the Taliban."

23. Allen, interview.

24. Gen. (Ret.) Joseph Votel, interview with author.

25. McRaven, correspondence.

26. This account of the Norgrove mission is based on the declassified CENT- COM investigation conducted by Votel and its supporting documents, including Votel's interviews with the SEALs involved in the mission, accessible at www3.centcom.mil/foia_rr/FOIA_RR.asp?Path=/5%20USC%20552 %28a%29%282%29%28D%29Records&Folder=NORGROVE.

27. CENTCOM investigation testimony of "TFE Commander," n.d.

28. CENTCOM investigation testimony of "Team Member 1 (A Team Leader)," Oct. 17, 2010.

29. CENTCOM investigation testimony of "TF East Command Master Chief," Oct. 16, 2010.

30. Votel, interview.

31. As remembered by Drew Poppas, in reference to a potential JSOC target in the Waygal valley that Poppas suggested during a visit by McRaven to Jalalabad Airfield in late 2010 or early 2011.

32. Votel, interview.

33. Brown, interview.

34. Wright and Brown, interviews.

35. Ibid.

36. Special operations source, interview.

37. Other than to confirm the period of time he led the Bagram JSOC task force in 2012 and that his responsibilities included approving strikes in Kunar and Nuristan, Ryan would not discuss Operation Haymaker for this book, saying he wasn't authorized to.

38. McChrystal describes the 2004 inception of JSOC's use of "kinetic strikes" in *My Share of the Task,* 136–46.

39. Ryan and Holliday, interviews.

40. Brown, interview.

41. Rankin, interview.

42. Wright, interview.

43. This number comes from a slide titled "TF [redacted] Aviation Disposition," depicting JSOC's aviation assets in Afghanistan as of August 2011, that was declassified with the CENTCOM investigation into the shootdown of Extortion 17, the Chinook carrying a strike force of Task Force East SEALs.

44. Special operations source, interview.

45. Requirements and Analysis Division, ISR Task Force, "ISR Support to Small Footprint CT Operations—Somalia/Yemen," Feb. 2013, theintercept.com/document/2015/10/15/small-footprint-operations-2-13/#page-1.

46. Special operations source, interview.

47. Ibid.

48. These and many other details about Operation Haymaker are drawn from a briefing slide deck leaked to and published by *The Intercept,* "OPN HAYMAKER Effects," March 2013, theintercept.com/document/2015/10/15/operation-haymaker/#page-1.

49. From its original home at Creech Air Force Base, Nevada, the Air Force's Predator and Reaper program had grown to include special operations drone squadrons at New Mexico's Cannon Air Force Base and Florida's Hurlburt Field and Air National Guard squadrons whose crews controlled their drones from bases in Missouri, Texas, New York, Ohio, North Dakota, and other states.

50. National Security Agency, "Finding Nuggets—Quickly—in a Heap of Voice Collection, from Mexico to Afghanistan," May 2011, firstlook.org/theintercept/document/2015/05/05/finding-nuggets-quickly-heap-voice-collection-mexico-afghanistan/.

51. "OPN HAYMAKER Effects" slide deck.

52. Under a division of labor established in 2009 and still largely in place a decade later, JSOC's three main elements split up the counterterrorist manhunting mission by theater: the SEALs ran the task force responsible for Yemen and East Africa, Delta Force ran the Iraq (and eventually the Syria) task force, and the Rangers headed the Afghanistan task force.

53. Special operations sources, interviews.

54. Special operations source, interview.

55. ISR Task Force, "ISR Support to Small Footprint CT Operations—Somalia/Yemen." "Combining FMV and SIGINT is key to successful fixes," the Pentagon study on Yemen and Somalia strikes advised, using the acronyms for full-motion video and signals intelligence.

56. Special operations sources, interviews.

57. Ibid.

58. Ibid.

59. Ibid.

60. Jamaluddin Badr, interview with author.

61. Burhan, Haji Abdul Qudus Nuristani, Jamaluddin Badr, and special operations sources, interviews; "OPN HAYMAKER Effects" slide deck; ISAF Joint Command, "Afghan Forces Conduct over 100 Special Operations Missions in May," June 5, 2012, www.nato.int/cps/en/natohq/news_88237 .htm?selectedLocale=en.

62. "OPN HAYMAKER Effects" slide deck; ISAF Joint Command, "Senior al-Qaida Leader Killed in Kunar Province Sunday," May 29, 2012, www .dvidshub.net/news/89103/senior-al-qaida-leader-killed-kunar-province -sunday.

63. ISAF Joint Command, "ISAF Joint Command Morning Operational Update," July 3, 2012, www.dvidshub.net/news/91032/isaf-joint-command -morning-operational-update.

64. ISAF Joint Command, "ISAF Joint Command Morning Operational Update," Aug. 5, 2012, www.dvidshub.net/news/92673/isaf-joint-command -morning-operational-update.

65. ISAF Joint Command, "ISAF Joint Command Morning Operational Update," Sept. 6, 2012, www.dvidshub.net/news/94287/isaf-joint-command -morning-operational-update.

66. Allen, interview.

67. The rare suicide bombings in Kunar over the years had included one in August 2007 that unsuccessfully targeted 2-503 Infantry's route-clearance platoon on a road across the Kunar River from Asadabad and another in June 2010, also in eastern Kunar outside the Pech, that killed two soldiers from the 101st Airborne's 2-327 Infantry. Other reports of impending suicide attacks against American bases had come in over the years through informants and signals intercepts, only for the attacks not to materialize.

68. Department of the Treasury, "Treasury Designates Senior al-Qaida Leader in Afghanistan."

69. Bain, interview.

70. Walrath and Capt. (Ret.) Flo Groberg, interviews with author; Groberg Medal of Honor citation and narrative.

71. ISAF Joint Command, "ISAF Joint Command Morning Operational Update," Sept. 17, 2012, www.dvidshub.net/news/94805/isaf-joint-command -morning-operational-update.

72. "OPN HAYMAKER Effects" slide deck.

73. What follows is largely a summary of the "OPN HAYMAKER Effects" slide deck.

74. During the fifteen months covered by the study, when Task Force East executed fifty-six Haymaker strikes in Kunar and Nuristan, the CIA is believed to have executed sixty-two strikes in Pakistan.

75. Intelligence source, interview.

76. Anayat Rahman Safi, interview.

77. ISR Task Force, "ISR Support to Small Footprint CT Operations—Somalia/Yemen." The study recommended reverting to raids by local forces with U.S. special operations advisers wherever possible.

78. Intelligence source, interview.

79. Special operations source, interview.

80. Intelligence source, interview.

81. Special operations source, interview.

82. Miller, interview.

83. "OPN HAYMAKER Effects" slide deck.

84. Resident of Gulsalak, interview with author.

85. Mawlawi Shahzada Shahid, interview.

86. ISAF Joint Command, "ISAF Joint Command April 6 Operational Update," April 6, 2013, www.dvidshub.net/news/104731/isaf-joint-command-april-6-operational-update.

87. Korengali influence in the Kunar insurgency was decreasing, not increasing; the Taliban's Peshawar *shura* had recently fired its longtime shadow governor for the province, Mawlawi Abdul Rahim, and replaced him with a non-Korengali. "Haji Matin was kind of retired," remembered one intelligence officer.

88. Intelligence source, interview.

89. Newkirk, interview.

90. Bullock, interview.

91. Walker, interview.

92. Ahmad Shah Ghanizada, "US Drone Strike Kill Top Taliban Leader in Kunar Province," Khaama Press News Agency, Oct. 21, 2013, www.khaama.com/us-drone-strike-kill-top-taliban-leader-in-kunar-province-1992/.

93. Poppas, interview. The description of the Kunar map on Brigadier General Erik Kurilla's office wall is from an interview with a special operations source.

94. Intelligence source, interview.

95. Ibid.

96. Special operations source, interview.

97. Intelligence source, interview.

98. Barack Obama, "Remarks by the President at the National Defense University," May 23, 2013, obamawhitehouse.archives.gov/the-press-office/2013/05/23/remarks-president-national-defense-university.

99. Ibid.

100. Allen, interview.

101. Gen. (Ret.) Joseph Dunford, interview with author.

102. "OPN HAYMAKER Effects" slide deck.

103. Special operations source, interview.

104. Intelligence source, interview.

105. Special operations source, interview.

106. Newkirk, interview.

107. UN Assistance Mission to Afghanistan and UN Office of the High Commissioner for Human Rights, "Afghanistan Annual Report 2012: Protection of Civilians in Armed Conflict," Feb. 2013, unama.unmissions.org /sites/default/files/2012_annual_report_eng_0.pdf.

108. Ibid.

109. Ibid.

110. Tommy Ryan, interview.

111. UNAMA and UNHCR, "Afghanistan Annual Report 2012."

112. UNAMA and UNHCR, "Afghanistan Mid-year Report 2013: Protection of Civilians in Armed Conflict," July 2013, unama.unmissions.org/sites/ default/files/2013_mid-year_report_eng.pdf.

113. Newkirk and Sherman, interviews.

114. Lt. Col. James DeOre, Maj. Scott Loria, and Capt. J. Hudson Page, interviews with author.

115. Loria, interview.

116. This description of the September 7, 2013, Haymaker strike near Gambir and its aftermath is based on interviews with special operations sources, Karzai, and Shahzada Shahid; UNAMA and UNHCR, "Afghanistan Annual Report 2013: Protection of Civilians in Armed Conflict," Feb. 2014, unama.unmissions.org/sites/default/files/feb_8_2014_poc-report_2013 -full-report-eng.pdf; David Zucchino, "Afghans Describe Relatives' Deaths in Recent U.S. Drone Strike," *Los Angeles Times,* Dec. 1, 2013, www.latimes .com/world/la-fg-afghanistan-drones-20131201-story.html; May Jeong, "Losing Sight: A 4-Year-Old Girl Was the Sole Survivor of a U.S. Drone Strike in Afghanistan. Then She Disappeared," *Intercept,* Jan. 27, 2018, theintercept.com/2018/01/27/a-4-year-old-girl-was-the-sole-survivor -of-a-u-s-drone-strike-in-afghanistan-then-she-disappeared/; Alice Ross, "Don't Ask Who's Being Killed by Drones in Afghanistan," *Vice,* July 24, 2014, www.vice.com/en_us/article/vbnjnd/dont-ask-whos-being-killed -by-drones-in-afghanistan; and "Afghan Officials Say NATO Air Strike Killed Nine Civilians," Associated Press, Sept. 8, 2013.

117. Jeong's sources say the truck was red, Zucchino's blue.

118. The information that Farouq sometimes stayed in Gambir and nearby Katar and Dehwuz comes from an interview with Anayat Rahman Safi.

119. ISAF statement quoted in Jeong, "Losing Sight."

120. Jeong, "Losing Sight."

121. ISAF statement quoted in Zucchino, "Afghans Describe Relatives' Deaths in Recent U.S. Drone Strike."

122. Jeong, "Losing Sight."

123. "Afghan Officials Say NATO Air Strike Killed Nine Civilians."

124. Dunford, interview.

125. Jeong, "Losing Sight."

126. UNAMA and UNHCR, "Afghanistan Annual Report 2013."

127. Zucchino, "Afghans Describe Relatives' Deaths in Recent U.S. Drone Strike."

128. Karzai, interview.

129. Shahzada Shahid, interview.

130. Ibid.

131. Dunford, interview.

132. Jeong, "Losing Sight."

133. Karzai, interview.

134. Shahzada Shahid, interview.

135. ISAF statement quoted in Ross, "Don't Ask Who's Being Killed by Drones in Afghanistan."

136. Kolenda et al., *Strategic Costs of Civilian Harm.*

137. Votel, interview.

138. See Maj. Gen. Joseph Osterman, quoted in Rob Taylor, "U.S. General Says al Qaeda Just Surviving in Afghanistan," Reuters, July 26, 2013, news.trust .org//item/20130726080544–ipi72/.

139. Obama, "Remarks by the President at the National Defense University."

140. Department of Defense, "Report on Progress Toward Security and Stability in Afghanistan," Nov. 2013, dod.defense.gov/Portals/1/Documents/pubs /October_1230_Report_Master_Nov7.pdf.

141. "OPN HAYMAKER Effects" slide deck.

142. Spiszer, interview.

143. Shahzada Shahid, interview.

CHAPTER 15: THE WAR THAT NEVER ENDS, 2014–2017

1. Former Special Forces captain who asked to be identified as Josh, interview with author.

2. Ibid.

3. Ibid.

4. Moeller, interview.

5. Special operations source, interview with author.

6. This description of the April 5–6, 2013, Unit 04 raid in Suno in the Shultan valley is based on the narrative accompanying the award of the Silver Star to Staff Sgt. Robert Ashwell; on Rod Nordland, "After Airstrike, Afghan Points to C.I.A. and Secret Militias," *New York Times,* April 18, 2013; and on UNAMA and UNHCR, "Afghanistan Mid-year Report 2013."

7. Jenkinson, interview.

8. Jenkinson and intelligence sources, interviews.

9. Dunford, interview.

10. Josh, interview.

11. Josh and intelligence source, interviews.

12. Rangers and other special operations sources, interviews with author.

13. Ranger source, interview.

14. Ibid.

15. Ranger sources, interviews.

16. Jenkinson, interview.

17. U.S. Forces—Afghanistan disclosed this air strike to the Bureau of Investigative Journalism, www.thebureauinvestigates.com/drone-war/data/get-the -data-a-list-of-us-air-and-drone-strikes-afghanistan-2015.

18. Kearney, interview.

19. Ranger source, interview.

20. Niamatullah Karyab and Rod Nordland, "Taliban Raid Afghan Army Base, Killing Soldiers in Their Sleep," *New York Times,* Feb. 23, 2014, www .nytimes.com/2014/02/24/world/asia/taliban-attack-afghan-army-base -killing-soldiers-in-their-sleep.html.

21. Ranger source, interview.

22. Trevithick and Seckman, "Heart of Darkness."

23. Mawlawi Shafiullah Nuristani, interview.

24. Obaidullah Nuristani, interview.

25. Group interview with Waygali men.

26. Obaidullah Nuristani, interview.

27. Mawlawi Shafiullah Nuristani, interview.

28. "NATO Drone Strike Leaves Six Militants Dead in Nuristan Province," *Khaama Press,* Dec. 8, 2014, www.khaama.com/nato-drone-strike-leaves -six-militants-dead-in-nuristan-province-8836/; Ahmad Shah Ghani Zada, "NATO Drone Strike Kills 8 Taliban Insurgents in Nuristan," *Khaama Press,* Dec. 16, 2014, www.khaama.com/nato-drone-strike-kills-8-taliban -insurgents-in-nuristan-9139/.

29. Fabrizio Foschini, "Classics of Conflict: Reviewing Some of Afghanistan's Most Notorious Hotspots," Afghanistan Analysts Network, July 9, 2015, www.afghanistan-analysts.org/classics-of-conflict-2-reviewing-some-of -afghanistans-most-notorious-hotspots/; Zeerak Fahim, "Taliban Mount Big Attack on District Center in Nuristan," *Pajhwok Afghan News,* June 25, 2015, www.pajhwok.com/en/2015/06/25/taliban-mount-big-attack -district-center-nuristan.

30. The Taliban website Voice of Jihad claimed on November 29 that two hundred security personnel surrendered during a Taliban attack on the district center. See Bill Roggio, "Taliban Claims Hundreds of Military Personnel, Government Officials Defect in Nuristan," *Long War Journal,* Dec. 1, 2015, www.longwarjournal.org/archives/2015/12/taliban-claims-hundreds-of -military-personnel-government-officials-defect-in-nuristan.php.

31. Ranger sources, interviews.

32. Ranger source, interview.

33. Ibid.

34. Haji Abdul Qudus Nuristani, interview.

35. Obaidullah, interview.

36. Waygali serving in the Kabul government, interview with author.

37. Mawlawi Shafiullah Nuristani, interview.

38. Morell, *Great War of Our Time,* 312–13.

39. Lt. Gen. Mike Flynn, interview with author.

40. ISAF's deputy chief of staff for operations offered an estimate of "less than 100" al-Qaida fighters in Kunar and Nuristan in July 2013, and a November

2013 Pentagon report to Congress cited "national estimates"—a veiled reference to the CIA—that put "the number of operatives in these groups in the dozens." Another report to Congress in June 2015 echoed the "fewer than 100" estimate, and the CIA director, John Brennan, said the same in a February 2016 interview.

41. Morell, interview.
42. Ranger source, interview.
43. Department of Defense, "Report on Enhancing Security and Stability in Afghanistan," June 2015, news.usni.org/wp-content/uploads/2015/06 /June_1225_Report_Final1.pdf.
44. In its February 2016 announcement of his addition to the Specially Designated Global Terrorist sanctions list, the Treasury Department described Farouq as "the al-Qaida emir for the Eastern Zone of Afghanistan reporting to al-Qaida's senior leadership," adding that in that role he was "responsible for planning attacks against U.S. and Coalition forces in Afghanistan, contributing to al-Qaida's external operations planning, and fundraising on al-Qaida's behalf." After Farouq's death, the Pentagon press secretary, Peter Cook, described him as "one of the terrorist group's plotters of attacks against the United States," while the Resolute Support and U.S. Forces—Afghanistan commander, Nicholson, called him an al-Qaida "external operations director." "Department of Defense Press Briefing by General Nicholson in the Pentagon Briefing Room," Dec. 2, 2016, www.defense .gov/Newsroom/Transcripts/Transcript/Article/1019029/department-of -defense-press-briefing-by-general-nicholson-in-the-pentagon-brief/; "Statement for the Record by Gen. John W. Nicholson, Commander, U.S. Forces—Afghanistan, Before the Senate Armed Services Committee on the Situation in Afghanistan," Feb. 9, 2017, www.armed-services.senate.gov /imo/media/doc/Nicholson_02-09-17.pdf; and in an interview with Brian Dodwell and Don Rassler, "A View from the CT Foxhole: General John W. Nicholson, Commander, Resolute Support and U.S. Forces—Afghanistan," *CTC Sentinel,* Feb. 2017, ctc.usma.edu/a-view-from-the-ct -foxhole-general-john-w-nicholson-commander-resolute-support-and-u -s-forces-afghanistan/.
45. Ranger source, interview.
46. Department of Defense, "Report on Enhancing Security and Stability in Afghanistan," June 2015. The same report also predicted that over the course of 2015 al-Qaida would likely try to take advantage of the reduced American military and intelligence presence and "attempt to rebuild its support networks and planning capabilities with the intention of reconstituting its strike capabilities against Western interests."
47. Flynn, interview.
48. Ranger source, interview.
49. Morell, interview.
50. Morell, *Great War of Our Time,* 312–13. "As in Yemen, there is one particular terrorist in South Asia whom I worry the most about—Farouq

al-Qahtani," Morell wrote, after writing of Asiri, "He may well be the most dangerous terrorist alive today. . . . He is a master at his craft and he is evil."

51. Former senior military officer and former counterterrorism official, interviews with author.
52. London, interview.
53. Eric Robinson, interview with author.
54. NSC source, interview.
55. Cmdr. (Ret.) Jeff Eggers, interview with author.
56. Lt. Gen. (Ret.) Michael Nagata, interview with author.
57. Department of Defense, "U.S. Airstrike Kills Senior Al-Qaida Leader," July 24, 2015, www.defense.gov/Explore/News/Article/Article/612696/.
58. This description of the October 11, 2015, Objective Thanos Lobo raid in Shorabak is based on interviews with three special operations sources who were involved in its planning and execution and on Dan Lamothe, " 'Probably the Largest' al-Qaeda Training Camp Ever Destroyed in Afghanistan," *Washington Post,* Oct. 30, 2015, www.washingtonpost.com /news/checkpoint/wp/2015/10/30/probably-the-largest-al-qaeda -training-camp-ever-destroyed-in-afghanistan/.
59. Ranger source, interview.
60. President Barack Obama, "Statement by the President on Afghanistan," Oct. 15, 2015, obamawhitehouse.archives.gov/the-press-office/2015/10/15 /statement-president-afghanistan; intelligence source, interview.
61. Ranger source, interview.
62. Blackmon, *Pale Horse,* 134.
63. Waygali serving in the Kabul government, interview with author.
64. Ranger source, interview.
65. Ibid.
66. Rohullah Anwari and Abubakar Siddique, "Drones Spread Fear in Remote Afghan Mountains," Radio Free Afghanistan, July 7, 2015.
67. Ranger source, interview.
68. Special operations source, interview.
69. Special operations sources, interviews.
70. London, interview.
71. This account of the October 23, 2016, air strike that killed Farouq al-Qahtani is based on interviews with American sources who, at the time of the event, were working at the JSOC task force headquarters at Bagram, the Special Operations Joint Task Force—Afghanistan headquarters in Kabul, Nicholson's headquarters in Kabul, JSOC headquarters, CENTCOM headquarters, and the NSC staff; interviews with Kunari sources, including Anayat Rahman Safi; Nicholson's December 2016 and February 2017 public statements referring to the strike; and three Pentagon public affairs statements: "Statement by Pentagon Press Secretary Peter Cook on Strikes Against Al-Qaeda Leaders in Afghanistan," Oct. 26, 2016, www.defense.gov /Newsroom/Releases/Release/Article/987885/statement-by-pentagon -press-secretary-peter-cook-on-strikes-against-al-qaeda-le/; "Statement

by Pentagon Press Secretary Peter Cook Confirming Death of Al-Qaeda Leader," Nov. 4, 2016, www.defense.gov/Newsroom/Releases/Release /Article/997111/statement-by-pentagon-press-secretary-peter-cook -confirming-death-of-al-qaeda-l/; and "Statement by Pentagon Press Secretary Peter Cook on Strikes Against al-Qaida Leaders in Afghanistan," Dec. 19, 2016, www.defense.gov/Newsroom/Releases/Release /Article/1033929/statement-by-pentagon-press-secretary-peter-cook-on -strikes-against-al-qaida-le/.

72. Lolita Baldor, "New War Rules Emphasize Need to Avoid Civilian Casualties," Associated Press, Dec. 13, 2016, www.militarytimes.com/news/your -military/2016/12/14/new-war-rules-emphasize-need-to-avoid-civilian -casualties/.

73. London, interview.

74. Senior military officer, interview.

75. NSC source, interview.

76. Nicholson briefing, Dec. 2, 2016. "All three were actively involved in carrying out and plotting terror attacks inside and outside Afghanistan," the Pentagon press secretary, Cook, agreed in a December 19 statement after Bilal's and Abd al-Wahid's deaths had been confirmed. "The deaths of these three al-Qaida leaders will significantly reduce the group's ability to threaten the United States, our interests and our allies."

77. Al-Qaida General Command, "Statement on the Martyrdom of Commander Farouq al-Qahtani and His Companions in Kunar Province," Nov. 2016.

78. Nagata, interview.

79. Anayat Rahman, interview.

80. Obaidullah Nuristani, interview.

81. Among the al-Qaida figures who arrived in Syria in 2015 were the group's number two leader, Abu al-Khayr al-Masri, who would be killed in a rare CIA drone strike near Idlib in 2017, and its top operational planner, Abu Mohammad al-Masri (Adrian Levy and Catherine Scott-Clark, "Al-Qaeda Has Rebuilt Itself—with Iran's Help," *Atlantic,* Nov. 11, 2017, www .theatlantic.com/international/archive/2017/11/al-qaeda-iran-cia /545576/). See also Don Rassler, "Al-Qaeda in South Asia: A Brief Assessment," in *How al-Qaeda Survived Drones, Uprisings, and the Islamic State,* Washington Institute for Near East Policy, June 2017, www.washington institute.org/uploads/Documents/pubs/PolicyFocus153-Zelin.pdf.

82. Antonio Giustozzi, *The Islamic State in Khorasan: Afghanistan, Pakistan, and the New Central Asian Jihad* (London: Hurst, 2018), 190–91.

83. Shahzada Shahid, interview.

84. Ranger source, interview. A second Ranger officer expressed a similar sentiment, saying that with the Islamic State mission in Nangarhar, "we have the okay to go after a target set with a lot of low-hanging fruit, and that's a lot more rewarding than developing al-Qaida targets for months and months and then having maybe one shot at them."

85. Nicholson, Feb. 2017 Senate Armed Services Committee testimony.

86. Ranger source, interview.

87. Giustozzi, *Islamic State in Khorasan,* 57.

88. "Notorious Daesh Commander Killed in Kunar Airstrike," *Pajhwok Afghan News,* May 16, 2016, www.pajhwok.com/en/2016/05/16/notorious-daesh-commander-killed-kunar-airstrike; "Top ISIS Commander Shafiq Abbas Killed in Afghan Air Force Raid," *Khaama Press,* May 16, 2016, www.khaama.com/top-isis-commander-shafiq-abbas-killed-in-afghan-air-force-raid-0953/.

89. Giustozzi, *Islamic State in Khorasan,* 56, 190–91; Antonio Giustozzi, "Daesh Moves House: Settling in to Life in Afghanistan," *RUSI Newsbrief* 38, no. 4 (May 2018).

90. Mohammad Afzal, Abdul Qudus, and a Waygali serving in the Kabul government, interviews with author.

91. Shahzada Shahid, interview.

92. Department of the Treasury, "Treasury Targets Pakistan-Based Terrorist Leaders and Facilitators," May 11, 2017, www.treasury.gov/press-center/press-releases/Pages/sm0080.aspx.

93. Shafiullah Nuristani and a Waygali serving in the Kabul government, interviews.

94. Intelligence source, interview.

95. Ranger source, interview.

96. Department of the Treasury, "Treasury Designates ISIS Financial, Procurement, and Recruitment Networks in the Middle East and South Asia," Nov. 18, 2019, home.treasury.gov/news/press-releases/sm831.

97. Kunari serving in the Kabul government, interview with author.

98. Special operations and CENTCOM sources, interviews.

99. The Pentagon described the Daesh leaders it killed in July 2016 and April 2017 in Nangarhar and in Kunar in July and August 2017 as the "emirs" of the caliphate's Afghan branch. But according to Giustozzi, the Italian Afghanistan scholar whose researchers interviewed members of the group, two Daesh figures always shared power in Afghanistan: the provincial governor, or wali, which was the real role of the slain "emirs," and the envoy of the caliph, a commissar-like post held by a succession of Afghan militants who were also veterans of the wars in Iraq and Syria.

100. Giustozzi, *Islamic State in Khorasan,* 197–98.

101. Bilal Sarwary, interview.

102. Yousuf Zarifi, "4 Daesh Militants Killed in Kunar Drone Strike," *Pajhwok Afghan News,* July 3, 2017, www.pajhwok.com/en/2017/07/03/4-daesh-militants-killed-kunar-drone-strike; "Top ISIS Leaders Reportedly Killed in Kunar Drone Strike in East of Afghanistan," *Khaama Press,* July 4, 2017, www.khaama.com/top-isis-leaders-reportedly-killed-in-kunar-drone-strike-in-east-of-afghanistan-03078.

103. Department of Defense, "Statement by Chief Pentagon Spokesperson Dana W. White on Death of ISIS-K Leader in Afghanistan," July 14, 2017, www.defense.gov/Newsroom/Releases/Release/Article/1248198/statement-by-chief-pentagon-spokesperson-dana-w-white-on-death-of-isis-k

-leader/; U.S. Forces—Afghanistan, "U.S. Forces—Afghanistan Identifies Additional ISIS-K Leaders Killed in July 11 Strike," July 30, 2017, rs.nato .int/news-center/press-releases/2017/us-forces-afghanistan-identifies -additional-isisk-leaders-killed-in-july-11-strike.aspx; Borhan Osman, "Another ISKP Leader 'Dead': Where Is the Group Headed After Losing So Many Amirs," Afghanistan Analysts Network, July 23, 2017, www .afghanistan-analysts.org/another-iskp-leader-dead-where-is-the-group -headed-after-losing-so-many-amirs/.

104. Khan Wali Salarzai, "7 Killed as Drone Hits Daesh Hideout in Kunar," *Pajhwok Afghan News,* July 31, 2017, www.pajhwok.com/en/2017/07/31 /7-killed-drone-hits-daesh-hideout-kunar; Noor Zahid and Zabihullah Ghazi, "Islamic State Seeks Foothold in Eastern Afghan Provinces," VOA, Aug. 6, 2017, www.voanews.com/extremism-watch/islamic-state-seeks -foothold-eastern-afghan-provinces; "Daesh Prisons Chief Among 3 Killed in Airstrike," *Pajhwok Afghan News,* Aug. 6, 2017, www.pajhwok.com /en/2017/08/06/daesh-prisons-chief-among-3-killed-airstrike; "A Dozen Daesh Militants Perish in Kunar Drone Blitz," *Pajhwok Afghan News,* Sept. 5, 2017, www.pajhwok.com/en/2017/09/05/dozen-daesh-militants-perish -kunar-drone-blitz.

105. U.S. Forces—Afghanistan, "Kunar Provincial ISIS-K Emir Killed in Air Strike," Aug. 13, 2017, twitter.com/USFOR_A/status/89663743671293 9520.

106. According to Giustozzi, *Islamic State in Khorasan,* 150, 157, when Hekmatyar announced his move to Kabul, he and other Hizb leaders encouraged some of their followers to join Daesh as a hedge in case the reconciliation process failed.

107. Chris Sands and Fazelminallah Qazizai, "How US Drone Strike, Political Betrayal Drove Aging Afghan Militant Closer to Daesh," *Arab News,* March 2, 2018, www.arabnews.com/node/1257321/world.

108. Shahzada Shahid, interview.

109. Sands and Qazizai, "How US Drone Strike, Political Betrayal Drove Aging Afghan Militant Closer to Daesh."

110. Shafiullah Nuristani, interview.

111. Waygali men, group interview with author.

112. Crowe, interview.

EPILOGUE: 2018–2020

1. Ryan, interview.

2. The assessment of Afghanistan as the world's deadliest conflict in 2018— with more deaths than the runners-up, Syria and Yemen, combined—is from Roudabeh Kishi and Melissa Pavlik, "ACLED 2018: The Year in Review," Armed Conflict Location and Event Data Project, January 11, 2019, https://acleddata.com/acleddatanew/wp-content/uploads/2019 /01/ACLED-2018-The-Year-in-Review_Final_Pub-1-1.pdf. The estimate that the share of the country's 407 districts "controlled" or "influenced" by the government fell in 2019 to 219 (or 53.8 percent) is from the

Special Inspector General for Afghanistan Reconstruction, "Quarterly Report to the United States Congress," January 30, 2019, https://www.sigar .mil/pdf/quarterlyreports/2019-01-30qr.pdf. For Afghan government casualties, see Special Inspector General for Afghanistan Reconstruction, "Quarterly Report to the United States Congress," January 30, 2017, https://www.sigar.mil/pdf/quarterlyreports/2017-01-30qr.pdf, which shows 6,785 deaths from January 1 through November 12 of 2016, the last year the U.S. military publicly reported the casualty estimates it was receiving from the Afghan government, and Rod Nordland, "The Death Toll for Afghan Forces Is Secret. Here's Why," *New York Times,* September 21, 2018, https://www.nytimes.com/2018/09/21/world/asia/afghanistan-security -casualties-taliban.html. The Pentagon's official estimate of its own troop increase in Afghanistan held that numbers rose from 11,000 to 14,000, but in October 2019, Gen. Scott Miller acknowledged to reporters that the true peak number in the fall of 2018 had been 15,000; see Susannah George, "U.S. Has Begun Reducing Troops in Afghanistan, Commander Says," *Washington Post,* October 21, 2019, https://www.washingtonpost.com/world /us-has-begun-reducing-troops-in-afghanistan-commander-says/2019 /10/21/d17a9e30-f3f1-11e9-8cf0-4cc99f74d127_story.html.

3. Ryan, interview.
4. Brennan, interview.
5. Ibid.
6. The Army Corps of Engineers had contracted an American construction company to build the thirty-acre base in Khas Kunar District using Afghan labor starting in 2012, with the idea that the ANA brigade would adopt it as its main headquarters and garrison. After work was finished in 2015, though, the ANA troops never moved from their existing headquarters, the old FOB Joyce, and the $110 million project lay mostly abandoned.
7. Adviser captain from Train-Advise-Assist Command East (TAAC East), interview with author.
8. TAAC-East adviser colonel, major, captain, and sergeant first class, interviews with author.
9. Brennan, interview.
10. TAAC-East adviser major, interview.
11. TAAC-East adviser major, captain, and sergeant first class, interviews.
12. TAAC-East adviser major, interview.
13. Ryan, interview.
14. Brennan, interview. Brennan wouldn't tell me that he was in Delta Force, only that he was a troop commander in a special operations unit, but his official Army biography makes it clear, and other special operations sources confirmed it to me.
15. Ostlund, interview.
16. Ostlund described this habitual answer in a videotaped conversation at West Point with *New York Times* reporter C. J. Chivers. "CJ Chivers on His New Book, 'The Fighters,'" Modern War Institute, September 27, 2018, https:// www.youtube.com/watch?v=FKJG3btYGkk.

17. 4th Infantry Division source, interview with author.

18. Ryan, interview.

19. Special operations sources, interviews.

20. Intelligence and special operations sources, interviews; Thomas Gibbons-Neff, Eric Schmitt, and Adam Goldman, "A Newly Assertive C.I.A. Expands Its Taliban Hunt in Afghanistan," *New York Times*, October 22, 2017, https://www.nytimes.com/2017/10/22/world/asia/cia-expanding -taliban-fight-afghanistan.html.

21. Special operations source, interview; Wesley Morgan, "U.S. Soldier Killed in Afghanistan Was Part of CIA Operation," *Politico*, July 24, 2018, https:// www.politico.com/story/2018/07/24/afghanistan-defense-cia-operation -704929.

22. Special operations source, interview.

23. Ibid.

24. "Foreign Forces Storm ISIS Hideouts in Kunar Province," *Khaama Press*, September 17, 2018, https://www.khaama.com/coalition-forces-storm-isis -hideouts-in-kunar-province-05977/; Department of Defense, "Annual Report on Civilian Casualties in Connection With United States Military Operations," May 2, 2019, https://media.defense.gov/2019/May/02 /2002126767/-1/-1/1/ANNUAL-REPORT-CIVILIAN-CASUALTIES -IN-CONNECTION-WITH-US-MILITARY-OPERATIONS.PDF.

25. Special operations source, interview.

26. Ryan, interview.

27. Brennan, interview.

28. Ali Soufan, "Hamza bin Ladin: From Steadfast Son to al-Qa`ida's Leader in Waiting," CTC Sentinel, September 2017, https://ctc.usma.edu/hamza -bin-ladin-from-steadfast-son-to-al-qaidas-leader-in-waiting/.

29. Douglas London, "The President, His Relationship with Intelligence, and the Soleimani Strike," *Just Security*, January 15, 2020, https://www.just security.org/68072/the-president-his-relationship-with-intelligence-and -the-soleimani-strike/.

30. Special operations source, interview.

31. Special operations sources, interviews; Bilal, interview; UNAMA and UNHCR, "Afghanistan Annual Report 2018," February 2019, https:// unama.unmissions.org/sites/default/files/unama_annual_protection_of _civilians_report_2018_-_23_feb_2019_-_english.pdf; Department of Defense, "Annual Report on Civilian Casualties in Connection With United States Military Operations."

32. President Donald Trump, "Statement from the President," September 14, 2019, https://www.whitehouse.gov/briefings-statements/statement-from -the-president-10/.

33. Department of Defense Inspector General, "Operation Freedom's Sentinel: Lead Inspector General Report to the United States Congress, October 1, 2018 to December 31, 2018," March 2019, https://media.defense.gov /2019/Mar/01/2002094845/-1/-1/1/FY2019_LIG_OCO_REPORT

.PDF; Department of Defense Inspector General, "Operation Freedom's Sentinel: Lead Inspector General Report to the United States Congress, January 31, 2019 to March 31, 2019," May 2019, https://media.defense .gov/2019/May/21/2002134153/-1/-1/1/FY2019_LIG_OCO _REPORT.PDF; Department of Defense, "Enhancing Security and Stability in Afghanistan," December 2018, https://media.defense.gov/2018 /Dec/20/2002075158/-1/-1/1/1225-REPORT-DECEMBER-2018. PDF; Senate Armed Services Committee confirmation hearing of Lt. Gen. Kenneth McKenzie and Lt. Gen. Richard Clarke, December 4, 2018, https://archive.org/details/CSPAN2_20181204_143000_Senate_Armed _Services_Military_Command_Confirmations.

34. Adam Taylor, "Even in the Midst of Afghan Peace Talks, the Taliban Still Deny al Qaeda Was Behind 9/11," *Washington Post,* August 22, 2019, https://www.washingtonpost.com/world/2019/08/22/even-midst -afghan-peace-talks-taliban-still-deny-al-qaeda-was-behind/; Jeff Seldin, "Concerns Mount as US Seen Downplaying Al-Qaida Threat in Afghanistan," Voice of America, October 16, 2020, https://www.voanews.com /south-central-asia/concerns-mount-us-seen-downplaying-al-qaida -threat-afghanistan.

35. McKenzie, SASC nomination hearing.

36. Ryan, interview; Thomas Gibbons-Neff and Julian Barnes, "U.S. Military Calls ISIS in Afghanistan a Threat to the West. Intelligence Officials Disagree," *New York Times,* August 2, 2019, https://www.nytimes.com/2019 /08/02/world/middleeast/isis-afghanistan-us-military.html.

37. Ryan, interview. "We're certainly aware of their presence," Ryan told me of Arab fighters in his battalion's sector in July 2010. "Some of it may be overstated because we focus so much on them from an intelligence standpoint."

38. According to the Italian scholar Giustozzi (*The Islamic State in Khorasan,* 70– 75) and two special operations sources I spoke with, evidence of Arab advisers on the battlefield was more common during the first two years of the battle against Daesh in Afghanistan, in 2015 and 2016, than it was later, as air strikes and raids picked the foreign fighters off or drove them underground.

39. Ryan, interview.

40. Intelligence source, interview.

41. Ryan, interview.

42. Franz Marty, "The Peculiar Presence of the Islamic State in Kunar," *The Diplomat,* May 14, 2019, https://thediplomat.com/2019/05/the-peculiar-presence-of-the-islamic-state-in-kunar/. For the relationship between the Taliban and the government in Chapa Dara in 2018, see Michael Semple, "Afghanistan's Islamic Emirate Returns: Life Under a Resurgent Taliban," *World Politics Review,* September 18, 2018, https://www.worldpolitics review.com/articles/25970/afghanistan-s-islamic-emirate-returns-life -under-a-resurgent-taliban.

43. Ayesha Tanzeem, "In One Afghan Province, the Taliban Safe-Guarded

the Elections," VOA, October 8, 2019, https://www.voanews.com/south-central-asia/one-afghan-province-taliban-safe-guarded-elections.

44. Special operations source, interview.
45. Department of Defense, "Transcript: Gen. McKenzie, Gen. Townsend and Acting ASD for International Security Affairs Wheelbarger at HASC," March 13, 2020, https://www.centcom.mil/MEDIA/Transcripts/Article/2111116/transcript-gen-mckenzie-gen-townsend-and-acting-asd-for-international-security/.
46. Special operations sources, interviews.
47. Special operations source, interview.
48. This section is based on an interview and correspondence with Frye and on a Facebook post he made on June 20, 2019.

INDEX

Afghan names generally do not adhere to the "surname, given name" indexing format designed for Western names. In Afghanistan, a person's name may change over time as new honorifics and descriptors are earned or gained, and a person may be known to some mainly by one part of his or her name and to others mainly by another part of it. The name Haji Abdul Qudus Nuristani, for example, indicates a person with the names Abdul and Qudus who has completed the pilgrimage to Mecca, known as the Haj, and who is from Nuristan, while the name Mawlawi Monibullah indicates a person named Munib who uses the religiously inspired suffix -ullah (meaning "of God") and is trained as a cleric. Some Afghans—such as Presidents Hamid Karzai and Ashraf Ghani—use versions of their names that fit more neatly into the common Western format, but because most do not, Afghan names are listed alphabetically here by their first word, even when that word is an honorific.

U.S. military units are arranged in descending order from largest (division) to smaller (battalion).

ABOUT THE AUTHOR

WESLEY MORGAN is a journalist who has covered the U.S. military and its wars in Afghanistan and Iraq since 2007. His reporting has appeared in *Politico*, *The Washington Post*, and *The New York Times*. This is his first book.